THE ECONOMIST WORLD ATLAS AND ALMANAC

THE ECONOMIST WORLD ATLAS AND ALMANAC

The
Economist
Books

Prentice Hall Press

New York London Toronto Sydney Tokyo

Prentice Hall Press
15 Columbus Circle
New York, New York 10023

Published simultaneously in Canada by Prentice Hall Canada Inc.
Published in Great Britain in 1989 by Hutchinson Business Books Ltd
(an imprint of Century Hutchinson Ltd)

PRENTICE HALL PRESS and colophon are registered trademarks of
Simon & Schuster Inc.

Library of Congress Cataloging-in-Publication Data

The Economist world atlas and almanac.

"World Maps © 1989. Esselte Map Service . . . World Comparisons and
World Encyclopedia maps and diagrams © 1989
The Economist Books" – Verso t.p.
Contents: World maps – World comparisons – World encyclopedia.
Bibliography: p.
Includes index and glossary.
1. Geography, Economic – Maps. 2. Geography, Economic.
3. World politics – Maps. I. Economist (London, England).
II. Esselte Map Service. III. The Economist Books.
IV. Title: World atlas and almanac.

G1046.G1E37 1989 330′.022′3 89-675252
ISBN 0-13-234964-7

Where opinion is expressed it is that of the author, and does not necessarily
coincide with the editorial views of The Economist newspaper.

Editorial Director Stephen Brough
Art Director Douglas Wilson
Editors Richard Platt, Brigid Avison, Penny Butler, Nicholas Denton,
Andrew Shaw, Miles Smith-Morris, Roger Thornham
Art Editor Alistair Plumb
Designers John Fitzmaurice, Stephen Moore, Jenny Sadler
Indexer Fiona Barr
Production Manager Rupert Wheeler
Production Assistant Shona Burns
Contributors Marjo Ahonen, John Ardagh, George Blazyca, Carl Bridge,
Peter Calvert, Simon Chapman, Geoffrey Denton, John Farndon,
Jim Fitzpatrick, Anthony Goldstone, Ray Granger, Philip Hanson,
John Hooper, Diana Hubbard, Mark Hudson, Philip Landau, Simon Long,
John McLachlan, John Marks, Trevor Mostyn, James Murphy,
Roger Murray, Jim Nail, Robert Parsons, David Perman, Philippa Potts,
Rod Prince, Alan Rake, Martin Rhodes, Gerald Roberts, Brian Slocock,
Raili Taylor, Nigel Wilkins, Dick Wilson, David Young

World Comparisons and World Encyclopedia maps and graphics
by Swanston Graphics Ltd, Derby, England
Typeset by MF Graphics Ltd, Hitchin, England
Color separation by Grafascan, Dublin and Colourscan, Singapore
Printed in Italy by Graphicom

10 9 8 7 6 5 4 3 2 1
First Prentice Hall Press Edition

CONTENTS

WORLD MAPS

MAP CONTENTS

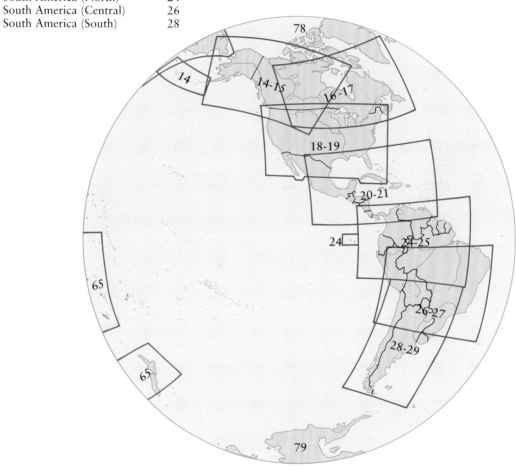

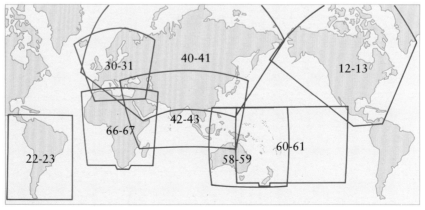

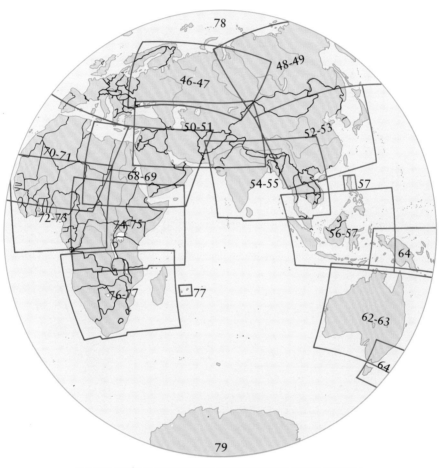

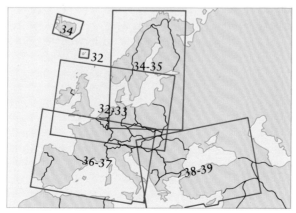

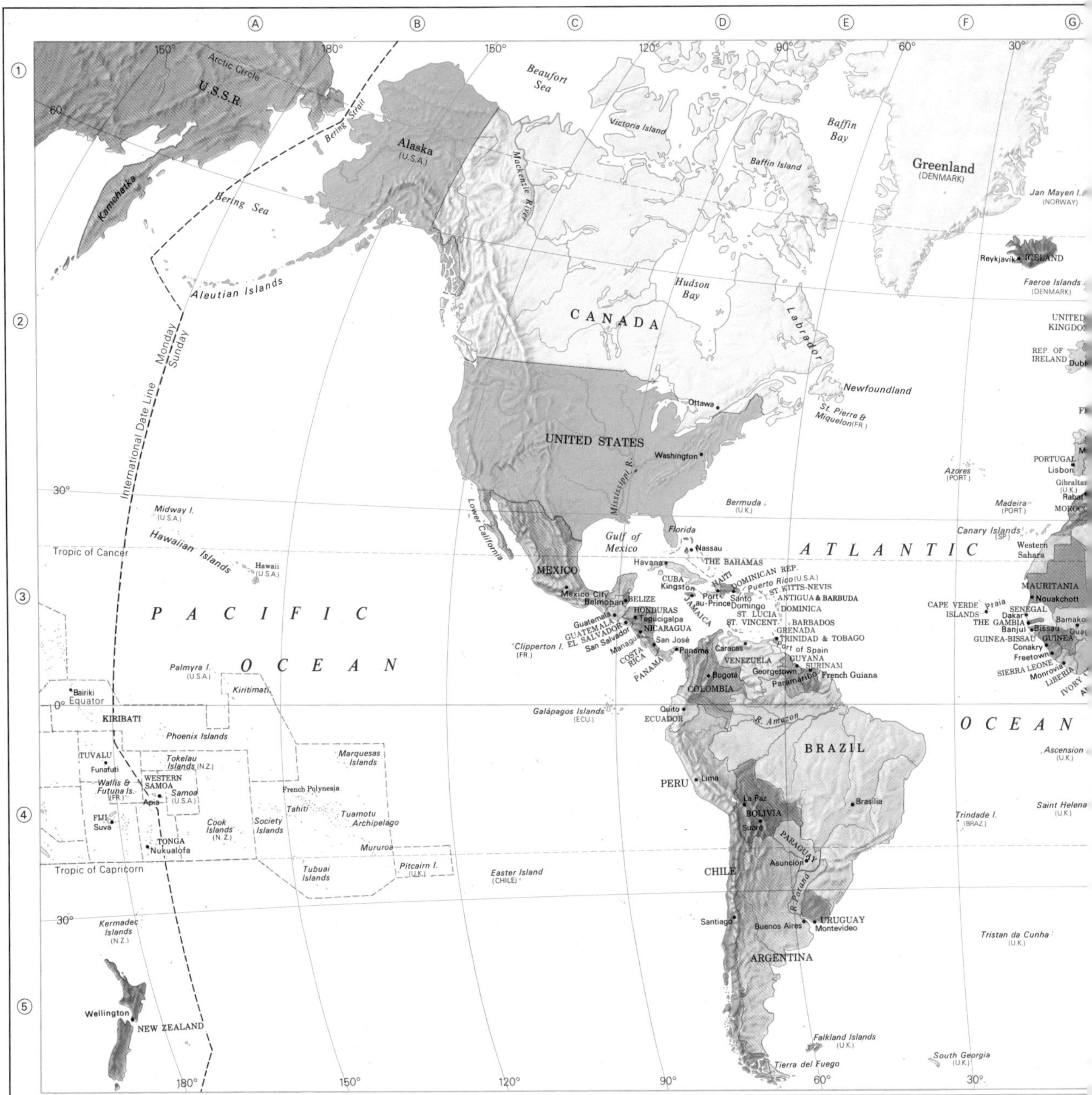

A
B
C
D
E
F
G
1
2
3
4
5
Arctic Circle
U.S.S.R.
Kamchatka
Bering Strait
Bering Sea
Aleutian Islands
Alaska
(U.S.A.)
Beaufort Sea
Victoria Island
Mackenzie River
Baffin Bay
Baffin Island
Greenland
(DENMARK)
Jan Mayen I.
(NORWAY)
Reykjavik
ICELAND
Faeroe Islands
(DENMARK)
Hudson Bay
CANADA
Labrador
Newfoundland
St. Pierre & Miquelon (FR.)
Ottawa
UNITED STATES
Washington
Mississippi R.
Lower California
International Date Line
Monday
Sunday
Midway I.
(U.S.A.)
Hawaiian Islands
Hawaii
(U.S.A.)
Tropic of Cancer
Bermuda
(U.K.)
Azores
(PORT.)
Madeira
(PORT.)
Canary Islands
(SP.)
Western Sahara
PORTUGAL
Lisbon
Gibraltar
(U.K.)
Rabat
REP. OF IRELAND
UNITED KINGDOM
Gulf of Mexico
Florida
Nassau
THE BAHAMAS
Havana
CUBA
Kingston
JAMAICA
HAITI
Port-au-Prince
DOMINICAN REP.
Santo Domingo
Puerto Rico (U.S.A.)
ST. KITTS-NEVIS
ANTIGUA & BARBUDA
DOMINICA
ST. LUCIA
ST. VINCENT
BARBADOS
GRENADA
TRINIDAD & TOBAGO
Port of Spain
ATLANTIC
OCEAN
MEXICO
Mexico City
BELIZE
Belmopan
HONDURAS
Tegucigalpa
GUATEMALA
Guatemala
EL SALVADOR
San Salvador
NICARAGUA
Managua
COSTA RICA
San José
PANAMA
Panamá
PACIFIC
OCEAN
Clipperton I.
(FR.)
Palmyra I.
(U.S.A.)
Kiritimati
Bairiki
Equator
KIRIBATI
Phoenix Islands
TUVALU
Funafuti
Tokelau Islands (N.Z.)
WESTERN SAMOA
Apia
Samoa
(U.S.A.)
Wallis & Futuna Is.
(FR.)
FIJI
Suva
TONGA
Nukualofa
Cook Islands
(N.Z.)
Society Islands
Tahiti
French Polynesia
Marquesas Islands
Tuamotu Archipelago
Mururoa
Tubuai Islands
Pitcairn I.
(U.K.)
Tropic of Capricorn
Easter Island
(CHILE)
Galápagos Islands
(ECU.)
Kermadec Islands
(N.Z.)
Wellington
NEW ZEALAND
Caracas
VENEZUELA
GUYANA
Georgetown
SURINAM
Paramaribo
French Guiana
Bogotá
COLOMBIA
Quito
ECUADOR
R. Amazon
BRAZIL
PERU
Lima
La Paz
BOLIVIA
Sucre
Brasília
PARAGUAY
Asunción
CHILE
Santiago
R. Paraná
Buenos Aires
URUGUAY
Montevideo
ARGENTINA
Falkland Islands
(U.K.)
Tierra del Fuego
South Georgia
(U.K.)
Trindade I.
(BRAZ.)
Tristan da Cunha
(U.K.)
Ascension
(U.K.)
Saint Helena
(U.K.)
CAPE VERDE
ISLANDS
Praia
MAURITANIA
Nouakchott
SENEGAL
Dakar
THE GAMBIA
Banjul
GUINEA-BISSAU
Bissau
GUINEA
Conakry
SIERRA LEONE
Freetown
LIBERIA
Monrovia
60°
30°
0°
150°
180°
120°
90°

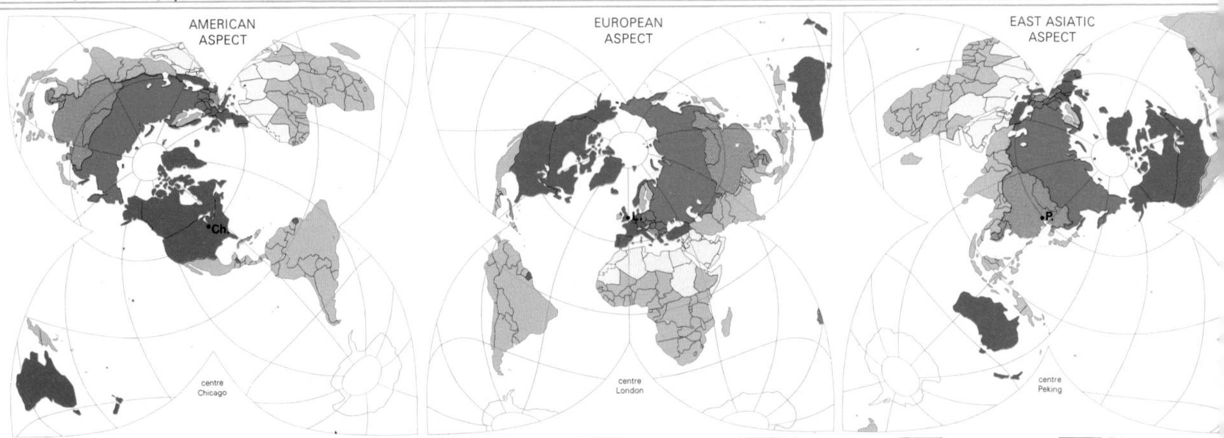

AMERICAN ASPECT
centre Chicago
EUROPEAN ASPECT
centre London
EAST ASIATIC ASPECT
centre Peking
Ch.
P.

MILITARY POLITICS

N.A.T.O., A.N.Z.U.S. | Warsaw Pact | Other communist states | Arab League | Other states | W. William- projection

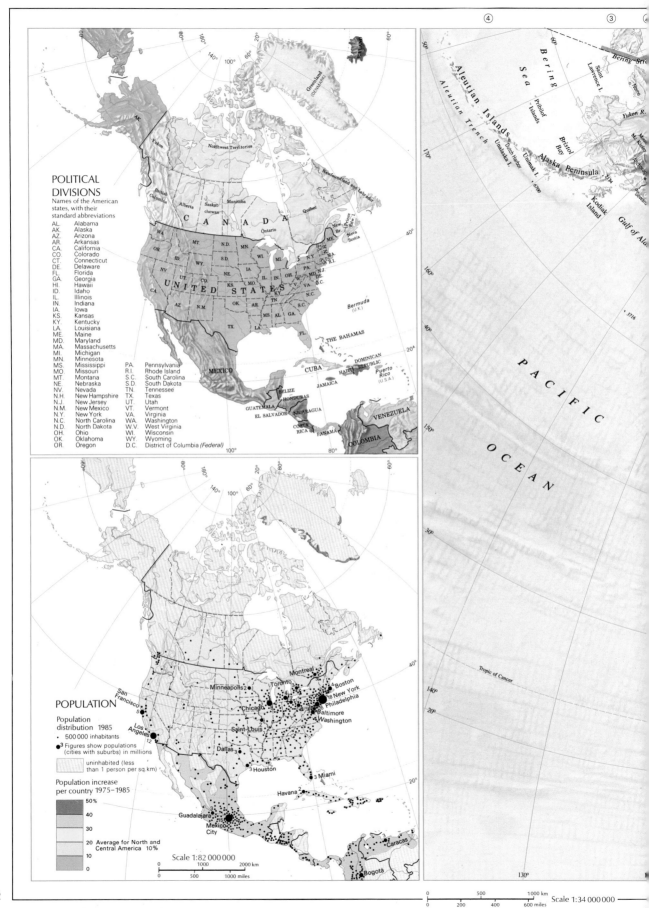

POLITICAL DIVISIONS

Names of the American states, with their standard abbreviations

AL.	Alabama	PA.	Pennsylvania
AK.	Alaska	R.I.	Rhode Island
AZ.	Arizona	S.C.	South Carolina
AR.	Arkansas	S.D.	South Dakota
CA.	California	TN.	Tennessee
CO.	Colorado	TX.	Texas
CT.	Connecticut	UT.	Utah
DE.	Delaware	VT.	Vermont
FL.	Florida	VA.	Virginia
GA.	Georgia	WA.	Washington
HI.	Hawaii	W.V.	West Virginia
ID.	Idaho	WI.	Wisconsin
IL.	Illinois	WY.	Wyoming
IN.	Indiana	D.C.	District of Columbia (Federal)
IA.	Iowa		
KS.	Kansas		
KY.	Kentucky		
LA.	Louisiana		
ME.	Maine		
MD.	Maryland		
MA.	Massachusetts		
MI.	Michigan		
MN.	Minnesota		
MS.	Mississippi		
MO.	Missouri		
MT.	Montana		
NE.	Nebraska		
NV.	Nevada		
N.H.	New Hampshire		
N.J.	New Jersey		
N.M.	New Mexico		
N.Y.	New York		
N.C.	North Carolina		
N.D.	North Dakota		
OH.	Ohio		
OK.	Oklahoma		
OR.	Oregon		

POPULATION

Population distribution 1985

· 500 000 inhabitants

●3 Figures show populations (cities with suburbs) in millions

uninhabited (less than 1 person per sq.km)

Population increase per country 1975–1985

	50%
	40
	30
	20 Average for North and Central America 10%
	10
	0

Scale 1:82 000 000

0 — 1000 — 2000 km
0 — 500 — 1000 miles

Scale 1:34 000 000

0 — 500 — 1000 km
0 — 200 — 400 — 600 miles

Beaufort Sea

Greenland (Denmark)

Queen Elizabeth Islands

Sverdrup Islands
Axel Heiberg Island
Ellesmere Island
Prince Patrick Island
Melville Island
Magnetic North Pole (1980)
Parry Islands
Devon Island
Banks Island
Somerset Island
Prince of Wales Island
Victoria Island
Boothia Pen.
Baffin Bay
Baffin Island
Davis Strait

Geographic North Pole

Godthåb
Frederikshåb
Julianehåb
C. Farewell

Brooks Range
Alaska
Yukon R.
Inuvik
Great Bear Lake
Mackenzie Mountains
Mackenzie River
Great Slave Lake
Yellowknife
Hay River
Northwest Territories
Melville Peninsula
Foxe Basin
Southampton Island
Hudson Strait
Cape Chidley
Labrador Sea

Coast Mountains
British Columbia
ROCKY MOUNTAINS
Peace R.
Dawson Creek
Lake Athabasca
CANADA
Alberta
Saskatchewan
Manitoba
Churchill
Hudson Bay
Ungava Peninsula
Ungava Bay
Newfoundland and Labrador
Labrador
Québec

Edmonton
Saskatoon
Regina
Lake Winnipeg
Lake Manitoba
Winnipeg
Brandon

Vancouver
Victoria
Seattle
Tacoma
Portland
Salem
Mount Rainier
Columbia River
Spokane
Missouri R.
Bismarck
Yellowstone R.
Billings
Snake R.
Great Salt Lake
Salt Lake City
Great Basin
Sierra Nevada
Sacramento
Oakland
San José
Death Valley
Mount Whitney
Los Angeles
Long Beach
San Bernardino
San Diego
Tijuana
Mexicali

Minneapolis
St. Paul
Madison
Milwaukee
Lake Superior
Lake Michigan
Lake Huron
Duluth
Sault Ste. Marie
Sudbury
Thunder Bay
Ottawa
Montreal
Toronto
Hamilton
Lake Ontario
Lake Erie
Detroit
Cleveland
Buffalo
Rochester
Niagara Falls
Boston
Cape Cod
New York
Newark
Philadelphia
Baltimore
WASHINGTON
Pittsburgh
Columbus
Cincinnati

Chicago
Des Moines
Omaha
Lincoln
North Platte R.
Cheyenne
Denver
Mount Elbert
Colorado Springs
UNITED STATES (USA)
Kansas City
St. Louis
Louisville
Nashville
Richmond
Norfolk
Cape Hatteras

Santa Fe
Albuquerque
Colorado R.
Grand Canyon
Colorado Plateau
Phoenix
Tucson
El Paso
Ciudad Juárez
Rio Grande
Oklahoma City
Tulsa
Arkansas R.
Wichita
Memphis
Little Rock
Birmingham
Atlanta
Charlotte
Charleston
Savannah
Jacksonville
Cape Canaveral

Lubbock
Fort Worth
Dallas
Pecos R.
Austin
San Antonio
Houston
Galveston
Beaumont
Baton Rouge
New Orleans
Mobile
Tampa
St. Petersburg
Florida
Miami
Key West
Straits of Florida

Bermuda Islands (U.K.)

ATLANTIC OCEAN

THE BAHAMAS
NASSAU
Tropic of Cancer

MEXICO
Hermosillo
Chihuahua
Culiacán
Mazatlán
Torreón
Saltillo
Monterrey
Matamoros
Gulf of Mexico
Corpus Christi
Tampico
San Luis Potosí
Aguascalientes
León
Guadalajara
MEXICO CITY
Morelia
Puebla
Veracruz
Mérida
Yucatán
Bay of Campeche
Acapulco
Southern Sierra Madre
Isthmus of Tehuantepec
Middle America Trench

HAVANA
CUBA
Santa Clara
Camagüey
Santiago de Cuba
Guantánamo
West Indies
Greater Antilles
JAMAICA
KINGSTON
HAITI
PORT-AU-PRINCE
DOMINICAN REPUBLIC
SANTO DOMINGO
Hispaniola
San Juan
Puerto Rico (U.S.A.)
Puerto Rico Trench

Caribbean Sea

BELIZE
BELMOPAN
GUATEMALA
San Pedro Sula
HONDURAS
TEGUCIGALPA
EL SALVADOR
SAN SALVADOR
NICARAGUA
MANAGUA
Lake Nicaragua
COSTA RICA
SAN JOSÉ
PANAMA
Panama Canal
Colón

Aruba I. (Neth.)
Curaçao I. (Neth.)
Bonaire I. (Neth.)
Maracaibo
Barquisimeto
CARACAS
Valencia
VENEZUELA
Barranquilla
Cartagena
Santa Marta
P. Gallinas
Bucaramanga
Medellín
Manizales
COLOMBIA
BOGOTÁ

13

Scale 1:14 000 000

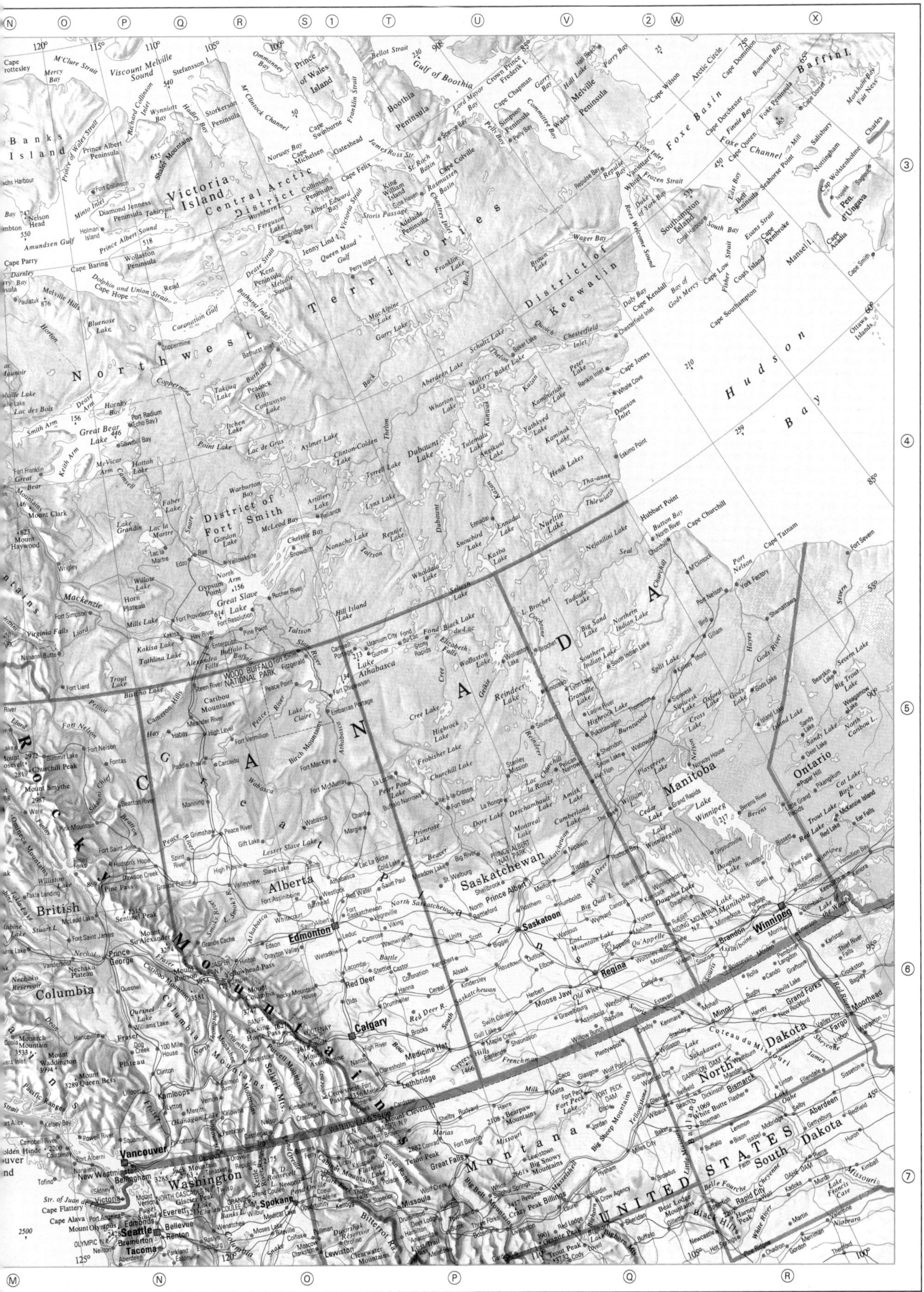

Banks Island

Victoria Island

Central Arctic District

Northwest Territories

District of Keewatin

District of Fort Smith

Baffin I.

Hudson Bay

Foxe Basin

Great Bear Lake

Great Slave Lake

Lake Athabasca

Reindeer Lake

Lake Winnipeg

C A N A D A

Mackenzie

British Columbia

Alberta

Saskatchewan

Manitoba

Ontario

Rocky Mountains

Edmonton

Calgary

Saskatoon

Regina

Winnipeg

Vancouver

Prince George

Moose Jaw

Medicine Hat

Lethbridge

Red Deer

Seattle

Tacoma

Spokane

Bellevue

Washington

Montana

North Dakota

South Dakota

UNITED STATES

Bismarck

Fargo

Grand Forks

Missoula

Great Falls

Billings

Olympic

Str. of Juan de Fuca

Gulf of Boothia

Boothia Peninsula

Melville Peninsula

Southampton Island

Prince of Wales Island

M'Clure Strait

Viscount Melville Sound

Arctic Circle

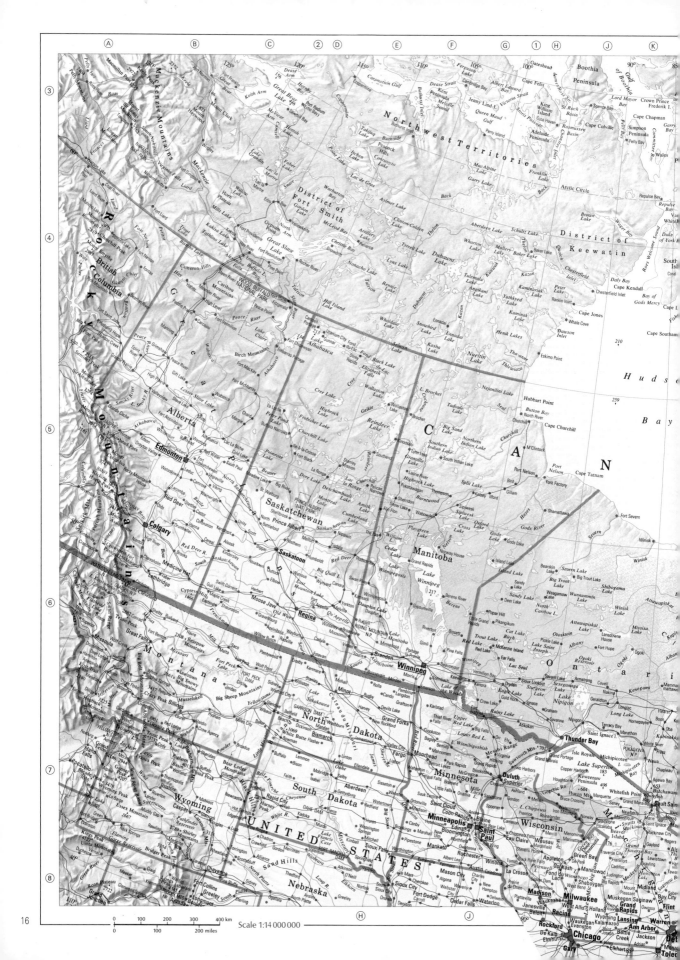

Baffin Island

Foxe Basin

Davis Strait

Kalaallit Nunaat
(Greenland)
(Denmark)

Cumberland Peninsula

Hudson Strait

Labrador Sea

Peninsule d'Ungava

Ungava Bay

CANADA

Coast of Labrador

Québec

Newfoundland and Labrador

James Bay

Akimiski Island

Labrador

Gulf of Saint Lawrence

Newfoundland

Saint John's
Cape Race

Saint Pierre et Miquelon (France)

Prince Edward Island

Cape Breton Island

New Brunswick

Nova Scotia

Maine

Vermont

ATLANTIC OCEAN

Gulf of Maine

Cape Sable

OTTAWA
Montréal
Québec
Toronto
Halifax
Rochester
Buffalo
New York
London
Hamilton

St. Lawrence R.

Île d'Anticosti

Cabot Strait

Arctic Circle

C 80° JAMAICA 70° Puerto Rico (U.S.A.) ST. KITTS AND NEVIS D 60° ANTIGUA AND BARBUDA Guadeloupe (France) Pointe-à-Pitre DOMINICA Martinique (France) Fort-de-France ST. LUCIA BARBADOS BRIDGETOWN E 50° F 40° G 30°

Caribbean Sea

Lesser Antilles ST. VINCENT GRENADA

P. Gallinas Aruba I. Curaçao I. (Neth.)
Santa Marta Barranquilla Maracaibo
Cartagena Mt. Cristóbal Colón Barquisimeto Maracay CARACAS Cumaná TRINIDAD AND TOBAGO PORT OF SPAIN
Colón PANAMÁ Valencia Ciudad Ojeda Barcelona
NAMÁ Cúcuta San Cristóbal Ciudad Bolívar Cerro Bolívar GEORGETOWN PARAMARIBO Cayenne

ATLANTIC OCEAN

Medellín Bucaramanga Tolima VENEZUELA Angel Falls Kaieteur Falls Mt. Roraima French Guiana
Manizales Ibagué BOGOTÁ Guiana Highlands GUYANA SURINAM
Buenaventura Cali COLOMBIA Guaviare R. Orinoco R. Boa Vista Roraima Amapá Macapá

QUITO Mt. Cotopaxi Putumayo R. R. Negro Amazon R. Marajó I. Belém St. Peter and St. Paul Rocks (Braz.)
JADOR Amazon R. Fonte Boa Manaus Santarém São Luís Parnaíba Equator 0°
Guayaquil Iquitos Leticia Amazonas Pará Maranhão Fortaleza Fernando de Noronha I. (Braz.)
PERU Marañón R. Juruá R. Selvas Madeira R. Tapajós R. Xingu R. Tocantins R. Teresina Ceará Sobral Mossoró C. São Roque Natal
Chiclayo Huánuco Acre Purus R. Porto Velho BRAZIL Caatingas Piauí Rio Grande do Norte João Pessoa Campina Grande
Trujillo Mt. Huascarán Cerro de Pasco Rio Branco Guajará Mirim Rondônia Piauí Pernambuco Recife
LIMA La Oroya Huancayo Cobija Mato Grosso Goiás Barreiras Bahia Aracaju Maceió
Callao Huancavelica Cuzco Trinidad Cuiabá Anápolis BRASÍLIA Distrito Federal São Francisco R. Alagoinhas Salvador
Arequipa Lake Titicaca Mt. Illampu LA PAZ Santa Cruz Goiânia Brazilian Itabuna Ilhéus
Mollendo BOLIVIA Oruro SUCRE Mato Grosso do Sul Uberlândia Minas Gerais Governador Valadares Teófilo Otoni Vitória
Tacna Arica Lake Poopó Campo Grande Uberaba Belo Horizonte Espírito Santo
Iquique Gran Chaco PARAGUAY Presidente Prudente São José Ribeirão Prêto Highlands Vitória Tropic of Capricorn 20°
Tocopilla Pilcomayo R. Campo ASUNCIÓN Bauru Sorocaba Campinas Juiz de Fora Rio de Campos Trindade I. (Braz.) Martin Vaz Is. (Braz.)
Antofagasta Bermejo R. Paraná R. Paraná Santos São Paulo Niterói Rio de Janeiro
Salta Formosa Paraná Ponta Grossa Santos Caxias do Sul
Copiapó Tucumán Resistencia Corrientes Posadas Curitiba Joinville
La Serena Santiago del Estero Salado R. Santa Catarina Blumenau Florianópolis
Mendoza Córdoba La Rioja Salinas Grandes Salado R. Río Grande do Sul Passo Fundo 4996
Valparaíso Mt. Aconcagua San Luis Santa Fe Rosario Paraná Uruguaiana Santa Maria Pôrto Alegre
SANTIAGO Río Cuarto Zárate Salto Paysandú L. dos Patos
CHILE Talca Junín BUENOS AIRES URUGUAY Lake Mirim Río Grande Pelotas
Concepción ARGENTINA La Plata MONTEVIDEO
Félix I. (Chile) S. Ambrosio I. (Chile) Juan Fernández Islands (Chile) Talcahuano Santa Rosa Azul Tandil Mar del Plata 5303

ATLANTIC OCEAN

Temuco Colorado R. Bahía Blanca
Valdivia Neuquén
Osorno Viedma
Puerto Montt Gulf of San Matías
Chiloé I. San Carlos de Bariloche Rawson
2652 Patagonia Gulf of San Jorge
Puerto Aisén Comodoro Rivadavia
Cerro San Valentín Puerto Deseado
6212 Río Gallegos Falkland Islands (U.K.) Stanley
Strait of Magellan Tierra del Fuego South Georgia (U.K.)
Ushuaia Horn 2915

© ESSELTE MAP SERVICE

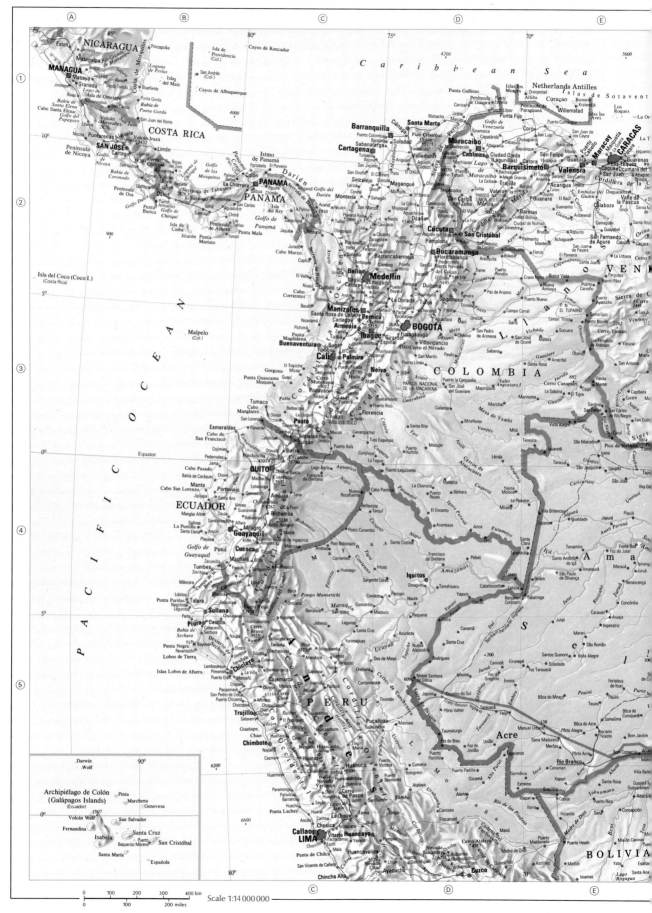

Scale 1:14 000 000

Map labels

Ocean / water:
ATLANTIC OCEAN

Grid / coordinates:
F · G · H · J · K
55° · 50° · 45°
10° · 5° · 0° Equator

Islands / Caribbean:
SAINT LUCIA — CASTRIES
SAINT VINCENT — KINGSTOWN
Mount Hillaby 340
BRIDGETOWN — BARBADOS
GRENADA — SAINT GEORGE'S
Tobago — Scarborough
Lesser Antilles — Windward Islands
4100 · 3000
Grenadines Islands

Venezuela / Trinidad region:
TRINIDAD AND TOBAGO
PORT OF SPAIN
Trinidad
San Fernando
Sangre Grande
Arima
Boca de la Serpiente
Golfo de Paria
Peninsula de Paria
Cumaná
Maturín
Carúpano
Güiria
Punta de Mata
Tigre
Ciudad Guayana
Ciudad Bolívar
Santo Tomé de Guayana
GURI DAM
Represa Raúl Leoni
San Pedro de las Bocas
El Dorado
Serranía de Imataca
Mouths of the Orinoco
Boca Grande
Orinoco
Morawhanna
Mabaruma
Arakaka
Matthew's Ridge
Charity
Suddie
Towakaima
Cuyuni
802 · 2500 · 2100
Cerro Guaiquinima
Auyán-Tepui
Churún Merú (Angel Falls)
La Gran Sabana
PARQUE NACIONAL CANAIMA
Cerro Roraima 2810
VENEZUELA
Kamaria Falls
Bartica
Kwakwani
New Amsterdam

Guyana / Surinam / French Guiana:
GEORGETOWN
GUYANA
Linden
Springlands
Nieuw Nickerie
PARAMARIBO
SURINAM
Wonotobo Falls
Kabalebo Reservoir
Van Blommestein Reservoir
King Edward VII Falls
Kaieteur Falls
Julianatop 1280
Brokopondo
Oranje Gebergte
Albina
Moengo
Saint-Laurent
FRENCH Guiana
Cayenne
Île du Diable (Devil's Island)
Kourou
Sinnamary
Iracoubo
Cabo Orange
Cabo Cassiporé
Saint-Georges
Oiapoque
Saül
Regina
Serra Tumucumaque

Brazil (north):
BRAZIL
Roraima
Boa Vista
Serra Pacaraima
Pico Rondón 1189
Caracaraí
Serra do Apiaú
Cachoeira do Pimenta
Catrimani
Amapá
Macapá
Pôrto Santana
Serra do Navio
Cachoeira Grande
Mouths of the Amazon
Canal do Norte
Cabo Norte
Ilha de Marajó
Belém
Bragança
São Luís
Maranhão
Bacabal
Imperatriz
Serra do Tiracambu
Serra do Gurupí
Pará
Santarém
Óbidos
Alenquer
Monte Alegre
Altamira
Manaus
Rio Negro
Arquipélago das Anavilhanas
Lago de Manacapuru
Carvoeiro
Barcelos
Serra dos Carajás
Serra do Cachimbo
Serra do Roncador
Serra das Alpercatas
Madeira
Rondônia
Goiás
Bahia
Mato Grosso
Serra dos Parecis
Serra do Tombador
PARQUE NACIONAL DO ARAGUAIA
Ilha do Bananal
PARQUE NACIONAL DA CHAPADA DOS VEADEIROS
Rio Grande
Xingu
Tapajós
Teles Pires
Araguaia
Tocantins

Publisher:
© ESSELTE MAP SERVICE
25

Scale 1:14 000 000

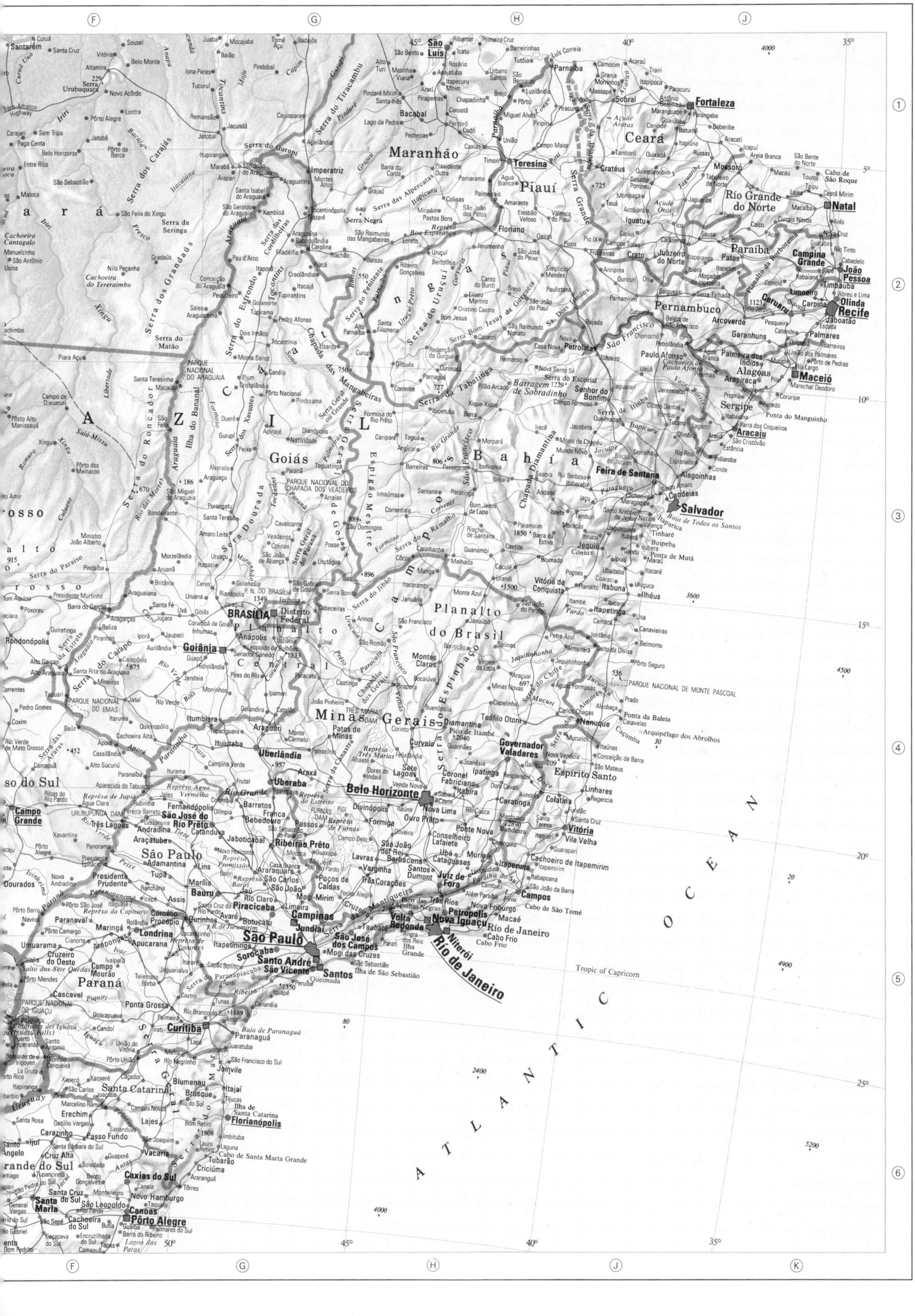

Maranhão
Piauí
Ceará
Rio Grande do Norte
Paraíba
Pernambuco
Alagoas
Sergipe
Bahia
Goiás
Minas Gerais
Espírito Santo
São Paulo
Paraná
Santa Catarina

Planalto do Brasil
Planalto Central

BRASÍLIA
Distrito Federal

Fortaleza
Teresina
Natal
João Pessoa
Recife
Olinda
Maceió
Aracaju
Salvador
Feira de Santana
Goiânia
Belo Horizonte
Uberlândia
Uberaba
Vitória
Campos
Rio de Janeiro
Niterói
Nova Iguaçu
Volta Redonda
São Paulo
Santo André
São Vicente
Santos
Campinas
Sorocaba
São José do Rio Prêto
Campo Grande
Londrina
Curitiba
Ponta Grossa
Joinville
Blumenau
Florianópolis
Caxias do Sul
Canoas
Pôrto Alegre
Santa Maria
São Luís

ATLANTIC OCEAN

Tropic of Capricorn

© ESSELTE MAP SERVICE

27

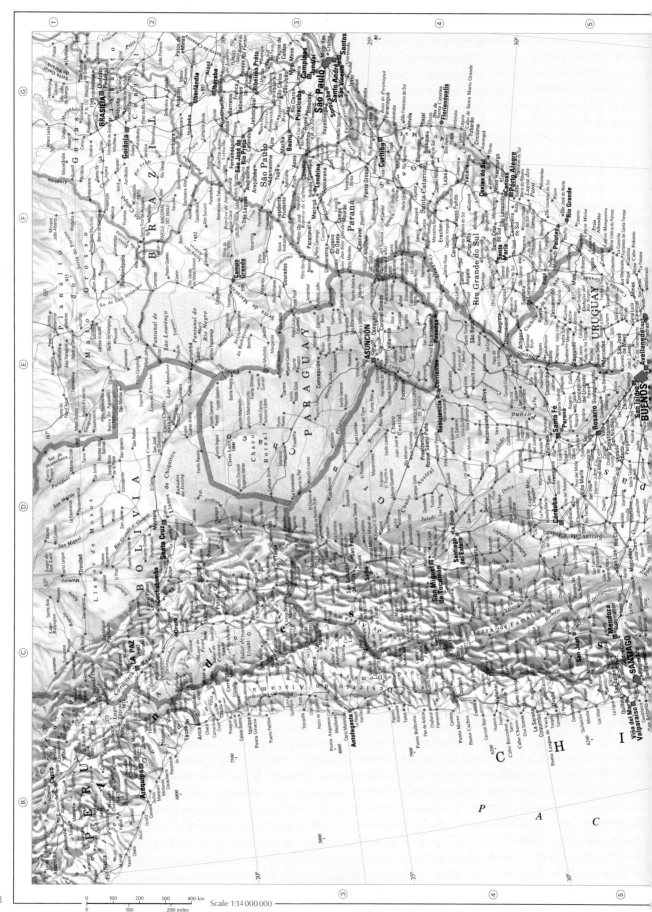

Scale 1:14 000 000

0 100 200 300 400 km
0 100 200 miles

A T L A N T I C

O C E A N

ARGENTINA

P a t a g o n i a

Mar del Plata
Necochea
Bahía Blanca
Bahía Blanca
Golfo San Matías
Península Valdés
Rawson
Trelew
Golfo San Jorge
Comodoro Rivadavia
Puerto Deseado
Río Gallegos
Bahía Grande

Falkland Islands
(Islas Malvinas)
(U.K.) Pebble Island
West Falkland
Jason Islands
Weddell
Mount Usborne
891
Stanley
Cape Pembroke
East Falkland
Cape Meredith

6200

5900

2000

Río Negro
Río Colorado
Colorado
Neuquén
San Carlos de Bariloche
Temuco
Osorno
Puerto Montt
Valdivia
Concepción
Talcahuano
Chillán
Talca

CHILE

Isla de Chiloé
Archipiélago de los Chonos
Península de Taitao
Golfo de Penas
Archipiélago Reina Adelaida
Tierra del Fuego
Isla Grande
Punta Arenas
Estrecho de Magallanes
Cabo de Hornos (Cape Horn)
Isla de los Estados (Staten Island)
Drake Strait

P A C I F I C   O C E A N

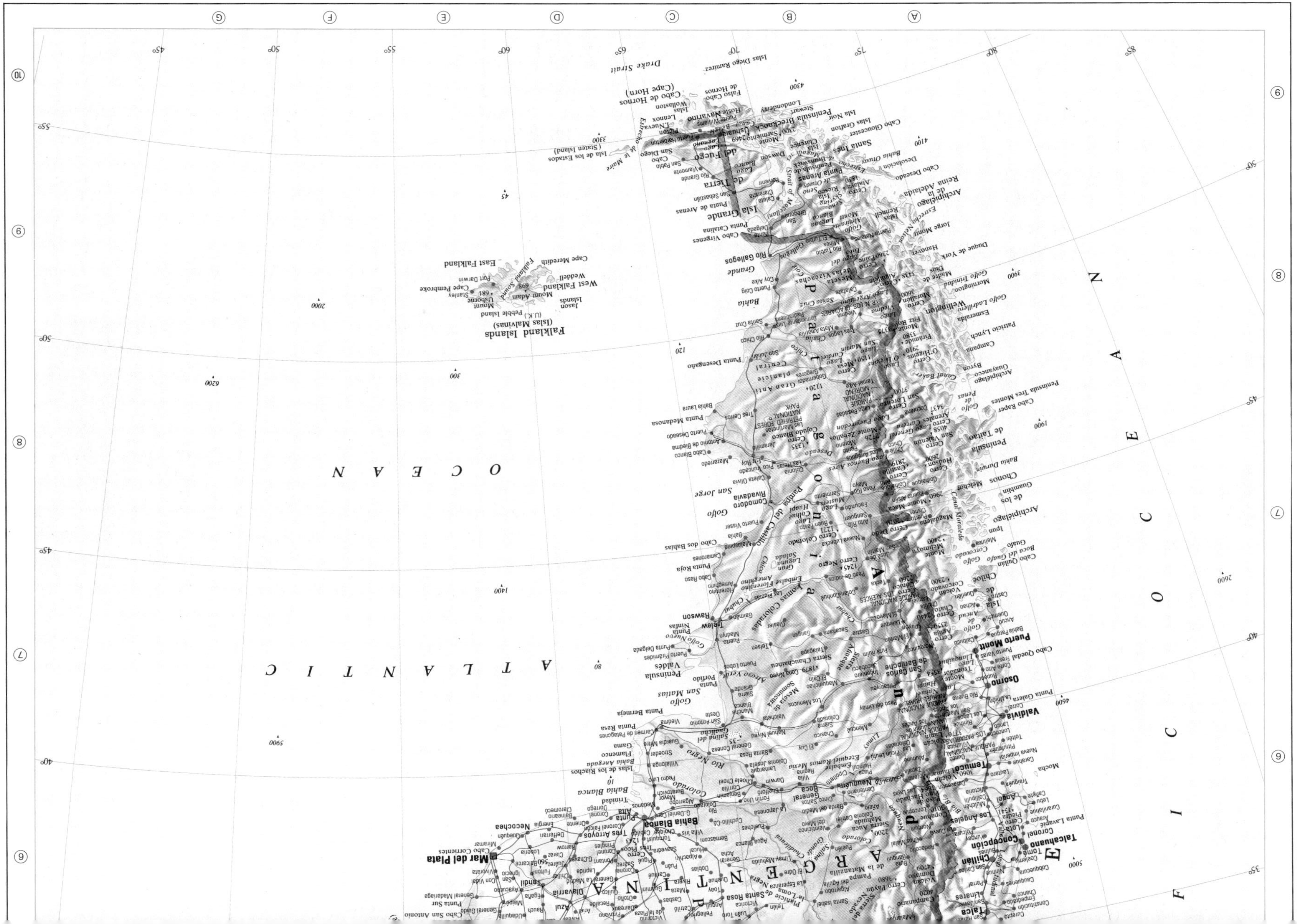

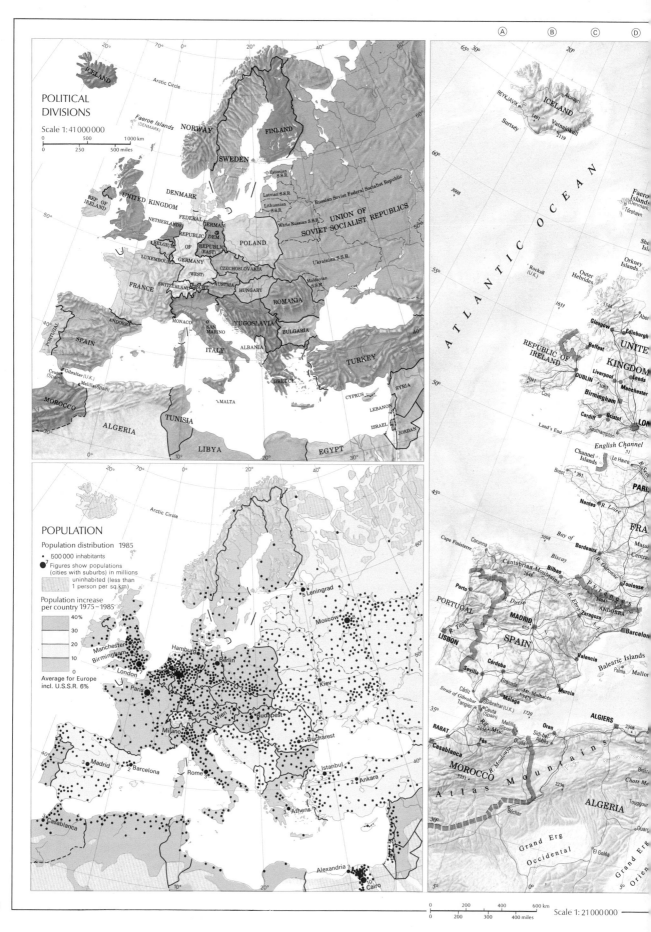

F G H J 1 K L M N O P Q R 2 S T U V

3

0° 10° North Cape 20° 30° 260 70° 50° 65° 70°

Norwegian Sea

Barents Sea

Tromsø

Kanin Peninsula R. Pechora Mt. Naroduaya 1894 R. Ob

Vesterålen Is. Murmansk

Ural Mountains Khanty-Mansiysk

Lofoten Is. Narvik 2111 Kiruna Kola Peninsula M91

Arctic Circle Kebnekaise Serov 4

Bodø 245 White Sea Arkhangel R. Ukhta 1569 Nizhniy Tagil 60°

Trondheim Severodvinsk North Dvina R. R. Vychegda Berezniki Sverdlovsk

L a p l a n d Oulu Syktyvkar R. Kama Zlatoust

NORWAY Perm 55°

Caldhøpiggen 2469 Östersund FINLAND Petrozavodsk R. Sukhona Kirov Ufa 5

Bergen SWEDEN 117 Lake Onega R. Vyatka Ustinov (Izhevsk) Sterlitamak Magnitogorsk

Sundsvall Umeå Gulf of Bothnia Lake Ladoga R. Volga Yoshkar Ola Kazan R. Kama

Stavanger 690 Leningrad Kazan Orenburg Uralsk 50°

Skagerrak OSLO Vänern 459 Turku HELSINKI Rybinsk Reservoir Yaroslavl Gorkiy Kuybyshev

Norrköping Saaremaa I. Estonian S.S.R. Novgorod 347 Ivanovo Ulyanovsk

Jutland Kattegat Gotland Riga Latvian S.S.R. Valdai Hills Kalinin Vladimir R. Oka Togliatti Ural R.

DENMARK Árhus Öland West Dvina R. Tver MOSCOW Ryazan Penza Saratov Kazakh S.S.R. 6

North Sea COPENHAGEN Malmö Lithuanian S.S.R. Smolensk Russian Soviet Federal Socialist Republic

Kiel Bornholm Kaliningrad Kaunas Vilnius Minsk Tula Tambov R. Ural Güryev

Hamburg Bremen Szczecin R. Neman Bryansk Orel R. Don R. Volga Astrakhan

ERDAM GERMAN Gdańsk White Russian S.S.R. Gomel Kursk Voronezh UNION OF SOVIET SOCIALIST REPUBLICS R. Volga -28

Hanover DEMOCRATIC Poznań WARSAW Pripet Marshes Kharkov 119 Voroshilovgrad Volgograd Caspian Sea

FEDERAL BERLIN R. Oder R. Vistula Kiyev Donets Basin R. Don

Essen Dortmund Leipzig Łódź POLAND Ukrainian S.S.R. Gorlovka Makeyevka Rostov na Donu 45°

Cologne REPUBLIC Dresden Wrocław Lvov Dnepropetrovsk Donetsk

BONN (EAST) Sudeten Mts. Katowice Vinnitsa Krivoy Rog Zaporozhye Zhdanov Stavropol

Frankfurt PRAGUE Brno Cracow 2663 R. Dniester Kishinev Nikolayev Sea of Azov Grozny

LUXEMBOURG CZECHOSLOVAKIA Bratislava R. Dnestr Odessa Krasnodar Caucasus Mts

Strasbourg GERMANY Nuremberg R. Dwod VIENNA BUDAPEST Moldavian S.S.R. Simferopol 2 Sochi Mt. Elbrus 5633

1149 (WEST) Stuttgart 518 AUSTRIA HUNGARY R. Tisza Cluj-Napoca 346 Crimea Sevastopol 1545 Georgian S.S.R. Tbilisi

Munich Graz Brasov Azerbaydzhan S.S.R.

SWITZERLAND LIECHTEN Zagreb ROMANIA 2543 Danube Constanta 2244 Armenian S.S.R. 40°

4810 Milan R. Po Venice YUGOSLAVIA BELGRADE R. Danube Iron Gate BUCHAREST Black Sea Yerevan Mt. Ararat

Turin Genoa Bologna SAN MARINO Sarajevo Split 307 2522 Varna Pontine Mountains 3365 Mt. Ararat Tabriz

MONACO Florence Adriatic Sea Balkan Mountains 2600 Samsun Drimurd

Ligurian Sea Mt. Musala SOFIA BULGARIA Istanbul Kizil Irmak R. Mosul R. Tigris

Corsica 2710 ROME Skopje 3925 Plovdiv Sea of Marmara ANKARA 870 Kayseri Kirkuk 8

ITALY Naples Vesuvio TIRANA Thessaloniki Bursa Eskişehir T U R K E Y 3916 Nineveh

Sardinia 3914 1277 ALBANIA Mt. Olympos 2911 Aegean A n a t o l i a Konya Taurus Mts R. Euphrates

Tyrrhenian 3550 GREECE Sea Izmir 3086 Adana Aleppo BAGHDAD

Palermo Messina Ionian Sea ATHENS Antalya 4100 S Y R I A IRAQ 9

Sicily Mt. Etna 3340 Catania Peloponnese 3864 Latakia Homs R. Euphrates

TUNIS VALLETTA Patras 4791 Rhodes NICOSIA 1463 DAMASCUS

MALTA Crete 2456 Iráklion CYPRUS 1952 LEBANON BEIRUT

Bizerta M e d i t e r r a n e a n S e a Sa ISRAEL AMMAN 30°

Sfax Gabès Tel Aviv-Yafo JERUSALEM JORDAN Nafud 10

TRIPOLI Misrātah Beida As Sallūm Alexandria Tanta Port Said SAUDI ARABIA

Tripolitania Gulf of Sirt Cyrenaica Benghazi Suez Canal 2637

Qattara Depression -134 Giza CAIRO Suez Sinai

L I B Y A EGYPT R. Nile Gulf of Suez

10° 15° 20° 25° 30° 40°

H J K L M N O P

31

© ESSELTE MAP SERVICE

OSLO
STOCKHOLM
Uppsala
Västerås
Eskilstuna
Örebro
Norrköping
Linköping
Jönköping
SWEDEN
Sveland
Dalarna
Värmland
Göteborg (Gothenburg)
Gotland
Öland
Tallinn
Estoniya
Tartu
Hiiumaa
Saaremaa
Latviya
Riga
Daugavpils
Ventspils
Liepāja
Klaipéda
Žemaitija
Litva (Lithuania)
Kaunas
Vilnius
Grodno
Brest
DENMARK (DANMARK)
Ålborg
Århus
Odense
KØBENHAVN (COPENHAGEN)
Malmö
Sjælland
Fyn
Bornholm
Kaliningrad
Gdańsk
Gdynia
Sopot
Elblag
Olsztyn
Białystok
Flensburg
Kiel
Lübeck
Rostock
Schwerin
Hamburg
Bremerhaven
Bremen
GERMAN DEMOCRATIC REPUBLIC
Mecklenburg
Szczecin
POLAND (POLSKA)
Bydgoszcz
Toruń
Poznań
WARSZAWA (WARSAW)
BERLIN (West) (Ost)
Potsdam
Magdeburg
Braunschweig
Hannover (Hanover)
Bielefeld
Münster
Hamm
Dortmund
Kassel
(DDR)
Halle
Leipzig
Dresden
Karl-Marx-Stadt
Erfurt
Zwickau
Łódź
Lublin
Radom
Wrocław
Legnica
Częstochowa
Kielce
FEDERAL REP. OF GERMANY
Frankfurt a. M.
Offenbach
Wiesbaden
Mainz
Darmstadt
Mannheim
Heidelberg
Würzburg
Nürnberg (Nuremberg)
Fürth
BUNDESREPUBLIK DEUTSCHLAND
Bayern (Bavaria)
Regensburg
Stuttgart
Karlsruhe
Augsburg
München (Munich)
Salzburg
PRAHA (PRAGUE)
Plzeň
Cechy (Bohemia)
CZECHOSLOVAKIA
Brno
Ostrava
Olomouc
Katowice
Kraków (Cracow)
Košice
Slovensko (Slovakia)
Karpackie (Carpathians)
Galicia
Rzeszów
Przemyśl
WIEN (VIENNA)
Linz
Graz
Bratislava
BUDAPEST
HUNGARY (MAGYARORSZÁG)
Győr
Miskolc
Debrecen
Szeged
Oradea
Arad
Timișoara
AUSTRIA
The Alps
Tirol
Innsbruck
Klagenfurt
Maribor
LIECHTENSTEIN
SWITZERLAND
BERN (BERNE)
Zürich
Winterthur
St. Gallen

33

© ESSELTE MAP SERVICE

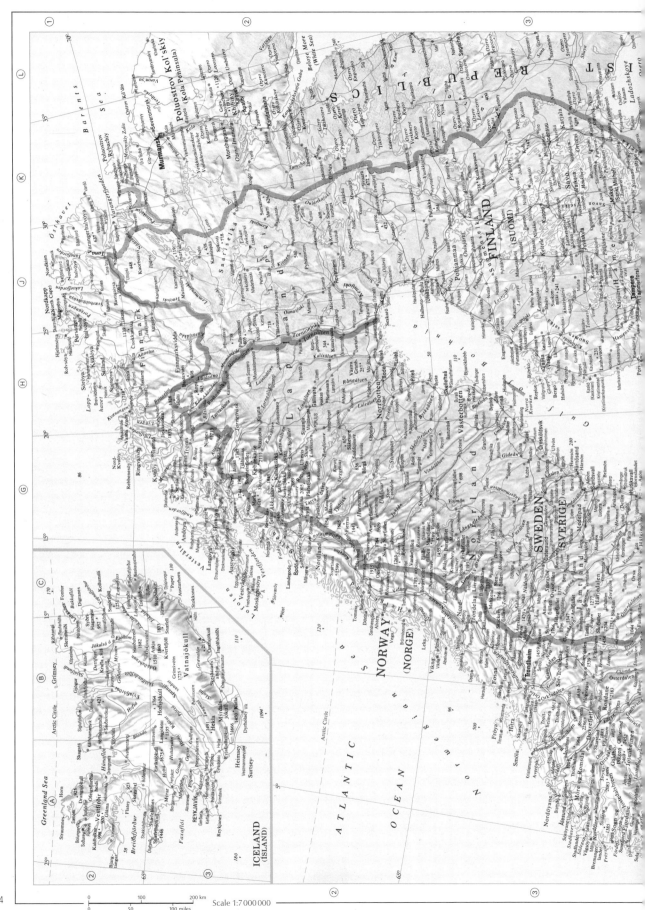

Scale 1:7 000 000

FEDERAL REP. OF GERMANY

BUNDESREPUBLIK DEUTSCHLAND

BONN · Frankfurt a. M · Wiesbaden · Mainz · Darmstadt · Mannheim · Heidelberg · Karlsruhe · Stuttgart · Nürnberg (Nuremberg) · Regensburg · Würzburg · Augsburg · München (Munich) · Bayern (Bavaria)

LUXEMBOURG · Trier · Saarbrücken · Kaiserslautern · Ludwigshafen

PRAHA (PRAGUE) · Plzeň (Pilsen) · České země (Bohemia) · Brno · CZECHOSLOVAKIA · Ostrava · Bielsko-Biała

Freiburg · Basel · Zürich · St. Gallen · SWITZERLAND · BERN (BERNE) · Winterthur · Innsbruck · Tirol · LIECHTENSTEIN · VADUZ

Salzburg · Linz · WIEN (VIENNA) · AUSTRIA · Graz · Bratislava · BUDAPEST · HUNGARY (MAGYARORSZÁG) · Szombathely · Pécs · Szeged

Mulhouse · Genève · Lausanne · Lyon · Grenoble

Bolzano · Belluno · Udine · Trieste · Ljubljana · Zagreb · Maribor · SLOVENIJA · Hrvatska (Croatia) · Osijek · Novi Sad

Torino (Turin) · Milano (Milan) · Como · Bergamo · Brescia · Verona · Vicenza · Padova · Venezia (Venice) · Gulf of Venice · Rijeka · YUGOSLAVIA · Sarajevo · Banja Luka · Tuzla

Nice · MONACO · Marseille · Toulon

Novara · Pavia · Cremona · Mantova · Ferrara · Bologna · Ravenna · Rimini · Forlì · Modena · Reggio nell'Emilia · Parma · Piacenza · Alessandria · Genova (Genoa) · La Spezia · Carrara · San Marino · SAN MARINO · Ancona · Split · Mostar · Hercegovina

Ligurian Sea · Genova · Pisa · Livorno · Firenze (Florence) · Prato · Arezzo · Siena · Perugia · Assisi · Zadar · Šibenik

Corse (Corsica) (Fr.) · Bastia · Ajaccio · Grosseto · Elba · Terni · Rieti · Pescara · Chieti · Vasto · Foggia · Dubrovnik

ROMA (ROME) · VATICAN STATE (CITTÀ DEL VATICANO) · ITALY (ITALIA) · L'Aquila · Avezzano · Bari · Mola di Bari · Monopoli · Brindisi · Taranto · Lecce

Sardegna (Sardinia) · Sassari · Nuoro · Oristano · Cagliari · Carbonia

Napoli (Naples) · Pozzuoli · Salerno · Benevento · Avellino · Caserta · Matera · Penisola Salentina · Golfo di Taranto

Tyrrhenian Sea · Cosenza · Catanzaro · Lamezia · Crotone

Stromboli · Isole Eolie o Lipari · Lipari · Vibo Valentia · Reggio di Calabria · Messina · Milazzo

Sicilia (Sicily) · Palermo · Bagheria · Trapani · Marsala · Agrigento · Gela · Caltanissetta · Enna · Catania · Siracusa · Ragusa · Modica · Etna

MEDITERRANEAN SEA · Ionian Sea · Adriatic Sea

Banzart (Bizerta) · TUNIS · TUNISIA · Annaba · Skikda · Constantine

MALTA · VALLETTA · Gozo · Pantelleria (Italy) · Canale di Malta · Canale di Sicilia

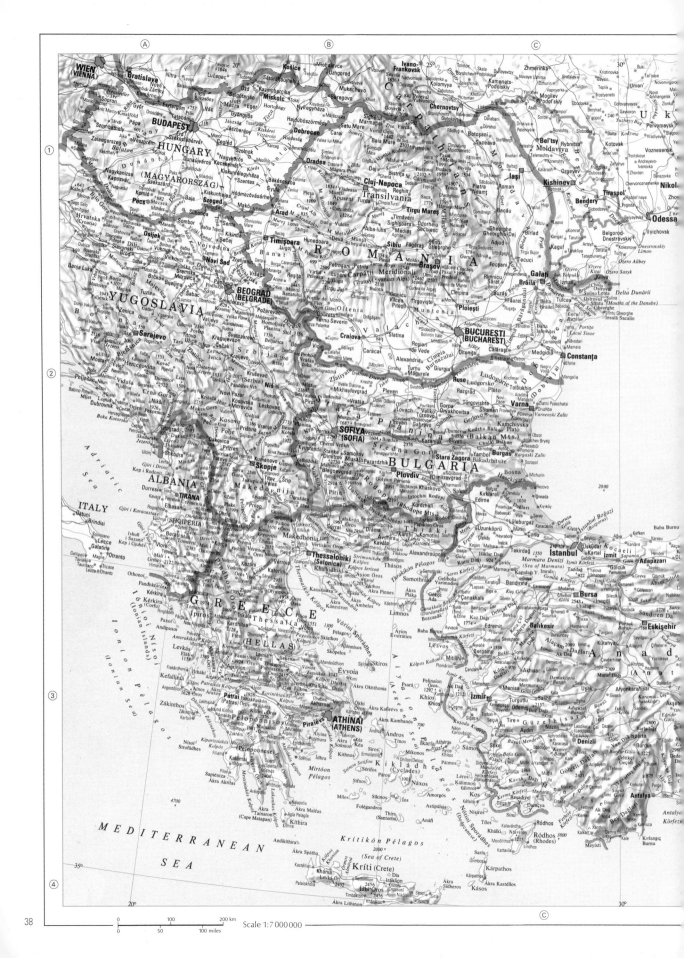

Scale 1:7 000 000

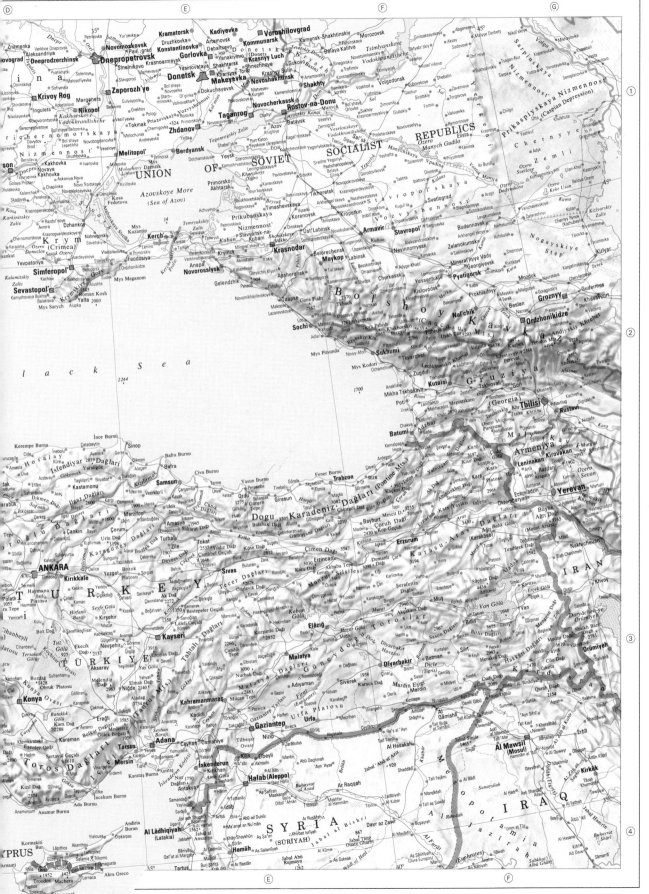

Pole

① ② ③ ④ ⑤

80° 70° 180° 60° 50°

Bering Strait
Chukotsk
Saint Lawrence I.
Peninsula
Providenya
Wrangel I.
Anadyr

OCEAN

East Siberian Sea

New Siberian Islands

3800

C. Chelyuskin

Laptev Sea

Pevek
Ambarchik

Koryak Range

Bering Sea

Aleutian Trench

Aleutian Islands (U.S.A.)

40°

Khatanga

Indigirka R.
Kolyma R.

Cheresky Range

Kamchatka

Komandorski Islands (Komandorskiye Ostrova) O. Medny

Central Siberian Plateau

R. Lena
Vilyuy R.
R. Lena
Yakutsk

Verkhoyansk Range

Kolyma Range

Petropavlovsk Kamchatskiy
Severo Kurilsk

Dzhugdzhur Range

PACIFIC

170°

1710
Lower Tunguska R.
Tura
Mirnyy
Lensk

Stanovoy Range

Sea of Okhotsk

2412
Okha
Nikolayevsk na Amure

Tunguska R.
R. Angara
Ust Kut
Kirensk

Great Khingan Mts

Aleksandrovsk
Sakhalin
Yuzhno Sakhalinsk

Kuril Islands

Japan Trench

30°

OCEAN

Kansk
Krasnoyarsk

SOCIALIST REPUBLIC

R. Angara
Bratsk
Cheremkhovo
Irkutsk
L. Baykal
Chita

Skovorodino
Blagoveshchensk
Svobodny
Belogorsk
Khabarovsk

Amur R.
Heilong Jiang

Soya Strait
Wakkanai
Asahikawa
Sapporo
Hokkaido
Hakodate

2290

SOCIALIST REPUBLICS

Sukhbaatar
ULAAN BAATAR

R. Selenga
R. Keralen

Hailar
Qiqihar

Manchuria

Sungari R.
Harbin
Changchun
Jilin
Mudanjiang
Vladivostok
Chongjin

Aomori
Akita
Sendai

Sea of Japan

JAPAN

Honshu

Niigata
Utsunomiya
TOKYO
Yokohama

7222

MONGOLIA

Gobi

Dalandzadgad

Nei Monggol (Inner Mongolia)
Hohhot
Zhangjiakou
BEIJING (PEKING)
Tangshan

Shenyang
Fushun
Benxi
Anshan
Dandong
PYONGYANG
NORTH KOREA
SEOUL
SOUTH KOREA
Taejon

Kyoto
Nagoya
Kobe
Osaka
Kitakyushu
Hiroshima
Matsuyama
Shikoku

Baotou
Datong

Tianjin
Lüda
Taegu
Pusan

Fukuoka
Kyushu

Ordos Plateau
Shijiazhuang
Qingdao

Yellow Sea

Kwangju
Nagasaki
Kagoshima

Taiyuan
Handan
Jinan
Lianyungang

Yellow R. Huang He

Yumen
Zhangye

Yinchuan
Yanan
Xinxiang
Kaifeng

Xining
Lanzhou
Xianyang

Luoyang
Zhengzhou
Xuzhou
Zhenjiang

CHINA

Baoji
Xian

Huainan
Nanjing
Wuxi
Shanghai

East China Sea

Ryukyu Islands

Naha
7507

Wuhan
Yangtze Kiang

Ningbo

Chengdu
Red Basin
Chongqing
Dongting Hu
Changsha
Nanchang
Wenzhou

Zigong
Luzhou
Zunyi
Hengyang
Fuzhou
TAIPEI

Nan Ling
Guiyang

TAIWAN
Kaohsiung

Kunming
Liuzhou
Guilin
Xiamen
Tainan
Kaohsiung

Nanning
Guangzhou
Shantou
Hong Kong (U.K.)
Macao (Port.)

Baoshan
Zhanjiang

Luzon Strait
Laoag
PHILIPPINES

BURMA
VIETNAM HANOI
Mandalay
LAOS
Haiphong

Tropic of Cancer

Ramapo Deep
10374

Bonin Is. (Japan)

20°

Kazan Is. (Japan)
Iwo Jima

150°

Mariana Trench
Mariana Islands (Adm. by U.S.A.)

Guam I. (U.S.A.)

140°

11034
Challenger Deep

⑥ ⑦ ⑧

130° 120° 110° 100° 140°

Ⓜ Ⓝ Ⓞ Ⓟ Ⓠ Ⓡ

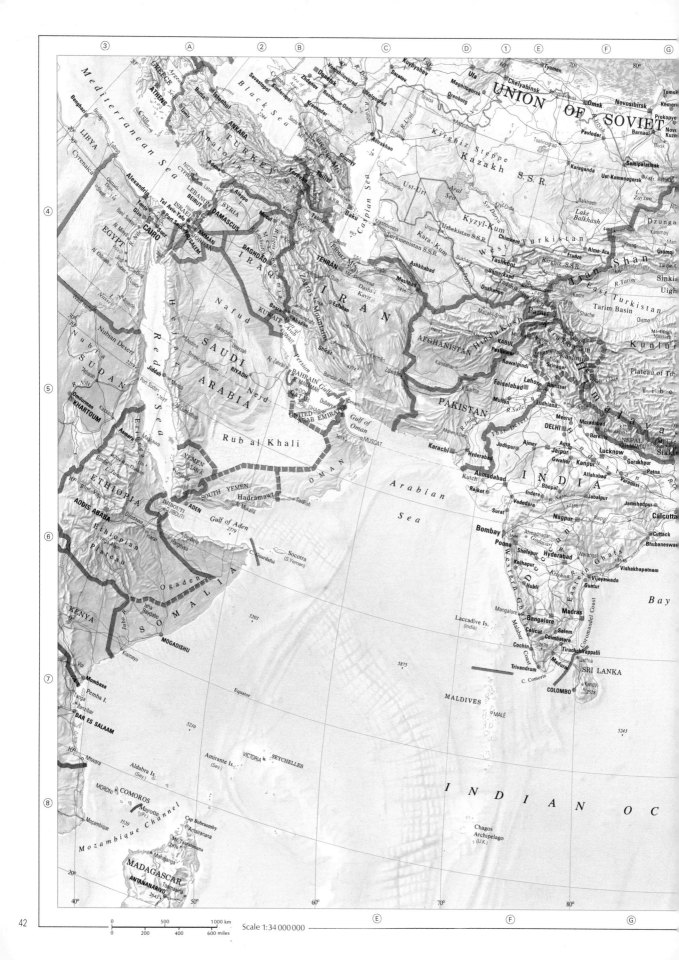

H J K L 1 L M N 2 O 3

CIALIST REPUBLICS

R. Angara
Kirensk
Ust-Kut
R. Lena
R. Shilka
R. Argun
Komsomolsk
na-Amure
Nikolayevsk
Gizhiga

Krasnoyarsk
Bratsk
L. Baykal
Chita
Heilong Jiang
Amur R.
Svobodnyy
Selemdzha
Stanovoy
Sakhalin I.
Soya Strait
Wakkana

an Ranges
Cheremkhovo
Angarsk
Ulan Ude
Kyakhta
Yablonovyy Range
Borzya
Nerchinsk
Blagoveshchensk
Bureya
Sikhote Alin
Khabarovsk
Yuzhno
Sakhalinsk
Asahikawa
Sapporo
HOKKAIDO
Hakodate

Irkutsk
Qiqihar
Sumari R.
Jiamusi
Nakhodka
Vladivostok
Aomori
Akita
Sendai

MONGOLIA
Saynshand
Changchun
Jilin
Chongjin
Niigata
Utsunomiya
Honshu
TOKYO
Yokohama

ULAAN BAATAR
Gobi
Nei Monggol (Inner Mongolia)
Shenyang
Anshan
Dandong
NORTH KOREA
PYONGYANG
Sea of Japan
JAPAN
Nagoya
Kyoto
Osaka

Dalandzadgad
Hohhot
Zhangjiakou
BEIJING (PEKING)
Tangshan
Luda
SEOUL
SOUTH KOREA
Taegu
Pusan
Kitakyushu
Hiroshima
Shikoku
Matsuyama

Baotou
Datong
Tianjin
Yellow Sea
Taejon
Fukuoka
Kyushu
Nagasaki
Kagoshima

Ordos Plateau
Yinchuan
Taiyuan
Shijiazhuang
Jinan
Qingdao
Lianyungang
Kwangju

Yumen
Zhangye
Huang Ho
Handan
Grand Canal
Bonin Is. (Japan)

Nan Shan
Koko Nor
Xining
Lanzhou
Xinxiang
Kaifeng
Zhengzhou
Xuzhou
Zhenjiang
Kazan Is. (Japan)
Iwo Jima

Tsaidam
Xianyang
Xian
Luoyang
Huainan
Nanjing
Wuxi
Shanghai

Bayan Har Shan
CHINA
Baoji
Wuhan
Yangtze Kiang
Hangzhou
Ningbo
East China Sea
PACIFIC

Chengdu
Red Basin
Nanchong
Yichang
Nanchang
Dongting Hu
Changsha
Wenzhou
Naha
OCEAN

Zigong
Chongqing
Mariana Islands (Adm. by U.S.A.)

Kunming
Guiyang
Nan Ling
Hengyang
Fuzhou
TAIPEI
Ryukyu Islands
Tropic of Cancer
Mariana Trench

Baoshan
Liuzhou
Guilin
Xiamen
TAIWAN
Guam I. (U.S.A.)

Gejiu
Nanning
Guangzhou
Shantou
Kaohsiung
Tainan

BURMA
Mandalay
HANOI
Haiphong
Hong Kong (U.K.)
Macao (Port.)
Zhanjiang
Luzon Strait
Challenger Deep
Ulithi
Trust Territory of the Pacific Islands (Adm. by U.S.A.)
Yap Is.
Sorol

RANGOON
THAILAND
VIETNAM
Gulf of Tonkin
Hainan
Paracel Islands (China)
Luzon
Cabanatuan
Quezon City
Palau Is.
Koror

Bassein
Moulmein
VIENTIANE
Savannakhet
Da Nang
Hue
Angeles
MANILA
Mindoro
PHILIPPINES
Palau (Adm. by U.S.A.)

Chiang Mai
Nakhon Ratchasima
Qui Nhon
South China Sea
Panay
Samar
Philippine Trench

Thon Buri
BANGKOK
KAMPUCHEA
Tonle Sap
Da Lat
Iloilo
Bacolod
Leyte
Cebu

Gulf of Thailand
PHNOM PENH
Ho Chi Minh (Saigon)
Palawan
Negros
Mindanao
Davao

Isthmus of Kra
Cape Ca Mau
Sulu Sea
Zamboanga
Basilan City

Andaman Sea
Surat Thani
Songkhla
Kota Kinabalu
Mt. Kinabalu
Sandakan
Sulu Archipelago
Celebes Sea
Halmahera
West Irian
Macke Mts.
New Guinea

Nicobar Is. (India)
Alor Setar
Kota Baharu
BANDAR SERI BEGAWAN
Sabah
BRUNEI
Manado
Ternate
Jayapura

George Town
MALAYSIA
Natuna Is. (Indonesia)
Kuching
Sarawak
Celebes
Molucca
Buru
Ceram
Aru Is.
Kolepom I.

Banda Aceh
Medan
Malaya
KUALA LUMPUR
Johor Baharu
Anambas I. (Indonesia)
Samarinda
Ambon
Banda Sea
Tanimbar Is.

Nias
Pematangsiantar
Melaka
SINGAPORE
Borneo
Balikpapan
INDONESIA
Arafura Sea

Bukittinggi
Pekanbaru
Pontianak
Greater Sunda Islands
Ujungpandang
Banda Sea
Cape Arnhem

Padang
Jambi
Banjarmasin
Flores Sea
Dili
Cape Arnhem

Mentawai Is.
Palembang
Belitung
Java Sea
Flores
Ende
Timor
Arnhem Land
AUSTRALIA

Bangka
JAKARTA
Semarang
Surabaya
Singaraja
Sumbawa
Lesser Sunda Islands
Kupang
Timor Sea
Darwin
Northern Territory

Krakatau
Bandung
Java
Yogyakarta
Bali
Lombok
Sumba
Cape Londonderry
Wyndham
Daly Waters

Christmas Island (Austr.)
Java Trench
Mount Isa
Tennant Creek

100°   110°   120°   130°

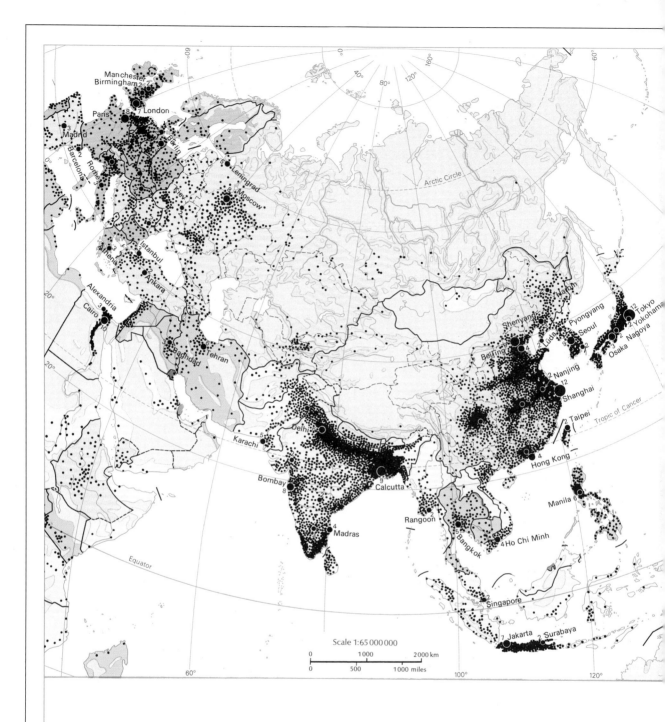

Manchester 2
Birmingham 2 2
Paris 8 7 London
Madrid 3
Barcelona 2
Rome 3
Berlin
Athens 3
Istanbul
Ankara 2
Leningrad 5
Moscow
Kiev
Alexandria
Cairo 3
10
Baghdad 3
Tehran
Karachi 5
Delhi
Bombay
8
Calcutta 9
Madras 4
Rangoon 4
Bangkok 5
Ho Chi Minh 4
Singapore
Jakarta 7
Surabaya 2
Harbin
Shenyang
Beijing
Luda
Pyongyang
Seoul 9
Nanjing 2
Shanghai 12
Taipei 2
Hong Kong 4
Manila 6
Tokyo 12
Yokohama 2
Nagoya 3
Osaka

Arctic Circle

Tropic of Cancer

Equator

Scale 1:65 000 000

| 0 | 1000 | 2000 km |
| 0 | 500 | 1000 miles |

POPULATION

Population
distribution 1985

· 500 000 inhabitants

●3 Figures show populations
(cities with suburbs) in millions

uninhabited (less than
1 person per sq. km)

Population increase
per country 1975–1985

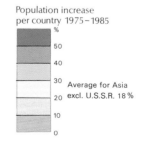

%
50
40
30   Average for Asia
20   excl. U.S.S.R. 18 %
10
0

POLITICAL DIVISIONS

Republics of the U.S.S.R.

1 Russian S.F.S.R.
2 Estonian S.S.R.
3 Latvian S.S.R.
4 Lithuanian S.S.R.
5 Belorussian S.S.R.
6 Ukrainian S.S.R.
7 Moldavian S.S.R.
8 Georgian S.S.R.
9 Armenian S.S.R.
10 Azerbaijan S.S.R.
11 Kazakh S.S.R.

12 Uzbek S.S.R.
13 Turkmen S.S.R.
14 Tadzhik S.S.R.
15 Kirgiz S.S.R.

Administrative regions in China
(Zizhiqu = Autonomous region)

1 Xinjiang Uygur Zizhiqu
2 Xizang Zizhiqu (Tibet)
3 Qinghai

4 Gansu
5 Nei Monggol Zizhiqu
6 Heilongjiang
7 Jilin
8 Liaoning
9 Hebei
10 Beijing Shi
11 Shanxi
12 Shaanxi
13 Ningxia Huizu Zizhiqu
14 Sichuan
15 Hubei
16 Henan

17 Shandong
18 Jiangsu
19 Anhui
20 Shanghai Shi
21 Zhejiang
22 Fujian
23 Jiangxi
24 Hunan
25 Guizhou
26 Yunnan
27 Guangxi Zhuangzu Zizhiqu
28 Guangdong
29 Tianjin Shi

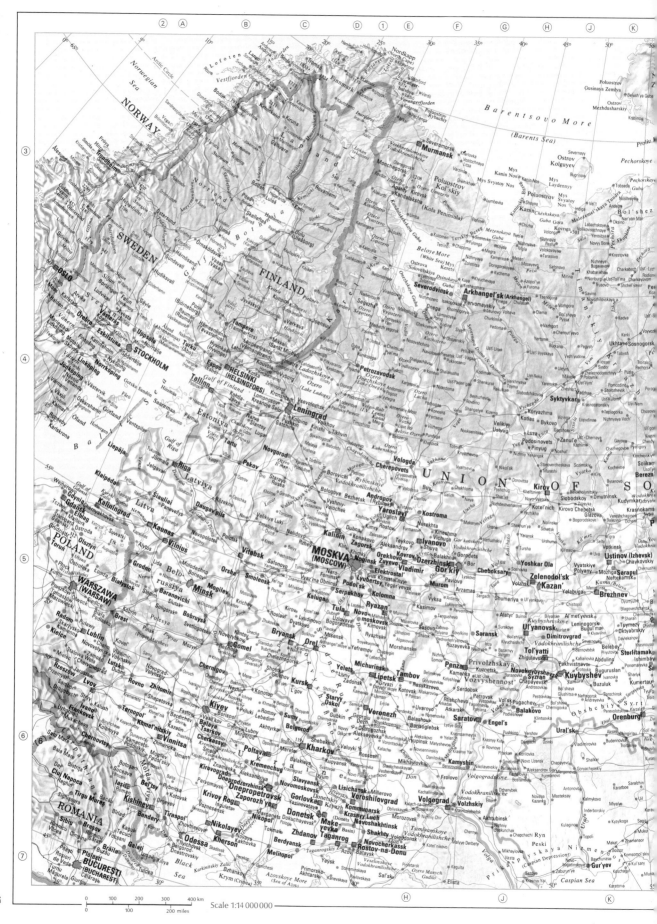

Scale 1:14 000 000

SOCIALIST REPUBLICS

Zapadno Sibirskoye Nizmennost'

(West Siberian Plain)

Sredne Sibirskoye Ploskogor'ye (Central Siberian Plateau)

Poluostrov Yamal (Yamal Peninsula)

Gydanskiy Poluostrov

Obskaya Guba (Gulf of Ob)

Skoye More (Kara Sea)

K A Z A K H S T A N

(Kirghiz Steppe)

Betpak-Dala

Kazakhskiy Melkosopochnik

Turgayskaya Stolovaya Strana

Barabinskaya Step'

Ishimskaya Step'

Kulundinskaya Step'

A L T A Y

T i a n S h a n

M O N G O L I A

C H I N A

Major places: Noril'sk · Vorkuta · Surgut · Nizhnevartovskoye · Khanty-Mansiysk · Nefteyugansk · Tobol'sk · Serov · Krasnotur'insk · Nizhniy Tagil · Sverdlovsk · Kamensk-Ural'skiy · Kurgan · Chelyabinsk · Kopeysk · Miass · Zlatoust · Troitsk · Kustanay · Rudnyy · Orsk · Novotroitsk · Tyumen · Omsk · Petropavlovsk · Tselinograd · Temirtau · Karaganda · Shakhtinsk · Pavlodar · Tatarsk · Barnaul · Biysk · Rubtsovsk · Semipalatinsk · Ust-Kamenogorsk · Tomsk · Kemerovo · Novosibirsk · Berdsk · Leninsk-Kuznetsk · Novokuznetsk · Prokop'yevsk · Kiselevsk · Belovo · Anzhero-Sudzhensk · Achinsk · Krasnoyarsk · Kansk · Abakan · Balkhash · Dzhezkazgan · Alma-Ata · Talgar · Przheval'sk

Ozero Balkhash · Ozero Tengiz · Ozero Chany · Ozero Zaysan · Aral'skoye More (Aral Sea)

Arctic Circle

© ESSELTE MAP SERVICE

47

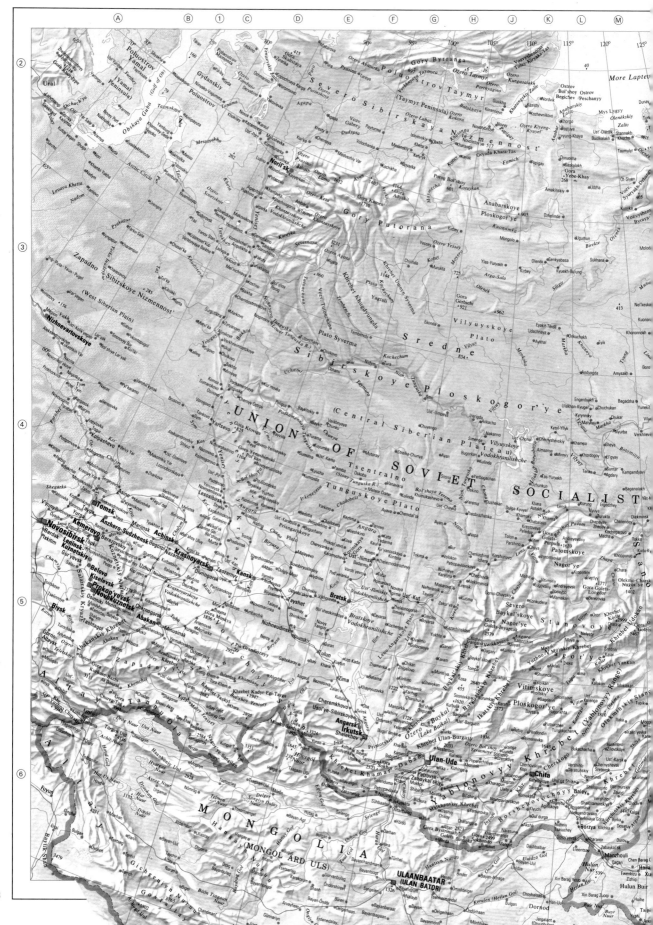

Vostochno Sibirskoye More
(East Siberian Sea)

Ostrov Kotel'nyy
Lyakhovskiye Ostrova
O. Malyy Lyakhovskiy
O. Bol'shoy Lyakhovskiy

Ostrov Semenovskiy

Mys Svatoy Nos

Yana-Indigirskaya Nizmennost'

Khrebet Polousnyy

Indigirskaya Nizmennost'

Alazeyskoye Ploskogor'ye

K o l y m s k a y a   N i z m e n n o s t'

Yukagirskoye Ploskogor'ye

Severnyy Anyuyskiy Khrebet

Yuzhnyy Anyuyskiy Khrebet

Oloyskiye Gory

Gory Ushurakchan

Anyuyskiy Zaliv

Arctic Circle

Khrebet Kolymskiy (Kolyma Range)

Khrebet Cherskogo
(Chersky Range)

Momskiy Khrebet

Verkhoyanskiy Khrebet

Khrebet Orulgan

Khrebet Suntar Khayata

Khrebet Dzhugdzhur

Khrebet (Stanovoy Range)

Penzhinskiy Khrebet

Koryakskiy Khrebet

Bering Sea

Zaliv Shelikhova

Zaliv Kresta

Magadan

Yakutsk

E P U B L I C S

Poluostrov Kamchatka

Petropavlovsk-Kamchatskiy

Okhotskoye More
(Sea of Okhotsk)

Ostrov Iony

Shantarskiye Ostrova

Khrebet Dzhagdy

Khrebet Bureinskiy

Khrebet Turana

Sikhote Alin

Sakhalin

Komsomol'sk-na-Amure

Svobodnyy
Belogorsk

Blagoveshchensk

Raychikhinsk

Khabarovsk

Nikolayevsk-na-Amure

Zaliv Akademii

Tatarskiy Proliv

Kuril'skiye Ostrova (Kuril Islands)

Kuril'skiy Proliv

O. Paramushir

O. Onekotan

O. Urup

O. Iturup

Yuzhno-Sakhalinsk

Kholmsk

Mys Aniva

C H I N A

Xiao Hinggan Ling (Lesser Khingan Mts)

Qiqihar
Hegang

Yilehuli Shan

Heilong Jiang

© ESSELTE MAP SERVICE

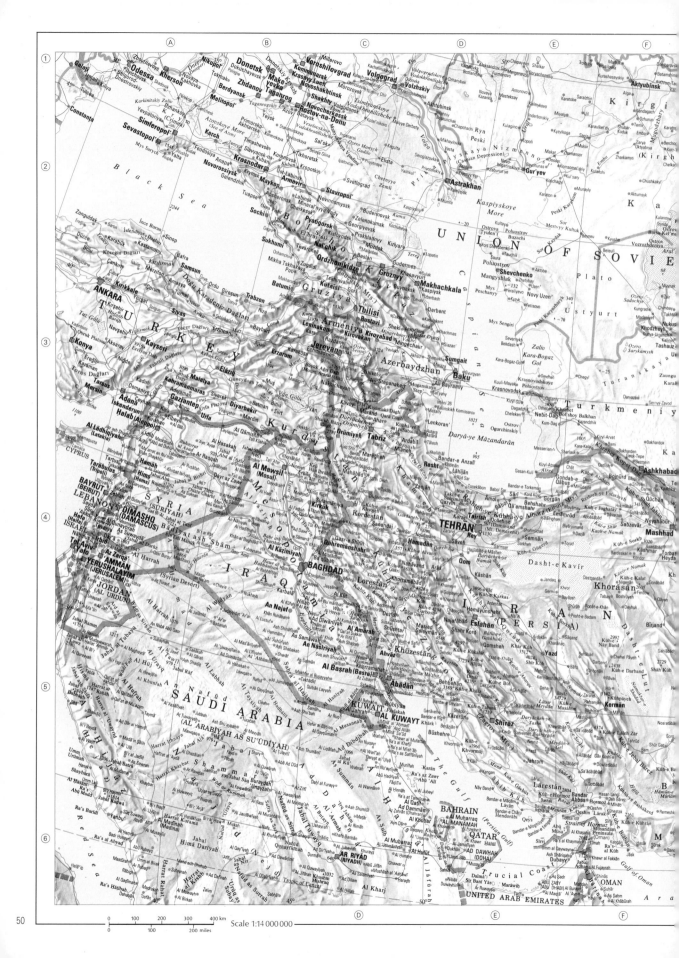

Scale 1:14 000 000

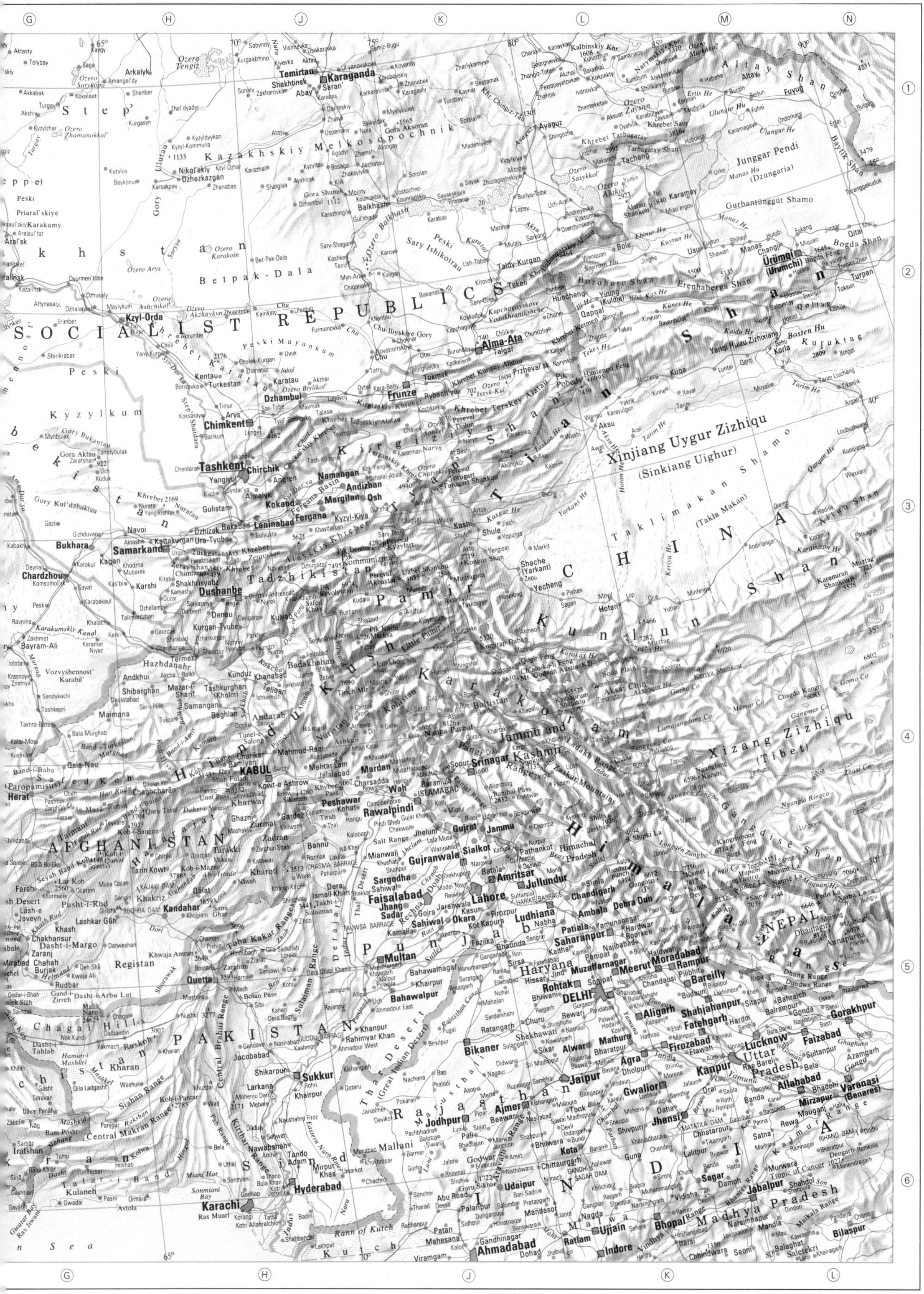

G H J K L M N

① ② ③ ④ ⑤ ⑥

SOCIALIST REPUBLICS

Step'

Kazakhskiy Melkosopochnik

Betpak-Dala

Peski Muyunkum

Kyzylkum

Peski Karakumy

Aral'sk

Temirtau **Karaganda**
Shakhtinsk Saran

Kzyl-Orda

Chimkent

Tashkent Chirchik

Frunze

Alma-Ata

Dzhambul

Namangan Andizhan
Kokand Margilan Osh
Fergana

Samarkand Leninabad

Bukhara

Chardzhou

Dushanbe

Kurgan-Tyube

Tadzhikistan

Pamir

Termez

Kabul

AFGHANISTAN

Herat

Kandahar

Quetta

PAKISTAN

Peshawar

Rawalpindi **ISLAMABAD**

Srinagar Jammu and Kashmir

Lahore

Faisalabad

Multan

Gujranwala Sialkot

Amritsar **Jullundur**
Ludhiana

Chandigarh

Himachal Pradesh

Punjab

Haryana

DELHI

Bikaner

Jaipur

Jodhpur

Rajasthan

Ajmer

Agra

Gwalior

Jhansi

Kanpur

Lucknow Faizabad

Uttar Pradesh

Allahabad

Varanasi (Benares)

Gorakhpur

NEPAL

CHINA

Xinjiang Uygur Zizhiqu
(Sinkiang Uighur)

Taklimakan Shamo
(Takla Makan)

Ürümqi (Urumchi)

Turpan

Kunlun Shan

Xizang Zizhiqu (Tibet)

Kun Lun Shan

Karakoram

Hindu Kush

Himalaya

Ahmadabad

Indore

Bhopal

Ujjain

Ratlam

Udaipur

Madhya Pradesh

Tropic of Cancer

Hyderabad

Karachi

Sukkur

Thar Desert

Great Indian Desert

Bahawalpur

Rann of Kutch

Kutch

Arabian Sea

INDIA

Altay Shan

Junggar Pendi (Dzungaria)

Tien Shan

Issyk-Kul

Balkhash

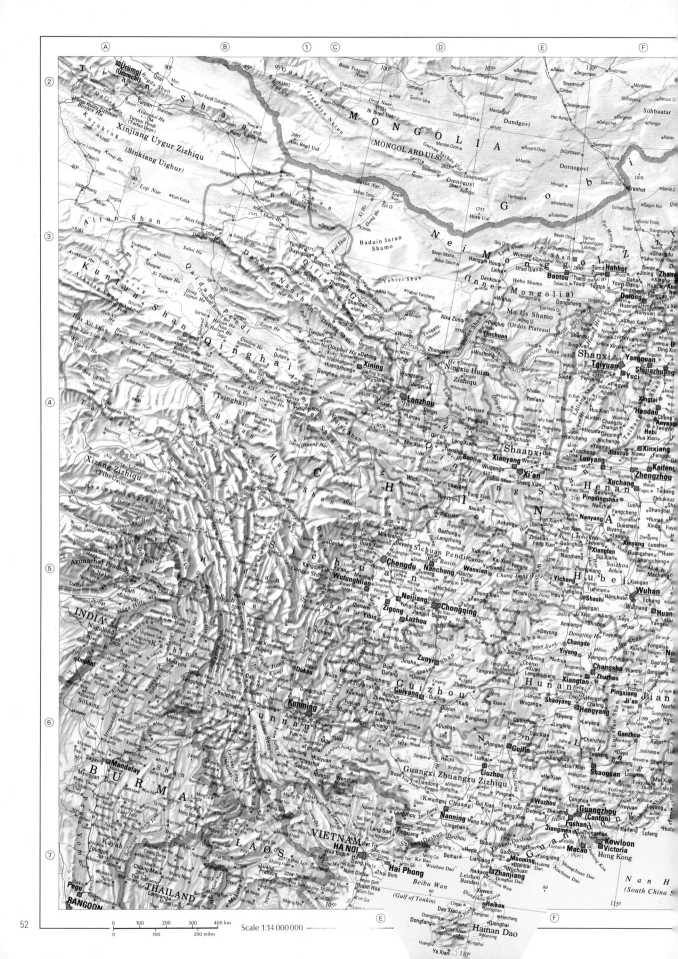

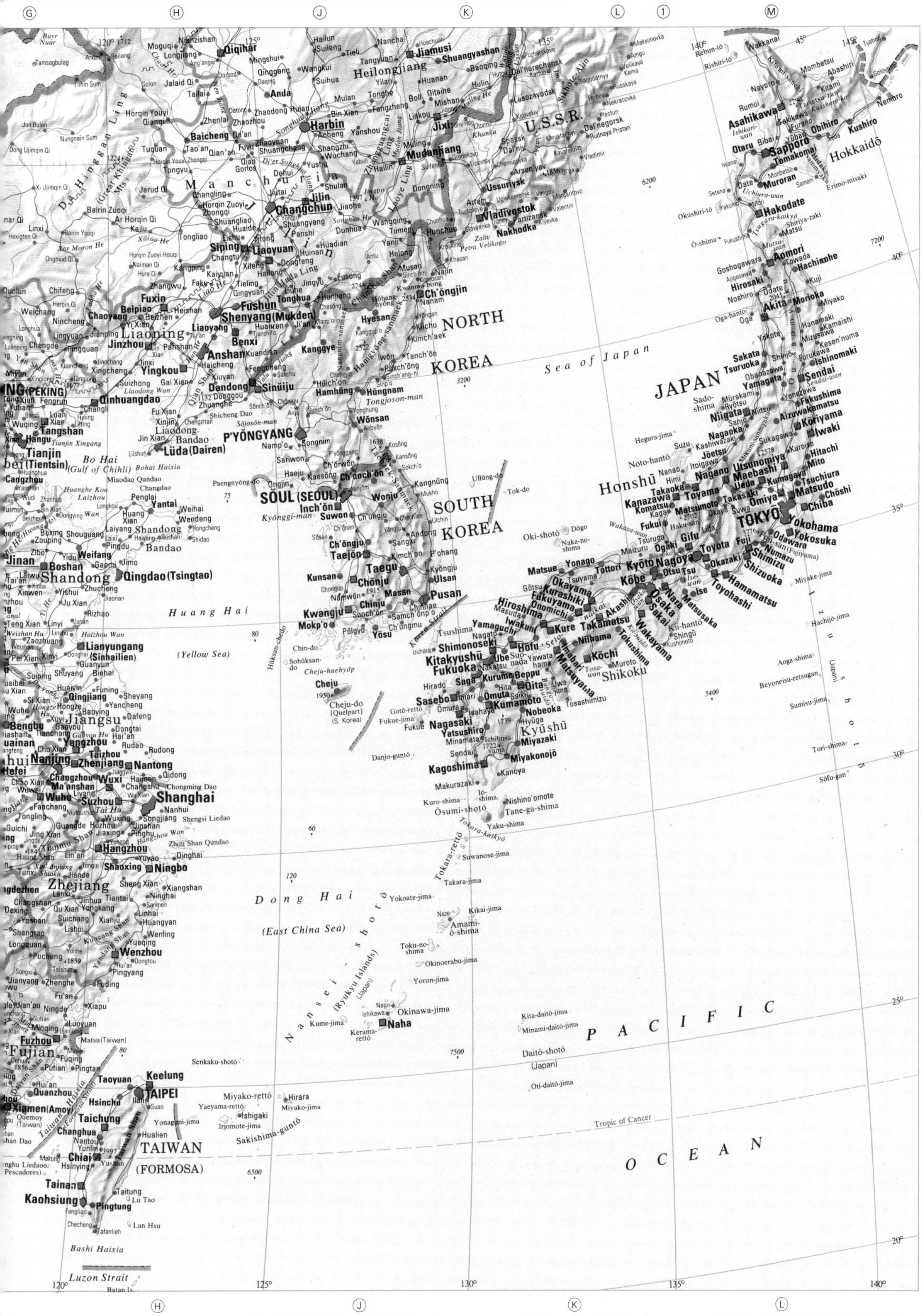

CHINA AND JAPAN

Qiqihar • Jiamusi • Shuangyashan
Heilongjiang
Harbin
Baicheng • Da'an
Manchuria
Jilin
Changchun
Siping • Liaoyuan
Mudanjiang
U.S.S.R.
Vladivostok
Nakhodka
Ch'ŏngjin

Fushun • Shenyang (Mukden)
Liaoning
Anshan
Jinzhou • Benxi
Yingkou
Dandong
Sinŭiju
Hamhŭng • Hŭngnam
NORTH KOREA

Wakkanai
Asahikawa
Otaru • Sapporo
Tomakomai
Hokkaidō
Muroran
Hakodate
Aomori
Hirosaki • Morioka
Akita

JAPAN
Sakata
Tsuruoka • Sendai
Fukushima
Niigata
Aizuwakamatsu • Kōriyama
Honshū
Nagaoka • Iwaki
Nagano • Utsunomiya
Maebashi • Mito
TOKYO
Kanazawa • Toyama
Matsumoto
Kōfu • Chiba
Yokohama
Nagoya • Yokosuka
Kyōto • Gifu • Shizuoka
Ōsaka • Hamamatsu
Kōbe • Nara • Toyohashi

P'YŎNGYANG
Namp'o
Haeju
Kaesŏng • Ch'unch'ŏn
SEOUL (SŎUL)
Inch'ŏn • Suwŏn
SOUTH KOREA
Wŏnju
Taejŏn
Kwangju • Taegu
Pusan
Masan
Mokp'o • Chinju
Yŏsu

Bo Hai (Gulf of Chihli)
Tianjin (Tientsin)
Tangshan
Cangzhou
Huang Hai (Yellow Sea)
Shandong
Qingdao (Tsingtao)
Jinan • Weifang
Boshan
Bandao
Lianyungang (Sinhailien)

Honshū
Matsue • Yonago
Okayama
Hiroshima
Fukuyama • Onomichi
Kure • Takamatsu
Shikoku
Kitakyūshū
Fukuoka • Kōchi
Saga • Kurume • Ōita
Sasebo • Kumamoto
Nagasaki • Miyazaki
Kyūshū
Kagoshima
Miyakonojō

Jiangsu
Nanjing
Yangzhou • Zhenjiang • Nantong
Wuxi
Shanghai
Suzhou
Hangzhou
Zhejiang
Shaoxing • Ningbo
Wenzhou

Dong Hai (East China Sea)

Nansei-shotō (Ryukyu Islands)
Amami-ō-shima
Okinawa-jima
Naha

PACIFIC OCEAN

Fujian
Fuzhou
Quanzhou
Xiamen (Amoy)
Keelung
TAIPEI
Hsinchu
Taichung
Changhua
TAIWAN (FORMOSA)
Tainan
Kaohsiung
Pingtung

Sea of Japan

Tropic of Cancer

Luzon Strait

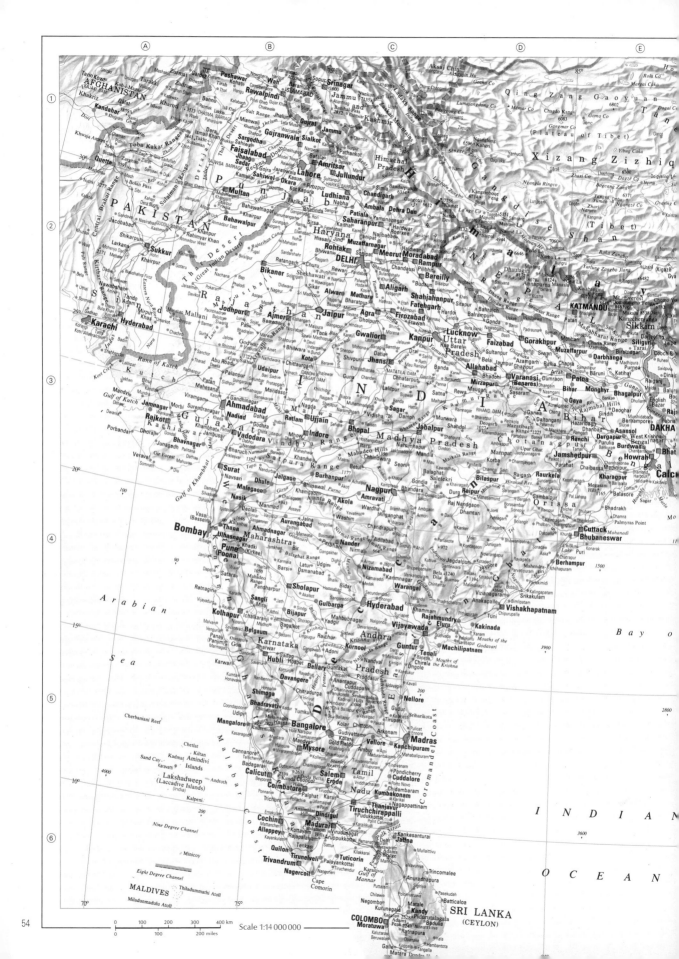

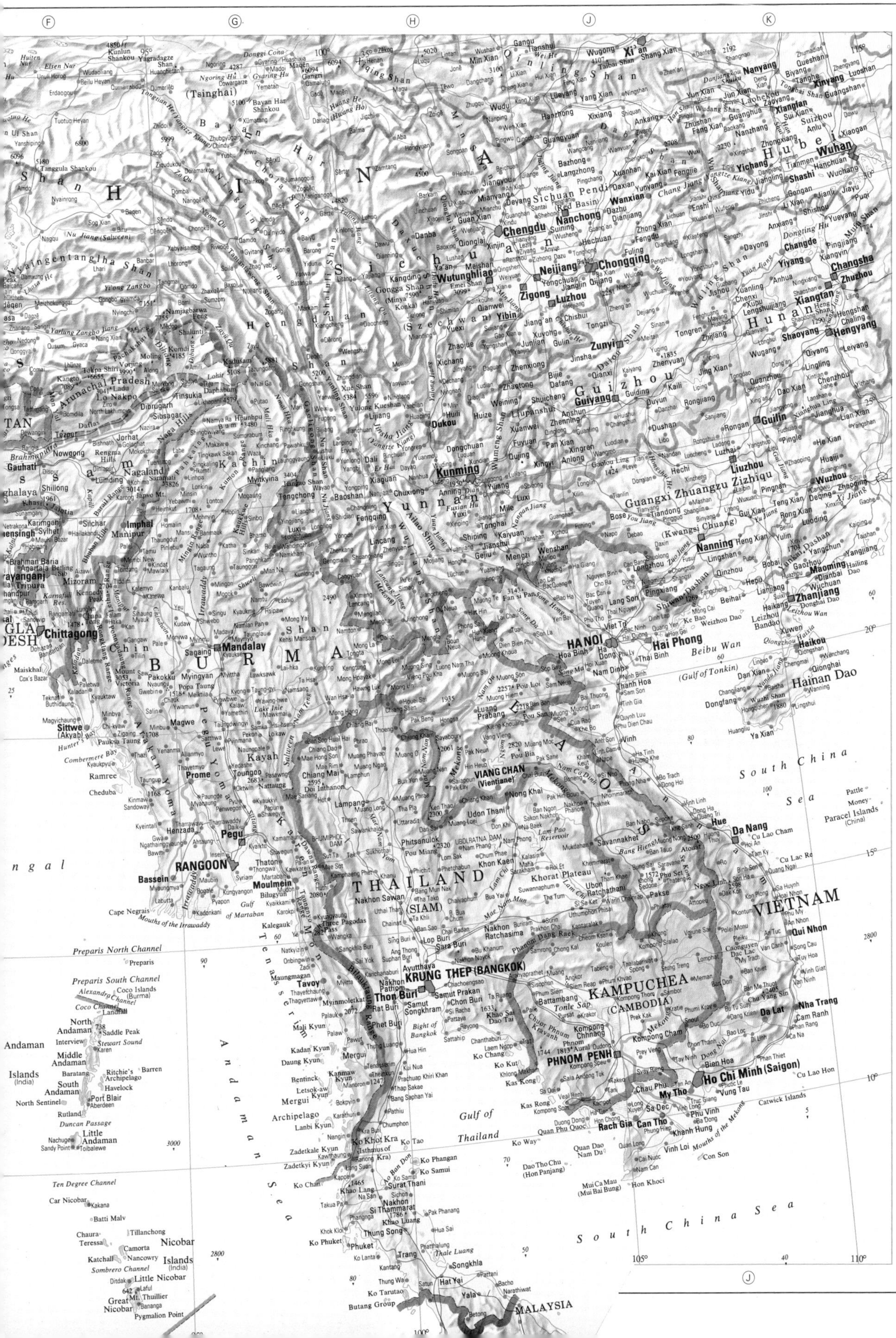

CHINA

Shan

(Tsinghai)

Sichuan (Szechwan)

Chengdu **Chongqing** **Neijiang** **Zigong** **Luzhou** **Wutunghliao**

Hubei **Wuhan** **Yichang** **Shashi** **Changde** **Changsha** **Xiangtan** **Zhuzhou** **Hengyang** **Hengshan** **Shaoyang**

Hunan

Guizhou **Guiyang** Zunyi **Dukou** **Kunming** Yunnan

Guilin Guangxi Zhuangzu Zizhiqu (Kwangsi Chuang) **Liuzhou** **Wuzhou** **Nanning** **Zhanjiang** **Beihai**

Maoming

Hainan Dao **Haikou**

Beibu Wan (Gulf of Tonkin)

Arunachal Pradesh Assam **Gauhati** **Shillong** Meghalaya Nagaland Manipur **Imphal** Mizoram Tripura

Chittagong Chin BANGLADESH **Sittwe (Akyab)**

BURMA **Mandalay** Sagaing Kachin **Myitkyina** Shan Kayah

Magwe **Prome** **Pegu** **RANGOON** **Bassein** **Moulmein** **Thaton**

Arakan Yoma

Andaman Islands (India) North Andaman Middle Andaman South Andaman **Port Blair**

Preparis North Channel Preparis South Channel Coco Channel Coco Islands (Burma)

Andaman Sea

Mergui Archipelago **Tavoy** **Mergui**

THAILAND (SIAM) **Chiang Mai** **Lampang** **Phitsanulok** **Nakhon Sawan** **KRUNG THEP (BANGKOK)** **Thon Buri** **Phet Buri** Khorat Plateau **Nakhon Ratchasima** **Ubon** **Khon Kaen**

Gulf of Thailand

LAOS **VIANG CHAN (Vientiane)** **Savannakhet** **Pakse**

VIETNAM **HANOI** **Hai Phong** **Thanh Hoa** **Vinh** **Hue** **Da Nang** **Qui Nhon** **Nha Trang** **Da Lat** **Ho Chi Minh (Saigon)** **Vung Tau**

Hoa Binh **Nam Dinh** **Lang Son**

KAMPUCHEA (CAMBODIA) **PHNOM PENH** **Battambang** **Kompong Cham** **Kompong Chhnang** Tonle Sap

My Tho **Rach Gia** **Can Tho** **Chau Phu** **Sa Dec**

Mouths of the Mekong Mui Ca Mau (Mui Bai Bung)

South China Sea

Paracel Islands (China)

Nicobar Islands (India) Car Nicobar Little Nicobar Great Nicobar Ten Degree Channel Sombrero Channel

Phuket **Ko Samui** **Surat Thani** **Nakhon Si Thammarat** **Songkhla** **Hat Yai**

MALAYSIA

Bay of Bengal

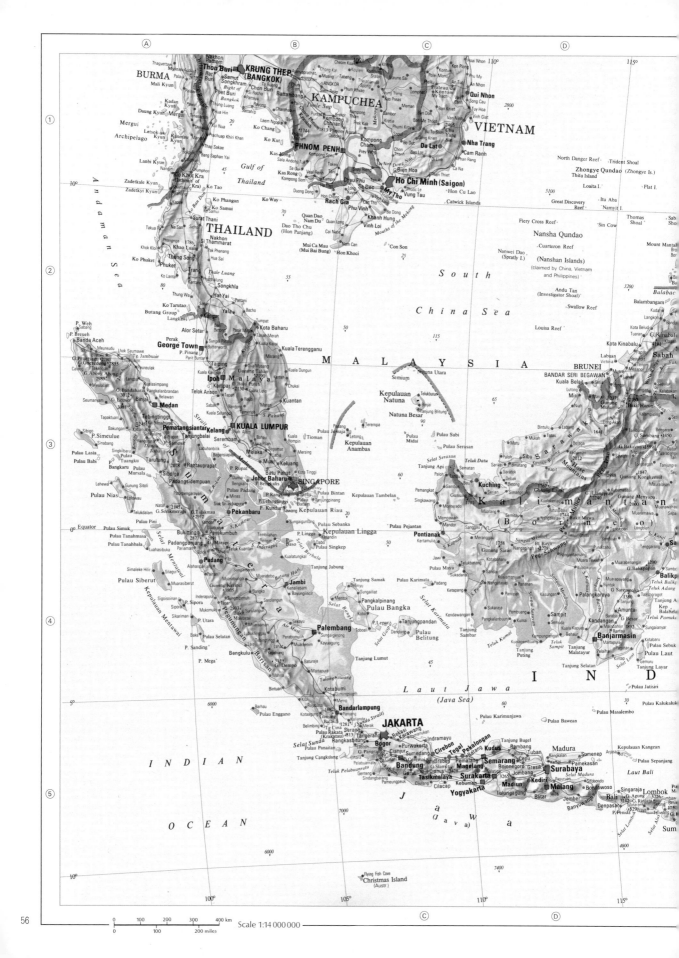

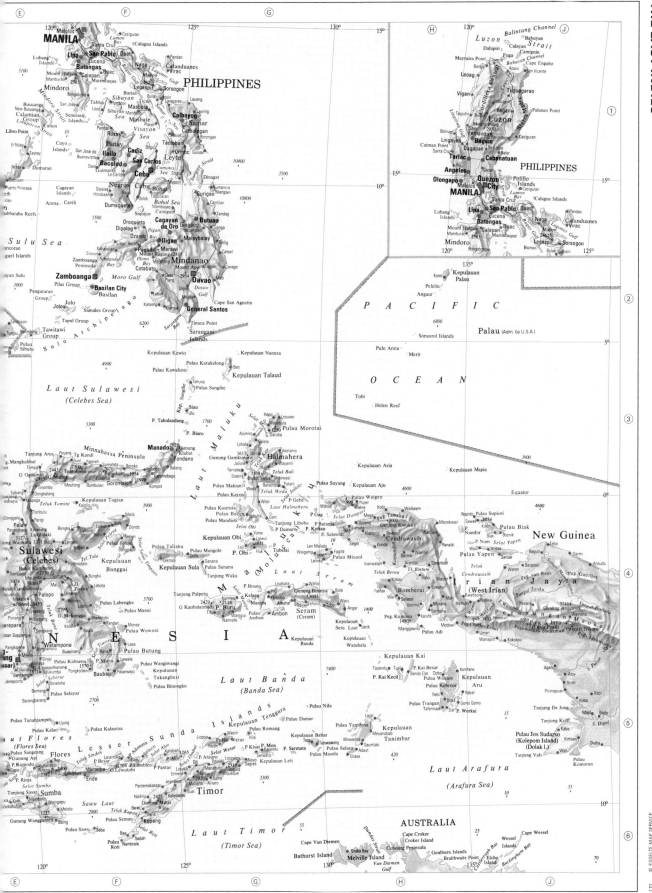

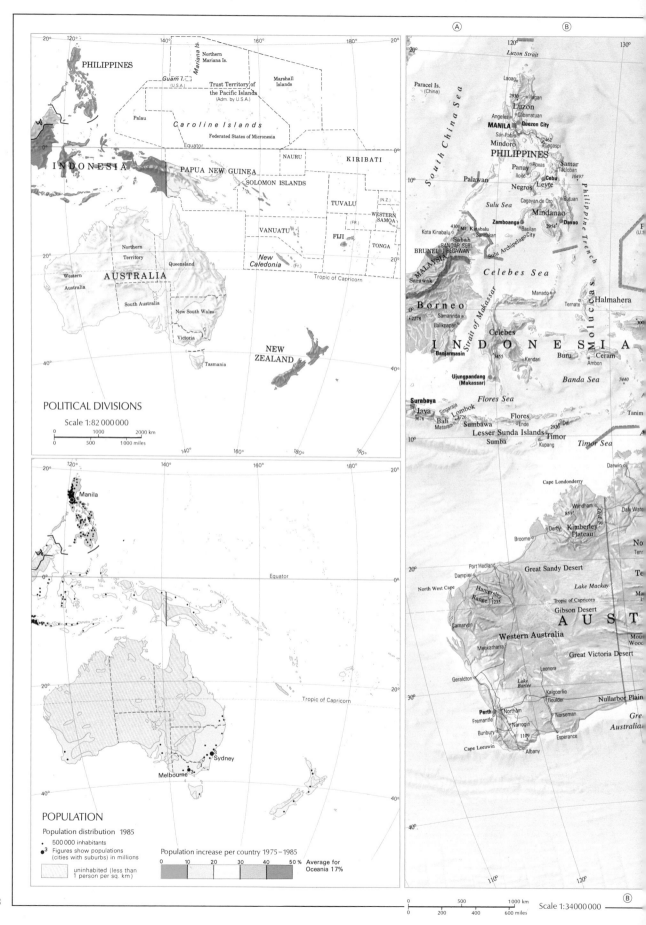

POLITICAL DIVISIONS

Scale 1:82 000 000

0 1000 2000 km
0 500 1000 miles

PHILIPPINES

Northern Mariana Is.

Guam 7. (U.S.A.)

Trust Territory of the Pacific Islands (Adm. by U.S.A.)

Marshall Islands

Palau

Caroline Islands

Federated States of Micronesia

Equator

INDONESIA

PAPUA NEW GUINEA

NAURU

KIRIBATI

SOLOMON ISLANDS

TUVALU

(N.Z.)

WESTERN SAMOA

VANUATU

(FR.)

FIJI

TONGA

New Caledonia (Fr.)

Tropic of Capricorn

Northern Territory

Queensland

Western Australia

AUSTRALIA

South Australia

New South Wales

Victoria

Tasmania

NEW ZEALAND

POPULATION

Population distribution 1985

• 500 000 inhabitants

•³ Figures show populations (cities with suburbs) in millions

uninhabited (less than 1 person per sq. km)

Population increase per country 1975–1985

0 10 20 30 40 50 %   Average for Oceania 17%

Manila

Sydney

Melbourne

Luzon Strait

Paracel Is. (China)

South China Sea

Laoag

Ilagan

Luzon

2930

Angeles Cabanatuan

MANILA Quezon City

San Pablo

Mindoro Legaspi

2462

PHILIPPINES

Panay Roxas Samar

Iloilo Tacloban

Palawan Cebu Leyte

Negros 10497

Cagayan de Oro Butuan

Sulu Sea Mindanao

Kota Kinabalu 4101 Mt. Kinabalu

Zamboanga Davao

2954

Sabah Basilan

BANDAR SERI Sandakan City

BEGAWAN Sulu Archipelago

BRUNEI

MALAYSIA

Sarawak *Celebes Sea*

Manado Ternate Halmahera

Borneo 300

2278

Samarinda Celebes

Balikpapan Strait of Makassar

Banjarmasin 3455 Buru Ceram

Kendari Ambon

I N D O N E S I A

Ujungpandang 7440

(Makassar) *Banda Sea*

Surabaya *Flores Sea*

Tanim

Java Singaraja

Bali 3676 Lombok Flores

3726 Sumbawa Ende Dili

Mataram 2920

Sumba Lesser Sunda Islands Timor

Kupang *Timor Sea*

Darwin

Cape Londonderry

Wyndham

853 Daly Water

Derby Kimberley Ord R.

Broome Plateau

No

Tenn

Port Hedland Great Sandy Desert

Dampier

Lake Mackay Te

North West Cape

Hamersley Tropic of Capricorn

Range 1235 Gibson Desert

Carnarvon A U S T

Mou

Western Australia Wood

Meekatharra Great Victoria Desert

Leonora

Geraldton

Luke Kalgoorlie

Barlee Boulder Nullarbor Plain

Perth Northam Norseman Gre

Fremantle Australi

Bunbury Narrogin

1109

Cape Leeuwin Albany Esperance

0 500 1000 km
0 200 400 600 miles

Scale 1:34000000

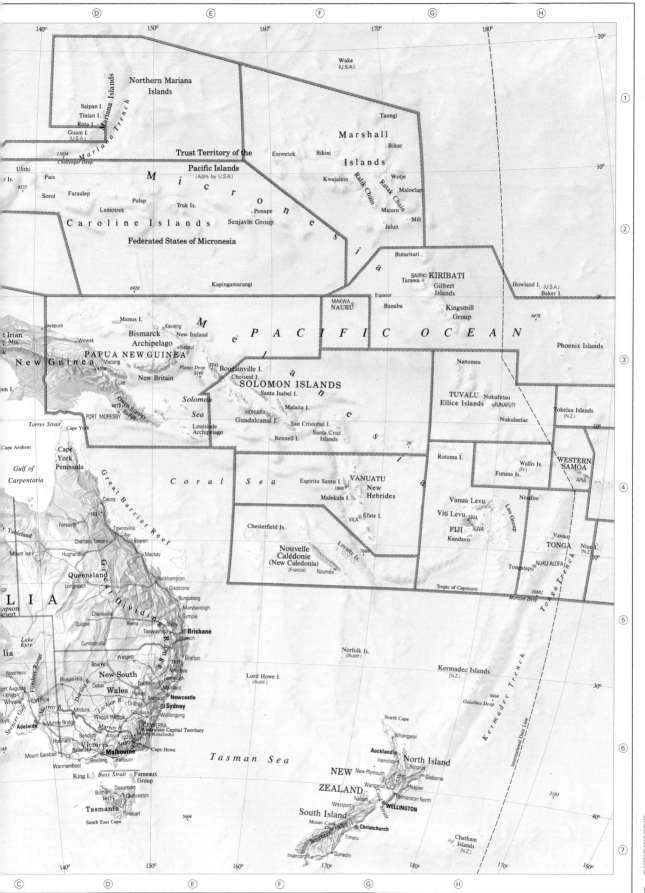

140° 150° 160° 170° 180° 20°

Wake
(U.S.A.)

Northern Mariana
Islands

Saipan I.
Tinian I.
Rota I.
Guam I.
(U.S.A.)

Taongi

M a r s h a l l

Trust Territory of the

Pacific Islands
(Adm. by U.S.A.)

I s l a n d s

Eniwetok   Bikini

Bikar

Ulithi
Is.
Fais
8527
Sorol   Faraulep

Kwajalein

Wotje
Maloelap

Ratak Chain
Ralik Chain

10°

11034
Challenger Deep

Mariana Trench

M i c r o n e s i a

Lamotrek
Pulap

Truk Is.

Majuro
Mili

Jaluit

Pulap
Ponape

C a r o l i n e   I s l a n d s
Senjavin Group

Federated States of Micronesia

Butaritari

BAIRIKI **KIRIBATI**
Tarawa
Gilbert
Islands

Howland I. (U.S.A.)
Baker I.

0°

Kapingamarangi

Equator
Banaba

Kingsmill
Group

6478

6920

MAKWA
NAURU

P A C I F I C   O C E A N

Manus I.
Kavieng
New Ireland

Phoenix Islands

Jayapura

Wewak

Bismarck
Archipelago
Rabaul

M e l a

Nanumea

New Guinea

PAPUA NEW GUINEA
Madang
4508

Planet Deep 2743
9140

Bougainville I.
Choiseul I.

3

Lae

New Britain

SOLOMON ISLANDS
Santa Isabel I.

4073 Owen Stanley
Range

Solomon
Sea

Malaita I.
HONIARA

TUVALU
Ellice Islands

Nukufetau
FUNAFUTI

Tokelau Islands
(N.Z.)

PORT MORESBY
Torres Strait
Cape York

Louisiade
Archipelago

Guadalcanal I.
San Cristobal I.

Santa Cruz
Islands

Nukulaelae

n e s i a

Cape Arnhem

Cape
York
Peninsula

Rennell I.

20

Rotuma I.

Wallis Is.
(Fr.)

**WESTERN
SAMOA**

10°

Gulf of
Carpentaria

C o r a l   S e a

Espiritu Santo I.
1880

VANUATU
New
Hebrides

Futuna Is.

APIA

Cairns
1611

Chesterfield Is.

Malekula I.

VILA Efate I.

Vanua Levu

Viti Levu 1324
SUVA

Niuafou

Lau Group

Forsayth
Tableland

Townsville
Ayr
Bowen
Charters Towers

FIJI
Kandavu

Niue I.
(N.Z.)

Mount Isa
Hughenden

Mackay

Nouvelle
Calédonie
(New Caledonia)
(France)

Loyalty Is.
7660

Vavau

TONGA

20°

Longreach

Rockhampton
Gladstone

Noumea

Tongatapu
NUKU'ALOFA

Tropic of Capricorn

Tonga Trench

10852
Horizon Deep

Queensland

Great Dividing Range

Bundaberg
Maryborough
Gympie

Charleville
Roma
Quilpie
Toowoomba
Dalby

Brisbane
Ipswich

5

Cunnamulla

Norfolk Is.
(Austr.)

Kermadec Islands
(N.Z.)

30°

Bourke
Walgett
Tamworth
Armidale

**New South
Wales**

Grafton
1615

Lord Howe I.
(Austr.)

Broken Hill
Cobar
Dubbo

Woomera
Flinders Range

Bathurst

Newcastle

9994
Galathea Deep

Wagga Wagga
Murray R.
Albury

Parkes
Orange

Goulburn

Sydney
Wollongong

CANBERRA
Australian Capital Territory

Kermadec Trench

International Date Line

Mildura

Bendigo

Australia

North Cape

Whangarei

Adelaide
Murray Bridge

Victoria
Ballarat
Melbourne

Mount Kosciusko
Cape Howe

Auckland
Hamilton

North Island
Rotorua

6

Horsham
Geelong
Yallourn

T a s m a n   S e a

New Plymouth

2797
Gisborne

Warrnambool

King I.
Bass Strait
Furneaux
Group

NEW

Wanganui
Napier
Palmerston North

Mount Gambier

Burnie
Devonport
Launceston
1617

ZEALAND

Nelson
Cook Strait
WELLINGTON

2103

Tasmania

Hobart

5604

South East Cape

South Island
Mount Cook
Southern Alps

Christchurch

Timaru

Chatham
Islands
(N.Z.)

40°

Invercargill
Dunedin

7

140° 150° 160° 170° 180° 170° 160°

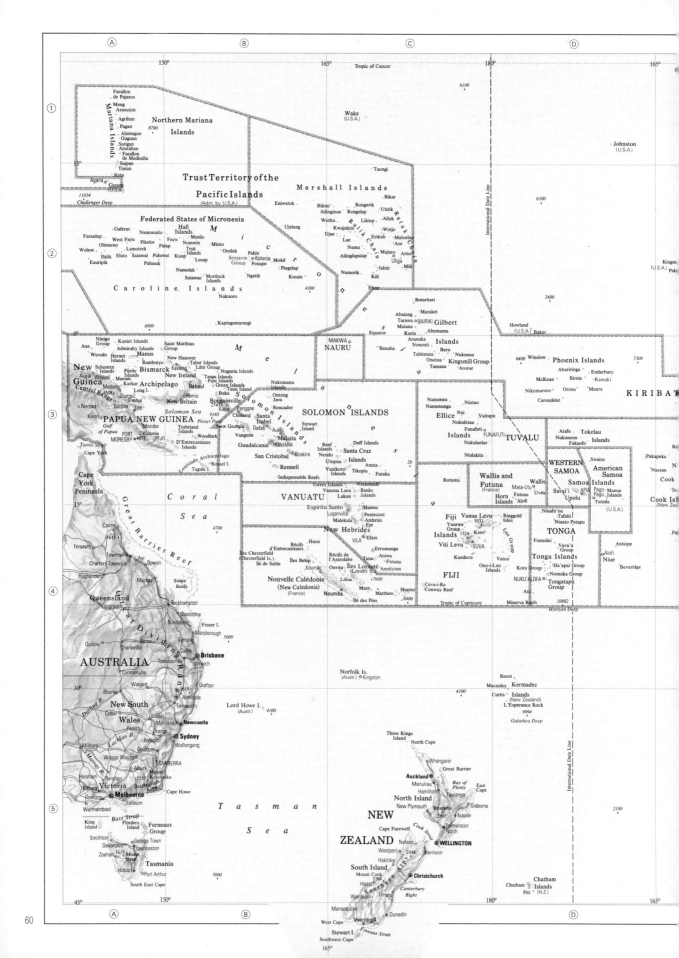

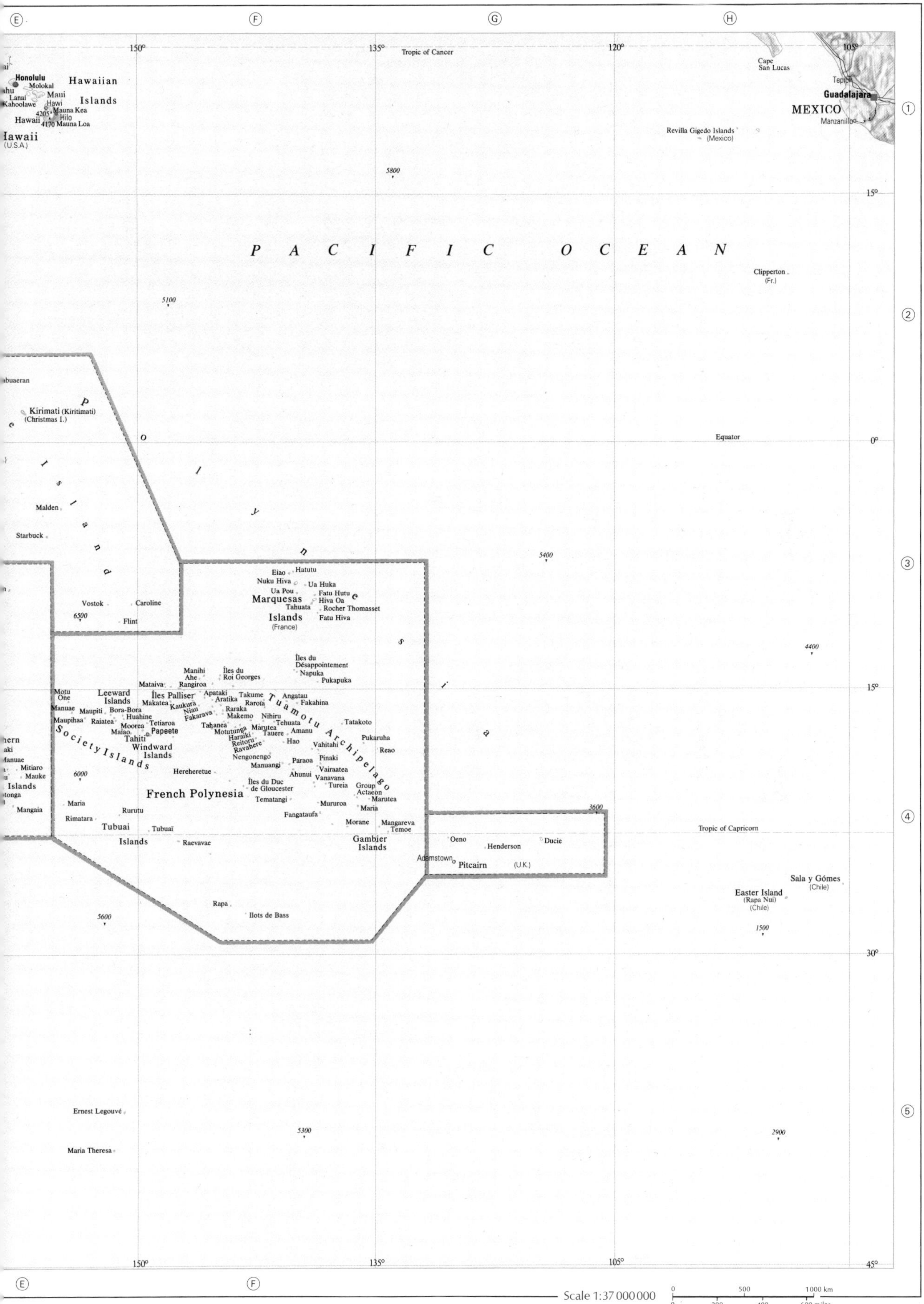

E   F   G   H

150°   135°   Tropic of Cancer   120°   105°

Cape
San Lucas

Tepic

Honolulu   Hawaiian   ①

Molokai   **Guadalajara**

Oahu   Maui   Islands   **MEXICO**

Lanai   Hawi   Manzanillo

Kahoolawe   4205 Mauna Kea

Hilo

Hawaii   4170 Mauna Loa

Hawaii
(U.S.A.)

Revilla Gigedo Islands
(Mexico)

15°

5800

P A C I F I C   O C E A N   Clipperton
(Fr.)

②

5100

P

abuaeran

Kirimati (Kiritimati)   o
(Christmas I.)

Equator   0°

I

s   l   y

Malden   a

n   ③

Vostok   Caroline   d   5400

6500   Flint

Eiao   Hatutu

Nuku Hiva

Ua Pou   Ua Huka

Fatu Hutu

Marquesas   Hiva Oa

Tahuata   Rocher Thomasset

Islands   Fatu Hiva
(France)

s   4400

Îles du
Désappointement

Manihi   Îles du   Napuka   15°

Ahe   Roi Georges   Pukapuka

Mataiva   Rangiroa   i

Motu   Leeward   Îles Palliser   Apataki   Takume   Angatau

One   Islands   Makatea   Kaukura   Aratika   Raroia   Fakahina

Manuae   Maupiti   Bora-Bora   Niau   Raraka   a

Maupihaa   Raiatea   Huahine   Fakarava   Makemo   Nihiru

Maiao   Moorea   Tetiaroa   Tahanea   Tehuata   Tatakoto

Society Islands   Tahiti   Motutunga   Marutea   Amanu

Haraiki   Tauere   Pukaruha

hern   Windward   Reitoru   Hao   r

aki   Islands   Ravahere   Vahitahi

Manuae   Hereheretue   Nengonengo   Pinaki   c

Mitiaro   Manuangi   Paraoa   Vairaatea

Mauke   Ahunui   Vanavana   h

Islands   Îles du Duc   Tureia   i

6000   de Gloucester   Group   p

onga   **French Polynesia**   Actaeon   e

Mangaia   Tematangi   Maria   Marutea   l

Maria   Fangataufa   a

Rurutu   Morane   Mangareva   g

Rimatara   Tubuai   Temoe   o   3600

Tubuai   Tubuai   Gambier   Oeno   Henderson   Ducie   Tropic of Capricorn

Islands   Raevavae   Islands   Adamstown   Pitcairn (U.K.)

Sala y Gómes
(Chile)

Rapa   Easter Island
(Rapa Nui)
(Chile)

5600   Ilots de Bass   1500   30°

Ernest Legouvé   ⑤

5300   2900

Maria Theresa

150°   135°   105°   45°

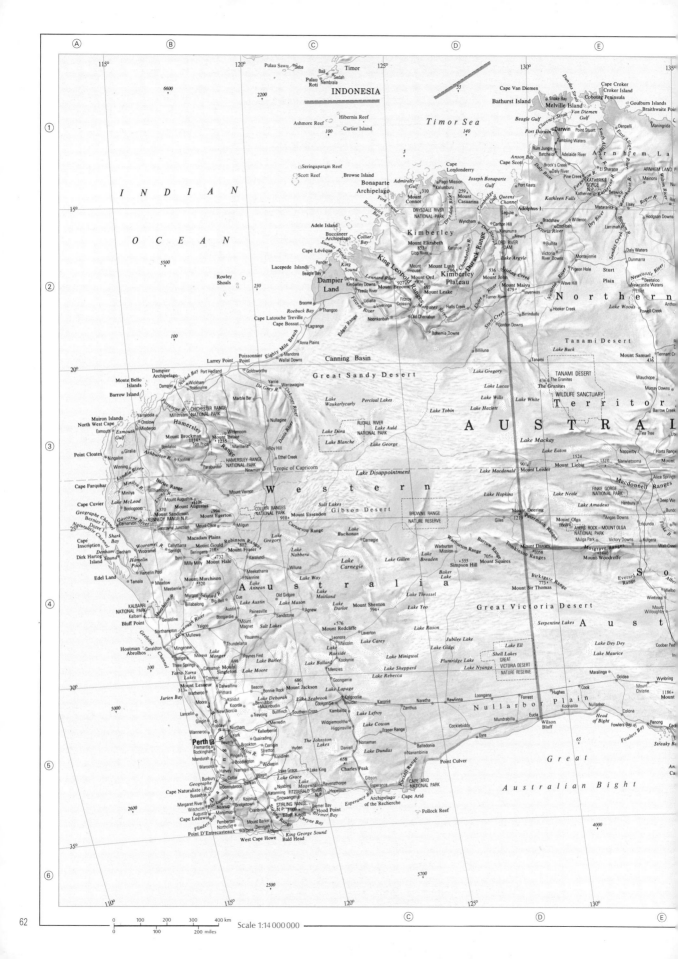

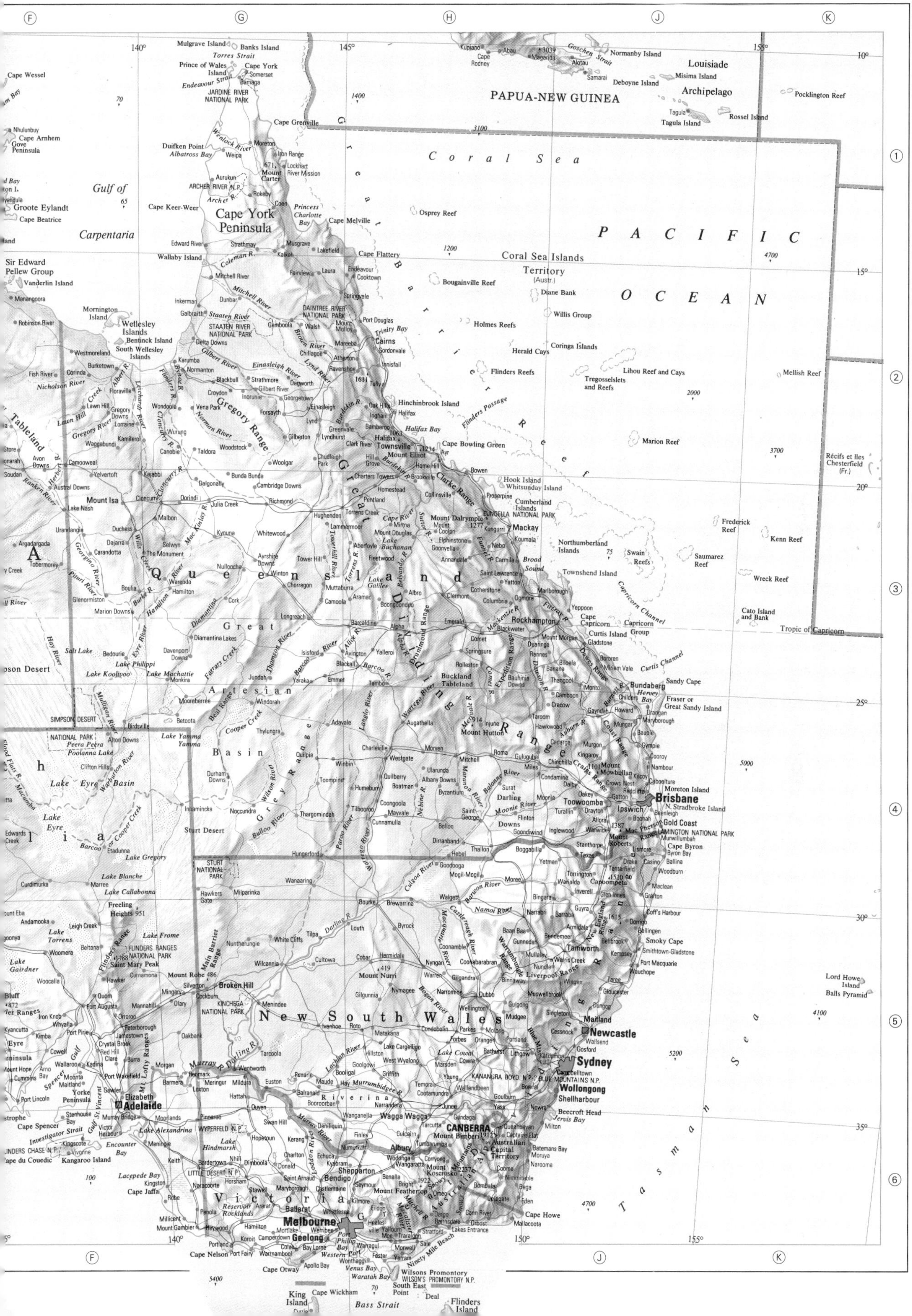

PAPUA-NEW GUINEA

Louisiade
Archipelago

Coral Sea

P A C I F I C

O C E A N

Gulf of
Carpentaria

Cape York
Peninsula

Coral Sea Islands
Territory
(Austr.)

Cairns

Q u e e n s l a n d

Townsville

Mount Isa

G r e a t
A r t e s i a n
B a s i n

SIMPSON DESERT
NATIONAL PARK

Rockhampton
Gladstone

Bundaberg

Tropic of Capricorn

Lake Eyre

Brisbane
Ipswich
Gold Coast

Toowoomba

N e w   S o u t h   W a l e s

Broken Hill

Newcastle

Sydney

Adelaide

Wollongong

CANBERRA
Australian
Capital
Territory

V i c t o r i a

Wagga Wagga

Albury

Bendigo
Shepparton

Melbourne
Geelong

Tasman
Sea

Bass Strait

Flinders
Island

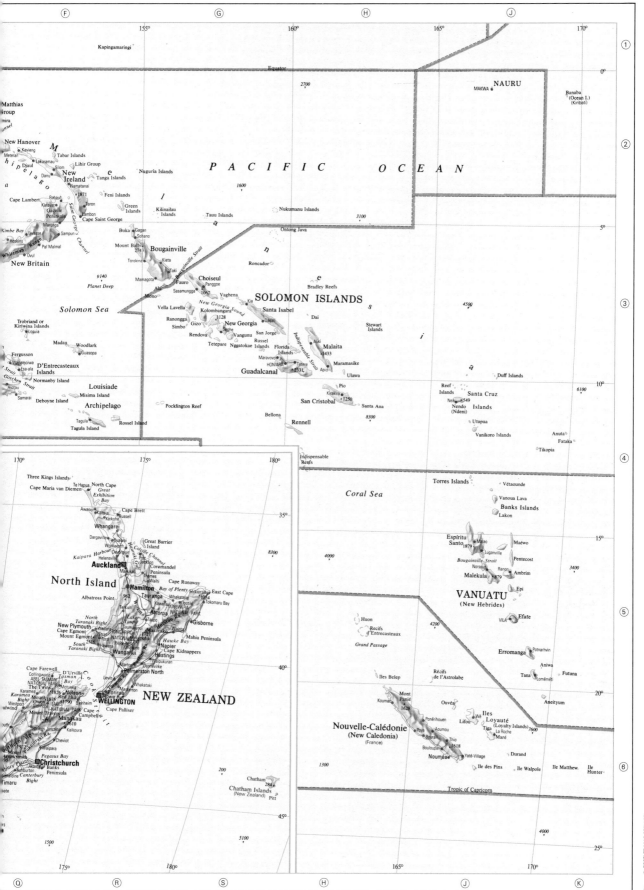

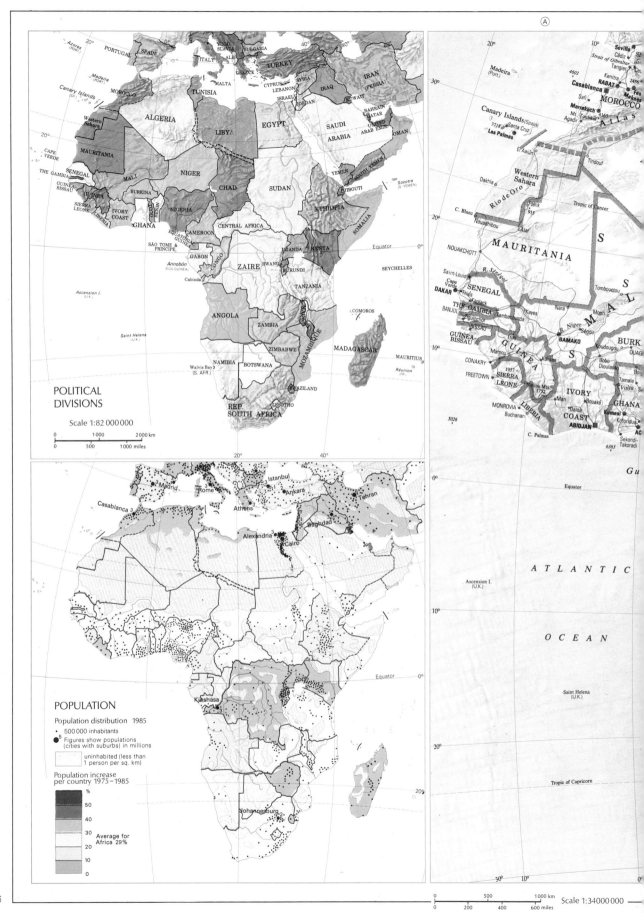

POLITICAL DIVISIONS

Scale 1:82 000 000

| 0 | 1000 | 2000 km |
| 0 | 500 | 1000 miles |

POPULATION

Population distribution 1985

• 500 000 inhabitants

●[5] Figures show populations (cities with suburbs) in millions

uninhabited (less than 1 person per sq. km)

Population increase per country 1975–1985

%
50
40
30 Average for
20 Africa 29%
10
0

Scale 1:34 000 000

| 0 | 500 | 1000 km |
| 0 | 200 | 400 | 600 miles |

(A)

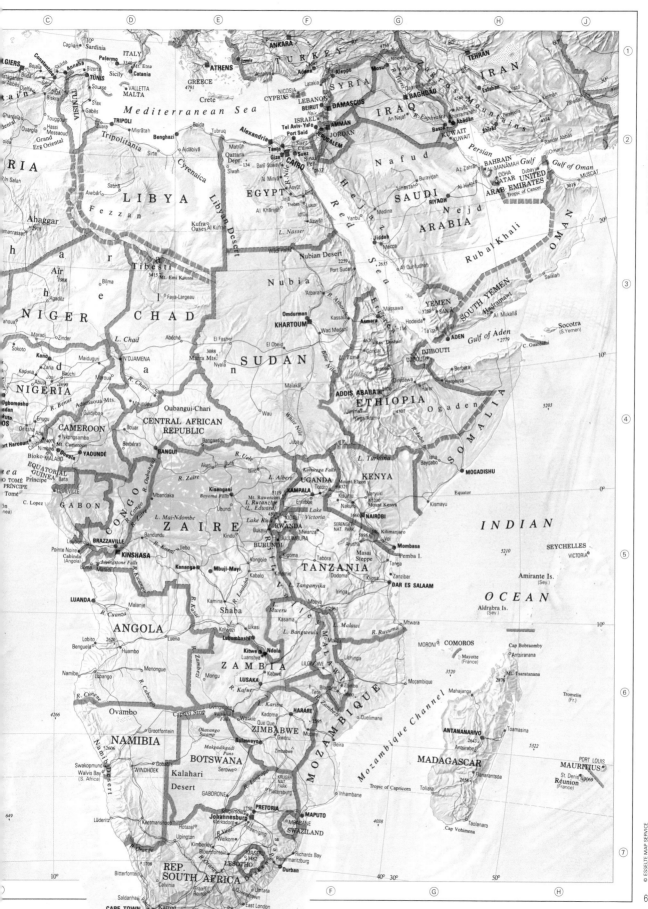

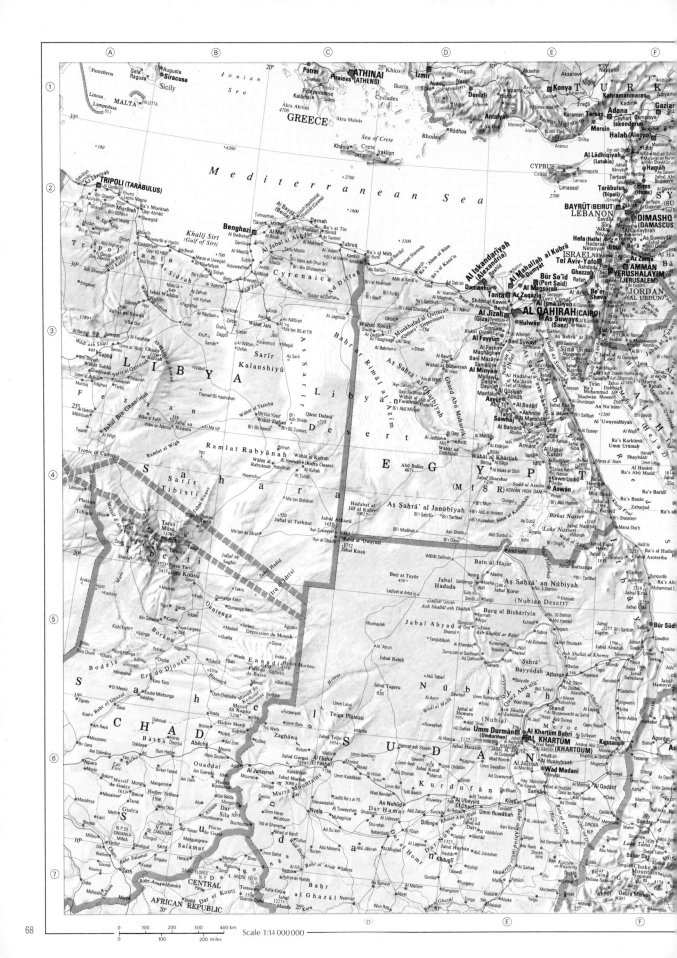

Scale 1:14 000 000

0   100   200   300   400 km
0   100   200 miles

Azores
(Port.)

Madeira
(Port.)

Islas Canarias
(Canary Islands)
(Spain)

ATLANTIC OCEAN

Tropic of Cancer

Western
Sahara

MAURITANIA

NOUAKCHOTT

SENEGAL

DAKAR

THE GAMBIA

BANJUL

GUINEA-
BISSAU

BISSAU

GUINEA

PORTUGAL

SPAIN

MOROCCO

RABAT

Dar el Beida (Casablanca)

Marrakech

ALG

MALI

BAMAKO

BURKINA

OUAGADOUGOU

GHANA

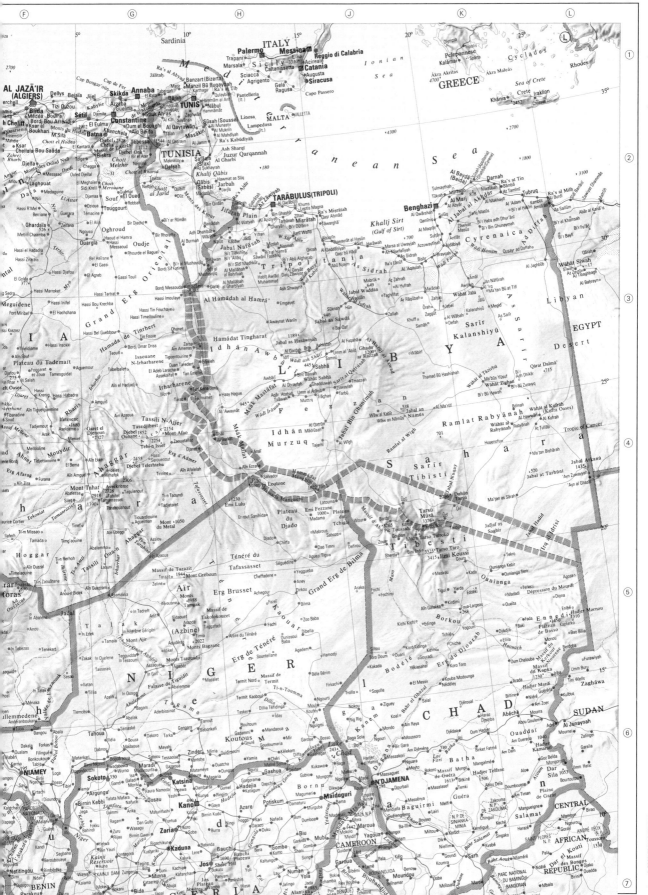

Scale 1:14 000 000

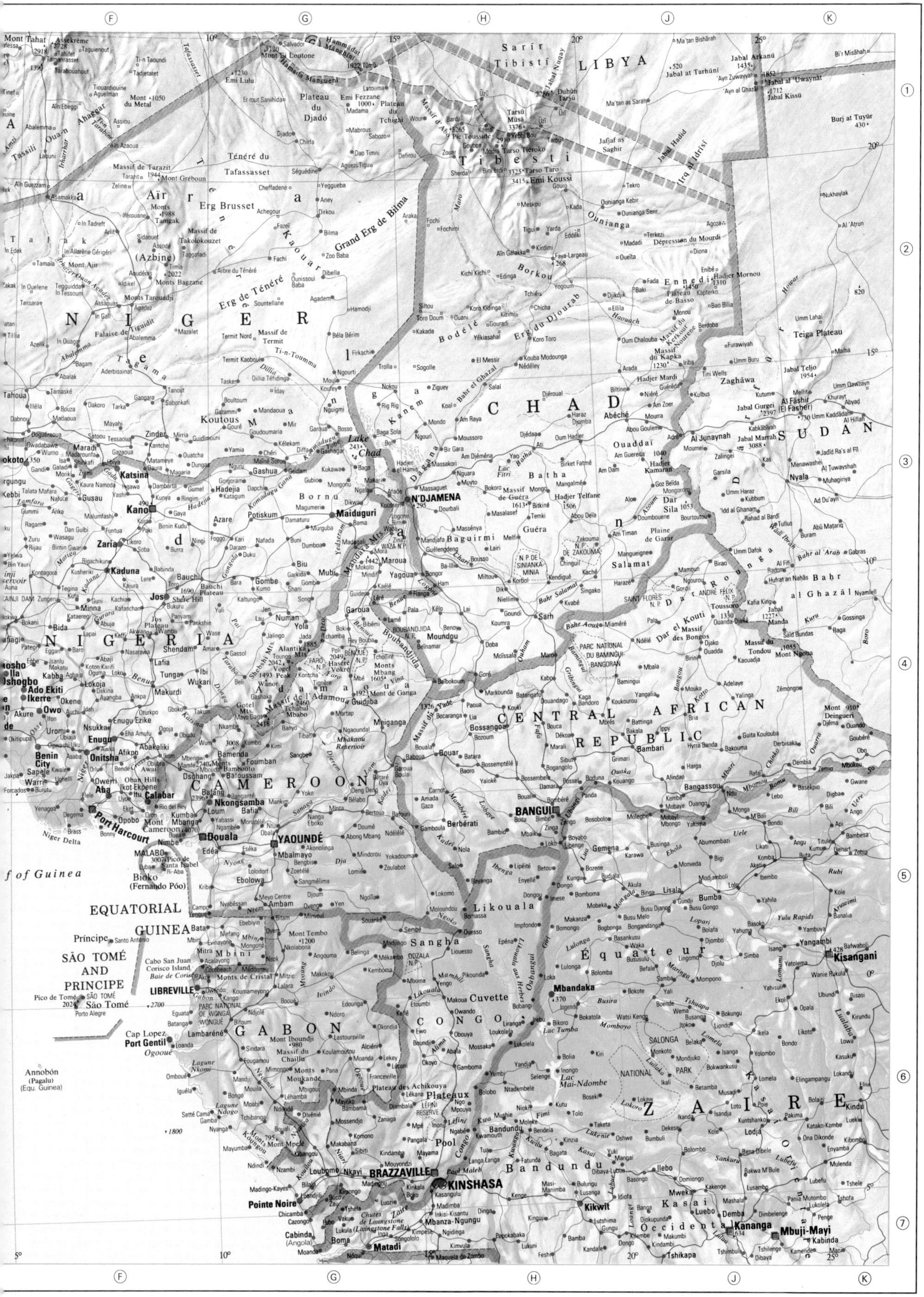

LIBYA
CHAD
NIGER
NIGERIA
CAMEROON
CENTRAL AFRICAN REPUBLIC
SUDAN
CONGO
GABON
ZAIRE
EQUATORIAL GUINEA
SÃO TOMÉ AND PRINCIPE
Tibesti
Emi Koussi
Aïr
Erg de Ténéré
Grand Erg de Bilma
Kaouar
Borkou
Ennedi
Ouaddaï
Bodélé
Kanem
Lake Chad
Bornu
N'DJAMENA
Abéché
Maiduguri
Kano
Katsina
Zaria
Kaduna
Jos
Zinder
Maradi
Agadez
Bilma
Faya-Largeau
Moundou
Sarh
Garoua
Maroua
Ngaoundéré
YAOUNDÉ
Douala
BANGUI
Bambari
Berbérati
Bangassou
Onitsha
Enugu
Port Harcourt
Calabar
MALABO
Bioko (Fernando Póo)
LIBREVILLE
Port Gentil
Lambaréné
Pointe Noire
BRAZZAVILLE
KINSHASA
Matadi
Kikwit
Kananga
Mbuji-Mayi
Mbandaka
Kisangani
Bandundu
Kasai
Équateur
Plateaux
Cuvette
Likouala
Sangha
Adamoua
Darfur
Al Fāshir (El Fasher)
Nyala
Al Junaynah
Jabal Marrah
Bight of Guinea
Annobón (Pagalu) (Equ. Guinea)
Cabinda (Angola)

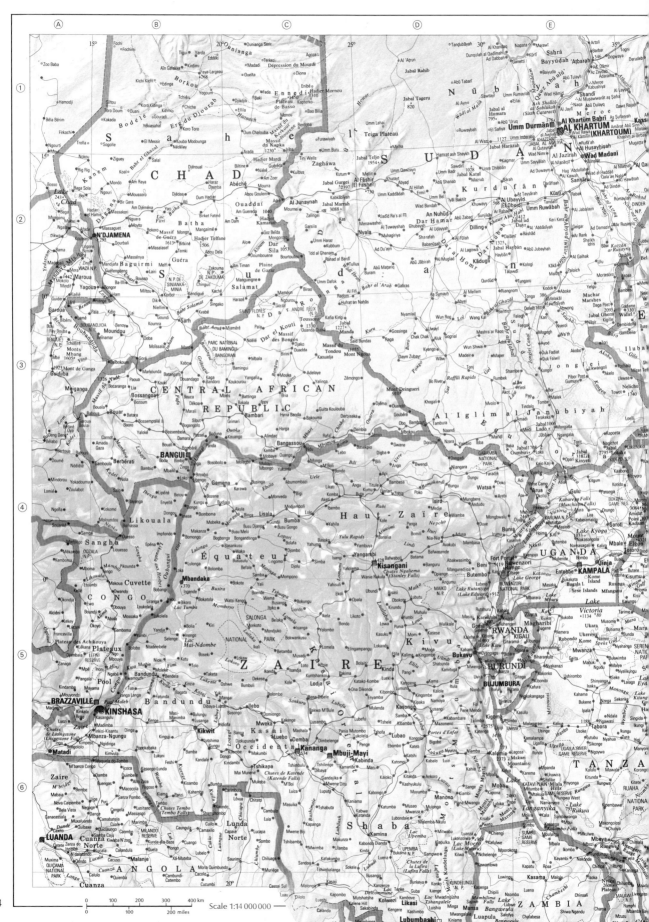

Scale 1:14 000 000

0   100   200   300   400 km

0   100   200 miles

AFRICA (EAST)

YEMEN
SOUTH YEMEN
SAN'A'
Hadramawt
Suquṭrā (Socotra) (S Yemen)
Ra's Fartak
'Abd al Kūri
Al Ikhwān
Ra's Āsir (Cape Guardafui)

BALADIYAT 'ADAN (ADEN)
Shaykh 'Uthmān
Gulf of Aden

Red Sea

Asmara
Massawa
Dahlak Archipelago
Dahlak Kebir

Kamaran
Al Hudaydah (Hodeida)
Ta'izz

Makale
Kobar Sink
Danakil Plain
Assab

DJIBOUTI
Lake Assale
Gulf of Tadjourah

Berbera
Migiurtinia
Karkār
Hadded
Al Madow
Ra's Ḥāfūn (Hāfūn) (Dante)

ADDIS ABABA
ETHIOPIA
Ethiopian Plateau
Dessye
Dessie

Harar
Diredawa
Hargeysa
Nugāl
Sōl

Jimma
Awasa
Hāud
Ogaden
Haud
Hararge

SOMALIA
Ogaden
Mudug

Bale
Webbe Shibeli
Sidamo
Webbe Gestro

Lake Stefanie
Gamud
Turkana (Lake Rudolf)

Chalbi Desert
MARSABIT NAT. RES.

MUQDISHO (MOGADISHU)
Marka
Baydabo
Koriolei

INDIAN OCEAN

KENYA
NAIROBI
Mount Kenya
MOUNT KENYA N.P.
ABERDARE N.P.

Kismāyu
Bajun Islands
Ra's Chiamboni
Kiunga

Lamu
Pate Island
Manda Island

Kilimanjaro
KILIMANJARO N.P.
Moshi
Arusha
TSAVO N.P.

Mombasa
Kilindini
Tanga

Equator 0°

SEYCHELLES
Praslin
La Digue
Silhouette
VICTORIA

African Is.
Eagle
Saint Joseph
Amirante Islands (Sey.)
Poivre Is.
Ile des Roches
Platte
Ile des Noefs

Pemba Island
Chake Chake
Wete

Zanzibar Island
Zanzibar

Morogoro
DAR ES SALAAM

Bijoutier
Alphonse
St. Francois
Coetivy (Sey.)

Mafia Island

SELOUS GAME RESERVE

Providence

Aldabra Islands (Sey.)
Assumption
Cosmoledo Group
Astove
Saint Pierre
Cerf
Farquhar Group

Mtwara
Cabo Delgado

© ESSELTE MAP SERVICE

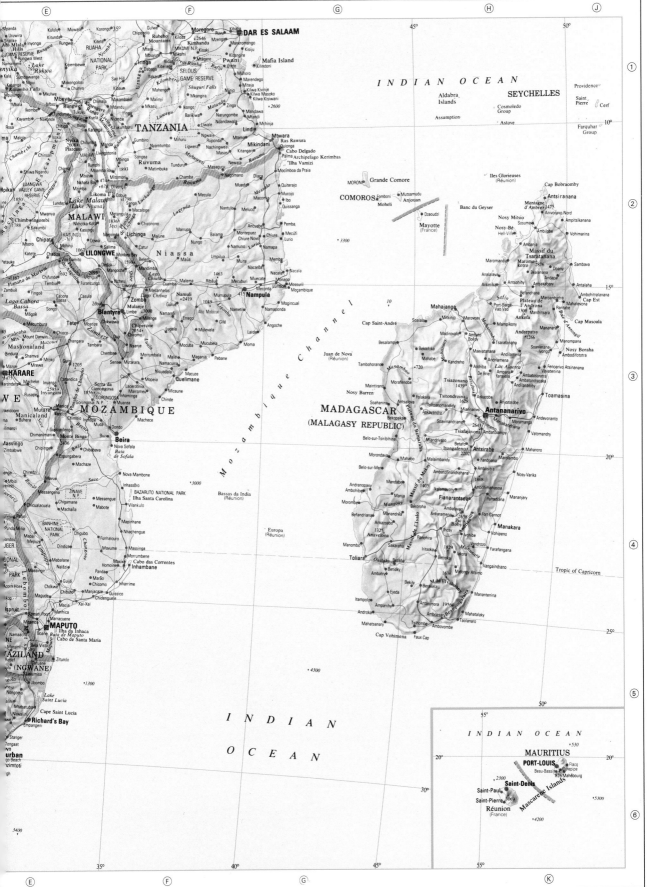

INDIAN OCEAN

SEYCHELLES

Aldabra
Islands

Providence

Saint
Pierre   Cerf

Cosmoledo
Group

Assumption

Astove

Farquhar
Group

TANZANIA

DAR ES SALAAM

Mafia Island

Mtwara
Ras Rawura
Cabo Delgado
Palma Archipelago Kerimbas
Ilha Vamizi
Moçimboa da Praia

Iles Glorieuses
(Réunion)

Cap Bobraomby

Antsiranana
Montagne
d'Ambre

Nosy Mitsio
Sosumava

Nosy-Bé
Hell-Ville

Ampitsikanana

Vohimarina

MORONI   Grande Comore

COMOROS   Fomboni   Anjouan
Moheli

Mutsamudu

Banc du Geyser

Mayotte
(France)

Dzaoudzi

MALAWI

LILONGWE

Niassa

Nampula

Massif du
Tsaratanana
Maromo-
kotro   Doany

Antsohihy
Analalava
Ankerika   Antsakabary

Sambava

Antalaha

Amborhitralanana   Cap Est
Maroantsetra   Mahalevona

Ankofa
Mandritsara

Cap Masoala

Antsiranana

Andrepatsy
Nosy Boraha

Mahajanga

Cap Saint-André

Soalala

Sofia   Plateau
d'Androna

Port-Bergé
Vao Vao

Maevatanana

Mampikony

Tsaratanana

Andilamena

Nosy Varika

Fenoarivo Atsinanana
Ambodifototra

Manompana

Soanierana-
Ivongo

Lac Alaotra

Antananarivo

Toamasina

BLANTYRE

Zomba

MOZAMBIQUE

Beira

MADAGASCAR
(MALAGASY REPUBLIC)

Mozambique Channel

Juan de Nova
(Réunion)

Nosy Barren

Maintirano

Morafenobe

Antsalova

Belo-sur-Tsiribihina

Belo-sur-Mer

Morondava

Mahabo

Miandrivazo

Antsirabe

Betafo

Fianarantsoa

Manakara

Antananarivo

MAPUTO

Cap Vohimena   Faux Cap

Toliara

Europa
(Réunion)

Bassas da India
(Réunion)

Andranopasy
Ambohibe

Manja

Mandabe

Befandriana

Ankazoabo

Anavelona

Manombo

Morombe

Ampanihy
Beloha

Androka

Itampolo

Ejeda

Ampanihy

Tropic of Capricorn

INDIAN

OCEAN

INDIAN OCEAN

MAURITIUS

PORT-LOUIS   Flacq

Beau-Bassin   Curepipe
Mahébourg

Saint-Denis

Saint-Paul

Saint-Pierre
Réunion
(France)

Mascarene Islands

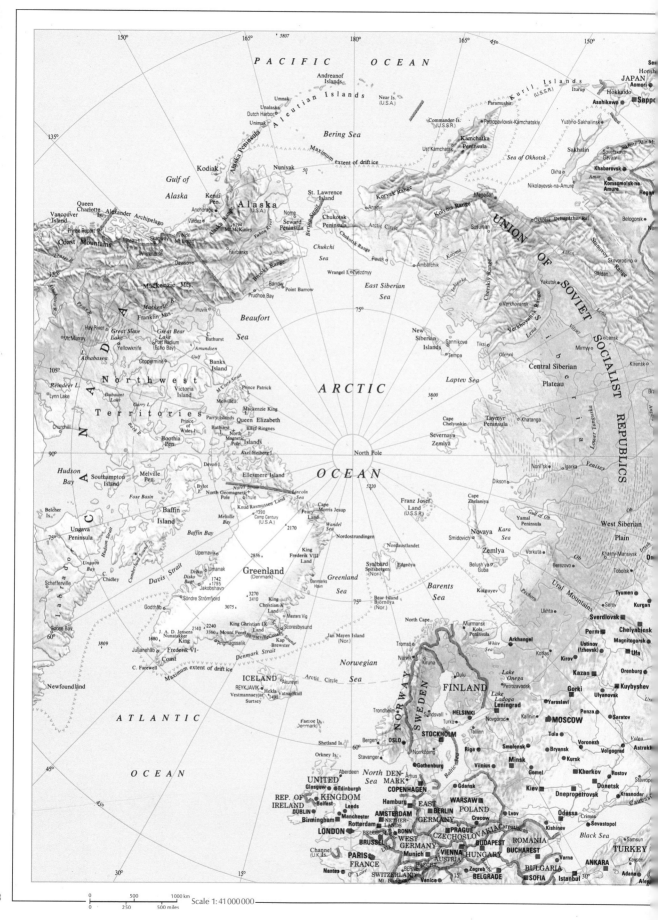

Scale 1:41 000 000

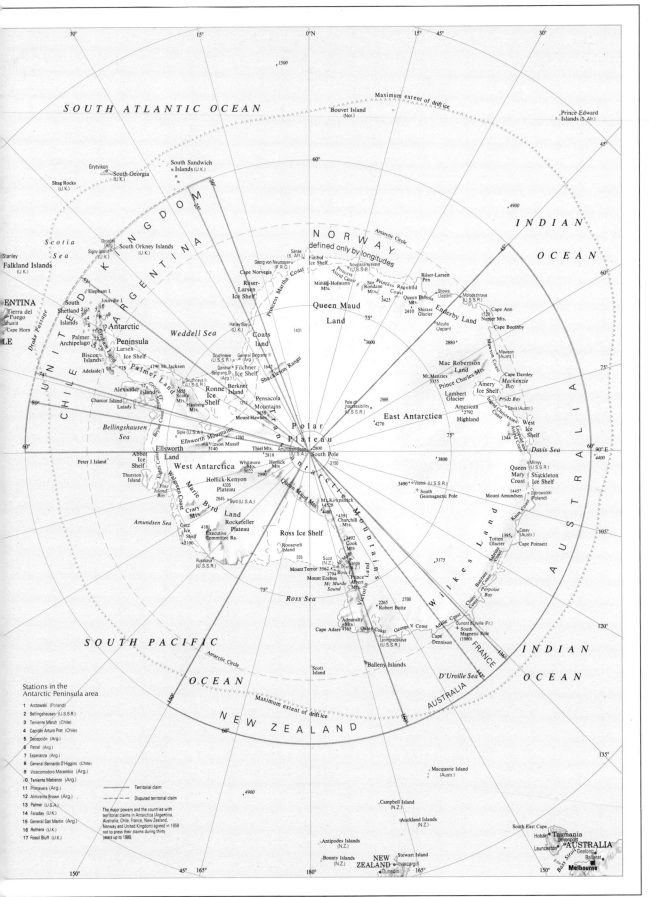

MAP LEGEND

Symbols
Scale 1:7 000 000, 1:14 000 000

Bombay — More than 5 000 000 inhabitants

Milano — 1 000 000 – 5 000 000 inhabitants

Zürich — 250 000 – 1 000 000 inhabitants

Dijon — 100 000 – 250 000 inhabitants

Dover — 25 000 – 100 000 inhabitants

Torquay — Less than 25 000 inhabitants

Tachiumet — Small sites

WIEN — National capital

Atlanta — State capital

——— Major road

——— Other road

– – – – Road under construction

——— Railway

– – – – Railway under construction

– – – – – Train ferry

National boundary

Disputed national boundary

State boundary

Disputed state boundary

Undefined boundary in the sea

4807 — Height above sea-level in metres

3068 — Depth in metres

National park

Niniveh — Ruin

Pass

KAINJI DAM — Dam

Wadi

Canal

Waterfall

Reef

Symbols
Scale 1: 21 000 000, 1:34 000 000, 1:37 000 000,
1:41 000 000

Shanghai — More than 5 000 000 inhabitants

Barcelona — 1 000 000 – 5 000 000 inhabitants

Venice — 250 000 – 1 000 000 inhabitants

Aberdeen — 50 000 – 250 000 inhabitants

Beida — Less than 50 000 inhabitants

Mawson — Scientific station

CAIRO — National capital

——— Major road

——— Railway

– – – – Railway under construction

National boundary

Disputed national boundary

State boundary

Disputed state boundary

Undefined boundary in the sea

8848 — Height above sea-level in metres

11034 — Depth in metres

2645 — Thickness of ice cap

Dam

Thebes — Ruin

Wadi

Canal

Waterfall

Reef

Colour Key

Tundra

Glacier

Coniferous forest

Mixed forest

Deciduous forest

Tropical rain forest

Chacos

Arable land

Grassland, pasture

Savanna

Steppe, semi-desert

Sand desert

Other desert

Mountain

Marshland

Salt lake

Intermittent lake

Salt desert, salt pan, dry lake

Lava field

WORLD COMPARISONS

ECONOMIC STRENGTH

The map plots Gross Domestic Product (GDP) per head of population for every country where data is available. GDP is generally regarded as the yardstick for the economic activity of a country; it measures the total value of the goods and services produced annually. GDP can be measured in a number of different ways; the commonest is GDP at market prices, which includes indirect taxes and subsidies. Subtracting these to give GDP at factor cost provides a picture of the income received by suppliers of goods and services. GDP is normally expressed at constant prices, which eliminates the effect of inflation.

Another frequently used measure of economic output is Gross National Product (GNP). It differs from GDP in that it includes residents' income from abroad, such as repatriated profits, minus the corresponding income of nonresidents.

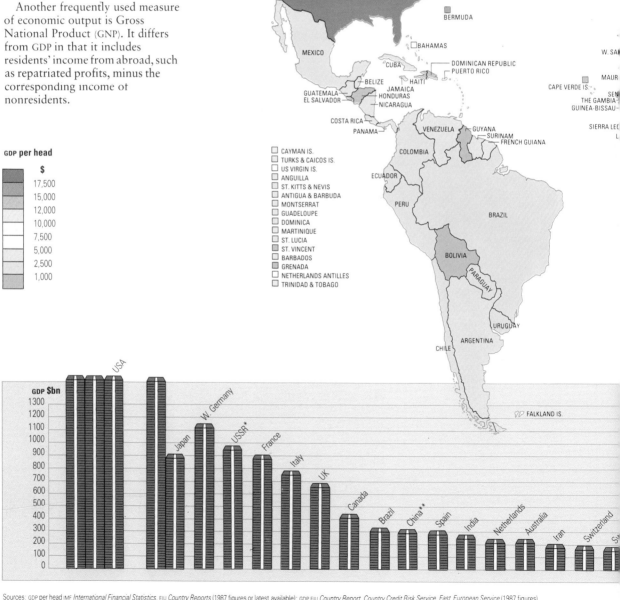

GDP per head

$
17,500
15,000
12,000
10,000
7,500
5,000
2,500
1,000

CAYMAN IS.
TURKS & CAICOS IS.
US VIRGIN IS.
ANGUILLA
ST. KITTS & NEVIS
ANTIGUA & BARBUDA
MONTSERRAT
GUADELOUPE
DOMINICA
MARTINIQUE
ST. LUCIA
ST. VINCENT
BARBADOS
GRENADA
NETHERLANDS ANTILLES
TRINIDAD & TOBAGO

Sources: GDP per head IMF *International Financial Statistics*, EIU *Country Reports* (1987 figures or latest available); GDP EIU *Country Report, Country Credit Risk Service, East European Service* (1987 figures).

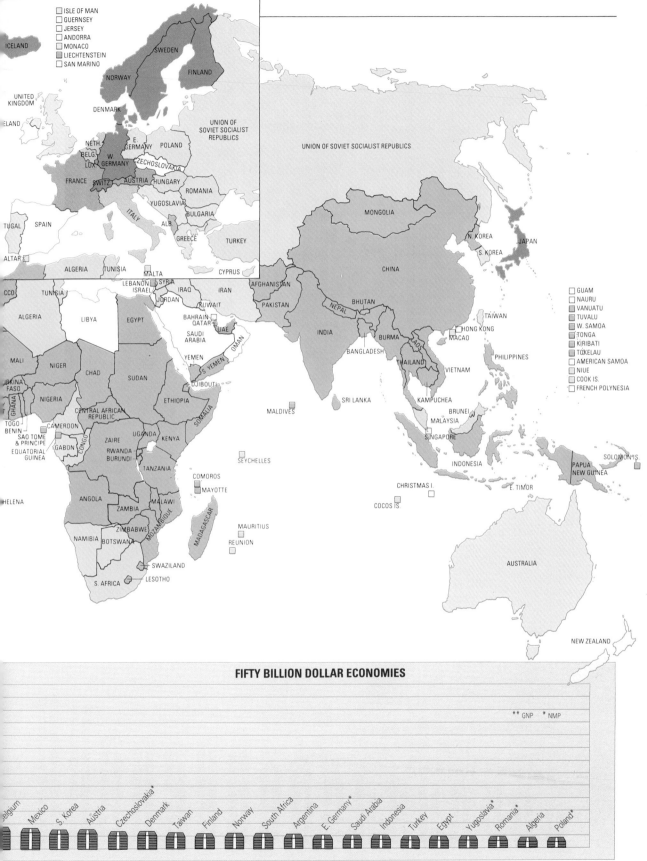

ICELAND

UNITED KINGDOM

IRELAND

TUGAL   SPAIN

ALTAR

CCO   TUNISIA

ALGERIA   TUNISIA

ALGERIA   LIBYA   EGYPT

MALI   NIGER   CHAD   SUDAN   ETHIOPIA

IRKINA FASO   NIGERIA   CENTRAL AFRICAN REPUBLIC

GHANA
TOGO
BENIN   CAMEROON
SAO TOME
& PRINCIPE   GABON   CONGO   ZAIRE   UGANDA   KENYA
EQUATORIAL GUINEA   RWANDA   BURUNDI   TANZANIA

HELENA   ANGOLA   ZAMBIA   MALAWI

NAMIBIA   BOTSWANA   ZIMBABWE   MOZAMBIQUE

SWAZILAND
S. AFRICA   LESOTHO

☐ ISLE OF MAN
☐ GUERNSEY
☐ JERSEY
☐ ANDORRA
☐ MONACO
☐ LIECHTENSTEIN
☐ SAN MARINO

SWEDEN   FINLAND
NORWAY

DENMARK

NETH.   E. GERMANY   POLAND
BELG.
LUX   W GERMANY   CZECHOSLOVAKIA
FRANCE   SWITZ   AUSTRIA   HUNGARY
ROMANIA
ITALY   YUGOSLAVIA
ALB.   BULGARIA
GREECE   TURKEY

UNION OF SOVIET SOCIALIST REPUBLICS

UNION OF SOVIET SOCIALIST REPUBLICS

MALTA   CYPRUS

LEBANON   SYRIA   IRAQ   IRAN   AFGHANISTAN
ISRAEL   JORDAN   KUWAIT   PAKISTAN   NEPAL   BHUTAN
BAHRAIN   QATAR   UAE   OMAN   INDIA   BURMA
SAUDI ARABIA
YEMEN   S YEMEN   BANGLADESH   LAOS
DJIBOUTI   THAILAND   VIETNAM

MONGOLIA

N. KOREA   JAPAN
S. KOREA

CHINA

TAIWAN   HONG KONG
MACAO
PHILIPPINES

SOMALIA   SRI LANKA   KAMPUCHEA
BRUNEI
MALAYSIA
SINGAPORE

MALDIVES   SEYCHELLES

COMOROS   MAYOTTE

CHRISTMAS I.

COCOS IS.

INDONESIA   E. TIMOR

PAPUA NEW GUINEA   SOLOMON IS.

MADAGASCAR   MAURITIUS   REUNION

☐ GUAM
☐ NAURU
☐ VANUATU
☐ TUVALU
☐ W. SAMOA
☐ TONGA
☐ KIRIBATI
☐ TOKELAU
☐ AMERICAN SAMOA
☐ NIUE
☐ COOK IS.
☐ FRENCH POLYNESIA

AUSTRALIA

NEW ZEALAND

FIFTY BILLION DOLLAR ECONOMIES

** GNP   * NMP

Belgium   Mexico   S. Korea   Austria   Czechoslovakia*   Denmark   Taiwan   Finland   Norway   South Africa   Argentina   E. Germany*   Saudi Arabia   Indonesia   Turkey   Egypt   Yugoslavia*   Romania*   Algeria   Poland*

FOREIGN DEBT

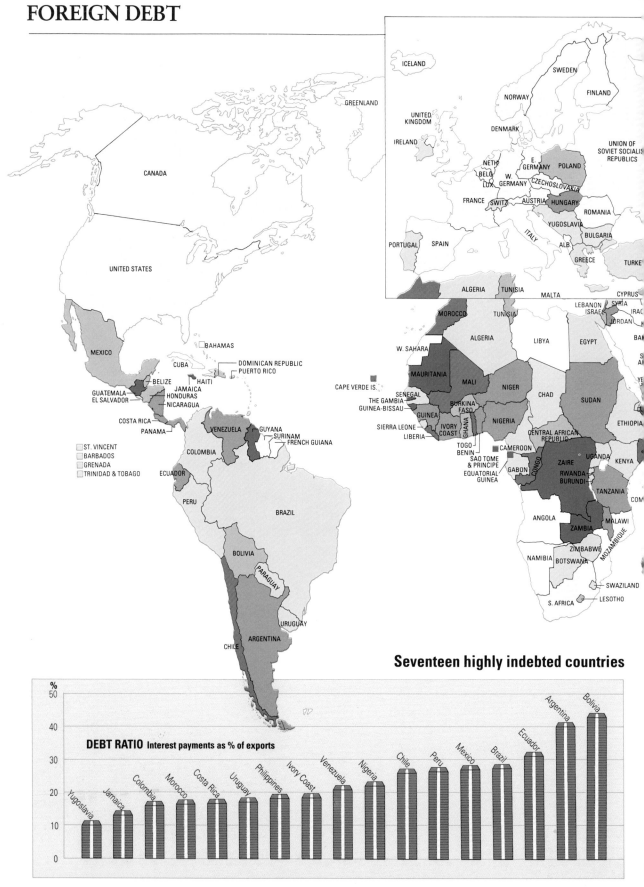

ICELAND

SWEDEN

NORWAY

FINLAND

GREENLAND

UNITED KINGDOM

DENMARK

UNION OF SOVIET SOCIALIST REPUBLICS

IRELAND

NETH.
BELG
LUX.
E. GERMANY
W. GERMANY
POLAND
CZECHOSLOVAKIA

FRANCE
SWITZ.
AUSTRIA
HUNGARY
ROMANIA

YUGOSLAVIA
BULGARIA

PORTUGAL
SPAIN
ITALY
ALB.
GREECE
TURKE

CANADA

UNITED STATES

MEXICO

BAHAMAS

CUBA

DOMINICAN REPUBLIC
PUERTO RICO

BELIZE
HAITI

GUATEMALA
EL SALVADOR
JAMAICA
HONDURAS
NICARAGUA

COSTA RICA
PANAMA

ST. VINCENT
BARBADOS
GRENADA
TRINIDAD & TOBAGO

VENEZUELA

GUYANA
SURINAM
FRENCH GUIANA

COLOMBIA

ECUADOR

PERU

BRAZIL

BOLIVIA

PARAGUAY

URUGUAY

ARGENTINA

CHILE

CAPE VERDE IS.

ALGERIA
TUNISIA
MALTA
CYPRUS

LEBANON
ISRAEL
SYRIA
IRAQ
JORDAN

MOROCCO
TUNISIA

W. SAHARA
ALGERIA
LIBYA
EGYPT

SI

MAURITANIA
MALI
NIGER
CHAD
SUDAN

SENEGAL
THE GAMBIA
GUINEA-BISSAU
GUINEA
BURKINA FASO
NIGERIA

SIERRA LEONE
IVORY COAST
GHANA

LIBERIA
TOGO
BENIN
CAMEROON

SAO TOME
& PRINCIPE
EQUATORIAL
GUINEA
GABON
CONGO

CENTRAL AFRICAN REPUBLIC
ETHIOPIA

ZAIRE
UGANDA
KENYA

RWANDA
BURUNDI

TANZANIA
COM

ANGOLA
MALAWI

ZAMBIA
MOZAMBIQUE

ZIMBABWE

NAMIBIA
BOTSWANA

SWAZILAND

S. AFRICA
LESOTHO

Seventeen highly indebted countries

DEBT RATIO Interest payments as % of exports

%
50
40
30
20
10
0

Yugoslavia
Jamaica
Colombia
Morocco
Costa Rica
Uruguay
Philippines
Ivory Coast
Venezuela
Nigeria
Chile
Peru
Mexico
Brazil
Ecuador
Argentina
Bolivia

Sources: World Bank *World Debt Tables* (1987 and 1988 figures); IMF *International Financial Statistics* (1986 figures); EIU *Country Profiles* (1986 and 1987 figures)

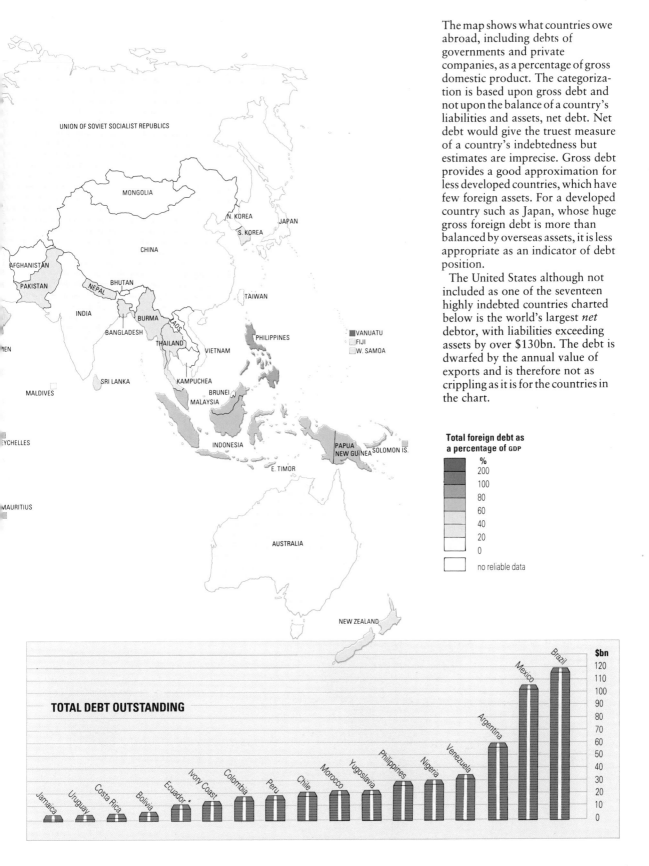

The map shows what countries owe abroad, including debts of governments and private companies, as a percentage of gross domestic product. The categorization is based upon gross debt and not upon the balance of a country's liabilities and assets, net debt. Net debt would give the truest measure of a country's indebtedness but estimates are imprecise. Gross debt provides a good approximation for less developed countries, which have few foreign assets. For a developed country such as Japan, whose huge gross foreign debt is more than balanced by overseas assets, it is less appropriate as an indicator of debt position.

The United States although not included as one of the seventeen highly indebted countries charted below is the world's largest *net* debtor, with liabilities exceeding assets by over $130bn. The debt is dwarfed by the annual value of exports and is therefore not as crippling as it is for the countries in the chart.

Total foreign debt as a percentage of GDP

%
200
100
80
60
40
20
0
no reliable data

TOTAL DEBT OUTSTANDING

THE BALANCE OF TRADE

A country which runs a deficit on the current account is usually consuming more than it produces. Deficits have to be financed by a capital inflow, which cannot continue indefinitely. Imbalances must be remedied sooner or later by measures such as devaluing the currency, raising taxes and cutting government spending.

The current account includes visible imports and exports (raw materials and manufactures) as well as invisibles (payments relating to services rather than goods, and investment income). The map shows the balance of visible trade. The chart showing the top trading nations is based on the sum of imports and exports.

The map also indicates which countries are signatories to the General Agreement on Tariffs and Trade (Gatt), which came into force in 1948 and is the world's major forum for negotiating the reduction of tariffs and other barriers to trade.

Sources: EIU International Economic Appraisal Service; EPL World in Figures;
IMF International Financial Statistics; Europa Year Book (1987 figures)

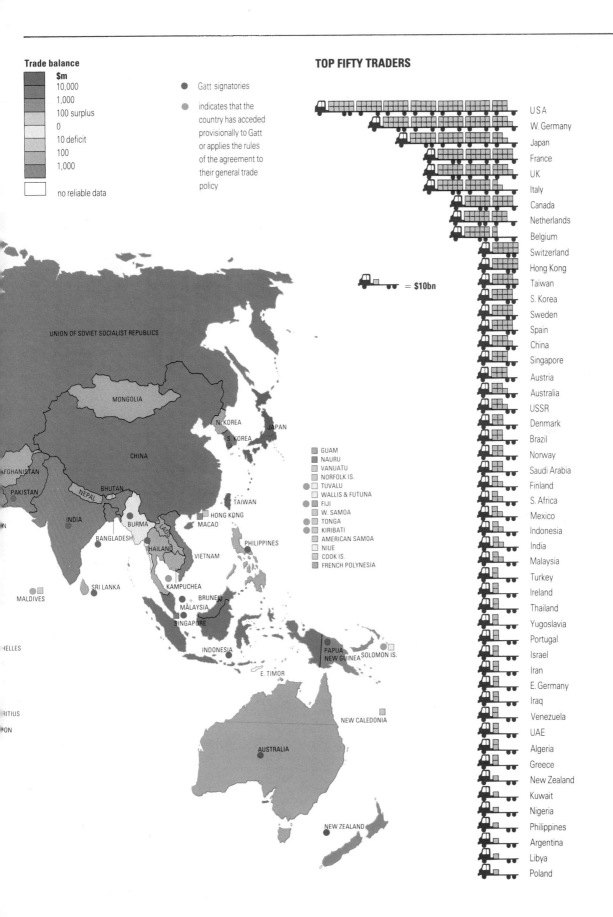

Trade balance

$m
- 10,000
- 1,000
- 100 surplus
- 0
- 10 deficit
- 100
- 1,000

no reliable data

● Gatt signatories

● indicates that the country has acceded provisionally to Gatt or applies the rules of the agreement to their general trade policy

TOP FIFTY TRADERS

= $10bn

USA
W. Germany
Japan
France
UK
Italy
Canada
Netherlands
Belgium
Switzerland
Hong Kong
Taiwan
S. Korea
Sweden
Spain
China
Singapore
Austria
Australia
USSR
Denmark
Brazil
Norway
Saudi Arabia
Finland
S. Africa
Mexico
Indonesia
India
Malaysia
Turkey
Ireland
Thailand
Yugoslavia
Portugal
Israel
Iran
E. Germany
Iraq
Venezuela
UAE
Algeria
Greece
New Zealand
Kuwait
Nigeria
Philippines
Argentina
Libya
Poland

GUAM
NAURU
VANUATU
NORFOLK IS.
TUVALU
WALLIS & FUTUNA
FIJI
W. SAMOA
TONGA
KIRIBATI
AMERICAN SAMOA
NIUE
COOK IS.
FRENCH POLYNESIA

UNION OF SOVIET SOCIALIST REPUBLICS
MONGOLIA
N. KOREA
S. KOREA
JAPAN
CHINA
AFGHANISTAN
PAKISTAN
NEPAL
BHUTAN
TAIWAN
INDIA
BURMA
HONG KONG
MACAO
BANGLADESH
LAOS
THAILAND
VIETNAM
PHILIPPINES
SRI LANKA
MALDIVES
KAMPUCHEA
BRUNEI
MALAYSIA
SINGAPORE
INDONESIA
PAPUA NEW GUINEA
SOLOMON IS.
E. TIMOR
HELLES
RITIUS
ON
NEW CALEDONIA
AUSTRALIA
NEW ZEALAND

TRADE IN MANUFACTURES

The chart at right ranks the principal categories of manufactured goods by the total dollar value of imports and exports, free on board (excluding transport and insurance costs). The other charts identify the biggest exporters and importers in each category. Only market economies are included because evaluations of trade with and between communist nations are blurred by the widespread use of barter and of nonconvertible currencies.

TOP ITEMS TRADED

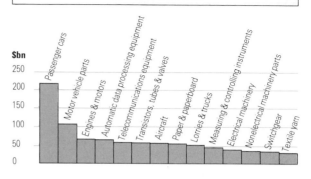

PASSENGER CARS

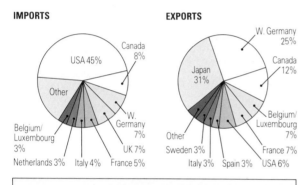

MOTOR VEHICLE PARTS

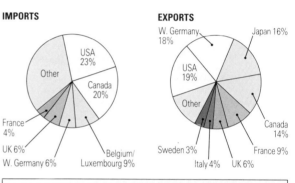

ENGINES & MOTORS

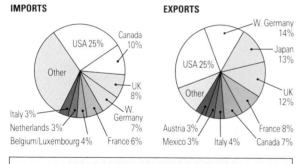

AUTOMATIC DATA PROCESSING EQUIPMENT

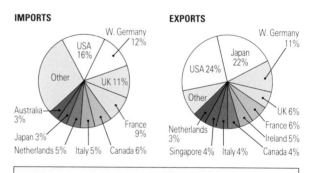

TELECOMMUNICATIONS EQUIPMENT

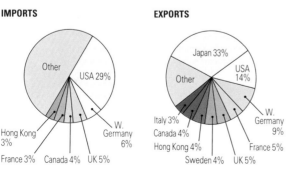

TRANSISTORS, TUBES & VALVES

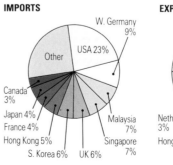
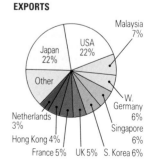

Source: UN *International Trade Statistics Yearbook* (1986 figures)

AIRCRAFT

IMPORTS

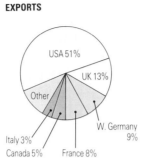

W. Germany 15%
USA 17%
Other
Saudi Arabia 3%
France 4%
Italy 4%
Canada 6%
UK 6%
Japan 7%

EXPORTS

USA 51%
UK 13%
Other
W. Germany 9%
Italy 3%
Canada 5%
France 8%

PAPER & PAPERBOARD

IMPORTS

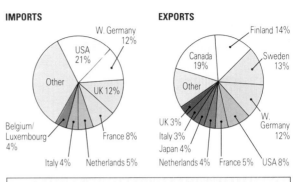

W. Germany 12%
USA 21%
Other
UK 12%
Belgium/Luxembourg 4%
France 8%
Italy 4%
Netherlands 5%

EXPORTS

Finland 14%
Canada 19%
Sweden 13%
Other
UK 3%
W. Germany 12%
Italy 3%
Japan 4%
Netherlands 4%
France 5%
USA 8%

LORRIES & TRUCKS

IMPORTS

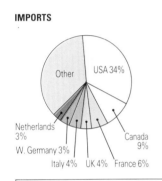

Other
USA 34%
Netherlands 3%
W. Germany 3%
Italy 4%
UK 4%
France 6%
Canada 9%

EXPORTS

W. Germany 13%
Canada 16%
Japan 36%
USA 9%
France 5%
Sweden 5%
Other
Belgium/Luxembourg 3%
Italy 4%

MEASURING & CONTROLLING INSTRUMENTS

IMPORTS

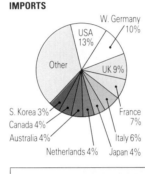

W. Germany 10%
USA 13%
Other
UK 9%
S. Korea 3%
Canada 4%
Australia 4%
France 7%
Netherlands 4%
Italy 6%
Japan 4%

EXPORTS

W. Germany 19%
USA 25%
Other
UK 12%
Italy 3%
Japan 10%
Netherlands 4%
Switzerland 6%
France 6%

ELECTRICAL MACHINERY

IMPORTS

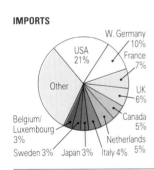

W. Germany 10%
USA 21%
France 7%
Other
UK 6%
Canada 5%
Belgium/Luxembourg 3%
Sweden 3%
Japan 3%
Italy 4%
Netherlands 5%

EXPORTS

W. Germany 19%
USA 14%
Japan 22%
UK 8%
France 7%
Other
Netherlands 6%
Belgium/Luxembourg 3%
Switzerland 4%
Italy 4%

NONELECTRICAL MACHINERY PARTS

IMPORTS

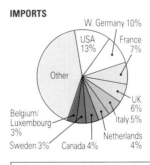

W. Germany 10%
USA 13%
France 7%
Other
UK 6%
Italy 5%
Belgium/Luxembourg 3%
Netherlands 4%
Sweden 3%
Canada 4%

EXPORTS

Japan 14%
Italy 10%
W. Germany 26%
France 9%
Other
USA 8%
UK 7%
Austria 3%
Switzerland 3%
Sweden 3%
Netherlands 3%

SWITCHGEAR

IMPORTS

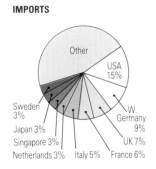

Other
USA 15%
Sweden 3%
Japan 3%
Singapore 3%
Netherlands 3%
Italy 5%
France 6%
UK 7%
W. Germany 9%

EXPORTS

Japan 17%
W. Germany 23%
USA 13%
Other
France 10%
UK 6%
Switzerland 5%
Netherlands 3%
Italy 4%
Singapore 4%

TEXTILE YARN

IMPORTS

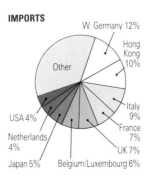

W. Germany 12%
Hong Kong 10%
Other
Italy 9%
France 7%
USA 4%
UK 7%
Netherlands 4%
Belgium/Luxembourg 6%
Japan 5%

EXPORTS

W. Germany 15%
Italy 10%
France 8%
Other
Japan 8%
Hong Kong 6%
USA 4%
Turkey 4%
Belgium/Luxembourg 5%
S. Korea 4%
UK 5%

BANKING AND FINANCE

Source: Morgan Stanley Capital International

STOCK MARKET GROWTH

$bn at the end of December

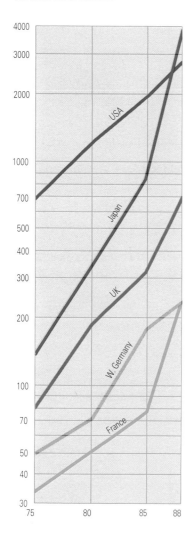

Plotting stock market capitalization in dollars - as here - provides the best comparison of the relative growth of the bourses of the top five countries, although currency fluctuations distort the picture. The figures use an index based on the performance of companies representing 60% of total market capitalization in the countries. The growth of the Japanese market has been spectacular, fuelled by investors who are attracted by the prospect of high capital gains rather than dividend earnings.

TOP INTERNATIONAL BANKS

Rank 1987	Rank 1982		Net assets ($bn) end 1987
1	8	Dai-Ichi Kangyo Bank (Tokyo)	270
2	13	Sumitomo Bank (Osaka)	251
3	10	Fuji Bank (Tokyo)	244
4	12	Mitsubishi Bank (Tokyo)	228
5	16	Sanwa Bank (Osaka)	218
6	21	Industrial Bank of Japan (Tokyo)	216
7	4	Crédit Agricole (Paris)	214
8	1	Citicorp (New York)	198
9	25	Norinchukin Bank (Tokyo)	187
10	3	Banque Nationale de Paris (Paris)	183
11	11	Deutsche Bank (Frankfurt)	169
12	5	Crédit Lyonnais (Paris)	168
13	38	Mitsubishi Trust & Banking (Tokyo)	166
14	6	Barclays Bank (London)	164
15	7	National Westminster Bank (London)	163
16	29	Tokai Bank (Nagoya)	162
17	47	Sumitomo Trust & Banking (Osaka)	154
18	23	Mitsui Bank	154
19	9	Société Générale	145
20	35	Long-Term Credit Bank of Japan (Tokyo)	139
21	40	Taiyo Kobe Bank (Kobe)	139
22	18	Bank of Tokyo (Tokyo)	137
23	48	Mitsui Trust & Banking (Tokyo)	131
24	22	Dresdner Bank (Frankfurt)	130
25	64	Yasuda Trust & Banking (Tokyo)	129
26	55	Daiwa Bank (Osaka)	126
27	31	Union Bank of Switzerland (Zürich)	126
28	32	Compagnie Financière de Paribas (Paris)	122
29	33	Swiss Bank Corporation (Basel)	122
30	81	Toyo Trust & Banking (Tokyo)	109
31	24	Hongkong & Shanghai Banking Corporation (Hong Kong)	106
32	39	Commerzbank (Frankfurt)	101
33	15	Chase Manhattan Bank (New York)	99
34	25	Westdeutsche Landesbank Girozentrale (Düsseldorf)	96
35	41	Banca Nazionale del Lavoro (Rome)	96
36	42	Bayerische Vereinsbank (Munich)	95
37	65	Nippon Credit Bank (Tokyo)	93
38	2	BankAmerica (San Francisco)	91
39	14	Midland Bank (London)	91
40	67	Kyowa Bank (Tokyo)	88
41	36	Algemene Bank Nederland (Amsterdam)	85
42	27	Lloyds Bank (London)	84
43	57	Crédit Suisse (Zürich)	84
44	73	Shokochukin Bank (Tokyo)	84
45	45	Rabobank (Utrecht)	82
46	–	Bank of China (Beijing)	81
47	43	Amsterdam-Rotterdam Bank (Amsterdam)	81
48	66	Deutsche Genossenschaftsbank (Frankfurt)	80
49	54	Bayerische Hypotheken & Wechsel Bank (Munich)	80
50	37	Chemical New York Corporation (New York)	77

The table shows the top 50 banks, ranked by the net dollar values of assets. The second column shows how each bank was ranked in 1982. The rise of Japan's banks has been as dramatic as the rise of the country's stockmarkets.

Source: *The Banker* (a *Financial Times* publication)

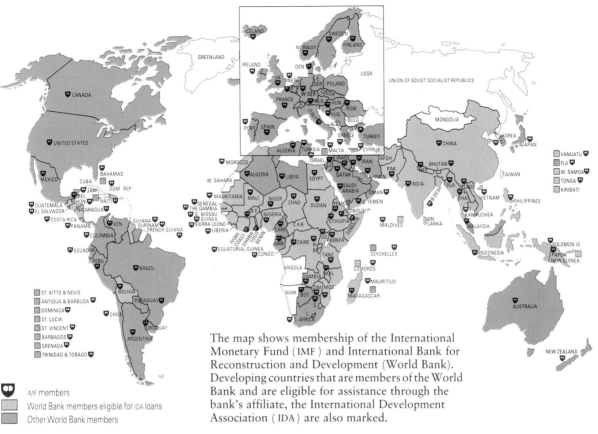

The map shows membership of the International Monetary Fund (IMF) and International Bank for Reconstruction and Development (World Bank). Developing countries that are members of the World Bank and are eligible for assistance through the bank's affiliate, the International Development Association (IDA) are also marked.

IMF members
World Bank members eligible for IDA loans
Other World Bank members

SPENDING ON INSURANCE

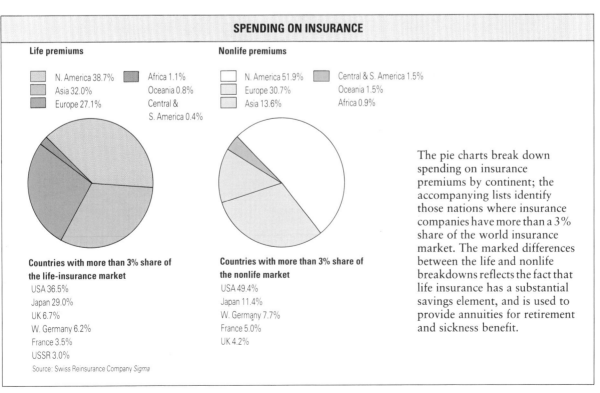

Life premiums

N. America 38.7%
Asia 32.0%
Europe 27.1%
Africa 1.1%
Oceania 0.8%
Central & S. America 0.4%

Nonlife premiums

N. America 51.9%
Europe 30.7%
Asia 13.6%
Central & S. America 1.5%
Oceania 1.5%
Africa 0.9%

Countries with more than 3% share of the life-insurance market

USA 36.5%
Japan 29.0%
UK 6.7%
W. Germany 6.2%
France 3.5%
USSR 3.0%

Source: Swiss Reinsurance Company *Sigma*

Countries with more than 3% share of the nonlife market

USA 49.4%
Japan 11.4%
W. Germany 7.7%
France 5.0%
UK 4.2%

The pie charts break down spending on insurance premiums by continent; the accompanying lists identify those nations where insurance companies have more than a 3% share of the world insurance market. The marked differences between the life and nonlife breakdowns reflects the fact that life insurance has a substantial savings element, and is used to provide annuities for retirement and sickness benefit.

INDUSTRIAL PRODUCTION

The map plots industrial growth
rates, averaged over the decade to
1987. Growth was rapid in parts of
East Asia; but output dropped in
states vulnerable to commodity
price falls or political upheaval.

The pie charts rank the top
producers of a selection of
manufactured goods.

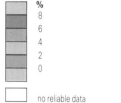

Average industrial growth rate

%
8
6
4
2
0

no reliable data

TOP PRODUCERS
1 tonne = 1.10 US (short) tons

Passenger cars Total 31.9m units

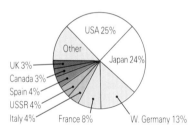

USA 25%
Other
UK 3%
Canada 3%
Spain 4%
USSR 4%
Italy 4%
France 8%
W. Germany 13%
Japan 24%

Crude steel Total 679.5m tonnes

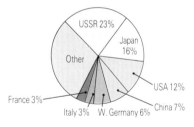

USSR 23%
Japan 16%
Other
USA 12%
France 3%
Italy 3%
W. Germany 6%
China 7%

Cigarettes Total 4,758 bn units

USA 14%
USSR 8%
Japan 7%
W. Germany 3%
Brazil 3%
Other

Ships (launched) Total 14.9m gross registered tons

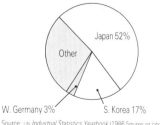

Japan 52%
Other
W. Germany 3%
S. Korea 17%

TV sets Total 84.9m units

Japan 21%
China 20%
Other
USA 16%
Brazil 3%
UK 3%
W. Germany 4%
S. Korea 9%
USSR 11%

Nitrogenous fertilizers Total 73.3m tonnes

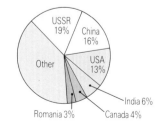

USSR 19%
China 16%
USA 13%
Other
India 6%
Romania 3%
Canada 4%

Source: UN *Industrial Statistics Yearbook* (1986 figures or latest available)

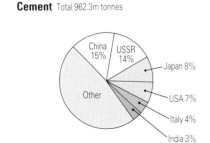

Cement Total 962.3m tonnes

- China 15%
- USSR 14%
- Japan 8%
- USA 7%
- Italy 4%
- India 3%
- Other

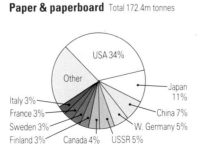

Paper & paperboard Total 172.4m tonnes

- USA 34%
- Japan 11%
- China 7%
- W. Germany 5%
- USSR 5%
- Canada 4%
- Finland 3%
- Sweden 3%
- France 3%
- Italy 3%
- Other

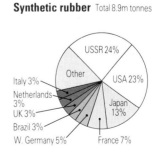

Synthetic rubber Total 8.9m tonnes

- USSR 24%
- USA 23%
- Japan 13%
- France 7%
- W. Germany 5%
- Brazil 3%
- UK 3%
- Netherlands 3%
- Italy 3%
- Other

ENERGY

The map plots energy consumption per head for fuels that are commercially exploited, and the charts show the biggest producers and consumers of energy, fuel by fuel as well as overall. Nuclear and hydroelectricity production is quantified on an output basis - the calorific value of the electricity produced. *Commercial* utilization of other energy resources satisfies an insignificant proportion of the world's energy needs, though wood is the principal fuel source for an estimated 80% of the population in the developing world.

COAL
Production 3.65bn tonnes

Consumption 3.57bn tonnes

OIL
Production 4.39bn tonnes of coal equivalent

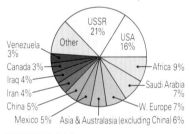

Consumption 4.40bn tonnes of coal equivalent

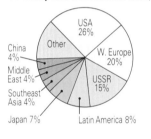

NATURAL GAS
Production 2.50bn tonnes of coal equivalent

Consumption 2.33bn tonnes of coal equivalent

NUCLEAR ENERGY
Production 606m tonnes of coal equivalent (output basis)

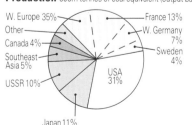

HYDROELECTRICITY
Production 792m tonnes of coal equivalent (output basis)

Energy consumption per head tonnes of coal equivalent per year

- 5.0
- 2.5
- 1.0
- 0.5
- 0.25

no reliable data

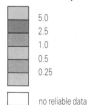

- CAYMAN IS.
- UK VIRGIN IS.
- ST. KITTS & NEVIS
- ANTIGUA & BARBUDA
- MONTSERRAT
- DOMINICA
- MARTINIQUE
- ST. LUCIA
- ST. VINCENT
- BARBADOS
- GRENADA
- NETHERLANDS ANTILLES
- TRINIDAD & TOBAGO

Sources: Top producers and consumers UN *Energy Statistics Yearbook* (1986 figures); Consumption per head UN *Energy Statistics Yearbook, Demographic Yearbook* (1985 figures); Fuels BP *Statistical Review of World Energy* (1987 figures)

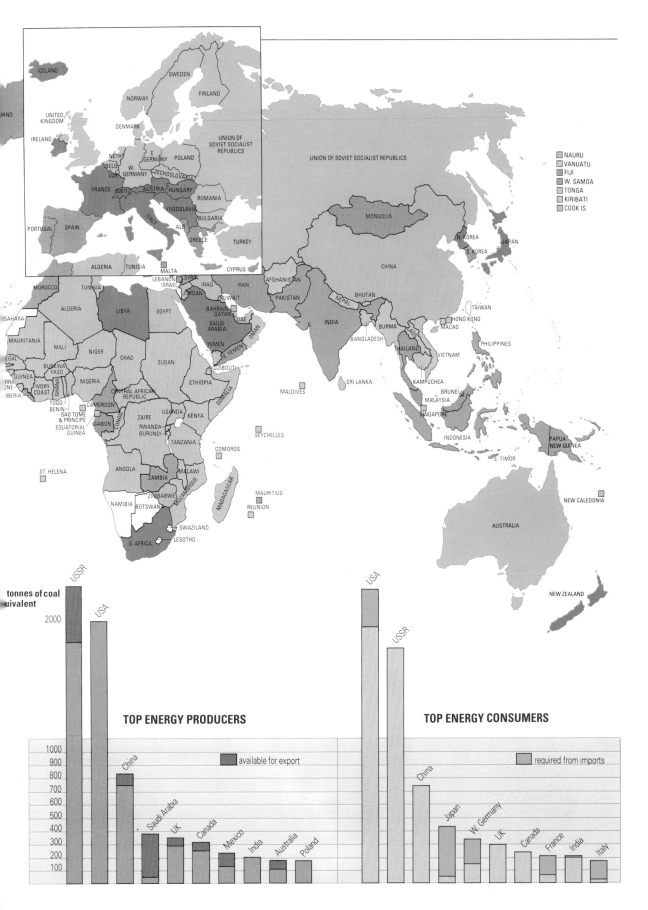

NAURU
VANUATU
FIJI
W. SAMOA
TONGA
KIRIBATI
COOK IS.

TOP ENERGY PRODUCERS

tonnes of coal
uivalent

2000

available for export

1000
900
800
700
600
500
400
300
200
100

USSR
USA
China
Saudi Arabia
UK
Canada
Mexico
India
Australia
Poland

TOP ENERGY CONSUMERS

required from imports

USA
USSR
China
Japan
W. Germany
UK
Canada
France
India
Italy

MINERAL WEALTH

The map symbols identify major producers of important minerals. The charts indicate total world mine output and the percentage mined by each of the larger producing countries. Production volumes for most minerals are for metal content, but output of iron, chromium and bauxite is instead measured as ore weight.

Figures for uranium production in the Eastern bloc are not available and even informed sources are reluctant to estimate output.

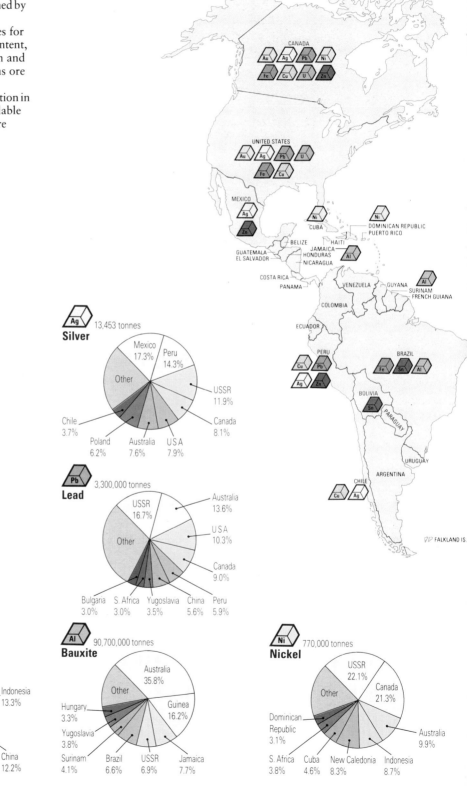

1 tonne = 1.1025 US tons

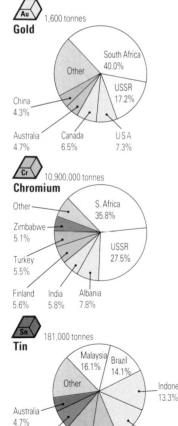

Au 1,600 tonnes
Gold

- South Africa 40.0%
- Other
- USSR 17.2%
- China 4.3%
- Australia 4.7%
- Canada 6.5%
- USA 7.3%

Ag 13,453 tonnes
Silver

- Mexico 17.3%
- Peru 14.3%
- Other
- USSR 11.9%
- Canada 8.1%
- Chile 3.7%
- Poland 6.2%
- Australia 7.6%
- USA 7.9%

Cr 10,900,000 tonnes
Chromium

- Other
- S. Africa 35.8%
- Zimbabwe 5.1%
- USSR 27.5%
- Turkey 5.5%
- Finland 5.6%
- India 5.8%
- Albania 7.8%

Pb 3,300,000 tonnes
Lead

- USSR 16.7%
- Australia 13.6%
- USA 10.3%
- Other
- Canada 9.0%
- Bulgaria 3.0%
- S. Africa 3.0%
- Yugoslavia 3.5%
- China 5.6%
- Peru 5.9%

Sn 181,000 tonnes
Tin

- Malaysia 16.1%
- Brazil 14.1%
- Other
- Indonesia 13.3%
- Australia 4.7%
- Bolivia 6.6%
- USSR 8.8%
- Thailand 9.4%
- China 12.2%

Al 90,700,000 tonnes
Bauxite

- Australia 35.8%
- Other
- Guinea 16.2%
- Hungary 3.3%
- Yugoslavia 3.8%
- Surinam 4.1%
- Brazil 6.6%
- USSR 6.9%
- Jamaica 7.7%

Ni 770,000 tonnes
Nickel

- USSR 22.1%
- Canada 21.3%
- Other
- Dominican Republic 3.1%
- Australia 9.9%
- S. Africa 3.8%
- Cuba 4.6%
- New Caledonia 8.3%
- Indonesia 8.7%

Sources: British Geological Survey *World Mineral Statistics*; *Mining Annual Review*; *Nuexco Annual Review* (1986 figures)

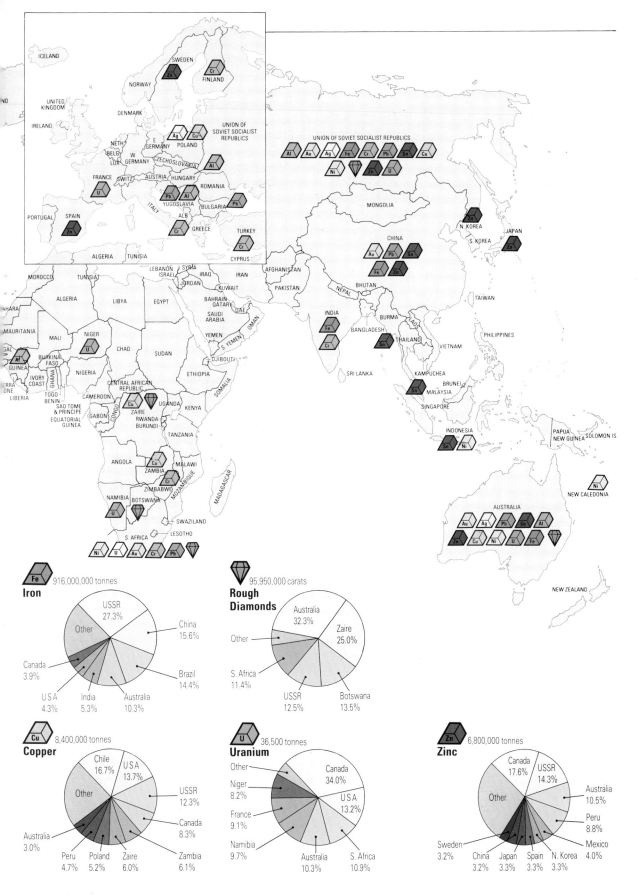

Iron 916,000,000 tonnes

USSR 27.3%
China 15.6%
Other
Brazil 14.4%
Canada 3.9%
Australia 10.3%
USA 4.3%
India 5.3%

Rough Diamonds 95,950,000 carats

Australia 32.3%
Zaire 25.0%
Other
S. Africa 11.4%
USSR 12.5%
Botswana 13.5%

Copper 8,400,000 tonnes

Chile 16.7%
USA 13.7%
USSR 12.3%
Other
Canada 8.3%
Zambia 6.1%
Zaire 6.0%
Poland 5.2%
Peru 4.7%
Australia 3.0%

Uranium 36,500 tonnes

Other
Canada 34.0%
Niger 8.2%
USA 13.2%
France 9.1%
Namibia 9.7%
Australia 10.3%
S. Africa 10.9%

Zinc 6,800,000 tonnes

Canada 17.6%
USSR 14.3%
Australia 10.5%
Other
Peru 8.8%
Mexico 4.0%
N. Korea 3.3%
Spain 3.3%
Japan 3.3%
China 3.2%
Sweden 3.2%

POLITICAL SYSTEMS

Source: Freedom House, NY, *Survey of Freedom 1988*

The map charts political rights, on a scale from 1 for the highest degree of political freedom to 7 for the lowest. Among criteria for a high rating are: recent free and fair elections; a parliament with effective power; a significant opposition and recent shifts in power through elections. Factors contributing to a lower rating include military or foreign control, the denial of self-determination to major population groups and lack of decentralized political power.

Human rights generally go hand-in-hand with political rights. A country that denies its citizens the right to participate in a free electoral process will often also deny them free assembly, demonstration and organization and freedom from political terror and unjustified imprisonment.

Countries which have become independent since 1945 are indicated, by the date of independence. Namibia was due to

become independent in 1990, after elections supervised by the UN in 1989. Aruba, formerly one of the Netherlands Antilles, was granted separate status in 1986 with a view to full independence by 1996.

Related territories of each country are listed separately, but their status and the degree of local autonomy varies widely. A few are under military occupation; some, such as the overseas departments of France, are considered to be integral parts of the sovereign state, while others have a large degree of self-determination.

Political freedom

1	Most free
2	
3	
4	
5	
6	
7	Least free

INTERNATIONAL GROUPINGS

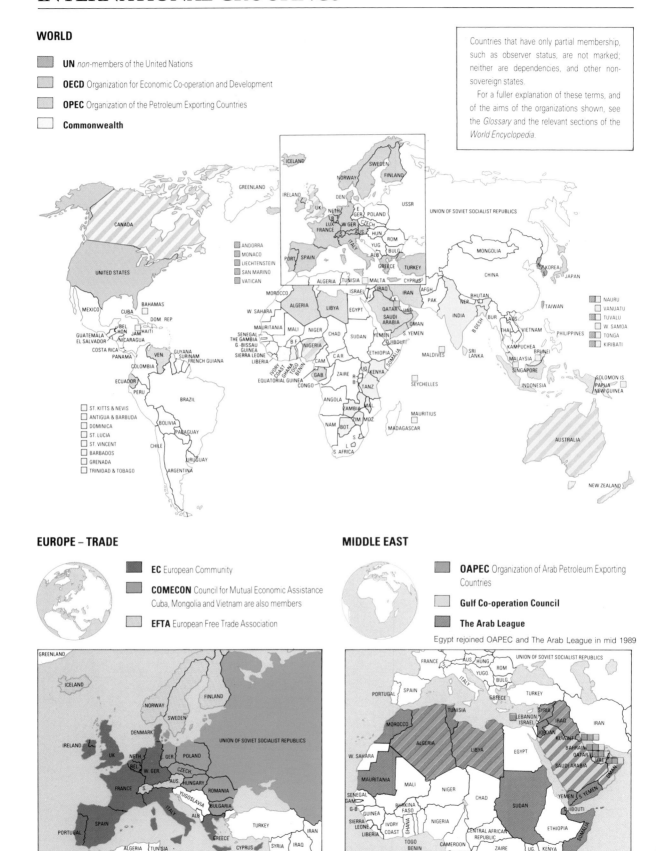

WORLD

UN *non*-members of the United Nations

OECD Organization for Economic Co-operation and Development

OPEC Organization of the Petroleum Exporting Countries

Commonwealth

Countries that have only partial membership, such as observer status, are not marked; neither are dependencies, and other non-sovereign states.

For a fuller explanation of these terms, and of the aims of the organizations shown, see the *Glossary* and the relevant sections of the *World Encyclopedia*.

EUROPE – TRADE

EC European Community

COMECON Council for Mutual Economic Assistance
Cuba, Mongolia and Vietnam are also members

EFTA European Free Trade Association

MIDDLE EAST

OAPEC Organization of Arab Petroleum Exporting Countries

Gulf Co-operation Council

The Arab League

Egypt rejoined OAPEC and The Arab League in mid 1989

THE NORTHERN HEMISPHERE – DEFENCE

NATO North Atlantic Treaty Organization

Warsaw Pact

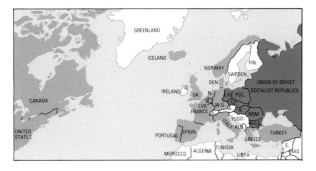

PACIFIC BASIN

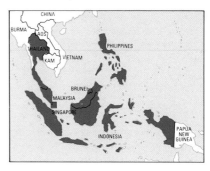

ASEAN Association of South East Asian Nations

LATIN AMERICA AND CARIBBEAN

ALADI Asociación Latinoamericana de Integración

Andean Pact

CARICOM Caribbean Community and Common Market

Organization of River Plate Basin Countries

AFRICA

OAU non-members of the Organization for African Unity

Franc Zone currency linked to the French Franc

SADCC Southern Africa Development Co-ordination Conference

PTA Preferential Trade Area for Eastern and Southern Africa

ECOWAS Economic Community of West African States

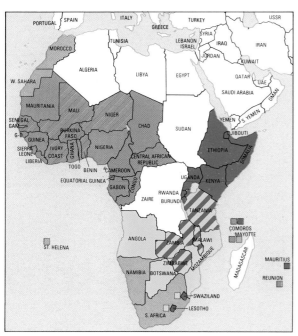

DEFENCE SPENDING

The map shows the proportion of national government expenditure allocated to defence. It gives an indication of the state's budgetary priorities, rather than absolute military strength. Comparisons are complicated by federal states such as Switzerland and Yugoslavia, which spend relatively little at a national level, thereby inflating the proportion of military spending. Where actual figures are unavailable, budgeted figures or, as a last resort, informed estimates have been used. For the USSR, these vary by as much as $100bn, because much of Soviet military procurement and research and development expenditure is not included in the published defence budget.

BILLION DOLLAR SPENDERS

$bn

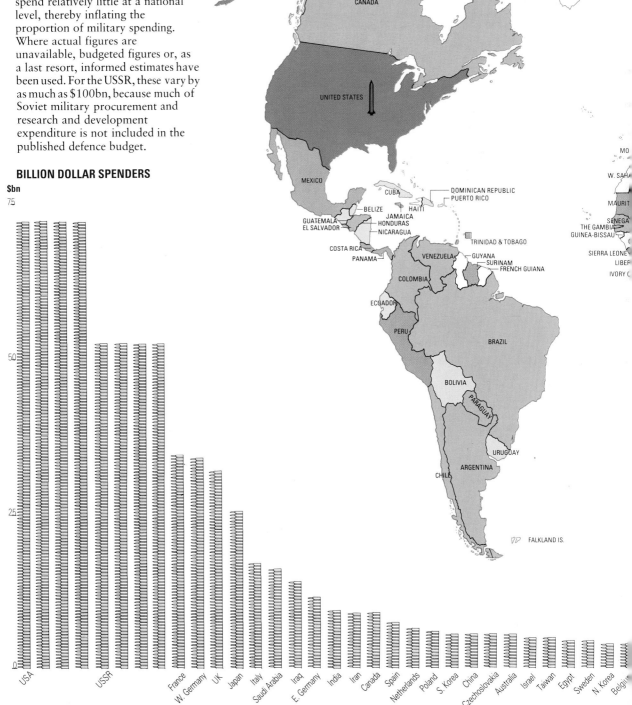

Source : International Institute for Strategic Studies *The Military Balance*

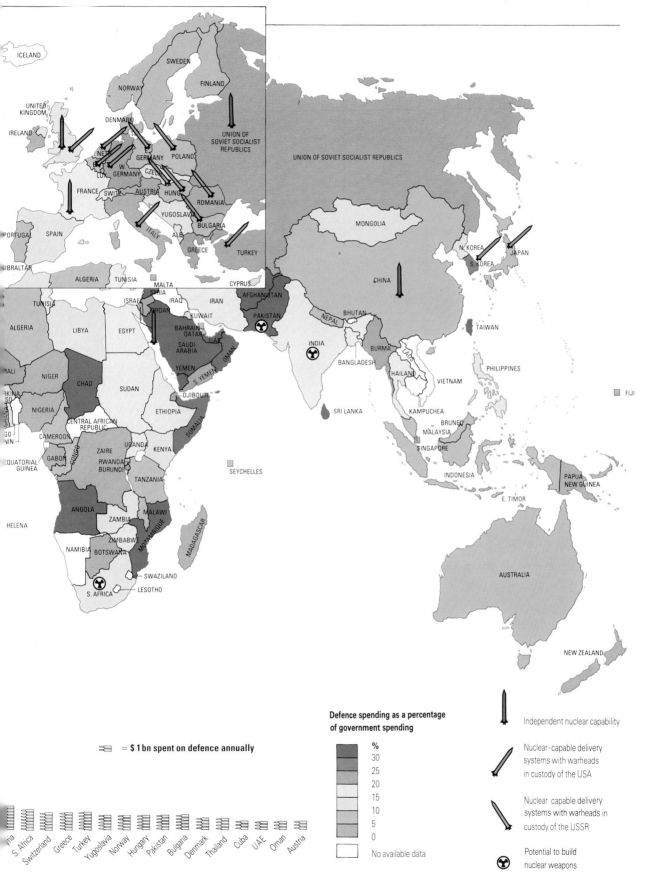

ICELAND

SWEDEN

NORWAY

FINLAND

UNITED
KINGDOM

IRELAND

DENMARK

UNION OF
SOVIET SOCIALIST
REPUBLICS

NETH

GERMANY

POLAND

UNION OF SOVIET SOCIALIST REPUBLICS

B
LUX

W
GERMANY

CZECH

FRANCE

SWITZ

AUSTRIA

HUNG

PORTUGAL

SPAIN

ITALY

YUGOSLAVIA

ROMANIA

BULGARIA

ALB

GIBRALTAR

GREECE

TURKEY

MONGOLIA

N. KOREA

JAPAN

ALGERIA

TUNISIA

MALTA

CYPRUS

S. KOREA

CHINA

TUNISIA

SYRIA

IRAQ

IRAN

AFGHANISTAN

ISRAEL

JORDAN

KUWAIT

PAKISTAN

NEPAL

BHUTAN

ALGERIA

LIBYA

EGYPT

BAHRAIN
QATAR

SAUDI
ARABIA

UAE

OMAN

INDIA

BURMA

TAIWAN

MALI

NIGER

CHAD

SUDAN

YEMEN

S. YEMEN

BANGLADESH

THAILAND

VIETNAM

PHILIPPINES

RKINA
SO

NIGERIA

DJIBOUTI

ETHIOPIA

SOMALIA

SRI LANKA

KAMPUCHEA

FIJI

CENTRAL AFRICAN
REPUBLIC

CAMEROON

GO
IN

EQUATORIAL
GUINEA

GABON

CONGO

ZAIRE

UGANDA

RWANDA
BURUNDI

KENYA

TANZANIA

SEYCHELLES

BRUNEI
MALAYSIA

SINGAPORE

INDONESIA

PAPUA
NEW GUINEA

E. TIMOR

HELENA

ANGOLA

ZAMBIA

MALAWI

MOZAMBIQUE

MADAGASCAR

NAMIBIA

ZIMBABWE

BOTSWANA

SWAZILAND

S. AFRICA

LESOTHO

AUSTRALIA

NEW ZEALAND

= $ 1bn spent on defence annually

ria
S. Africa
Switzerland
Greece
Turkey
Yugoslavia
Norway
Hungary
Pakistan
Bulgaria
Denmark
Thailand
Cuba
UAE
Oman
Austria

**Defence spending as a percentage
of government spending**

%
30
25
20
15
10
5
0

No available data

Independent nuclear capability

Nuclear-capable delivery
systems with warheads
in custody of the USA

Nuclear capable delivery
systems with warheads in
custody of the USSR

Potential to build
nuclear weapons

FOREIGN AID

The map shows the amount of official aid received by each country per head of population. The figures, in US dollars, cover grants, loans and technical assistance and show actual disbursements, rather than commitments. Both bilateral — government-to-government — and multilateral aid through agencies such as the World Bank group is included. Military aid is excluded.

The aid is all provided by members of the OECD Development Assistance Committee (DAC), Opec and Comecon; aid from countries that do not belong to these organizations is excluded.

The pie chart shows the share of aid contributed by major donors, including the individual shares of EC members and the proportion of French aid that goes to its overseas departments and territories.

Total foreign aid received per head per year

$
	1000
	500
	200
	100
	50
	20
	0 or net donor

Source: OECD (1987 figures)

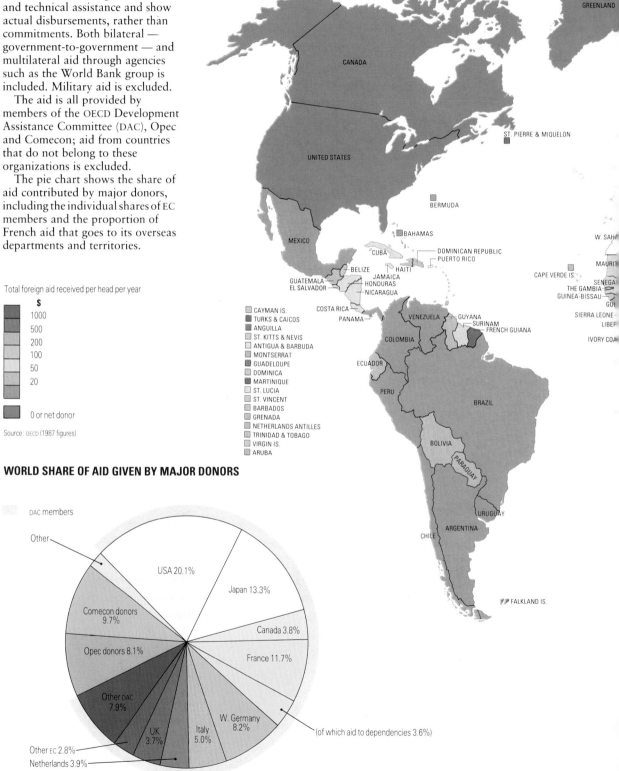

CAYMAN IS.
TURKS & CAICOS
ANGUILLA
ST. KITTS & NEVIS
ANTIGUA & BARBUDA
MONTSERRAT
GUADELOUPE
DOMINICA
MARTINIQUE
ST. LUCIA
ST. VINCENT
BARBADOS
GRENADA
NETHERLANDS ANTILLES
TRINIDAD & TOBAGO
VIRGIN IS.
ARUBA

WORLD SHARE OF AID GIVEN BY MAJOR DONORS

DAC members

Other

USA 20.1%
Japan 13.3%
Canada 3.8%
France 11.7%
(of which aid to dependencies 3.6%)
W. Germany 8.2%
Italy 5.0%
UK 3.7%
Netherlands 3.9%
Other EC 2.8%
Other DAC 7.9%
Opec donors 8.1%
Comecon donors 9.7%

Source: OECD (1986-87 average figures)

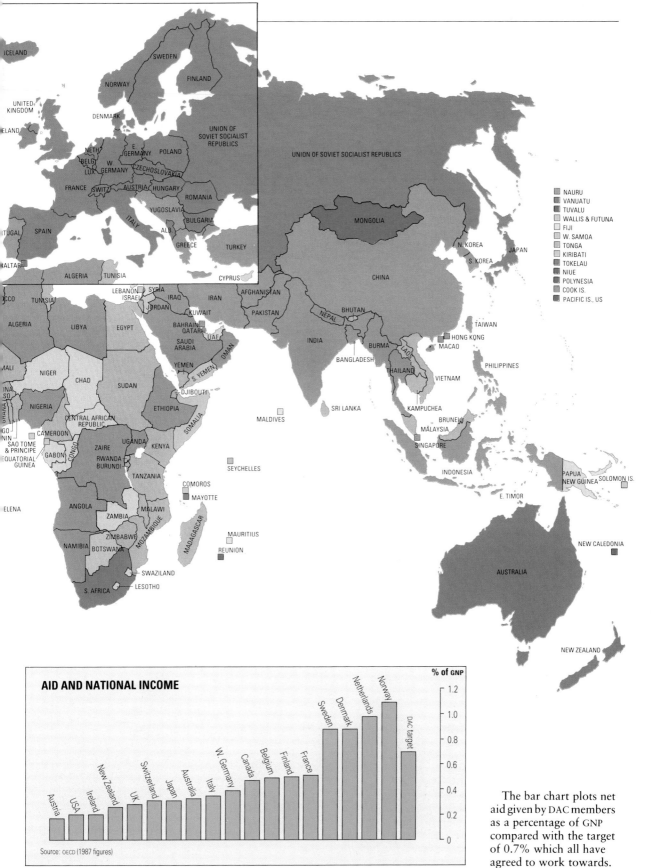

NAURU
VANUATU
TUVALU
WALLIS & FUTUNA
FIJI
W. SAMOA
TONGA
KIRIBATI
TOKELAU
NIUE
POLYNESIA
COOK IS.
PACIFIC IS., US

AID AND NATIONAL INCOME

% of GNP

Austria
USA
Ireland
New Zealand
UK
Switzerland
Japan
Australia
Italy
W. Germany
Canada
Belgium
Finland
France
Sweden
Denmark
Netherlands
Norway
DAC target

1.2
1.0
0.8
0.6
0.4
0.2
0

Source: OECD (1987 figures)

The bar chart plots net aid given by DAC members as a percentage of GNP compared with the target of 0.7% which all have agreed to work towards.

FOOD AND HUNGER

The map shows the calorie consumption per head of population, and countries where on average people do not get enough protein. A moderately active man needs to consume about 3,000 calories per day, a sedentary one 2,500. Their female counterparts require respectively 2,200 and 2,000 calories per day.

The use this century of fertilizers, pesticides and new hybrids has meant that the world now produces enough to feed everyone. But the production of food is unevenly distributed, while as a commodity its transport costs are usually high in relation to its market price. Most foodstuffs are subject to price fluctuations, related to weather. Few government attempts to stabilize prices by subsidies, controls or international stockpiling have met with much long-term success.

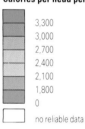

Calories per head per day

- 3,300
- 3,000
- 2,700
- 2,400
- 2,100
- 1,800
- 0
- no reliable data
- ● average daily protein consumption per head per day less than 45 gm

ST. KITTS & NEVIS
ANTIGUA & BARBUDA
GUADELOUPE
DOMINICA
MARTINIQUE
ST. LUCIA
ST. VINCENT
BARBADOS
GRENADA
NETHERLANDS ANTILLES
TRINIDAD & TOBAGO

STAPLE FOOD PRODUCTION

The charts show world production of staple foods. Figures indicate the yield in kilograms per hectare.
1,000 kg ha = 8·92 US cwt acre

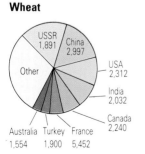

Wheat

USSR 1,891
China 2,997
USA 2,312
India 2,032
Canada 2,240
Other
Australia 1,554
Turkey 1,900
France 5,452

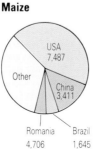

Maize

USA 7,487
China 3,411
Other
Romania 4,706
Brazil 1,645

Millet

India 523
China 2,045
Nigeria 945
Other
Mali 856
Niger 427
USSR 1,132

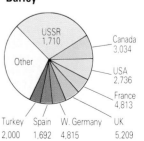

Barley

USSR 1,710
Canada 3,034
USA 2,736
France 4,813
Other
Turkey 2,000
Spain 1,692
W. Germany 4,815
UK 5,209

Sources: Food and Agriculture Organizations. Consumption 1983-85 average; production 1979-81 average.

Sorghum

- USA 4,251
- India 656
- Sudan 736
- Argentina 3,000
- Nigeria 1,087
- Mexico 3,706
- China 3,484
- Other

Oats

- USSR 1,598
- USA 2,008
- Sweden 3,413
- Australia 1,259
- Poland 2,452
- W. Germany 4,442
- Canada 2,511
- Other

Rice

- China 5,372
- India 2,195
- Japan 6,322
- Burma 3,125
- Vietnam 2,857
- Thailand 1,916
- Bangladesh 2,350
- Indonesia 3,979
- Other

Rye

- USSR 1,714
- Poland 2,537
- China 1,538
- W. Germany 4,281
- E. Germany 3,536
- Other

POPULATION DENSITY AND GROWTH

Populations are hard to measure and change constantly, so all figures are estimates. Even the more reliable ones may be based on a census carried out up to 10 years ago.

The map shows population density, obtained by dividing population by land area. However, the larger and more geographically varied a country, the cruder this measure becomes. In the USSR the vast majority of the population lives west of the Urals. Even in a small country the density figure can be deceptive; if you exclude the uninhabitable areas of Japan, population density increases from 324 people per sq km to 1,500.

Also indicated on the map are the world's biggest cities, based on central areas only. A list based on greater metropolitan areas would be very different. For example, the population of central Paris is only 2.2m but some 10m people live within the official boundaries of greater Paris, making it the world's fifth biggest metropolitan area.

People per sq km

500
250
100
50
25
10
0

Largest cities
Population (m)

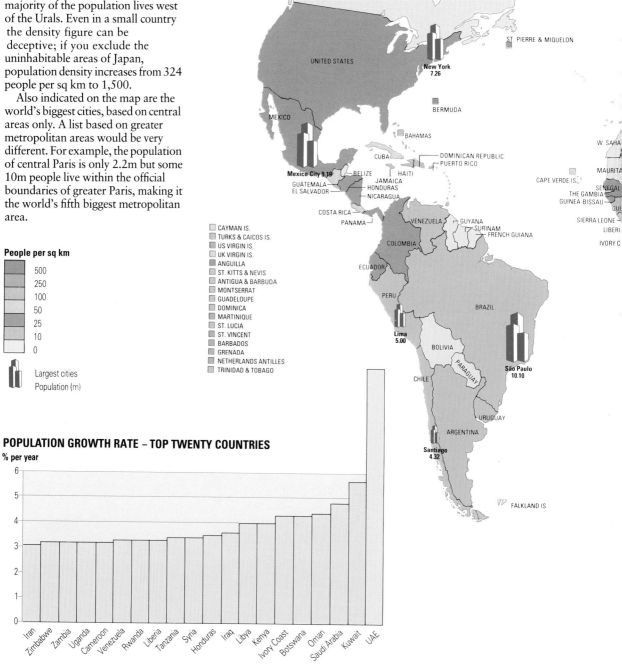

CAYMAN IS.
TURKS & CAICOS IS.
US VIRGIN IS.
UK VIRGIN IS.
ANGUILLA
ST. KITTS & NEVIS
ANTIGUA & BARBUDA
MONTSERRAT
GUADELOUPE
DOMINICA
MARTINIQUE
ST. LUCIA
ST. VINCENT
BARBADOS
GRENADA
NETHERLANDS ANTILLES
TRINIDAD & TOBAGO

POPULATION GROWTH RATE – TOP TWENTY COUNTRIES

% per year

6
5
4
3
2
1
0

Iran, Zimbabwe, Zambia, Uganda, Cameroon, Venezuela, Rwanda, Liberia, Tanzania, Syria, Honduras, Iraq, Libya, Kenya, Ivory Coast, Botswana, Oman, Saudi Arabia, Kuwait, UAE

Sources: Density EPL *World in Figures* (1985 figures); Growth rates World Bank (1980-87 average figures)

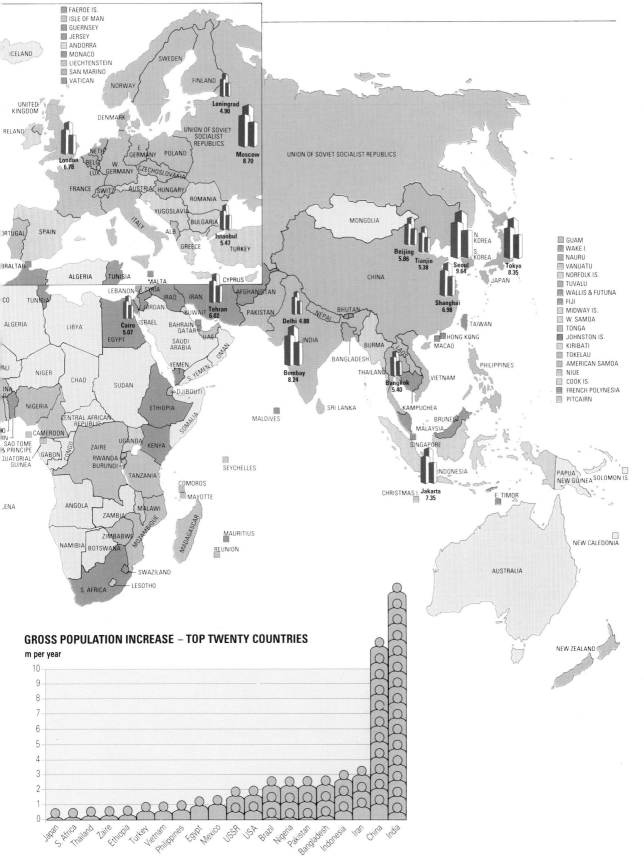

FAEROE IS.
ISLE OF MAN
GUERNSEY
JERSEY
ANDORRA
MONACO
LIECHTENSTEIN
SAN MARINO
VATICAN

ICELAND

SWEDEN

NORWAY

FINLAND

UNITED KINGDOM

DENMARK

Leningrad 4.90

IRELAND

NETH.
BELG.
LUX.

E. GERMANY

POLAND

UNION OF SOVIET SOCIALIST REPUBLICS

Moscow 8.70

London 6.78

W GERMANY

CZECHOSLOVAKIA

UNION OF SOVIET SOCIALIST REPUBLICS

PORTUGAL

SPAIN

FRANCE

SWITZ.

AUSTRIA

HUNGARY

ROMANIA

ITALY

YUGOSLAVIA

BULGARIA

ALB.

GREECE

Istanbul 5.47

TURKEY

MONGOLIA

CHINA

GIBRALTAR

ALGERIA

TUNISIA

MALTA

CYPRUS

LEBANON

SYRIA

IRAQ

IRAN

AFGHANISTAN

Tehran 6.02

PAKISTAN

NEPAL

BHUTAN

Beijing 5.86

Tianjin 5.38

Shanghai 6.98

Seoul 9.64

N. KOREA

S. KOREA

Tokyo 8.35

JAPAN

CO

TUNISIA

JORDAN

ISRAEL

KUWAIT

BAHRAIN

QATAR

UAE

Delhi 4.88

INDIA

TAIWAN

ALGERIA

LIBYA

EGYPT

Cairo 5.07

SAUDI ARABIA

OMAN

BURMA

BANGLADESH

HONG KONG

MACAO

ALI

NIGER

CHAD

SUDAN

YEMEN

S. YEMEN

Bombay 8.24

THAILAND

LAOS

VIETNAM

Bangkok 5.40

PHILIPPINES

NIGERIA

DJIBOUTI

ETHIOPIA

SRI LANKA

KAMPUCHEA

SAO TOME & PRINCIPE

CENTRAL AFRICAN REPUBLIC

CAMEROON

UGANDA

ZAIRE

KENYA

SOMALIA

MALDIVES

BRUNEI

MALAYSIA

SINGAPORE

GABON

CONGO

EQUATORIAL GUINEA

RWANDA

BURUNDI

TANZANIA

COMOROS

MAYOTTE

SEYCHELLES

INDONESIA

PAPUA NEW GUINEA

SOLOMON IS.

LENA

ANGOLA

ZAMBIA

MALAWI

MOZAMBIQUE

MADAGASCAR

MAURITIUS

REUNION

CHRISTMAS I.

Jakarta 7.35

E. TIMOR

ZIMBABWE

NAMIBIA

BOTSWANA

SWAZILAND

S. AFRICA

LESOTHO

NEW CALEDONIA

AUSTRALIA

GUAM
WAKE I.
NAURU
VANUATU
NORFOLK IS.
TUVALU
WALLIS & FUTUNA
FIJI
MIDWAY IS.
W. SAMOA
TONGA
JOHNSTON IS.
KIRIBATI
TOKELAU
AMERICAN SAMOA
NIUE
COOK IS.
FRENCH POLYNESIA
PITCAIRN

NEW ZEALAND

GROSS POPULATION INCREASE – TOP TWENTY COUNTRIES

m per year

10
9
8
7
6
5
4
3
2
1
0

Japan
S. Africa
Thailand
Zaire
Ethiopia
Turkey
Vietnam
Philippines
Egypt
Mexico
USSR
USA
Brazil
Nigeria
Pakistan
Bangladesh
Indonesia
Iran
China
India

LIFE EXPECTANCY & HEALTH

LIFE EXPECTANCY

The map shows average female life expectancy. Men generally have a lower life expectancy, but the gap between the sexes varies widely. It is greatest – up to 10 years, more commonly 6 or 7 – in several Eastern European countries and in the developed nations, and smallest on average, 2-3 years – in less developed countries. In a few countries, notably those of the Indian subcontinent, men have a slightly higher life expectancy than women.

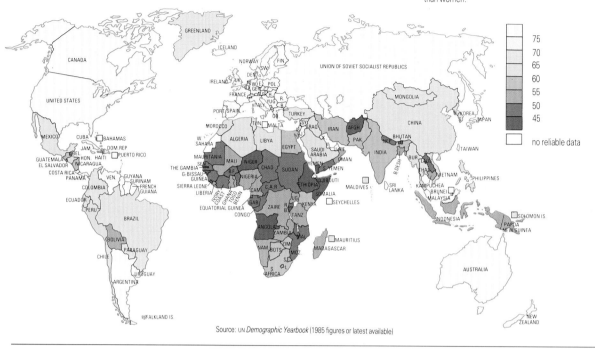

	75
	70
	65
	60
	55
	50
	45
	no reliable data

Source: UN *Demographic Yearbook* (1985 figures or latest available)

INFANT MORTALITY

The map shows the number of children per 1,000 who die before reaching their first birthday. Many of the deaths in countries with high infant mortality rates are caused by poor water and sanitation, disease and a lack of health education.

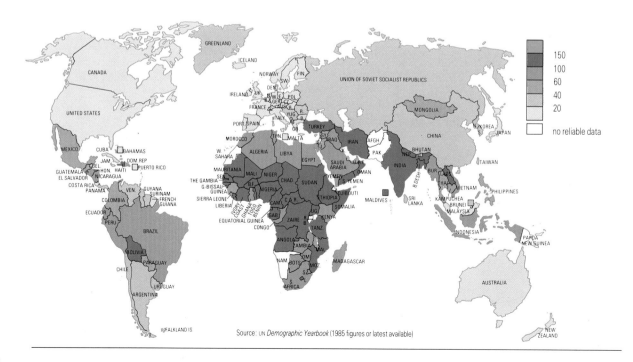

	150
	100
	60
	40
	20
	no reliable data

Source: UN *Demographic Yearbook* (1985 figures or latest available)

PEOPLE PER PHYSICIAN

Comparing this map with those showing infant mortality and life expectancy reveals that the number of physicians is not a straightforward indicator of a state's standards of health; for example, the USSR has more physicians per head of population than any other country, yet ranks 39th in the life expectancy table. The available figures are for all qualified physicians, not just those in medical practice, and exclude paramedics who play a significant role in primary health care, particularly in developing countries.

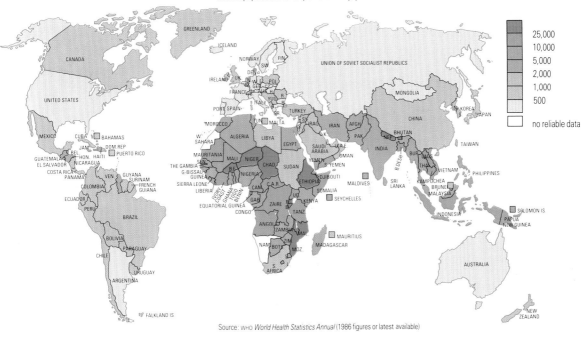

	25,000
	10,000
	5,000
	2,000
	1,000
	500
	no reliable data

Source: WHO *World Health Statistics Annual* (1986 figures or latest available)

NUMBER OF PENSIONERS

Developed countries are preoccupied by the ageing of their populations. They face an awkward combination of declining birth rates and high and rising life expectancy. The prospect is an unbalanced age profile: a large number of people over 65, born in an era of high fertility and living much longer than previous generations, supported by too few economically active citizens. Current levels and conditions of pensions provision will be increasingly expensive to maintain, and difficult, politically, to erode.

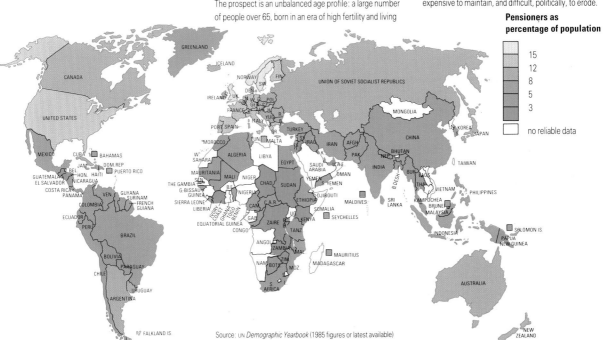

Pensioners as percentage of population

	15
	12
	8
	5
	3
	no reliable data

Source: UN *Demographic Yearbook* (1985 figures or latest available)

ENVIRONMENT

Burning fossil fuel releases large quantities of carbon dioxide which, with other gasses, traps heat in the atmosphere and is causing a slow increase in global temperatures. This "greenhouse effect" could have disastrous consequences: widespread crop failures and flooding of population centres. The first chart identifies the countries that generate the most carbon dioxide from fossil fuels. The second chart shows global temperature rise, with future predictions based on three models.

Burning of tropical rain forests releases yet more carbon dioxide; this is just one of many problems of deforestation. The third chart shows the scale of forest loss and the map identifies where the destruction is taking place.

The meagre environment on the fringes of the world's deserts is being destroyed by over-grazing and deforestation. The map indicates where the threat of desertification is most serious.

Acid rain, the product of industrial emissions of sulphur dioxide and nitrogen oxides, is a major contributor to forest destruction and water pollution in the northern hemisphere. The map shows the regions of great acidity. Some countries, the members of the "30% club" (Austria, Canada, Denmark, Finland, France, the Netherlands, Norway, Sweden, Switzerland and West Germany), have begun to tackle the problem with an agreement to cut sulphur emissions to 70% of present levels by 1993.

DESERTIFICATION

Very high degree of desertificaiton hazard

High degree of desertification hazard

Source: United Nations *Map of desertification*

RAIN FOREST DESTRUCTION

Present distribution of forest area

Area originally forested

Source: Smithsonian Institute *Tropical Rainforests: A Disappearing Treasure*

ACID DEPOSITION

Estimated acidity of precipitation in the northern hemisphere

ph

5.0 least acid

4.5

4.0 most acid

Source: World Metereological Organisation *Long-Range Transport of Sulphur in the Atmosphere and Acid Rain*

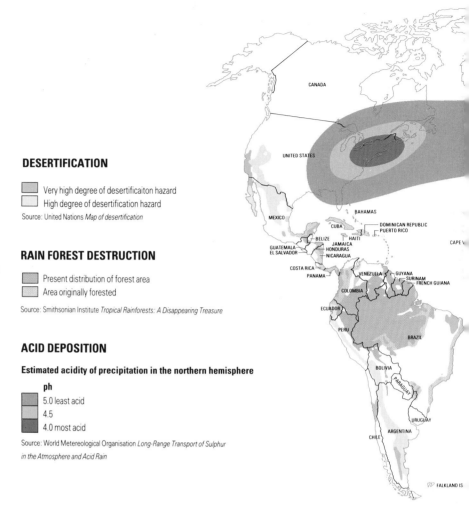

CARBON DIOXIDE EMISSIONS

Figures indicate tonnes of carbon per head per year

% of total world CO$_2$ emissions

1 tonne = 1.102 US tons

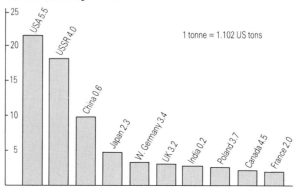

USA 5.5 · USSR 4.0 · China 0.6 · Japan 2.3 · W. Germany 3.4 · UK 3.2 · India 0.2 · Poland 3.7 · Canada 4.5 · France 2.0

Source: Carbon Dioxide Information Analysis Centre (1986 figures)

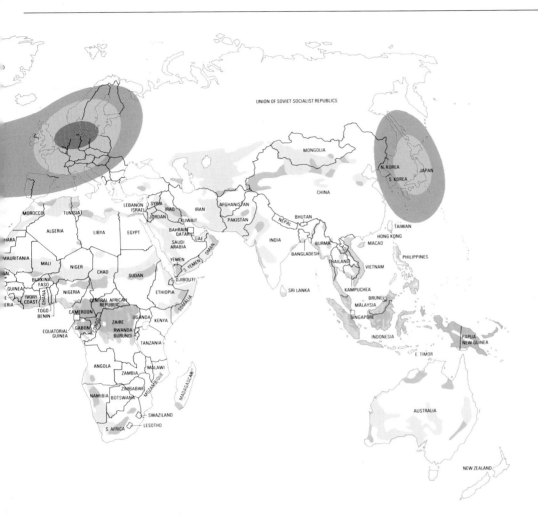

GLOBAL WARMING

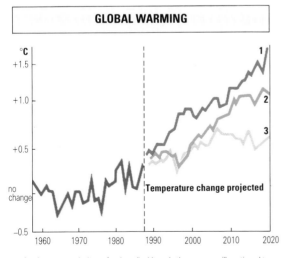

1 Assumes emissions of carbon dioxide and other gasses will continued to grow at the current rate

2 Assumes emissions of carbon dioxide continue at the current level

3 Assumes drastic cuts in emissions in the 1990s

Source: Nasa Goddard Institute for Space

DEFORESTATION IN TROPICAL COUNTRIES

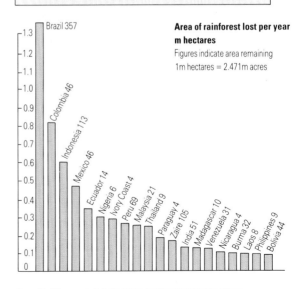

Area of rainforest lost per year m hectares

Figures indicate area remaining
1m hectares = 2.471m acres

Source: World Resources Institute *World Resources Report* (1981-85 average figures)

EDUCATION

The map shows government spending on education as a percentage of GDP, averaged over the five years 1982-86, while the chart ranks those independent countries which spend most per head on education, rounding figures to the nearest $50. In countries where many are educated privately the actual spending on education is, of course, significantly higher.

Average education spending as a percentage of GDP

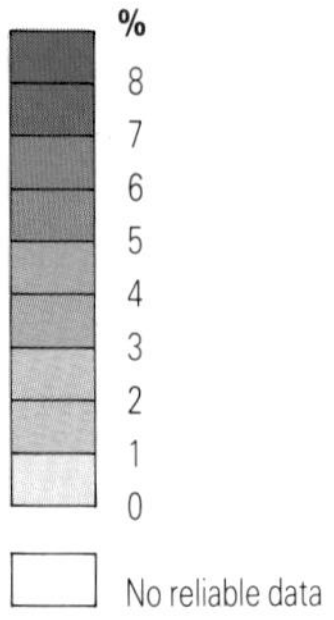

%
8
7
6
5
4
3
2
1
0

No reliable data

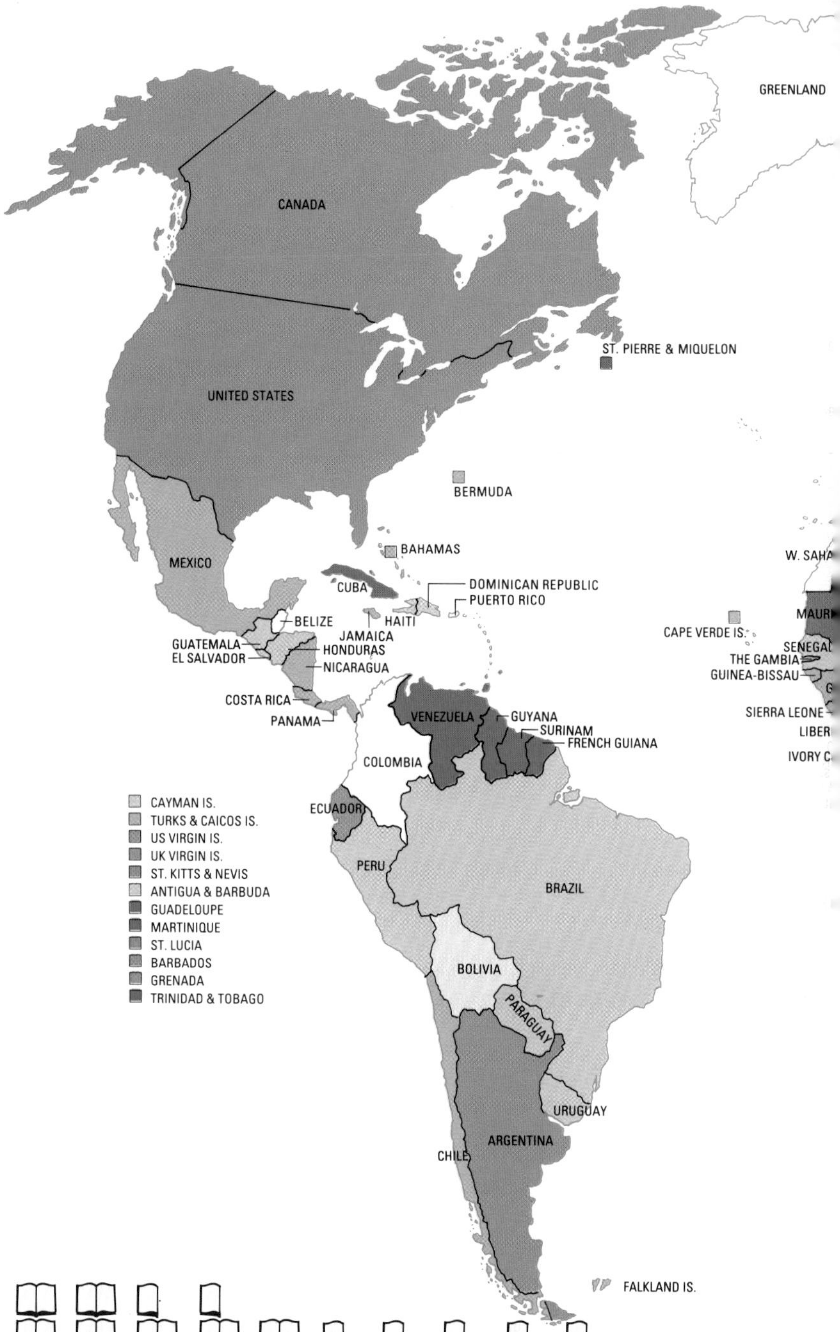

GOVERNMENT SPENDING PER HEAD

= $100

CAYMAN IS.
TURKS & CAICOS IS.
US VIRGIN IS.
UK VIRGIN IS.
ST. KITTS & NEVIS
ANTIGUA & BARBUDA
GUADELOUPE
MARTINIQUE
ST. LUCIA
BARBADOS
GRENADA
TRINIDAD & TOBAGO

GREENLAND

CANADA

ST. PIERRE & MIQUELON

UNITED STATES

BERMUDA

BAHAMAS

W. SAHA

MEXICO

CUBA
DOMINICAN REPUBLIC
PUERTO RICO
HAITI
JAMAICA
BELIZE
GUATEMALA
HONDURAS
EL SALVADOR
NICARAGUA
COSTA RICA
PANAMA

CAPE VERDE IS.
MAUR
SENEGAL
THE GAMBIA
GUINEA-BISSAU
G
SIERRA LEONE
LIBER
IVORY C

VENEZUELA
GUYANA
SURINAM
FRENCH GUIANA

COLOMBIA

ECUADOR

PERU

BRAZIL

BOLIVIA

PARAGUAY

URUGUAY

ARGENTINA

CHILE

FALKLAND IS.

Qatar · USA · Canada · Sweden · Norway · Switzerland · Luxembourg · Saudi Arabia · Australia · Denmark · Kuwait · Netherlands · France · Finland · Libya · UAE · Japan · Israel · Austria · Belgium · W. Germany

Source: Unesco *UN Demographic Survey* (1982-86 average figures)

LANGUAGE

Countries are coloured according to their *lingua franca*, the language most widely spoken, but the accompanying graphic gives a breakdown of world population by mother tongue. The contrast between the two is striking, reflecting the tension between the official and the colloquial. The map could be one of the great empires, with six international languages, English, French, Spanish, Portuguese, Arabic and Russian, covering most of the globe. Yet, as the chart shows, a majority have as their native tongue one spoken by fewer than 1% of the world's population. These minor languages are included in 'Others'.

It is in Africa that the dichotomy between *lingua franca* and mother tongue is strongest. Nations divided along tribal lines have tended to adopt the language of their colonisers, a common denominator, as their official language: inhabitants thus fall into one category and the country into another. Similarly, in Canada, the USSR, India, Peru and Paraguay there are large linguistic minorities which often find it expedient to understand the dominant language, but do not adopt it as a mother tongue.

- CAYMAN IS.
- TURKS & CAICOS IS.
- US VIRGIN IS.
- UK VIRGIN IS.
- ANGUILLA
- ST. KITTS & NEVIS
- ANTIGUA & BARBUDA
- MONTSERRAT
- GUADELOUPE
- DOMINICA
- MARTINIQUE
- ST. LUCIA
- ST. VINCENT
- BARBADOS
- GRENADA
- NETHERLANDS ANTILLES
- TRINIDAD & TOBAGO

MOTHER TONGUES

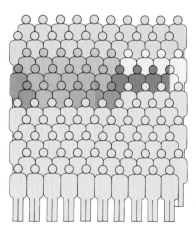

Source: Larrouse *Atlas Geostrategique*

FAEROE IS.
ISLE OF MAN
GUERNSEY
JERSEY
ANDORRA
MONACO
LIECHTENSTEIN
SAN MARINO
VATICAN

ICELAND

UNITED
KINGDOM

IRELAND

SWEDEN

NORWAY

FINLAND

DENMARK

NETH.
BELG.
LUX.

E.
GERMANY

POLAND

W.
GERMANY

CZECHOSLOVAKIA

UNION OF
SOVIET SOCIALIST
REPUBLICS

UNION OF SOVIET SOCIALIST REPUBLICS

FRANCE

SWITZ.

AUSTRIA

HUNGARY

RTUGAL

SPAIN

ITALY

YUGOSLAVIA

ROMANIA

BULGARIA

ALB.

GREECE

TURKEY

RALTAR

MALTA

CYPRUS

ALGERIA

TUNISIA

MONGOLIA

N. KOREA

JAPAN

S. KOREA

GUAM
PACIFIC IS., US
WAKE I.
NAURU
VANUATU
NORFOLK IS.
TUVALU
WALLIS & FUTUNA
FIJI
MIDWAY IS.
W. SAMOA
TONGA
JOHNSTON IS.
KIRIBATI
TOKELAU
AMERICAN SAMOA
NIUE
COOK IS.
FRENCH POLYNESIA
PITCAIRN

LEBANON
SYRIA
ISRAEL
IRAQ
JORDAN
KUWAIT

IRAN

AFGHANISTAN

PAKISTAN

CHINA

TAIWAN

TUNISIA

ALGERIA

LIBYA

EGYPT

BAHRAIN
QATAR
UAE

SAUDI
ARABIA

OMAN

NEPAL

BHUTAN

INDIA

BURMA

BANGLADESH

HONG KONG

MACAO

NIGER

CHAD

SUDAN

YEMEN

S. YEMEN

LAOS

THAILAND

VIETNAM

PHILIPPINES

KRNA
SO

NIGERIA

DJIBOUTI

ETHIOPIA

SOMALIA

MALDIVES

SRI LANKA

KAMPUCHEA

BRUNEI
MALAYSIA

CENTRAL AFRICAN
REPUBLIC

O
VIN
AO TOME
PRINCIPE

CAMEROON

GABON

JATORIAL
GUINEA

CONGO

ZAIRE

RWANDA
BURUNDI

UGANDA

KENYA

TANZANIA

SEYCHELLES

CHAGOS ARCHIPELAGO

CHRISTMAS I.

COCOS IS.

SINGAPORE

INDONESIA

E. TIMOR

PAPUA
NEW GUINEA

SOLOMON IS.

ANGOLA

ZAMBIA

MALAWI

COMOROS

MAYOTTE

MOZAMBIQUE

MADAGASCAR

MAURITIUS

REUNION

NEW CALEDONIA

NAMIBIA

ZIMBABWE

BOTSWANA

AUSTRALIA

SWAZILAND

S. AFRICA

LESOTHO

NEW ZEALAND

Mandarin
English
Hindi
Russian
Spanish
Portuguese
Japanese
Arabic
French
German
Other

LIVING STANDARDS

CAR OWNERSHIP

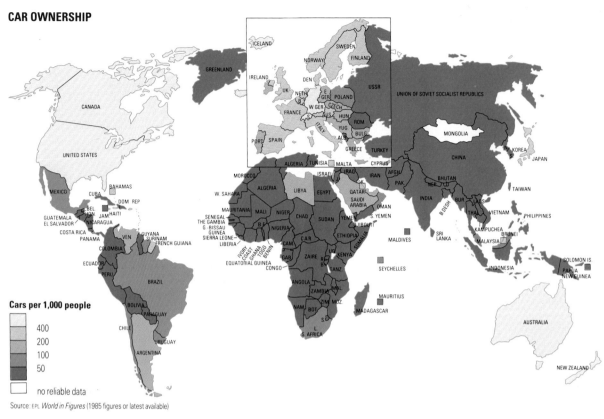

Cars per 1,000 people

- 400
- 200
- 100
- 50
- no reliable data

Source: EPL *World in Figures* (1985 figures or latest available)

TELEPHONE OWNERSHIP

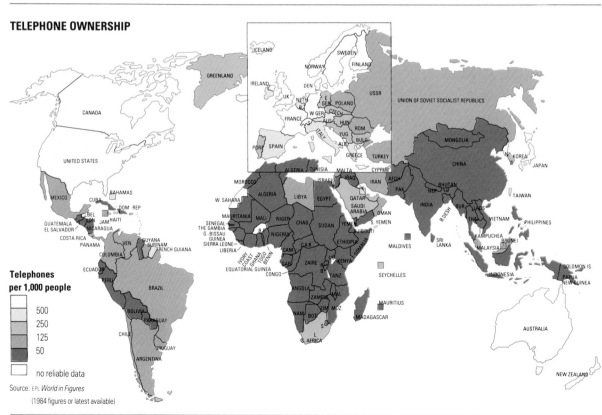

Telephones per 1,000 people

- 500
- 250
- 125
- 50
- no reliable data

Source: EPL *World in Figures*
(1984 figures or latest available)

WORLD ENCYCLOPEDIA

NORTH AMERICA

Climate

North American climatic conditions range from tropical desert to Arctic. The central plains have a continental climate with cold winters and hot summers; temperatures range from below -15°C (5°F) in winter to above 30°C (86°F) in summer. Temperature ranges are less extreme on the west coast; the Gulf coast has a sub-tropical climate, subject to hurricanes and tornadoes moving northeast from the Caribbean. Most regions can be affected by depressions from the west bringing cloud, rain and changeable weather. Most of the northern coast of Canada is ice-bound throughout the year.

Canadian-US trade

The proportion of Canadian exports going to the USA has doubled to nearly 80% since World War II. Canadian manufacturers are increasingly dependent on US demand, so the Canadian economy generally mirrors recession and boom in its neighbour. The high degree of integration of the North American economy also dampens relative currency movements. The free-trade agreement between Canada and the USA, ratified in 1989, will reinforce the North American trade bloc and the tendency of the two economies to run in parallel.

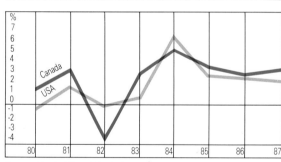

GDP GROWTH

Source: EIU *International Economic Appraisal Service*

CURRENCY TRENDS

$Can/$US exchange rate

Sources: EIU *Country Profile*; IMF *International Financial Statistics*

Alaska

The territory was purchased by the USA from Russia for $7.2m in 1867. This was regarded by many Americans as a waste of money until gold was discovered at Nome in 1889.

Alaska received territorial status in 1912 and became the 49th state of the union in 1959. Large oil reserves were discovered in 1968; the Trans-Alaska oil pipeline, from the North Slope field to the ice-free port of Valdez, was built in the 1970s. Oil production is expected to peak in 1990.

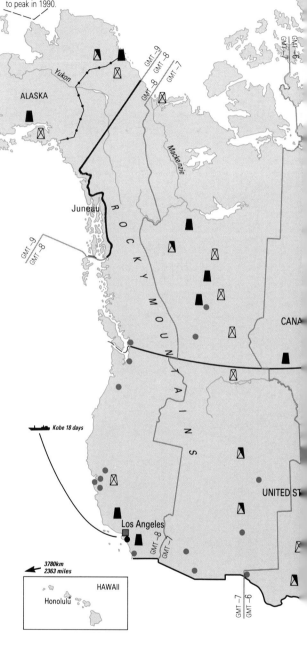

Hawaii

Hawaii became the 50th US state in 1959, some 60 years after it was formally annexed. Food processing, fishing and tourism are the main industries. Pearl Harbor remains an important naval base. Hopes for future growth rest on financial services and scientific research.

The Arctic

Since the discovery of oil and USS *Nautilus's* crossing under the ice in 1958, the Arctic has gained considerable economic and political significance. The world's smallest ocean has become both an arena and a possible cause of conflict, patrolled by Soviet and US ballistic missile submarines. Territorial claims by Canada to what the USA insists is an international waterway have led to disputes over the transit of US vessels. US economic interest in the region focuses on the large oil reserves, which would help to reduce dependence on foreign energy supplies; but there are logistical difficulties in production and mounting international concern for a fragile ecology.

The St Lawrence Seaway and the Great Lakes

The St Lawrence Seaway, a 3,500km (2,200-mile) system of canals, locks and dams, was built in the late 1950s to open up navigation between the Atlantic and the Great Lakes for ocean-going vessels.

The seaway is closed by ice for about four months of the year; from May to December it carries huge volumes of bulk commodities from the industrial areas on the shores of the Great Lakes. The seaway was built jointly by the USA and the Canada but US cargo is the main beneficiary of its subsidized tolls.

The Great Lakes – Superior, Michigan, Huron, Erie and Ontario – are the largest group of freshwater lakes in the world. They have a total surface area of 245,000 sq km (95,000 sq miles), of which about one-third is in Canada; only Lake Michigan is entirely within the USA.

St Pierre and Miquelon

These eight islands 25km (16 miles) from the coast of Newfoundland are a territorial collectivity of France. The French-speaking, Roman Catholic population of 6,200 is almost entirely dependent on the sea, with fishing and chandlery the only industries. The islands also attract tourists, mainly from the USA and Canada.

♦	Major oil field
⊠	Major gas field
◭	Oil & gas field
←→	Alaska oil pipeline
■	More than 1 million
●	250,000 – 1 million

Oil and gas

US oil production is concentrated in four states, Texas, Louisiana, California and Alaska; the first two, along with Oklahoma, are also the leading natural gas producers. Dependence on imports is increasing. Low prices have made many small wells unprofitable and there have been few substantial new discoveries. Alaskan production, which came to the rescue in the late 1970s, is expected to go into a rapid decline in the 1990s.

Canada, on the other hand, is producing more oil than it needs and exports have grown during the 1980s. Alberta is the main oil-producing province. Substantial new reserves await exploitation in the Arctic but low prices have discouraged exploration and recovery costs will be high.

Map labels: GMT –4, GMT –5, London 7 hours, Rotterdam 12 days, to 14½ hours, St Lawrence, Montreal, Ottawa, Toronto, L. Superior, L. Huron, L. Ontario, L. Michigan, L. Erie, Detroit, Chicago, Mississippi, New York, Philadelphia, Washington, Ohio, AMERICA, Houston, GMT –6, GMT –5

THE AMERICAS

UNITED STATES OF AMERICA

At the end of World War II the United States commanded a pre-eminence in world affairs. The period since has been crowded with challenges and crises. The twin goals have been continued economic and technological progress and the avoidance of major conflict. Yet it has lived through a deeply unpopular war, social turmoil arising from the pressure for greater equality, the assassination of one president and the near impeachment of another, and the humiliation of being subjected to blackmail during the Iran hostage crisis of the late 1970s. The election of Ronald Reagan in 1980 marked a turning point. Exploiting the president's personal popularity, his administration reasserted the United States' confidence in its role in the world and injected new vigour into the economy.

The US economy has always been firmly hitched to the star of free enterprise and a great deal of its vitality springs from the entrepreneurial spirit and the long-standing business ethos of the American people. During the postwar years the United States enjoyed steady underlying growth but when Ronald Reagan took office in 1981 the economy was causing concern: inflation had hit 18% the previous year and industry was in decline. President Reagan's policy of personal and corporate tax cuts, combined with the Federal Reserve's firm control of the money supply, resulted in one of the swiftest economic booms the USA has ever enjoyed, with a growth rate reaching nearly 7% in 1984 and inflation less than 2% in 1986. But Reaganomics had its downside as well as its supply side. The surge in domestic demand sucked in imports, while US exports became increasingly uncompetitive because of the rise in the value of the dollar. The trade deficit soared. So, too, did the federal budget deficit, as a result of the administration's lax fiscal policy. In 1985 the USA became a net debtor nation.

The huge inherited budget, trade and current account deficits – and the need to control inflation – are the economic priorities of the Bush administration. Many believe that the only way to balance the budget is by raising taxes, a course of action steadfastly repudiated by Ronald Reagan and also by George Bush on the 1988 campaign trail. The trade deficit may have peaked but bringing it down to an acceptable level will require changes in economic management that will inevitably be controversial. Calls for tough protectionist measures have so far been resisted, the administration pursuing instead hard-nosed agreements with countries that have a large trade surplus with the USA.

Economically and demographically the country continues to move to the west and southwest. California and Texas now rank as the most important manufacturing states in terms of the value of their shipments, having attracted

OFFICIAL NAME United States of America.

CAPITAL CITY Washington DC.

GEOGRAPHY The great plains that are the USA's agricultural – and in the north industrial – heartland sweep down from the Canadian Shield to the Gulf of Mexico. To the east they are bordered by the old rocks of the Appalachians, to the west by the younger Rockies. South and east of the Appalachians is a coastal plain, often swampy, and with generally poor soils except around the Mississippi. West of the Rockies a series of intermontane plateaus and basins rises up into the coastal ranges of the Sierras and the Cascades. The USA also includes the mountainous Arctic region of Alaska and the volcanic Pacific islands of Hawaii. *Highest point* Mt McKinley 6,190 metres (20,300 feet). *Area* 9,372,570 sq km (3,618,700 sq miles).

PEOPLE *Population* 239m. *Density* 262 per sq km. *Ethnic groups* White 76.8%, Afro-Caribbean 11.7%, Hispanic 6.4%, Asian/Pacific 1.5%, Amerindian/Inuit/Aleut 0.6%.

RELIGION Protestant 33%, RC 22%, Jewish 2%.

LANGUAGE English. Also Spanish and other minority languages.

EDUCATION Free to age 18, generally compulsory for ages 7–16. Mostly organized at state and local level, with some federal funding. Enrolment in private schools is around 13% at primary level, 9.5% at secondary level.

CLIMATE Enormous variety, from sub-tropical in Florida – annual average temperature 29°C (84°F) – to arctic in Alaska – annual average temperature -13°C (9°F). Most of the country is temperate, though the centre gets continental extremes. Average annual rainfall 735mm (29ins); large deserts in southwest and south.

CURRENCY Dollar ($).

PUBLIC HOLIDAYS (*some states only) Jan 1, 3rd Mon in Jan*, 3rd Mon in Feb*, Good Fri, last Mon in May, Jul 4, 1st Mon in Sep, 2nd Mon in Oct*, Nov 11, 4th Thu in Nov, Dec 25. Also many regional, state and city holidays.

GOVERNMENT Federal republic. There are 50 states and one federal district (Columbia), all internally self-governing; the federal government is responsible for defence, foreign affairs, internal security, the posts and the coinage. The chief executive is the president, elected for a 4-year term by a college elected by direct vote in each state. He appoints the rest of the executive, subject to Senate approval. The legislative Congress has two elected houses: the Senate has 2 members for each state elected for a 6-year term (elections for a third of the seats are held every 2 years), while the 435 members of the House of Representatives are elected for 2-year terms. The judiciary is headed by the Supreme Court, which can veto legislation and overturn executive decisions on constitutional grounds. The written constitution, drawn up in 1787, is the oldest in existence. Subsequent amendents include 10 made in 1791 and known as the Bill of Rights.

WAGES AND PRICES

1980 = 100

138.1
136.3
119.5
114.5

1981
1982 1983
1984
1985
1986
1987

Consumer prices
Wages
Producer prices
Productivity

Source: IMF *International Financial Statistics*

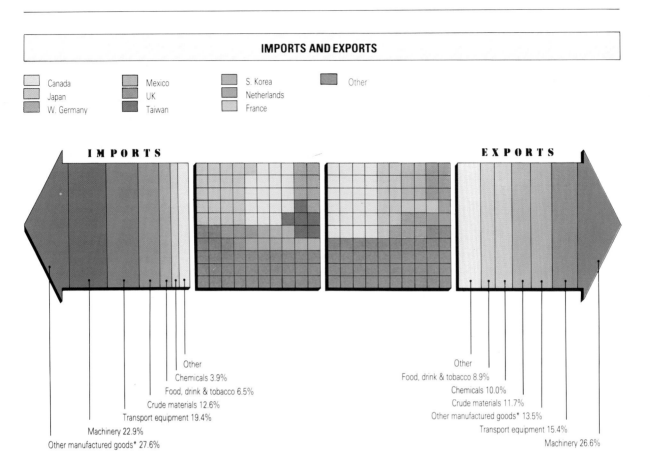

IMPORTS AND EXPORTS

Legend:
- Canada
- Japan
- W. Germany
- Mexico
- UK
- Taiwan
- S. Korea
- Netherlands
- France
- Other

IMPORTS

- Other manufactured goods* 27.6%
- Machinery 22.9%
- Transport equipment 19.4%
- Crude materials 12.6%
- Food, drink & tobacco 6.5%
- Chemicals 3.9%
- Other

EXPORTS

- Other
- Food, drink & tobacco 8.9%
- Chemicals 10.0%
- Crude materials 11.7%
- Other manufactured goods* 13.5%
- Transport equipment 15.4%
- Machinery 26.6%

Source: EIU *Country Report* (Imports/Exports 1986 figures; Trading partners 1987 figures) * Excluding machinery, transport equipment & chemicals

WORK FORCE

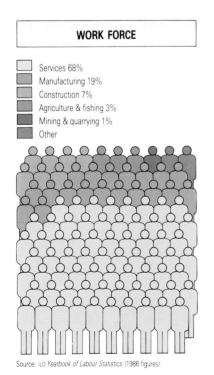

- Services 68%
- Manufacturing 19%
- Construction 7%
- Agriculture & fishing 3%
- Mining & quarrying 1%
- Other

Source: ILO *Yearbook of Labour Statistics* (1986 figures)

BALANCE OF PAYMENTS

Source: EIU *International Economic Appraisal Service*

FEDERAL BUDGET DEFICIT

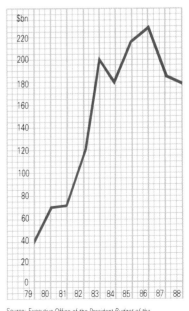

Source: Executive Office of the President *Budget of the United States Government*.

THE AMERICAS

POPULATION - THE BIG SEVEN

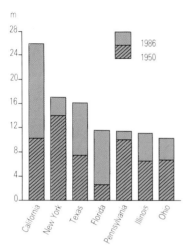

Legend: 1986, 1950

Seven states in the USA have a population of more than 10m. They dominate the winner-takes-all presidential election: a candidate who took California, New York, Texas, Pennsylvania, Illinois, Florida and Ohio would be more than two-thirds of the way to victory. In evenly balanced presidential elections the seven are usually split; the Sun Belt states now lean towards the Republicans and those of the Rust Belt towards the Democrats. The Sun belt is an increasingly valuable prize for the Republicans: in terms of population – and thus electoral weight – Florida has overtaken Ohio, Illinois and Pennsylvania in the 1980s, Texas will soon surpass New York and California remains comfortably the most populous state.

Source *Statistical Abstract of the United States* (1986 figures)

THE MELTING POT

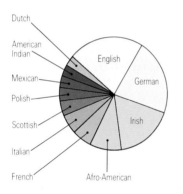

Statistically, the inhabitants of the USA are demonstrably heterogeneous: no ancestry group accounts for much more than a fifth of the total. As the identities of the various European communities become blurred, continuing immigration of Central Americans and Asians sustains ethnic variety. The official breakdown under-represents these groups because they have grown fast since the last census in 1980, and many of the new immigrants are illegal and so unrecorded.

Source *Statistical Abstract of the United States* (1980 figures)

mainly high-technology and light industry; heavy industry remains concentrated along the Great Lakes and in the northeast. Although only a small percentage of American citizens were born outside the USA, modern America is as much a melting pot as it ever was; nearly half the population of Miami, for example, is of Hispanic origin. Much immigration is illegal; even by conservative estimates, over 5m Mexicans living in the USA entered it unofficially.

Drug-related crime and the degeneration of many inner-city areas are two of present-day America's most serious social problems. The polarization between rich and poor in urban areas is a major cause of tension. In 1989 the level of crime in Washington DC became so serious that the authorities resorted to imposing a night-time curfew on young people. Yet US society and politics have displayed considerable stability. At the root of the national consciousness is a civic orthodoxy which places personal liberty above the claims of authority, awards the right of privacy to individuals but denies it to bureaucracy, and encourages suspicion of all who exercise power. Americans have made astute use of the governmental checks and balances laid down by the constitution by frequently electing a president from one party while giving control of Congress to the other.

In both world wars it was the entry of the USA that assured victory for the allies, and since the end of war in the Pacific in 1945 the United States has

Rust Belt to Sun Belt

The shift in the US economy from manufacturing to services over the past 30 years has been accompanied by a movement of output and workers from the old industrial heartland, the northern "Rust Belt" states, to the booming south and west, the "Sun Belt."

The proportion of America's population living in the Rust Belt has fallen from 47% to 41% since 1970 Arizona, Nevada and Florida have been the fastest-growing states in population terms over the past 20 years; the populations of states like Iowa, Michigan, Ohio and Pennsylvania have remained static or declined slightly.

Immigration

The USA practised an open-door policy on immigration from independence until the 1960s. Since 1970 immigration, estimated at about 500,000 a year, has accounted for about 20% of population growth but official figures give no idea of the extent of illegal immigration, mostly across the Mexican border from Central America.

Drugs

American politicians regard the war against drugs as one of the most important problems they face. About 30m Americans are thought to take an illegal drug regularly. About 2m are thought to be addicts: about a quarter to heroin, the rest to cocaine. Drug-related deaths are on the increase, but, at about 10,000 a year, still fall short of deaths linked to the use of tobacco (390,000) or alcohol (100,000). The cost of America's drug habit is estimated at anywhere from $50bn to $100bn a year. Concern is focused on the growing availability and low price of cocaine – despite all efforts at control – and the crime and violence associated with it.

Agriculture

The US agricultural sector is a victim of its own success. It is immensely productive; of the world's exports, it provides a quarter of the wheat, a half of the maize and three-quarters of soyabeans, at prices with which most other producers cannot fairly compete. Widespread international agricultural protectionism, the USA's greatest trade grievance, constrains the country's capacity to export more. The government, at substantial cost and against its *laissez-faire* instincts, has mitigated the consequences through subsidies and price support, sustained by production quotas. But its efforts to expand the overseas market for US produce have not had significant effect. So improvements in productivity have manifested themselves in a shrinking work force and a declining share of GDP – falling to just over 2% in the late 1980s – rather than in increased output.

Smaller farmers have taken the brunt of the contraction but larger businesses have also suffered. Many borrowed heavily in the late 1970s and early 1980s on the security of property which has since fallen in value. Their financial predicament extends to the banks to which they owe a crippling debt of over $40bn.

▪	Rust Belt
▪	Sun Belt
◼	More than 1 million
●	250,000–1 million

The Mississippi

The Mississippi and its major tributaries, the Missouri and Ohio, form the largest river system in the USA. The Missouri is the country's longest river: 3,725km (2,320 miles) from its source in Montana to its confluence with the Mississippi north of St Louis. The Mississippi itself is the second longest, flowing for 1,884km (1,170 miles) from Lake Itasca in Minnesota to the Gulf of Mexico. The rivers form a major transport artery: the Mississippi is navigable as far as Minneapolis, the Ohio for its entire length from Pittsburgh to Cairo, Illinois, and the Missouri as far as Fort Benton, Montana.

assumed the role of defender of the free world. In recent years, however, many Americans have felt that the country was being expected to carry more than its fair share of the defence burden. For three decades at least the main threat was seen as communism. In the 1950s suspected "reds" were ostracized at home and a war against communism fought abroad, on the other side of the world. In 1962 the government sent the first US troops into Vietnam and it was not until 1972 that the last ones left. But the late 1970s saw a shift in policy with the recognition by the USA of mainland "Red" China. Events in the late 1980s in the Soviet Union now pose the challenge of a fundamental reappraisal of relations with the other great communist power.

As the USA is having to adjust to the easing of the Cold War it is also having to come to terms with the changing shape of the economic and industrial world. The current account deficit has been funded to a large extent by Japan, and Japanese investment in the US economy increased more than twentyfold between 1977 and 1987. Industrialization continues apace in East Asia, the USSR is striving to modernize its economy and Europe is moving towards a single market. But Americans have never been a people with a tendency to live in the past. They are less concerned with their lost pre-eminence than with the new challenges and opportunities that lie ahead.

GNP BY ORIGIN

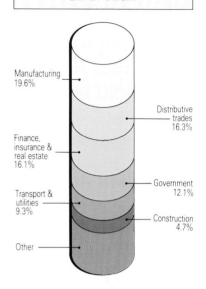

Manufacturing 19.6%
Distributive trades 16.3%
Finance, insurance & real estate 16.1%
Government 12.1%
Transport & utilities 9.3%
Construction 4.7%
Other

INCOME DISTRIBUTION

Average income of families with children
% change in real terms, 1979-87

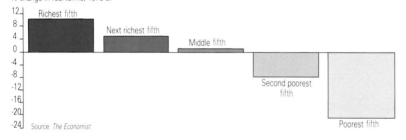

Richest fifth
Next richest fifth
Middle fifth
Second poorest fifth
Poorest fifth

Source: *The Economist*

COMPONENTS OF GNP

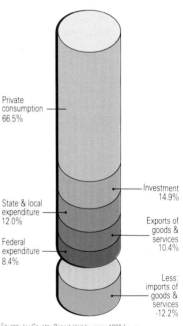

Private consumption 66.5%
Investment 14.9%
State & local expenditure 12.0%
Exports of goods & services 10.4%
Federal expenditure 8.4%
Less: imports of goods & services -12.2%

Source: EIU *Country Report* (GNP by origin 1986 figures;
Components of GNP 1987 figures)

ECONOMIC PROFILE

The world's most enduringly successful economy by some measures; past its peak by others. Output dwarfs that of Japan, its closest economic rival, but now makes up less than a quarter of world output, down from 40% in 1945. Low tax rates foster and reflect entrepreneurial ethos but contribute to high budget deficit, much of it funded abroad. Capital inflow demonstrates confidence in the vitality of the US economy but mirrors a destabilizing current account deficit: foreign competition and investment have provoked calls for trade protection and limits on foreign ownership. Inflation fell to 2–5% in the 1980s but only by a tight monetary policy of high interest rates and an overvalued dollar. Increased employment rather than productivity has fuelled growth since early 1980s' recession; most new jobs are in the low-wage, low-productivity service industries

rather than in manufacturing, which is the largest tradeable sector but in substantial deficit and relative decline.

Growth Dynamic computer industry, but imports rising even faster than exports. High world demand for commercial aircraft has helped maintain 20% annual growth and a $10bn-plus trade surplus in aerospace sector. Pharmaceutical industry very profitable.

Problems Agricultural production hit by falling world demand. Oil price fall of over 50% since 1970s has made unprofitable many fields developed then; import dependence rising again. Safety fears have effectively halted expansion of nuclear power. Defence industry set to contract as defence spending stagnates. Saturated market for motor vehicles has forced US automobile industry to scale down investment and modernization.

CANADA

The world's second largest country has a lower population density than virtually any other nation. Almost 90% of the country is uninhabited and 85% of the population live within 100 miles of the US border. This proximity to the vast US market and Canada's wealth of natural resources contribute greatly to the country's prosperity. Yet, despite close economic links with the USA, Canada has assiduously maintained a separate political and cultural identity, retaining its ties with other Commonwealth countries and the francophone world.

Domestic economic activity and prosperity are as unevenly distributed as the population. Ontario has both the largest manufacturing base and agricultural sector, and its capital, Toronto, is the country's business and financial centre; the province contributes about 40% of GNP. The Canadian economy has recovered well from the recession of the early 1980s, the country's worst for half a century; and supporters of the 1988 free-trade agreement with the USA argue that the removal of the remaining barriers between the two countries could boost GDP by 5% over ten years. But the agreement has been the subject of intense debate which dominated the 1988 election, won by the pro-free trade Progressive Conservative Party but on a minority vote. Those who oppose it fear increasing domination of the economy by the USA and the dissipation of Canada's cultural identity and its liberal social philosophy. The question of closer ties with the USA is likely to continue to be a hot issue.

The Inuit

About 14,500 Inuit, or Eskimos, live in the Canadian Arctic. In 1974 they demanded the creation of an autonomous state, Nunavut, consisting of part of the mainland of the Northwest Territories and several Arctic islands, including Baffin Island. The area, covering 2.4m sq km (930,000 sq miles), is rich in minerals, including iron ore, gold, lead, zinc and copper, and offshore oil and natural gas. A referendum in the territory in 1982 supported the move, which was approved in principle by the federal government. The division of the Northwest Territories into Nunavut and Denendeh, to the west, is expected to be completed in 1991.

The Canadian provinces

Canada is more truly federal in its political structure than its southern neighbour. Its ten provinces have responsibility for most social services, labour matters and the civil law. But the federal parliament can involve itself in provincial areas of jurisdiction if it considers proposals to be "for the general advantage of Canada". The division of powers is enshrined in the 1982 constitution but Québec did not agree until 1987 to provincial status.

OFFICIAL NAME Canada.

CAPITAL CITY Ottawa.

GEOGRAPHY The second largest country in the world, half its area is the central Canadian Shield, a glaciated platform of ancient rock centred on Hudson Bay which is largely covered by lakes and forests. Only 8% of Canada is suitable for cultivation. There are three lowland zones: the sparsely populated western plains, the ice-covered Arctic plains, and the area around the Great Lakes and the St Lawrence where most of the population live. In the far west are the Cordillera, parallel mountain ranges whose westernmost outriders make up Vancouver and the Queen Charlotte Islands. The Appalachians run from Quebec through the Gaspé peninsula to Newfoundland. *Highest point* Mt Logan 6,050 metres (19,850 feet). *Area* 9,976,139 sq km (3,851,810 sq miles).

PEOPLE *Population* 25m. *Density* 3 per sq km. *Ethnic groups* UK/Irish 44%, French 27%, German 5%, Italian 3%, Ukrainian 2%, Amerindian/Inuit 2%, Dutch 2%.

RELIGION Christian 90% (RC 47%, Protestant 41%, other 2%), Jewish 1%.

LANGUAGE English and French.

EDUCATION Free and compulsory; ages vary by province, though 85% of ages 12–17 attend secondary school.

CLIMATE Continental: fairly dry inland, monthly average temperature range -17–19°C (1–66°F) in the prairies; very cold in north. Pacific coast mild and wet.

CURRENCY Canadian dollar (C$).

PUBLIC HOLIDAYS Jan 1, Good Fri, Easter Mon, penultimate Mon in May, Jul 1, 1st Mon in Sep, 2nd Mon in Oct, Nov 11, Dec 25, Dec 26.

GOVERNMENT Parliamentary and federal monarchy. There are 10 provinces, each with their own legislature, and 2 territories. The British monarch, represented by the governor-general, is head of state. The legislature has a 104-member Senate nominated by the provinces and a 282-member House of Commons elected from single-member constituencies for a term of up to 5 years. Executive power is held by a prime minister and cabinet drawn from the majority party in the Commons.

Québec

Separatism in the French-speaking province of Québec reached a peak in 1976, when the Parti Québecois came to power in provincial elections. The party campaigned for a separate status for the province and for the use of French as the official language, but its support declined and it lost power in Québec to the Liberals in 1985. The Meech Lake Accord of 1987 recognized Québec as a "distinct society" within the Canadian federation - despite the initial opposition of some English-speaking provinces - and restored some important new powers to the provinces which they had lost in the 1982 Constitution Act.

- ■ More than 1 million
- ● 250,000 – 1 million
- • 100,000 – 250,000
- ▲ Proposed new district

IMPORTS AND EXPORTS

USA
Japan
UK
W. Germany
S. Korea
Taiwan
USSR
Other

IMPORTS   **EXPORTS**

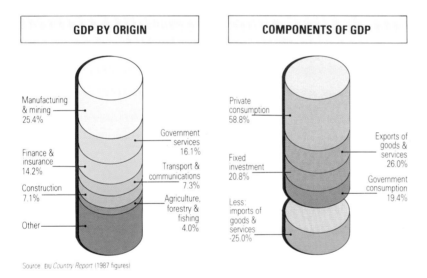

Other
Crude oil & gas 5.8%
Food 7.1%
Other minerals 13.1%
Machinery & equipment 14.0%
Forest products 16.3%
Motor vehicles & parts 26.7%

Other
Food 6.8%
Other consumer goods 10.9%
Industrial materials 16.7%
Motor vehicles & parts 28.4%
Machinery & equipment 28.8%

Source: EIU *Country Report* (1987 figures)

GDP BY ORIGIN

Manufacturing & mining 25.4%
Finance & insurance 14.2%
Construction 7.1%
Other

Government services 16.1%
Transport & communications 7.3%
Agriculture, forestry & fishing 4.0%

Source: EIU *Country Report* (1987 figures)

COMPONENTS OF GDP

Private consumption 58.8%
Fixed investment 20.8%
Less: imports of goods & services -25.0%

Exports of goods & services 26.0%
Government consumption 19.4%

ECONOMIC PROFILE

Rich resource base gives Canada capacity to outperform most industrial economies. Exports substantial volumes of energy – oil, natural gas, coal, hydroelectricity – as well as metals such as copper, nickel, lead, zinc and iron ore and other natural resources including timber. Major agricultural exporter, especially of wheat. Industry, largely resource-based, closely linked to US market.

Growth Free-trade agreement will effectively expand domestic market tenfold. Sales of all forms of energy to USA are expanding rapidly. Sales of metal products also strong.

Problems Worldwide surpluses have hit agriculture. Industry faces problems competing in high-technology sectors, particularly electronics. Persistent deficit in invisible trade, including investment income, travel and financial services. Heavy government borrowing.

The last decade has seen considerable wrangling over constitutional reform. Canada's ten provinces have considerable autonomy, and it was a difficult task for the federal government to persuade the provincial governments to relinquish some of their independence and agree to the terms of the Constitution Act of 1982. Its provisions include a charter of rights and a new procedure for constitutional amendments; it also did away with the anachronistic requirement that such amendments had to be passed by the UK parliament.

For most of the 1960s right up until the early 1980s Canadian politics at a national level were dominated by the Liberal Party. Since 1984 the Progressive Conservatives under Brian Mulroney have held power, and a third party, the left-of-centre New Democrats, has been gaining support. Brian Mulroney's first term of office was affected by ministerial scandals and the government was accused of being indecisive. His second term started on a more confident note. Radical tax reforms and a policy of deregulation are under way, and the key objective of reducing the budget deficit looks more feasible.

MEXICO

"So far from God and so close to the United States:" Mexico, the world's largest Spanish-speaking country, sits uneasily in the shadow of its powerful neighbour. The fact that it now spends only 4% of its national budget on defence belies a bitter past. Half a million people died in the great Mexican revolution of 1910–20. Since the 1930s, when an extensive land reform was hurried through, workers on cooperative farms (*ejidos*) have formed the bulk of the agrarian labour force. They, the trade unions and the state bureaucracy form the three "pillars" of the ruling party, now called the Party of the Institutionalized Revolution which has monopolized political power since 1929.

Today, the system is breaking up. The president who took office for a six-year term in December 1988, Carlos Salinas de Gortari, won only narrowly in a bitterly contested election amid well-founded allegations of fraud. A career bureaucrat, Salinas is also a Harvard-trained economist, but opposition was spearheaded from within the system by Cuauhtémoc Cárdenas, son of a reforming president of the 1930s, and his government faces a difficult time in the new congress.

Oil was nationalized in 1938, since when the government has continued to dominate the economy. But vast new discoveries in the early 1970s were squandered and, in 1982, Mexico gave the world the term "debt crisis" when it admitted that the task of servicing a debt of more than $100bn was beyond its resources.

OFFICIAL NAME United Mexican States.
CAPITAL CITY Mexico City.
GEOGRAPHY Most of Mexico is highland, a complex of mountains – some volcanic – and plateaus criss-crossed by valleys and canyons. The only extensive lowlands are the long, narrow, desert peninsula of Baja California and the limestone Yucatán Peninsula. *Highest point* Orizaba 5,700 metres (18,700 feet). *Area* 1,972,547 sq km (761,610 sq miles).
PEOPLE *Population* 78.5m. *Density* 40 per sq km. *Ethnic groups* Mestizo 55%, Amerindian 30%, European 15%.
RELIGION RC 93%, Protestant 3%.
LANGUAGE Spanish. Also some Amerindian dialects.
EDUCATION Free to age 18; compulsory for ages 6–12. There are 82 universities. The government has invested heavily in drives to improve adult literacy.
CLIMATE Temperate in the north and central highlands, with an average temperature of 15°C (59°F) – though winters can be severe – and tropical in the south and the coastal lowlands, with an annual average temperature of 18°C (64°F). Extensive deserts in the north and west.
CURRENCY Mexican peso (Mex$).
PUBLIC HOLIDAYS Jan 1, Feb 5, Mar 21, Good Fri-Easter Mon, May 1, 5, Sep 1, 16, Oct 12, Nov 2, 20, Dec 12, 24-25.
GOVERNMENT Federal republic. There are 31 states, each with its own governor and legislature, and a federal district. Both houses of the national congress are directly elected: the 64 members of the senate – 2 from each confederation member – for 6 years, and the 400-member chamber of deputies – 300 deputies come from single-member constituencies, the remainder from PR lists – for 3 years. The chief executive and head of state is the president, directly elected every 6 years. The president appoints the cabinet.

Unemployment and immigration
The unemployment rate, virtually a state secret, is estimated at around 18m; but only workers covered by the state-affiliated trade unions enjoy full benefits and perhaps 20m more are underemployed. Illegal immigration to the USA helped to relieve social pressures until 1987; measures to curb this have serious implications for Mexico's industrial stability.

CALIFORNIA

UNITED STATES OF AMERICA

ARIZONA

NEW MEXICO

SONORA

TEXAS

Chihuahua

Rio Grande

Monterrey ■

MEXICO

New York 2½ hours

London 9 hours

Rotterdam 17½ days

Bay of Campeche

Guadalajara ■

Mexico City ■

Coatzacoalcos

BELIZE

Kobe 24½ days

Acapulco

GUATEMALA

GMT -8
GMT -7
GMT -7
GMT -6

□ More than 1 million
● 250,000 – 1 million
• 100,000 – 250,000

Minerals
Only an estimated 15% of the country's mineral wealth has been exploited. The Sonora region's copper resource is of world significance, but precious metals, mined there and at Chihuahua and Zacatecas, account for 45% by value of mineral reserves. The state controls 42% of mine output.

Mexico City
Mexico City was built on the site of the old Aztec capital on the edge of a lake, now drained. The city, centre of Mexico's culture, trade and industry, lies a mile above sea level in a basin that traps rising air and pollution. The city has long spread outside the federal district and 15m people live in the metropolitan area, creating horrendous problems of overcrowding, insufficient water supply, and inadequate drainage and sewage disposal.

Oil
The largest oil-producing region is the Bay of Campeche, source of 65% of Mexico's oil output.

THE AMERICAS

Since then, austerity has been the official watchword as the government has striven to master the debt crisis, but success looks as far away as ever. For five years, the government pursued a conventional course of successive austerity programmes tailored to avoid choking off demand. Rising oil prices in 1987 swelled reserves but an ambitious debt retirement plan launched in December of that year, backed by a zero-coupon bond issue from the US Treasury, failed to meet high expectations. The wages and prices freeze of early 1988 checked gathering inflation, which had reached 159% the previous year; but, as a former finance minister said, "The problem with asking Mexicans to tighten their belts is that so few of them have belts to tighten."

The question of whether to continue the freeze after the 1988 election posed the same problem as in Argentina and Brazil: how to unfreeze without inflation again taking off. The Salinas government's first cautious economic package did little to reconcile the conflicting demands of a disgruntled population and a vigorous anti-inflationary policy. Privatization plans, though widely considered essential to reduce the swollen state bureaucracy, have run into difficulties because buyers have been hard to find.

The new government can in theory use its mandate to carry out even more drastic reforms. In practice, it depends for its support on the very interests it needs to curb.

GDP BY ORIGIN

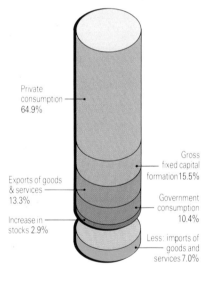

Manufacturing 25.5%
Commerce & hotels 23.8%
Services 21.4%
Agriculture 9%
Transport & utilities 8.4%
Oil and mining 7.2%
Construction 4.7%

Source: EIU *Country Report* (1986 figures)

COMPONENTS OF GDP

Private consumption 64.9%
Gross fixed capital formation 15.5%
Exports of goods & services 13.3%
Government consumption 10.4%
Increase in stocks 2.9%
Less: imports of goods and services 7.0%

BALANCE OF PAYMENTS

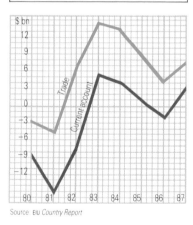

Source: EIU *Country Report*

IMPORTS AND EXPORTS

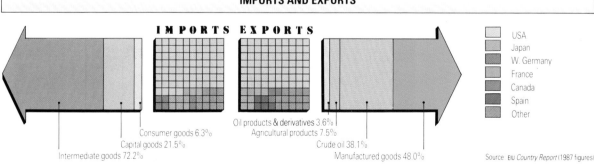

IMPORTS   EXPORTS

Consumer goods 6.3%
Capital goods 21.5%
Intermediate goods 72.2%

Oil products & derivatives 3.6%
Agricultural products 7.5%
Crude oil 38.1%
Manufactured goods 48.0%

USA
Japan
W. Germany
France
Canada
Spain
Other

Source: EIU *Country Report* (1987 figures)

CENTRAL AMERICA

Independent from Spain since 1821, Central America split into five separate states more than a century ago. Many Central Americans, however, see economic and political arguments for reunification. The last serious attempt to bring the states together was the Central American Common Market (CACM) set up in 1961. This increased intra-regional trade three times in seven years, but fell apart in 1969. The major obstacle to unification as a single market, with the benefits that would bring, is that the region's economies tend to be competitive rather than complementary. All remain backward, linked too closely for comfort to the fortunes of a single export crop such as coffee, bananas or sugar. Growth has been achieved through new export crops, notably cotton, but development remains threatened by political instability and periodic outbursts of violence in an area also notoriously prone to natural disasters.

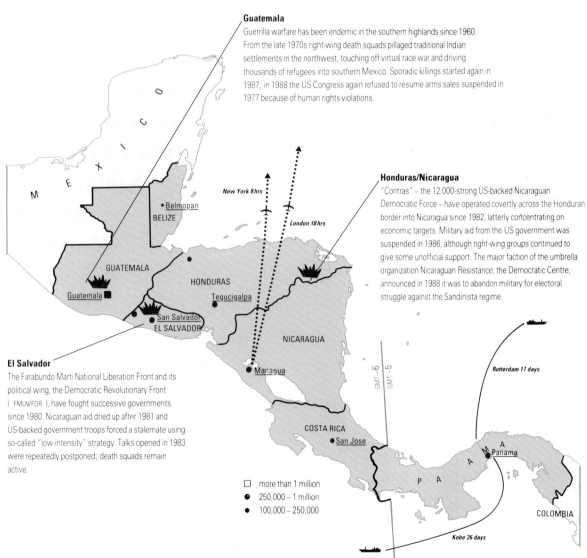

Guatemala

Guerrilla warfare has been endemic in the southern highlands since 1960. From the late 1970s right-wing death squads pillaged traditional Indian settlements in the northwest, touching off virtual race war and driving thousands of refugees into southern Mexico. Sporadic killings started again in 1987; in 1988 the US Congress again refused to resume arms sales suspended in 1977 because of human rights violations.

Honduras/Nicaragua

"Contras" – the 12,000-strong US-backed Nicaraguan Democratic Force – have operated covertly across the Honduran border into Nicaragua since 1982, latterly concentrating on economic targets. Military aid from the US government was suspended in 1986, although right-wing groups continued to give some unofficial support. The major faction of the umbrella organization Nicaraguan Resistance, the Democratic Centre, announced in 1988 it was to abandon military for electoral struggle against the Sandinista regime.

El Salvador

The Farabundo Marti National Liberation Front and its political wing, the Democratic Revolutionary Front (FMLN/FDR), have fought successive governments since 1980. Nicaraguan aid dried up after 1981 and US-backed government troops forced a stalemate using so-called "low-intensity" strategy. Talks opened in 1983 were repeatedly postponed; death squads remain active.

- ☐ more than 1 million
- ● 250,000 – 1 million
- • 100,000 – 250,000

Panama

Because of its canal, Panama is at the centre of US strategic interests in the Caribbean basin. Although the USA's power in the region would seem unchallenged, Central America has dominated the concerns of its policymakers during the 1980s because of growing fears that Cuba, as the Soviet Union's representative, was exploiting latent unrest to gain a strategic advantage.

Fears that unrest will spread from state to state are shared by the region's governments, but they see US involvement as the problem rather than the solution. Their concerns lie behind two major recent efforts to bring peace to the region: the Contadora plan, sponsored by Mexico, Panama, Colombia and Venezuela, and the Arias plan, mooted by President Oscar Arias of Costa Rica and accepted by all the Central American governments.

The Panamanian flag flies from the masts of over 11% of the world's merchant fleet – only in Liberia is there a greater shipping tonnage registered.

THE AMERICAS

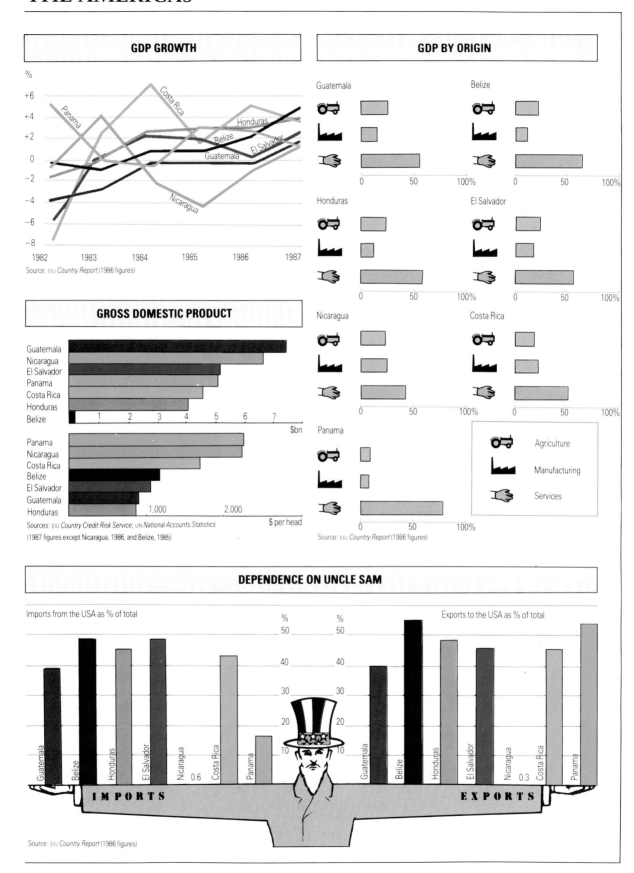

GDP GROWTH

%
+6
+4
+2
0
-2
-4
-6
-8

Panama
Costa Rica
Honduras
Belize
El Salvador
Guatemala
Nicaragua

1982   1983   1984   1985   1986   1987

Source: EIU *Country Report* (1986 figures)

GROSS DOMESTIC PRODUCT

Guatemala
Nicaragua
El Salvador
Panama
Costa Rica
Honduras
Belize

1   2   3   4   5   6   7

$bn

Panama
Nicaragua
Costa Rica
Belize
El Salvador
Guatemala
Honduras

1,000   2,000

$ per head

Sources: EIU *Country Credit Risk Service*; UN *National Accounts Statistics*
(1987 figures except Nicaragua, 1986, and Belize, 1985)

GDP BY ORIGIN

Guatemala   Belize

0   50   100%   0   50   100%

Honduras   El Salvador

0   50   100%   0   50   100%

Nicaragua   Costa Rica

0   50   100%   0   50   100%

Panama

Agriculture
Manufacturing
Services

0   50   100%

Source: EIU *Country Report* (1986 figures)

DEPENDENCE ON UNCLE SAM

Imports from the USA as % of total

%
50
40
30
20
10

Guatemala
Belize
Honduras
El Salvador
Nicaragua   0.6
Costa Rica
Panama

IMPORTS

Exports to the USA as % of total

%
50
40
30
20
10

Guatemala
Belize
Honduras
El Salvador
Nicaragua   0.3
Costa Rica
Panama

EXPORTS

Source: EIU *Country Report* (1986 figures)

GUATEMALA

Guatemala, the "land of eternal spring," is torn by bitter and seemingly irreconcilable tensions. Once the centre of a major world civilization, it remains primarily an Indian society, with Indian languages such as Quiché and Poko-mam still widely spoken. But the Indians' ancestors were driven off the best lands onto the less productive uplands, and land reform, frustrated in the 1950s, remains a bitter issue. The start of oil production has only exacerbated the struggle over land rights in the northwest highlands.

A decade ago, the armed forces turned on the civilian population in an effort to stamp out the persistent guerrilla activity which had spluttered on since the early 1960s. Instead, they nearly set off a race war. After a century and a half of almost unbroken dictatorship, often by military men, the government elected in 1986 for a four-year term is nominally headed by a civilian, the Christian Democrat, Vinicio Cerezo Arévalo; but political power remains dependent on the support of the army, which continues to stand in the way of essential economic changes such as tax reform.

The largest economy in Central America, Guatemala still depends to an unhealthy degree on exports of primary agricultural products, especially coffee. Chicle, the raw material for chewing gum, is also important. Diversification of the economy received a significant boost in the late 1970s from Guatemala's unexpected transformation into an oil producer, with a surplus for export. Among new crops, cotton has been the most successful. Forestry has expanded dramatically in the past decade, with worrying ecological consequences.

Guatemala's only outlet to the sea for exporting these surpluses is a narrow strip off the Gulf of Honduras. A deal with Belize allowing easier access to the Caribbean would do much to help develop the interior, but has hitherto been blocked by Guatemala's claims to its neighbour's territory.

OFFICIAL NAME Republic of Guatemala.

CAPITAL CITY Guatemala City.

GEOGRAPHY Most of the population live in the central highlands. To the north is the sparsely populated limestone tableland of the Petén and to the south is a fertile region of alluvial and volcanic soils. *Highest point* Tajumulco 4,220 metres (13,850 feet). *Area* 108,889 sq km (42,040 sq miles).

PEOPLE *Population* 7.9m. *Ethnic groups* Amerindian 50%, Mestizo 42%, European 4%.

RELIGION Christian 100% (RC 80%, other 20%).

LANGUAGE Spanish. Also Amerindian languages.

EDUCATION Free for ages 7–14, compulsory in urban areas only. There are 5 universities.

CURRENCY Quetzal (Q).

CLIMATE Sub-tropical in the lowlands, with an average annual temperature of 28°C (82°F); milder – 20°C (68°F) – in the highlands. The rainy season is May–Nov, except on Caribbean coast where it falls year-round.

PUBLIC HOLIDAYS Jan 1, 6, Good Fri-Easter Mon, May 1, Jun 30, Aug 15, Sep 15, Oct 12, 20, Nov 1, Dec 24, 25, 31.

GOVERNMENT The head of state is a president, elected for 5 years, who shares executive power with a cabinet appointed from the 100 members of the legislative national congress. Congress members are also elected for a 5-year term, 75 of them from single constituencies, the rest by PR.

BELIZE

A former British colony, independent since 1981, Belize is a parliamentary democracy. Its Prime Minister, Manuel Esquivel, took over from George Price, who had ruled for almost 25 years, in free and fair elections in 1984. Belize has still to be recognized by its neighbour, Guatemala, which has trimmed its traditional claim to the entire territory but remains a threat, with an army more than one-fifth the size of Belize's population. A small defence force is being trained by the USA, and the UK maintains a small "trip-wire" force in the area.

Belize's economy has suffered in the 1980s as a result of its sugar industry, which replaced the traditional major export, timber, and which still accounts for a quarter of total employment. Efforts at diversification have encouraged a small but growing industrial base, founded primarily on processing of crops – especially citrus fruits – but with growing emphasis on other light industries such as shoes and textiles. Purchase by the Coca-Cola Corporation of large areas of land to develop citrus fruit production touched off a national debate about the desirability of new foreign – that is, US – influence and investment in this once sleepy backwater of empire, and the implications for the local environment. This culminated in Coca-Cola's withdrawal of the scheme in September 1987, ostensibly for economic reasons.

Another sector of the economy which has attracted an increasing amount of foreign investment, and with it a growing fear of foreign dominance, is tourism, which has considerable potential as a foreign-exchange earner.

OFFICIAL NAME Belize.

CAPITAL CITY Belmopan.

GEOGRAPHY Most is jungle; the southern half is dominated by the Maya Mountains, an ancient plateau with deep-cut valleys, while the northern half is lowland, much of it swamp. *Highest point* Victoria Peak 1,222 metres (3,680 feet). *Area* 22,963 sq km (8,870 sq miles).

PEOPLE *Population* 170,000. *Density* 7 per sq km. *Ethnic groups* Creole 40%, Mestizo 33%, Garifuna 8%, Maya 7% European 4%, Ketchi 3%, East Indian 2%.

RELIGION RC 62%, Protestant 18%.

LANGUAGE English 56%, Spanish 28%, Carib 6%, Maya 5%.

EDUCATION Free for ages 6–19, compulsory to age 14.

CLIMATE Sub-tropical. Dry season Feb–May, wet season Jun–Nov. Annual rainfall in the south is 1,290mm (51ins), three times as much as in the north.

CURRENCY Belizean dollar (Bz$).

PUBLIC HOLIDAYS Jan 1, 1st Mon in Mar, Good Fri-Easter Mon, May 1, Mon after Jun 7, Sep 10, 21, Oct 12, Nov 19, Dec 25, 26.

GOVERNMENT Parliamentary democracy. Effective power lies with the house of representatives. The titular head of state is the British monarch, represented by a governor-general.

HONDURAS

Formerly neglected by Spain and still sparsely populated, Honduras has assumed increasing strategic significance. The US-backed "Contras" have operated across the border into Nicaragua and, since 1984, US troops have been stationed in the country, officially on exercises. The Honduran army, traditionally reticent in politics, is torn between the economic advantages of continued involvement in the long-running dispute and its fears for the future. Honduras has been less willing to participate in US efforts to defeat the rebels in El Salvador, who have their strongholds in territory disputed between the two countries. The territorial dispute led to a 10-day war in 1969 and has not been fully resolved despite a peace treaty signed in 1980.

Forty years ago, one-third of Honduras belonged to no one. Bananas, the major export crop, are grown in an enclave of US enterprise on the north coast, linked to the ports of Tela and San Pedro Sula by the country's few railways. Guatemala straddles the Pan American highway and so has benefited from US involvement in the transport infrastructure, previously a growth area but with an uncertain future.

The banana interests, although small by US standards, have been overwhelmingly powerful in Honduras; in the mid-1970s a president fell because it was revealed he had accepted a bribe to keep banana prices down. Production of coffee began as recently as the 1950s, but it has quickly become the second largest export, although Honduras is still one of the smaller Central American producers.

OFFICIAL NAME Republic of Honduras.

CAPITAL CITY Tegucigalpa.

GEOGRAPHY 70% of the population lives in the central highlands where there are sheltered valleys with fertile soils. The east of the country is thickly forested. There are extensive alluvial plains to the north, and good harbours on the long Caribbean coast. *Area* 112,088 sq km (43,280 sq miles).

PEOPLE *Population* 4.4m. *Density* 39 per sq km. *Ethnic groups* Mestizo 90%, others (Amerindians, Europeans, Africans) 10% .

RELIGION RC 96%, Protestant 3%.

LANGUAGE Spanish. Also Indian dialects.

EDUCATION Free to age 18, compulsory for ages 7–13. There are 3 universities.

CLIMATE Tropical on the coast but more moderate inland. Rainy season May–Nov.

CURRENCY Lempira (La).

PUBLIC HOLIDAYS Jan 1, Maundy Thu-Easter Sun, Mar 14, May 1, Sep 15, Oct 3, 12, 21, Dec 25.

GOVERNMENT The 134-member legislature is elected every 4 years. Executive power is in the hands of the president; he is elected, also for a 4-year term, but in practice is the leader of the majority party.

NICARAGUA

A beautiful land of lakes and volcanoes, Nicaragua could have been the richest of the Central American republics. But it failed to be chosen as the site for the isthmian canal, became a US protectorate for 20 years and for more than 30 years was looted by the Somoza family, who came to control more than 40% of the economy.

The revolution of 1979 ousted the Somozas at a cost of 50,000 lives. The provisional Sandinista government, a coalition of left-wing, Christian and moderate democratic groups, used the family's wealth to alleviate poverty, carried out a major literacy campaign and abolished the death penalty. Since 1981, however, the USA – fearing left-wing influences – has waged undeclared war on Nicaragua by sponsoring the so-called Nicaraguan Democratic Force or "Contras." The government of the popularly elected President Daniel Ortega, fearing US intervention, maintains a disproportionately large army and militia. Each tends to confirm the other's worst suspicions.

Contra activity, focused on economic targets, has been damaging, although it has waned since the Iran–Contra scandal undermined the credibility of US support for the guerrillas and the Bush administration elected to confine its actions to economic and political pressure on the Sandinistas.

Shortages exist in almost every sector, there is rampant inflation (10,000% in 1988), and only improvization and willpower enable the vital coffee crop to be harvested and exported. Sugar and cotton are other significant export crops. Despite aid from both Eastern and Western Europe to what remains a mixed economy with great scope for private enterprise, recovery has been frustrated by US economic pressure to cut trade and block loans. Left with no alternative, the government has pressed on with drastic adjustment policies, including currency devaluation and tax increases, in an effort to turn the economy around, even though these policies have provided the domestic opposition with a rallying point in advance of the elections promised for 1990.

OFFICIAL NAME Republic of Nicaragua.

CAPITAL CITY Managua.

GEOGRAPHY The eastern plains are largely jungle, and the Caribbean coast is marked by sandbanks, lagoons and reefs. Most settlement is in the west, in a triangular mountainous area with fertile valleys and basins. In the south a large basin contains lakes Managua and Nicaragua, the largest in Central America. A range of volcanoes separates the lakes from the Pacific. *Highest point* Pico Mogoton 2,107 metres (6,910 feet). *Area* 130,000 sq km (50,000 sq miles).

PEOPLE *Population* 3.3m. *Density* 25 per sq km. *Ethnic groups* Mestizo 69%, European 14%, African 8%, Zambo 5%, Amerindian 4%.

RELIGION RC 90%, Protestant 5%.

LANGUAGE Spanish. Some English is spoken.

EDUCATION Free to age 18, compulsory for ages 7–13.

CLIMATE Tropical, with an average temperature of 26°C (79°F), milder in the highlands and the east. Annual rainfall 3,800mm (150ins) in the east, half as much in the west.

CURRENCY Córdoba (C).

PUBLIC HOLIDAYS Jan 1, Maundy Thu, Good Fri, May 1, Jul 19, Aug 10, Sep 14, 15, Nov 2, Dec 25.

GOVERNMENT The 1987 constitution provides for an executive of president and vice-president, elected every 6 years, and their appointed cabinet. The 96-member legislative assembly is to be elected by PR.

EL SALVADOR

Smallest but most densely populated of the traditional Central American states, El Salvador has a long history of frequent coups and political violence.

The country has been torn by civil war since 1980, when left-wingers sought to emulate events in neighbouring Nicaragua. US backing for the armed forces brought about a stalemate and the insurgents have been prepared to negotiate. US support for a democratic outcome has foundered, however, on the weakness of the political centre and the public intransigence of the extreme right, which shocked world opinion with the assassination of Archbishop Romero at mass in 1980. The election victory in early 1989 of the far-right Arena party added to uncertainty about the future.

El Salvador has much to gain from peace in Central America. Historically a coffee-planters' oligarchy, it also has a strong artisan tradition and industrial potential, notably in food processing, textiles and clothing.

OFFICIAL NAME Republic of El Salvador.
CAPITAL CITY San Salvador.
GEOGRAPHY Most people live in the lake-strewn central plain, bounded by mountains and volcanoes. *Area* 21,041 sq km (8,120 sq miles).
PEOPLE *Population* 4.8m. Ethnic groups Mestizo 94%, Amerindian 5%, European 1%.
RELIGION RC 96%, Protestant 3%.
LANGUAGE Spanish.
EDUCATION Free and compulsory for ages 7–16.
CURRENCY El Salvador colón (ESC).
PUBLIC HOLIDAYS Jan 1, Good Fri-Easter Mon, May 1, Corpus Christi, Aug 5, 6, Sep 15, Oct 12, Nov 2, 5, Dec 24, 25.
GOVERNMENT Executive power lies with an elected president and a council of ministers appointed from a 60-member elected national assembly.

COSTA RICA

For 100 years Costa Rica has been an oasis of democracy in Central America. Rich volcanic soil, relatively evenly distributed, is the foundation of both its fine coffee – the major export – and its stable social structure.

The abolition of the armed forces in 1948 by the far-sighted José Figueres and his colleagues has so far saved the country from the scourge of militarism. Power changes hands in free elections which are keenly contested. Educational levels are high by regional standards and extreme poverty is rare. Long-term stability lies in strict neutrality and keeping out of regional conflicts. US pressure to re-arm, however well-intentioned, is seen as a threat to a unique way of life.

OFFICIAL NAME Republic of Costa Rica.
CAPITAL CITY San José.
GEOGRAPHY There are three mountain chains and swampy lowlands on the Caribbean shore. *Area* 50,700 sq km (19,600 sq miles).
PEOPLE *Population* 2.6m. Ethnic groups European 85%, Mestizo 10%.
RELIGION RC 92%, Protestant 7%.
LANGUAGE Spanish.
CURRENCY Costa Rican colón (CRC).
PUBLIC HOLIDAYS Jan 1, Mar 19, Maundy Thu, Good Fri, Apr 11, May 1, Corpus Christi, Jun 29, Jul 25, Aug 2, 15, Sep 15, Oct 12, Dec 1, 8, 25.
GOVERNMENT The head of state is a president elected every 4 years, at the same time as the 57 members of the legislative assembly.

PANAMA

Panama is regarded as being in South America since until 1903 it was part of Colombia, but it shares many characteristics with the Central American states. What sets it apart is the canal. Its other sources of revenue, such as flags of convenience and offshore banking, depend on its unique position as a cross-roads of world trade. The canal – like the country – was the creation of the USA, which retains a controlling interest until December 31, 1999. The future of the canal is problematic because of silting and the size of supertankers.

Panama is nominally a presidential democracy but in practice the National Guard calls the shots. The guard's commander, General Omar Torrijos, effectively controlled the country for 13 years until his death in an air crash in 1981. Torrijos took a tough stand on renegotiation of the canal agreements and improved relations with Cuba, to US displeasure. The USA tried various means, including an economic boycott, to dislodge General Manuel Noriega, who took over as National Guard commander in 1983, after allegations that he had long been involved in international drug trafficking. The US boycott disrupted offshore banking, a major growth area in recent years. Potential also lies in large recent finds of copper, which await exploitation.

OFFICIAL NAME Republic of Panama.
CAPITAL CITY Panama City.
GEOGRAPHY Apart from volcanic mountains in the south, most of the land is below 700 metres (2,300 feet). The majority of people live on the Pacific side. *Area* 77,082 sq km (29,760 sq miles).
PEOPLE *Population* 2.2m. Ethnic groups Mulatto/Mestizo 70%, African 12%, European 12%.
RELIGION RC 89%, Protestant 5%, Muslim 4%.
LANGUAGE Spanish.
EDUCATION Free to university level, compulsory for ages 6–15.
CURRENCY Balboa (Ba).
PUBLIC HOLIDAYS Jan 1, 9, Shrove Tue, Good Fri, May 1, Aug 15, Oct 11, Nov 1-5, 10, 28, Dec 8, 12, 25.
GOVERNMENT There are 9 provinces and 3 Indian reservations. The elected president forms the executive with two vice-presidents and a cabinet. There is an elected 67-member legislative assembly.

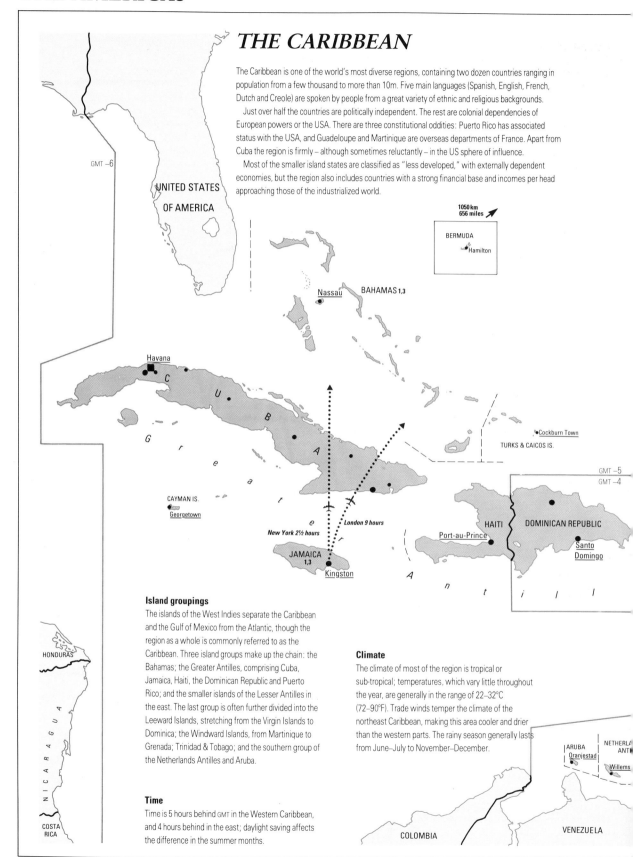

THE CARIBBEAN

The Caribbean is one of the world's most diverse regions, containing two dozen countries ranging in population from a few thousand to more than 10m. Five main languages (Spanish, English, French, Dutch and Creole) are spoken by people from a great variety of ethnic and religious backgrounds.

Just over half the countries are politically independent. The rest are colonial dependencies of European powers or the USA. There are three constitutional oddities: Puerto Rico has associated status with the USA, and Guadeloupe and Martinique are overseas departments of France. Apart from Cuba the region is firmly – although sometimes reluctantly – in the US sphere of influence.

Most of the smaller island states are classified as "less developed," with externally dependent economies, but the region also includes countries with a strong financial base and incomes per head approaching those of the industrialized world.

Island groupings

The islands of the West Indies separate the Caribbean and the Gulf of Mexico from the Atlantic, though the region as a whole is commonly referred to as the Caribbean. Three island groups make up the chain: the Bahamas; the Greater Antilles, comprising Cuba, Jamaica, Haiti, the Dominican Republic and Puerto Rico; and the smaller islands of the Lesser Antilles in the east. The last group is often further divided into the Leeward Islands, stretching from the Virgin Islands to Dominica; the Windward Islands, from Martinique to Grenada; Trinidad & Tobago; and the southern group of the Netherlands Antilles and Aruba.

Time

Time is 5 hours behind GMT in the Western Caribbean, and 4 hours behind in the east; daylight saving affects the difference in the summer months.

Climate

The climate of most of the region is tropical or sub-tropical; temperatures, which vary little throughout the year, are generally in the range of 22–32°C (72–90°F). Trade winds temper the climate of the northeast Caribbean, making this area cooler and drier than the western parts. The rainy season generally lasts from June–July to November–December.

Trade and industry

The USA is the main trading partner of almost all countries in the region. A large proportion of tourists are American, and US companies are increasing their investment in tourism, manufacturing, mining, energy and agri-business. The USA has promoted duty-free access to its market through the Caribbean Basin Initiative, launched in 1984, but benefits have been fewer than expected; the region's trade balance with the USA has gone from surplus to deficit during the 1980s, principally because of reduced oil imports, but also because of protectionist measures such as the slashing of sugar import quotas.

Tourism and the supply of raw materials and agricultural produce to the developed world remain the main economic activities. Only the larger countries have significant industrial sectors, often based on a single commodity, such as bauxite in Jamaica. During the 1980s, though, new export industries developed, notably electronic components assembly and garment manufacturing.

Almost every country runs a trade deficit, and the earnings from tourism and financial sector services are badly needed to correct the overall payments balance. A shortage of low-cost development finance has meant frequent resort to commercial borrowing, resulting in a heavy repayment burden. Structural adjustment programmes overseen by the IMF have been adopted by the Dominican Republic, Jamaica and Dominica.

Caricom

Founded in 1973 to replace the Caribbean Free Trade Association, the Caribbean Community and Common Market aims to promote unity and economic integration in the region. However, the economic difficulties of the member states have hindered this attempt at regional cooperation, and moves towards free trade have made slow progress. Wider integration involving the non-English-speaking countries that are not members of Caricom is an even more distant prospect. Member states are marked on the map; the Dominican Republic, Surinam and Haiti have observer status.

The Organization of Eastern Caribbean States

The seven members of this associate institution of Caricom formerly comprised the West Indies Associated States. The organization was formed in 1981 to foster economic and political ties between the member states in the Windward and Leeward Islands.

The Lomé Convention

Ten Caribbean states are parties to the Lomé Convention, which provides privileged access to the European Community for (mainly agricultural) exports from former French and British possessions in Africa, the Caribbean and the Pacific (ACP states). Lomé conventions signed in 1976, 1981 and 1984 also provide aid for these territories.

Eastern Caribbean geography

The Windward and Leeward Islands are so called because they are swept by the prevailing NE trade winds. The islands vary in size from over 60km (37 miles) across to tiny low-lying islands without lakes or rivers. Many are formed from coral, but some are volcanic in origin – Montserrat has seven active volcanoes; they are often thickly forested.

GROSS DOMESTIC PRODUCT

	$m
Puerto Rico	20,200
Cuba	20,000
Dominican Republic	5,427
Trinidad & Tobago	5,113
Jamaica	2,757
Haiti	1,970
Bahamas	1,500
Barbados	1,230
Netherlands Antilles	1,100
Guadeloupe	1,100
US Virgin Is.	1,030
Bermuda	900
Cayman Is.	240
Antigua & Barbuda	170
St Lucia	160
St Vincent & the Grenadines	103
Grenada	96
Dominica	90
British Virgin Is.	80
St Kitts & Nevis	65
Montserrat	37
Martinique	37
Turks & Caicos Is.	30
Anguilla	8

GDP PER HEAD

	$
Bermuda	16,071
Cayman Is.	11,429
US Virgin Is.	9,279
British Virgin Is.	6,667
Bahamas	6,494
Puerto Rico	6,155
Netherlands Antilles	5,446
Guadeloupe	5,446
Barbados	4,862
Trinidad & Tobago	4,191
Turks & Caicos Is.	3,750
Montserrat	3,083
Martinique	3,083
Antigua & Barbuda	2,125
Cuba	1,982
St Kitts & Nevis	1,413
St Lucia	1,231
Dominica	1,184
Jamaica	1,149
Anguilla	1,143
St Vincent & the Grenadines	990
Grenada	857
Dominican Republic	822
Haiti	374

Sources: UN *National Account Statistics*; EIU *Country Credit Risk Service*

ork 5 days

Rotterdam 13½ days

VIRGIN IS.
US BRITISH

San Juan

PUERTO RICO

Road Town
Charlotte Amalie

ANGUILLA
The Valley

ANTIGUA & BARBUDA 1, 2, 3

NETHERLANDS ANTILLES

Basseterre

ST KITTS & NEVIS 1, 2, 3

St John's

Plymouth
MONTSERRAT 1, 2

GUADELOUPE
Basse-Terre

DOMINICA 1, 2, 3
Roseau

Fort-de-France   MARTINIQUE

Castries   ST LUCIA 1, 2, 3

BARBADOS 1, 3
Bridgetown

ST VINCENT 1, 2, 3
Kingstown

St George's   GRENADA 1, 2, 3

Port of Spain   TRINIDAD & TOBAGO 1, 3

Leeward Islands
Lesser Antilles
Windward Islands

■ More than 1 million
● 250,000 – 1 million
• 100,000 – 250,000

1 Caricom
2 Organization of Eastern Caribbean States
3 EEC ACP states

CUBA

Since 1959 Cuba has been the Caribbean's only one-party socialist state, with a highly centralized economy. Its achievements include strong economic growth which tapered off only in the late 1980s; a creditable health and education system; determined efforts to eliminate racial inequality; and a strong national identity. Problems include a distorted economy heavily dependent on favourable Soviet trade terms; a severe external debt burden; a pervasive and lethargic bureaucracy; and persistent inefficiency.

To remedy some of the difficulties, President Fidel Castro has eschewed the Soviet road of *perestroika*, and instead launched a "rectification" campaign involving a reduction in privileges enjoyed by communist party and government officials, as well as a drive for greater economic efficiency. The government has less leverage on external economic difficulties, which have largely arisen through adverse world sugar and oil prices.

Since the 1959 revolution, relations with the USA have ranged from dangerous to lukewarm, and no breakthrough to normalization can be foreseen. Cuba has, however, restored relations with almost all Latin American countries, and has gained international respect for its role in Angola. Yet in the Caribbean its influence is small. Instead, Cuba's pattern of trade is closely integrated with the Soviet Union and other Comecon members. Sugar accounts for four-fifths of export earnings; but in hard-currency terms it has been outstripped by the resale to the world market of oil imported from the USSR. Other important earners are tobacco, nickel and other minerals, seafood and agricultural produce.

The drive to industrialize has undergone several changes of emphasis; it is now concentrated on minerals, oil, nuclear power, steel and engineering, including equipment for the sugar industry. Plans are also being pushed to increase tourism.

In recent years, the political structure has been reshaped, with older ministers and party leaders giving way to younger appointees. Castro nevertheless still dominates with no successor in sight.

OFFICIAL NAME Republic of Cuba.

CAPITAL CITY Havana.

GEOGRAPHY A long narrow island with a complex of eroded mountain ranges interspersed with small plains, Cuba is the summit of a marine tableland. The highest mountains are the Sierra Maestra on the southeast coast. There is a well-developed underground river system and a long coastline of bays, beaches, swamps and cliffs. *Highest point* Turquino 2,005 metres (6,580 feet). *Area* 110,861 sq km (42,800 sq miles).

PEOPLE *Population* 10.1m. *Density* 91 per sq km. *Ethnic groups* European 72%, Mulatto 15%, African 12%.

RELIGION RC 40%.

LANGUAGE Spanish.

EDUCATION Free and compulsory for ages 6–12. Schooling combines study and manual work.

CURRENCY Cuban peso (Cub$).

PUBLIC HOLIDAYS Jan 1, May 1, Jul 25-27, Oct 10.

GOVERNMENT Communist republic. The only authorized party is the Partido Comunista de Cuba. The 1976 constitution provides for a 499-member national assembly of people's power, elected for 5 years by municipal assemblies. The national assembly appoints 31 members as the council of state, whose president is head of state and head of government.

JAMAICA

Throughout the 1970s, during the charismatic Michael Manley's socialist experiment, the Caribbean's largest English-speaking country suffered from negative domestic growth. Inflation reached 30% and, by the time Edward Seaga took over in 1980, GDP per head was down to just over $1,200. Seaga made friends with the USA and embarked upon a course designed to cut public spending, increase exports, constrain demand and liberalize the economy. In 1986 there was a modest recovery; in 1987 the economy grew by over 5%. But Seaga's policies had become increasingly unpopular and the country remained plagued by huge debt, a persistent trade deficit and periodic outbursts of violence. In 1988 a hurricane wrecked half of Jamaica's housing stock, damaged public utilities and destroyed key cash crops. In February 1989 the electorate returned Michael Manley to power.

Manley, who now eschews the "jobs for votes" political largesse that has been a major cause of electoral violence, is committed to expanding social services and "normalizing" relations with Cuba, his soul-mate of the 1970s. But he cannot afford to antagonize the USA – which among other things wants a much more concerted effort to cut back the trade in cannabis on which so many Jamaicans rely – and he can only manoeuvre within the fairly tight strictures laid down by the IMF. However, earnings from tourism are increasing, bauxite production is rising and the manufacturing sector is showing signs of growth.

OFFICIAL NAME Jamaica.

CAPITAL CITY Kingston.

GEOGRAPHY The island has a spine of limestone mountains and plateaus, much of it covered in rain forest. Most settlement is on the coastal plains. *Area* 10,991 sq km (4,240 sq miles).

PEOPLE *Population* 2.3m. *Ethnic groups* African 76%, mixed 15%, European 3%, Asian Indian 2%.

RELIGION Church of God 18%, Baptist 10%, Anglican 7%, Seventh Day Adventist 7%, Pentecostal 5%, RC 5%, Presbyterian 5%, Methodist 3%. There are also many Rastafarians.

LANGUAGE English. Also English/African patois.

CURRENCY Jamaica dollar (J$).

PUBLIC HOLIDAYS Jan 1, Ash Wed, Good Fri-Easter Mon, May 23, Aug 6, Oct 15, Dec 25, 26.

GOVERNMENT Parliamentary monarchy. A governor-general, representing the British monarch, is appointed on the recommendation of the prime minister. The prime minister is the head of the majority party in the 60-member house of representatives, elected every 5 years. The upper house, the senate, has 21 members.

HAITI

Political turmoil has gripped Haiti for much of its history since Toussaint L'Ouverture led the slaves to freedom from France in 1804, making Haiti the Caribbean's first independent state. Sporadic conflict between the mulatto and black populations led the USA to intervene in 1915 and take control of the country for nearly 20 years. The 29-year dictatorship of the Duvalier family, which ended with the flight of Jean-Claude Duvalier in 1986, kept the majority of Haitians in wretched poverty, with the worst housing, health and education record in the Caribbean, while millions of dollars were embezzled by the presidential elite.

Attempts to establish a constitutional elected government have been frustrated by partisans of the old regime, using every means including open terror. The November 1987 general election was cancelled after voters were shot down at the polling stations. The army, itself by no means united, has resumed its habit formed before the Duvalier regime of intervening in politics. The second of 1988's two military coups departed from the norm: it was led by sergeants, although they installed a former Duvalier confidant, Lt-Gen Prosper Avril, as president. Many officers were arrested and drummed out of the army.

The country's troubles have hardly helped the economy. Agriculture and fishing provide a bare level of subsistence for 65% of the population. A number of US-owned manufacturers provide employment in the Port-au-Prince area, but several have moved to other countries in the region, increasing the ranks of the capital's unemployed.

The suspension of US and other foreign aid has brought severe cash problems for the government, which has long depended on overseas funds for budgetary support as well as for development projects. Widespread smuggling has weakened official control of the state finances.

OFFICIAL NAME Republic of Haiti.

CAPITAL CITY Port-au-Prince.

GEOGRAPHY Haiti is the western part of Hispaniola, with two long, rocky, calcareous peninsulas joined by an alluvial plain and a central plateau. Earthquakes are common. *Highest point* Pic de la Selle 2,674 metres (8,770 feet). *Area* 27,750 sq km (10,710 sq miles).

PEOPLE *Population* 5.3m. *Density* 190 per sq km. *Ethnic groups* African 95%, Mulatto 5%.

RELIGION RC 80%, Protestant 14%; Voodoo recognized by the state but no available figures.

LANGUAGE French. Also Creole.

EDUCATION Compulsory for ages 7–13. State system supplemented by many fee-paying RC schools.

CURRENCY Gourde (Gde).

PUBLIC HOLIDAYS Jan 1, 2, Shrove Mon-Tue, Good Fri, May 1, 18, 22, Nov 1, 18, Dec 5, 25.

GOVERNMENT Republic since 1804. Haiti has veered between democracy and dictatorship. The March 1987 constitution provides for a president, elected every 5 years, to form the executive with a prime minister and cabinet drawn from the majority party in the legislature. There is a 27-member senate and a 77-member chamber of deputies.

DOMINICAN REPUBLIC

A booming tourist industry, rapid expansion of duty-free industrial zones and a grandiose programme of public works have produced a high economic growth rate and new employment opportunities for the Dominican Republic. Forcing the pace, though, has brought problems. A headlong fall of the national currency set off a sharp rise in food and fuel prices which led to widespread rioting in early 1988. The government subsequently reasserted control over the exchange rate by closing the privately run exchange offices and banning street currency trading.

Despite the achievement of octogenarian President Joaquín Balaguer in setting the economy on an upward growth path without a new IMF agreement, income from tourism and the industrial zones may still not be enough to stave off a debt crisis. External debt is over $4bn, and payments arrears are growing. The government has so far failed to persuade creditors to agree to a rescheduling without an IMF programme.

The government's dilemma is that an earlier IMF-led austerity drive in 1984 brought an explosion of angry demonstrations, violently repressed at the cost of 100 lives. If the attempt to buy time and goodwill with the public works programme fails, severe social conflict could lie ahead. Though a divided and demoralized opposition party makes electoral upheaval seem unlikely, the ghost of military intervention – thought to have been laid to rest since 1979 – reappeared briefly in mid-1988, when Balaguer sacked defence minister General Antonio Imbert Barrera after a flurry of coup rumours.

OFFICIAL NAME Dominican Republic.

CAPITAL CITY Santo Domingo.

GEOGRAPHY The relief is dominated by a series of hills and mountain ranges running northwest to southeast. There is an abundance of fertile soils, especially the alluvia of the southeastern lowlands. *Highest point* Pico Duarte 3,175 metres (10,420 feet). *Area* 48,374 sq km (18,820 sq miles).

PEOPLE *Population* 6.2m. *Density* 128 per sq km. *Ethnic groups* Mulatto 75%, European 15%, African 10%.

RELIGION RC 98%, Protestant 1%.

LANGUAGE Spanish.

EDUCATION Free to university level; compulsory for ages 7–14.

CURRENCY Dominican Republic peso (DR$).

PUBLIC HOLIDAYS Jan 1, 6, 21, 26, Feb 27, Good Fri, Apr 4, May 1, Jul 16, Aug 16, Sep 24, Oct 12, 24, Nov 1, Dec 25.

GOVERNMENT Republic since 1821. It has remained free of military coups in the 1980s. The chief executive, the president, is directly elected for a 4-year term and is assisted by a vice-president and a cabinet. The national congress has a 30-member senate and 120-member chamber of deputies.

THE BAHAMAS

Tourism contributes more than 50% of GNP and provides jobs for almost half the working population; 90% of the 1.5m tourists who visit every year come from the USA. Offshore banking, insurance and one of the largest "open-registry" shipping fleets in the world help to offset a substantial trade deficit: 80% of food is imported. Attempts are being made to develop fishing and agriculture, particularly growing citrus fruit for export.

The country's exposed position close to the US coast, with its 700 widely dispersed islands (of which only 29 are inhabited), makes it a haven for international drug traffickers. Officials up to ministerial level have been implicated in drug-related corruption. Prime Minister Sir Lynden Pindling has denied accusations of involvement; his Progressive Liberal Party won a fifth consecutive term in the 1987 elections. The government has sought increased US assistance in its anti-smuggling efforts.

OFFICIAL NAME Commonwealth of the Bahamas.
CAPITAL CITY Nassau.
GEOGRAPHY An archipelago, there are more than 700 low-lying islands, 29 of them inhabited. *Area* 13,935 sq km (5,380 sq miles).
PEOPLE *Population* 230,000. *Ethnic groups* African 70%, mixed 14%, European 13%.
RELIGION Christian 95% (Protestant 47%, RC 25%, Anglican 21%, other 2%).
LANGUAGE English.
CURRENCY Bahamian dollar (Ba$).
PUBLIC HOLIDAYS Jan 1, Good Fri, Easter Mon, Whit Mon, 1st Sat in Jun, Jul 10, Aug 8, Oct 12, Dec 25, 26.
GOVERNMENT Parliamentary monarchy. A governor-general represents the British monarch and acts on the advice of the prime minister and cabinet.

PUERTO RICO

Puerto Rico is subject to US law, with the US administration responsible for defence, taxation and immigration procedures. It has a measure of internal self-government, electing its own congress and governor, but Puerto Ricans cannot vote in US presidential elections.

The island is largely industrialized, and about a third of the population lives in the San Juan urban area. Agriculture plays only a small part in the economy; the two major growth areas are tourism and manufacturing.

The US internal revenue code grants tax exemption to US companies based in Puerto Rico, provided that they pay 10% of their profits into the government development bank. These funds amount to more than $7bn, and the Puerto Rican administration has offered to use $840m to assist industrial development in countries benefiting from the Caribbean Basin Initiative, by setting up twin plants for the finishing of semi-manufactured goods.

Past controversy over the island's status appears to have waned, with the current position gaining support over the extremes of US statehood or independence.

OFFICIAL NAME Commonwealth of Puerto Rico.
CAPITAL CITY San Juan.
GEOGRAPHY A rugged, hilly island. Mountains slope steeply to the sea on the south, but give way in the north to a plateau and rain forest cut by deep valleys. *Area* 9,104 sq km (3,520 sq miles).
PEOPLE *Population* 3.3m. *Ethnic groups* European (mostly Spanish) 75%, African 15%, Mulatto 10%.
RELIGION RC 85%, Protestant 5%.
LANGUAGE Spanish and English.
CURRENCY US dollar ($).
PUBLIC HOLIDAYS Jan 1, 6, 12, 3rd Mon in Feb, 4th Wed in Mar, Apr 16, Good Fri, last Mon in May, Jul 4, 17, 25, 27, 1st Mon in Sep, Oct 12, Nov 11, 19, last Thu in Nov, Dec 25.
GOVERNMENT "Free associated state" of the USA. The chief executive is the governor. There is a cabinet of 15 appointed secretaries. The legislature is a 27-member senate and 51-member house of representatives.

TRINIDAD & TOBAGO

The fall in international oil prices during the 1980s wrought havoc in Trinidad and Tobago's economy. Petroleum products account for about 70% of exports, and falling production brought a steady decline in GDP, coupled with adverse trade and payments figures. At the same time, rising interest payments on loans contracted for extravagant and badly managed development projects helped almost exhaust once ample reserves. Structural adjustment, debt rescheduling and IMF assistance have become the order of the day, as the government grapples with finances burdened by a loss-making state sector.

An abrupt change in political direction came in December 1986, when the electorate turned its back on the People's National Movement after 30 years in power. The incoming government, headed by Prime Minister Arthur Robinson, was an uneasy coalition of conflicting interests under the banner of the National Alliance for Reconstruction; by 1988, a prolonged internal wrangle had led to the expulsion of its pro-labour representatives. With the party taking a more orthodox business-oriented stance, the stage seems set for a political realignment along clearer left – right lines than hitherto.

OFFICIAL NAME Republic of Trinidad and Tobago.
CAPITAL CITY Port of Spain.
GEOGRAPHY Trinidad has mountains on the north, a central plain and volcanic hills to the south. Tobago is surrounded by coral reefs. *Area* 5,128 sq km (1,980 sq miles).
PEOPLE *Population* 1.2m. *Ethnic groups* African 41%, Asian Indian 40%, mixed 17%.
RELIGION Christian 62%, Hindu 25%, Muslim 6%.
LANGUAGE English.
CURRENCY Trinidad & Tobago dollar (TT$).
PUBLIC HOLIDAYS Jan 1, Shrove Mon-Tue, Good Fri-Easter Mon, Id al-Fitr, Whit Mon, Corpus Christi, Jun 19, Aug 1, 31, Sep 24, Divali, Dec 25, 26.
GOVERNMENT Republic since 1962. The president is elected by a college of the legislature which comprises an elected 36-member house of representatives and a 31-member senate.

CAYMAN ISLANDS

OFFICIAL NAME Colony of the Cayman Islands.
CAPITAL CITY Georgetown.
GEOGRAPHY An archipelago of low-lying rocky islands surrounded by coral reefs. There are no rivers.
PEOPLE *Population* 21,000. *Ethnic groups* Mixed 50%, African 25%, European 25%.
RELIGION Protestant 85%, RC 5%.
LANGUAGE English.
CURRENCY Cayman Islands dollar (CI$).
PUBLIC HOLIDAYS Jan 1, Ash Wed, Good Fri-Easter Mon, 3rd Mon in May, Mon after Jun 8, 1st Mon in Jul, 2nd Mon in Nov, Dec 25, 26.
GOVERNMENT UK colony administered by Jamaica until 1962. A governor represents the British monarch. Small executive council and legislative assembly.

The Cayman Islands has become the world's largest offshore financial centre, offering secrecy and freedom from taxes to more than 18,000 companies. Since 1986, however, US law enforcement agencies have been allowed access to banking records, as part of a crackdown on drug-trafficking. The islands' thriving tourist industry, based overwhelmingly on the US market, accounts for 70% of GDP and 75% of foreign exchange earnings. A property boom shows no signs of slackening, and a labour shortage is met by the employment of foreigners, who make up a third of the population.

TURKS & CAICOS Is

OFFICIAL NAME Colony of Turks and Caicos Islands.
CAPITAL CITY Cockburn Town.
GEOGRAPHY More than 30 islands, 8 inhabited, in two groups.
PEOPLE *Population* 8,000. *Ethnic groups* Mixed 63%, African 33%.
RELIGION Protestant 78%.
LANGUAGE English.
CURRENCY US dollar ($).
PUBLIC HOLIDAYS Jan 1, Easter (4 days), May 30, Jun 13, Aug 1, Oct 10, Dec 25, 26.
GOVERNMENT UK colony. A governor represents the British monarch. Executive and legislative councils.

The Turks and Caicos Islands regained an elected government in 1988; a period of direct rule by a council headed by the British governor had followed the conviction in 1986 of three ministers on drugs charges in the USA. The new government, headed by Chief Minister Oswald Skippings, negotiated a £15m aid package from the UK, aiming to eliminate the need for budgetary support over three years. Tourism and offshore financial services are being developed to supplement the main foreign exchange earner, lobster.

BERMUDA

OFFICIAL NAME Colony of Bermuda.
CAPITAL CITY Hamilton.
GEOGRAPHY An archipelago of 120 coral islands, 20 of them inhabited.
PEOPLE *Population* 56,000. *Ethnic groups* African 61%, European 37%.
RELIGION Christian 88%, Muslim 1%.
LANGUAGE English.
CURRENCY Bermuda dollar (Bda$).
PUBLIC HOLIDAYS Jan 1, Good Fri, 2nd Mon in Jun, last Thu and Fri in Jul, 1st Mon in Sep, Nov 11, Dec 25, 26.
GOVERNMENT UK colony. A governor represents the British monarch. House of assembly and senate.

A British colony since 1620, Bermuda lies in the Atlantic Ocean, 1,450km (900 miles) northeast of Nassau. Like several of the Caribbean islands, it makes handsome earnings from tourism and offshore financial services; GNP per head is among the highest in the world. Income from services offsets a severe trade deficit; the island imports 80% of its food – much of it eaten by the tourists – and manufactured goods. Almost all tourist and commerical business originates in the USA and the economy has followed that of the USA in and out of recession in recent years.

The government is discussing constitutional issues with the UK, USA and Canada, but a referendum is promised before any moves are made towards independence, which public opinion has traditionally opposed.

US VIRGIN ISLANDS

OFFICIAL NAME Virgin Islands of the United States.
CAPITAL CITY Charlotte Amalie.
GEOGRAPHY A group of more than 50 islands.
PEOPLE *Population* 111,000. *Density* 322 per sq km. *Ethnic groups* African 80%, European 15%.
RELIGION Christian 98%.
LANGUAGE English. Also Spanish, French, Creole.
CURRENCY US dollar ($).
GOVERNMENT Unincorporated US territory with a measure of self-government.

Tourism is the dominant industry in the 68-island group, a US possession of which St Thomas, St John and St Croix are the main islands. Condominium and hotel construction is continuing rapidly, and industry is also expanding, helped by the extension of US tax concessions.

BRITISH VIRGIN Is

OFFICIAL NAME Colony of British Virgin Islands.
CAPITAL CITY Road Town.
GEOGRAPHY Four large islands and about 36 islets and cays.
PEOPLE *Population* 12,000. *Density* 78 per sq km. *Ethnic groups* African 88%, European 7%.
RELIGION Protestant 73%, RC 6%.
LANGUAGE English.
CURRENCY US dollar ($).
GOVERNMENT UK colony. A governor represents the British monarch. Two councils.

A successful drive to promote luxury tourism has brought substantial foreign earnings to this British dependency. A recent growth sector has been offshore business, with nearly 6,000 companies registered by early 1988.

ANGUILLA

OFFICIAL NAME Dependent Territory of Anguilla.
CAPITAL CITY The Valley.
GEOGRAPHY Low-lying coral island covered in scrub.
PEOPLE *Population* 7,000. *Density* 47 per sq km. *Ethnic groups* Mainly African or mixed.

RELIGION Mainly Christian.
LANGUAGE English.
CURRENCY East Caribbean dollar (EC$).
GOVERNMENT UK colony. A governor represents the British monarch. Council and assembly.

Anguilla has achieved a balanced budget virtually without taxation. Most revenue comes from customs duties, and income from a fast-growing tourist industry and other services offsets a big trade deficit. Unemployment of about 27% is the outstanding problem.

ST KITTS-NEVIS

OFFICIAL NAME Federation of Saint Christopher and Nevis.
CAPITAL CITY Basseterre.
GEOGRAPHY Three mountainous islands: St Kitts, Nevis and Sombrero.
PEOPLE *Population* 46,000. *Ethnic groups* African 94%, Mulatto 3%, European 1%.
RELIGION Protestant 85%, RC 7%.
LANGUAGE English.
CURRENCY East Caribbean dollar (EC$).
GOVERNMENT Parliamentary monarchy. A governor-general represents the British monarch. Elected parliament and prime minister.

Tourism is replacing the declining sugar industry; manufacturing and service sectors are also growing fast. Development plans include a new road to open up the southeast peninsula of St Kitts for housing, industrial and tourist construction, funded by US aid.

ANTIGUA & BARBUDA

OFFICIAL NAME Antigua & Barbuda.
CAPITAL CITY St John's.
GEOGRAPHY The main islands of the group are Antigua and Barbuda. Redonda is uninhabited.
PEOPLE *Population* 77,000. *Ethnic groups* African 94%, European 1%.
RELIGION Christian 96%, mainly Anglican.
LANGUAGE English.
CURRENCY East Caribbean dollar (EC$).
GOVERNMENT Parliamentary monarchy. A governor-

general represents the British monarch. Senate and house of representatives.

Governed almost without interruption since 1956 by the Antigua Labour Party, the islands have relied for growth on luxury tourism. There is some manufacturing, but farming is at an ebb; food imports add to the chronic trade deficit, and the health services and infrastructure are in poor condition. Borrowing to finance development projects has built up a large external debt and debt service takes almost a fifth of state revenue. The government has been repeatedly accused of corruption.

MONTSERRAT

OFFICIAL NAME Colony of Montserrat.
CAPITAL CITY Plymouth.
GEOGRAPHY A mountainous island with active volcanoes.
PEOPLE *Population* 12,000. *Ethnic groups* African 96%, European 3%, mixed 1%.
RELIGION Christian 97%.
LANGUAGE English.
CURRENCY East Caribbean dollar (EC$).
GOVERNMENT UK colony. A governor represents the British monarch. Legislative council includes 12 elected members.

Tourism is the island's mainstay, but it is not allowed to dominate. Electronic components make up over half of exports; agricultural produce is also exported and the island aims to be self-sufficient in food. Opinion is divided on independence, but no decision will be taken without a referendum.

GUADELOUPE

OFFICIAL NAME Department of Guadeloupe.
CAPITAL CITY Basse-Terre.
GEOGRAPHY The main islands in the seven-island group are Grande-Terre and Basse-Terre.
PEOPLE *Population* 330,000. *Ethnic groups* Mulatto 77%, African 10%, Mestizo 10%, European 2%.
RELIGION Christian, mainly RC.
LANGUAGE French.
CURRENCY French franc (Fr).
GOVERNMENT French overseas department.

Guadeloupe has a strong independence movement which has mounted sporadic bombings. French aid has ensured a high living standard, but unemployment is almost 40%. Main exports are sugar, rum and bananas, mostly to France. Tourism is thriving.

DOMINICA

OFFICIAL NAME Commonwealth of Dominica.
CAPITAL CITY Roseau.
GEOGRAPHY A ridged volcanic island. Two-thirds of the land is forested.
PEOPLE *Population* 76,000. *Ethnic groups* African 90%, Mulatto 7%, American Indian 2%, Carib 0.5%.
RELIGION RC 90%, Protestant 8%.
LANGUAGE English. Also French patois.
CURRENCY East Caribbean dollar (EC$).
GOVERNMENT Republic since 1978. Chief executive and head of state is a president, elected by 30-member house of assembly.

Dominica is developing its roads and public utilites to support future industrial growth, aided by an IMF loan. Agriculture is the mainstay, and bananas the leading export crop. Specialized tourism is being encouraged.

MARTINIQUE

OFFICIAL NAME Department of Martinique.
CAPITAL CITY Fort-de-France.
GEOGRAPHY The island rises steeply from the sea to the northern volcanic massif of Mount Pelôe.
PEOPLE *Population* 330,000. *Ethnic groups* Mulatto 95%, European 2%, Asian Indian 2%.
RELIGION RC 91%, Protestant 5%.
LANGUAGE French. Also Creole.
CURRENCY French franc (Fr).
GOVERNMENT French overseas department.

French government expenditure on the island accounts for 70% of GNP, providing jobs and social services to cushion high unemployment. Bananas, rum and pineapples are the chief exports, but tourism is important, and the industrial sector includes an oil refinery, cement works and agro-processing.

ST LUCIA

OFFICIAL NAME Saint Lucia.
CAPITAL CITY Castries.
GEOGRAPHY A mountainous volcanic island.
PEOPLE *Population* 130,000. *Ethnic groups* African 90%, Mulatto 6%, Asian Indian 3%, European 1%.
RELIGION RC 86%, Protestant 11%.
LANGUAGE English. Also French patois.
CURRENCY East Caribbean dollar (EC$).
GOVERNMENT Parliamentary monarchy. A governor-general represents the British monarch. Senate and house of representatives.

Vigorous infrastructure development is taking place as St Lucia strives to overcome a persistent trade deficit and chronic unemployment. Tourism, bananas and manufacturing are the main sources of foreign exchange. There are plans to exploit thermal energy reserves to reduce oil imports.

ST VINCENT & THE GRENADINES

OFFICIAL NAME Saint Vincent and the Grenadines.
CAPITAL CITY Kingstown.
GEOGRAPHY The group comprises St Vincent, Bequia, Mustique, Canouan, Mayreau and Union.
PEOPLE *Population* 100,000. *Ethnic groups* African 65%, Mulatto 19%, Asian Indian 5%, European 3%.
RELIGION Protestant 77%, RC 19%.
LANGUAGE English.
CURRENCY East Caribbean dollar (EC$).
GOVERNMENT Parliamentary monarchy. A governor-general represents the British monarch. House of assembly.

Conservative budgeting and infrastructure development – notably the construction of an international airport – are the main planks of the government's programme. Foreign aid supports land reform and other projects, but unemployment remains a problem. The trade gap is narrowing, thanks to increased agricultural exports. Luxury tourism is developing on the smaller islands.

BARBADOS

OFFICIAL NAME Barbados.
CAPITAL CITY Bridgetown.
GEOGRAPHY A rugged island ringed by a reef.
PEOPLE *Population* 250,000. *Ethnic groups* African 92%, European 3%, mixed 3%.
RELIGION Protestant 88%, RC 6%.
LANGUAGE English.
CURRENCY Barbados dollar (Bds$).
GOVERNMENT Parliamentary monarchy. A governor-general represents the British monarch. Senate and house of assembly.

Tourism has taken over as Barbados's leading industry but the island still produces about 80,000 tonnes (88,200 US tons) of sugar a year, mostly for the UK. Offshore fields produce oil and natural gas; manufacturing has suffered from depressed markets, and hopes of economic growth are pinned on service industries. Barbados is an important air transport and communications centre for the eastern Caribbean, and houses several regional institutions. Foreign debt, unemployment and a widening trade gap are serious problems, but the country enjoys political stability and good welfare services.

GRENADA

OFFICIAL NAME Grenada.
CAPITAL CITY St George's.
GEOGRAPHY Main island and arc of smaller islands running north to St Vincent.
PEOPLE *Population* 112,000. *Ethnic groups* African 84%, Mulatto 11%, Indian 3%.
RELIGION Christian 99% (RC 64%).
LANGUAGE English.
CURRENCY East Caribbean dollar (EC$).
GOVERNMENT Parliamentary monarchy. A governor represents the British monarch. Senate and house of representatives.

The traumatic events of 1983, when the violent overthrow of Prime Minister Maurice Bishop's government led to armed intervention by the USA, are still keenly felt in Grenada, which remains a fragmented society, marked by strong personal as well as political differences.

Despite US financial support, the government has found it hard to balance the budget, largely because tax reform has not raised the expected revenue. Some mooted development schemes involving foreign partners have come badly unstuck. While the nutmeg industry has been helped by a trade pact with Indonesia, cocoa and bananas – the other traditional export crops – are in a more difficult position.

NETHERLANDS ANTILLES

OFFICIAL NAME Netherlands Antilles.
CAPITAL CITY Willemstad.
GEOGRAPHY Comprises the Leeward and Windward groups some 800km (500 miles) apart.
PEOPLE *Population* 200,000. *Ethnic groups* Mulatto 84%, European 6%.
RELIGION RC 87%, Protestant 10%.
LANGUAGE Dutch. Also Spanish, English, patois.
CURRENCY Netherlands Antillian guilder (NAGld).
GOVERNMENT Netherlands dependency. A governor represents the Dutch monarch. Council and parliament.

The federation of six islands became five in 1986 when Aruba seceded; the others are expecting to hold referenda on independence. The federation is heavily dependent on Dutch aid; tourism, finance and, to a decreasing extent, oil refining are the main economic activities.

ARUBA

OFFICIAL NAME Aruba.
CAPITAL CITY Oranjestad.
GEOGRAPHY The dry and flat limestone island lies 25km (16 miles) north of Venezuela.
PEOPLE *Population* 68,000. *Ethnic groups* Dutch, mixed, American Indian, Portuguese.
RELIGION RC 80%.
LANGUAGE Dutch. Also a patois, Papiamento.
CURRENCY Aruba guilder (AGld).
GOVERNMENT Netherlands dependency.

Falls in US demand and cuts in Venezuelan production have forced the closure of Aruba's oil refinery, leaving the island reliant on its expanding tourism industry and Dutch aid. Independence is scheduled for 1996.

SOUTH AMERICA

Cocaine

US government agencies estimate that in 1987 retail sales of South American cocaine totalled $22bn-worth. Bolivia and Peru are the main producers and Colombia the centre for refining and export. After middlemen have taken their cut and the money is laundered, only about $1.5bn in foreign exchange is actually reinvested in the producer nations, often in real estate. As a proportion of GDP therefore cocaine revenue is relatively small. Nevertheless, the crop reduces the countries' balance of payment deficits, and provides employment for an estimated 5% of the working population.

The Galapagos islands

The Galapagos islands, on the Equator 970km (610 miles) west of the South American mainland, have been administered by Ecuador since 1832. Four of the islands are inhabited. The Galapagos' unique wildlife, particularly iguanas and giant tortoises, has made the islands a focus of scientific study since Charles Darwin visited in 1835. Isabela, the largest island, was a prison colony until 1958.

Trade

Prospects of South American states uniting to repudiate their debt are much reduced by the fact that they depend on the outside world much more than they do on each other. Trade between the 11 member countries of the Asociación Latinoamericana de Integración (Aladi) runs at only about 10% of their total exports and imports.

This may be starting to change. Brazil and Argentina, which once competed for dominance of the sub-continent, are edging towards a customs union, which Uruguay will also join. Both are looking at bilateral agreements with other countries that could greatly reduce their dependence on traditional US and European markets.

Aladi, whose members are the 10 Portuguese and Spanish-speaking South American states, plus Mexico, was set up in 1980 to promote freer trade and economic integration.

The Falkland Islands/Malvinas

The question of whose flag should fly over the Falklands/Malvinas Islands dates from long before Argentina and the UK went to war in 1982. Costly in lives and physical damage, the war did not end the dispute.

The population was dwindling through emigration before the war and the sheep-based economy was in a parlous state. Commercial quantities of oil and natural gas may exist offshore and, under British protection, a fishing industry is beginning to flourish. The presence of 3,000 British troops has more than compensated for the end of Argentine duty-free shopping trips to Port Stanley, but this is hardly a stable foundation for longer-term economic development.

Tierra del Fuego

At the southern tip of the continent, Tierra del Fuego is split between Argentina and Chile. The two countries' territorial dispute over the Beagle Channel, south of the island, was settled in 1984, after Vatican mediation.

GALAPAGOS IS.

Kobe 30 days

The Amazon basin

The Amazon, the world's largest river by volume and the second longest, rises in the Peruvian Andes only 150km (95 miles) from the Pacific and flows into the Atlantic through a huge delta; its total length is 6,750km (4,218 miles). The Amazon has more than 1,100 tributaries, draining a basin of 7m sq km (2.7m sq miles); together they carry one-fifth of the world's running water.

Burning the Amazon forest, the world's largest, for new settlements and agriculture is estimated to reduce its area by 4% a year. The global environmental implications of this destruction are causing mounting concern.

Indigenous peoples

Latin America's indigenous peoples are becoming the victims of the race for development. The Indians of the Amazon basin, once insulated from the outside world by impenetrable forest, are increasingly exposed as new roads open up their homelands to development and settlement. Hundreds of thousands of landless migrants have settled in Rondonia and Acre provinces, on Brazil's western border, invading Indian land, destroying the forest and polluting the rivers. Farther east, the state of Para has been opened up by huge mining projects, hydroelectric dams and cattle ranches. Amazonia is thought to have supported an Indian population of 2m in 230 tribal groups 500 years ago. Today the number has dwindled to less than 50,000, many tribes have vanished altogether.

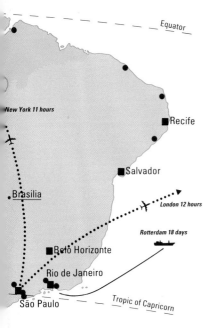

■ More than 1 million
● 250,000 – 1 million
▨ Natural extent of tropical rainforest

EXTERNAL DEBT

The debt crisis

The focus of concern about Latin American debt has shifted. In the early 1980s the future of the world financial system seemed to be at stake, as debtors could no longer repay the huge loans banks had been eager to make in the heyday of Opec surpluses. By the end of the decade the problem was the stability of Latin America. Banks have written down the value of their debt, traded some of it on the secondary market, often at huge discounts, and frequently put up new loans to help debtors pay off old loans. The banks have survived, but South American countries have had their prospects for growth squeezed by the struggle to service debt.

Various schemes have been tried to reduce indebtedness. With debt trading at a deep discount, debtors can buy back their debt for a quarter or half its face value. Debt can be swapped for equity: a company will buy debt in foreign currency in exchange for an agreed amount of local currency to invest in businesses in the debtor country. Some countries have tried debt-for-nature swaps: an environmentalist group buys debt at a discount, then sells it back to the debtor at a premium, using the proceeds for local conservation projects. Debt reduction schemes like these reduced the $300bn debt of the big four Latin American debtors by around $18bn in 1988.

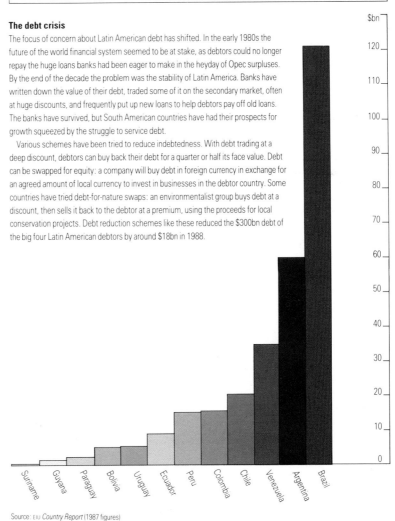

Source: EIU *Country Report* (1987 figures)

ECUADOR

Ecuador's history has been one of coups and counter-coups, but civilians have ruled since 1979. Rodrigo Borja Cevallos, inaugurated as president in August 1988, enjoys a majority in the legislature unlike his civilian predecessors – although this has been engineered by an alliance between his own Izquierda Democrática party and other left and centre-left parties. Ecuador has always been notorious for the shifting allegiances of its numerous political parties. Dr Borja has – unlike his two predecessors – become president without winning over Guayaquil, Ecuador's commercial centre, rival of the capital, Quito.

President Borja's immediate challenge is to turn round an economy on which a supply-side experiment was made by his predecessor, inopportunely as it turned out, for oil prices were about to collapse. An earthquake in March 1987 disrupted oil production, making matters worse. The external account became so weak that debt service payments fell behind, even though the commercial bank component had been rescheduled.

The 1980s have generally been a much tougher time for Ecuador than the previous decade, when the start of oil exports in 1972 set off a burst of prosperity. Before that, the economy had been banana-based – Ecuador is still top of the world banana exporters' league.

OFFICIAL NAME Republic of Ecuador.
CAPITAL CITY Quito.
GEOGRAPHY The Andes run north–south through the country in three parallel ranges separated by wide basins; one of the peaks is Cotopaxi, the highest active volcano in the world. On the Pacific coast is a lowland area, part cultivated, part rain forest. Almost all the population live on the coast or in the mountain valleys; the east of the country, an impenetrable forest lowland at the edge of the Amazon basin, is nearly empty. *Highest point* Chimborazo 6,267 metres (20,560 feet). *Area* 283,561 sq km (109,480 sq miles).
PEOPLE *Population* 9.4m. *Density* 33 per sq km. *Ethnic groups* Amerindian (mainly Quechua) 50%, Mestizo 40%, European 8%.
RELIGION RC 96%, Protestant 2%.
LANGUAGE Spanish. Also Amerindian languages, especially Quechua.
EDUCATION Compulsory for six years for ages 6–14. Free in state schools, but there is a large private sector. There are 16 universities. State-run literacy centres and adult schools boost government educational spending to 28% of the total budget.
CLIMATE Tropical, but moderated by altitude and the Humboldt current. Coastal temperature 23–25°C (73–77°F), wet season Jan-May. Beyond the mountains, temperature 23–27°C (73–81°F), 90% humidity and 6,000mm (240ins) annual rainfall.
CURRENCY Sucre (Su).
PUBLIC HOLIDAYS Jan 1, 6, Shrove Mon-Tue, Maundy Thu-Easter Sat, May 1, 24, Jul 24, Aug 10, Oct 9, 12, Nov 1-3, Dec 6, 25.
GOVERNMENT Republic since 1830. The head of state and chief executive is a president elected for a 4-year term. For the literate, voting is compulsory. The legislative congress has 71 members, 12 elected nationally for 4 years, the remainder elected regionally for 2 years.

ECONOMIC PROFILE

Traditionally a producer of cocoa, coffee, pyrethrum and Panama hats; world's leading banana exporter. Oil produced since 1917 but exports began only after new discoveries in early 1970s; natural gas and hydroelectric resources ensure plentiful energy supplies. Intermediate and capital goods imported.

Growth Fruit, vegetables and cut flowers increasingly important exports. Fishing industry, particularly shrimps, growing rapidly. Gold production also rising.

Problems Sugar, once exported, now has to be imported. Manufacturing in decline in 1980s, due to small domestic market, inadequate investment and shortage of skilled labour.

IMPORTS AND EXPORTS

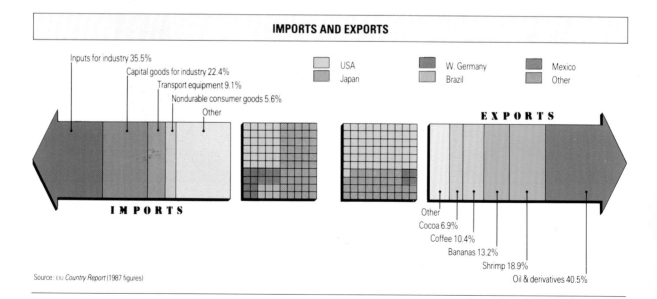

Inputs for industry 35.5%
Capital goods for industry 22.4%
Transport equipment 9.1%
Nondurable consumer goods 5.6%
Other

USA
Japan
W. Germany
Brazil
Mexico
Other

IMPORTS

EXPORTS

Other
Cocoa 6.9%
Coffee 10.4%
Bananas 13.2%
Shrimp 18.9%
Oil & derivatives 40.5%

Source: EIU *Country Report* (1987 figures)

COLOMBIA

Colombia's unhappy record of political strife and violence goes back as far as its emergence as a republic in 1830. Bitter civil wars between federalist liberals and centralist conservatives punctuated much of the 19th century. Blood was spilled again on an epic scale between 1948 and 1957, the period known as "La Violencia." About 300,000 died in this final outburst of conflict between the two parties before they agreed to govern as a coalition. This arrangement remained intact, in some form or another, until Virgilio Barco became president in 1986. But by then violence had plenty of new authors: guerrillas, death squads, drug traffickers, and common criminals.

President Barco has been concerned more with the causes than with the symptoms of the Colombian malady. Potentially one of his most important actions was to allow the local election of mayors. This could encourage some feeling of direct involvement with government among people, particularly those in remoter areas, and begin a trend towards greater regional autonomy.

Mr Barco has also embarked on a programme to eradicate desperate poverty and rehabilitate areas hit by guerrilla violence; and he has attempted to get an agrarian reform bill through congress. On the first count there have been financial constraints, on the second congress has been obstructive. The president has been forced to take more direct action, offering to renew talks with guerrillas begun by his predecessor, Belisario Betancur. But he has yet to clamp down on the death squads, known to have military connections, or take on the *capos* of the Medellín and Cali drug trafficking cartels. The government has been energetic in trying to stamp out production and trafficking of cocaine; but the *capos* have escaped extradition to the USA by terrorizing the judiciary and corrupting many politicians.

Colombia is broadening its economic base. Development of the Guajira and other coal deposits, the increase in oil production and plans to mine gold offer a much brighter future than coffee and cocaine alone could have done. However, Colombia needs foreign capital to realize its potential; investors will not be queuing up to put money into Colombia until violence is curbed.

OFFICIAL NAME Republic of Colombia.

CAPITAL CITY Bogotá.

GEOGRAPHY 80% of Colombians live in the high valleys and intermontane plateaus of the Andes. Most of the coastal plains and the lowlands of the interior, stretching from the Andes to the Orinoco, are covered in tropical rain forest. *Highest point* Colón 5,775 metres (18,950 feet). *Area* 1,138,914 sq km (439,740 sq miles).

PEOPLE Population 26.6m. *Density* 25 per sq km *Ethnic groups* Mestizo 50%, Mulatto 23%, European 20%, African 5%.

RELIGION RC 97%, Protestant 1%.

LANGUAGE Spanish.

EDUCATION Free and compulsory for five years to be taken between ages 6 and 12. Education takes up nearly 20% of the nation's budget.

CLIMATE Tropical, with a range of 23–27°C (73–81°F) on the coast, less at altitude; temperatures seldom exceed 18°C (64°F) in Bogotá. Annual rainfall 2,500mm (100ins) in the Amazon basin and on the coast, less in other regions.

CURRENCY Colombian peso (Col$).

PUBLIC HOLIDAYS Jan 1, 6, Mar 19, Maundy Thu, Good Fri, May 1, Ascension, Corpus Christi, Jun 9, 29, Jul 20, Aug 7, 15, Oct 12, Nov 1, 11, Dec 8, 25.

GOVERNMENT Republic since 1830. The chief executive is a president elected for a 4-year term. He governs with the help of a cabinet drawn from the bicameral congress which is a 112-member senate and a 199-member house of representatives.

ECONOMIC PROFILE

Economy based on growing coffee and, to a much lesser extent, cotton and bananas. Well endowed with mineral resources – gold, oil, emeralds, coal, nickel, platinum and silver. Some manufactures exported to Andean neighbours. Major supplier of cocaine to US and other markets.

Growth Resurgence of oil production; exports resumed in 1986. Development of Cerrejón Norte coalfields could mean coal overtakes coffee as leading export.

Problems Agriculture has suffered from violence in rural areas; food imported although Colombia has capacity to feed itself. Financial sector still recovering from crisis in early 1980s. Disorder deters investors.

IMPORTS AND EXPORTS

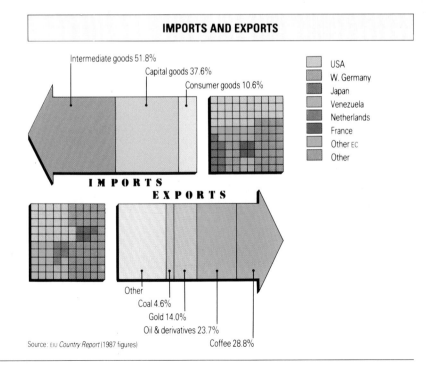

Intermediate goods 51.8%
Capital goods 37.6%
Consumer goods 10.6%

USA
W. Germany
Japan
Venezuela
Netherlands
France
Other EC
Other

IMPORTS
EXPORTS

Other
Coal 4.6%
Gold 14.0%
Oil & derivatives 23.7%
Coffee 28.8%

Source: EIU *Country Report* (1987 figures)

147

VENEZUELA

Venezuela has enjoyed stable democracy for the past 30 years, with power alternating between the slightly left-of-centre Acción Democrática (AD) and the Christian Democrat Copei. Although the country has had its share of dictatorships and military governments since independence, the armed forces have not constituted a threat in the past three decades, when they have concentrated on border disputes with Guyana and Colombia and, more recently, the unwelcome overspill of Colombian guerrillas. Venezuela's own guerrillas have been persuaded to give up their guns and seek the people's votes instead.

The picture has less rosy aspects. Occasional outbursts of unrest have been dealt with harshly and, on a seamier note, there are periodic allegations of corruption in high places. Some involve drug trafficking, given Venezuela's position as a link in the cocaine trade between its Andean neighbours and North America. Some result from the use of the country's oil wealth to erect a vast state machine.

Until oil was discovered in commercial quantities in 1914, Venezuela's economy was based on coffee and, to a lesser extent, cocoa and cattle. By 1930 the country had become the world's first major oil exporter, and the largest producer after the USA. Oil gave Venezuela the chance to develop into a modern nation; it also lined many a personal pocket. In the 1950s and 1960s Venezuela was the richest Latin American country in terms of GDP per head; it was also well ahead of the future economic giants of Asia.

The state took an increasing share of oil profits, finally nationalizing the oil industry in 1976. Its role grew throughout the heady 1970s, as oil prices rose to undreamed-of heights. But Venezuela was already beginning to feel the effects of excessive dependence on a single commodity.

The fall in oil price forced the AD government of President Jaime Lusinchi, despite the party's strong links with labour, to impose austerity in seeking respite from debt servicing. However, the adjustments were not stringent enough, even though they brought increased inflation and a higher level of unemployment.

When the new AD president, Carlos Andrés Pérez, was inaugurated in February 1989, he announced much more swingeing measures which met with a violent reaction from many Venezuelans. Hundreds died in riots which were a bad omen for Mr Pérez's second term of office.

OFFICIAL NAME Republic of Venezuela.

CAPITAL CITY Caracas.

GEOGRAPHY In the west two arms of the Andes enclose the shallow, freshwater coastal Lake Maracaibo, whose basin is a large oilfield. East of the lake is a range of coastal mountains containing most of the population and the capital. From here a wide plain stretches to the swampy delta of the Orinoco. Inland is the heavily forested and sparsely populated granite mass of the Guiana highlands. *Highest point* Pico Bolívar 5,007 metres (16,430 feet). *Area* 912,050 sq km (352,140 sq miles).

PEOPLE *Population* 17.3m. *Density* 19 per sq km. *Ethnic groups* Mestizo 69%, European 20%, African 9%, Amerindian 2%.

RELIGION RC 92%.

LANGUAGE Spanish.

EDUCATION Free and compulsory for ages 7–14. There are 11 universities.

CLIMATE Tropical, with a rainy season Apr–Oct. On the coast, average temperature 28°C (82°F), appreciably lower rainfall. Cooler in the highlands, with an average of 21°C (70°F) in Caracas.

CURRENCY Bolívar (B).

PUBLIC HOLIDAYS (* not universally observed) Jan 1, 6*, Mar 10*, 19*, Good Fri–Easter Mon, Apr 19, May 1, Ascension*, Jun 24, 29*, Jul 5, 24, Aug 15*, Sep 4, Oct 12, 24*, Nov 1*, Dec 8*, 24, 25, 31.

GOVERNMENT Federal republic since 1830. The head of state and chief executive is a president, elected for a single 5-year term, as is the legislative national congress, made up of a 199-member chamber of deputies and a senate of 44 elected members and all past presidents.

ECONOMIC PROFILE

Oil provides 80% of export earnings, although Venezuela no longer world's largest exporter due to Opec constraints. Overseas refining and distribution facilities have been bought. Iron and steel and aluminium are also exported.

Growth Bauxite reserves and abundant hydroelectricity could encourage aluminium production. Iron ore, coal, natural gas and gold being developed. Agriculture beginning to revive with investment.

Problems Manufacturing, hampered by foreign-exchange shortages, unable to meet domestic demand. Investment needed to diversify economy threatened by oil slump and heavy foreign debt.

IMPORTS AND EXPORTS

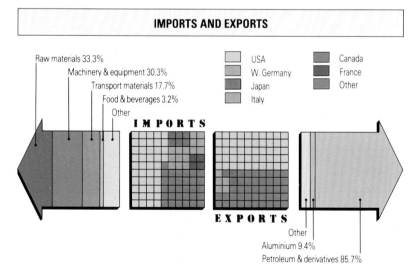

Raw materials 33.3%
Machinery & equipment 30.3%
Transport materials 17.7%
Food & beverages 3.2%
Other

USA
W. Germany
Japan
Italy
Canada
France
Other

IMPORTS

EXPORTS

Other
Aluminium 9.4%
Petroleum & derivatives 85.7%

Source: EIU *Country Report* (Imports/Exports 1986 figures; Trading partners 1987 figures)

GUYANA

A former British territory, Guyana was ruled by Forbes Burnham from before independence in 1966 until his death in 1985. Mr Burnham, a member of the Afro-Guyanese minority in a racially divided country, steadily increased his own and the state's influence. He had less and less truck with opposition and incurred the wrath of human rights activists.

Burnham's successor, Desmond Hoyte, has been preoccupied with the economy, which has been stifled by lack of foreign exchange for most of the 1980s. This has led to food shortages, nurtured a black market, made foreign debt repayments impossible and compounded the problems of financing large budget deficits.

Devaluation and rationalization of some state industries were among Mr Hoyte's first steps. Privatization and a welcome to foreign investors scared away by Mr Burnham's nationalizations are likely to follow, as Guyana tries to regain IMF and other international support.

Bauxite, rice and sugar are Guyana's economic foundations. Considerable potential also lies in huge timber reserves, livestock, gold and diamonds. Dependence on imported oil could be reduced by exploiting hydroelectricity.

OFFICIAL NAME Co-operative Republic of Guyana.
CAPITAL CITY Georgetown.
GEOGRAPHY Much is rain forest. A fertile coastal strip with a central plateau supports most of the population. There are mountains in the south and west. *Area* 215,000 sq km (83,000 sq miles).
PEOPLE *Population* 790,000. *Ethnic groups* Asian Indian 51%, African 31%, mixed 12%, Amerindian 4%.
RELIGION Protestant 34%, Hindu 34%, RC 18%, Muslim 9%.
LANGUAGE English. Also Amerindian and Creole.
EDUCATION Free and compulsory for ages 6–14.
CLIMATE Tropical, with a rainy season Apr–Aug.
CURRENCY Guyana dollar (G$).
PUBLIC HOLIDAYS Jan 1, Feb 23, Good Fri-Easter Mon, May 1, Id al-Fitr, Jul 1, Id al-Adha, 1st Mon in Aug, Mouloud, Dec 25, 26.
GOVERNMENT Republic since 1966. The leader of the majority party of the 65-member national assembly is the president who appoints the prime minister and cabinet.

SURINAM

The former Dutch Guiana gained independence as recently as 1975, but has been under military domination for most of the 1980s. Lieutenant-Colonel Desi Bouterse, leader of a 1980 coup, so outraged world opinion by murdering 15 opponents two years later that Dutch, US and EC aid was cut off. At a time of falling commodity prices the economic consequences were disastrous. The financial squeeze forced Bouterse gradually to move back to a more democratic posture. After elections were held in November 1987, Ramsewak Shankar became president but Bouterse remained on the scene, his role ill-defined. A rebellion by the *bosneger* (Bush Negro) descendants of African slaves provided excellent cover for continued military involvement in day-to-day affairs.

The elections brought the resumption of Dutch aid, made all the more vital because of rebel disruption of the all-important bauxite/aluminium industry. The sugar industry is now a shadow of its former self and rice is much more important.

OFFICIAL NAME Republic of Suriname.
CAPITAL CITY Paramaribo.
GEOGRAPHY Much is jungle. Most people live in a narrow coastal zone. *Area* 163,265 sq km (63,040 sq miles).
PEOPLE *Population* 380,000. *Ethnic groups* Asian Indian 35%, Creole 32%, Indonesian 15%, Bush Negro 10%, Amerindian 3%, Chinese 3%.
RELIGION Hindu 27%, RC 23%, Muslim 20%, Protestant 19%.
LANGUAGE Dutch. Also English.
EDUCATION Free to age 18 and compulsory 6–14.
CLIMATE Sub-tropical; high rainfall on coast.
CURRENCY Surinam guilder (SGld).
PUBLIC HOLIDAYS Jan 1, Feb 25, Phagwa (Mar), Good Fri-Easter Mon, May 1, Id al-Fitr, Jul 1, Nov 25, Dec 25, 26.
GOVERNMENT Military-dominated republic. The 1987 constitution provides for a 51-member elected national assembly and a joint civilian-military council of state.

FRENCH GUIANA

The only remaining European colony on the South American mainland, French Guiana is sparsely inhabited, with most people confined to the coastal strip; the interior is heavily forested. A French overseas department, it houses the Kourou base of the European Ariane satellite-launching rocket, together with a French military base.

Except for rice, agriculture is little developed; the interior has valuable reserves of tropical hardwoods and large deposits of bauxite and kaolin but transport difficulties have limited their exploitation. The territory is overwhelmingly dependent on French aid and on imports from France and the USA. The government is by far the largest employer, but unemployment is high.

OFFICIAL NAME Department of French Guiana.
CAPITAL CITY Cayenne.
GEOGRAPHY Most is tropical rain forest. *Area* 91,000 sq km (35,000 sq miles).
PEOPLE *Population* 82,000. *Density* 0.9 per sq km. *Ethnic groups* Creole 43%, Chinese 14%, French 11%.
RELIGION RC 87%, Protestant 4%, Animist 4%.
LANGUAGE French. Also a Creole patois.
EDUCATION Compulsory for ages 6–16.
CURRENCY French franc (Fr).
PUBLIC HOLIDAYS Jan 1, Shrove Mon-Tue, Good Fri-Easter Mon, May 1, Ascension, Whit Mon, Jul 14, Nov 11, Dec 25.
GOVERNMENT French overseas department. 2 deputies are sent to the French national assembly.

BRAZIL

For all its boundless potential, Brazil has still not crossed the divide between the developing and developed worlds. Almost as large as the USA, with about half South America's population, Brazil has the eighth largest economy in the world, is a prime producer of coffee and sugar and has barely begun to exploit its vast mineral and energy resources. Its manufacturing sector has experienced phenomenal growth, particularly in the late 1960s and early 1970s, when Brazil enjoyed its economic miracle.

One reason Brazil remains part of the Third World is its failure to find the right political structure. The country took a step towards democracy in 1985, after two decades of military rule, when an electoral college picked a civilian president. Unfortunately, the man they chose, Tancredo Neves, died before inauguration day. José Sarney, who took his place, lacked Neves' charisma and faced a new constituent assembly dominated by the dead man's supporters. The assembly set about writing a constitution which, besides having strong nationalist elements, gave more power to the states at the expense of the president. The mix was no solution to balance of payments and budget crises.

Another obstacle to Brazil's membership of the developed world is the extreme poverty of much of the country: the contrast between opulence in Rio de Janeiro and destitution in the northeast being only the most glaring example of skewed income distribution. Children are frequently abandoned: about one fifth of all boys under 15 are forced to look for work.

OFFICIAL NAME Federative Republic of Brazil.
CAPITAL CITY Brasília.
GEOGRAPHY Two-thirds of Brazil is covered by forest. The great majority consists of plateaus, low mountain ranges and tablelands. The only large lowland area is the upper Amazon basin; farther east, the Amazon flows through a narrow floodplain between two highland regions. There is no coastal plain, but sheltered bays provide several excellent deep-water harbours, especially in the southeast. *Highest point* Pico da Neblina 3,014 metres (9,890 feet). *Area* 8,511,965 sq km (3,286,490 sq miles).
PEOPLE *Population* 135.6m. *Density* 16 per sq km. *Ethnic groups* Mulatto 22%, Portuguese 15%, Italian 11%, Spanish 10%, other European 17%, Mestizo 12%, African 11%, Japanese 1%.
RELIGION RC 89%, Protestant 7%.
LANGUAGE Portuguese.
EDUCATION Free to age 19, and compulsory for ages 7–14. There is a parallel private system. There are 47 state and 21 private universities.
CLIMATE Tropical, wet and unchanging in the Amazon basin, average temperature around 25°C (77°F). Cooler in highlands and on coast, with more definite seasons and rainfall of 1,000–1,500mm (40–60ins), most falling in Dec–Apr.
CURRENCY Cruzado (Cz).
PUBLIC HOLIDAYS Jan 1, Apr 24, May 1, Ascension, Corpus Christi, Sep 7, Oct 12, Nov 2, 15, Dec 25.
GOVERNMENT Federal republic of 23 states and 3 territories. The legislative national congress has a 49-member senate representing the regions and a 487-member chamber of deputies elected for 4 years by compulsory popular vote. The executive president is in future to be elected by direct ballot for a 5-year term.

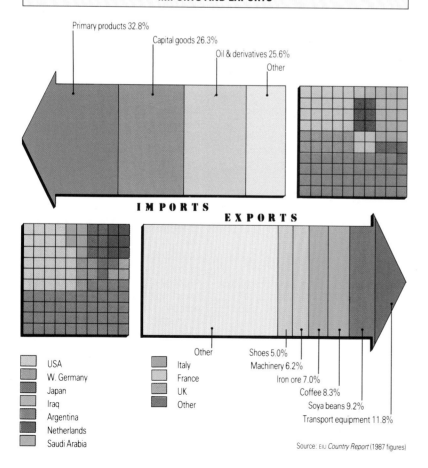

IMPORTS AND EXPORTS

Primary products 32.8%
Capital goods 26.3%
Oil & derivatives 25.6%
Other

IMPORTS

EXPORTS

USA	Italy
W. Germany	France
Japan	UK
Iraq	Other
Argentina	
Netherlands	
Saudi Arabia	

Other
Shoes 5.0%
Machinery 6.2%
Iron ore 7.0%
Coffee 8.3%
Soya beans 9.2%
Transport equipment 11.8%

Source: EIU *Country Report* (1987 figures)

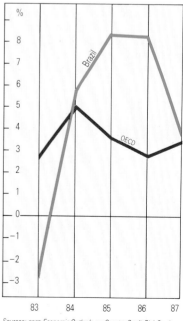

GDP GROWTH

%
8
7
6
5
4
3
2
1
0
−1
−2
−3

Brazil

OECD

83 84 85 86 87

Sources: OECD *Economic Outlook*; EIU *Country Credit Risk Service*

Poverty is compounded by the country's relatively high rate of population growth and by deteriorating education standards. In 1980, one quarter of the adult population was estimated to be illiterate, although the situation in the northeast was worse than in the wealthiest states, Rio de Janeiro, São Paulo and Minas Gerais.

The northeast is prone to drought, but its poverty is also caused by the structure of land holding; holdings of less than 10 hectares represent 68% of all titles, those of 1,000 hectares barely 1%. The nine states of the region, home to 40m people, have the highest rates of infant mortality and malnutrition. Not surprisingly they have become a hotbed of political unrest.

In the past, governments tried to defuse such tensions by encouraging landless peasants and the urban unemployed to move into the vast virgin territories of the Amazon region. The tax incentives and government funds designed for this purpose have been misused, however, and no greater equity has resulted. More constitutional land reforms have been strongly resisted by those who stood to lose. Now the government has decided to inhibit the expansion of agriculture in the Amazon region because of the ecological consequences of slash-and-burn farming.

Brazil's foreign debt, at over $100bn, is higher than that of any other South American country and on a par with Mexico's. Servicing this debt is beyond Brazil's means: if it had been able to repay all principal and interest due in 1987, it would have been looking at a bill of about $24bn. Instead, it has muddled through the 1980s with a mixture of new loans, reschedulings and rollovers, not to mention a temporary moratorium on interest payments to commercial banks in 1987. Policies linked to the new loans have been undermined by political and social considerations. Hyperinflation – reaching close to 1,000% in 1988 – has been one result. A package of economic measures introduced at the beginning of 1989, including a wage and price freeze and currency devaluation, represented the Sarney government's last chance to push through effective economic reforms before the presidential election due at the end of the year. But the immediate prospects of a return to growth were bleak.

ECONOMIC PROFILE

World's largest coffee producer for over 100 years, growing about one third of world total. Sugar and cocoa are other important traditional crops; soya and oranges are new crops developed as part of export drive. Manufacturing has grown rapidly since the 1960s, with heavy government involvement, first to meet domestic requirements and then for export.

Growth New agricultural exports have captured strong market share – Brazil supplies 85% of the world's orange juice concentrates. Need to notch up large trade surpluses has stimulated exploitation of mining and energy resources, particularly oil, hydroelectricity and nuclear power. Use of new technology is increasing industrial productivity.

Problems Agriculture neglected as investment went to industry; coffee harvest perennially vulnerable to drought and frost. Food, oil and many raw materials imported. Capital to sustain development is in short supply. Falling oil prices have made alcohol fuel programme uneconomic.

GDP BY ORIGIN

Manufacturing 25.9%
Commerce 13.5%
Agriculture 9.1%
Construction 5.7%
Other

COMPONENTS OF GDP

Private consumption 67.6%
Gross domestic investment 19.0%
Government consumption 10.4%
Exports of goods & services 10.2%
Less: imports of goods & services −7.2%

Source: EIU *Country Report* (GDP by origin 1986 figures; Components of GDP 1987 figures)

BALANCE OF PAYMENTS

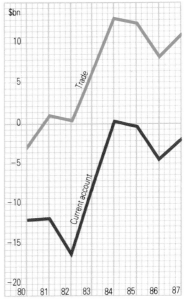

Source: EIU *Country Credit Risk Service*

PERU

Alán García's days of rousing speeches from the balcony of the presidential palace seem to be over. His radical economic plans have taken the country rapidly from boom to bust and his government is edging towards a reconciliation with the international community, estranged when President García decided in 1985 unilaterally to limit overseas debt repayments. The reversal of economic policy has cost the president popularity and the toll can only be expected to increase if adjustment measures are seen to be at the behest of the IMF and World Bank.

But Peru faces a still more insidious problem in its Maoist Sendero Luminoso (Shining Path) terrorists. Since 1980, the organization has widened its theatre of operations from the department of Ayacucho to Lima itself. More than 11,000 have died as a result of the guerrilla war, but the security forces are no nearer defeating the insurgents. With the economy flagging, Sendero Luminoso is finding many new recruits.

In these circumstances it is not surprising that coup rumours have surfaced. The military has been, if not actually in power, then not far from it for most of this century. They reluctantly accepted Mr García and his left-wing Alianza Popular Revolucionaria Americana in 1985 and now see that even more radical elements could win 1990 elections.

ECONOMIC PROFILE

Silver, gold, copper, lead and zinc main foreign-exchange earners, followed by coffee, cotton, fishmeal, textiles; also coca and cocaine. Agriculture has declined as manufacturing has expanded.

Growth Recovery in metal prices should help export earnings.

Problems Once-important fishing industry in decline, because of overfishing and appearance of warm Niño current. Oil production dwindling due to inadequate investment in exploration. Manufacturing initially responded well to government stimulation of demand but there are foreign-exchange constraints.

OFFICIAL NAME Republic of Peru.

CAPITAL CITY Lima.

GEOGRAPHY A narrow strip of desert lowland along the coast has less rainfall than the Sahara, but still maintains the bulk of the population. Most of the country is the high Andes, with some cultivation and pastureland up to 4,000 metres (13,000 feet). To the east are the lower forested slopes of the Montaña, giving way to marshy jungle lowlands at the edge of the Amazon basin. *Highest point* Nevado Huascarán 6,768 metres (22,200 feet). *Area* 1,285,216 sq km (496,230 sq miles).

PEOPLE *Population* 19.7m. *Density* 15 per sq km. *Ethnic groups* Amerindian 54% (mainly Quechua), Mestizo 32%, European 12%.

RELIGION RC 92%, other Christian 2%.

LANGUAGE Spanish and Quechua. Also Aymará and Autoctonos.

EDUCATION Free and compulsory for ages 6–15. There are 25 state and 10 private universities.

CLIMATE Tropical, but moderated by altitude. Cool Humboldt current makes coast temperate; rainfall is negligible. Monthly average temperatures in Lima in the range 16–23°C (61–73°F).

CURRENCY Inti (I).

PUBLIC HOLIDAYS Jan 1, Maundy Thu, Good Fri, May 1, Jun 29, Jul 28, 29, Aug 30, Oct 8, Nov 1, Dec 8, 25.

GOVERNMENT Republic since 1824. The head of state and chief executive is a president elected every 5 years. The legislative national congress has a 60-member senate elected nationally and a 180-member chamber of deputies elected from constituencies. Both houses are elected every 5 years.

IMPORTS AND EXPORTS

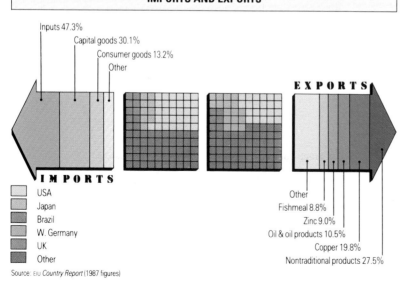

Inputs 47.3%
Capital goods 30.1%
Consumer goods 13.2%
Other

EXPORTS

IMPORTS

- USA
- Japan
- Brazil
- W. Germany
- UK
- Other

Other
Fishmeal 8.8%
Zinc 9.0%
Oil & oil products 10.5%
Copper 19.8%
Nontraditional products 27.5%

Source: EIU *Country Report* (1987 figures)

BALANCE OF PAYMENTS

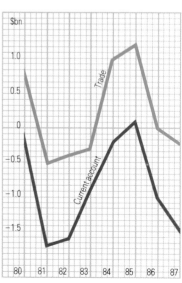

$bn

Trade

Current account

Source: EIU *Country Credit Risk Service*

BOLIVIA

After no fewer than 189 coups in 154 years, Bolivian politics has been relatively stable in the 1980s. Civilian presidents have held power from 1982. Víctor Paz Estenssoro, president from 1985 to 1989, inherited a dizzying rate of inflation driven by enormous budget and balance of payments deficits. To make matters worse, the price of tin, the most important export after gas, soon collapsed. The new president, who in the 1950s nationalized tin mines and made sweeping agrarian reforms, decided on drastic cuts in government spending and lifted restrictions on foreign trade.

The policy paid dividends in as much as the rot of five years' economic decline was stopped, inflation fell from its 1985 rate of nearly 12,000% and foreign loans began to flow in again. But it was only the start of a long and painful restructuring process which persisted beyond Dr Paz's term of office.

Agriculture is the main sector of the economy, employing one-half of the working population. It is largely labour-intensive and in the central highlands subsistence farming predominates, so productivity levels are low. The sector has been hard hit in the 1980s by a succession of droughts and floods. Large reserves of petroleum and natural gas remain unexploited because of lack of investment, and official figures make Bolivia the poorest country in South America. There is, however, another side to the story: a vast black economy run on dollars earned by the cocaine trade and, to a lesser extent, contraband. Bolivia not only grows coca but now produces paste and unrefined cocaine, and more than half a million people make a living from the drugs trade, which is thought to contribute around 6% of GNP.

OFFICIAL NAME Republic of Bolivia.
CAPITAL CITY La Paz (administrative), Sucre (legal).
GEOGRAPHY Most Bolivians live in the high Altiplano, with Lake Titicaca at its northern end. The Oriente, east of the Andes, is a sparsely populated lowland area. *Highest point* Nevado Sajama 6,520 metres (21,390 feet). *Area* 1,098,581 sq km (424,160 sq miles).
PEOPLE *Population* 6.4m. *Density* 6 per sq km. *Ethnic groups* Amerindian 45% (Quechua 25%, Aymará 17%), Mestizo 31%, European 15%.
RELIGION RC 94%.
LANGUAGE Spanish. Also Quechua and Aymará.
EDUCATION Free and compulsory for ages 6–14.
CLIMATE Annual mean temperature of 10°C (50°F) in the Altiplano, with dry winters and wet summers; southern Altiplano is desert. Hot, 25°C (77°F), and wet year-round in the Oriente.
CURRENCY Boliviano (B).
PUBLIC HOLIDAYS Jan 1, Good Fri, May 1, Corpus Christi, Aug 6, Nov 1, Dec 25.
GOVERNMENT Republic since 1825. Bolivian political history is a succession of military coups interspersed with occasional elections. The constitution provides for a 27-member senate and 130-member chamber of deputies, both elected for 4 years, and an executive president also elected for 4 years by popular vote.

PARAGUAY

After 34 years in power, General Alfredo Stroessner was sent into Brazilian exile in February 1989 after a coup engineered by his own supporters. The general had remained in power only partly by dint of his control over the ruling Colorado party; more important had been the prizes for those loyal to him and the repression – at times brutal – of opposition. The system he created finally dislodged him: as two factions within the ruling party jostled to secure the succession, one – led by General Andrés Rodriguez – seized the initiative by ousting the man at the top. The convincing victory of General Rodriguez in the 1989 election for president legitimised the takeover. With the opposition weak and divided, the Colorado Party's monopoly of power and patronage seemed secure.

Rapid economic growth in the 1970s and early 1980s had undoubtedly helped to keep Stroessner in power. It came about mainly as a result of the $20bn Itaipú hydroelectric project, a joint venture with Brazil that brought millions of dollars and thousands of jobs to Paraguay.

As work on Itaipú tailed off, another hydroelectric scheme, Yacyretá, was planned to take up the slack but this was delayed by financial difficulties. As a result, slower – and occasionally negative – growth, fiscal deficits, high inflation and balance of payments difficulties have become as familiar in Paraguay as elsewhere in the sub-continent, although wholesale debt reschedulings have so far been avoided.

The government has begun a process of readjusting the economy whose fortunes now once again rest on agriculture and, to an unknown extent, on the contraband trade with Brazil and Argentina.

OFFICIAL NAME Republic of Paraguay.
CAPITAL CITY Asunción.
GEOGRAPHY The country is landlocked, but has access by river to the Atlantic. The eastern third is a forested plateau, bounded by low mountains to the north and by the Paraná river to the south and east. In the west is the flat scrub of the Northern Chaco. Most people live in the centre. The Paraguay basin is swampy. *Highest point* 700 metres (2,300 feet). *Area* 406,752 sq km (157,050 sq miles).
PEOPLE *Population* 3.7m. *Density* 9 per sq km. *Ethnic groups* Mestizo 90%, Amerindian 3%.
RELIGION RC 96%, Protestant 2%.
LANGUAGE Spanish. Also Guaraní.
EDUCATION Free and compulsory for 6 years.
CLIMATE Sub-tropical, with monthly average temperatures in the range 17–29°C (63–84 °F). Annual rainfall 1,250mm (50ins) in the west and 800mm (30ins) in the east.
CURRENCY Guaraní (G).
PUBLIC HOLIDAYS Jan 1, Feb 3, Mar 1, Maundy Thu, Good Fri, May 1, 14, 15, Ascension, Jun 12, Corpus Christi, Aug 15, 25, Sep 29, Oct 12, Nov 1, Dec 8, 25.
GOVERNMENT Military-dominated republic. The country is usually under a state of siege or emergency. The current military government has promised open elections.

URUGUAY

Once a model of democracy, Uruguay had a traumatic period of military domination from 1973 to 1985. The return to civilian rule has not been easy; President Julio María Sanguinetti has had to face a crescendo of demands for prosecutions, on the Argentine model, of those in the military accused of horrendous human rights abuses. Fears that such trials would provoke renewed military intervention have caused deep divisions within the two main parties, the Colorados and the Blancos.

Mr Sanguinetti has had some success on the economic front: rescheduling foreign debt, raising exports, reducing the fiscal deficit and achieving positive growth, albeit with relatively high inflation rates. To an extent, though, he has fallen victim to his own success because, although unemployment has fallen and real wages have risen, the population – used to social security and other benefits unparalleled in Latin America – demands more. Strikes have been frequent.

The main challenge facing Mr Sanguinetti, and whoever succeeds him in 1990, is the diversification of an economy largely dependent on two export commodities: beef and wool. Capital investment in agriculture will be needed to introduce new technology and – since the domestic market is so small – new export industries must be encouraged. Another, perhaps more formidable task is to reduce the country's vulnerability to events in neighbouring Argentina and Brazil, which can cause violent fluctuations in export earnings, tourism receipts and capital flows.

OFFICIAL NAME Oriental Republic of Uruguay.
CAPITAL CITY Montevideo.
GEOGRAPHY The smallest country in South America, it has a plateau to the north and west and a region of low, granitic hills to the east and south. There is lowland around the coast, where there are tidal lakes and dunes, and along the valleys of the Uruguay and the Negro. Almost half of the population live in the capital. *Highest point* Cerro de las Animas 501 metres (1,640 feet). *Area* 176,215 sq km (68,040 sq miles).
PEOPLE *Population* 3m. *Density* 17 per sq km. *Ethnic groups* European 92%, Mestizo 3%, Mulatto 2%.
RELIGION RC 60%, Protestant 2%, Jewish 2%.
LANGUAGE Spanish.
EDUCATION Free and compulsory for ages 6–15.
CLIMATE Temperate, with a monthly average temperature range of 10–22°C (50–72°F). Annual rainfall of around 900mm (35ins), evenly distributed through the year.
CURRENCY Uruguayan new peso (UrugN$).
PUBLIC HOLIDAYS Jan 1, 6, Apr 19, May 1, 18, Jun 19, Jul 18, Aug 25, Oct 12, Nov 2, Dec 8, 25.
GOVERNMENT Republic since 1825. The new civilian government has undertaken to overhaul the constitution, which currently provides for an executive president elected for 5 years and a bicameral legislative congress – a 30-member senate and a 99-member chamber of deputies – elected for 5 years by PR.

ECONOMIC PROFILE

Abundant good grassland fostered livestock industry. Beef and wool production brought prosperity until 1950s, and are still the leading exports. Rice, citrus and dairy products also exported. No oil and gas, but hydroelectric power provides 90% of energy; electricity exported to Argentina. Few mineral resources. Principal industries process agricultural produce.

Growth Developing nontraditional exports including textiles, leather, plastics and chemicals. Fishing and free trade zones offer potential.

Problems Badly hit by loss of European and US markets for beef, although new buyers have been found in Middle East and Asia. Small domestic market restricts growth.

BALANCE OF PAYMENTS

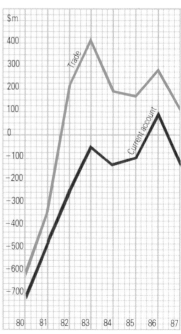

Source: EIU *Country Credit Risk Service*

IMPORTS AND EXPORTS

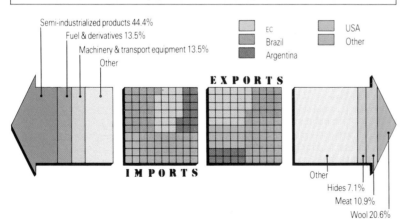

Semi-industrialized products 44.4%
Fuel & derivatives 13.5%
Machinery & transport equipment 13.5%
Other

EC
Brazil
Argentina
USA
Other

EXPORTS

IMPORTS

Other
Hides 7.1%
Meat 10.9%
Wool 20.6%

Source: EIU *Country Report* (1987 figures)

CHILE

After 15 years of authoritarian military rule, Chileans were given a chance to vote for change in 1988. They did so by rejecting the idea that General Augusto Pinochet, leader of the *junta*, should remain president for a further eight years. The vote obliged the *junta* to call open presidential elections in December 1989 and to hold the first legislative elections for 15 years at the same time.

The people's rejection of a further term for Pinochet was by no means a foregone conclusion, despite the repressive nature of his regime. The economy was in tatters when the military seized power from the Marxist Salvador Allende in 1973. The *junta*, daringly adopting the free-market policies of the "Chicago boys," US-educated technocrats, turned it around. By 1988, Chile was in far better shape economically than its Latin American neighbours: the budget almost in balance, inflation at tolerable levels, exports booming and debt repayments well in hand. For business, the Pinochet years were good, with the ground rules clearly and favourably established. For others, General Pinochet's anti-communist stand was important, although – perhaps more than anything – his appeal was that he had brought strong government after a long period when coalitions had steered an uncertain course.

Not everyone benefited from the boom years. There was concern that the open-door investment policy was just too open and, isolated by its lack of a democratically elected government, Chile plumped for change even though fragmented party politics made a return to coalition government likely.

OFFICIAL NAME Republic of Chile.

CAPITAL CITY Santiago.

GEOGRAPHY The Atacama desert in the north is one of the driest places on earth, while the southern region of islands, lakes and mountains is one of the bleakest and wettest. The population is concentrated in the centre, mostly in the mineral-rich sedimentary plains that lie between the high Andes and the coastal mountains that block access to the sea. Chile is seismically active, with frequent earth tremors and several active volcanoes. *Highest point* Ojos del Salado 6,880 metres (22,570 feet). *Area* 756,945 sq km (292,260 sq miles).

PEOPLE *Population* 12.1m. *Density* 16 per sq km. *Ethnic groups* Mestizo 90%, Amerindian 6%, European 4%.

RELIGION RC 80%, Protestant 6%.

LANGUAGE Spanish.

EDUCATION Free and compulsory for ages 6–14. A 1981 law banned all political activity in universities, reduced funding and encouraged the setting up of private technical universities.

CLIMATE Generally temperate, moderated by the cool Humboldt current. Desert-dry in the north, but over 4,000mm (160ins) of rain a year in extreme south, most falling in winter. Average annual temperature in Santiago is 15°C (59°F).

CURRENCY Chilean peso (Ch$).

PUBLIC HOLIDAYS Jan 1, Good Fri, Easter Sat, May 1, 21, Aug 15, Sep 18, Oct 12, Nov 1, Dec 8, 25, 31.

GOVERNMENT Military-dominated republic. Since the military coup of 1973 Chile has suffered a succession of states of emergency and siege.

IMPORTS AND EXPORTS

- USA
- Japan
- W. Germany
- Brazil
- Argentina
- UK
- Italy
- Venezuela
- Other

Intermediate goods 54.5% Capital goods 25.0% Consumer goods 20.5%

IMPORTS

EXPORTS

Agriculture & fish products 15.3%
Industrial products 34.9%
Mining products 49.8%

Source: EIU *Country Report* (1987 figures)

BALANCE OF PAYMENTS

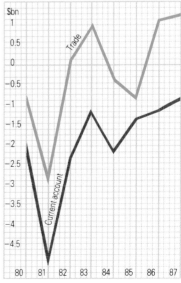

Trade

Current account

Source: EIU *Country Credit Risk Service*

ECONOMIC PROFILE

Agriculture and mining most important sectors. Exports of copper, also fruit, timber products, fishmeal. Nearly self-sufficient in many basic foods. Diverse manufacturing sector.

Growth Output of gold, silver, molybdenum and cobalt; La Escondida copper reserves, world's largest, start production in 1992. Coal, natural gas and hydroelectricity resources are being tapped.

Problems Economy still vulnerable to drop in copper prices. Oil production is declining. Industry shaken by impact of trade liberalization and increased foreign competition.

GDP BY ORIGIN

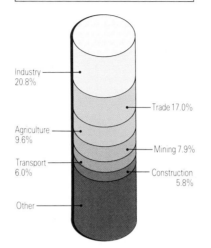

Industry 20.8%
Trade 17.0%
Agriculture 9.6%
Mining 7.9%
Transport 6.0%
Construction 5.8%
Other

COMPONENTS OF GDP

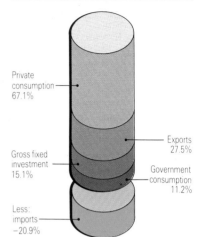

Private consumption 67.1%
Exports 27.5%
Gross fixed investment 15.1%
Government consumption 11.2%
Less: imports −20.9%

Source. EIU *Country Report* (GDP by origin 1987 figures; Components of GDP 1986 figures)

ARGENTINA

The election of Raúl Alfonsín as president in December 1983 represented a new beginning for Argentina. A military coup in 1930, some 80 years after the foundation of the federal republic, marked the start of a long period of military intervention. The country enjoyed a brief period of democracy in the early 1970s but had been under military rule since 1976 and was badly demoralized by its defeat in the Falklands/Malvinas war in 1982 as well as by the brutal campaign waged against alleged subversives in the late 1970s. The new president bravely decided to bring the armed forces to book; many military leaders were put on trial, though the decision not to let the indictments extend beyond a certain deadline or to those acting under orders was widely criticized.

Argentina's main preoccupation now is falling living standards. Inflation has become intolerable, even by Argentine standards, and the country is burdened with an acute balance of payments position and a huge $56bn external debt. These problems are the symptoms of a maladjusted economy painfully slow to grow out of dependence on a handful of agricultural products. Even today, the

ECONOMIC PROFILE

Traditionally based on rich agricultural produce of the *pampas* – beef, grains and wool. Industry developed to cut imports of consumer goods but still heavily based on agricultural processing. Some capital goods and manufactures imported. Abundant energy resources.

Growth Natural gas being developed to supply growing petrochemicals industry. Burgeoning computer industry. Great potential, as yet untapped, in fishing, forestry, and copper and uranium mining.

Problems Motor assembly and textiles industries have suffered from foreign competition and inadequate investment. Oil production has declined due to lack of incentives for exploration and competition from other energy sources. Troubled financial sector cannot mobilize sufficient development funds; capital flight a serious problem and foreign investment disappointing.

OFFICIAL NAME Argentine Republic.

CAPITAL CITY Buenos Aires.

GEOGRAPHY Most consists of an alluvial plain between the Andes and the Atlantic, covered in the north by forest and savannah and in the south by the rolling, fertile grasslands and marshes of the pampas. In the west are the Andes, high and wild in the north, but lower in Patagonia, a glaciated region of forests, lakes and meadows. Much of the coast is swampy, especially around the mouth of the Plata. *Highest point* Aconcagua 6,960 metres (22,830 feet). *Area* 2,766,889 sq km (1,068,300 sq miles).

PEOPLE *Population* 30.6m. *Density* 11 per sq km. *Ethnic groups* European 98%, Mestizo 2%.

RELIGION RC 92%, Protestant 3%, Jewish 2%.

LANGUAGE Spanish.

EDUCATION Free to university level and compulsory for ages 6–14. There are 29 state and 23 private universities.

CLIMATE Mostly temperate, though sub-tropical in the northeast and sub-Arctic in the extreme south. Temperatures in Buenos Aires around 23°C (73°F) in summer, 9°C (48°F) in winter. Widespread winter frosts. Most rain falls in the east.

CURRENCY Austral (A).

PUBLIC HOLIDAYS Jan 1, Good Fri, May 1, 25, Jun 10, Jul 9, Aug 17, Dec 8, 25.

GOVERNMENT Federal republic with 23 provinces and one national territory. The legislative congress has a senate whose 46 members are appointed for 9 years by the provinces and a chamber of deputies whose 254 members are elected every 4 years. The chief executive and head of state, the president, is chosen by an electoral college every 6 years.

beef, grains and wool that made Argentina the richest country in Latin America and one of the richest in the world in the early part of this century account for nearly half of export earnings. But investment in agriculture has been inadequate and the manufacturing sector, built up in the 1960s behind high tariff barriers, is still reeling from the shock of exposure to foreign competition. Another deep-rooted problem is the state's pervasive involvement in many areas of the economy, which makes both balancing the budget and meeting external debt repayments difficult.

Dr Alfonsín failed to come up with very effective prescriptions for the economic malady, apart from a brief and optimistic time in 1985, when his government applied shock treatment and froze prices and wages. He was hamstrung by opposition from the Peronists – the party founded in the 1940s by General Juan Domingo Peron, husband of Eva Duarte Peron (Evita) – and their ally, the labour movement, and from entrenched business interests. Winning votes in congressional and provincial elections was given priority, resulting in compromises on economic policy. The dilemma was made more acute by the anxiety not to give the armed forces any pretext to return to the political stage. Even though the military was discredited, its strength could not be ignored, as several revolts by sections of the army made clear.

The failure of Dr Alfonsín and the Radical Party to make progress on the economy led to the election of Peronist Carlos Menem as president in 1989. Menem has the advantage that the Peronists have traditionally had a close relationship with the military; but the economic problems he faces are immense and will take many years to solve.

GDP BY ORIGIN

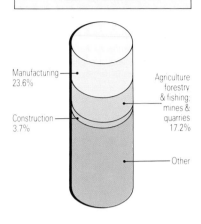

COMPONENTS OF GDP

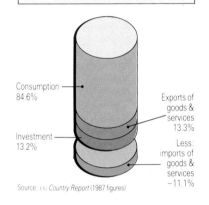

Source: EIU *Country Report* (1987 figures)

IMPORTS AND EXPORTS

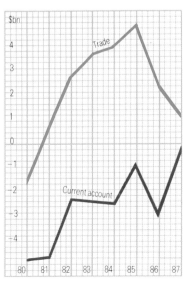

Source: EIU *Country Report* (1986 figures)

BALANCE OF PAYMENTS

Source: EIU *Country Credit Risk Service*

157

EUROPEAN COMMUNITY

EC institutions

The **Commission** initiates, implements and supervises community action. Its 17 members are appointed by member governments, but their loyalty is pledged to the community as a whole.

The **Council of Ministers** directly represents governments and takes final decisions on proposals presented by the Commission. Its composition depends on the subject under discussion. Each state is represented by one minister but states are allocated voting rights in proportion to their size.

The 518-member **European Parliament** was directly elected for the first time in 1979. Elections are held every five years. The parliament has joint responsibility with the Council of Ministers for finalizing the EC's annual budget; its role in legislation is mainly advisory. In theory, it also has the power to dismiss the Commission. Parliamentary sessions are held in Strasbourg, its secretariat is based in Luxembourg, most committees sit in Brussels. In January 1989 the parliament voted to move to Brussels, but the final decision rests with the member governments.

The **Economic and Social Committee** is purely an advisory body but it is consulted by the Commission and the Council of Ministers on a variety of issues. Its members come from interest groups, including employers, trade unions, consumers and farmers.

The **European Council**, consisting of the heads of government of member states, meets twice a year.

Regional development

EC regional policy aims to direct funds to areas most in need. These fall into two categories: underdeveloped rural areas, mainly in Mediterranean regions but also including Ireland and French overseas departments, and areas of industrial decline, mainly in the UK, France and Belgium. Regional spending is channelled through the European Regional Development Fund, set up in 1975, and the European Social Fund.

1992 and the internal market

A white paper prepared by the Commission lists some 300 actions to be taken to achieve a single market. They fall into three categories.

● Removal of physical barriers. The abolition of frontier controls by 1992.

● Removal of technical barriers. The programme to harmonize national manufacturing standards should be replaced by mutual recognition of national standards, pending the adoption of European standards.

● Removal of fiscal barriers. Levels of VAT and excise duty should be adjusted to fall within 2.5% of a target level.

1951 Treaty of Paris establishers European Coal & Steel Community (members: Belgium, France, West Germany, Italy, Luxembourg, Netherlands)
1955 Six ECSC members form committee to investigate feasibility of a common market.
1957 Treaty of Rome establishes European Economic Community (EEC); European Atomic Energy Community (Euratom) set up
1961 UK, Ireland, Denmark, Norway apply for EEC membership.
1962 Common market in agriculture established.
1963 France vetoes UK membership of EEC; Ireland, Denmark and Norway withdraw applications
1966 UK again applies for membership; France again vetoes
1967 EEC, ECSC and Euratom amalgamated as European Community (EC)
1972 Renewed applications for membership from UK, Ireland, Denmark and Norway accepted; Norway rejects membership in referendum, other three become members on January 1 1973
1979 European Monetary System established. First direct elections to European Parliament
1981 Greece becomes a member of EC
1986 Spain and Portugal join. Single European Act signed
1987 Turkey and Morocco apply to join.

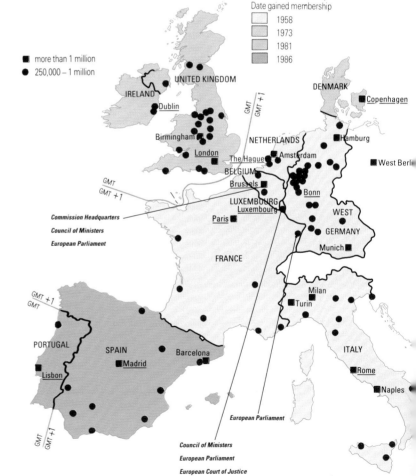

NET RECEIPTS

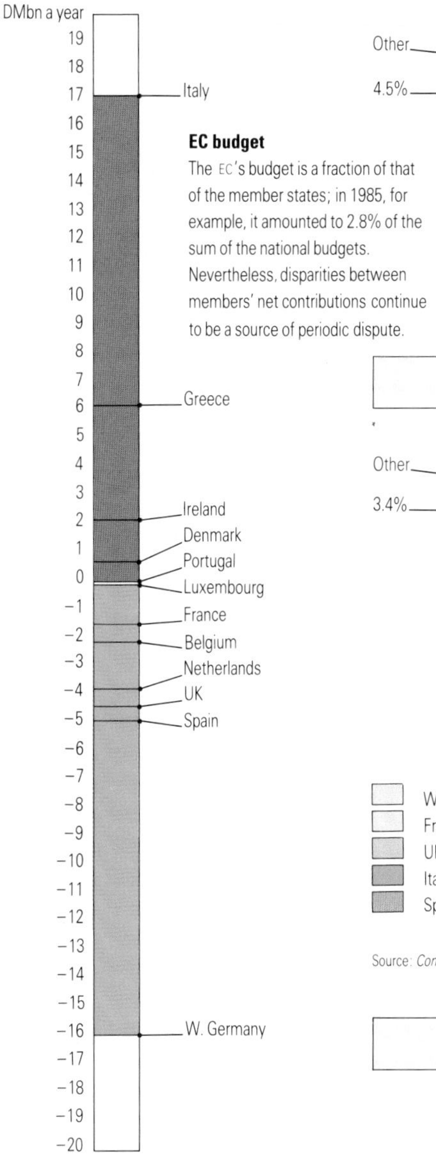

DMbn a year

19	
18	
17	Italy
16	
15	
14	
13	
12	
11	
10	
9	
8	
7	
6	Greece
5	
4	
3	
2	Ireland
1	Denmark
0	Portugal / Luxembourg
−1	France
−2	Belgium
−3	Netherlands
−4	UK
−5	Spain
−6	
−7	
−8	
−9	
−10	
−11	
−12	
−13	
−14	
−15	
−16	W. Germany
−17	
−18	
−19	
−20	

EC budget
The EC's budget is a fraction of that of the member states; in 1985, for example, it amounted to 2.8% of the sum of the national budgets. Nevertheless, disparities between members' net contributions continue to be a source of periodic dispute.

Source: *Commission of the European Communities* (1987 figures)

GROSS CONTRIBUTION

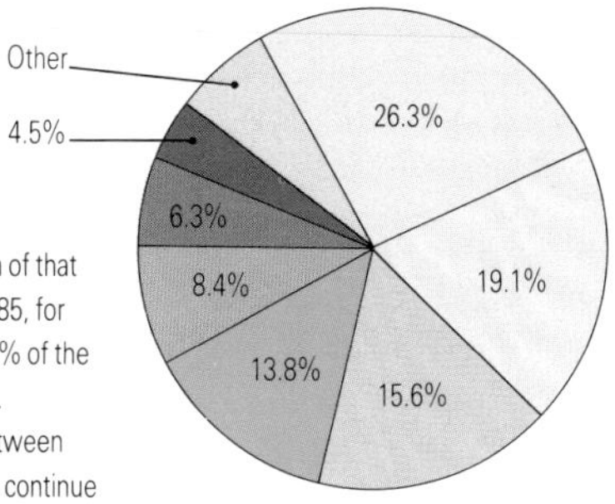

Other 4.5%

26.3%
19.1%
15.6%
13.8%
8.4%
6.3%

GROSS RECEIPTS

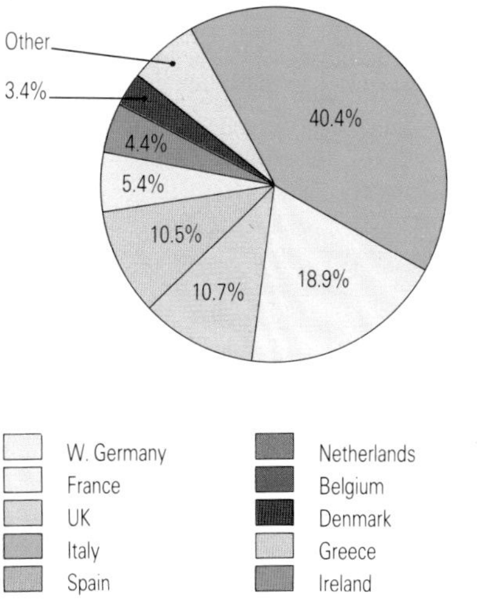

Other 3.4%

40.4%
18.9%
10.7%
10.5%
5.4%
4.4%

☐ W. Germany	☐ Netherlands
☐ France	☐ Belgium
☐ UK	☐ Denmark
☐ Italy	☐ Greece
☐ Spain	☐ Ireland

Source: *Commission of the European Communities* (1987 figures)

SPENDING BREAKDOWN

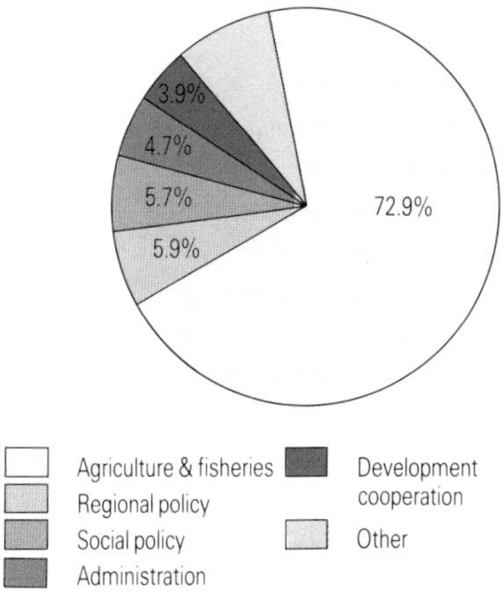

72.9%
5.9%
5.7%
4.7%
3.9%

☐ Agriculture & fisheries	☐ Development cooperation
☐ Regional policy	☐ Other
☐ Social policy	
☐ Administration	

Source: *Commission of the European Communities* (1985 figures)

GMT +2
GMT +1

GREECE

GMT +2

Athens

UNITED KINGDOM

As friend and foe alike recovered from World War II, Britain sank into a 30-year decline. In the 1950s economic policy lurched between stop and go, as every attempt to match the growth rates of the USA or West Germany foundered in a balance of payments crisis. By the 1970s, Britain's reputation was a far from proud one: low productivity, poor management, soaring inflation and an appalling strike record. Socialism had been tried and found wanting. The once great imperial power had become a distinctly second-rank nation.

Since then the tide has turned. Cushioned by oil revenues from the North Sea, the Thatcher government, elected in 1979 for the first of three consecutive terms, has presided over a remarkable economic recovery. In the 1980s Britain's productivity growth outpaced many of its competitors, union power was curtailed and strikes much reduced, income tax rates were cut dramatically, and towards the end of the decade the government was even running a budget surplus.

An unswerving commitment to the virtues of the free market appears to have paid economic dividends, yet great uncertainties remain as to whether the economic recovery can be sustained. The increasing prosperity of the south has done nothing to close the traditional north–south divide, and there is concern that the balance will tip still further in favour of the south after the creation of a single European market, if only for geographical reasons. Business complains that it is hampered by the financial sector's short-term approach to profits and there are many who doubt that the continuing growth of service industries and the uneven but undeniable recovery of manufacturing have compensated for the erosion in the early 1980s of the nation's industrial base. Others bemoan a lack of public investment in infrastructure and worry about the shortage of adequately skilled people coming out of Britain's schools and universities. The treasury must also live with the economic facts that North Sea oil production is declining and the list of companies and industries available for privatization is getting shorter (between 1979 and 1988 asset sales raised nearly $24bn). And towards the end of the 1980s it became clear that two old demons of the 1970s – high inflation and a constraining trade deficit – had not been laid to rest.

Mrs Thatcher has undeniably changed the economic and political ground rules by which the country is run, but Britain has still to decide what role it wants to play in the world. It still exercises, or thinks it exercises, an influence disproportionate to that of a second-class power – perhaps because London is

OFFICIAL NAME United Kingdom of Great Britain and Northern Ireland.

CAPITAL CITY London.

GEOGRAPHY The UK's varied landscape ranges from the relatively undeveloped uplands of North Wales and Scotland to the intensively farmed lowlands of southeast England. Over 75% of land is used for agriculture. The UK's largest lake, Lough Neagh, is in Northern Ireland, most of which is lowland. Major ports are dotted around the long, indented coastline. A tunnel under the English Channel, due for completion in 1993, will provide the first road and rail link between Great Britain and the rest of Europe. The highly urbanized population is densest in the southeast; around 12% live in Greater London. The other main cities are in the more heavily industrialized areas of the centre and north. *Highest point* Ben Nevis 1,343 metres (4,410 feet). *Area* 244,100 sq km (94,250 sq miles).

PEOPLE *Population* 56.6m. *Density* 232 per sq km. *Ethnic groups* White 94%, Indian 1%, West Indian/Guyanese 1%, Pakistani 1%, mixed 0.4%, Chinese 0.2%, African 0.2%, Bangladeshi 0.2%.

RELIGION Christian 85% (Church of England 50%, RC 13%, Church of Scotland 4%, Methodist 2%, Baptist 1%, other 18%), Muslim 2%, Jewish 1%, Hindu 1%, Sikh 1%.

LANGUAGE English. Also Welsh and Gaelic.

EDUCATION Compulsory for ages 5–16 and free at all levels. Some 6% of pupils attend private schools. There are 45 universities. Scotland and Northern Ireland have separate educational systems.

CLIMATE Temperate and variable. Monthly average temperatures 15°C (60°F) in summer, 5°C (40°F) in winter. Annual rainfall 900–1,000mm (35–40ins), less in London, heaviest Oct–Feb.

CURRENCY Pound sterling (£).

PUBLIC HOLIDAYS Jan 1, Good Fri, Easter Mon, first and last Mon in May, last Mon in Aug, Dec 25, Dec 26.

GOVERNMENT Parliamentary monarchy. There is no written constitution. The legislature has two houses: the House of Commons has 650 members elected for a term of up to 5 years from single-member constituencies; the less important House of Lords consists of hereditary and appointed life peers. Executive power is in the hands of the prime minister, usually leader of the majority party in the Commons, and a Cabinet drawn mainly from the House of Commons.

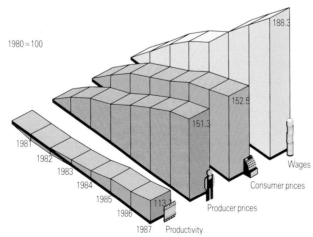

WAGES AND PRICES

1980 = 100

188.3
152.5
151.3
113.

1981
1982
1983
1984
1985
1986
1987 Productivity

Wages
Consumer prices
Producer prices

Source: IMF *International Financial Statistics*

Northern Ireland

The six northeastern counties of Ulster remained part of the UK when the rest of Ireland won its independence in 1921. About 60% of the population is Protestant. Anti-Catholic discrimination led to increasingly violent opposition. In an attempt to quell the violence, the British government sent troops to the province in 1969. In the years to 1989 over 830 members of the security forces and 1,830 civilians lost their lives as the result of the "troubles."

The devolved parliament at Stormont was prorogued and direct rule imposed from Westminster in 1972. Subsequent attempts to create a new administrative structure have fallen foul of growing religious and political polarization.

The Anglo-Irish agreement, signed in November 1985, allows the Irish government the right of consultation on Northern Ireland's affairs. It is vigorously opposed by Northern Ireland's Unionists but, for the time being at least, is positively supported by the government of the southern republic.

Isle of Man

A dependency of the crown, and not part of the United Kingdom, the Isle of Man has its own legislative assembly and legal system. The Manx government controls direct taxation and the island has developed as a tax shelter and financial centre.

North Sea oil

North Sea oil transformed Britain from an oil importer to the world's fifth largest oil exporter within a decade. Benefits to the economy included savings on imports of around $10bn a year and export earnings of $8bn a year by the mid-1980s and an oil industry employing 100,000 people. Oil also fuelled the growth of Britain's foreign assets, income from which will assume greater importance as the oil runs out. On the negative side, oil gave a boost to the exchange rate at a time when manufacturers were struggling to compete in export markets. Between 1979 and 1984, the UK changed net exporter of manufactures to a net importer.

Oil production passed its peak in 1985, but the UK is expected to remain a significant producer well into the 1990s and self-sufficient into the next century. The prospects of discovering and exploiting new fields depend on the price of oil.

Regional tensions

Despite the UK's small size and relatively long history as a unified state, national and regional differences persist in many areas of social, political, economic and cultural life. Some differences are enshrined in law; Scotland, for example, has separate legal and educational systems. National sentiment in Scotland and Wales and support for devolution are fuelled by an increasingly marked political divide; in the 1987 general election, the Conservatives won a majority in parliament but took only 10 of the 72 Scottish seats and 8 of the 38 Welsh seats.

The gap in living standards between north and south is more perceived than actual; regional income variations are less marked in the UK than in most other Western European countries. However, the divide is growing, partly as a result of the reorientation of trade from overseas to EC partners. As the map illustrates, the economies of the Southeast, Southwest and East Anglia grew roughly twice as fast over the decade to 1987 as those of outlying regions. Projections show no weakening of the overall trend, although the divide is moving north as the Midlands attracts investment deterred by high property costs and skilled labour shortages in the Southeast.

Channel Islands

The only part of the Duchy of Normandy retained by the English crown after 1204, the Channel Islands do not form part of the United Kingdom and have their own legislative assemblies and legal systems. Low income tax has encouraged the development of Jersey and Guernsey, the largest islands, as financial centres, supplementing tourism and agriculture as the islands' main sources of income.

SCOTLAND

Edinburgh

UNITED KINGDOM

NORTHERN IRELAND

Belfast

Isle of Man

NORTH

YORKSHIRE AND HUMBERSIDE

NORTH WEST

Dublin

IRELAND

EAST MIDLANDS

WEST MIDLANDS

EAST ANGLIA

E N G L A N D

Birmingham

WALES

London

Cardiff

SOUTHEAST

SOUTHWEST

New York 7 hours

Tokyo 15 hours

New York 11½ days

Kobe 38 days (via Suez canal)

Channel Is.

- More than 1 million
- 250,000 – 1 million
- 100,000 – 250,000

GDP growth (1977–1987)
20%
15%

one of the world's key financial centres, sterling is a reserve currency and English is one of the world's dominant languages.

The withdrawal from empire, which began in earnest after World War II, was relatively painless and successful, though absorption of immigrants from the colonies has not been without tensions. Ties with Commonwealth countries become weaker as the years pass, while those with Europe strengthen only gradually. Britain has never been an enthusiastic member of the EC, preferring the special relationship with the USA. It alone among EC countries refused to join the European Monetary System when it was founded and the Thatcher government's approach to the legislation of the single European market is likely to be highly selective. On defence, however, particularly under Mrs Thatcher, Britain has been a vigorous member of Nato, and has maintained its independent nuclear deterrent. Living on an island, like the Japanese, the British have always stood somewhat apart from the rest of the world – and believed in their superiority.

There is also great controversy over the kind of society Britain should be. The British people have largely respected Mrs Thatcher for her firm hand on the tiller, for restoring Britain's image abroad and for getting the economy back on course. But critics accuse her of encouraging selfish attitudes and promoting "bourgeois triumphalism," and it is doubtful whether there is the same level of support for her radical proposals for the health service and for replacing the system of financing local government through property taxes with a community charge or "poll tax."

Class divisions remain substantial and, with the increase in those opting for private rather than state education and healthcare, the gap between the haves and have-nots is becoming more marked. Thatcherism has challenged the postwar consensus on the welfare state head-on and the stripping back of the welfare safety-net is a subject of great debate.

In the new environmentally conscious age, there is also great scepticism about Mrs Thatcher's commitment to green issues. It is not for nothing that Britain is known as "the dirty man of Europe" and the privatization programme has now moved on to the more sensitive public utilities sectors such as water and electricity supply (including nuclear power). There are also complaints that the Thatcher government, which was elected on a promise of less government, has actually assumed more power for itself and that it is too cavalier in deciding what the people have a right to know.

After a decade of rule by the world's most visible stateswoman there are signs that the British are beginning to weary of radical conservatism and its high activity quotient. But is there an alternative? Britain's electoral system and the division of the opposition gave Mrs Thatcher more than a 100-seat parliamentary majority in both the 1983 and 1987 elections, despite the fact that the Conservative Party's share of the popular vote was only 42%. Only now that the Labour Party has reestablished itself as the main contender for power might it deny Mrs Thatcher the fourth term she has declared that she is ready for and looking forward to.

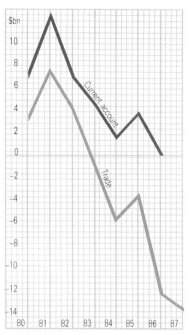

BALANCE OF PAYMENTS

Source: EIU *International Economic Appraisal Service*

ECONOMIC PROFILE

Manufacturing has declined in importance since 1960s, while service sector has grown to become mainstay of economy. Severe contraction of traditional industries – textiles, coal, steel, engineering, transport equipment. Recovery in 1980s of some manufacturing industries due in part to greater productivity, also evident in shrinking agricultural sector which provides efficiently for two-thirds of food needs. Level of state ownership in industry greatly reduced.

Growth Chemicals, expanding into high-technology, high value-added rather than bulk products. Financial services, particularly through strengthening of London's global position. UK is favourite location for Japanese and US investment in EC.

Problems Oil production now declining. Further rationalization still needed in capital goods, shipbuilding, truck and coal industries. High unemployment persists despite skilled labour shortages. Symptoms of overheating economy, with widening trade deficit and retail price inflation.

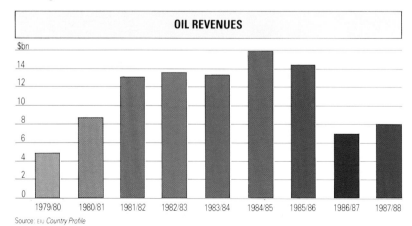

OIL REVENUES

Source: EIU *Country Profile*

IMPORTS AND EXPORTS

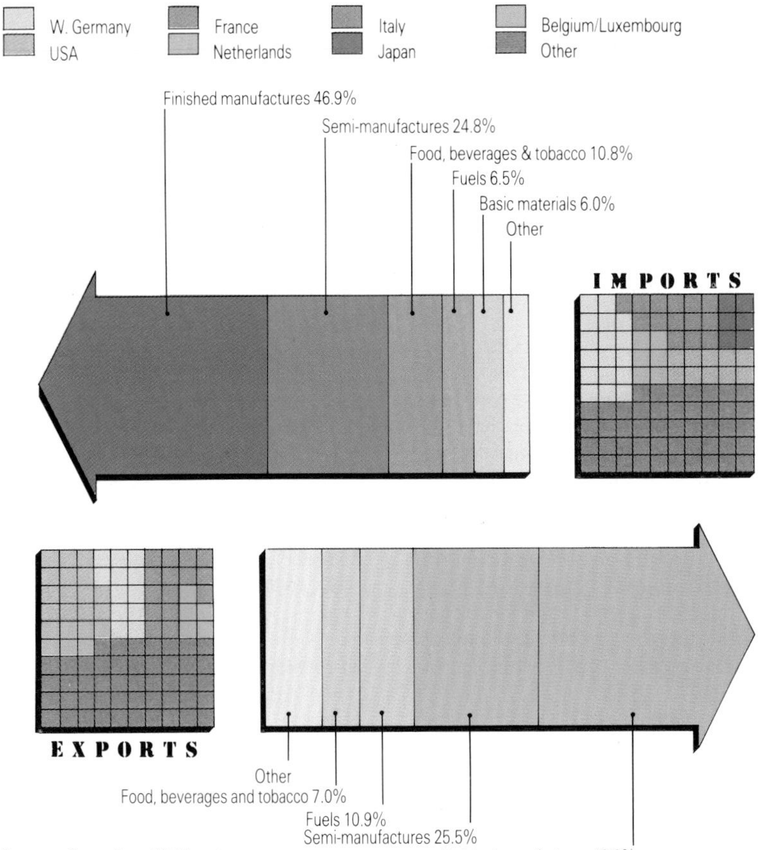

W. Germany
USA
France
Netherlands
Italy
Japan
Belgium/Luxembourg
Other

Finished manufactures 46.9%
Semi-manufactures 24.8%
Food, beverages & tobacco 10.8%
Fuels 6.5%
Basic materials 6.0%
Other

IMPORTS

EXPORTS

Other
Food, beverages and tobacco 7.0%
Fuels 10.9%
Semi-manufactures 25.5%
Finished manufactures 43.9%

Source: EIU *Country Report* (1987 figures)

GDP BY ORIGIN

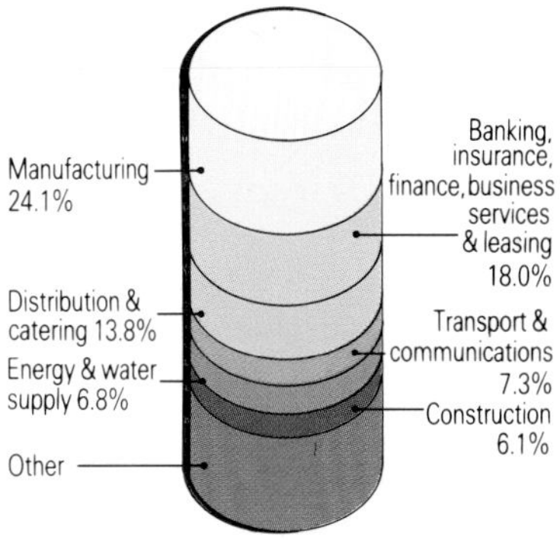

Manufacturing
24.1%

Distribution &
catering 13.8%

Energy & water
supply 6.8%

Other

Banking,
insurance,
finance, business
services
& leasing
18.0%

Transport &
communications
7.3%

Construction
6.1%

COMPONENTS OF GDP

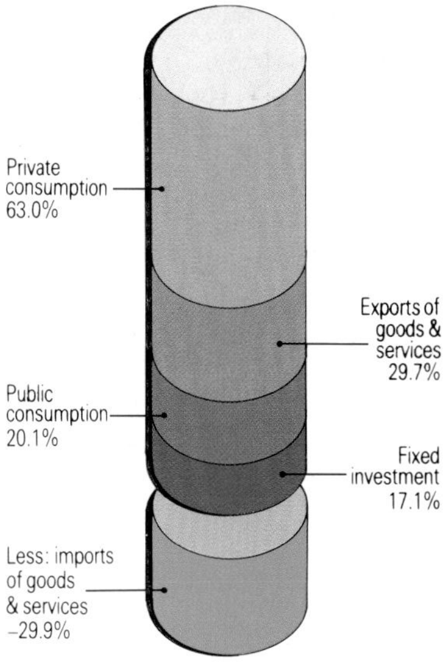

Private
consumption
63.0%

Public
consumption
20.1%

Less: imports
of goods
& services
−29.9%

Exports of
goods &
services
29.7%

Fixed
investment
17.1%

Source: EIU *Country Report* (1987 figures)

GDP GROWTH

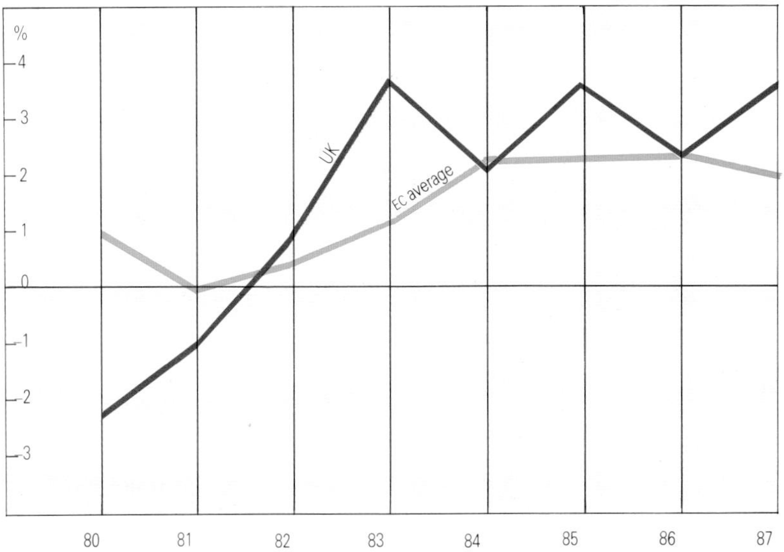

%
—4
—3
—2
—1
0
—-1
—-2
—-3

UK
EC average

80 81 82 83 84 85 86 87

Source: EIU *International Economic Appraisal Service*

EMPLOYMENT BY SECTOR

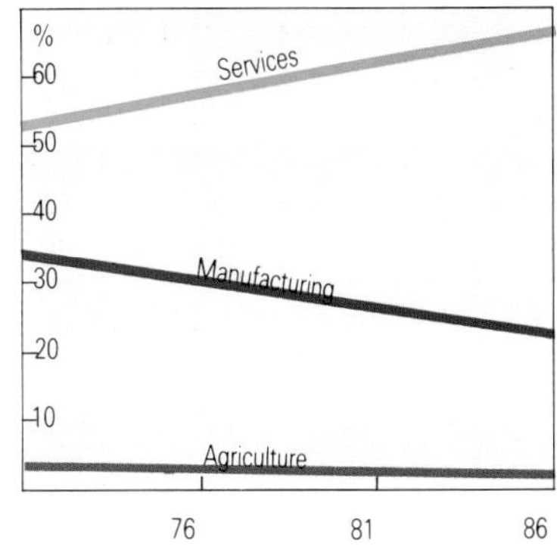

%
—60
—50
—40
—30
—20
—10

Services
Manufacturing
Agriculture

76 81 86

Source: ILO *Yearbook of Labour Statistics*

IRELAND

In 1921, after a war of independence, the Anglo-Irish treaty was signed conceding dominion status within the British Commonwealth to the 26 counties of the Irish Free State; the six northern counties had been given their own parliament within the UK the year before. Opposition to partition continued and two years of civil war ensued. In 1949 the last remaining constitutional ties with Britain were cut and the Free State became a republic.

Ireland's economy has always lagged behind that of the industrialized countries of Western Europe. The 1960s was a period of growth, then in 1973 Ireland joined the EC; but after the oil price rises of the same year, it soon ran into the problems of recession, rising inflation and a mounting balance of payments deficit. In the late 1970s the Fianna Fail government borrowed heavily to finance an ambitious programme of public spending. The habit continued in the early 1980s when governments came and went in quick succession. Ireland has been paying for this profligacy ever since: cutting public spending and borrowing are now the government's main priorities. Several years of austerity seemed to be paying off by the end of the 1980s, with strong growth forecast alongside low inflation and a widening balance of payments surplus.

The country has a tradition of mass emigration dating back to the great famine of 1847–50 when a million people left for Britain and the USA. Its demographic structure is similar to that of many developing nations – half the population is under 25. Industrial growth, encouraged by government incentives, has been greatest in high-technology rather than more labour-intensive sectors; with the work force growing faster than the number of jobs, emigration is once again rising.

Irish unity remains high on the political agenda. The Anglo-Irish agreement signed in 1985 is, for the moment at least, seen as the vehicle for progress in this direction. Recent governments have taken stronger measures against terrorism and can claim some success in stopping the IRA from using bases in the south for incursions into the north. Meanwhile, thousands of southerners cross the border every week to shop where prices are considerably lower.

OFFICIAL NAME Republic of Ireland.

CAPITAL CITY Dublin.

GEOGRAPHY Most of Ireland's high ground is around the coast; the centre is a lush, sometimes boggy, limestone plain dotted with lakes and low hills and drained by slow, winding rivers. The west coast is wild and rocky, with wide bays, while the east is much more sheltered. *Highest point* Carantuohill 1,041 metres (3,420 feet). *Area* 70,283 sq km (27,140 sq miles).

PEOPLE *Population* 3.6m. *Density* 51 per sq km. *Ethnic groups* Irish 96%, English and Welsh 2%, Northern Irish 1%.

RELIGION RC 94%, Church of Ireland 3%, Presbyterian 1%.

LANGUAGE Irish and English. Irish is the official first language but is rarely spoken.

EDUCATION Compulsory for ages 6–15 and free to university level, in either state or subsidized private schools. There are 2 universities.

CLIMATE An equable maritime climate greatly influenced by the Gulf Stream. Average temperatures around 5°C (40°F) in winter, rising to not more than 16°C (60°F) in summer. Annual rainfall around 1,500mm (60ins) in the west, half that in the east.

CURRENCY Punt, or Irish pound (I£).

PUBLIC HOLIDAYS Jan 1, Mar 17, Good Fri, Easter Mon, 1st Mon in Jun, 1st Mon in Aug, last Mon in Oct, Dec 25, 26.

GOVERNMENT Republic since 1949. The head of state is a president elected by direct vote every 7 years. There is a bicameral legislature. The upper house, the Senate, which has no power of veto, has 60 members, 11 nominated by the prime minister, the others indirectly elected. The lower house, the Dail, has 166 members elected by PR every 5 years. The chief executive, the Taoiseach (prime minister), is leader of the majority party in the Dail; the Taoiseach appoints the cabinet.

IMPORTS AND EXPORTS

Machinery & transport equipment 33.5%
Manufactured goods 15.8%
Misc. manufactures 12.8%
Chemicals 12.3%
Other

UK
USA
W. Germany
France

Netherlands
Belgium/Luxembourg
Japan
Other

I M P O R T S

E X P O R T S

Other
Misc. manufactures 12.2%
Chemicals 12.2%
Food & live animals 24.9%
Machinery & transport equipment 31.4%

Source: EIU *Country Report* (1987 figures)

ECONOMIC PROFILE

Agriculture, traditionally dominant, now less important. Industrial expansion, largely financed by foreign capital, based on producing high-value goods for export.

Growth High-tech industries such as electronics, pharmaceuticals. Service industries, particularly tourism.

Problems Older industries such as textiles and footwear hit by foreign competition. Job creation not keeping pace with growth of labour force.

FRANCE

France has been described as an "idea necessary to civilization." It is also a nation essential to Europe. With both Atlantic and Mediterranean coastlines, it is the only country that belongs to northern and to southern Europe, and its national culture embraces both mercurial Latin flair and the methodical industriousness more usually associated with northern societies. For centuries, France has played a focal role in European affairs, and not only politically: Paris has long paraded as the cultural champion of the West, the arbiter of artistic fashion and the melting-pot of new ideas. Economically, France has been slower to develop: despite a notable record of scientific invention in the 19th century, it has only recently become a major industrial power in the forefront of technology. This remarkable postwar modernization has also helped it to secure the *de facto* political leadership of the EC.

Since the 1950s, France has become a dynamic, prosperous and confident country, with a well-balanced and open society. But the earlier part of the century was not a happy period. The 1914–18 war drained French strength. The interwar years were a time of decline, unrest and economic stagnation, leading to the defeat of 1940 and the German occupation. This humiliation spurred postwar renewal, though the recovery was obscured by political instability and divisive colonial wars (notably in Algeria) until General de Gaulle returned to power in 1958.

Postwar modernization has shifted the economic focus from farming to industry, as more than 6m people have moved off the land and cities have swelled. Agriculture still plays an important role, in this fertile and relatively spacious country, but the peasant has been replaced by the business-minded farmer. With many ups and downs, and despite recurrent problems with inflation and trade balances, the economy has moved steadily forward, especially in high-tech fields.

In foreign affairs and defence, General de Gaulle has left France with a strong legacy of independent-mindedness, coupled with dislike of American dominance of the Western alliance. De Gaulle took France out of the military structure of Nato in 1966, though it remains part of the political wing. But the French have skilfully managed to identify EC interests with their own; they are

OFFICIAL NAME French Republic.

CAPITAL CITY Paris.

GEOGRAPHY The geography and economy of France are centred on five great river systems, those of the Rhine, the Rhône, the Seine, the Loire – whose fertile valley is known as the Garden of France – and the Garonne. In the centre are the old, eroded, largely forested ranges of the Massif Central and the Massif Armoricain. In the east are newer mountains, the Alps and the Jura; and the Pyrénées form the border with Spain in the southwest. To the north are the fertile, rolling hills and plateaus of the Paris basin. The Aquitaine basin forms a lowland area in the southwest and southeastern lowlands surround the valley and delta of the Rhône. *Highest point* Mont Blanc 4,810 metres (15,780 feet). *Area* 547,062 sq km (211,210 sq miles).

PEOPLE *Population* 55.2m. *Density* 101 per sq km. *Ethnic groups* French 93%, Algerian 1.5%.

RELIGION RC 76%, Muslim 3%, Protestant 2%, Jewish 1%.

LANGUAGE French. Also Breton and Basque.

EDUCATION Compulsory for ages 6–16 and free in state schools; private schools, mainly RC, highly subsidized. 9.2% of government spending is on education.

CLIMATE Temperate and wet on north coast; long hot summers and dry winters in the south; wet springs and autumns in the west; a continental climate in the centre and east. Temperatures in Paris are generally between 0°C (32°F) and 24°C (75°F).

CURRENCY Franc (Fr).

PUBLIC HOLIDAYS Jan 1, Easter Mon, May 1, May 8, Ascension, Whit Mon, Jul 14, Aug 15, Nov 1, Nov 11, Dec 25.

GOVERNMENT Republic. The head of state and chief executive is the president, elected by a simple majority in a 2-round election every 7 years. He appoints the prime minister, and with him the rest of the council of ministers. The 577-member national assembly is elected for 5 years; PR has been used, but the current system is on the basis of single-member constituencies. The second chamber, the senate, is elected by a college of local councillors and members of the national assembly.

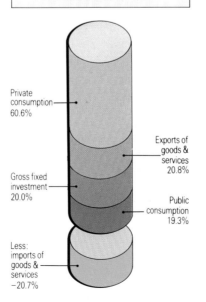

GDP BY ORIGIN

Services 63.2%
Industry 27.1%
Construction 5.9%
Agriculture 3.8%

COMPONENTS OF GDP

Private consumption 60.6%
Gross fixed investment 20.0%
Exports of goods & services 20.8%
Public consumption 19.3%
Less: imports of goods & services −20.7%

Source: EIU *Country Report* (1987 figures)

among the most dedicated and enthusiastic of "Europeans." Not only has French agriculture benefited greatly from the EC, but French vision and dynamism have enabled France to dominate many high-tech projects, such as Eureka, Airbus and the Ariane space programme. By retaining close economic ties with its former African possessions, France has kept a good deal of influence in the Third World.

In a highly centralized country with a tradition of state intervention, the postwar renewal certainly benefited from intelligent state planning and the dynamic leadership of state technocrats, especially in regional development. France has been centralized since medieval times, when the Capetian monarchs forged its diverse elements into one nation. Napoleon continued the process, setting up the system of government by local state-appointed prefects. But Paris tended to suck the life-blood from the provinces, leaving them lethargic and resentful. The postwar revival brought new life to the regions and with it a new regional awareness and demands for more autonomy. In the 1980s, these demands finally began to be met by the Socialists' devolutionary reforms.

Today, many argue that the *étatiste* tradition, once valuable, is a liability in an age of open frontiers. Recent governments, of both the right and left, have begun to reduce state power in local affairs and the economy. This trend seems likely to continue, even though in 1988 the Socialist government halted the extensive privatization programme begun by its right-of-centre predecessor. But state influence remains strong, both structurally and informally: much real power is still in the hands of graduates of a handful of state colleges, who hold many key posts in the upper civil service and in both public and private agencies and corporations.

Class divisions remain strong. Wealth is still very unevenly shared and trade unions are weak. Yet in many other ways society has changed enormously since the war. Social formality has given way to a new free-and-easiness. Moral attitudes have relaxed, abortion has been legalized, the influence of the Catholic church has waned. Parental authority too has declined and parent-child

BALANCE OF PAYMENTS

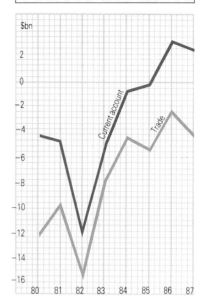

Source: EIU *International Economic Appraisal Service*

ECONOMIC PROFILE

Industry traditionally strong in heavy engineering, including railways, bridges and power stations; also vehicles, aircraft and weapons. Agriculture now modernized and very diverse; a big net exporter of food, notably cereals, and drinks. Perfumes and other quality goods still play a role.

Growth Ambitious state-backed telecommunications and aerospace developments still progressing, as is already highly developed nuclear power industry. Public works contractors and telecommunications companies particularly well placed to benefit from single European market. Service and leisure industries growing fast.

Problems Older industries – textiles, steel, shipbuilding – in decline; car industry menaced by competition and saturated markets. Coal mines nearing exhaustion; still heavy reliance on imported oil and gas, despite growth of nuclear power. Financial markets slow to expand and vulnerable to competition post-1992.

IMPORTS AND EXPORTS

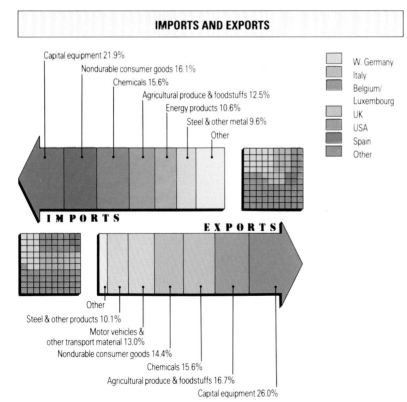

Capital equipment 21.9%
Nondurable consumer goods 16.1%
Chemicals 15.6%
Agricultural produce & foodstuffs 12.5%
Energy products 10.6%
Steel & other metal 9.6%
Other

W. Germany
Italy
Belgium/Luxembourg
UK
USA
Spain
Other

IMPORTS
EXPORTS

Other
Steel & other products 10.1%
Motor vehicles & other transport material 13.0%
Nondurable consumer goods 14.4%
Chemicals 15.6%
Agricultural produce & foodstuffs 16.7%
Capital equipment 26.0%

Source: EIU *Country Report* (1987 figures)

Population

As a population centre, Paris still dominates the country: about 10m of France's 55m people live within the boundaries of Greater Paris. Only three other conurbations – Lyons, Marseilles and Lille – have populations over the 1m mark.

The past few years have seen a drift in population away from the capital for the first time. The new growth areas are where high-tech industries are expanding, in cities like Toulouse, Montpellier and Grenoble, coinciding with a southward shift in the centre of economic gravity as heavy industry in the Nord–Pas-de-Calais region has declined.

Railways

The high-speed passenger train (TGV) has transformed French rail travel. The first TGV line from Paris to Lyons is being followed by lines linking the capital with Bordeaux and Brest on the west coast. A northern route will divide at Lille, with one branch going on to the Channel tunnel, the other to Brussels.

With journey times from Paris of two hours to Lyons and three hours to Bordeaux, the TGV is offering strong competition to domestic air services.

■	more than 1 million	
●	250,000 – 1 million	
•	100,000 – 250,000	

TGV lines
⊢—⊢ existing
⊢--⊢ under construction

Monaco

An outpost of Genoa in the 12th century, Monaco has since been more or less continuously independent and ruled by members of the Grimaldi family. It occupies about 1.5 sq km (0.6 sq miles) on France's Mediterranean coast, subsisting largely off the money spent by visitors in its casinos and hotels.

Corsica

The fourth largest island in the Mediterranean was in turn under Arab, Pisan and Genoan rule until France annexed it in 1768, a few months before the birth of Napoleon Bonaparte, the island's most famous son.

Corsica gained the status of *collectivité territoriale* in 1982, with increased autonomy and its own directly elected assembly. This did not satisfy separatist movements, which continued to mount sporadic terrorist attacks.

relations have become more equal, while rigid classroom discipline has been replaced by cheerful informality, sometimes at the cost of high academic standards. In the cultural field, this seems to be the age of the dazzling performing arts, full of visual fireworks, rather than solid creativity: literature, philosophy and painting are all somewhat in the doldrums.

Despite class divisions, society has become more cohesive, less polarized, and this is reflected in recent political changes. General de Gaulle, during his term as president from 1958 to 1969, did much to give the French new self-confidence and political stability, but the old French tendency to split into warring camps of right and left survived. In the 1980s, however, the trend was towards consensus. Not only has the once-powerful Communist Party declined, now representing a mere 10% of the electorate; but the Socialist Party, largely as a result of its experience of power in 1981–86, has shifted from doctrinaire crypto-Marxism towards a moderate social-democratic stance that accepts the market economy. This change has loosened the old left/right divide and made possible hitherto unimaginable forms of partnership, such as "cohabitation" between a Socialist president and a right-wing government. The constitution devised for the Fifth Republic by de Gaulle gives substantial powers to a directly elected president and seems well suited to the age-old French love of strong leaders. But the problem of relations between president and parliament has yet to be resolved.

Now that the Socialists have abandoned nationalization, a bipartisan approach has emerged towards solving France's economic problems, some of which still cause great concern. Despite the progress in key modern sectors, and the growth of successful corporate giants, France still has too many inefficient older industries and has failed to put adequate stress on capital investment. This helps to explain why exports recently have been falling, and why structural unemployment remains so high. Added to this are the traditional weakness of the financial markets, still slow to develop despite recent reforms; the inadequacies of French middle-grade technical education as compared with that provided `in West Germany; and the continuing malaise of the overcrowded universities.

Yet the French enjoy such challenges. There is no lack of enthusiasm for new projects, and old chauvinistic attitudes have been abandoned in favour of a new international outlook. Modernism is welcomed and enjoyed, and the latest gadgets find a ready market. But traditional values have not been forsaken. Good food and wine are still important, as are style and elegance, albeit in a new, more informal interpretation.

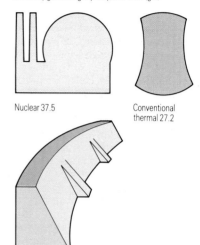

NUCLEAR POWER

Electricity generating capacity, end-1985 (gw)

Nuclear 37.5

Conventional thermal 27.2

Hydro 22.0

Net production by primary energy source (twh)

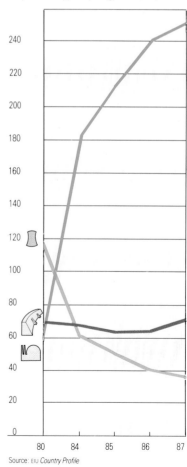

Source: EIU *Country Profile*

WAGES AND PRICES

1980 = 100

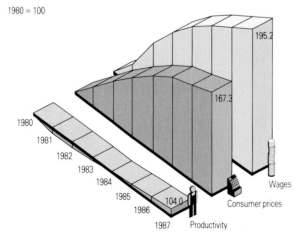

195.2

167.3

104.0

1980
1981
1982
1983
1984
1985
1986
1987

Wages

Consumer prices

Productivity

Source: IMF *International Financial Statistics*

BELGIUM

The Dutch-speaking Flemings and the French-speaking Walloons have shown every sign of regretting at leisure a union created in haste in 1830. And yet, despite some superficial indications to the contrary, the Belgian state is unlikely to fall apart. Rather, new coherence and new emphasis on what the two linguistic communities have in common can be expected now that agreement has largely been reached on a federal solution to the country's internal divisions. In the process, the unitary state will progressively disappear; in the 1990s around 40% of public funds will be controlled at regional level.

With an undeveloped sense of national identity by general European standards, Belgium has rarely attempted to limit movement of goods or people across its boundaries. Instead, capitalizing on its position as a crossroads of Europe, Belgium has become a machine for making money out of foreigners. Typically, exports and imports are each equivalent to around 90% of GDP. Not unexpectedly, Belgium plays a leading role in European economic integration, both physically by virtue of the presence in Brussels of the EC's headquarters, and in terms of strong popular and government commitment.

Governments, whose composition reflects not only the electorate's verdict on political parties' performance but also a delicate balance between the two main communities, find themselves with relatively few policy choices. The enormous public deficit will determine the direction of economic policy well into the 1990s, as governments focus their energies on curbing public spending and improving the balance of payments. The consequent lack of intervention will mean that Belgium should remain the most *laissez-faire* economy in Europe, after Switzerland.

This means that much of Belgian business is moving towards 1992 with considerable trepidation. In the absence of clear government policies, there is still too much emphasis on relatively low added-value industries, generally at the heavy end of the spectrum, where market growth and margins are below average. Increased competition, in a market wide open to countries with much lower labour costs, could prove deeply problematic.

This vulnerability betokens a certain element of inflexibility in Belgium's industrial structure. Company ownership is concentrated among a few large

OFFICIAL NAME Kingdom of Belgium.

CAPITAL CITY Brussels.

GEOGRAPHY Except for the forested plateau and foothills of the Ardennes in the southeast, most of the country is low-lying, an extension of the Paris basin, with sandy and clay soils; much of the coastal region has been reclaimed from the sea. *Highest point* Botrange 694 metres (2,270 feet). *Area* 30,513 sq km (11,780 sq miles).

PEOPLE *Population* 9.8m. *Density* 323 per sq km. *Ethnic groups* Belgian 91%, Italian 3%, Moroccan 1%, French 1%, Dutch 1%, Turkish 1%.

RELIGION RC 96%.

LANGUAGE Dutch (Flemish) 57%, French (Walloon) 42%, German 1%.

EDUCATION Free and compulsory for ages 6–18. 15% of the government's budget goes on education, through either the state secular system or subsidies to the parallel private denominational system.

CLIMATE Temperate, with mild, foggy winters and cool summers. Monthly temperature range is 0–23°C (32–73°F). Annual rainfall from 750mm (30ins) on the coast to 1,000mm (40ins) inland.

CURRENCY Belgian franc (BFr).

PUBLIC HOLIDAYS Jan 1, Easter Mon, May 1, Ascension, Whit Mon, Jul 21, Aug 15, Nov 1, Nov 11, Dec 25.

GOVERNMENT Parliamentary monarchy. The 212-member chamber of representatives is elected for 4 years, while the senate has 106 directly elected members plus 50 from the provincial councils, 25 co-optees and the heir to the throne. Voting, through PR, is compulsory. The chief executive is the prime minister.

IMPORTS AND EXPORTS

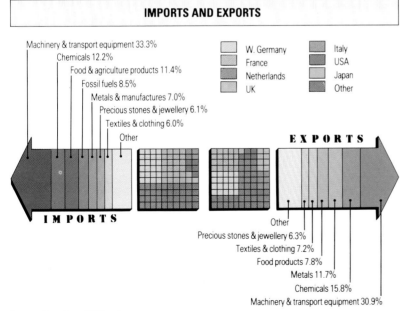

Machinery & transport equipment 33.3%
Chemicals 12.2%
Food & agriculture products 11.4%
Fossil fuels 8.5%
Metals & manufactures 7.0%
Precious stones & jewellery 6.1%
Textiles & clothing 6.0%
Other

W. Germany
France
Netherlands
UK
Italy
USA
Japan
Other

EXPORTS

IMPORTS

Other
Precious stones & jewellery 6.3%
Textiles & clothing 7.2%
Food products 7.8%
Metals 11.7%
Chemicals 15.8%
Machinery & transport equipment 30.9%

Source: EIU *Country Report* (1987 figures)

ECONOMIC PROFILE

Decline in older industries – coal, steel, textiles, heavy engineering, chemicals and food – and rapid expansion of service industries. Agriculture, small in scale, provides meat, fruit, vegetables and dairy products for domestic consumpion. Few mineral or energy resources; nuclear power replacing coal as main energy source.

Growth Light industry expanding, backed by government incentives. Brussels continues to grow as centre for European and international institutions.

Problems Large industrial combines lack flexibility in competitive environment.

groups whose interlocking structures of holding companies and operational subsidiaries and affiliates reach into most parts of industry, finance and trade. Seen as under-utilizing their assets, these big corporations are likely increasingly to become targets for foreign takeover attempts, which could turn out to be the catalyst for change that govemment policies have so far failed to be. Already, Belgian industry is taking up the challenge and investing heavily in new machinery and technology.

BALANCE OF PAYMENTS

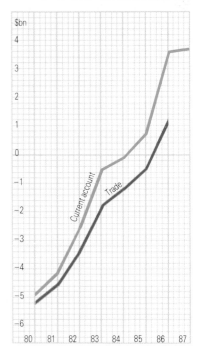

Source: EIU *International Economic Appraisal Service*

GDP BY ORIGIN

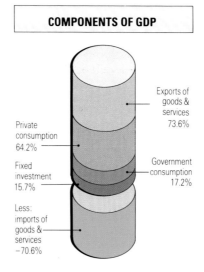

Commerce & finance 25.7%

Manufacturing 25.5%

Transport & communications 8.0%

Construction 5.1%

Other

COMPONENTS OF GDP

Private consumption 64.2%

Fixed investment 15.7%

Less: imports of goods & services −70.6%

Exports of goods & services 73.6%

Government consumption 17.2%

Source: EIU *Country Report* (1986 figures)

BENELUX COUNTRIES

Benelux and Bleu

The Benelux treaty, signed in 1958 by Belgium, Luxembourg and the Netherlands, created the first free international labour market and established free movement of services and capital; most border formalities were abolished in 1971. Benelux serves as a model for the EC's internal market after 1992.

Belgium and Luxembourg also form a tighter economic union, Bleu. Their foreign trade and payments accounts are amalgamated and the two currencies circulate freely.

Devolution

Differences between the Flemish-speaking community in the north of Belgium and the French-speaking Walloons in the south led to the creation in 1982 of three regional assemblies: one for Flanders, one for Wallonia and one for largely French-speaking Brussels.

- ■ More than 1 million
- ● 250,000 – 1 million
- • 100,000 – 250,000
- ☐ French speaking
- ▨ Dutch and Flemmish speaking

NETHERLANDS

The Dutch obsession with consensus could only be found in a country fearful of the internal diversity that has threatened to pull it apart. Differences of political and religious orientation, singly and in every conceivable combination, have been resolved by allowing the major groups to become pillars of society. Nowhere is this seen more clearly than in the television networks: Protestants, Catholics, Socialists and Liberals each have their own station. Perhaps not surprisingly, the government has rejected plans to introduce independent television.

At the political level, consensus tends to mean that differences rarely become polarized. Compromise always has to prevail in the end, not least because no single party ever gets enough votes to rule alone.

Economic policies are often, as a result, equivocal and nebulous in both conception and implementation. The economy's fundamental strength may have prevented any real disasters, but indecision has recently carried the penalty of slow growth, well below the EC average. The need to improve economic performance receives lip service but action would call for forceful growth policies that could be provocative and unacceptable to some key members of the governmental coalition. Thus the political agenda is headed by subjects such as education, the environment and the state welfare system. One consequence is that the state sector accounts for over half the GNP, the largest proportion in the EC. Almost inevitably, personal taxation and social security contributions are higher than in any other OECD country and will remain high even after planned reductions.

The Netherlands has always been more environmentally aware than most countries. The need to create and protect land from the sea has ensured that green issues are given considerable attention. Pollution of the Rhine, which provides nearly three-quarters of the country's fresh water for drinking and agriculture, is a major concern.

The most pressing challenge facing the Netherlands is whether it can become competitive enough for success in Europe after 1992 without damaging its elaborate welfare state. To do so, it will be necessary for its disparate interest groups to risk a greater degree of political confrontation than has hitherto been acceptable.

OFFICIAL NAME Kingdom of the Netherlands.
CAPITAL CITY Amsterdam.
GEOGRAPHY With the exception of a small area on the southern border, the Netherlands is totally flat and criss-crossed with canals. Much of it, especially in the west, is below sea level and protected by dykes and dunes. 7,700 sq km (3,000 sq miles) of land have been reclaimed from the sea. *Highest point* Vaalserberg 321 metres (1,050 feet). *Area* 41,785 sq km (16,130 sq miles).
PEOPLE *Population* 14.5m. *Density* 347 per sq km. *Ethnic groups* Dutch 96%, Turkish 1%, Moroccan 1%.
RELIGION RC 36%, Dutch Reformed Church 19%, other Reformed Church 8%.
LANGUAGE Dutch.
EDUCATION Free and compulsory for ages 5–16. There are 21 universities. Education takes up 10.9% of the government's budget.
CLIMATE Generally temperate, though winter temperatures can fall to -17°C (0°F). Summers warm but unsettled and windy. Driest in spring; annual rainfall is around 800mm (32ins).
CURRENCY Guilder (Gld) or florin (Fl).
PUBLIC HOLIDAYS Jan 1, Good Fri-Easter Mon, Apr 30, May 5, Ascension, Whit Mon, Dec 25.
GOVERNMENT Parliamentary monarchy. The bicameral legislature, the states-general, has a 75-member upper chamber elected for 6 years by 12 provincial councils and a 150-member lower chamber directly elected by PR for 4 years. Executive power lies with a council of ministers headed by the prime minister. Every postwar government has been a coalition, and few have lasted a full term. There are 15 active parties; the 3 main ones, all more or less centrist, are the Christian Democrats, the Labour Party and the People's Party for Freedom and Democracy.

GDP BY ORIGIN

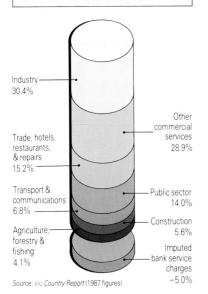

Industry 30.4%
Trade, hotels, restaurants, & repairs 15.2%
Transport & communications 6.8%
Agriculture, forestry & fishing 4.1%
Other commercial services 28.9%
Public sector 14.0%
Construction 5.6%
Imputed bank service charges −5.0%

Source: EIU *Country Report* (1987 figures)

COMPONENTS OF GDP

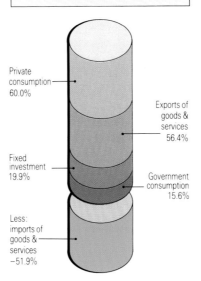

Private consumption 60.0%
Fixed investment 19.9%
Less: imports of goods & services −51.9%
Exports of goods & services 56.4%
Government consumption 15.6%

BALANCE OF PAYMENTS

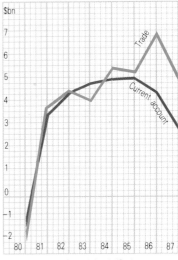

$bn

Trade
Current account

Source: EIU *International Economic Appraisal Service*

IMPORTS AND EXPORTS

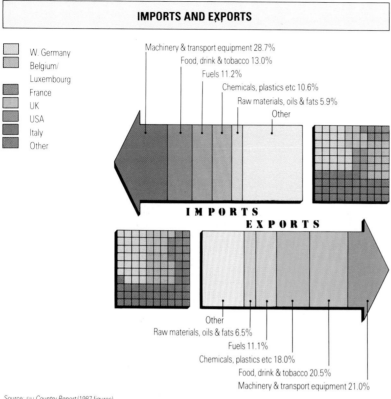

- W. Germany
- Belgium/ Luxembourg
- France
- UK
- USA
- Italy
- Other

Machinery & transport equipment 28.7%
Food, drink & tobacco 13.0%
Fuels 11.2%
Chemicals, plastics etc 10.6%
Raw materials, oils & fats 5.9%
Other

IMPORTS

EXPORTS

Other
Raw materials, oils & fats 6.5%
Fuels 11.1%
Chemicals, plastics etc 18.0%
Food, drink & tobacco 20.5%
Machinery & transport equipment 21.0%

Source: EIU *Country Report* (1987 figures)

ECONOMIC PROFILE

Historically a major trading nation, importing raw materials for processing and manufacture and re-exporting the products; today, exports and imports each equivalent to about 60% of GDP. Efficient, high-yielding agriculture, specializing in horticulture and dairy products. Europe's leading producer and exporter of natural gas; almost self-sufficient in energy.

Growth Chemicals, rubber, paper, food and drink have led economic growth. Service industries growing strongly. Slick marketing and advanced technology have boosted worldwide flower and bulb exports.

Problems Falling gas prices have forced public spending cutbacks. Textiles and heavy engineering contracting in face of competition from low-cost producers.

LUXEMBOURG

Unabashed by its anachronistic status as a grand duchy, Luxembourg sees itself as spectator, rather than participant, in the relationships between nations.

Emphasis is placed on playing a full role in an integrated Europe, notably as a home for European institutions, and neutrality has been abandoned in favour of commitment to Nato; but such moves represent Luxembourg's public face. Official and private attitudes are often inward-looking and almost reclusive, possibly as a means of preserving a national identity otherwise defended only by 630 regular soldiers.

Continuity is provided by a succession of coalition governments whose policies differ as marginally as their composition. Inflation is low, unemployment negligible, public finances and the balance of payments healthy. The perpetually troubled iron and steel industry, however, will preoccupy government well into the 1990s until the growth of financial services, manufacturing and chemicals deprive it of its central role in the economy.

Banking and financial services have also become increasingly important, as Luxembourg has established a leading role in the Eurocurrency markets and in offshore Deutschmark deposits. A high number of holding companies – over 5,000 – are registered in the duchy, attracted by a law exempting them from tax on dividends or interest and capital gains tax. Portfolio management services have been doing well, boosted by legislation to guarantee Swiss-style banking secrecy and the absence of stamp duty on security transactions.

OFFICIAL NAME Grand Duchy of Luxembourg.
CAPITAL CITY Luxembourg-Ville.
GEOGRAPHY Luxembourg is a landlocked upland. The northern section, the Oesling, is part of the plateau of the Ardennes, a windswept area cut by rocky valleys. The southern section, the Gutland, is heavily wooded and contains most of the important towns and industries. Almost all the rivers drain into the Moselle on the southeastern boundary. *Highest point* 559 metres (1,830 feet). *Area* 2,586 sq km (1,000 sq miles).
PEOPLE *Population* 370,000. *Density* 142 per sq km. *Ethnic groups* Luxembourger 74%, Portuguese 8%, Italian 6%, French 3%, German 2%.
RELIGION RC 93%, Protestant 1%.
LANGUAGE French, German and Letzeburgish.
EDUCATION Compulsory and free for ages 6–15. There is 1 university.
CLIMATE Temperate. Annual rainfall is 750–1000mm (30–40ins).
CURRENCY Luxembourg franc (LFr).
PUBLIC HOLIDAYS Jan 1, Easter Mon, May 1, Ascension, Whit Mon, Jun 23, Aug 15, Nov 1, Dec 25, Dec 26.
GOVERNMENT Parliamentary monarchy. The grand duke appoints a council of ministers responsible to an elected chamber of deputies. The 64-member chamber of deputies is elected by PR for 5 years.

SCANDINAVIA

Åland (Ahvenanmae)

This group of 6,554 islands, 80 of them inhabited, lies between Sweden and Finland at the south end of the Gulf of Bothnia. The islands form an autonomous district of Finland, although Swedish is the main language, and send two representatives of their own to meetings of the Nordic Council.

Nordic Council

The five Nordic countries cooperate through the Nordic Council, an assembly that meets annually, and the Nordic Council of Ministers, whose membership consists of ministers responsible for the issue under discussion. The Nordic Council's 87 members are elected annually by and from the parliaments of the various countries. The Faroes, Greenland and the Finnish Åland islands are each represented by two members of their own.

The Nordic Council countries form a common labour market, with reciprocal welfare benefits and a passport union.

Finland and the USSR

Since World War II, when Finland lost one-tenth of its territory to invading Soviet forces, it has practised a policy of peaceful coexistence with its huge neighbour. In the 1948 friendship treaty between the two countries, Finland agreed to resist any attack on the USSR through its territory, if necessary with Soviet help.

The USSR is Finland's most important trading partner, although most business is done on countertrade terms, designed to balance out over five-year periods. The USSR supplies virtually all Finland's oil, gas and coal, taking Finnish machinery in exchange.

Lakes

Both Finland and Sweden are dotted with lakes, with 60,000 in Finland alone making up about 10% of the land area. Lake Vänern in Sweden is Western Europe's largest, with an area of 5,585 sq km (2,160 sq miles).

Seasonal ice

Ice blocks the Gulf of Bothnia for several months of the year. Farther north, the coast of Norway remains ice-free, warmed by the Gulf Stream.

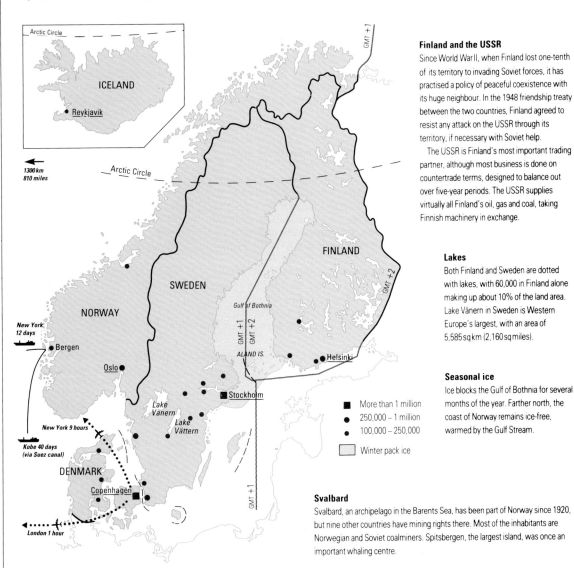

Legend:
- More than 1 million
- 250,000 – 1 million
- 100,000 – 250,000
- Winter pack ice

Svalbard

Svalbard, an archipelago in the Barents Sea, has been part of Norway since 1920, but nine other countries have mining rights there. Most of the inhabitants are Norwegian and Soviet coalminers. Spitsbergen, the largest island, was once an important whaling centre.

Efta

Finland, Iceland, Norway and Sweden belong to the European Free Trade Association, whose other members are Austria and Switzerland.

Efta was set up in 1960 with the aim of creating a single market including all countries in Western Europe. Free trade in manufactured goods was established among its members in 1966 and with European Community members in 1970. The UK and Denmark left to join the EC in 1972, Portugal in 1986.

The Efta states are, collectively, the EC's most important trading partner. There are fears in Efta that the removal of internal barriers in the EC after 1992 will widen the gaps between the EC and its neighbours.

DENMARK

Danes want more than anything to enjoy life. For years the welfare state has supported their lifestyle and Denmark has ranked highest in European surveys of personal satisfaction with life. But this attitude has led to suggestions that the nation lives way beyond its means.

Denmark has had a current account deficit for over 20 years; this persists even though the government has managed to slow down inflation, reduce unemployment and turn a large budget deficit into a sizeable surplus. Throughout the 1970s, the welfare state and the extension of the public sector were increasingly financed by borrowing on the international capital markets. Tighter economic policies have been adopted in the 1980s, but balancing the national economy will require several more years of austerity. There are calls for restrictions on consumption and an increase in domestic savings; cuts in welfare payments, higher charges for medicines and labour-saving productivity increases in the public sector have also been discussed.

Political fragmentation has undoubtedly made matters worse. There have been 19 general elections since World War II but no party has had an absolute majority. Minority and coalition governments have had to look for support from other parties often reluctant to share responsibility for painful measures.

Denmark nevertheless remains one of the most prosperous members of the EC, which it joined in 1973. The creation of a single European market in 1992 may cause problems for Denmark, however, as its high marginal tax rates and indirect taxation come into conflict with the EC Commission's objective of fiscal harmonization. The defeat in parliament in 1986 of a programme of EC reforms on internal trade barriers led to a national referendum in which only a narrow majority supported the reforms.

Danish opponents of the EC base their arguments on the sense of Nordic unity. They feel the country belongs to Scandinavia and do not like to see Denmark being drawn into the European cultural sphere. The other Nordic countries, by contrast, view Denmark as their gateway to the European market.

Although Denmark is generally a loyal EC member, it has long been regarded

OFFICIAL NAME Kingdom of Denmark.
CAPITAL CITY Copenhagen.
GEOGRAPHY Denmark is the Jutland Peninsula and a total of 483 low-lying islands, 97 inhabited. The number of islands and the fjords of Jutland give Denmark a disproportionately long coastline. Average elevation is less than 30 metres (100 feet); much of the land is sandy or moraine gravels, though the peninsula has much fertile loam. *Highest point* Yding Skovhöj 179 metres (590 feet). *Area* 43,069 sq km (16,630 sq miles).
PEOPLE *Population* 5.1m. *Density* 119 per sq km. *Ethnic groups* Danish 99%.
RELIGION Evangelical Lutheran 96%, RC 1% .
LANGUAGE Danish.
EDUCATION Free and compulsory for ages 7–16. 90% of children are educated at municipal schools.
CLIMATE Temperate and changeable, moderated by the North Atlantic Drift. Average temperatures 16°C (61°F) in Jul, 0°C (32°F) in Feb. Rainfall all year round, with most in summer and autumn; annual totals around 800mm (31ins) in the west, half that in the eastern islands.
CURRENCY Danish krone (DKr).
PUBLIC HOLIDAYS Jan 1, Maundy Thu, Good Fri, Easter Mon, 4th Fri after Good Fri, Ascension, Jun 5, Whit Mon, Dec 25–26.
GOVERNMENT Constitutional monarchy. The legislature, the Folketing, has 179 members elected for 4 years by PR. A fragmented party structure has led to a string of coalition and minority governments; defeats are common, but do not necessarily lead to resignation.

IMPORTS AND EXPORTS

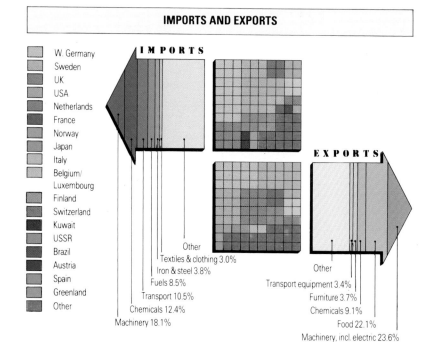

W. Germany
Sweden
UK
USA
Netherlands
France
Norway
Japan
Italy
Belgium/Luxembourg
Finland
Switzerland
Kuwait
USSR
Brazil
Austria
Spain
Greenland
Other

IMPORTS

Other
Textiles & clothing 3.0%
Iron & steel 3.8%
Fuels 8.5%
Transport 10.5%
Chemicals 12.4%
Machinery 18.1%

EXPORTS

Other
Transport equipment 3.4%
Furniture 3.7%
Chemicals 9.1%
Food 22.1%
Machinery, incl. electric 23.6%

Sources: Imports/Exports EIU *Country Report* (1986 figures); Trading partners UN *International Trade Statistics Yearbook* (1986 figures)

BALANCE OF PAYMENTS

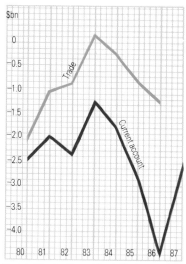

$bn

Trade

Current account

Source: EIU International Economic Appraisal Service

as ideologically unsound on basic strategy within Nato. It has not met Nato's targets for military spending and is firmly opposed to the presence of nuclear weapons on its territory – a position that Nato accepts but that has caused some internal political controversy.

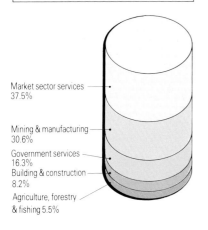

GDP BY ORIGIN

Market sector services 37.5%

Mining & manufacturing 30.6%

Government services 16.3%

Building & construction 8.2%

Agriculture, forestry & fishing 5.5%

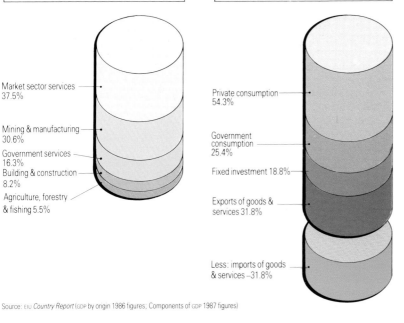

COMPONENTS OF GDP

Private consumption 54.3%

Government consumption 25.4%

Fixed investment 18.8%

Exports of goods & services 31.8%

Less: imports of goods & services –31.8%

Source: EIU *Country Report* (GDP by origin 1986 figures; Components of GDP 1987 figures)

ECONOMIC PROFILE

Agricultural exports – cheese, beef, bacon – declining in importance since 1945, although Danish farmers still produce enough to feed three times the population. Fishing hit by falling prices, quota disputes and overcapacity. Most exports now manufactured goods, particularly in high-technology sectors. Agricultural machinery, cement, bricks and tiles are important.

Growth Electronics is fastest-growing industry, 90% of production for export. Development of offshore hydrocarbon resources helping to reduce dependence on imported energy.

Problems Need to import most raw materials contributes to recurrent balance of payments problems and high external debt. Decline of fishing and shipbuilding industries has increased unemployment.

THE FAROE ISLANDS

OFFICIAL NAME Faroe Islands.

CAPITAL CITY Tórshavn.

GEOGRAPHY An archipelago. *Area* 1,399 sq km (540 sq miles).

PEOPLE *Population* 46,000. *Density* 33 per sq km. *Ethnic groups* Scandinavian.

RELIGION Protestant 99% (Evangelical Lutheran 74%, Plymouth Brethren 20%, other 5%).

LANGUAGE Faroese and Danish.

EDUCATION Danish system. One university.

CLIMATE The Gulf Stream moderates the Arctic climate. Wet and cool winters, mild summers.

CURRENCY Faroese krone (FKr). Parity with Danish krone, also used.

PUBLIC HOLIDAYS As Denmark, plus Apr 25.

GOVERNMENT Some home rule since 1948; sends 2 members to the Danish parliament.

The 18 Faroe Islands, lying between Scotland and Iceland, have been administered by Denmark since 1380, although they have their own government and parliament and decided not to join the EC with Denmark in 1973. Seventeen of the islands are inhabited, although one-third of the population lives on the main island, Streymoy. Fishing dominates the economy, accounting for 90% of exports, and the Faroes government's imposition of stringent conservation measures within 200 nautical miles of the coast in 1977 brought it into conflict with the EC.

GREENLAND

OFFICIAL NAME Greenland.

CAPITAL CITY Godthåb.

GEOGRAPHY Most is ice with some sandy or clay plains in the ice-free areas. *Area* 2,175,600 sq km (840,000 sq miles); ice-free area 341,700 sq km (131,930 sq miles).

PEOPLE *Population* 53,000. *Ethnic groups* Greenlander (includes Inuit) 82%, Danish 14%.

RELIGION Evangelical Lutheran 88%, other Protestant 10%.

LANGUAGE Danish and Greenlandic (Inuit).

EDUCATION Based on the Danish model, free, and compulsory to age 16.

CLIMATE Cold and bleak. Average monthly temperatures range from -8°C (18°F) to 10°C (50°F) in the south, from -22°C (-8°F) to 5°C (41°F) in the north.

CURRENCY Danish krone (DKr).

PUBLIC HOLIDAYS As Denmark, plus Jun 12.

GOVERNMENT 21-member legislature and 5-member executive; 2 members sent to the Danish parliament.

The world's largest island, Greenland came under Danish rule in 1380 and got some independence in 1953. Resentment of Danish domination led to the growth of a nationalist movement; a referendum in 1979 produced a large majority in favour of a degree of home rule and the island has since been gradually taking control of its internal affairs. A further referendum in 1982 supported Greenland's withdrawal from the EC, which took effect in 1985. Seal-hunting, fishing and sheep-rearing are the main economic activities. The economy still depends on substantial subsidies from Denmark, which remains by far the largest trading partner. Exploitation of mineral resources has begun on a limited scale.

ICELAND

Like its Nordic fellows, Iceland has a standard of living that is among the highest in the world, and provides a comprehensive social security system. Fish sales provide 70% of export earnings and fishing and related industries are the only large-scale source of employment. As a consequence, falling fish prices have forced several devaluations of the currency in recent years. Very little land is arable, but the wool industry has expanded in the 1980s.

Iceland is the most seismically active nation in the world, with earthquakes, active volcanoes and solfataras in abundance. The tourist trade is growing, based on the scenery, thermal springs and geysers. Almost unlimited reserves of thermal and hydroelectric power have stimulated plans to export electricity.

Political life is fragmented, with up to seven parties represented in the 63-seat parliament. The composition of coalition governments has been influenced in recent years by a series of political scandals, generally connected with fish.

Iceland is a member of Nato and provides the USA with an important military base at Keflavik.

OFFICIAL NAME Republic of Iceland.
CAPITAL CITY Reykjavik.
GEOGRAPHY The interior is a glaciated tableland and most settlement is on the rocky coasts, whose fjords provide safe harbours for the fishing fleet. *Area* 103,000 sq km (39,800 sq miles).
PEOPLE *Population* 241,000. *Density* 2 per sq km. *Ethnic groups* Icelander 97%.
RELIGION Church of Iceland (Lutheran) 93%, other Lutheran 4%, RC 1%.
LANGUAGE Icelandic.
EDUCATION Free and compulsory for ages 7–16.
CURRENCY Icelandic króna (IKr).
PUBLIC HOLIDAYS Jan 1, Maundy Thu, Good Fri, Easter Mon, Ascension, Whit Mon, Jun 17, Aug 8, Dec 24–26, Dec 31.
GOVERNMENT Republic since 1944. The president is elected every 4 years as are the 63 members of the legislature, the Althing, by PR; one-third forms an upper chamber.

SWEDEN

Sweden is the key Scandinavian state, with the largest population, a wide industrial base, long experience of democracy and a strategic central position. As a neutral country it has enjoyed a long period of peace, as well as political stability; the Social Democrats have been in power for all but six years since 1932.

Swedes have one of the highest standards of living in the world; extremes of wealth and poverty have been eliminated by a combination of taxation policy and a highly developed welfare state. Like the other Nordic countries, Sweden has also been an open society, in which political leaders are expected to be accessible. This partly explains why the assassination of Prime Minister Olof Palme in the spring of 1986 – a crime of the sort that many felt could not happen in Scandinavia – had such a deep impact.

Swedish society felt another shock only two months after Mr Palme's death, when radioactive clouds from the Chernobyl nuclear disaster in the Soviet Union passed across the country. The risks of atomic energy became all too apparent, and the country was forced to reappraise its own nuclear programme, on which it relies for about 40% of its electricity supplies. Before Chernobyl, the nuclear industry had been convinced that its image was improving: a national referendum in 1980 had narrowly backed a continued nuclear reactor building programme, to be phased out by 2010 as alternative energy resources were developed. Chernobyl, however, turned attention to the environment and encouraged the Swedish electorate to vote members of the Green Party into parliament.

The economy has continued to do well. A recession in the late 1970s and early 1980s was brought to an end by falling oil prices, a general upturn in trade and two drastic devaluations of the krona. For much of the 1980s the economy has enjoyed a boom, with rapidly rising production, low unemployment and industry working close to capacity, accompanied by fears of overheating.

Sweden does not want to be left out of the single European market, although Swedish politicians think membership of the EC is ruled out because of Sweden's neutrality. Instead, they are seeking closer relations with the EC in all areas except security and foreign policy, with the emphasis on a special relationship through Efta, of which it is a member.

OFFICIAL NAME Kingdom of Sweden.
CAPITAL CITY Stockholm.
GEOGRAPHY 15% of Sweden lies inside the Arctic Circle; the Norrland, the northern region of mountains, forests and finger lakes, is almost uninhabited. The fertile central lowlands, where wide lakes and gravel ridges bear witness to glaciation, contain most of the population. The southern tip of the country has the stony uplands of Småland and the major agricultural region, Skåne. *Highest point* Kebnekaise 2,111 metres (6,930 feet). *Area* 449,964 sq km (173,730 sq miles).
PEOPLE *Population* 8.4m. *Density* 19 per sq km. *Ethnic groups* Swedish 95%, Finnish 2%.
RELIGION Church of Sweden (Evangelical Lutheran) 68%, RC 1%.
LANGUAGE Swedish. Also Finnish and Lapp.
EDUCATION Free and compulsory for ages 7–16. There are 34 universities and colleges.
CLIMATE Monthly average temperature ranges vary according to latitude: in south, from -3°C (27°F) to 18°C (64°F); in far north, from -14°C (7°F) to 14°C (57°F). Average rainfall is 400mm (16ins) in north, 550mm (22ins) in south.
CURRENCY Swedish krona (SKr).
PUBLIC HOLIDAYS Jan 1, Jan 6, Good Fri, Easter Mon, May 1, Ascension, Whit Mon, Jun 24, Nov 1, Dec 25–26.
GOVERNMENT Constitutional monarchy. The 349-member Riksdag is elected for 3 years; the Riksdag elects a prime minister, whose cabinet is the executive power. The administration is fairly decentralized.

IMPORTS AND EXPORTS

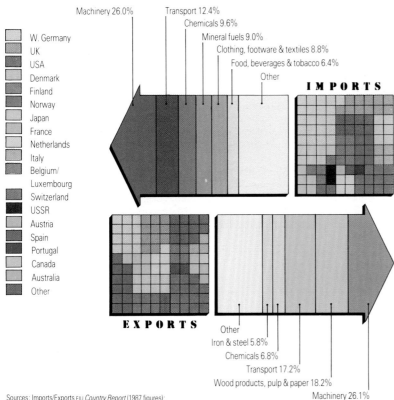

Machinery 26.0%
Transport 12.4%
Chemicals 9.6%
Mineral fuels 9.0%
Clothing, footware & textiles 8.8%
Food, beverages & tobacco 6.4%
Other

IMPORTS

W. Germany
UK
USA
Denmark
Finland
Norway
Japan
France
Netherlands
Italy
Belgium/Luxembourg
Switzerland
USSR
Austria
Spain
Portugal
Canada
Australia
Other

EXPORTS

Other
Iron & steel 5.8%
Chemicals 6.8%
Transport 17.2%
Wood products, pulp & paper 18.2%
Machinery 26.1%

Sources: Imports/Exports EIU *Country Report* (1987 figures);
Trading partners UN *International Trade Statistics Yearbook* (1986 figures)

ECONOMIC PROFILE

Manufacturing the most important economic sector, particularly metallurgy, engineering, timber and pulp and paper industries. One of the world's largest iron ore producers; copper, zinc, uranium also important. Decline in agriculture this century, but government striving to maintain 80% self-sufficiency in basic foods.

Growth Sophisticated high-technology goods – vehicles, electronics, telecommunications – finding wide export markets. Changes to financial regulations attracting foreign banks.

Problems Most energy supplies imported; nuclear power being phased out because of public pressure. Heavy subsidies have failed to save shipbuilding industry, once second largest in the world.

BALANCE OF PAYMENTS

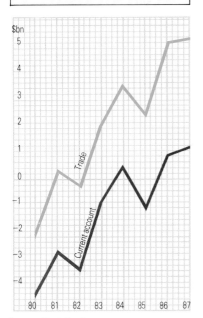

$bn

Trade

Current account

80 81 82 83 84 85 86 87

Source: EIU *Country Report*

COMPONENTS OF GDP

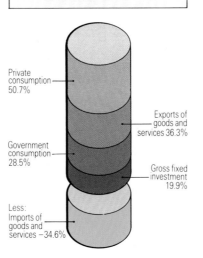

Private consumption 50.7%
Exports of goods and services 36.3%
Government consumption 28.5%
Gross fixed investment 19.9%
Less: Imports of goods and services −34.6%

Source: EIU *Country Report* (1987 figures)

GDP BY ORIGIN

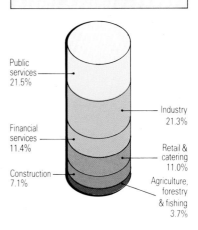

Public services 21.5%
Industry 21.3%
Financial services 11.4%
Retail & catering 11.0%
Construction 7.1%
Agriculture, forestry & fishing 3.7%

NORWAY

Discovery of the Ekofisk oil field in the North Sea in 1970 meant Norwegians were finally able to have it all: to cut taxes and maintain high public spending at the same time. Today Norwegians enjoy a high standard of living, with an excellent national health care and social security system. Unemployment has been around 2% for many years.

But the oil bonanza has brought its problems. The collapse of oil prices in 1986 plunged Norway into an economic crisis. An austerity programme was adopted, aimed at halting the consumer boom and righting the trade balance, but recovery has been slow and painful. More emphasis is being placed on traditional industries, to make the economy less vulnerable to fluctuating oil prices.

The approach of the single European market has forced Norwegians again to consider the possibility of joining the EC. In a 1972 referendum they voted by a narrow majority to stay out of the EC, revealing that they were deeply divided on the issue. As moderation and consensus dominate Norwegian politics, EC membership is unlikely to come about without broad agreement among the people.

OFFICIAL NAME Kingdom of Norway.

CAPITAL CITY Oslo.

GEOGRAPHY As well as the mountainous western half of the Scandinavian peninsula, it includes the Svalbard Archipelago inside the Arctic Circle and several uninhabited northern islands. Glaciations have scoured out plateaus inland and hundreds of fjords on the coastline. There are 160,000 lakes; the interior is forested. *Highest point* Glittertind 2,472 metres (8,110 feet). *Area* Mainland 324,219 sq km (125,180 sq miles); islands 62,422 sq km (24,100 sq miles).

PEOPLE *Population* 4.2m. *Density* 13 per sq km (excluding islands). *Ethnic groups* Norwegian 98%.

RELIGION Church of Norway (Evangelical Lutheran) 88%, Pentecostalist 1%.

LANGUAGE Bokmål (Old Norwegian) and Landsmål or Nynorsk (New Norwegian).

EDUCATION Free and compulsory for ages 7–16. 4 universities and 10 colleges.

CLIMATE West coast has marine climate with cool summers and mild, rarely freezing winters, moderated by the Gulf Stream; coastal rainfall can be as much as 2,000mm (80ins) a year. Inland has warmer summers, colder winters and less rain.

CURRENCY Norwegian krone (NKr).

PUBLIC HOLIDAYS Jan 1, Maundy Thu, Good Fri, Easter Mon, May 1, May 17, Ascension, Whit Mon, Dec 25–26.

GOVERNMENT Constitutional monarchy. The 157-member Storting is elected for 4 years by PR. The Storting divides into the Lagting and Odelsting. Executive power lies with a prime minister and state council.

IMPORTS AND EXPORTS

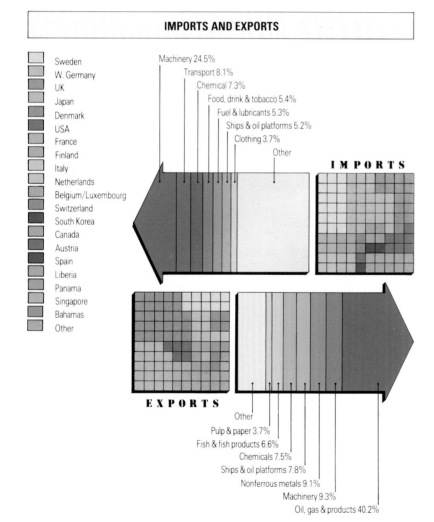

Sweden
W. Germany
UK
Japan
Denmark
USA
France
Finland
Italy
Netherlands
Belgium/Luxembourg
Switzerland
South Korea
Canada
Austria
Spain
Liberia
Panama
Singapore
Bahamas
Other

Machinery 24.5%
Transport 8.1%
Chemical 7.3%
Food, drink & tobacco 5.4%
Fuel & lubricants 5.3%
Ships & oil platforms 5.2%
Clothing 3.7%
Other

IMPORTS

EXPORTS

Other
Pulp & paper 3.7%
Fish & fish products 6.6%
Chemicals 7.5%
Ships & oil platforms 7.8%
Nonferrous metals 9.1%
Machinery 9.3%
Oil, gas & products 40.2%

Source: EIU *Country Report* (1987 figures)

COMPONENTS OF GDP

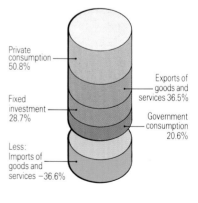

Private consumption 50.8%

Fixed investment 28.7%

Less: Imports of goods and services −36.6%

Exports of goods and services 36.5%

Government consumption 20.6%

Source: EIU *Country Report* (1988 figures)

ECONOMIC PROFILE

Older industries based on local raw materials – iron ore, timber, fish. Large oil and gas producer. Rugged terrain makes agriculture difficult – less than 3% of land area cultivated.

Growth Engineering, chemical and fish exports helping to make up for drop in oil earnings.

Problems Oil output likely to fall after 1990s unless new discoveries made. Concentration on oil allowed other productive sectors to stagnate. Shipbuilding, once a major industry, in severe decline.

GDP BY ORIGIN

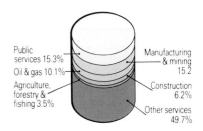

Public services 15.3%
Oil & gas 10.1%
Agriculture, forestry & fishing 3.5%
Manufacturing & mining 15.2
Construction 6.2%
Other services 49.7%

Source: EIU *Country Report* (1987 figures)

FINLAND

The Finns are keenly aware of their unique position in the shadow of the Soviet Union, linked to Scandinavia by a long shared history but separated from it by different ethnic and linguistic origins.

Fairly rapid industrialization has created a demographic imbalance, as the small farms cease to be viable, with people moving to the urban centres of the south. Yet a high level of agricultural self-sufficiency is regarded as vital, and Finland faces the problem of trying to protect domestic production while observing international agreements that limit government subsidies.

Increasingly dependent on foreign trade, Finland is keenly aware that even good housekeeping is no insulation against fluctuations in international markets. Adjustments in trading relations may be needed; Finland has taken a leading role in negotiations between Efta and the EC and follows changes in Soviet trade policy with keen interest. Financial and exchange controls have been loosened in recent years, bringing about a radical change in the financial market.

Like their Nordic neighbours, Finns benefit from a level of education as good as anywhere else and living standards and life expectancy among the highest in the world. The biggest challenge they face is how to maintain their prosperity. It is unlikely that this will involve radical change: a high value is put on consensus in decision-making. The large number of parties in parliament keeps them interdependent and trade unions are expected to act as much for the common good as in their members' interests.

OFFICIAL NAME Republic of Finland.

CAPITAL CITY Helsinki.

GEOGRAPHY Most is forested; 30% of the land is marshy and 10% is taken up by 55,000 mainly shallow lakes. Apart from mountains in the extreme northwest, the country is low-lying. One-third lies within the Arctic Circle. *Highest point* Haltia 1,324 metres (4,340 feet). *Area* 337,032 sq km (130,130 sq miles).

PEOPLE *Population* 4.9m. *Density* 15 per sq km. *Ethnic groups* Finnish 92%, Swedish 7%.

RELIGION Lutheran 90%, Greek Orthodox 1%.

LANGUAGE Finnish and Swedish.

EDUCATION Comprehensive system, free and compulsory for ages 7–16. There are 22 universities and colleges of further education.

CLIMATE In the far north temperatures range from -30°C (-22°F) to 27°C (81°F); extremes less marked farther south. The Baltic freezes most years. Annual rainfall around 600mm (24ins).

CURRENCY Markka (FMk).

PUBLIC HOLIDAYS Jan 1, Jan 6, Good Fri, Easter Mon, May 1, Ascension, Whit weekend, Jun 21, Nov 1, Dec 6, Dec 25–26.

GOVERNMENT Republic since 1917. The chief executive is the president, elected every 6 years by a college of 301 electors chosen by popular vote. The 200-member legislature, the Eduskunta, is elected by PR for a 4-year term, subject to dissolution by the president, who also appoints the prime minister and administrative council of state. Coalitions and minority governments are the rule. The average life expectancy of an administration is less than 1 year.

ECONOMIC PROFILE

Forests are mainstay of Finland's prosperity, covering 65% of land area and providing about 40% of export earnings, although foreign competition and reduced demand have taken a toll. Shipbuilding and manufacture of machinery for timber and paper industries are important. Highly mechanized cereal and dairy farming meets domestic requirements. Large copper reserves only major mineral resources.

Growth Forestry companies looking for expansion overseas. The emphasis domestically is on diversification. Grain surplus produced in recent years, leading to start of exports. Rapid growth in tourism.

Problems Industrial expansion constrained by shortage of skilled labour and need to import a major part of energy needs and many raw materials.

WEST GERMANY

Over 40 years ago Germany lay in ruins, devastated by war and divided by the allies' postwar settlement. Now the Federal Republic, the nation created from the portion that fell within the Western sphere, is the world's third largest economy and biggest exporter; and its role in international relations, far from being an antagonistic one, is mature and reassuring.

Postwar success was built on the *Wirtschaftswunder*, the economic miracle, of the 1950s. Determined to put the horrors of the Nazi years behind them, Germans worked tirelessly to rebuild their shattered country and, aided by entrepreneurial dynamism, succeeded to such an extent that the infant nation's economy grew by 8% a year. German firms such as BMW, Bayer and Bosch earned an international reputation for quality products that they retain today.

Underlying the country's prosperity is a degree of political stability and consensus remarkable in the shadow of earlier events. Fifteen years under the steady guiding hand of the first chancellor, Konrad Adenauer, paved the way for gentle swings of the political pendulum between alternating moderate coalitions of left and right. The liberal Social Democrats held the balance of power during the 1970s, giving way to the Christian Democrats under Helmut Kohl in 1982. Between the two are the Free Democrats, the kingmakers of German politics, whose fickle allegiance has a powerful influence on the fate of governments. In the late 1980s, however, there were signs of a threat to the status quo from a resurgence of support for right-wing parties.

Society is characterized by a degree of orderliness that some other Europeans find stifling, but which is crucial to the German success. Orderliness may bring with it a rather legalistic, bureaucratic society, but it has also helped sustain a record of harmonious labour relations that is the envy of the Western world and allows a degree of worker participation in management that might threaten disaster elsewhere.

But it is no longer accurate, if it ever was, to see Germans as overdisciplined and authoritarian. Prosperity has eroded class differences and encouraged a more relaxed and easy-going outlook. It has also brought a quality of life matched by few people in the world. Germans pay themselves well, buy

OFFICIAL NAME Federal Republic of Germany.

CAPITAL CITY Bonn.

GEOGRAPHY The northern third of the country is a plain cut by rivers and canals; both the North Sea and Baltic coastlines are indented with estuaries leading to major ports. More rivers intersect the central uplands, an area of forested low ranges and plateaus. In the south, the land rises to an extension of the Jura Mountains, which merge into the Bavarian Alps and the coniferous Black Forest. Dominating the west is the highly polluted Rhine; older heavy industry is concentrated in and around the Ruhr valley, the most densely populated area. *Highest point* Zugspitze 2,963 metres (9,720 feet). *Area* 248,577 sq km (95,980 sq miles).

PEOPLE *Population* 61m. *Density* 245 per sq km. *Ethnic groups* German 93%, Turkish 2%, Yugoslavian 1%, Italian 1%, Greek 0.5%.

RELIGION Protestant 47%, RC 44%, Muslim 2%.

LANGUAGE German.

EDUCATION Compulsory and free for 9 years between 6 and 18. Education is the responsibility of the Länder rather than the federal government. There are 48 universities and 9 technical universities.

CLIMATE Temperate and variable. Temperature -3–1°C (27–34°F) in Jan, 16–19°C (61–66°F) in July, higher in southern valleys. Spring and autumn often overcast. Rainfall around 600mm (25ins) in the north, 2,000mm (80ins) in the Alps.

CURRENCY Deutschmark (DM).

PUBLIC HOLIDAYS (* some Länder only) Jan 1, Jan 6*, Good Fri, Easter Mon, May 1, Ascension, Whit Mon, Corpus Christi*, Jun 17, Aug 15*, Nov 1*, Repentance Day, Dec 25, Dec 26.

GOVERNMENT Federal republic, consisting of 10 regions (Länder) and West Berlin. The federal government deals only with defence, foreign affairs and finance. The legislature has 2 houses: the 45-member federal council appointed by the governments of the Länder and the 518-member federal assembly largely elected in a mixed system of PR and single-member constituencies. The assembly elects the chief executive, the federal chancellor, who appoints the cabinet. The head of state is a president elected by a college of the assembly and regional legislatures.

ECONOMIC PROFILE

Prosperity built on manufacturing; cars, machinery, electrical equipment and chemicals are key exports. High farm productivity; Germany is the world's fourth largest exporter of food and drink, but also one of the biggest importers. Fuel resources and basic raw materials always in short supply; 94% of oil is imported.

Growth Advanced chemicals, electrical engineering, optics and machine tools tipped for healthy expansion. Frankfurt developing as Europe's second financial centre.

Problems Coal deposits running out. Steel, shipbuilding and textile industries suffering from Asian competition. Consumer goods and services sector underdeveloped. Industrial structure unsuited to technological innovation.

BALANCE OF PAYMENTS

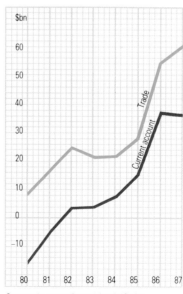

Source: EIU *International Economic Appraisal Service*

The Länder

The short history of the German nation state has done little to erode attachment to region. The pre-1918 German Empire, the Weimar Republic, its successor and the Federal Republic of Germany all made allowance for this in a federal structure of government. The Federal Republic, founded in 1949, consists of ten Länder (states) and West Berlin. The Länder have many of the features of an independent country. Each has its own constitution, government and legislative assembly. Education, police and culture are their responsibility; only defence, foreign affairs and finance are reserved for the federal government in Bonn.

Their influence on the federal government is strong, as they appoint the members of the federal upper house, the Bundesrat; and the composition of the Land governments often points towards new patterns of coalition. For example, the Christian Democrat–Free Democrat coalition was first tested at the state level. The Social Democrat–Green state governments are trials for a possible "red–green" alliance at the 1990 federal election.

West Berlin

Isolated in East German territory, West Berlin is politically unique. Technically a Land of the Federal Republic, its deputies in Bonn have limited voting rights. It has its own parliament, but supreme authority over the city still rests with the "protecting powers," France, the UK and the USA. Most major German companies have moved their headquarters elsewhere but, even though unemployment is above the national average, the decline in Berlin's population has been reversed, helped by lower personal taxation and exemption from military service for the city's inhabitants.

The Rhine

The Rhine, 1,320km (825 miles) long, is Western Europe's leading commercial waterway, linked by canals to the Rhône and the Danube. The river is a major transport link from southern Germany and Switzerland to the North Sea; Germany's industrial heartland is on its banks and those of tributaries such as the Ruhr and Main.

Defence

West Germany is on the front line between East and West. Some 400,000 foreign troops — from the USA, the UK, Belgium, the Netherlands, Canada and Denmark — are permanently stationed there, each contingent responsible for defending a section of the eastern border. It is enshrined in the German constitution that its armed forces are purely for defensive purposes; nevertheless, it has the largest army in Western Europe, 495,000-strong.

Bonn

Bonn became the West German capital by a quirk of history in 1949. The country's 18th largest city, with only 290,000 inhabitants, it has retained its provincial atmosphere. Parliament and all ministries are in Bonn and foreign diplomats are based there, but there is little commercial activity apart from banking.

Immigration

West Germany's booming economy sucked in migrant workers, many of them from Turkey, in the 1960s and 1970s. Official estimates show a foreign population of 4.1m, compared with 57m native Germans. Continuing high levels of immigration, resulting in part from the country's liberal asylum laws and the growing number of ethnic Germans who are being allowed to leave Eastern Europe and the Soviet Union, threaten to set off a political backlash. In early 1989, the far right made its biggest gains since the 1960s in local elections in West Berlin where foreigners account for 10% of the population.

Map labels:
DENMARK
SCHLESWIG-HOLSTEIN
New York 12½ days
Kobe 39 days (via Suez canal)
HAMBURG
Hamburg
BREMEN
NIEDERSACHSEN
NETHERLANDS
Rhine
NORDRHEIN WESTFALEN
Ruhr
London 1½ hours
New York 9 hours
Bonn
BELGIUM
HESSE
Frankfurt
EAST GERMANY
WEST BERLIN
RHEINLAND-PFALZ
Main
SAARLAND
FRANCE
CZECHOSLOVAKIA
FEDERAL REPUBLIC OF GERMANY
BAVARIA
Danube
BADEN-WURTTEMBERG
Munich
AUSTRIA
SWITZERLAND
Elbe

Routes to West Berlin
— Road
+—+ Rail
■ More than 1 million
● 250,000 – 1 million
• 100,000 – 250,000

expensive cars and high-quality consumer goods and take long holidays abroad. German cities, clean and affluent, are increasingly well-provided with cultural and leisure facilities.

Yet, as a generation grows up unable to remember the traumas of the war, new tensions are appearing. Young people, while enjoying the benefits of prosperity, are starting to reject their elders' comfortable, complacent politics. Liberal immigration policies have led to an influx of settlers from the Eastern bloc and parts of the Middle East and Far East, which has exacerbated the housing shortage in urban areas. Growing awareness of environmental issues focuses on the ravages of acid rain in Germany's forests. At the same time, Germans – sensitive to their warlike past – question the militarization of their country, and the large American military presence in particular. Support for environmental and antinuclear causes brought the Green Party into parliament for the first time in 1983 and ensured that these issues remain at the forefront of German concerns. Older Germans, meanwhile, are beginning to wonder whether political consensus has bred not stability but paralysis.

The smooth German economic engine has also begun to vibrate a little. True, inflation is typically low (although increasing), the trade surplus remains substantial and the Deutschmark is consistently strong. Yet economic growth ambled through the 1980s at less than 2% a year, as traditional industries ran into trouble because of high labour costs and low investment at home and cheap competition abroad. Another worry is the ageing, and diminishing, population and its ability to sustain prosperity. At the end of the century, 47 people will be of pensionable age for every 100 in work.

These worries seem less disturbing in the light of the continued success of much of German industry, its determination to stay in the vanguard of modern technology and its flexibility in responding to changing world markets. Growth may not be rapid but it is reassuringly steady. Moreover, West Germany is setting the pace in the EC on many environmental issues. The country's economic might will ensure that it retains a leading role in the Community after the creation of the single European market.

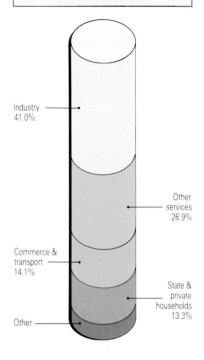

GDP BY ORIGIN

Industry 41.0%

Other services 26.9%

Commerce & transport 14.1%

State & private households 13.3%

Other

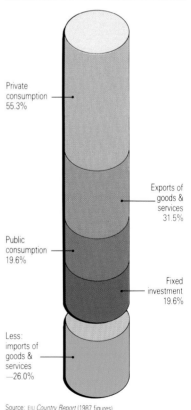

COMPONENTS OF GDP

Private consumption 55.3%

Exports of goods & services 31.5%

Public consumption 19.6%

Fixed investment 19.6%

Less: imports of goods & services —26.0%

Source: EIU *Country Report* (1987 figures)

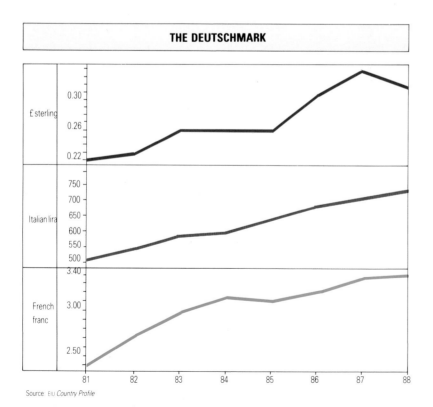

THE DEUTSCHMARK

£ sterling

0.30
0.26
0.22

Italian lira

750
700
650
600
550
500

French franc

3.40
3.00
2.50

81 82 83 84 85 86 87 88

Source: EIU *Country Profile*

IMPORTS AND EXPORTS

Agricultural products, food, drink & tobacco 13.7%
Chemicals 9.8%
Electrical engineering products 9.1%
Road vehicles 7.8%
Mechanical engineering products 5.8%
Crude oil & natural gas 5.5%
Other

	France		Austria
	Netherlands		Japan
	Italy		Spain
	USA		Sweden
	UK		Denmark
	Belgium/Luxembourg		USSR
	Switzerland		Other

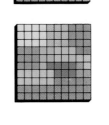

IMPORTS

EXPORTS

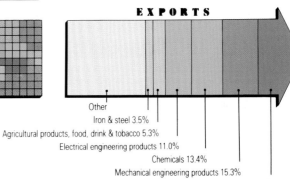

Other
Iron & steel 3.5%
Agricultural products, food, drink & tobacco 5.3%
Electrical engineering products 11.0%
Chemicals 13.4%
Mechanical engineering products 15.3%
Road vehicles 18.7%

Source: EIU *Country Report* (1987 figures)

WAGES AND PRICES

1980 = 100

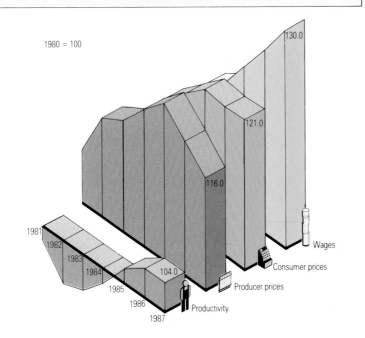

130.0
121.0
116.0
104.0

1981
1982
1983
1984
1985
1986
1987

Wages
Consumer prices
Producer prices
Productivity

Source: IMF *International Financial Statistics*

WORK FORCE

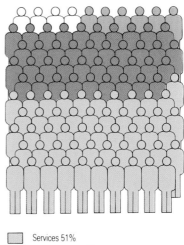

Services 51%
Manufacturing 41%
Construction 6%
Other

Source: EIU *Country Profile* (1987 figures)

SWITZERLAND & AUSTRIA

Neutrality

Switzerland's long tradition of neutrality was recognized internationally when its borders were fixed by treaty in 1815. Its state of "permanent neutrality" has kept it at peace ever since but the policy of not entering into alliances is leaving it ever more isolated in an increasingly integrated Europe. Although a founder member of Efta, Switzerland has made it clear its neutrality precludes membership of the EC.

Austria enshrined permanent neutrality in its constitution in 1955. Unlike Switzerland, it has used its neutral stance to act as a bridge between East and West and has taken a forthright stand on many world issues. Development of the single European market has also persuaded Austria to move towards membership of the EC.

The neutral status of Switzerland and Austria has made them popular sites for the headquarters of international organizations. Ten UN agencies, including the International Labour Organization, World Health Organization and High Commission for Refugees, are based in Geneva, as are the International Red Cross, General Agreement for Tariffs and Trade and European Free Trade Association. The Bank for International Settlements, the central banks' bank, has its headquarters in Basel. Vienna is home to the Organisation of Petroleum Exporting Countries, International Atomic Energy Agency and Industrial Development Organization, among others. Geneva has often been the site of sensitive political talks, including negotiations to end the Vietnam and Iran-Iraq wars.

Liechtenstein

The Principality of Liechtenstein lies on the foothills of the Alps and the floodplain of the Rhine between Austria and Switzerland, with which it has a postal and customs union. There is some industry, including machinery, precision instruments and dentistry, and postal stamps make up 7.5% of government income, but most revenue derives from its status as a company tax haven.

Liechtenstein is a constitutional democracy with a prince as head of state. Only two parties, the Progressive Citizens' Party and Fatherland Union, are represented in the 15-member Landtag or legislature. Referenda are called on all important issues. Diplomatic representation is via Switzerland, with which there are strong links.

Other Swiss Cantons

1	SCHAFFHAUSEN	8	NEUCHATEL
2	THURGAU	9	GLARUS
3	BASEL-LAND	10	NIDWALDEN
4	SOLOTHURN	11	OBWALDEN
5	APPENZELL-AUSSER RHODEN	12	FRIBOURG
6	APPENZELL-INNER RHODEN	13	URI
7	ZUG	14	GENEVA

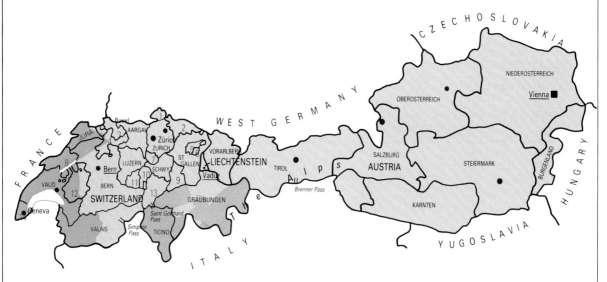

The Alps

Europe's principal mountain range, the Alps stretch in parallel chains for over 1,000km (625 miles) from northeast Italy to eastern Austria. The Alps are the source of many great European rivers, including the Rhine, Rhône and Po. Mont Blanc, at 4,807 metres (15,770 feet), is the highest peak. There are railway tunnels at Col de Fréjus, Lotschberg, Simplon and St Gotthard; major passes are at Mont Cenis, Simplon, St Bernard, Gemmi, St Gotthard, Splugen, Stilfserjoch and Brenner. These attract long-distance road traffic between Italy and the rest of Western Europe. The environmental damage caused has led to moves, particularly in Switzerland, to impose restrictions on lorries in transit.

Languages

The historic isolation of different communities in Switzerland's mountainous terrain is reflected in its linguistic divisions. Six of the 26 cantons are French-speaking, there is one Italian-speaking canton on the Italian border, one with a sizeable community that uses Romansch and the rest of the country speaks German.

German-speaking
French-speaking
Italian-speaking
Romansch-speaking
■ More than 1 million
● 250,000 – 1 million
• 100,000 – 250,000

SWITZERLAND

For more than 170 years, Switzerland has held itself aloof from the wars and diplomatic skirmishes that have washed around it. The Swiss are deeply proud of their neutrality – in a recent survey 87% of Swiss youth said it should be maintained in all circumstances – and it has made the confederation a haven for political refugees and a headquarters for international organizations.

Neutrality also left the Swiss free to make money in their own quiet, business-like way. The economy has become a model of steady prosperity, the richest in Europe in terms of income per head, and remarkably resilient in riding the ups and downs of world markets. Without natural resources, the Swiss have made the most of their human ones, using a skilled, highly paid work force to develop a diversified industrial base, famous for quality products. The sophisticated and secretive banking system is enabling Switzerland to remain an international financial centre through the wave of deregulation in the 1980s.

The country's business success owes much to a profound work ethic and a record of industrial harmony: a no-strike agreement with the largest trade union has lasted since 1937. Politically, Switzerland is as stable, or as immobile, as an alpine rock. Four parties – the Radicals, Christian Democrats, Social Democrats and Swiss People's Party – have run the country in harness along the same cautious lines since the late 1950s. Most of its citizens are apolitical or uninterested in change, despite a tradition of democracy in which local issues may be decided by a show of hands in the town square and national issues by referendum. Such is the depth of conservatism that women did not get the vote in national elections until 1971, and are still excluded from some local elections.

On the face of it, life is good. Unemployment is almost nonexistent, wages are high and Swiss towns display an affluence matched in few other countries. Swiss business continues to thrive, although it has been slow to exploit high-growth areas such as electronics and computers. But many young Swiss are disillusioned by their parents' bourgeois complacency and the lack of political change. The environment is becoming an issue and Green politics may be a force in future. The Swiss are under growing economic pressure to abandon their tradition of noninvolvement; but the commitment to neutrality is unlikely to be surrendered while the country continues to thrive and prosper.

OFFICIAL NAME Swiss Confederation.
CAPITAL CITY Berne.
GEOGRAPHY Landlocked and mountainous, Switzerland is the source of many of Europe's great rivers. The west is bounded by the Jura, a wooded limestone range with upland meadows, while the Alps – split by the Rhône and Rhine valleys – cover the southern half of the country. Most of the population live on the central plateau, the Mittelland, which runs from Lake Geneva in the southwest to Lake Constance in the northeast. *Highest point* Dufourspitze 4,634 metres (15,200 feet). *Area* 41,293 sq km (15,940 sq miles).
PEOPLE *Population* 6.5m. *Density* 157 per sq km. *Ethnic groups* Swiss 86%, Italian 4%, French 2%, Spanish 2%, West German 2%.
RELIGION RC 48%, Protestant 44%, Jewish 0.3%.
LANGUAGE German, French and Italian. Also Romansch.
EDUCATION Compulsory and free for ages 7–15. Education is administered at canton level and there are 26 different systems, with many private schools catering to overseas as well as Swiss students.
CLIMATE Wide variations: Atlantic in the west, Mediterranean in the south, continental in the east. Temperature varies with altitude. Annual rainfall over 1,000mm (39ins), except in dry pockets such as the Valais.
CURRENCY Swiss franc or franken (SFr).
PUBLIC HOLIDAYS (* some cantons only) Jan 1, Jan 2, Good Fri, Easter Mon, Ascension, Whit Mon, May 1*, Aug 1*, Dec 25, Dec 26.
GOVERNMENT Federal republic. The 20 cantons and 6 half-cantons have their own governments and legislatures. The federal assembly – a 46-member council of states and a 200-member national council – is elected by PR. Some cantons still have no female suffrage. The assembly appoints the federal council as an executive and a president as head of state for a 1-year term. Referenda are often used at both state and cantonal level.

IMPORTS AND EXPORTS

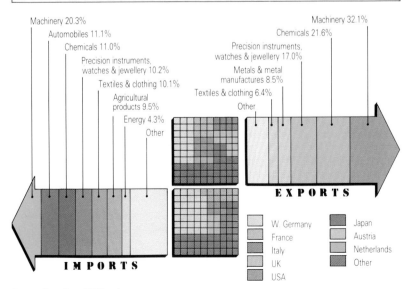

Machinery 20.3%
Automobiles 11.1%
Chemicals 11.0%
Precision instruments, watches & jewellery 10.2%
Textiles & clothing 10.1%
Agricultural products 9.5%
Energy 4.3%
Other

Machinery 32.1%
Chemicals 21.6%
Precision instruments, watches & jewellery 17.0%
Metals & metal manufactures 8.5%
Textiles & clothing 6.4%
Other

EXPORTS

IMPORTS

W. Germany
France
Italy
UK
USA
Japan
Austria
Netherlands
Other

Source: EIU *Country Report* (1937 figures)

COMPONENTS OF GDP

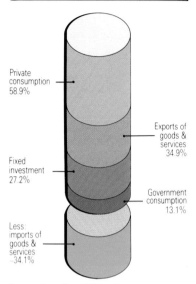

Private consumption 58.9%

Exports of goods & services 34.9%

Fixed investment 27.2%

Government consumption 13.1%

Less: imports of goods & services -34.1%

Source: EIU *Country Report* (1987 figures)

BALANCE OF PAYMENTS

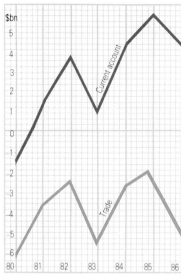

Current account

Trade

Source: EIU *International Economic Appraisal Service*

ECONOMIC PROFILE

Highly dependent on foreign trade: earns more than a third of GNP from exports; imports energy and more food per head than any other country. Economy mixed but traditionally strong in high-quality manufactured goods, especially precision instruments, machinery and chemicals, and in banking. Tourists also bring in foreign currency.

Growth Machinery and chemical industries benefiting from rationalization and shift towards specialized, high-technology products such as pharmaceuticals and medical equipment.

Problems Traditional exports such as textiles cut by acute labour shortages, high labour costs, currency fluctuations and changing world markets.

AUSTRIA

At the centre of the Austro-Hungarian empire until its dissolution in 1918, Austria was occupied by Nazi Germany in 1938; not until 1955, after 10 years of occupation by allied forces, did it formally regain its independence.

Austria's postwar reconstruction was almost as remarkable as that of West Germany, if on a smaller scale. Its success was due not least to the willingness of the partners in successive coalitions, the Socialist Party and Austrian People's Party, to play down ideological differences for the sake of social cohesion. About one-quarter of manufacturing industry was nationalized and, with generous government support, was a key factor in the consistent achievement of one of the highest growth rates in Europe.

But the success of state industry bred complacency; left largely to its own devices, it became cumbersome and inflexible, and the country is now paying for years in which it doled out subsidies, regardless of efficiency or profitability. The growth rate is among Europe's lowest and Austria is burdened with a chronic budget deficit and huge public debt.

The coalition has begun to tackle this problem with determination. For the state sector, it is a case of restructure or go under. Subsidies have been suspended and jobs trimmed. The success of an initially cautious privatization programme may yet lead the coalition, in which the Socialist Party is the senior partner, to seek to broaden the popular appeal of share ownership.

The policies have begun to bite, but much depends on the Austrian people's reactions to higher unemployment and reduced spending on the comprehensive social security system. Austrians are already aware that changes are needed to maintain prosperity after the establishment of the single European market: two-thirds of the country's trade is with the EC and there have been hints from the Community that associated countries will not enjoy the same trade advantages as full members after 1992. In March 1989 the Austrian government announced its intention to apply for EC membership but there is opposition both from within the EC and from critics at home who doubt Austria's readiness to withstand greater competition.

OFFICIAL NAME Republic of Austria.

CAPITAL CITY Vienna.

GEOGRAPHY Most of the country is alpine or sub-alpine, with heavily wooded mountains and hills cut by the valleys of fast-flowing rivers. The plains around Vienna and the valley of the Danube in the northeast are the only lowland areas, and contain most of the population. *Highest point* Grossglockner 3,798 metres (12,460 feet). *Area* 83,849 sq km (32,370 sq miles).

PEOPLE *Population* 7.5m. *Density* 90 per sq km. *Ethnic groups* Austrian 96%, Yugoslavian 2%, Turkish 1%.

RELIGION RC 89%, other Christian 8%, Muslim 1%.

LANGUAGE German.

EDUCATION Free and compulsory for ages 6–15. There are 6 universities and 14 specialist university colleges.

CLIMATE Varies with altitude: in lowlands, average monthly temperatures -1–20°C (34–68°F); above 3,000 metres (9,800 feet) -11–2°C (12–36°F). Annual rainfall up to 1,000mm (39ins) in west, less in east.

CURRENCY Schilling (Sch).

PUBLIC HOLIDAYS Jan 1, Jan 6, Easter Mon, May 1, Ascension, Whit Mon, Corpus Christi, Aug 15, Oct 26, Nov 1, Dec 8, Dec 25, Dec 26.

GOVERNMENT Federal republic consisting of 9 provinces. The federal assembly consists of a 183-member national council elected every 4 years by PR and a 63-member federal council elected by the provincial assemblies. The head of state, the president, is elected every 6 years by popular vote and is advised by a council of ministers, led by a chancellor.

ECONOMIC PROFILE

Manufacturing is economy's mainstay.
Agricultural production meets most food
needs, with some surplus for export.
Heavily dependent on Eastern Europe
for energy supplies; environmentalist
groups have delayed development of
hydroelectric resources and nuclear
power. Substantial foreign earnings from
tourism.

Growth Chemicals, electronics and
vehicles. Amendments to banking laws
have helped financial sector improve
profit margins.

Problems State-owned heavy industries –
textiles, steel, machinery – face declining
markets and sometimes painful
restructuring.

IMPORTS AND EXPORTS

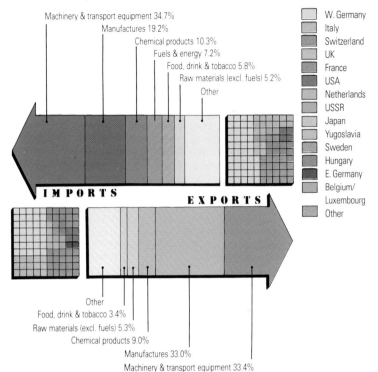

Machinery & transport equipment 34.7%
Manufactures 19.2%
Chemical products 10.3%
Fuels & energy 7.2%
Food, drink & tobacco 5.8%
Raw materials (excl. fuels) 5.2%
Other

IMPORTS

EXPORTS

Other
Food, drink & tobacco 3.4%
Raw materials (excl. fuels) 5.3%
Chemical products 9.0%
Manufactures 33.0%
Machinery & transport equipment 33.4%

W. Germany
Italy
Switzerland
UK
France
USA
Netherlands
USSR
Japan
Yugoslavia
Sweden
Hungary
E. Germany
Belgium/
Luxembourg
Other

Source: EIU *Country Report* (1987 figures)

BALANCE OF PAYMENTS

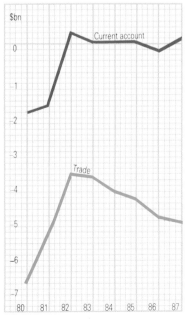

$bn

Current account

Trade

80 81 82 83 84 85 86 87

Source: EIU *International Economic Appraisal Service*

GDP BY ORIGIN

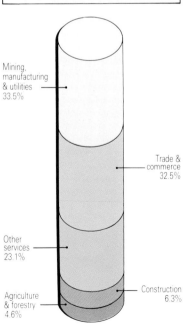

Mining,
manufacturing
& utilities
33.5%

Trade &
commerce
32.5%

Other
services
23.1%

Construction
6.3%

Agriculture
& forestry
4.6%

Source: EIU *Country Report* (1987 figures)

COMPONENTS OF GDP

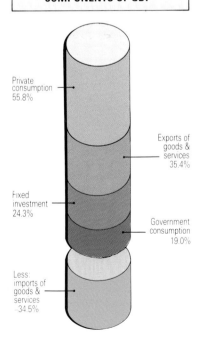

Private
consumption
55.8%

Exports of
goods &
services
35.4%

Fixed
investment
24.3%

Government
consumption
19.0%

Less:
imports of
goods &
services
–34.5%

ITALY

The home of one of Europe's oldest civilizations, Italy is also one of its newest nations. It has been politically united only since 1870, and city or region is still the primary unit of allegiance for many. Its people rank among the most prosperous in the world, yet there is an acute disparity between the wealthy industrial north and the poor, less developed south.

The paradoxes and contradictions do not end there. Its business people are among Europe's most adaptable and entrepreneurial, and its engineers and designers among Europe's most inventive, but it is saddled with a chronically inefficient bureaucracy and public sector. It is a major industrial power, ranking alongside the UK and France, but its governments lurch from crisis to crisis, unable to cope with a growing national debt and chaotic public finances.

Italy emerged from World War II with its economy in ruins and its political leaders in disgrace after two decades of fascism and Mussolini's alliance with Hitler. The discredited monarchy – which first collaborated with Mussolini, then helped to overthrow him – was abolished by popular referendum in 1946. The new republic's constitution was drawn up two years later, a compromise between the competing forces of liberalism, socialism and Christian Democracy. The first elections for the chamber of deputies that year brought a government dominated by the Christian Democrats to power; the Communists and Socialists were consigned to opposition.

The pattern of political power since has changed little. The Christian Democrats have remained the largest party, followed by the Communists; but the Communists have been excluded from government. The Christian Democrats have dominated all postwar governments, even if the loss of their absolute majority after 1953 forced them to govern with the help of smaller centre parties – the Liberals, Republicans and Social Democrats – and to allow the Socialists into the fold since the mid-1960s.

But coalitions have not delivered stability. Between 1945 and 1988 there were some 50 different governments; some lasted a few years, many only a matter of weeks. Not only has each government been formed from between three and five political parties but the major parties are themselves coalitions of competing factions. The Christian Democrats form a precariously balanced

OFFICIAL NAME Italian Republic.

CAPITAL CITY Rome.

GEOGRAPHY Much of Italy is upland, with the Alps in the north and the limestone Apennines making up the spine of the country and extending into Sicily. Earthquakes are common in southern and central regions, and there are active volcanoes in Sicily and on the Bay of Naples. The most important lowland area is the valley of the Po, containing the industrial centres of Turin and Milan. *Highest point* Mont Blanc 4,810 metres (15,780 feet). *Area* 301,225 sq km (116,300 sq miles).

PEOPLE *Population* 57.1m. *Density* 190 per sq km. *Ethnic groups* Italian 98%.

RELIGION RC 83%.

LANGUAGE Italian.

EDUCATION Free and compulsory for ages 6–14.

CLIMATE Temperate in the north, Mediterranean in the south and centre, with mild winters and long dry summers. Average temperatures around 25°C (77°F) in summer, 8°C (46°F) in winter, with local variations according to altitude.

CURRENCY Lira (L).

PUBLIC HOLIDAYS Jan 1, Jan 6, Easter Mon, Apr 25, May 1, May 12, Aug 15, Nov 1, Nov 6, Dec 8, Dec 25, Dec 26.

GOVERNMENT Republic since 1946. Italy has 20 regions, with varying degrees of autonomy. The head of state, the president of the republic, is elected for 7 years by a college of parliament and regional representatives. Parliament has 2 chambers, the 630-member chamber of deputies and the 315-member regional senate, both elected by PR; the 2 chambers have equal powers. The chief executive is a council of ministers, whose leader is known as president of the council.

IMPORTS AND EXPORTS

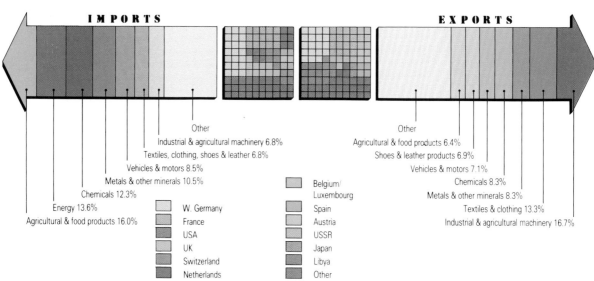

Other
Industrial & agricultural machinery 6.8%
Textiles, clothing, shoes & leather 6.8%
Vehicles & motors 8.5%
Metals & other minerals 10.5%
Chemicals 12.3%
Energy 13.6%
Agricultural & food products 16.0%

Other
Agricultural & food products 6.4%
Shoes & leather products 6.9%
Vehicles & motors 7.1%
Chemicals 8.3%
Metals & other minerals 8.3%
Textiles & clothing 13.3%
Industrial & agricultural machinery 16.7%

W. Germany
France
USA
UK
Switzerland
Netherlands

Belgium/Luxembourg
Spain
Austria
USSR
Japan
Libya
Other

Source: EIU *Country Report* (1987 figures)

The black economy

Italy has long been famous for its *economia sommersa*; estimates of the black economy's contribution to GDP range from 10% to 50%. One study found that 54% of civil servants had second jobs, 33% sold goods within their ministries and 27% ran other businesses during working hours. The hidden economy boomed during the 1970s thanks to a combination of rigid labour laws and high taxes at a time when the official economy was in trouble. In 1987 a revision of government statistics to bring some informal economic activity into the official figures added 18% to estimates of national income at a stroke.

The regions

Italy's 20 regions have considerable autonomy, with powers over health, education and the police, although revenue comes from the central government as they cannot levy taxes. Each region has a legislative council, elected every five years. Five older regions have more autonomy than the rest: the two large islands, Sicily and Sardinia, French-speaking Valle D'Aosta, Trentino-Alto Adige, with its large German-speaking population, and Friuli-Venezia Giulia.

Differences between the regions reflect the country's north-south divide. The eight southern regions, the *mezzogiorno*, cover 40% of the land area, contain 35% of the population but account for only about 25% of GDP. Even here there are wide disparities, with Calabria and Sardinia lagging far behind more developed regions such as Apulia. About a third of the work force in parts of the south is still engaged in agriculture, compared with only 4% in Lombardy, the most densely populated region, which alone is responsible for one-third of the country's total GDP and 30% of exports.

San Marino

Tourism accounts for 60% of revenue for this small, landlocked republic within Italy, and postage stamp sales for a further 10%. There is also some agriculture and light industry. The lack of customs restrictions makes San Marino an outlet for the illegal export of Italian currency and avoidance of value-added tax.

Vatican

An enclave in Rome, seat of the Holy See of the Roman Catholic church, the Vatican is sustained entirely by investment income and voluntary contribution. With a total area of less than 1 sq km it is the smallest nation in the world, as well as the only one where Latin is an official language.

Energy

Italy is more dependent on imported energy than any other European country, meeting only 20% of its needs from domestic sources, primarily natural gas. The oil price shocks of the 1970s encouraged diversification to reduce vulnerability although oil still accounts for about 60% of demand. Algeria, for example, is a major supplier of natural gas, through the Transmed pipeline from Tunisia to Sicily, although Italy also plans to increase gas purchases from the Soviet Union, piped through Austria. Electricity is imported from France, Switzerland, Austria and Yugoslavia.

■ More than 1 million
● 250,000 – 1 million
· 100,000 – 250,000
▨ The mezzogiorno

federation led by warring political barons. Small wonder, then, that governments are so fragile.

In the absence of any real transfer of power, Italy's is a badly flawed democracy. Corruption has become endemic in a system in which Christian Democrat parliamentary dominance is complemented by a vast and complex network of patronage. Other parties, particularly the Socialists, have followed suit, making the contest for political appointments as important as that for electoral success. Linked to instability, this is perhaps the major problem of Italian government, one which constantly obstructs attempts at reform, whether of the institutions of government itself or of the vast and sprawling public sector.

Italy's economy has developed regardless of these and other handicaps, including a paucity of natural resources and a dependence on imported raw materials and fuels second only to that of Japan among major industrial nations. Output doubled during the economic miracle of the 1950s and 1960s; by the 1970s income per head was approaching that of Italy's wealthier neighbours. Taking into account a massive black economy – estimated at 10–50% of GDP – the Italians were by 1987 claiming that they had overtaken the UK to become the world's fifth largest industrial power. Italy had become one of the most dynamic exporting nations in the OECD and the names of Italian companies such as Fiat and Olivetti had gained global recognition.

The decades since the war have seen a major social, economic and demographic upheaval as Italy has been transformed by massive migration into an urbanized, industrial society; but the impact of growth remains unbalanced. The south is still poor and relatively undeveloped, with an inadequate infrastructure, although its problems have been alleviated by state investment. In the late 1980s, the south's unemployment rate was over 20%, almost three times that of the more prosperous north. Its image remains tarnished by the power and influence of organized crime: the Sicilian Mafia and the Neapolitan Camorra still undermine social and political order.

The south is more traditional than the urbanized north, but everywhere the transformation of social attitudes has been profound. Sexual mores have been revolutionized since the 1960s; despite the opposition of the Roman Catholic church, abortion and contraception are widely accepted and practised. However, the divorce rate remains low, despite its approval by more than 60% of the population in a 1974 referendum.

More generally, modernization has been incomplete and often very costly. An alienated work force was one of the prices paid for the rapidity with which many Italians were transferred from agricultural to industrial labour in the

ECONOMIC PROFILE

Economic growth led by manufacturing; export strengths lie mainly in medium- and low-tech products – industrial and office equipment, domestic appliances, vehicles, textiles, clothing, chemicals. Agriculture accounts for only 5% of GDP, producing mainly wheat, maize, rice, olives, wine and citrus fruit.

Growth White goods now account for third of European sales. Fiat vies with Audi/vw for leadership of European car market. Machine tools industry overtook USA in terms of total sales in 1988. Textiles and clothing moving successfully upmarket.

Problems Highly reliant on imported mineral and energy supplies, a dependence likely to increase following rejection of nuclear power programme by popular referendum; also on food imports. Some traditional products – steel, textiles, clothing – suffering from Asian competition. Financial system remains fragmented; small, regionally based banks will have to merge to compete after 1992.

COMPONENTS OF GDP

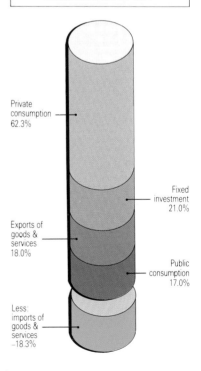

Private consumption 62.3%

Fixed investment 21.0%

Exports of goods & services 18.0%

Public consumption 17.0%

Less: imports of goods & services –18.3%

BALANCE OF PAYMENTS

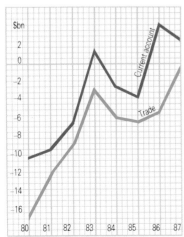

$bn

Current account

Trade

Source: EIU *International Economic Appraisal Service*

GDP BY ORIGIN

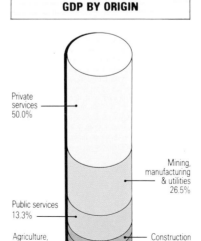

Private services 50.0%

Mining, manufacturing & utilities 26.5%

Public services 13.3%

Agriculture, forestry & fishing 4.6%

Construction 5.6%

Source: EIU *Country Report* (1987 figures)

1950s and 1960s. Urban terrorism, from both left and right, has been one of the consequences of Italy's blocked democracy, though it has subsided since reaching a peak in the 1970s.

Italy's institutional development has failed to keep pace with that of its economy: unstable governments, a politicized bureaucracy and a public debt equal to annual GDP in the late 1980s are the major impediments to success in the more competitive context of the single European market. The 1990s will show whether the flexibility of Italian private industry, which has shown an enviable ability to recognize and exploit new opportunities, is sufficient to overcome these handicaps.

WORK FORCE

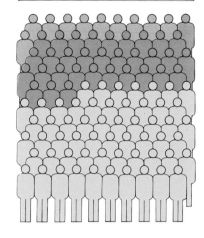

☐ Services 57%
☐ Industry, including construction 32%
☐ Agriculture, forestry & fishing 10%
☐ Other

Source: EIU *Country Profile* (1987 figures)

WAGES AND PRICES

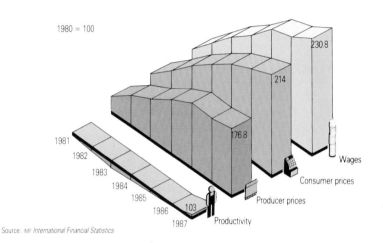

1980 = 100

230.8
214
176.8
103

1981
1982
1983
1984
1985
1986
1987

Wages
Consumer prices
Producer prices
Productivity

Source: IMF *International Financial Statistics*

MALTA

The 1970s and 1980s have been a period of reorientation for Malta. Under the Labour Party, led by Dom Mintoff, in power for 16 years until its narrow electoral defeat by the Nationalist Party in 1987, the islands withdrew from the close colonial relationship with the UK. A new position of nonalignment allowed improved relations with the USSR and Libya; the latter supplied Malta with cheap crude oil, although the two countries fell out for a time in the early 1980s over a maritime boundary dispute, settled in 1987 in Libya's favour.

The final departure of British forces in 1979 lost Malta a major source of income and hastened economic restructuring. Former naval dockyards became the centre of a ship-repair industry. The Nationalist Party, led by Prime Minister Eddie Fenech Adami, has pledged to reduce state involvement in the economy and liberalize trade; construction of a container port is intended to strengthen Malta's role as a transshipment point, and there are plans to promote Malta as an offshore business centre. It has also announced its intention of applying for membership of the EC which, despite attempts to find new markets, accounts for some 70% of Malta's exports. In the meantime, light industry – notably textiles and clothing, food, tobacco and beverages, and electrical and electronic machinery – remains, with tourism, the mainstay of the economy.

OFFICIAL NAME Republic of Malta.
CAPITAL CITY Valletta.
GEOGRAPHY The limestone archipelago lies 93km south of Sicily and 200km north of Libya. Only Malta, Gozo and Comino are inhabited. Malta's rugged north and west coasts give way to good deep harbours on the east. There are few streams and no permanent lakes. *Highest point* 249 metres (820 feet). *Area* 316 sq km (120 sq miles).
PEOPLE *Population* 380,000. *Density* 1,212 per sq km. *Ethnic groups* Maltese 96%, British 2%.
RELIGION RC 97%, Anglican 1%.
LANGUAGE Maltese and English. Also Italian.
EDUCATION Free and compulsory for ages 5–16. There is 1 university.
CLIMATE Mediterranean, with average annual temperature of 18°C (64°F), around 25°C (77°F) in summer. Annual rainfall 560mm (22ins), most falling in winter.
CURRENCY Maltese lira (ML).
PUBLIC HOLIDAYS Jan 1, Mar 31, Good Fri, May 1, Aug 15, Dec 13, Dec 25.
GOVERNMENT Independent since 1964, republic since 1974. The 65-member legislature, the house of representatives, is elected every 5 years by a form of PR. The house elects a president as head of state and he appoints, on advice, the prime minister and the cabinet.

SPAIN

Spain is an old country that feels young. The death of the dictator General Franco in 1975 and the restoration of the monarchy in the person of his chosen. successor as head of state, King Juan Carlos, gave a new lease of life to a nation traditionally among the most backward and reactionary in Europe. The years since have witnessed sweeping political changes, numerous social reforms and, most recently, rapid economic development.

Once described as a land of oases and deserts, Spain is the second largest country in Europe in size but only the fifth largest in terms of population; and a strikingly large proportion of its people live in provincial capitals and a handful of other industrial and commercial centres. This has been particularly true since the mid-1930s, when large-scale migration from the countryside to the towns began, a trend which also increased yet further the number of Spaniards living on the coasts and in the largest river valleys, the Ebro and Guadalquivir. The principal exception to this rule is Madrid, the capital arbitrarily chosen in the 16th century by King Philip II. Under General Franco, Madrid grew from a purely administrative capital into an industrial and business centre.

Spain is also an unusually varied country, in both its landscapes and its people. The province of Almeria contains Europe's only desert; Cantabria has snow-capped peaks and mountain valleys. The flamboyant Andalusian is as Spanish as the sober Castilian. Almost a quarter of the population speak languages other than Castilian Spanish, including Basque, Europe's only pre-Indo-European language, Catalan and Galician. Their survival has further reinforced the strong regional feelings that have been characteristic of Spaniards for centuries. Historically, these have their roots in the invasion of Spain and the destruction of the Visigothic kingdom by Muslim invaders in the early 8th century. The reconquest of the country, culminating in the overthrow of the kingdom of Granada in 1492, was accomplished by a number of Christian states acting, for the most part, independently and evolving distinctive cultures and institutions.

OFFICIAL NAME Kingdom of Spain.
CAPITAL CITY Madrid.
GEOGRAPHY The centre of Spain is a wide semi-arid plateau, the Meseta, bounded on the north and east by mountains and cut by a central range. The most extensive lowlands are in the northeast around the valley of the Ebro, on the east coast around Valencia and in the south around the valley of the Guadalquivir. *Highest point* (mainland) Mulhacén 3,478 metres (11,410 feet). *Area* 504,782 sq km (194,900 sq miles).
PEOPLE *Population* 38.6m. *Density* 76 per sq km. *Ethnic groups* Spanish 73%, Catalan 16%, Galician 8%, Basque 2%.
RELIGION RC 97%.
LANGUAGE Spanish (Castilian). Also Catalan, Galician, Basque, Andalusian.
EDUCATION Free and compulsory for ages 6–14. More than 30% of pupils are in private, mainly RC, schools, subsidized by the state. There are 33 universities.
CLIMATE Temperate in the north, 9–18°C (48–64°F), with annual rainfall of over 1,000mm (39ins). More extreme in the centre, with hot, dry summers and cold winters; average temperatures 24°C (26°F) in July, 5°C (41°F) in Jan. Mediterranean in south.
CURRENCY Peseta (Pta).
PUBLIC HOLIDAYS (* not all areas) Jan 1, Jan 6, Maundy Thu*, Good Fri, Easter Mon*, May 1, May 15*, Corpus Christi, Jun 24, Jul 25, Aug 15, Oct 12*, Nov 1, Dec 6, Dec 8*, Dec 25, Dec 26*.
GOVERNMENT Parliamentary monarchy. The king has more influence than most constitutional monarchs. The legislature, the Cortes, has a 350-member congress of deputies elected for a 4-year term, and a senate with 208 directly elected members and 49 regional representatives.

IMPORTS AND EXPORTS

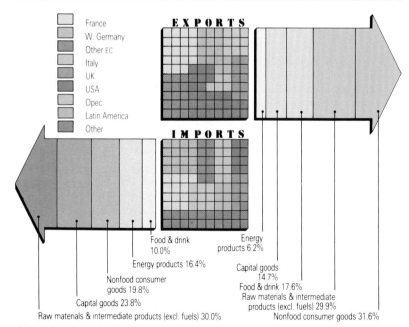

France
W. Germany
Other EC
Italy
UK
USA
Opec
Latin America
Other

EXPORTS

IMPORTS

Food & drink 10.0%
Energy products 16.4%
Nonfood consumer goods 19.8%
Capital goods 23.8%
Raw materials & intermediate products (excl. fuels) 30.0%

Energy products 6.2%
Capital goods 14.7%
Food & drink 17.6%
Raw materials & intermediate products (excl. fuels) 29.9%
Nonfood consumer goods 31.6%

Source: EIU *Country Report* (1987 figures)

BALANCE OF PAYMENTS

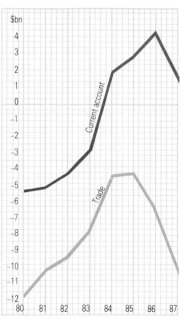

Source: EIU *International Economic Appraisal Service*

Unification of the country in the 16th century was achieved only by restoring to the regions privileges that it had taken centuries to eliminate; some survive still. Local resentment of central government, which evolved during the last century into nationalist sentiment in the Basque country, Catalonia and Galicia, is still a source of friction. Its most violent manifestation is in the Basque guerrilla movement, Eta. Elsewhere, however, the thirst for self-rule has been largely slaked by the devolution of substantial powers to regional governments in the 1978 constitution.

That constitution marked the culmination of a sometimes tense transition from dictatorship to democracy. It did not, however, prevent a backlash. In 1981, a civil guard officer, Lieutenant Colonel Antonio Tejero, led an assault on the lower house of parliament that formed part of a much broader, but abortive, coup attempt by officers who regarded the reform of Franco's institutions as a betrayal.

Under the socialist government of Felipe Gonzalez, which took power the following year, the threat of military intervention evaporated as it became clear that Spain's commitment to democracy was permanent. In 1986, Spain joined the EC and later that year confirmed in a referendum its membership of Nato, which it had joined in 1982, although it has remained outside Nato's military structure.

The early years of socialist rule also saw sweeping rationalization of the economy, in particular of older industries. This, together with the boost provided by EC membership, brought an abrupt end to a longer and tougher recession than that endured by almost any other advanced Western nation. In 1987, Spain grew faster than any other state in the EC.

The unresolved challenge is how to provide Spain with a social structure and amenities more in keeping with its political maturity and economic development. During the early years of the monarchy many Spanish institutions were modernized, divorce was reintroduced and a limited abortion law was passed. But health and social services, schools and universities and the legal system are, in parts, chaotic. The level of unemployment is the highest in the EC; the youth unemployment rate is above 40%. Social effects are acute because provision of welfare benefits is well below the standard considered a minimum elsewhere in Europe. Reform lost momentum after the early years of socialist rule. The almost total support for a national one-day strike in 1988 – Spain's first for more than half a century – owed much to public discontent with the government's performance in this area.

Nevertheless, Spaniards can – and usually do – look to the future with hope. In their case, there is a specific date on which to fix: 1992. It will mark the completion of the transition period of Spain's EC membership, coinciding with the planned introduction of the single European market. Spain will also host the Olympic Games in Barcelona and Expo '92 in Seville. And it will be the 500th anniversary of the discovery of America.

GDP BY ORIGIN

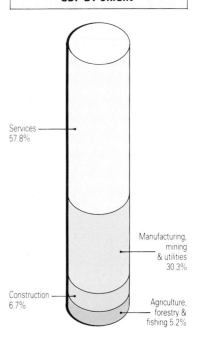

Services 57.8%

Manufacturing, mining & utilities 30.3%

Construction 6.7%

Agriculture, forestry & fishing 5.2%

COMPONENTS OF GDP

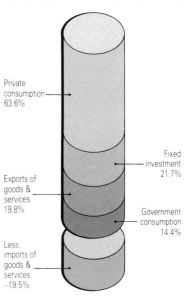

Private consumption 63.6%

Fixed investment 21.7%

Exports of goods & services 19.8%

Government consumption 14.4%

Less: imports of goods & services –19.5%

Source: EIU *Country Report* (1987 figures)

ECONOMIC PROFILE

Services, except for tourism, less important than in most other EC countries. Composition of GDP stable; major changes within sectors. Industrial reconversion programme begun in early 1980s. Agricultural sector still substantial, increasingly specializing in high-value products for exports. Spain is the world's prime tourist destination; tourism income helps balance persisting trade deficit.

Growth Surge of investment in industry since EC membership; expanding sectors include transport equipment, electrical machinery. Tourism revenue increasing. Fruit and vegetable exports growing fast.

Problems Heavily dependent on imported oil. Steel, shipbuilding, chemicals and light engineering have contracted in the 1980s.

THE IBERIAN PENINSULA

The Basque country

The Basques, who speak Europe's only surviving pre-Indo-European language, remained largely independent, living in parts of southern France and northern Spain, until the 19th century. The Basque separatist movement, Euscadi ta Askatasuna (Eta), has been active in Spain since the late 1960s; more than 600 people have died as a result of its actions. An extradition agreement reached with France in 1984 has led to the capture of many Eta leaders.

Andorra

The Principality of Andorra is a land-locked enclave in the Pyrénées under the joint sovereignty of France and Spain. Agriculture and tourism are the main occupations of the population, though low taxes have made it a centre of international finance and duty-free trading.

Gibraltar

An awkward relic of empire, Gibraltar is a continuing irritant in relations between Spain and the UK. The Rock has been a British colony since 1713 and the 20,000 native Gibraltarians are determined that it will remain one. The British government has repeatedly reassured them that there will be no change in the colony's status without their consent, despite the reduction in the British military presence and the closure of the naval dockyard. The opening of the border with Spain in 1985 has brought significant benefits, however, giving the tourist industry a boost and helping to end labour shortages. Further potential lies in the development of an offshore financial centre and expansion of the port.

Balearic Islands

Five large islands, including Mallorca, Menorca and Ibiza, and 11 islets form the Baleares autonomous region. The economy is based on agriculture, fishing and tourism.

Tourism

Tourism has been Spain's major growth industry in the past two decades: by the mid-1980s it had become the most popular destination in the world, with arrivals exceeding 50m for the first time in 1987, bringing in around $13bn in foreign exchange. Most visitors go to the beaches of the Costa Brava in Catalonia and Costa del Sol in Andalucia and the Canary and Balearic islands, but the historical and cultural attractions of the cities of the interior are being heavily promoted. The vast majority of tourists come from other European countries, led by France, Portugal, the UK and West Germany, but efforts to attract visitors from elsewhere focus on 1992 when Barcelona hosts the Olympic Games and the Seville Expo marks the 500th anniversary of Columbus's voyage to the New World.

Portugal's tourist industry is on a much smaller scale, with around 12m visitors a year, more than half of them day-trippers from Spain, but it is growing rapidly. The Algarve region in the south is the most popular destination, especially with visitors from northern Europe.

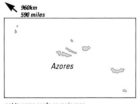

The Azores and Madeira

Two groups of volcanic islands in the eastern Atlantic, the Azores and Madeira have been Portuguese colonies since their discovery in the 15th century. None of the islands had an indigenous population. Their colonists have relied on agriculture, fishing and, more recently, tourism. Since 1976 the two archipelagos have been autonomous regions within the Portuguese republic, with their own assemblies.

Canary Islands

An archipelago of seven large and numerous small islands off the Moroccan coast, the Canaries have been under Spanish rule since 1479. Agriculture and tourism are the main sources of income and employment. The islands belong to the EC, but do not participate in its common agricultural policy or customs union.

PORTUGAL

Entry into the EC in 1986 let a strong, cold wind into the musty anteroom that Portugal had inhabited since it was temporarily absorbed into Spain in 1580. It will take more than a few years to alter mental attitudes inculcated by centuries of disillusion; but the fear of being overrun by foreign interests and, more positively, the example set by other countries, are spurring changes.

Politically, Portugal has made enormous strides since the Salazar era ended in 1974. The church and the army, bastions of the dictatorship, have lost almost all their influence. However, political parties have so far failed to evolve identities independent of the personalities of their leaders.

Membership of the EC has provided a substantial jolt to an economy that has relied heavily on protectionist measures. Portugal is moving to complete integration into the Community by the mid-1990s and this is no easy matter for the poorest EC member, where GDP per head is only half that of neighbouring Spain. In the mid-1980s a fifth of Portugal's work force was employed in agriculture, and one in six households had no electricity. This backwardness is a legacy of the long years of dictatorship, when private entrepreneurs were discouraged and both human resources and the physical infrastructure were neglected. The brief period of revolutionary fervour after the 1974 coup made matters worse. A quarter of the economy was nationalized and resources were pumped into building up white elephants in heavy industries such as steel, shipbuilding and oil refining. Political squabbles and instability absorbed the country's attention, leaving fundamental imbalances largely uncorrected.

These problems are now being faced following the marked electoral success in 1987 of the aggressive right-wing economist, Aníbal Cavaco Silva, whose conservative Social Democrats won over half the vote and an absolute majority in parliament. Liberalization is removing the dead hand of the state from much of the economy, while Community initiatives and grants are stimulating investment. Foreign firms are attracted to an EC member with exceptionally low labour costs. Social expectations have been raised, putting greater pressures on government. The main economic challenge lies in moving production from low valued-added areas, where competition is becoming too fierce, to specialist niches. The national debt is over $17bn; the repayments keep the budget deficit high. But in the new mood of optimism such obstacles are no longer regarded as insurmountable.

OFFICIAL NAME Portuguese Republic.

CAPITAL CITY Lisbon.

GEOGRAPHY The River Tagus splits Portugal into 2 zones. To the north, 90% of the land is over 400 metres, with most of the population in low, sheltered east–west valleys cut through plateaus and mountains. To the south, there are rolling lowlands. Much of the country is forested; soil is generally poor and droughts common. The coast is marked by capes and sandbars, with few good harbours. *Highest point* Estrela 1,993 metres (6,540 feet). *Area* 92,072 sq km (35,550 sq miles).

PEOPLE *Population* 10.3m. *Density* 111 per sq km. *Ethnic groups* Portuguese 99%.

RELIGION RC 95%, Protestant 1%.

LANGUAGE Portuguese.

EDUCATION Free and officially compulsory for 9 years, to be taken between ages 6 and 15; secondary education attendance well below EC average.

CLIMATE Mild and wet in winter, warm and dry in summer, with droughts in south. Rainfall highest in north, over 1,000mm (39ins) a year; around 700mm (27ins) in Lisbon. Average temperatures range from 7°C (45°F) in north in Jan to around 20°C (68°F) in south in Aug.

CURRENCY Escudo (Esc).

PUBLIC HOLIDAYS Jan 1, Shrove Tue, Good Fri, Apr 25, May 1, Corpus Christi, Jun 10, Jun 13 (Lisbon), Jun 24 (Oporto), Aug 15, Oct 5, Nov 1, Dec 1, Dec 8, Dec 25.

GOVERNMENT Republic. The head of state is the president, elected for a 5-year term by majority popular vote. The 250-member assembly of the republic is elected for a 4-year term. The president appoints the leader of the majority party in the assembly as prime minister and also, on his recommendation, the council of ministers. Madeira and the Azores have been autonomous units within the republic since 1976.

ECONOMIC PROFILE

Traditional export-oriented businesses such as textiles and tourism are the mainstays. High level of imports, including three-fifths of food, most machinery and transport equipment and all oil. Remittances from migrant workers help to bridge trade deficit.

Growth Paper companies and automotive and electrical component affiliates expanding fast. Services sector being modernized, with much of the impetus coming from foreign banks and retailing concerns providing impetus for modernization. Tourism booming.

Problems Heavy industry – steel, chemicals, oil refining – uncompetitive in world markets, as are many traditional small-scale manufacturing and retailing companies.

IMPORTS AND EXPORTS

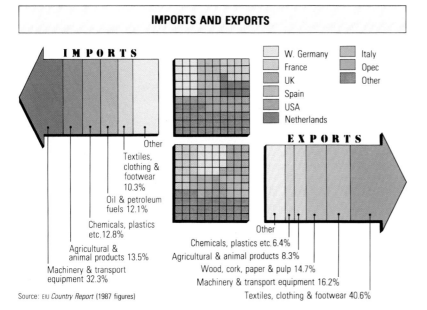

IMPORTS

W. Germany · France · UK · Spain · USA · Netherlands · Italy · Opec · Other

Other

Textiles, clothing & footwear 10.3%

Oil & petroleum fuels 12.1%

Chemicals, plastics etc. 12.8%

Agricultural & animal products 13.5%

Machinery & transport equipment 32.3%

EXPORTS

Other

Chemicals, plastics etc. 6.4%

Agricultural & animal products 8.3%

Wood, cork, paper & pulp 14.7%

Machinery & transport equipment 16.2%

Textiles, clothing & footwear 40.6%

Source: EIU *Country Report* (1987 figures)

GREECE, TURKEY & CYPRUS

The Kurds

Kurdish speakers make up some 14% of Turkey's total population and are in a majority in eight southeastern provinces flanking Syria, Iran and Iraq. However, the Kurds are not officially recognized as a separate ethnic group and it is illegal to speak Kurdish.

The separatist Workers' Party of Kurdistan (the PKK) supports the creation of a Kurdish national homeland within Turkey and is engaged in a violent guerrilla campaign against the Turkish authorities. The lifting of martial law imposed in 1979 and its replacement by a state of emergency under a district governor was designed to reduce tensions. However, continuing army repression, the economic backwardness of the south eastern regions and an underlying clash between the secular Turkish state tradition and Islamic fundamentalism ensure that support for the PKK persists.

Tourism

Greece has been one of Europe's most popular destinations since the 1960s. The number of visitors has continued to expand – to around 7.5m a year – but the amount spent by each has declined. The average American visitor is estimated to spend three times as much as the typical European but American tourists have been discouraged by security scares in recent years.

As Greek tourist resorts near saturation point, the country is losing business to Turkey, which has been one of the fastest-growing tourist destinations in the 1980s, with receipts exceeding $16m for the first time in 1985. Most of the 2.5m tourists visiting each year have come from Western Europe, but the government is also trying to attract visitors from the Middle East.

The Dardanelles and Bosporus

The straits separating European and Asiatic Turkey have long been of strategic significance. The Dardanelles (Turkish name Canakkale Bogazi) linking the Aegean Sea with the Sea of Marmara are 65km (40 miles) long and 1.6km (1 mile) wide at their narrowest point. The Bosporus (Istanbul Bogazi), from the Sea of Marmara to the Black Sea, is 32km (20 miles) long and narrows to only 640m (2,100 feet). The Bosporus is spanned at Istanbul by two suspension bridges; a third is planned.

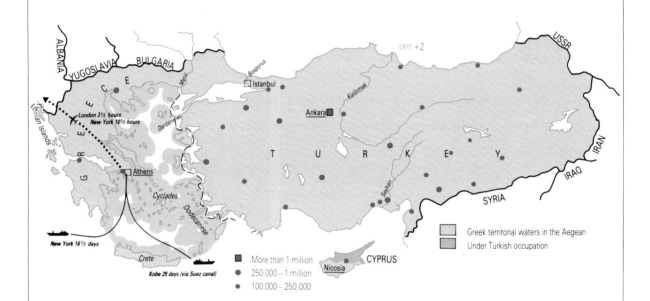

Greek territorial waters in the Aegean

Under Turkish occupation

More than 1 million

250,000 – 1 million

100,000 – 250,000

The Aegean

The territorial dispute between Greece and Turkey over the Aegean Sea centres on two issues: the continental shelf and airspace. Turkey does not claim Greek islands in the Aegean close to its coast, but does claim half the continental shelf, partly for its mineral resources, partly for security reasons. This runs counter to Greece's desire to extend its territorial waters to a 12-mile limit, which would bring the area it controls within a few kilometres of the Turkish coast in places and block Turkey's access to international waters. The question of airspace follows on from this issue: the extent of national airspace is defined in international law as being the same as that of territorial waters.

Both countries depend heavily on the USA for military aid. The USA maintains bases in both countries in exchange for military assistance, provided in a 7:10 ratio to allow Greece, with a smaller standing army, to achieve a balance of power.

Divided island

Cyprus's 1960 constitution provided for a Greek president and Turkish vice-president, and a council of ministers containing seven Greeks and three Turks. Tension between the two communities came to a head in 1963, after President Makarios declared his intention of revising the constitution; since then, the Turkish community has not participated in government. The coup that overthrew Archbishop Makarios in 1974 was swiftly followed by the Turkish invasion and effective partition of the island. The Turkish north unilaterally declared independence in 1983 as the Turkish Republic of North Cyprus, so far recognized only by Turkey. Each community has its own president, ministers, judiciary and education system.

Cleaning up the Mediterranean

All but one (Albania) of the 18 Mediterranean countries signed the Barcelona convention in 1976, setting aside national rivalries in a concerted effort to combat pollution. Further agreements followed on cleaning up discharges of sewage, industrial waste and agricultural pesticides; marine reserves have been designated to protect wildlife. Over 80 marine laboratories carry out long-term monitoring of pollution. The programme has made considerable progress: by the late 1980s, four out of five Mediterranean beaches were regarded as being safe for swimmers. But the migration every summer of 100m tourists to shores where 130m people already live will continue to put enormous pressure on local efforts to fight pollution.

GREECE

Greece is on the periphery of Western Europe in more than just a geographical sense. Ostracized during the dictatorship of the colonels from 1967 to 1974, it eventually joined the EC in 1981; but later that year an election victory for the Panhellenic Socialist Movement (Pasok) gave Greece its first socialist government, led by Andreas Papandreou, and there were early promises of taking Greece out of Nato and of a referendum on EC membership.

Such fundamental changes to Greece's relationships with its neighbours and allies failed to materialize, but there have been intermittent signs of discord. The Pasok administration blew hot and cold on the question of US bases, and the Reagan administration countered with accusations that Greece was soft on Middle East terrorism and not pulling its weight as a Nato member. Relations with Turkey, already blighted by the 1974 Turkish invasion of Cyprus, were further shaken by arguments over territorial waters and mineral exploration of the Aegean. By the late 1980s, however, tensions had diminished as Greece's allies learned to distinguish between internal politicking and serious policy statements, and the Pasok government became more conciliatory, to the extent that Mr Papandreou initiated a dialogue with Turkey in 1988.

Traditionally a largely agricultural economy, Greece had begun to industrialize in earnest under the military dictatorship. The major problem after the restoration of democracy was attracting investment to sustain both industrial growth and popular consumption. Greece has chronically weak external balances, and consumer demand, sucking in imports, increased rapidly in the early 1980s. Grants from the EC temporarily alleviated problems in the countryside, but a severe austerity programme, imposed in 1985–87, lost the government political support and led to strikes in the public sector.

The approach of the single European market has galvanized Greek industry into unprecedented activity. There has been a spate of acquisitions and mergers, and foreign companies are starting to invest. Shipping, the biggest earner after tourism, is showing real signs of emerging from the recession of the early 1980s. Tourism, although it has suffered ups and downs – like the terrorist scare that kept Americans away for a year – is becoming more solidly based and more evenly spread throughout the country.

The area most resistant to change is the bureaucracy, the bane of both foreign investors and the Greek business community which has some longstanding grievances about the tax regime. But here too there is confidence that events in Europe will be the engine for change, and lead the government to streamline the cumbersome bureaucratic machine.

OFFICIAL NAME Hellenic Republic.

CAPITAL CITY Athens.

GEOGRAPHY Greece is a country of mountainous peninsulas and rugged islands, themselves the tops of submerged ranges. River valleys, small basins in the mountains and coastal plains are the only lowland areas and contain most of the population. Agriculture is limited to less than 25% of the land. Much of the bedrock is porous limestone, and rivers tend to be short, with erratic flows. There are frequent earthquakes. *Highest point* Mt Olympus 2,917 metres (9,570 feet). *Area* 131,957 sq km (50,950 sq miles).

PEOPLE *Population* 9.9m. *Density* 75 per sq km. *Ethnic groups* Greek 95%, Macedonian 2%, Turkish 1%, Albanian 1%.

RELIGION Greek Orthodox 98%, Muslim 1%.

LANGUAGE Greek.

EDUCATION Free and officially compulsory for ages 6–15, though enrolment is below 75%. There are 14 universities.

CLIMATE Mediterranean, with hot, dry summers. Average temperatures in Athens 28°C (82°F) in July, 9°C (48°F) in Jan; cooler in north of country. West has highest rainfall.

CURRENCY Drachma (Dr).

PUBLIC HOLIDAYS Jan 1, Jan 6, Mon before Shrove Tue, Mar 25, Greek Orthodox Good Fri–Easter Mon, May 1, 7th Mon after Easter Mon, Aug 15, Oct 28, Dec 25, Dec 26.

GOVERNMENT Republic. A 300-member parliament is elected for a 4-year term. The president, ceremonial head of state, is elected by parliament for 5 years; he appoints the majority leader in parliament as prime minister and chief executive. Recent legislation has been aimed at creating greater autonomy for Greece's 13 regions.

ECONOMIC PROFILE

Agriculture and manufacturing are mainstays. Large balance of payments deficit; foreign exchange earnings mainly from tourism, also shipping. Olive oil, citrus fruits, sugar and wine exported.

Growth Mining and quarrying, oil refining, clothing, some agricultural products such as yoghurt. Tourism continues to expand.

Problems Tobacco, footwear and leather, machinery and transport equipment industries are in decline. Increasing demand for imported manufactured goods.

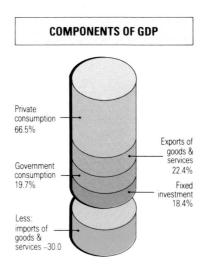

GDP BY ORIGIN

Manufacturing 17.5%
Wholesale & retail trade 15.8%
Construction 6.4%
Other
Agriculture, forestry & fishing 16.3%
Transport & communications 8.0%
Electricity, gas & water 3.2%

COMPONENTS OF GDP

Private consumption 66.5%
Government consumption 19.7%
Less: imports of goods & services –30.0
Exports of goods & services 22.4%
Fixed investment 18.4%

Source: EIU *Country Report* (1897 figures)

IMPORTS AND EXPORTS

W. Germany
Italy
France
Netherlands
UK
Saudi Arabia
USA
Other

EXPORTS

IMPORTS

Other
Iron & steel 4.3%
Chemicals & fertilizers 5.1%
Crude oil 11.1%
Machinery 15.6%
Food 16.2%
Manufactured consumer goods 29.6%

Other
Minerals 3.8%
Petroleum products 11.4%
Food & beverages 25.5%
Manufactures 50.0%

Source: EIU *Country Report* (1986 figures)

BALANCE OF PAYMENTS

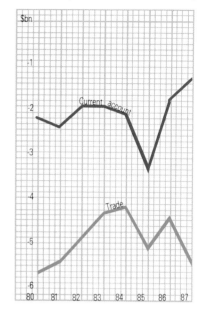

Current account

Trade

$bn
+1
-2
-3
-4
-5
-6
80 81 82 83 84 85 86 87

Source: EIU *Country Credit Risk Service*

TURKEY

For much of the postwar period, Turkey has alternated between the excesses of democratic party politics and the repression of military rule. The last, and most lasting, military intervention took place in 1980, when the armed forces under General Kenan Evren took power to deal with widespread terrorism and economic problems.

With the old parties and their leaders banned, the 1983 elections were only a partial restoration of democracy, but the victory of the centrist Motherland Party (Anap), under the technocrat Turgut Ozal, heralded a new era of stability and economic vigour. Re-elected in 1987, and braving the return of some former leaders to the political arena, Mr Ozal boldly applied for membership of the EC.

The response from Brussels was sympathetic but hardly encouraging. Turkey's political qualifications were called into question, with evidence of the repression and torture of political dissidents and ethnic minorities such as the Kurds, and many countries find the presence of Turkish troops in Cyprus unacceptable. But it was the economic balance sheet that drained the colour from Western European faces.

On the credit side, economic growth in the 1980s has been spectacular: industrial output almost doubled in value between 1982 and 1987; and, although the importance of agriculture declined, farm output more than trebled in value in the same period. Yet average income remained far below that of Portugal, the EC's poorest member; and Turkey's population is growing fast. Some areas of the economy have failed to share in the economic miracle, and its sustainability is under threat from steep inflation and a heavy debt burden.

Just as anti-inflationary measures began to take effect in early 1989, Turkey's political future was thrown into doubt by the result of local elections in which Anap polled only 22% of the vote, less than either of the two main opposition parties, leading to widespread calls for an early general election.

OFFICIAL NAME Republic of Turkey.

CAPITAL CITY Ankara.

GEOGRAPHY Thrace, the area northwest of the Bosporus, is mostly lowland, but the bulk of the country, Anatolia, is made up of seismically active young mountain chains, highest in the east of the country. Less than 10% of Turkey, mostly around the coasts, is level or gently sloping. *Highest point* Mt Ararat 5,165 metres (16,950 feet). *Area* 780,576 sq km (301,380 sq miles).

PEOPLE *Population* 50.3m. *Density* 64 per sq km. *Ethnic groups* Turkish 87%, Kurdish 9%, Arab 2%.

RELIGION Sunni Muslim 99%, Christian 0.5%.

LANGUAGE Turkish. Also Kurdish and Arabic.

EDUCATION Officially compulsory for 5 years, to be taken between ages 6 and 14; free to university level. Around 20% of secondary pupils attend private schools. There are 28 universities.

CLIMATE Much of interior is semi-arid, with continental extremes of temperature. Winters cold, around 0°C (32°F) in Ankara in Jan, down to -40°C (-40°F) in eastern mountains; summers warm, around 23°C (71°F) in Ankara in July, hotter on Mediterranean coast.

CURRENCY Turkish lira (TL).

PUBLIC HOLIDAYS Jan 1, Apr 23, May 1, Seker Bayram, May 19, Kurban Bayram, Aug 30, Oct 29.

GOVERNMENT Republic. The 1982 constitution provides for a 450-member national assembly, elected for a 5-year term by a form of PR. The powers of the government, led by a prime minister, are limited by a constitutional court and a national security council, dominated by the military and headed by the president, elected for a 7-year term by the national assembly.

BALANCE OF PAYMENTS

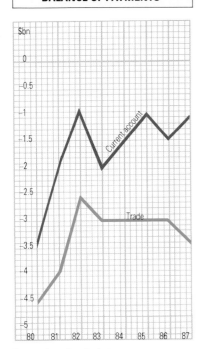

Source: EIU *Country Credit Risk Service*

IMPORTS AND EXPORTS

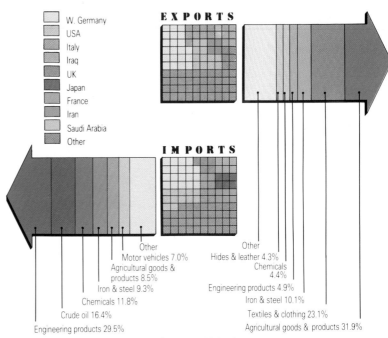

W. Germany
USA
Italy
Iraq
UK
Japan
France
Iran
Saudi Arabia
Other

EXPORTS

IMPORTS

Other
Motor vehicles 7.0%
Agricultural goods & products 8.5%
Iron & steel 9.3%
Chemicals 11.8%
Crude oil 16.4%
Engineering products 29.5%

Other
Hides & leather 4.3%
Chemicals 4.4%
Engineering products 4.9%
Iron & steel 10.1%
Textiles & clothing 23.1%
Agricultural goods & products 31.9%

Source: EIU *Country Report* (Imports/Exports 1986 figures: Trading partners 1987 figures)

ECONOMIC PROFILE

Agriculture overtaken by manufacturing, though still important: key crops are cotton, tobacco, wheat, hazelnuts, dried fruit, silk, olives. Remittances from migrant workers in Western Europe, notably West Germany, declining.

Clothing and textiles important exports, following industrialization.

Growth Machinery, iron and steel, chemicals. Tourism set to continue as growth area.

Problems Dependent on imports of oil and other fuels. High inflation rates and foreign debt burden threaten recent high growth rates. Fiscal difficulties arise from the failure to effectively tax agricultural incomes.

CYPRUS

This small but strategically placed Mediterranean island gained independence from the UK in 1960. Its partition dates from 1974 when Turkish troops invaded the north, responding both to a Greek right-wing coup that had overthrown President Makarios and to the beleaguered state of the Turkish Cypriot minority.

Since then, the Greek south has prospered as never before and annual income per head is more than $4,000. Wealth has been generated by manufacturing (clothing, shoes, plastics) and specialized agriculture (potatoes, avocados, exotic fruits), although these products all face rising tariff barriers in the main EC markets. Substantial income comes from the British bases, UN personnel and the Cypriot community in the UK; but the most spectacular growth has been in offshore banking, shipping and, above all, tourism. The Turkish north, by contrast, has had only limited success in breaking out of its diplomatic isolation to market its agricultural produce and undeniable tourist potential.

OFFICIAL NAME Republic of Cyprus.

CAPITAL CITY Nicosia.

GEOGRAPHY A hot central plain is flanked by the Kyrenian Mountains to the north, which drop to a fertile coastal plain, and the Troödos Massif to the south. *Area* 9,251 sq km (3,570 sq miles).

PEOPLE *Population* 670,000. *Density* 72 per sq km. *Ethnic groups* Greek 81%, Turkish 19%.

RELIGION Greek Orthodox 77%, Muslim 18%.

LANGUAGE Greek and Turkish. Also English.

EDUCATION Free, and compulsory for ages 5–11.

CLIMATE Mediterranean with above-average rainfall.

CURRENCY Cyprus pound (C£), also Turkish lira (TL).

PUBLIC HOLIDAYS (* Greek; † Turkish) Jan 1, 6*, 19*, Mon before Shrove Tue*, Mar 25*, Apr 23†, Greek Orthodox Good Fri–Easter Mon*, May 1†, Ramazam Bayram†, May 19†, Jul 20†, Kurban Bayram†, Aug 30†, Oct 1*, Birth of the prophet†, Oct 28*, 29†, Nov 15†, Dec 25, 26*.

EASTERN EUROPE

The states of Eastern Europe were carved in the course of two world wars from the remains of the Austro-Hungarian Empire, which dominated the map in 1913.

Eastern Europe clustered around the Soviet Union to form a united front against what was perceived as a Western threat. Yugoslavia's assertion of independence in 1948 made the Soviet Union more concerned to keep a tight hold on its allies, particularly in the strategically sensitive north of the region, where its forces confronted those of Nato. Twice it has had to intervene to preserve the alliance – in Hungary in 1956 and Czechoslovakia in 1968.

The thaw in Soviet politics in the 1980s is unlikely to change the map of Eastern Europe, where the nationalist aspirations of ethnic minorities have often been harshly suppressed. But changing economic relationships may weaken the ties between Moscow and its satellites.

1913 BORDERS

- Russian Empire
- German Empire
- Austro-Hungarian Empire
- Romania
- Bulgaria
- Montenegro
- Serbia
- Albania
— 1989 borders

Climate

Most of the region has a continental climate, with warm summers and cold winters, but within this pattern there are wide variations. Poland has cold snowy winters and short summers. Yugoslavia's Mediterranean coast has a climate similar to that of Greece but its mountains have snow cover throughout the year. Summer temperatures can be as high as 28°C (82°F) in Bulgaria, winter ones as low as −60°C (−76°F) in Poland. Most rainfall is in the warmer months. East Germany and western Poland have a more equable, temperate climate.

RELATIVE SIZE OF ECONOMIES

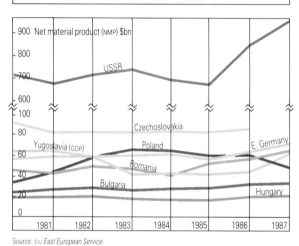

Source: EIU *East European Service*

PASSENGER CARS PER 1,000 PEOPLE

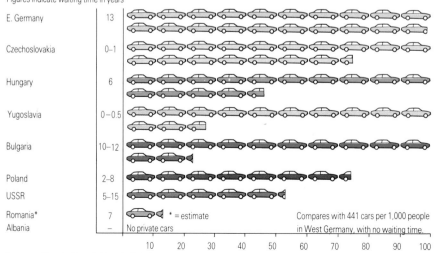

Source: ECHO (Hungarian Economic Information Service)

TRADE INTERDEPENDENCE

Trade with other Comecon as % of all external trade

	exports	imports
Bulgaria		
Czechoslovakia		
E. Germany		
Hungary		
Poland		
Romania		
USSR		

Source: UN *Monthly Bulletin of Statistics* (1986 figures)

Warsaw Pact

The Warsaw "treaty of friendship, cooperation and mutual assistance" was signed in May 1955, partly in response to West Germany's decision to join Nato the previous year. It provided for a single military command to be set up in Moscow, and obliged signatories to assist each other in the event of an attack.

The treaty was last renewed, for 20 years, in 1985, with the terms unchanged. Over the years, several members have sought changes: Hungary unsuccessfully tried to leave the pact in 1956; Romania and Czechoslovakia have both argued for change in the command structure; Albania withdrew in 1968.

Joint manoeuvres are carried out every year, but Warsaw Pact forces have gone into action together only once, in Czechoslovakia in 1968. Soviet army divisions are stationed in Czechoslovakia, East Germany, Hungary and Poland but sharp reductions in Warsaw Pact forces have been promised as part of the new climate of *détente* in Eastern Europe.

Comecon

Formed in 1949, the Council for Mutual Economic Assistance aims to share resources to help member states' development. One way of doing this was by enabling individual states to specialize in particular industries, but its achievement of this aim has been modest, limited to isolated examples like Hungary's buses and Bulgaria's fork-lift trucks.

About 60% of Comecon trade is with other members. There have been disputes over pricing of goods because of the lack of a convertible currency for trade between members. The "convertible socialist currency," the transferable ruble, functions only as a unit of account. This also complicates comparisons between Comecon economies and those of Western nations.

EAST GERMANY

East Germany is the "small Germany," not only in size, population, political and economic position, but also in its self-image. For decades after World War II, its leaders were preoccupied with gaining recognition as a sovereign state, a goal realized only in 1972 through West German Chancellor Willy Brandt's *Ostpolitik*. Even today, much of importance about East Germany can be expressed by reference to the larger and more powerful Federal Republic.

Aside from language, tradition and family ties, the West German influence is present in the accessible and very popular radio and television, with their messages of consumer satisfaction and political pluralism. The potential of these cultural factors to cause unrest helps to explain the regime's determination to stick to its hard-line stance. The leadership shows little tolerance of dissent, although it does make efforts to get on with the sometimes outspoken Lutheran church.

The economy, by contrast, relies heavily on the Federal Republic, which classifies trade with East Germany as "internal" and erects no trade barriers, providing a welcome back door into the EC. A special clearing agreement between the two means that East Germany does not need to generate hard currency for its purchases in the Federal Republic, which also pays hard currency for communal services and for the use of transport routes to West Berlin.

These advantages have helped East Germany become the most developed and efficient economy in Eastern Europe, enabling it to retain its highly centralized economic management at a time when such systems are becoming discredited among its eastern neighbours.

OFFICIAL NAME German Democratic Republic.
CAPITAL CITY East Berlin.
GEOGRAPHY The northern half is a plain; the extreme north is marked by sandy soils, lakes and forested moraine ridges. The southern and southwestern uplands bear metals and spruce forest, and include the fertile and populous Elbe valley. *Highest point* Fichtelgebirge 1,214 metres (3,980 feet). *Area* 108,333 sq km (41,830 sq miles).
PEOPLE *Population* 16.6m. *Density* 154 per sq km. *Ethnic groups* German 99%, Wendish 1%.
RELIGION Protestant 80%, RC 10%.
LANGUAGE German.
EDUCATION Free and compulsory for ages 6–16. Well-developed higher education system.
CLIMATE Temperate in the lowlands: monthly average temperatures 0–17°C (32–63°F); rainfall moderate. Wetter and cooler in the mountains.
CURRENCY Mark (M), known as DDR-Mark.
PUBLIC HOLIDAYS Jan 1, Good Fri, May 1, Whit Mon, Oct 7, Dec 25–26, Dec 31 (half-day).
GOVERNMENT Communist republic since 1949. The Socialist Unity (communist) Party dominates the National Front, which approves candidates for the Volkskammer. Its 500 members elect a council of state, whose chairman is *de facto* head of state.

IMPORTS AND EXPORTS

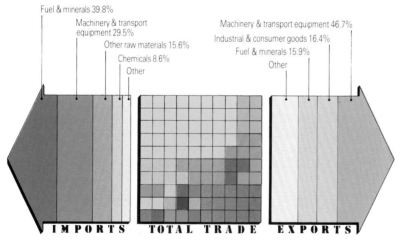

Fuel & minerals 39.8%
Machinery & transport equipment 29.5%
Other raw materials 15.6%
Chemicals 8.6%
Other

Machinery & transport equipment 46.7%
Industrial & consumer goods 16.4%
Fuel & minerals 15.9%
Other

IMPORTS   TOTAL TRADE   EXPORTS

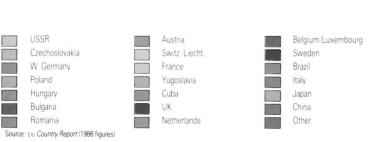

USSR
Czechoslovakia
W. Germany
Poland
Hungary
Bulgaria
Romania

Austria
Switz./Liecht.
France
Yugoslavia
Cuba
UK
Netherlands

Belgium/Luxembourg
Sweden
Brazil
Italy
Japan
China
Other

Source: EIU *Country Report* (1986 figures)

ECONOMIC PROFILE

A fully industrialized economy, without significant natural resources but with a highly skilled, mainly urban work force. Steel, vehicles, fertilizers, textiles, agricultural and electrical equipment among main sectors.

Growth Priorities include expansion of robotics and industrial automation technologies, electrical engineering and instrument building.

Problems Agriculture stagnant. Older technologies used in steel, mechanical engineering and automotive industries only slowly being upgraded. Industry makes inefficient use of energy; conversion to coal and nuclear power taking longer than expected.

POLAND

The wheel has come full circle for the Polish government. A fresh round of price rises early in 1988 sparked off widespread industrial unrest, putting the regime under great pressure to review social and economic policies after the confrontation with the unions at the start of the 1980s.

Economic reforms adopted in 1982 had disappointing results. Growth began again after the slump of 1980–81 but the leadership made the mistake of raising expectations too high. Increased industrial production made headlines in the official press but had little impact on stocks in the shops. With 60% of the population living below the poverty line people's patience was wearing thin.

Without effective reform, the debt-ridden Polish economy is in deep trouble. Even by Eastern European standards, Polish industry is inefficient.

The new government formed in October 1988 made a clear commitment to "economic pluralism," envisaging a much larger role for the private sector. The new mood in the USSR and the support of the IMF and World Bank helped bolster this commitment to change; Poland may soon be rehabilitated as a member of the international financial community.

But the great bugbear is the domestic political situation. By the late 1980s it was clear that the economic reform demanded a measure of social support to make it work properly. The government has signalled its desire for social compromise. In 1989 it removed the ban on Solidarity, the opposition union organizaton, and allowed free elections to 35% of the seats of the Sejm, the lower house, and all the seats of the Senate, the new upper house. Solidarity's overwhelming victory in the seats it could contest embarrassed both government and opposition. The landslide threatened the communist party's legitimacy, if not its formal control, prompting fears of a backlash from party conservatives. Solidarity seemed reluctant to accept the unaccustomed responsibility which accompanied its new, but limited, power.

OFFICIAL NAME Polish People's Republic.
CAPITAL CITY Warsaw.
GEOGRAPHY Most is lowland, part of the Central European Plain, though to the south there are the Sudety Mountains and the Carpathians. The Baltic coast consists of swamps and dunes; inland, there is a belt of lakes. Most agriculture and industry is in the centre. *Highest point* Tatry 2,499 metres (8,200 feet). *Area* 312,677 sq km (120,730 sq miles).
PEOPLE *Population* 37.9m. *Density* 119 per sq km. *Ethnic groups* Polish 99%.
RELIGION RC 81%, Polish Orthodox 1%.
LANGUAGE Polish.
EDUCATION Free and compulsory for ages 7–14. There are 11 universities and 18 technical universities.
CLIMATE Temperate in the west; continental in the east. Summers short and hot, autumns mild, winters long, cold and snowy. Monthly average Warsaw temperature -6–24°C (21–75°F).
CURRENCY Zloty (Zl).
PUBLIC HOLIDAYS Jan 1, Easter Mon, May 1, May 9, Corpus Christi, Jul 22, Nov 1, Dec 25–26.
GOVERNMENT Communist republic since 1945. The Polish United Workers' Party is constitutionally the leading political force in the state. 65% of the seats of the Sejm, the lower house, are reserved for the communists and their allies. The freely-elected upper house, the Senate, has important blocking powers.

ECONOMIC PROFILE

Largest East European economy, a major source of raw materials and fuel, especially coal. Loss-making heavy industries – shipbuilding, steel – eat up government subsidies at expense of newer sectors. Farming still largely in private hands, but food supplies inadequate. Exports manufactured goods to East; raw materials, food and light industrial products to West.

Growth Potential for growth in small but vibrant private sector, if freed from government controls. Joint ventures with Western partners to be encouraged.

Problems Industry needs re-equipping and restructuring away from reliance on heavy metals and fuel. Shortages of energy – 80% supplied by coal – inevitable unless efficiency improves.

IMPORTS AND EXPORTS

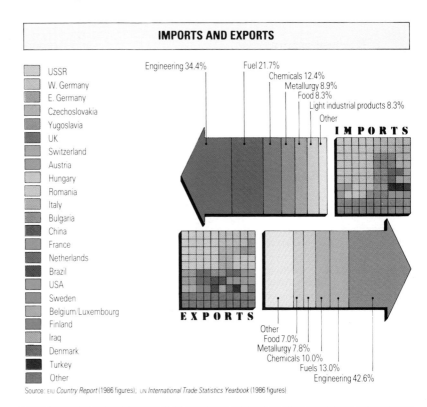

Source: EIU *Country Report* (1986 figures); UN *International Trade Statistics Yearbook* (1986 figures)

CZECHOSLOVAKIA

Czechoslovakia is not quite grinding to a halt but it is plainly slowing down: growth rates are slipping and plan targets have been revised down. At the same time, Czechoslovaks are demanding a better standard of living and more political freedom. Neither is likely to be delivered by the government; the Czechoslovak communist party is one of the most orthodox in the region, led by men of exceptionally limited vision.

Yet Czechoslovakia is of immense importance to the rest of Eastern Europe as a supplier of relatively modern machinery and equipment. Its industrial base, well developed before World War II, did not need central planning to accelerate development. Indeed, the Czech economy was the first, back in the early 1960s, to run into problems of over-centralization. As growth slipped, economic and political reform appeared on the agenda, briefly, in the "Prague spring" of 1968. Warsaw Pact tanks banished Alexander Dubcek's vision of "socialism with a human face" in favour of a return to conformity, managed on Moscow's behalf by Gustáv Husák.

Conservatism became entrenched over the next two decades. Economic growth and output quality faltered as the overdue modernization of economy and society was further postponed. Frustration grew, and not just in Prague. Mikhail Gorbachev's new gospel of *glasnost* and *perestroika* penetrated Czechoslovak orthodoxy slowly, received without enthusiasm by the same men who had overseen the obliteration of the reform movement 20 years earlier.

When Mr Husák fell from grace in 1987 his successor, Milos Jakes, inherited a country with the potential for rapid economic growth. Exceptionally low foreign debt made extra borrowing to finance industrial reconstruction feasible. As with other centrally planned economies, potential resources could be released by decentralization and policy changes, and by harnessing market forces. But few believe the unadventurous Mr Jakes can retrieve policies so forcefully rejected in 1968 though so urgently needed today.

OFFICIAL NAME Czechoslovak Socialist Republic.
CAPITAL CITY Prague.
GEOGRAPHY Around 65% is upland, 20% mountains and 10% lowland. The west is dominated by the Bohemian massif, a hilly, undulating basin surrounded by mountain ranges; the Carpathian Mountains are the major feature of the eastern area. *Highest point* Gerlachovsky 2,663 metres (8,740 feet). *Area* 17,869 sq km (49,370 sq miles).
PEOPLE *Population* 15.6m. *Density* 121 per sq km. *Ethnic groups* Czech 64%, Slovak 31%, Magyar 4%.
RELIGION RC 66%, Czechoslovak church 4%.
LANGUAGE Czech and Slovak (very similar).
EDUCATION Free and compulsory for ages 6–16.
CLIMATE Mixed. Mean annual temperatures of -4°C (25°F) in the highlands, 10.5°C (51°F) in the lowlands. Rainfall is highest in summer.
CURRENCY Koruna or Crown (Kcs).
PUBLIC HOLIDAYS Jan 1, Easter Mon, May 1, May 9, Dec 25–26.
GOVERNMENT Communist republic since 1948. All candidates are sponsored by the National Front, which is dominated by the Communist Party of Czechoslovakia. The elected bicameral federal assembly elects a president, who appoints a prime minister and other ministers to form an executive. The presidium of the central committee of the Communist Party directs political policy.

ECONOMIC PROFILE

Extensive but increasingly obsolete industrial capacity, including vehicles, glass, footwear, textiles and ceramics. Large coal deposits, plus copper, zinc. Agriculture a long way short of self-sufficiency. Forests large and productive.

Growth Large gold deposits discovered mid-1980s. Cautious reforms allowing more private enterprise.

Problems Failure to modernize industry hitting quality and export demand. Poor harvests, labour and energy shortages also contributing to slackening growth rate. Hydro-power potential not fully exploited, so oil has to be imported. Much food imported, for both consumption and processing.

IMPORTS AND EXPORTS

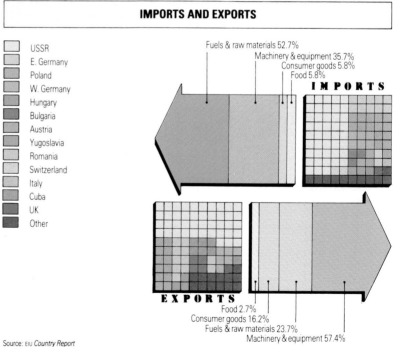

USSR
E. Germany
Poland
W. Germany
Hungary
Bulgaria
Austria
Yugoslavia
Romania
Switzerland
Italy
Cuba
UK
Other

IMPORTS
Fuels & raw materials 52.7%
Machinery & equipment 35.7%
Consumer goods 5.8%
Food 5.8%

EXPORTS
Food 2.7%
Consumer goods 16.2%
Fuels & raw materials 23.7%
Machinery & equipment 57.4%

Source: EIU *Country Report*

(Imports/Exports 1986 figures; Trading partners 1987 figures)

HUNGARY

In May 1988 János Kádár, leader of Hungary's communist party for almost 32 years, was removed amid general dissatisfaction with his final years in office. Mr Kádár came to power in 1956 as Soviet tanks crushed his country's doomed revolution, but had become a truly popular leader, allowing a modicum of political freedom and overseeing reforms to dismantle central planning. Yet by the mid-1980s years of half-hearted reform and heavy borrowing had brought on an economic crisis that proved his downfall.

His successor, Károly Grosz, is a flexible man who promises major political and economic change. Although Mr Grosz's commitment to radical reform is still questioned, he has been joined in the party leadership by several strong advocates of both political and economic liberalization. Moreover, parliament, until now a rubber stamp for party policies, is beginning to assert its rights and numerous independent political groups are challenging the party's authority.

But the task ahead is immense. For too long, scarce resources were directed towards "white elephant" energy and heavy industry projects. Profitable enterprises are heavily taxed to subsidize loss-making firms, and the dynamic private sector suffers from the uncertain business environment. In agriculture, as in industry, production is oriented towards bulk products as opposed to goods with higher value added. This must change if Hungary is to boost exports to the West and meet debt service payments, which in 1988 accounted for over half of convertible-currency merchandise export earnings.

Recent efforts to shift resources into exports have led to an austerity programme; a new income tax has also cut purchasing power and most people hold two or three jobs to get by. However, the economy's fundamental problems persist and there is a consensus that the old, corrupt political system impedes the implementation of new policies. In response, Hungary's leaders promise political liberalization, as part of a clear move towards a more market-oriented economy. The pressure from society for such change is mounting.

OFFICIAL NAME Hungarian People's Republic.
CAPITAL CITY Budapest.
GEOGRAPHY A lowland country, mostly 80–200 metres (250–650 feet) in altitude, surrounded by mountains. The Great and Little Hungarian Plains are separated by the Hungarian highlands, but the geography is dominated by the Danube and its tributary the Tisza, which flood regularly in spring and summer. One-sixth of the country is forested. *Highest point* Kékes 1,015 metres (3,330 feet). *Area* 93,030 sq km (35,920 sq miles).
PEOPLE *Population* 10.6m. *Density* 114 per sq km. *Ethnic groups* Magyar (Hungarian) 93%.
RELIGION Christian 83% (RC 54%, Protestant 22%, other 7%), Jewish 1%.
LANGUAGE Magyar (Hungarian).
EDUCATION Free from the age of 3 and compulsory for ages 6–16. There are 9 universities and 9 technical universities.
CLIMATE Continental, with an annual rainfall of 500–750mm (20–30ins); average temperatures around 0°C (32°F) in winter, 20°C (68°F) in summer.
CURRENCY Forint (Ft).
PUBLIC HOLIDAYS Jan 1, Mar 15, Apr 4, Easter Mon, May 1, Aug 20, Nov 7, Dec 25–26.
GOVERNMENT Communist republic since 1945. The Patriotic People's Front, dominated by the Hungarian Socialist Workers' (communist) Party, approves a list of candidates for the 387-member national assembly, elected for 5 years; 35 members are elected unopposed from a national list. The assembly elects a presidential council, chaired by a president, that functions as executive and collective head of state.

IMPORTS AND EXPORTS

Raw materials & semi-finished goods 46.6%
Machinery & transport equipment 17.6%
Fuels & energy 16.3%
Industrial & consumer goods 12.2%
Food 7.3%

IMPORTS

USSR
W. Germany
E. Germany
Austria
Czechoslovakia
Italy
China
Switzerland
Yugoslavia
UK
Japan
Other

EXPORTS
Fuel & energy 3.7%
Consumer goods 16.5%
Food 19.2%
Machinery & transport equipment 28.8%
Raw materials & semi-finished goods 31.8%

Source: EIU *Country Report* (1987 figures)

ECONOMIC PROFILE

Heavy industry and agriculture mainstays of economy. Major producer and exporter of buses, bulk agricultural products – world's largest exporter of broiler chickens – and computer software. Limited mineral resources apart from bauxite and recently discovered copper.

Growth Western joint ventures growing fast, bringing in new technology and management styles. Tourism growing rapidly. Ambitious nuclear power programme.

Problems Much industry energy-inefficient and unprofitable, saddled with outdated equipment and hopelessly uncompetitive in the West. Energy resources cannot meet demand because of inefficient use.

YUGOSLAVIA

Yugoslavia has not disintegrated, as many predicted it would after the death of Tito in 1980, but its fragile unity is under intense pressure. In the absence of Tito's personal authority, the central state and party bodies find it difficult to balance the divergent interests of the six republics and two autonomous regions. Growing antagonism between Serbs and Montenegrins on the one hand and Kosovar Albanians, Croatians and Slovenes on the other gives rise to fears that the federation will break up or that the Serbs, the largest nationality, will attempt to regain their former hegemony.

Modern Yugoslavia emerged from the victory of Tito's partisans in 1945 and the communist party's split with the USSR three years later. Isolated from the international communist movement, Yugoslavia developed unique forms of party, state and economic organization, with power devolved to the regions and workers gaining at least theoretical control over their places of work.

In the hope of preventing ethnic rivalry, Tito was replaced by a collective presidency rotated annually among the republics and regions. In practice, this procedure weakened the political centre. Few decisions can be taken without the consent of the republics and regions. Real authority rests with the League of Communists; here too, power has shifted away from the centre.

Since Yugoslavia's break with the communist block it has sought the middle way in international relations and was instrumental in forming the nonaligned movement. It goes to great lengths to ensure its military independence, designing and producing much of its own equipment.

After a period of rapid growth, the economy faces a severe balance of payments problem, foreign debt of $22bn, an inflation rate of 220% and high unemployment. The IMF's agreement to provide further credit in 1988 carried stringent conditions, including the freeing of prices, removal of import restrictions, radical changes in foreign exchange policy and curbs on government spending. As a consequence, labour unrest added to and fuelled ethnic conflict. Economic reforms introduced in late 1988 seemed at best a limited response to pressure for a move towards a full market economy.

OFFICIAL NAME Socialist Federal Republic of Yugoslavia.
CAPITAL CITY Belgrade.
GEOGRAPHY Most people live in the Pannonian lowlands drained by the Danube in the northeast. Forested mountains run behind the other population centre of the Adriatic coast. *Highest point* Triglav 2,864 metres (9,400 feet). *Area* 225,804 sq km (98,770 sq miles).
PEOPLE *Population* 23.3m. *Density* 90 per sq km. *Ethnic groups* Serbian 36%, Croatian 20%, Muslim 9%, Slovene 8%, Albanian 8%, Macedonian 6%, Montenegrin 3%, Hungarian 2%, Gypsy 1%.
RELIGION Serbian Orthodox 35%, RC 26%, Muslim 9%.
LANGUAGE Serbo-Croatian. Also Slovene, Macedonian, Albanian and Hungarian.
EDUCATION Free and compulsory for ages 7–15. There are 19 universities.
CLIMATE Mediterranean on coast, continental inland. Temperatures are around 20°C (70°F) in summer, close to freezing in winter. Rainfall is steady.
CURRENCY Yugoslav dinar (YuD).
PUBLIC HOLIDAYS (* in certain republics only) Jan 1–2, Apr 27*, May 1–2, Jul 4, Jul 7*, Jul 13*, Jul 22*, Jul 27*, Aug 2*, Oct 11*, Nov 1*, Nov 29–30.
GOVERNMENT Communist federal republic. The duties of head of state are rotated among the members of the collective presidency. The bicameral federal assembly has regional groupings.

ECONOMIC PROFILE

Manufacturing, with emphasis on assembly and processing, and mining are backbone of economy. Textiles, transport and electrical equipment and chemicals are among main exports. Leading European producer of copper, bauxite, silver, bismuth, mercury. Agriculture, largely cereals and livestock, labour-intensive, employing quarter of work force; the world's ninth largest wine producer. Tourism helps offset trade deficit.

Growth Potential for export-led growth with liberalization of trade/foreign exchange regime. Exports of iron and steel products increasing as competing EC industries decline. Lower labour costs benefit shipbuilding. Joint ventures promoted.

Problems Stress on import substitution created industries that find it hard to compete on world markets. Oil and gas reserves cannot meet demand. Many raw materials and manufactured goods imported.

IMPORTS AND EXPORTS

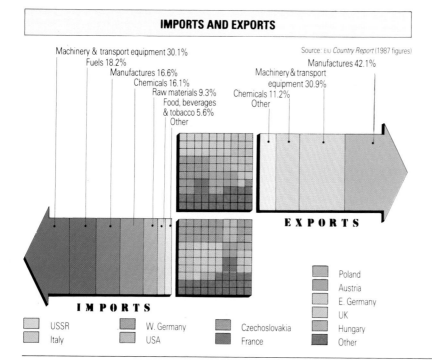

Source: EIU *Country Report* (1987 figures)

Machinery & transport equipment 30.1%
Fuels 18.2%
Manufactures 16.6%
Chemicals 16.1%
Raw materials 9.3%
Food, beverages & tobacco 5.6%
Other

Manufactures 42.1%
Machinery & transport equipment 30.9%
Chemicals 11.2%
Other

IMPORTS

EXPORTS

- USSR
- Italy
- W. Germany
- USA
- Czechoslovakia
- France
- Poland
- Austria
- E. Germany
- UK
- Hungary
- Other

ALBANIA

Albania achieved independent statehood for the first time in 1912 after centuries as a subject of the Ottoman empire. The staunchly pro-Stalinist Albanian Workers' Party has ruled since 1944 with Enver Hoxha at the helm until his death in 1985. The party still maintains extensive control over government and social activity and in 1967 abolished religion.

Albania takes perverse pride in its isolation. Since severing relations with Yugoslavia, the USSR and China, it has described itself as the world's sole surviving bastion of Marxism-Leninism, dividing the world into "bourgeois" and "revisionist" camps. But Hoxha's successor, Ramiz Alia, though showing no sign of abandoning hostility to the two superpowers, has been more willing to establish relations with other states, regardless of their political systems, and seeks a more active role in Balkan affairs.

The country's achievements in expanding and diversifying industrial production and developing agriculture have been considerable, but growth rates are falling rapidly. Modernization of its antiquated industrial base, much of it built by the Soviets in the 1950s, has been impeded by a constitutional ban on the acceptance of foreign credits, and food production is failing to keep pace with the fastest population growth in Europe. The need for economic reform has become pressing.

OFFICIAL NAME People's Socialist Republic of Albania.
CAPITAL CITY Tirana.
GEOGRAPHY The Balkan Mountains take up 70%; 40% is forest. Clay and sand lowlands along the coast and valleys are the most populous parts. *Area* 28,748 sq km (11,100 sq miles).
PEOPLE *Population* 3.2m. *Ethnic groups* Albanian 93%, Gypsy 2%, Greek 2%.
RELIGION Muslim 20%, Christian 5%.
LANGUAGE Albanian.
EDUCATION Free and compulsory for ages 7–15.
CLIMATE Mediterranean along the coast; more extreme inland. Average July temperature 25°C (77°F). Average annual rainfall 1,400mm (55ins).
CURRENCY Lek (Lk).
PUBLIC HOLIDAYS Jan 1, Jan 11, May 1, Nov 7, Nov 28–29.
GOVERNMENT Communist republic. The party controls · elections to the 250-member people's assembly. There is a presidium whose president is head of state, and a council of ministers whose chairman is head of government.

ROMANIA

Romania is enduring a test of fire personally initiated by Nicolae Ceausescu, state and party leader since 1965. Widely regarded as the most repressive communist leader in the world, Mr Ceausescu was for many years something of a hero in the West because of his independent stance. The only Warsaw Pact member never to break diplomatic ties to Israel, Romania does not allow Soviet troops on its territory, refused to endorse the 1968 invasion of Czechoslovakia and presents a diplomatic annoyance to the USSR.

Romania's maverick stance was enhanced by emphasizing trade and cooperation with the West. Its own oil and natural gas reserves freed it from dependence on Soviet supplies of these vital raw materials and enabled it to steer its own economic course. Heavy investment in industry and a variety of prestige schemes brought rapidly rising debts, however, culminating in rescheduling agreements requiring IMF assistance in 1982 and 1983.

Mr Ceausescu has since condemned the country to an unrelenting repayment effort, subordinating all national aims to export promotion. Even the IMF found his austerity programme too rigid. At the same time he has embarked on major construction schemes and relocation projects which the West has condemned as wasteful and inhumane. His plans to bulldoze 7,000 villages and rehouse their inhabitants in massive new agro-industrial complexes, ostensibly to make more efficient use of agricultural land, have led to charges that the real aim is to disperse the 2m Hungarian minority. Relations with Hungary worsened in 1988 when thousands of refugees crossed the border, but Mr Ceausescu continued his policy and unilaterally revoked most-favoured-nation trading status with the USA rather than suffer criticism of his human rights policies.

With the foreign debt due to be fully repaid by 1991, Romania intends to become less vulnerable to international financial pressure. But the cost of years of privation is revealed by the dropping of most measurements of consumer welfare from the statistical records. Mr Ceausescu's narrow path to self-sufficiency may leave Romania's hungry, poorly clothed and inadequately sheltered population with little to show for their sacrifices.

OFFICIAL NAME Socialist Republic of Romania.
CAPITAL CITY Bucharest.
GEOGRAPHY The Carpathians and Transylvanian alps run across the centre; to their west and north lie the Transylvanian tablelands. The population is concentrated in the fertile plains of the south and east, especially the Danube valley. The delta on the Black Sea has fishing and tourist industries. *Highest point* Moldoveanu 2,543 metres (8,340 feet). *Area* 237,500 sq km (91,700 sq miles).
PEOPLE *Population* 22.8m. *Density* 97 per sq km. *Ethnic groups* Romanian 89%, Hungarian 8%, German 2%.
RELIGION Orthodox Christian 80% (Romanian 70%, Greek 10%), Muslim 1%.
LANGUAGE Romanian.
EDUCATION Free and compulsory for ages 6–16. There are 7 universities and 5 technical universities.
CLIMATE Variations according to altitude; the climate in the southeast lowlands is almost Mediterranean. Generally, summers hot and humid with a monthly average temperature of 23°C (73°F); winter average -3°C (27°F). Average annual rainfall 660mm (26ins).
CURRENCY Leu; plural Lei (L).
PUBLIC HOLIDAYS Jan 1–2, May 1–2, Aug 23–24.
GOVERNMENT Communist republic. The general secretary of the Romanian Communist Party is head of government. The 369-member assembly elects 21 of its members as a state council, whose president is head of state.

BULGARIA

Bulgaria is historically the USSR's closest ally in Eastern Europe. The friendship between the two nations dates back to 1875, when Tsarist Russia liberated Bulgaria from 500 years of Turkish domination. Linguistic affinity reinforces the friendship. In the 1960s there was talk of making Bulgaria the 16th Soviet republic.

That the temptation was resisted may give Bulgaria's conservative political leaders some satisfaction as they look east across the Black Sea. The rigidly Stalinist response to dissent since Todor Zhikov took over in 1956 is more to their taste than the greater democracy now being enthusiastically pursued by Moscow.

Nevertheless, mass demonstrations were permitted in early 1988, and these and other apparent moves towards political liberalization were reported upon positively in the national press and obtained support from young party representatives. But the flirtation with democracy was slapped down again within months; reformers were ousted and the leadership reaffirmed its conservative stance. The men who had engineered nationwide repression of the Turkish minority in 1985 were clearly still in charge.

Calls for economic reform were heeded, however, prompted by Bulgaria's erratic performance on world markets and growing foreign debt. Management has been decentralized and profit and loss accounting introduced, although the difficult issue of stimulating agricultural production through more flexible pricing has still to be tackled. The emphasis is on small high-technology production units which planners hope will stimulate economic growth in the priority fields of electronics, new materials and biotechnology. But success is hampered by the way in which these new priorities have been grafted on to traditional industrial sectors developed somewhat haphazardly since the 1950s, when Bulgaria was still a peasant economy.

OFFICIAL NAME People's Republic of Bulgaria.
CAPITAL CITY Sofia.
GEOGRAPHY The north of the country is taken up by the rolling, fertile plain of the Danube, rising to the Balkans. Farther south are other mountain ranges, all running east–west. In the mountains are deep gorges and sheltered upland basins, in one of which lies Sofia. The sandy beaches of the Black Sea coast support a thriving tourist industry. *Area* 110,912 sq km (42,820 sq miles).
PEOPLE *Population* 9m. *Density* 81 per sq km. *Ethnic groups* Bulgarian 87%, Turkish 8.5%, Macedonian 2.5%, Gypsy 2%.
RELIGION Eastern Orthodox 27%, Muslim 8%, Protestant 1%, RC 1%.
LANGUAGE Bulgarian, written in Cyrillic script. Also Turkish and Macedonian.
EDUCATION Free from the age of 3 and compulsory for ages 6–16.
CLIMATE A country of extremes of temperature. In Sofia, averages range from -5°C (23°F) in winter to 28°C (82°F) in summer. Annual rainfall varies from 450mm (18ins) in the northeast to 1,200mm (48ins) in the mountains. Hail and thunderstorms common in spring and summer.
CURRENCY Lev (Lv).
PUBLIC HOLIDAYS Jan 1, Mar 3, May 1–2, May 24, Sep 9–10, Nov 7.
GOVERNMENT Communist republic since 1946. The Bulgarian Communist Party dominates the Fatherland Front which puts up all the unopposed candidates to the 400-member national assembly. The assembly elects a state council whose president is head of state.

IMPORTS AND EXPORTS

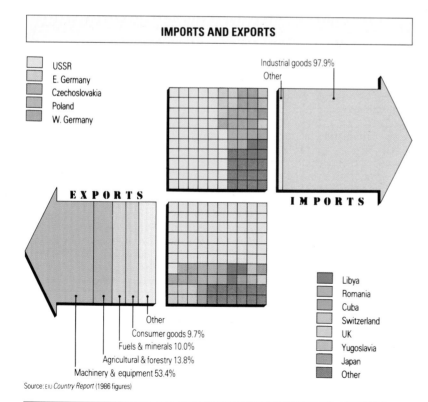

USSR
E. Germany
Czechoslovakia
Poland
W. Germany

Industrial goods 97.9%
Other

EXPORTS

IMPORTS

Libya
Romania
Cuba
Switzerland
UK
Yugoslavia
Japan
Other

Other
Consumer goods 9.7%
Fuels & minerals 10.0%
Agricultural & forestry 13.8%
Machinery & equipment 53.4%

Source: EIU *Country Report* (1986 figures)

ECONOMIC PROFILE

Agriculture and basic manufacturing still the core of the economy. New high-tech industries starting to make a contribution. Sales of agricultural products to West – canned fruit and vegetables, cigarettes, wine – bring in hard currency. Other major exports include construction steels, aluminium ingots, refined oil products, machinery and equipment.

Growth Electronics is fastest-growing sector. Promotion of joint ventures and tourism. High priority given to nuclear programme and expansion of the biotechnology industry.

Problems Shortages of energy (supplying only one third of needs). Fork-lift truck production, the largest industry, in long-term decline, and other established industries – chemicals, engineering – allowed to stagnate.

THE USSR

The Soviet people have long been aware of two facts about their country: that it has the resources, both natural and human, to dominate Europe and play a leading role on the world stage; and that it has remained, compared with North America and most of Europe, a backward nation, unable to realize its potential.

It is one of history's ironies that the Soviet Union has been the pioneer of centrally planned socialism. Neither the country's size and ethnic diversity nor the disorderly tendencies of the prevailing Russian national culture suit it for this role. Soviet history is as much about the pursuit of modernization as it is about the pursuit of a social ideal. Catching up and overtaking the leading capitalist nations has always been a prime objective of Soviet policy.

The USSR began with a lot of ground to make up and some real gains have been made. When Stalinist command methods became the norm in the late 1920s, Soviet output per head was about one-fifth that of the USA; now most estimates put it around two-fifths. An industrial base has been built to support, in the 1970s, strategic parity with the USA.

Yet, by 1986, when party leader Mikhail Gorbachev described the economy as being close to crisis, there had been a striking loss of momentum. From around 1974, even Soviet official figures ceased to show output catching up with that of the USA, admitting in effect that the gap in output per head was growing. Central planning, successful in marshalling resources for the drive to industrialize, proved a blunt instrument when it came to adapting to the complexities of a modern economy.

Agriculture received growing subsidies, but farmers had no incentives to produce more. Food consumption levels stagnated in the early 1980s and shortages in the state shops got worse. Precious hard currency had to be spent on importing some of the EC surpluses. These signs of economic debility were accompanied by widespread, growing corruption and cynicism in the administration and general apathy. The population might put up with privation indefinitely – it had had plenty of practice – but, if trends were not reversed, the Soviet Union would slide gradually down the international economic league table and lose its status as a military superpower. President Gorbachev's policies have been based on a refusal to accept this outcome, and a readiness to take risks to avert it. Since 1985, his remedies of *perestroika* (reconstruction) and *glasnost* (openness) have entered the world's vocabulary. The efficacy of

OFFICIAL NAME Union of Soviet Socialist Republics.
CAPITAL CITY Moscow.
GEOGRAPHY The Soviet Union is the largest country in the world, occupying one-sixth of the land surface. Most people live in the great western plain bounded in the south by the Caucasus and Carpathians and in the east by the Urals. Beyond the Urals are the low, featureless and relatively uninhabited Siberian plains. The mountain chains marking the length of the southern border extend into plateaus in central Siberia and rise again in the mountainous peninsula of Kamchatka. Several areas, especially the far east, are volcanically active. Northern USSR falls inside the Arctic Circle and forms a continuous, largely uninhabited belt of tundra. *Highest point* Communism Peak 7,495 metres (24,590 feet). *Area* 22,402,200 sq km (8,649,500 sq miles).
PEOPLE *Population* 288m. *Density* 12 per sq km. *Ethnic groups* Russian 52%, Ukrainian 16%, Uzbek 5%, Belorussian 4%, Kazakh 2%, Tatar 2%, Azerbaijan 2%, Armenian 2%, Georgian 1%, Moldavian 1%, Tadzhik 1%, Lithuanian 1%, Turkmen 1%.
RELIGION Russian Orthodox 22%, Muslim 11%, Protestant 2%, RC 1%, Jewish 1%.
LANGUAGE Russian (59%), Ukrainian (15%), Uzbek (4%). There are 112 recognized languages in all and 5 alphabets.
EDUCATION Free at all levels and compulsory for ages 7–17, with proposals to bring the starting age down to 6. There are 894 institutes of higher education.
CLIMATE An enormous climatic range, but predominantly a continental, extreme climate; temperatures range from -70°C (-94°F) in Siberia to 50°C (122°F) in the central deserts. Average temperatures in Moscow vary from -12°C (10.5°F) in Jan to 18°C (64.5°F) in July.
CURRENCY Ruble (Rub).
PUBLIC HOLIDAYS Jan 1, Feb 23, Mar 8, May 1–2, May 9, Oct 7, Nov 7–8, 3rd Sun in Nov.
GOVERNMENT Communist federal republic since 1917. The USSR is a federation of 15 separate republics. The CPSU is the only legal party. Under the constitutional changes introduced in 1989 a congress of people's deputies is chosen in national elections in which nonpolitical groups may stand against CPSU candidates. The congress elects the country's legislature, the 500-member Supreme Soviet, which elects a presidium (over 20 members) and a chairman who is acting head of state. The Supreme Soviet may initiate legislation and veto the presidium. Whether the new constitution will reduce the power of the CPSU remains to be seen.

TRADE

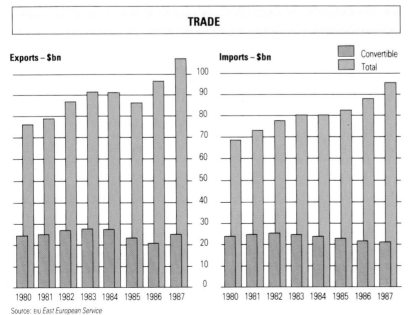

Exports – $bn

Imports – $bn

Convertible
Total

Source: EIU *East European Service*

EUROPE

the cures has yet to be proved, but their radicalism is undeniable.

Traditionally run like a single giant corporation, the economy has been bedevilled by two problems: the information overload on central planners and the lack of incentives for producers to cut costs, introduce new products and maintain quality. So long as the centre had access to substantial revenue and could mobilize a rapidly growing labour force and exploit cheap raw materials, wastefulness and lack of innovation were masked by throwing additional resources at the problems.

This system's weakness has been exposed as the growth of the labour force has slowed and the more accessible reserves of fuel, minerals and metals have been depleted. To counter this, Mr Gorbachev and his allies have deployed an array of economic measures. Some of these have been fairly conventional remedies: firing corrupt officials and replacing them with a younger generation keen to make its mark; singling out certain sectors – notably high-technology industries – for accelerated development and pumping in extra resources to achieve high targets. Others have been novel and controversial. One aim is to decentralize the state economy, moving towards so-called market socialism.

Urals

The traditional border between European and Asiatic Russia, this mineral-rich mountain range stretches 2,000km (1250 miles) from the Arctic to the Kazakh steppes. Highest point Mt Narodnaya, 1,894 metres (6,210 feet).

Baltic states

The three Baltic states, independent between World Wars I and II, were occupied by Soviet forces in 1940, ostensibly to protect them from the Germans, actually as part of the Nazi-Soviet pact, which assigned the Baltic area to the USSR.

Estonia is closely related linguistically and ethnically to Finland. Estonian SSR founded 1940. **Population 2m, area 45,100 sq km (17,400 sq miles).**

Latvia was successively under German, Polish and Swedish rule before coming under Russian domination in the 18th century. Latvian SSR founded and included in USSR 1940. **Population 3m, area 63,700 sq km (24,600 sq miles).**

Western republics

Moldavia Formed when Bessarabian region of Romania was occupied by Soviet army in 1940. Moldavian, claimed by Soviet scholars as a distinct romance language, is the local dialect of Romanian written in Cyrillic. Moldavian SSR founded 1940.

Population 4m, area 33,700 sq km (13,000 sq miles).

Ukraine Second most populous Soviet republic. Slavic nation occupying territory of former Kievan Rus princedom. Holds own seat at UN. Ukrainian SSR founded 1917, included in USSR since 1922.

Population 51m, area 603,700 sq km (233,100 sq miles).

Belorussia Slavonic nation, once part of Lithuania. Holds own seat at UN. Belorussia SSR founded January 1919, included in USSR since 1922. **Population 10m, area 207,600 sq km (80,200 sq miles).**

Population

70% of the population lives west of the Urals, less than 10% in Siberia and the Far East. Russians are still largest ethnic group, but the population growth rate in Central Asian republics is close to 3%, compared with less than 1% in the Russian Federation.

Languages

About 75% of population speak Slavic languages; a knowledge of Russian is vital to career advancement. Turkic, spoken by about one-eighth of the population, is the next largest language group. There are 112 recognised languages; five alphabets are used.

Climate

Most Soviet territory is far from the sea, so the climate is continental – warm summers, cold winters. The difference between the warmest and coldest months is most marked in Central Asia and eastern Siberia, where temperatures rise and fall by 45–65°C (113–149°F) in the course of the year. Most precipitation is in the warmest months.

Climatic zones range from arctic to sub-tropical, but in winter it is cold almost everywhere. Average January temperatures range from 6°C (43°F) on the Black Sea to –50°C (–58°F) in the Far East. Summer temperatures can be as high as 50°C (122°F) in Central Asia. The Black Sea region has a more temperate climate.

Caucasus

Armenia The Armenians, an ancient Indo-European people, have lived in Transcaucasia since 6th century BC. Claim to have been first Christian kingdom. Persian part of Armenia conquered by Russians in 1828. Short-lived independent Armenian Republic overrun by Soviet army 1920 and Armenian SSR founded. **Population 3m, area 29,800 sq km (11,500 sq mile).**

Azerbaijan Original Iranian population turkicized by Seljuk Turks in 8th century. Persian khanate of Gulistan ceded to Russia 1813. Independent republic fell to Soviet forces and Azerbaijan SSR founded April 1920. **Population 7m, area 86,600 sq km (33,400 sq miles).**

Georgia Ancient people speaking unique Caucasian language. Allied with Russia under Treaty of Georgievsk 1783. Independent Menshevik republic from 1918 until conquered by Soviet forces and Georgian SSR founded 1920. **Population 5m, area 69,700 sq km (26,900 sq miles).**

Arctic Circle

The longest sea coast – over 6,000km (3,700 miles) – is by the Arctic Ocean. The coast is sparsely settled and the sea to the north frozen over for nine months of the year, from October to June.

Baikal

The world's deepest lake, at 1,620 metres (5,310 ft). 636km (395 miles) long and an average 50km (30 miles) wide, it contains one-fifth of all fresh water in the world's lakes. It has unique flora and fauna, but cellulose factories at the southern end have caused severe pollution since the 1960s.

Russian Federation

Russian Soviet Federal Socialist Republic Largest Soviet republic, stretching from Baltic to Arctic and Pacific. Includes Moscow, Leningrad and most other large Soviet cities. RSFSR founded 1917, included in USSR 1922. **Population 144m, area 17,075,400 sq km (6,592,800 sq miles).**

Central Asia

Most of the region became part of Russia in the second half of the 19th century, by either conquest or alliance. Four of the five republics are Turkic speaking.

Uzbekistan Conquered by imperial Russia 1865–84. After 1917 revolution part of Soviet Turkestan. Uzbek SSR founded 1924. **Population 18m, area 447,400 sq km (172,700 sq miles).**

Turkmenistan Last Central Asian territory to be conquered by Russia, 1878–85. After October revolution part of Soviet Turkestan. Turkmen SSR founded 1924. **Population 3m, area 488,100 sq km (188,500 sq miles).**

Kirgizia Small Turkic people closely related to Kazakhs. Accepted Russian protection in 1855; conquest completed 1876. After the revolution an autonomous *oblast* (province), then an autonomous republic within Russian Federation. Kirgiz SSR founded 1936. **Population 4m, area 198,500 sq mk (76,600 sq miles).**

Kazakhstan The second largest Soviet republic in area. In 1731 the khan of the Little Horde (one of three Kazakh hordes) accepted Russian rule in return for military aid. Russians established control by 1850s. In 1920 became an autonomous republic within the Russian Federation. Kazakh SSR founded 1936. **Population 16m, area 2,717,300 sq km (1,049,200 sq miles).**

Tadzhikistan Tadzhiks speak a language linked to Persian. Conquered by Russians in 1860s–70s. Part of Soviet Uzbekistan until 1924. Tadzhik SSR founded 1929. **Population 5m, area 143,100 sq km (55,300 sq miles).**

BAM

The Baikal–Amur Mainline, completed in 1984, was built to relieve pressure on Trans-Siberian railway, with which it connects at both ends. Running for 3,145km, some 400km north of the Trans-Siberian, it has also opened up access to new mineral resources. A branch is being built to Yakutsk.

Mineral wealth

Much of the Soviet Union's mineral wealth lies in inhospitable and barely accessible Siberia; vast areas have yet to be properly surveyed. Deposits nearer the industrial centres are rapidly being worked out. Oil and gas have accounted for up to 70% of exports in recent years, but oil fields around the Caspian Sea are almost exhausted, newer fields in western Siberia are in difficult terrain and struggling to maintain their production level. Most gas reserves are in western Siberia, Central Asia or the Far East. Huge pipelines have been built to ship the gas across the country and to Western Europe. Coal tells the same story – Ukrainian reserves running out, but there are huge deposits in Central Siberia.

Huge copper deposits exist in Kazakhstan and the Urals are rich in iron, copper, bauxite, titanium, chromite and platinum. Gold, tin and iron ore can be found in eastern Siberia.

EUROPE

Another is to expand the non-state sector – privatization, in a word.

By 1988, the Soviet Union had more liberal laws on cooperatives than Hungary or Poland, and a return to family farming – on 50-year leases – was being facilitated. There were moves to make the economy less insulated from the outside world, with joint Soviet-Western ventures on Soviet soil being encouraged and a target of making the ruble partially convertible towards the end of the century.

On the ground, these measures have yet to make much impact. Growth remains slow. The non-state sector is still small. Shortages are still routine. The bulk of output continues to be centrally allocated, and prices still controlled. Real change has been most visible in politics and social life.

President Gorbachev aims to keep the party's monopoly of power, but to make officials more accountable and to allow conflicting views to be expressed. The 1989 election and first sitting of the new congress of people's deputies emphasized dramatically these intentions. The obstacles are numerous: officials who do not want their power diluted; workers who prefer secure and slothful subsistence to effort, insecurity and the promise, but not the guarantee, of greater material reward. There are also signs that change is bringing instability: nationalists in the republics are seizing the opportunity to push for greater autonomy; East European liberals see a chance to abandon the Soviet model.

Mr Gorbachev has also seized the initiative in international affairs, withdrawing from overseas entanglements such as Afghanistan and giving new impetus to negotiations on arms control. In a very short time, he has transformed his country's image in the eyes of many Westerners. Transforming the country itself will take a lot longer.

ECONOMIC PROFILE

Comprehensive natural resource base makes self-sufficiency feasible, at a cost, and permits large net energy exports; world's largest oil producer and second largest producer of natural gas, coal and gold. Well-developed traditional heavy industries – iron and steel, shipbuilding, vehicles, machine tools, chemicals – but modernization struggling against entrenched bureaucracy and corruption. Agriculture, largely collectivized, suffers from labour shortages and lack of incentives. Exports to West largely fuels and raw materials; sells manufactured goods to rest of eastern bloc. Massive food imports in recent years.

Growth Natural gas output rising fast. Service sector growing rapidly, albeit from small base. Joint ventures with Western partners promoted to transfer technology.

Problems No-growth economy for 20 years. Technological change sluggish and export performance in competitive markets weak. Lower oil prices hit hard-currency earnings. Depletion of mineral resources forcing development of high-cost Siberian reserves.

NMP BY ORIGIN

Mining & manufacturing 44%
Agriculture, forestry & fishing 21%
Wholesale & retail trade 17%
Construction 12%
Transport, storage & communications 6%

Source: EIU *Country Report* (1986 figures)

COMPONENTS OF NMP

Consumption 74%
Investment 26%

Soviet statisticians and those from some other Comecon countries publish fiscal data in the form of net material product. NMP has no exact parallel in Western financial figures, and is most useful for internal analysis as shown here, and for comparison between Comecon countries that use the same index. It is of less value for year-on-year comparisons, because NMP does not allow for inflation, resulting in growth figures that are artificially high.

WORK FORCE

Services 41%
Manufacturing 29%
Agriculture & fishing 19%
Construction 9%
Other 2%

Source: ILO *Yearbook of Labour Statistics* (1987 figures)

212

NATIONALITIES

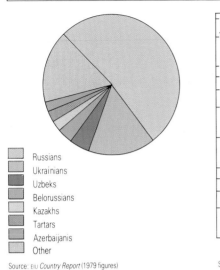

Russians
Ukrainians
Uzbeks
Belorussians
Kazakhs
Tartars
Azerbaijanis
Other

Source: EIU *Country Report* (1979 figures)

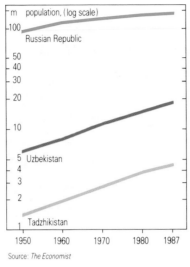

m population, (log scale)
100 Russian Republic
50
40
30
20
10
5 Uzbekistan
4
3
2
1 Tadzhikistan
1950   1960   1970   1980   1987

Source: *The Economist*

Demographic patterns

In the 1970s the population of the Muslim republics grew more than 2.5 times faster than that of the USSR as a whole, and during the 1980s the Russian proportion of the total population fell to below half. The composition of the army has provided a focus for Russian concerns about the changing ethnic balance; Muslims now make up 30–40% of soldiers and their loyalty is questioned. Reportedly, some were unwilling to fight against fellow Muslims in Afghanistan.

NATIONAL INCOME

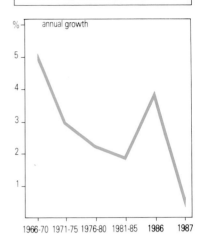

% annual growth
5
4
3
2
1
1966-70 1971-75 1976-80 1981-85 1986 1987

Plotting national income illustrates the urgency of *perestroika*. Most informed Western estimates – and even some Soviet official figures – show that real income growth rates have been slowing for nearly two decades.

Source: CIA estimates

IMPORTS AND EXPORTS

E. Germany
Czechoslovakia
Bulgaria
Poland
Hungary
Cuba
W. Germany
Yugoslavia
Romania
Finland
Japan
Italy
India
USA
France
China
Austria
Libya
UK
Mongolia
N. Korea
Other

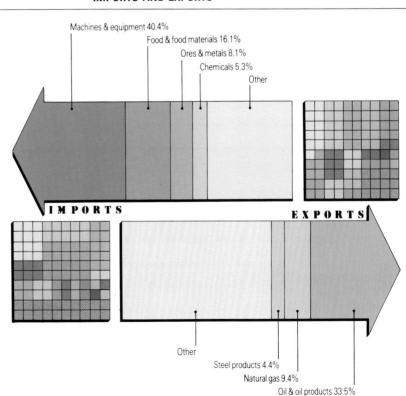

Machines & equipment 40.4%
Food & food materials 16.1%
Ores & metals 8.1%
Chemicals 5.3%
Other

IMPORTS

EXPORTS

Other
Steel products 4.4%
Natural gas 9.4%
Oil & oil products 33.5%

INDIAN SUBCONTINENT

Afghan refugees

At least 5m refugees have left Afghanistan since the Soviet invasion in 1979 and the subsquent guerrilla war; over 3m are in Pakistan, the rest in Iran. The refugee communities have been a focus for resistance to the Soviet occupation and a channel for foreign military aid to the *mujahideen* fighting within Afghanistan. Continued fighting after the Soviet withdrawal condemned the refugees to more years in exile.

Drugs

The troubled border between Pakistan and Afghanistan has been fertile ground for the drug trade in the past decade. Pakistan became the world's biggest heroin producer and exporter in the early 1980s, after the Islamic revolution in Iran and tough action against producers in the Burma–Thailand Golden Triangle cut off other sources of supply. Under US pressure, the Pakistan government has made efforts to crack down on the trade, but it has been unable to do much about opium grown across the border in Afghanistan, which helped to finance the guerrilla war against the Soviet occupation.

Language

India's official languages are Hindi and English, spoken by 30% of the population. The constitution also recognizes 16 regional languages of which the most widely spoken are Telugu, Bengali, Marathi, Tamil, Urdu and Gujarati.

Food and climate

Indian agriculture depends on the monsoon, which brings 80% of annual rainfall between June and September. India once suffered catastrophic famines when the monsoon failed but the "green revolution" has transformed food supplies over the past 20 years through use of irrigation, fertilizers and improved seed varieties. India is now self-sufficient in food grains, with surpluses to see it through the bad years, but the benefits of the green revolution have been uneven, favouring the medium-sized farm and failing to ensure a supply of food for the rural, landless poor.

Islands

Three groups of islands form part of India. The Andaman and Nicobar islands in the Bay of Bengal became an Indian state in 1950. The two groups contain over 300 islands. The Andaman islands were a British penal colony until 1945; the mountainous Nicobar group to the south was occupied by Denmark for almost a century before being annexed by the British in 1869. The Lakshadweep or Laccadive islands lie 300km (190 miles) off India's southwest coast. Ten of the 27 coral islands are inhabited.

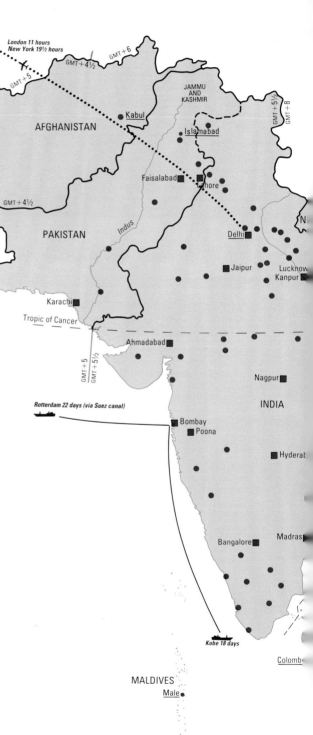

Kashmir

The northern state of Jammu and Kashmir, which at the time of India's independence in 1947 had a Hindu ruler and a Muslim majority population, has remained a bone of contention between India and Pakistan ever since. The state sought separate status but attached itself to India after an attack by Pakistan. Fighting ended in 1949 after a UN-negotiated ceasefire and effective partition. The two countries went to war again over the issue in 1965 and 1972; the border in Kashmir follows the ceasefire line. Relations again deteriorated in the 1980s after accusations that Pakistan was supporting the Sikh separatist movement in Punjab.

The Himalayas

A series of parallel mountain ranges, rising towards the Tibetan plateau in the north, the Himalayas stretch from the Pamir Mountains in the Soviet Union to the borders of Assam and China in the east, about 2,400km (1,500 miles) away. The Himalayas contain the world's highest mountains, with peaks over 8,000 metres (26,250 feet) high.

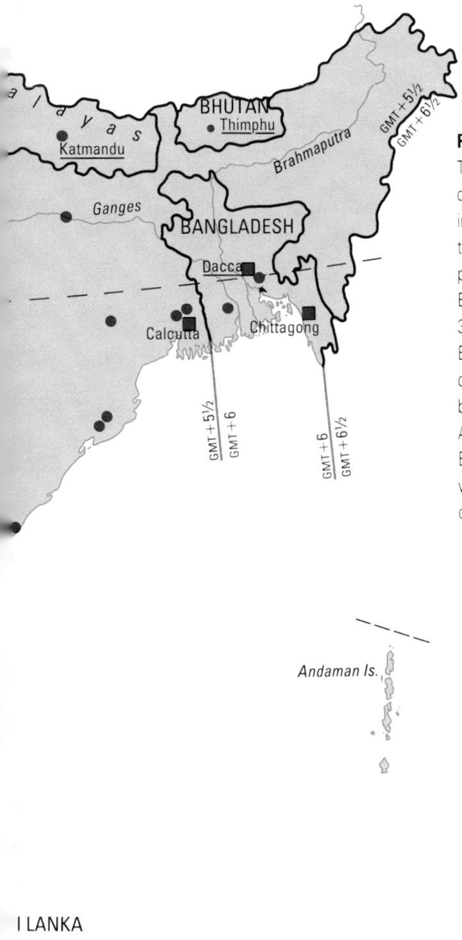

BHUTAN
Thimphu
Katmandu
Brahmaputra
Ganges
BANGLADESH
Dacca
Calcutta
Chittagong
GMT+5½
GMT+6½
GMT+5½
GMT+6
GMT+6
GMT+6½

Rivers

The disastrous flooding of the Ganges/Brahmaputra delta in recent years has been blamed on deforestation in the Himalayas in India and Nepal but plans to control the flow of water have run up against political problems. Mutual suspicion between India and Bangladesh has so far prevented the construction of a 320km (200-mile) canal to transfer water from the Brahmaputra to the Ganges to increase supplies to drought-affected regions of India. India also plans to build dams on the upper reaches of the Brahmaputra in Arunachal Pradesh state; the scheme would protect Bangladesh from floods but has antagonized China where the Brahmaputra has its source and which claims Arunachal Pradesh as its own territory.

Andaman Is.

Religion

- Sunni Muslim
- Predominantly Hindu
- Southern Buddhist
- Lamaist Buddhist

I LANKA

- ■ More than 1 million
- ● 250,000 – 1 million

AFGHANISTAN

Throughout its history Afghanistan has balanced uncomfortably between Russia and the Western powers. The British invaded twice in the 19th century to maintain the country's status as a buffer between India and the advancing Russian empire. British and Russian recognition of Afghan independence in 1921 temporarily removed the country from the arena of great power conflict.

A left-wing coup in 1972 deposed the monarchy and in 1973 established a republic. Disenchantment with the pace of reform led to a further military coup in April 1978, which handed power to the Moscow-oriented People's Democratic Party of Afghanistan (PDPA). Clumsy implementation of radical policies, conservative opposition and internal divisions produced political chaos. In September 1979, PDPA leader Nur Muhammad Taraki was replaced by his hardline deputy, Hafizullah Amin. Two months later, Soviet forces invaded.

The Soviet action aroused intense internal and international opposition. With extensive military assistance from the USA, the cooperation of the Pakistani government and a secure base among more than 4m refugees in Pakistan and Iran, opposition groups – though divided by regional, religious and political differences – fought an unrelenting war of resistance.

The *mujahideen* (holy warriors) undermined government control over large areas and inflicted heavy losses on Soviet forces, whose numbers rose to some 115,000. In 1988 the Soviet Union began a full-scale withdrawal, which it completed the following year, leaving the PDPA's Dr Najibullah to pursue a political formula based on "national reconciliation" to forestall an outright *mujahideen* victory. The war severely disrupted Afghanistan's predominantly agricultural economy, based on growing wheat and rearing sheep; natural gas, fruit and carpets are the main exports.

OFFICIAL NAME Republic of Afghanistan.
CAPITAL CITY Kabul.
GEOGRAPHY The south of the country is a desert plateau. Most people live in the north, in the fertile plains and foothills beneath the high mountains of the Hindu Kush. *Area* 647,500 sq km (250,000 sq miles).
PEOPLE *Population* 18.1m. *Density* 28 per sq km. *Ethnic groups* Pushtun or Pathan 50%, Tadzhik 25%, Uzbek 9%, Hazarah 3%.
RELIGION Muslim 99% (Sunni 87%, Shia 12%).
LANGUAGE Pushtu and Dari, a dialect of Persian. Also many local languages.
EDUCATION Compulsory for ages 7–15.
CLIMATE Continental, with extreme temperatures, especially at altitude. At Kabul, average monthly temperature range is -3°C (27°F) to 25°C (77°F). Annual rainfall ranges from 75mm (3ins) to 1,300mm (50ins).
CURRENCY Afghani (Af).
PUBLIC HOLIDAYS Mar 21, 1st day of Ramadan, Apr 27, May 1, Id al-Fitr, Id al-Adha, Aug 18, Ashoura, Mouloud.
GOVERNMENT Republic since 1973. The communist People's Democratic Party of Afghanistan has been the only permitted party since 1978. Under the 1987 constitution the main organ of government is a 165-member revolutionary council, represented by a 21-member presidium. The chairman of the council is head of state.

PAKISTAN

Created by the partition of British India into Muslim and Hindu areas, the state that came into being in August 1947 comprised two widely separated regions, West and East Pakistan. Conflict between the two led to a bitter civil war in 1971. After Indian intervention, East Pakistan seceded and became Bangladesh. Regional tensions persisted in West Pakistan. Violent conflicts between rival groups have been aggravated by an influx of arms resulting from the war in neighbouring Afghanistan.

In 1977, the army overthrew the first elected civilian government, led by Zulfikar Ali Bhutto. Chief of staff General Zia ul-Haq ruled for eight years under martial law. Bhutto was convicted of murder and hanged. A controlled move towards civilian institutions culminated in 1985 in the lifting of martial law, but Zia remained president and commander of the army.

Zia's death in an air crash in 1988 accelerated the transition to civilian rule. Bhutto's daughter Benazir was appointed prime minister after elections in November, but a strong showing by Zia's followers in the Punjab promised heightened regional tensions. As in the past, the survival of civilian leadership depended on the consent of the army. The army has enjoyed a ready supply of sophisticated weaponry from the USA during the Afghan conflict, despite differences over Pakistan's covert efforts to develop a nuclear military capacity. Benazir Bhutto's election offered the hope of improved relations with India, with which Pakistan has gone to war three times.

The economy has grown rapidly but depends heavily on external resources. A chronic trade deficit is funded by remittances from workers abroad and by heavy foreign lending. A severe fiscal crisis has resulted from a combination of tax evasion and exemptions for the agricultural sector. As a result, social spending is low and investment is crowded out by borrowing to cover deficits.

OFFICIAL NAME Islamic Republic of Pakistan.
CAPITAL CITY Islamabad.
GEOGRAPHY The Himalayas in the far north feed rivers that run through a scrubby plateau to Pakistan's heartland: the flat and featureless alluvial flood plain of the Indus. In the west the mountainous border with Afghanistan gives way to the Baluchistan plateau and deserts in the south. *Highest point* Mt Godwin Austen (K2) 8,611 metres (28,250 feet). *Area* 769,095 sq km (307,370 sq miles).
PEOPLE *Population* 96.2m. *Density* 121 per sq km. *Ethnic groups* Punjabi 66%, Sindhi 13%, Pushtun 8%.
RELIGION Muslim 97%, Hindu 2%, Christian 1%.
LANGUAGE Urdu. Also English, Punjabi, Pushtu, Sindhi, Saraiki and others.
EDUCATION Free for ages 5–18 but noncompulsory.
CLIMATE Continental, with daily temperature ranges of 15°C (60°F); average 4°C (39°F) in Jan, over 40°C (105°F) in summer. Rainfall 750–900mm (30–35ins) in the mountains, but less than 500mm (20ins) elsewhere, with some desert regions.
CURRENCY Pakistan rupee (PR).
PUBLIC HOLIDAYS (* for Christians only) Mar 23, Good Fri*, Easter Mon*, 1st day of Ramadan, May 1, Id al-Fitr, Id al-Adha, Aug 14, Muharram, Ashoura, Sep 6, 11, Mouloud, Nov 9, Dec 25, 26*.
GOVERNMENT Federal republic since 1947. The bicameral legislature consists of an 87-member senate elected by the 4 provincial assemblies for 6 years, and a 237-member national assembly elected for 5 years.

ECONOMIC PROFILE

Wheat is main food crop; cotton is grown for domestic market and for export. Industry is dominated by textiles and food processing. Remittances from overseas workers have shrunk in recent years, but still bring in more income than any single commodity export.

Growth Output of both food and cash crops has grown significantly, if erratically. Natural gas production has risen sharply, as has output of food processing and chemical industries.

Problems Production of cotton cloth in decline. External demand for cotton and rice exports fluctuates dramatically. Dependence on oil contributes to trade deficit. Heavy debt service burden.

IMPORTS AND EXPORTS

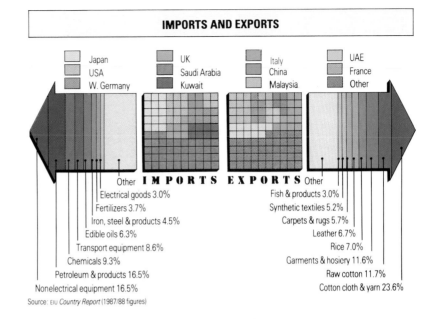

Japan
USA
W. Germany

UK
Saudi Arabia
Kuwait

Italy
China
Malaysia

UAE
France
Other

IMPORTS

Other
Electrical goods 3.0%
Fertilizers 3.7%
Iron, steel & products 4.5%
Edible oils 6.3%
Transport equipment 8.6%
Chemicals 9.3%
Petroleum & products 16.5%
Nonelectrical equipment 16.5%

EXPORTS

Other
Fish & products 3.0%
Synthetic textiles 5.2%
Carpets & rugs 5.7%
Leather 6.7%
Rice 7.0%
Garments & hosiery 11.6%
Raw cotton 11.7%
Cotton cloth & yarn 23.6%

Source: EIU *Country Report* (1987/88 figures)

INDIA

Today, as at independence in August 1947, the vast majority of India's people work small plots of land and live in simple village communities. For them, poverty and insecurity are still the dominant facts of life. Yet India has also developed a complex urban society and a sizeable middle class. Social divisions are eased somewhat by nationalist political traditions and democratic institutions. Indians are more firmly attached to their own culture than many in the Third World. Internationally, these attitudes translated in the early years of independence into a pioneering role in the nonaligned movement, although border tensions with China and Pakistan drew India towards the Soviet Union. At home, a tradition of concern for the poor is upheld by both individuals and government. There have been significant advances in extending literacy, education and healthcare, although huge inequalities remain.

Economic progress has been slow but sure. Growth has not been rapid but it has firm foundations. Heavy foreign debt has been avoided by financing investment largely from domestic savings; both industry and government have made determined efforts to promote technological self-sufficiency. The country can now maintain food reserves to meet demand even in shortage years. On the other hand, poor environmental management has caused serious problems with deforestation and loss of vital top soils.

India's democratic institutions have survived, but the Indian National Congress, architect of independence, is a shadow of its former self. Congress was split by the radical economic policies of Indira Gandhi, who took office in 1966, two years after the death of her father, India's first prime minister Jawaharlal Nehru. Politics became bitterly factionalized and Mrs Gandhi's response was authoritarian, culminating in the declaration of a state of emergency in 1975. The Janata party ousted Mrs Gandhi in the 1977 elections, but she was returned to power two years later.

Divisions in the body politic have been paralleled by tensions among the diverse linguistic, religious and cultural groups. In the northern state of Punjab, economic prosperity generated a new political assertiveness among the Sikh people, building upon their well-established sense of cultural identity. Their grievances increasingly found expression in violence against the Punjab's Hindu minority. In 1984, Mrs Gandhi herself became a casualty, when her Sikh

OFFICIAL NAME India.

CAPITAL CITY New Delhi.

GEOGRAPHY To the south of the Himalayas a wide and densely populated alluvial plain contains the Ganges, Indus and Brahmaputra. Peninsular India consists of the Deccan plateau fringed by a coastal plain. *Highest point* Nanda Devi 7,817 metres (25,650 feet). *Area* 3,287,590 sq km (1,269,350 sq miles).

PEOPLE *Population* 751m. *Density* 228 per sq km. *Ethnic groups* Mainly Indo-Aryan and Dravidian. Also Mongoloid and Australoid.

RELIGION Hindu 83%, Muslim 11%, Christian 3%, Sikh 2%, Buddhist 1%, Jain 1%.

LANGUAGE Hindi and English. Also many local languages.

EDUCATION Government aiming at free and compulsory education for ages 6–14 by 1990.

CLIMATE Tropical, monsoon season Jun–Oct. Annual rainfall 750–1,500mm (30–60ins) in most areas. Average annual temperatures from around 13°C (55°F) in northern highlands to 25–30°C (77–86°F) on coast.

CURRENCY Indian rupee (IR).

PUBLIC HOLIDAYS Vary from state to state. In New Delhi: Pongal (Jan), Jan 26, Maha Shivaratri, Holi (Mar), Good Fri, Ram Navami, Buddha Purinama (May), Id al-Fitr, Id al-Adha, Muharram, Aug 15, 20, 28, Oct 2, 18-20, Divali, Nov 1, Dec 25, 26.

GOVERNMENT Federal republic. Each of the 25 states has its own elected legislature and governor appointed by the federal president. The legislative parliament has a 245-member council of states (Rajya Sabha) elected for 6 years by the state assemblies and a 544-member house of the people (Lok Sabha) elected for 5 years from single-member constituencies. The chief executive is the prime minister. Head of state is the president, elected by a college of parliament and the state assemblies.

IMPORTS AND EXPORTS

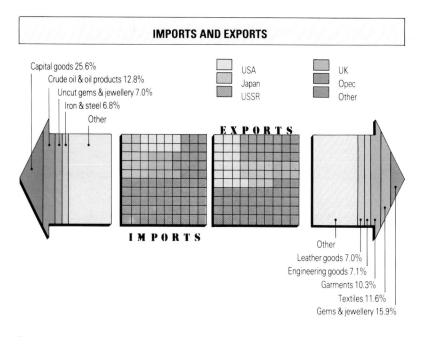

Capital goods 25.6%
Crude oil & oil products 12.8%
Uncut gems & jewellery 7.0%
Iron & steel 6.8%
Other

USA
Japan
USSR

UK
Opec
Other

EXPORTS

IMPORTS

Other
Leather goods 7.0%
Engineering goods 7.1%
Garments 10.3%
Textiles 11.6%
Gems & jewellery 15.9%

GDP BY ORIGIN

Agriculture, forestry, mining & fisheries 34.7%

Industry 24.3%

Miscellaneous services 22.5%

Transport, communications & trade 18.5%

Source: EIU *Country Report* (1986 figures)

COMPONENTS OF GDP

Private consumption 66.0%

Gross fixed capital formation 24.3%

Government consumption 11.9%

Exports of goods & services 6.2%

Less: imports of goods & services –8.4%

ECONOMIC PROFILE

Most people work on the land, but the industrial sector is large and diverse, its contribution to GDP almost as great as that of agriculture. "Green revolution" technologies have boosted crop yields, especially of wheat, but much agriculture still on a subsistence basis, dependent on annual monsoon. Exports account for only a small proportion of output; efforts being made to diversify into sectors such as clothing, engineering, chemicals.

Growth Development of new reserves boosted oil production in early 1980s. Wide range of consumer and capital goods industries expanding fast. Services, particularly tourism, contributing a growing share of GDP.

Problems Traditional exports such as tea and jute declining, as is cotton textile industry. Many more sophisticated capital goods still imported. Higher foreign borrowing likely to be needed to sustain worsening current account deficit.

BALANCE OF PAYMENTS

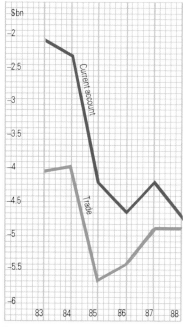

Source: EIU *Country Credit Risk Service*

bodyguards took revenge for the storming of the Golden Temple, the Sikhs' holiest shrine and stronghold of militants. The terrible violence that followed her death did enormous damage to national unity.

Rajiv Gandhi took his mother's place and for a brief period embodied popular sentiment in favour of a cleansing of political life. But eventually he became tarnished by involvement in the established pattern of power-broking and manoeuvring. The crusade for clean government found a new leader as the main opposition parties united behind Vishwanath Pratap Singh, a disillusioned former finance minister in Gandhi's government.

Indian politics is in a state of flux and the exact pace and direction of change remains uncertain. Many attack authoritarianism and corruption as the causes of India's troubles; others see the solution in greater autonomy for the 25 states of the union. Still others invoke a strident Hindu nationalism that would consign the various minorities to second-class status.

NEPAL

OFFICIAL NAME Kingdom of Nepal.
CAPITAL CITY Kathmandu.
GEOGRAPHY Three-quarters of Nepal is ruggedly mountainous. The only lowland is the flat, fertile Tarai plain along the southern border; the plain is marshy in the north and susceptible to flooding. The land rises through forested foothills marked by steep scarps to a system of mountain ranges divided by glacial basins where snow-fed rivers run and most of the population live. The high Himalayas in the north are uninhabited. *Highest point* Mt Everest 8,848 metres (29,030 feet). *Area* 140,797 sq km (54,360 sq miles).
PEOPLE *Population* 16.6m. *Density* 118 per sq mile. *Ethnic groups* Nepali 54%, Bihari 19%, Tamang 6%, Newari 4%, Tharu 4%.
RELIGION Hindu 90%, Buddhist 5%, Muslim 3%.
LANGUAGE Nepali. Also Bihari, Tamang and other languages.
EDUCATION Free and officially compulsory for ages 6–11; few girls are educated. There is 1 university.
CLIMATE Sub-tropical on the plain, temperate in the mountain valleys, alpine or arctic on the peaks. Annual rainfall 1,500–2,000mm (60–80ins) in the east, half that in the west. Kathmandu temperatures range between around 2°C (35°F) and 30°C (86°F).
CURRENCY Nepalese rupee (NR).
PUBLIC HOLIDAYS Feb 18, Shivaratri, New Year (Apr), Buddha's Birthday, Indra Jatra, Dasain Durga-Puja festival (one week in Oct), Tihar (2 days in Nov), Dec 16, 28.
GOVERNMENT Constitutional monarchy. The head of state and chief executive is the king, usually acting on the recommendation of the prime minister. The prime minister is elected by the legislative national assembly, 112 of whose members are directly elected for 5 years, while the remaining 28 are appointed by the king.

Nepal is one of the dwindling number of states in which a monarch holds real political power. King Birendra remains the principal executive authority, although since 1980 the prime minister has been responsible to a national nonparty assembly, the *panchayat*. Opposition to this system is led by the banned Nepali Congress Party; there are no legal parties.

Nepal's subsistence economy is precariously dependent on the rains and liberal amounts of foreign aid, and is threatened by ecological damage caused primarily by deforestation. Periodic Indian border restrictions underline Nepal's economic reliance on its southern neighbour and expose the fragility of its nonaligned foreign policy.

BHUTAN

OFFICIAL NAME Kingdom of Bhutan.
CAPITAL CITY Thimphu.
GEOGRAPHY Most of the people live in flat, broad, fertile valleys, often thickly forested, that run north–south through the centre of the country. Farther north, by the ill-defined border with Tibet, the peaks are over 7,000 metres (23,000 feet) and the lower ground is pastureland. Along the southern border runs the Duars plain, a strip of semi-tropical forest, bamboo jungle and savannah. *Highest point* Kula Kangri 7,554 metres (24,780 feet). *Area* 47,000 sq km (18,000 sq miles).
PEOPLE *Population* 1.4m. *Density* 30 per sq km. *Ethnic groups* Bhutia 61%, Gurung 15%, Assamese 13%.
RELIGION Buddhist 70%, Hindu 25%, Muslim 5%.
LANGUAGE Dzongkha (Tibetan/Burmese).
EDUCATION Noncompulsory; free where available. Teaching is in English, with a British-style syllabus.
CLIMATE Temperate, varying with altitude. Dry in the extreme north, hot and humid on the Duars plain. Average monthly temperatures in the valleys from around 5°C (41°F) in Jan to around 17°C (63°F) in July.
CURRENCY Ngultrum (Nu). Indian rupee (IR) also used.
PUBLIC HOLIDAYS Nov 11, Dec 17. Buddhist lunar holidays also observed.
GOVERNMENT Constitutional monarchy. The legislative national assembly has 106 elected members and 45 appointees and shares power with the king and his advisors, a council of ministers and the Buddhist head abbot. There are no political parties.

Bhutan is a landlocked kingdom in the eastern Himalayas. King Jigme Singye Wangchuk is head of state and government, advised by a national assembly. External affairs are "guided" by India, under a 1949 treaty.

The economy is based on maize and rice cultivation. Only some 9% of the land is cultivated. Cement, stamps and tourism earn foreign exchange but not enough to avert dependence on grants from India and elsewhere.

CHAGOS ARCHIPELAGO

OFFICIAL NAME British Indian Ocean Territory.
GEOGRAPHY The isolated series of small coral atolls lies some 1,800km (1,100 miles) east of the Seychelles. *Area* 60 sq km (20 sq miles).
PEOPLE *Population* 4,000. *Density* 77 per sq km.
LANGUAGE English.
CURRENCY US dollar ($) and UK pound (£).

GOVERNMENT UK territory. It is administered jointly by a commissioner in the British Foreign and Commonwealth Office and a Royal Navy commander.

The British Indian Ocean Territory now consists only of the Chagos archipelago, which is held by the UK, despite Mauritian claims, to maintain the US military base on Diego Garcia. The original inhabitants were evacuated before the construction of the base; it has a temporary British and US population.

MALDIVES

OFFICIAL NAME Republic of Maldives.
CAPITAL CITY Male.
GEOGRAPHY The archipelago consists of more than 1,000 coral islands, none of them very large and only 210 inhabited. They are grouped into 19 atolls for administrative purposes. *Area* 298 sq km (120 sq miles).
PEOPLE *Population* 180,000. *Density* 594 per sq km. *Ethnic groups* Mainly Sinhalese.
RELIGION Sunni Muslim.
LANGUAGE Divehi. Also English, Arabic and Hindi.
EDUCATION Noncompulsory. There are three systems: traditional Koranic schools, Divehi primary schools, and English primary and secondary schools.
CLIMATE Tropical and humid, with annual average temperature around 27°C (81°F). Rainfall varies between 2,500mm (100ins) and 4,000mm (160ins).
CURRENCY Rufiyaa (Rf).
PUBLIC HOLIDAYS Jan 7, Id al-Fitr, Id al-Adha, Jul 26, Muharram, Mouloud, Nov 11, Dec 10.
GOVERNMENT Republic, independent since 1965. Executive power is in the hands of a president elected for 5 years after nomination by the citizens' council, a 48-member legislature. Each atoll is partly self-governing and there are no political parties.

Consistent with its isolation in the Indian Ocean, the Maldives remains economically dependent on the sea. Tourism has supplemented the mainstays of fishing and shipping, but this source of income could be threatened by instances of political instability such as the 1988 coup attempt which was suppressed with Indian help.

SRI LANKA

Communal violence has blighted the prospects of Sri Lanka, which has come some way in diversifying an economy traditionally based on rice growing and tea exports through the development of light industry and tourism.

The conflict between the Sinhalese majority of the north (74% of the population) and the northern Tamil people (18%) is the most serious political problem facing the country. Heavy-handed government treatment of demands for local autonomy caused young Tamils to turn to violence. After anti-Tamil riots in 1983 the conflict escalated into civil war. Under pressure from India, the government met many Tamil demands in 1987 and allowed an Indian peace-keeping force into the country; the Indians took control of Tamil areas after a campaign against the main separatist group, the Tamil Tigers, and secured the cooperation of more moderate Tamil groups in holding elections for new provincial councils in late 1988.

President Junius Jayawardene retired at the beginning of 1989, after dominating Sri Lankan politics for more than a decade. His conservative United National Party won a decisive electoral victory in 1977 over the Sri Lanka Freedom Party of Mrs Sirimavo Bandaranaike and her populist programme. The UNP introduced a new constitution based on a presidential system of government and in 1982 used a national referendum to postpone a general election for a further six years.

Mr Jayawardene leaves the country deeply divided. Tamil separatists remain a force in the north, while in the south the Janatha Vimukti Peramuna, which combines fierce Sinhalese nationalism with crude Marxism, has been waging a campaign of violence against concessions to the Tamils. Despite violence and intimidation, the election of Mr Jayawardene's successor took place on schedule, resulting in a narrow victory for Ranasinghe Premadasa, the former prime minister, who promised to send the Indian forces home.

OFFICIAL NAME Democratic Socialist Republic of Sri Lanka.

CAPITAL CITY Colombo.

GEOGRAPHY The largest and most populous area, north and east, is a lush, rolling plain. South and central highlands fall off in scarps to uplands and there are numerous short, swift rivers. Lagoons, dunes, marshes and sandy beaches on the coast are separated by peninsulas. *Highest point* Pidurutalagala 2,524 metres (8,280 feet). *Area* 65,610 sq km (25,330 sq miles).

PEOPLE *Population* 15.8m. *Density* 241 per sq km. *Ethnic groups* Sinhalese 74%, Tamil 18%, Moor 7%.

RELIGION Buddhist 70%, Hindu 15%, Christian 8%, Muslim 7%.

LANGUAGE Sinhala. Also Tamil and English.

EDUCATION Free and compulsory for ages 5–15.

CLIMATE Tropical monsoon; monthly temperatures 25–29°C (77–84°F). Main rainy season is May–Oct, with a secondary season Dec–Mar.

CURRENCY Sri Lanka rupee (SLR).

PUBLIC HOLIDAYS Jan 1, Feb 4, Good Fri, Easter Mon, Apr 12–13, May 1, Id al-Fitr, Id al-Adha, Mouloud, Deepavali, Dec 25–26 and every full moon.

GOVERNMENT Republic since 1948. The chief executive and head of state is a president who is not accountable to parliament; he appoints the prime minister and the cabinet. Parliament is elected by PR; there are no by-elections.

BANGLADESH

Bangladesh, the former eastern region of Pakistan, has had an unsettled history since its birth in 1971 out of a bitter civil war, resolved by Indian intervention. Four military coups have followed and two heads of state – including Shaikh Mujib ur Rahman, the country's founding father – have died violently in office.

President Hossain Mohammad Ershad, who came to power in a military coup in 1982, is a skilful politician who resigned as army chief of staff to take up the civilian presidency in 1986. Opposition comes from political parties founded by the two murdered presidents: Shaikh Mujib's Awami League and the Bangladesh National Party of General Zia, who was killed in 1981. Their regular mass protests and boycott of political institutions only add to the instability of political life.

In recent years such conflicts have been overshadowed by the elements. Storms and flooding during the monsoon season have taken a terrible toll in loss of life and destruction of homes and crops. Discussion of flood control schemes with India, begun in the mid-1970s, has been repeatedly bogged down in an atmosphere of mutual suspicion.

Bangladesh is one of the poorest and most densely populated countries in the world, heavily dependent on foreign aid, with an agricultural economy based on rice growing in the densely populated Ganges delta. International demand for jute, the principal export crop, has long been in decline, but substantial reserves of coal, oil and natural gas await development.

OFFICIAL NAME People's Republic of Bangladesh.

CAPITAL CITY Dhaka.

GEOGRAPHY Most of the country is flat, low-lying and extremely fertile alluvial flood plains and deltas of the Ganges and Brahmaputra. The southeast is hilly and thickly forested. *Area* 143,998 sq km (55,600 sq miles).

PEOPLE *Population* 98.7m. *Density* 685 per sq km. *Ethnic groups* Mainly Bengali.

RELIGION Muslim 85%, Hindu 7%, Buddhist 0.6%, Christian 0.3%.

LANGUAGE Bangla.

EDUCATION Noncompulsory. Only primary education (5–10) is free. There are 6 universities.

CLIMATE Tropical monsoon; monthly temperatures 21–28°C (70–82°F). Rainy season Jun–Sep. Cyclonic storms occur in the Bay of Bengal.

CURRENCY Taka (Tk).

PUBLIC HOLIDAYS Jan 1, Feb 21, Mar 26, Good Fri, Easter Mon, May 1, Buddha Purinama (May), Id al-Fitr, Jamat Wida (Jul), Id al-Adha, Muharram, Shab-i-Bharat (Sep), Durga Puja (Sep), Mouloud, Nov 7, Dec 16, Dec 25–26.

GOVERNMENT Republic since 1971. The elected president is head of state and chief executive; the 330-member parliament includes 30 nonelected women.

CHINA

Home to more than one-fifth of the human race, China is the world's most populous country. It is also one of the poorest, and the outcome of its desperate search for the fast lane to economic growth will have global repercussions. The Chinese have immense pride staked on their success. Their civilization was ahead of Europe for most of recorded history. Traditionally, they see themselves as the "Middle Kingdom" of refinement and technology, surrounded by ignorant barbarians.

A decline set in roughly 200 years ago, steep enough to rank them now among the poverty-stricken nations of the world. Gross national product is only about $300 per head; that of the USA is 50 times bigger. It will be a long and arduous haul before China can achieve the modernity and prosperity that the West now takes for granted.

Emperors, increasingly effete, ruled China until well into the 20th century, by which time national weakness and breakdown had allowed Western and Japanese imperialism to nibble away at China's edges – Britain in Hong Kong, Japan in Taiwan, the Tsars in Siberia. Sun Yat-sen led the republican forces to victory in 1912 but could not unify them. Precious time and resources were wasted fighting regional warlords, in civil war between the right-wing Kuomintang (or Nationalist) party and the communists, and in resisting Japan's invasion in the 1930s. By the time peace returned with the communist victory in 1949, at least 10m lives had been lost and the stock of infrastructure and productive assets was gravely depleted. Revolution has not destroyed China's unity, though many of its 30 provinces and municipalities are as large and populous as Britain or France.

The communists began by alienating the country's entrepreneurial talent and then, impatient with slow economic growth, in 1958 launched Mao Zedong's Great Leap Forward, an ill-prepared campaign to accelerate development by lengthening working hours and using second-rate materials. The resulting chaos was compounded by exceptional weather setbacks, leading to famine. Similar failure attended Mao's Cultural Revolution in the late 1960s, which aimed to re-establish socialist ideals; its actual result was a costly suspension of all education for a decade and the loss of the regime's credibility. Only after Mao's death in 1976 were more pragmatic policies adopted, less interventionist

OFFICIAL NAME People's Republic of China.

CAPITAL CITY Beijing.

GEOGRAPHY The plateau of Tibet in the southwest, where many great Asian rivers have their sources, is the highest in the world at over 4,000 metres (13,120 feet). Around it to the north and east is a wide arc of basins and plateaus from the desert of Takla Makan in the northwest to the rocky southeastern shore. To the east rolling hills and plains are drained and shaped by the Huang He, Chang Jiang and Xi Jiang rivers. They are most cultivated – and most heavily populated – in the northern half, where flatter terrain makes up for lower rainfall. Extensive coastal plains end in flat, sandy beaches north of Shanghai and a rugged shore marked by bays and islands to the south. *Highest point* Mt Everest 8,848 metres (29,030 feet). *Area* 9,561,000 sq km (3,692,000 sq miles).

PEOPLE *Population* 1,041m. *Density* 109 per sq km. *Ethnic groups* Han 93%, Zhuang 1.3%.

RELIGION Confucian 20%, Buddhist 6%, Taoist 2%, Muslim 2%.

LANGUAGE Mandarin Chinese. Also local languages and dialects.

EDUCATION Noncompulsory, and fee-paying at all levels.

CLIMATE Sub-tropical in the southeast, but continental in the interior. 4,000mm (1,579ins) of rain can fall in the southeast, less than 250mm (10ins) in large areas of the arid northwest. Winter temperatures range from -28°C (-18.5°F) in the extreme north, dominated by the Siberian air-mass, to 20°C (68°F) in the sheltered south. The summer range is much smaller. Typhoons hit the southern coast every summer.

CURRENCY Yuan (¥).

PUBLIC HOLIDAYS Chinese New Year, Mar 8, May 1, Aug 1, Oct 1–2.

GOVERNMENT Communist republic since 1949. There are 21 provinces, 5 autonomous regions and 3 municipalities. All power is concentrated in the Chinese Communist Party, whose quinquennial congress elects a 175-member central committee and 18-member politburo. The main constitutional body is the national people's congress (NPC), whose 2,970 deputies are elected indirectly for 5 years by regional bodies and the People's Liberation Army. The NPC elects a standing committee, an administrative state council of premier and ministers, and a president who is head of state.

CONSUMERISM

Until the early 1980s, heavy industry dominated Chinese manufacturing, but current policies put more emphasis on consumer goods. Initially volume was a priority, but Chinese consumers are now more discerning and growth in terms of numbers is slowing in favour of improvements in quality.

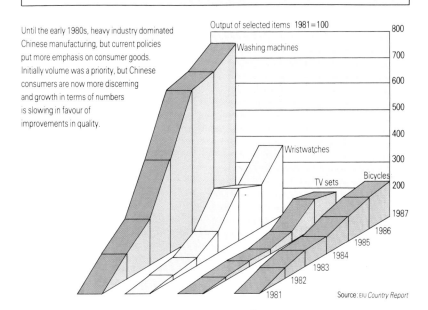

Output of selected items 1981=100

Source: EIU *Country Report*

and more output-oriented. In the countryside these have largely been successful, but the cities contain more officials – and beneficiaries – with a vested interest in state control. The urban population is quicker to produce a political backlash if its immediate interests are harmed by change.

The pursuit of growth is hampered by the fact that China is governed by a communist party more dedicated to the distribution than to the creation of wealth – and no practical alternative to the party exists. Even its fiercest critics concede that the only hope of policy change must come from factional realignments within the 46m-strong party, which has been entrenched in power for over 40 years and which, after Mao's death, continued to be dominated by veteran revolutionaries led by Deng Xiaoping.

Farming is still conducted on lease of collectively owned land, but by families free from bureaucratic fetters. Heavy industry remains state-owned but with management increasingly independent of central controls. Light industry, with the service trades, has become the preserve of small collectives, cooperatives and a new army of private entrepreneurs and self-employed. Yet many politically powerful party members cling to the old socialist dreams – hoping to be more prudent than Mao, but aiming for the same goal.

Freeing the peasants from the dead hand of Mao's People's Commune released sufficient energy (and greed) to hoist the major grain harvests – rice, wheat and maize – by 40% in the decade after Mao's death. But the other side of the coin is neglect of irrigation works, coupled with industry's inability to produce enough chemical fertilizer for the farms.

The government has fought shy of sharply raising staple food crop prices for farmers, fearing the spectre of inflation. Whether the official target of 500m tonnes (550m US tons) of cereals a year by 1999 can be achieved is therefore uncertain. Other agricultural sectors, especially cash crops and vegetables, are in a very healthy state. Farmers as a whole have never been better off. Only a return to the polarization of incomes, as the state ceases either to protect the weak or to curb the resourceful cultivators, mars the picture.

Loosening the reins for market-led production has involved more social and political freedom as well, to the delight of the albeit small professional middle class. It has also led to higher crime figures and unprecedented levels of official

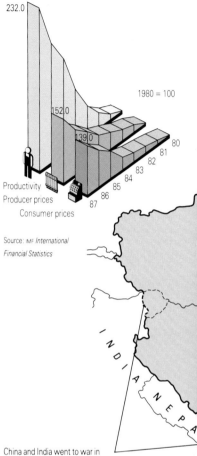

PRICES AND PRODUCTION

1980 = 100

Productivity
Producer prices
Consumer prices

Source: IMF *International Financial Statistics*

China and India went to war in 1962 over their disputed border in the Himalayas. The issue has not been settled, although India has recently shown willingness to yield its claim to land China took in 1962 if China gives up its claim to part of the Indian state of Arunchal Pradesh.

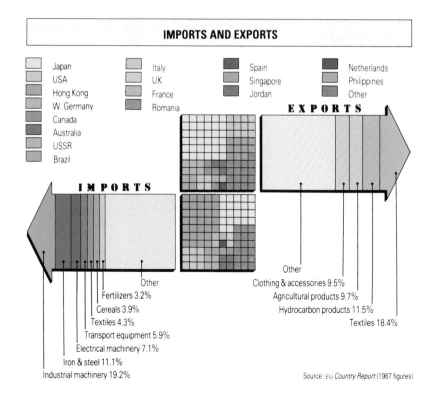

IMPORTS AND EXPORTS

Japan
USA
Hong Kong
W. Germany
Canada
Australia
USSR
Brazil

Italy
UK
France
Romania

Spain
Singapore
Jordan

Netherlands
Philippines
Other

EXPORTS

IMPORTS

Other
Fertilizers 3.2%
Cereals 3.9%
Textiles 4.3%
Transport equipment 5.9%
Electrical machinery 7.1%
Iron & steel 11.1%
Industrial machinery 19.2%

Other
Clothing & accessories 9.5%
Agricultural products 9.7%
Hydrocarbon products 11.5%
Textiles 18.4%

Source: EIU *Country Report* (1987 figures)

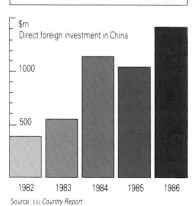

FOREIGN INVESTMENT

$m
Direct foreign investment in China

1000

500

1982   1983   1984   1985   1986

Source: EIU *Country Report*

Population distribution

Population is heavily concentrated in the fertile plains and river basins of the southeast; by comparison, the arid northwest is virtually uninhabited. 90% of the population inhabits 15% of the land and nearly three-quarters of Chinese live in cities. Population densities range from over 600 people per square kilometre in Jiangsu province, north of Shanghai, to only two in Xizang autonomous region (Tibet). Over twenty Chinese cities have populations exceeding one million, the number is much higher if suburbs are included.

Climate

Beijing and northern China have cold winters with temperatures below freezing. Summers are hot and thundery. In the far north, snow lies and rivers are frozen for four to six months of the year. Central China has mild winters, with hot and humid summers broken by prolonged heavy rain. The south has a sub-tropical climate, with summer temperatures rising to 30°C (86°F).

Talks on delineating the 8,000km (5,000-mile) border with the USSR have progressed since 1986, when Soviet leader Mikhail Gorbachev accepted China's definition of the Amur river boundary in the north.

■ More than 1 million
● 250,000 – 1 million

Major cities

(population in millions)

Shanghai	12.2
Beijing	9.6
Tianjin	8.1
Shenyang	7.5
Wuhan	6.4
Guangzhou	5.9

Tension has been high on the border with Vietnam since 1979, fuelled by Vietnam's treatment of its Chinese population and its invasion of Kampuchea. China and Vietnam have also clashed over their claims to the Spratly and Paracel islands in the South China Sea.

Special Economic Zones

The four Special Economic Zones (SEZs) were set up in 1979, aiming to attract foreign investment through tax and other incentives. Growth rates have been disappointing, particularly in the largest zone, Shenzhen, bordering Hong Kong's New Territories. Two of the other zones, Shantou and Zhuhai, are, like Shenzhen, in Guangdong province; the fourth, Xiamen, is in neighbouring Fujian.

Time zones

All of China is eight hours ahead of GMT.

Mineral resources

Coal is still by far the largest energy source but major reserves are in the northwest, far from the southern industrial consumers, causing acute transport problems.
Oil output from onshore fields grew rapidly in the 1950s and 1960s but has stagnated in recent years. Offshore exploration in the South China Sea in the 1980s produced disappointing results.

Iron ore mines are spread across the country, as are the steel works they supply. Exploitation of nonferrous metals, including copper, tin, lead, zinc and titanium, is growing rapidly. Tungsten, mined in the Linguan mountains in the southwest, gives China 40% of the world market.

Languages

Putonghua (Mandarin) has been adopted as the national language; seven main Chinese dialects exist, although the written language is the same throughout China. The Pinyin system of transliteration for Mandarin was officially adopted in 1958.

corruption and bribery. Even top party officials have voiced their concern about tumbling public morality.

Corruption, nepotism and censorship were the principal targets of the students who led the remarkable uprising on Tienanmen Square in Beijing in May 1989. But the party leadership, despite internal tensions between reformers and conservatives, was able to use the army to re-establish its authority. An altogether less liberal regime emerged, committed to basic economic reforms but not the political reforms which intellectuals want.

The Chinese do not drink ethics from the cup of religion as most other countries do. There is no universal ethic in the Buddhism or indigenous religions that China practises, and Confucianism limits its demands to relations within the family. The extended family is so strong and tight, in spite of communist intrusions, that its web of obligation overrides those to party or state. (That is one reason why the government has had difficulty enforcing its strict family planning policy to contain damaging population growth.) The practical response to adversity tends to be superstition. The Chinese are unusually addicted to charms, rituals, lucky numbers, lucky days, lucky years, astrology and geomancy.

Isolated for millennia from other civilizations, China was again cut off under Mao. Deng opened the door to the West, facilitating trade, investment, travel, training and other forms of foreign intercourse. But the violent events of mid-1989 only served to remind the world of the power of those within the party who are worried about the social and political effects of pursuing western ideas of freedom.

GDP GROWTH

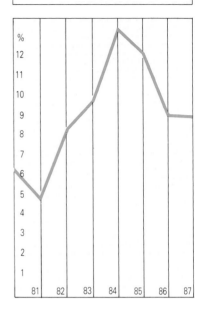

Source: EIU *Country Credit Risk Service*

ECONOMIC PROFILE

Primarily an agricultural economy; rice, wheat and pigs the main products. Industry mostly developed in few centres around Beijing, Shanghai, Wuhan and Guangzhou; primitive and highly labour-intensive elsewhere. Textiles and consumer electrical goods are important exports, along with rice, processed meat and vegetables, oil and coal. Superabundance of manpower, exported for construction projects overseas.

Growth Farming was biggest beneficiary of economic reforms in 1980s, but all-round growth trend strong. Chemical (especially fertilizer), vehicle, power and construction industries likely to be growth leaders in 1990s.

Problems Urgent need to encourage enterprise in society used to bureaucracy. Serious energy shortage hampers industry. Transport infrastructure poorly developed. Economic reforms in 1980s made cash crops more profitable than cereals, leading to major cereal imports.

FOREIGN EXCHANGE RESERVES

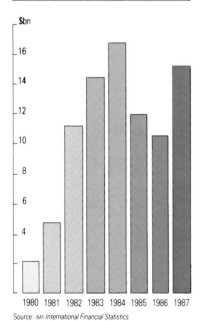

Source: IMF *International Financial Statistics*

BALANCE OF PAYMENTS

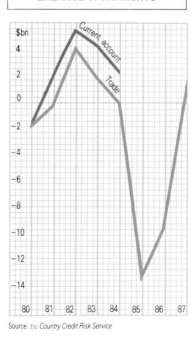

Source: EIU *Country Credit Risk Service*

China has in recent years run a trade surplus; the current account plunged into deficit in 1985, when imports surged after a poor grain harvest and relaxation of curbs on imports of consumer goods. Efforts to boost exports, including devaluation, and strong inflows from tourism helped reduce the deficit in subsequent years. The deficits ate into foreign exchange reserves, which had reached an all-time high in 1984, but these resumed a rising trend after an export boom in 1987.

WORK FORCE

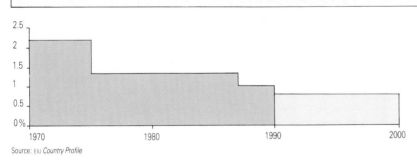

	Agriculture & fishing 74%
	Manufacturing 12%
	Services 10.5%
	Construction 2%
	Mining & quarrying 1.5%

Source: ILO *Yearbook of Labour Statistics* (1987 figures)

GDP BY ORIGIN

Agriculture 45%

Total industrial activity 42%

Construction 5%

Transport & communications 3%

Wholesale & retail trade 5%

Source: UN *National Accounts Statistics* (1985/86 figures)

COMPONENTS OF GDP

Private expenditure 63%

Gross fixed capital formation 30%

Government consumption 8%

POPULATION GROWTH

The graph shows that China's population growth rate slowed from 2.2% a year in 1970–75 to 1.3% in 1980–87. The government's population target for 1990 is 1.1bn but it does not look feasible. If the government is to achieve its year 2000 population target of 1.2bn the growth rate must slow dramatically to 0.8% a year.

Source: EIU *Country Profile*

MONGOLIA

An area half the size of India wedged in the high central Asian plateau between the USSR and China, Mongolia is too weak to be neutral. Before an agreement with China to reduce its presence the USSR stationed about 200,000 troops and advisers in Mongolia. Nevertheless, normal relations are enjoyed with the USA and China, although the latter claimed sovereignty over Mongolia until 1950; and there are more people of Mongolian origin in China than in Mongolia itself. Language and culture are distinctive; the traditional form of Lamaistic Buddhism is similar to that of Tibet.

The economy is traditionally based on animal husbandry; there are 22m sheep, goats, cattle and horses. Steady industrial development has taken place in recent decades based on indigenous coal and oil. Wool, hides, fluorspar and copper are exported; oil, vehicles, fertilizer, sugar and consumer goods are the chief imports.

OFFICIAL NAME Mongolian People's Republic.
CAPITAL CITY Ulan Bator.
GEOGRAPHY The country consists largely of high, rolling steppes, with mountains to the north and the Gobi Desert in the south. *Area* 1,565,000 sq km (604,000 sq miles).
PEOPLE *Population* 1.9m. *Density* 1.2 per sq km. *Ethnic groups* Khalkha 84%, Kazakh 5%, Durbet 3%.
RELIGION Shamanist 31%, Buddhist 2%, Muslim 1%.
LANGUAGE Khalka Mongolian.
EDUCATION Compulsory for ages 6–16.
CLIMATE Continental, with very cold, dry winters and warm summers; low rainfall.
CURRENCY Tugrik or Tögrög (Tug).
PUBLIC HOLIDAYS Jan 1, Mar 8, May 1, Jul 11, Nov 7.
GOVERNMENT Communist republic since 1924.

EASTERN ASIA

The four "Little Dragons"

Asia's four "Little Dragons" – Hong Kong, Singapore, South Korea and Taiwan – have achieved impressive export-led growth and rapid development of manufacturing and services. Their approach has been characterized by a high level of government intervention in their economies, high spending on education and training and pragmatic, mildly authoritarian government.

Investment by Japan, which took advantage of lower labour costs in the four newly industrializing countries to set up plants for the assembly of electronic and other goods, helped to set these countries on the road to rapid economic growth. They are now trying to emulate Japan's shift from labour-intensive manufacturing to more capital-intensive sectors such as electronics. With small domestic markets, they must export to survive; protectionism in major markets, such as the USA, and loss of competitiveness are the major threats to continued growth. They must also meet the growing demands of their people for more democracy and a fairer share of the benefits of prosperity.

The Mekong

The longest river in Southeast Asia, the Mekong has its source in China's Qinghai province. It forms the border between Laos and both Burma and Thailand. In Cambodia to the south, a huge freshwater lake, Tonle Sap, acts as a natural flood reservoir for the Mekong. During the rainy season the Tonle Sap river linking the Mekong to the lake reverses its flow and the lake floods an area three times its normal size. In Vietnam the Mekong separates into four main branches and enters the South China Sea through a delta.

Climate

Southeast Asia has a tropical climate strongly influenced by monsoon winds. Thailand, Malaysia, the Philippines, Vietnam, Cambodia and Laos have heavy rainfall during the May–October southwest monsoon; Indonesia's rainy season runs from December to March. Temperatures vary little from month to month, averaging 22–32°C (72–90°F), and humidity is high throughout the year.

Korea has an extreme continental climate, with cold winters and hot summers. Winter winds bring cold dry air from Siberia; in summer, warm moist winds blow from the Pacific. June to September are the wettest months. North Korea has severe winter weather, with temperatures as low as –13°C (9°F).

The golden triangle

The area where Thailand, Burma and Laos meet on the banks of the Mekong River has long been notorious as a source of opium and heroin. Parts of eastern Burma are controlled by warlords who use drug smuggling to finance their struggle against the government; in Laos the government itself is alleged to be involved in the drugs business. The Thai government, with backing from the USA, has taken the lead in attempts to control the trade.

Macao

An enclave on the Chinese coast that was once Portuguese, Macao is now Chinese under Portuguese administration and due to be ceded fully to China in 1999. The Portuguese-appointed governor acts on domestic affairs in consultation with the legislative assembly, 6 of whose 17 members are directly elected. Foreign affairs are the preserve of the Portuguese president. Macao's industry centres on textile manufacture; tourism and gambling are also important sources of revenue.

480 miles
790 km

5 days

GMT +9
GMT +8

IWAN

Los Angeles 22 days

ON

Manila   PHILIPPINES

New York
21 hours

MINDANAO

Equator

IRIAN
JAYA   PAPUA
NEW GUINEA

CELEBES

GMT +9

EAST TIMOR
Dili

GMT +9
GMT +8

■ More than 1 million
● 250,000 – 1 million

Asean

Founded in 1967, the Association of Southeast Asian Nations (Asean) has proved one of the more successful regional organizations in the developing world. Asean has given its members a collective say in world affairs, through a regular dialogue with the USA, the EC and Japan. It has been particularly prominent in seeking a settlement in Cambodia although here the aims of Indonesia, which seeks to contain Chinese influence, have conflicted with those of its Asean partners, whose priority is curbing Vietnam. Economic cooperation has been less fruitful as most Asean members produce a similar range of commodities and thus compete on world markets. Intra-Asean trade is only about 30% of the total. Founder members were Indonesia, Malaysia, the Philippines, Singapore and Thailand; Brunei joined in 1984. Papua New Guinea is an observer.

The Spratlys and Paracels

The Spratlys, or Nanshan Islands, in the South China Sea probably rank as the most disputed scraps of land in the world. No less than five nations have a claim to some or all of the islands, which lie on major international trade routes in an area regarded as promising for oil exploration. Vietnam, the Philippines, Malaysia and Taiwan all maintain garrisons on various islets; in early 1988, the arrival of Chinese marines near Vietnamese-held islands led to a brief naval battle followed by angry diplomatic exchanges. Earlier, the Chinese ousted Vietnam from the Paracels, another island group farther north.

Japanese investment

Japan is the leading trading partner and source of foreign investment for many Eastern Asian countries. Japanese investment in the four "Little Dragons" grew by 15–25% a year during the 1980s. Increasingly, however, as the four "Little Dragons'" labour costs rise and their currencies appreciate against the dollar, Japan is turning to other countries in the region, which offer lower costs. Indonesia, Malaysia, the Philippines and Thailand are following in the "Little Dragons'" wake, capitalizing on lower labour costs to make a competitive play in world markets. But all remain dependent on raw material exports, making them vulnerable to fluctuating world commodity prices.

SOUTH KOREA

The Koreans, an ethnically cohesive, linguistically united people, enjoyed many centuries as an independent kingdom until the Japanese annexation of 1910. After Japan's defeat in 1945, Korea was divided into Soviet and American zones of occupation and then in 1948 into two republics. The north's invasion of the south in 1950 led to three years of war, in which the UN saved the south and China the north from total defeat. The two sides were left glaring at each other across a ceasefire line not far from the original border.

South Korea gave priority to education and made owner-occupation by smallholders the basis of land tenure. In 1962 a military government based a new strategy of export-oriented industrialization on the country's one major advantage: cheap but well-educated labour. The next quarter century was one barely interrupted boom, with GNP growth averaging well over 8% a year. A green revolution maintained self-sufficiency in food grains, with some of the world's highest rice yields.

South Korea at the start of the 1990s is very much in a state of transition. In domestic politics, it is moving from military dictatorship to a more democratic system. In international relations, communist countries are moving towards recognition of South Korea, after decades of backing the north's claim to the whole peninsula. In economic terms, the question is not *if* South Korea will leave behind developing country status and join the OECD but *when*: 1992 looks the likely answer.

Before then, however, the government of President Roh Tae-Woo wants to effect a further transition, whereby market forces take over from government the main role of allocating resources. This would in turn help transform the country's position in world markets, making it rely less on manufactures sold

OFFICIAL NAME Republic of Korea.
CAPITAL CITY Seoul.
GEOGRAPHY Most of the country is mountainous, and its population is concentrated in the arable river valleys and along the coastal plain. The plain is wider on the west coast, where there are many rias and offshore islands, than on the east, where the Taebaek range often falls sheer into the sea. *Highest point* Halla San 1,950 metres (6,400 feet). *Area* 98,484 sq km (38,030 sq miles).
PEOPLE *Population* 41.2m. *Density* 418 per sq km. *Ethnic groups* Korean.
RELIGION Buddhist 37%, Christian 30%, Confucian 17%, Chundo Kyo 4%.
LANGUAGE Korean.
EDUCATION Free and compulsory for ages 6–12. 90% of those eligible are enrolled in higher education; there are more than 100 university-level institutions. Education accounts for 20% of total government expenditure.
CLIMATE Continental, with an average temperature range from -5°C (23°F) in winter to 27°C (81°F) in summer, more extreme in the interior. Annual rainfall is 1,000–1,400mm (40–55ins).
CURRENCY South Korean won (SKW).
PUBLIC HOLIDAYS Jan 1-3, Chinese New Year, Mar 1, Apr 5, May 5, Buddha's birthday, Jun 6, Jul 17, Aug 15, Choo-Suk (Sep), Oct 1, Oct 3, Oct 9, Dec 25.
GOVERNMENT Republic since 1948. The latest constitution, promulgated in 1987, gives executive power to a president directly elected for a single term of 5 years; the legislative national assembly is elected for 4 years. Serving military officers are banned from membership of the state council, which consists of the president, prime minister and their appointees.

ECONOMIC PROFILE

Export-led growth dominated by labour-intensive manufactures, especially textiles, clothing and footwear. Agriculture protected from market forces to maintain self-sufficiency in food.

Growth Motor vehicles, aerospace, computers, advanced materials, nuclear power, financial services are all growth areas. Government R&D spending to double in real terms in less than five years.

Problems Oil and most industrial raw materials imported. The problems of success: rising labour costs, inflationary pressures.

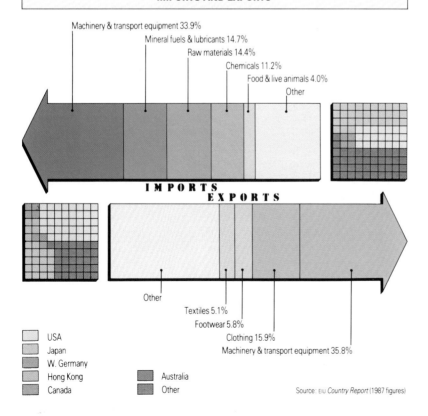

IMPORTS AND EXPORTS

Machinery & transport equipment 33.9%
Mineral fuels & lubricants 14.7%
Raw materials 14.4%
Chemicals 11.2%
Food & live animals 4.0%
Other

IMPORTS
EXPORTS

Other
Textiles 5.1%
Footwear 5.8%
Clothing 15.9%
Machinery & transport equipment 35.8%

USA
Japan
W. Germany
Hong Kong
Canada
Australia
Other

Source: EIU *Country Report* (1987 figures)

on the basis of cheap labour, more on high-quality, high-technology goods sold under the brand names of major South Korean corporations. Already, with some difficulty, it is coping with a swing from current account deficit to surplus. The world's fourth largest debtor in the early 1980s will soon take on the role of international creditor.

These simultaneous shifts interlock. South Korea's new role as a developed economy is likely to affect its relations with China, whose cheap labour it may seek to employ in joint ventures, and even with the USSR, whose Siberian raw materials it may help to develop. Its determination to reach the first rank almost requires a successful transition to democracy, since it depends not just on training but on persuading people with internationally marketable skills that South Korea is a country worth staying in, or returning to. On the other hand, the shift to democracy makes the technological priority inevitable: now that it is no longer politically possible to suppress workers' demands for a larger share of the new prosperity, South Korea's days as a cheap labour market are numbered; it will have to rely on nimble minds, not nimble fingers. The move into current account surplus is only a problem – posing a choice between unwanted currency appreciation and an inflationary growth of foreign exchange reserves – because of the restrictions that prevent South Koreans investing abroad as they wish: economic liberalization is being forced on South Korea by the very successes of a quasi-command economy.

With political luck, both at home and in relation to a still hostile North Korea, the South Korea of the 1990s will reflect the dominant trends of the late 1980s. An overwhelmingly urban community, with a falling and ageing rural population, it will make its way in the world as a highly successful exporter of goods such as cars and consumer electronics, and will be a major importer of raw materials. It will be a much more open economy, with tariffs on manufactures down to the OECD norm, although it will ape the worst OECD practice in protecting its agriculture. Its citizens will demand a bigger social element in a social market economy; its highly educated work force will be able to provide the wherewithal.

GDP GROWTH

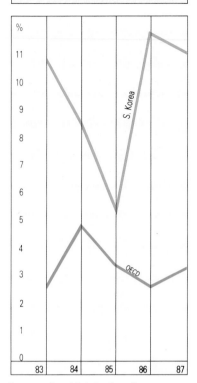

Sources: OECD *Economic Outlook*; EIU *Country Report*

BALANCE OF PAYMENTS

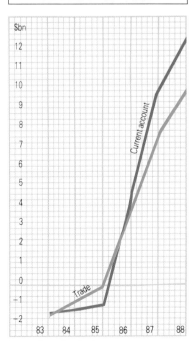

Source: EIU *Country Credit Risk Service*

GDP BY ORIGIN

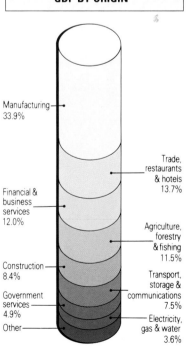

Manufacturing 33.9%

Financial & business services 12.0%

Construction 8.4%

Government services 4.9%

Other

Trade, restaurants & hotels 13.7%

Agriculture, forestry & fishing 11.5%

Transport, storage & communications 7.5%

Electricity, gas & water 3.6%

Source: EIU *Country Report* (1987 figures)

COMPONENTS OF GDP

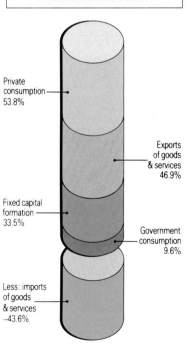

Private consumption 53.8%

Fixed capital formation 33.5%

Less: imports of goods & services −43.6%

Exports of goods & services 46.9%

Government consumption 9.6%

NORTH KOREA

The communist regime of North Korea, imposed by the USSR in 1945 and rescued by China in 1951, has managed to play off one communist power against the other. The regime is one of unreconstructed Stalinism; the cult of personality surrounding its leader, Kim Il Sung, and to a lesser extent his son and designated successor Kim Jung Il, might seem grotesque even by Stalin's standards.

Agriculture is collectivized and has been fairly successful, at least in grain production. The emphasis in development has been on heavy industry, not least to support a formidable war machine that absorbs, according to some Western estimates, about 25% of GNP. Industry produces virtually nothing that can be sold on world markets. Exports, primarily to other communist countries and at a low level, are dominated by raw materials and refined metals, notably zinc. Exports in 1986, for example, were worth $65 per head of population, compared with $816 per head in South Korea. Imports on credit from the non-communist world are largely ruled out by North Korea's default on its debt to Western creditors. The debt resulted from a bid in the early 1970s to modernize with the help of Western capital goods. When exports failed to rise sufficiently to service the debt, North Korea simply stopped paying.

There are few signs of the reforming trend now evident in both China and the USSR. This and any measure of *détente* with South Korea may have to wait until the regime changes.

OFFICIAL NAME Democratic People's Republic of North Korea.
CAPITAL CITY Pyongyang.
GEOGRAPHY Mountains run down the eastern side of the country. Major settlements – more than half the population is urbanized – are on the wide west and narrow east coastal plains. *Area* 120,538 sq km (46,540 sq miles).
PEOPLE *Population* 20.4m. *Density* 169 per sq km. *Ethnic groups* Predominantly Korean.
RELIGION Shamanist 16%, Chundo Kyo 14%, Buddhist 2%, Christian 1%.
LANGUAGE Korean.
EDUCATION Free and compulsory for ages 5–16.
CLIMATE Continental, with monthly average temperatures ranging from -3°C (27 °F) to 24°C (75°F). Annual rainfall is 1,000mm (40ins), most in Jun–Sep.
CURRENCY North Korean won (NKW).
PUBLIC HOLIDAYS Jan 1, Apr 15, May 1, Aug 15, Sep 9, Oct 10, Dec 27.
GOVERNMENT Communist republic since 1948. The Korean Workers' Party (KWP) has been in power since 1949. The president is elected by the supreme people's assembly, whose 655 members are elected unopposed.

HONG KONG

After flourishing for 150 years as a British colony, Hong Kong will become a "special administrative region" of China in mid-1997. China, in need of Hong Kong's commercial, technical and marketing skills, has pledged that the territory will be free to pursue capitalism for at least 50 years.

Ironically, much of Hong Kong's prosperity is based on the efforts of refugees from Canton and Shanghai who, following the creation in 1949 of the People's Republic of China, exchanged communism for the *laissez-faire* policies of a British colonial government that viewed Hong Kong primarily as a free port.

OFFICIAL NAME Colony of Hong Kong.
CAPITAL CITY Victoria.
GEOGRAPHY The mainland and islands of Hong Kong are a partly drowned old mountain range. Between Hong Kong island and the Kowloon peninsula is one of the great deep-water harbours of the world. The terrain is steep and hilly, with sheer cliffs; land is at such a premium that some has been reclaimed from the sea. Inland, north of the Kowloon ridge, are the agricultural New Territories, where there are no large towns. *Highest point* Tai Mo Shan 957 metres (3,140 feet). *Area* 2,916 sq km (1,130 sq miles).
PEOPLE *Population* 5.5m. *Density* 5,110 per sq km. *Ethnic groups* Chinese 97%, British 0.5%.
RELIGION Buddhist 18%, Christian 18%, Taoist 14%, Confucian.
LANGUAGE English and Chinese.
EDUCATION Free and almost universal for ages 6–14. There are 2 universities.
CLIMATE Sub-tropical, with an annual average temperature of 21°C (70°F) and a rainfall of 2,160mm (85ins), more than half of which falls in Jun–Aug. Winters are dry and sunny, summers humid.
CURRENCY Hong Kong dollar (HK$).
PUBLIC HOLIDAYS Jan 1, Chinese New Year, Good Fri, Easter Mon, Apr 5, Queen's birthday, Tuen Ng (Jun), last Sat in Aug, Aug 29, mid-autumn festival (Sep), Chung Yeung festival (Oct), Dec 25-27.
GOVERNMENT UK colony. It is administered by a British-appointed governor with a nominated executive council and a legislative council of 56 members, 24 of them elected.

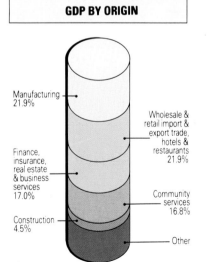

GDP BY ORIGIN

Manufacturing 21.9%
Finance, insurance, real estate & business services 17.0%
Construction 4.5%
Wholesale & retail import & export trade, hotels & restaurants 21.9%
Community services 16.8%
Other

COMPONENTS OF GDP

Export of goods 104.9%
Gross fixed capital formation 24.1%
Net export of services 5.9%
Private consumption 62.2%
Government consumption 7.1%
Less: imports of goods –104.5%

Source: EIU *Country Report* (GDP by origin 1986 figures; Components of GDP 1987 figures)

IMPORTS AND EXPORTS

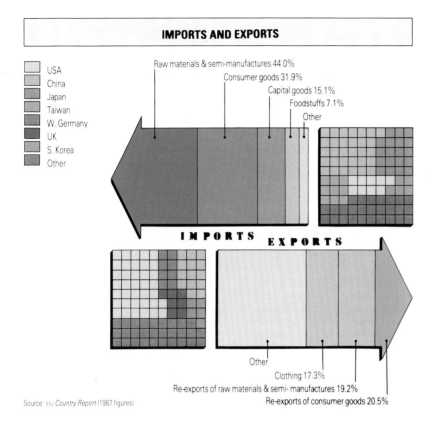

USA
China
Japan
Taiwan
W. Germany
UK
S. Korea
Other

Raw materials & semi-manufactures 44.0%
Consumer goods 31.9%
Capital goods 15.1%
Foodstuffs 7.1%
Other

IMPORTS   EXPORTS

Other
Clothing 17.3%
Re-exports of raw materials & semi- manufactures 19.2%
Re-exports of consumer goods 20.5%

Source: EIU *Country Report* (1987 figures)

ECONOMIC PROFILE

No resources save deep-water port and people, so trade is mainstay and ingenuity in adding value is crucial. Manufacturing – garments, electronics, toys, plastics – developed only in post-war years, unbalanced and beset by high costs. Services, especially banking and tourism, now strong.

Growth Upswing in activities oriented towards China: trade, industrial subcontracting to Chinese labour; provision of services and technology. Construction, printing and publishing also thriving.

Problems Uncertainty about future leading to drain of skills and investment. All energy supplies and raw materials, most food and water are imported, largely from China. Land is short and has to be reclaimed from the sea. Several industries past competitive peak; shipping fleet mothballed because of world contraction. Offshore currency markets favour Singapore.

With only half the population and area of London, Hong Kong has become the world's biggest container port, largest garment exporter and 13th biggest trader. GDP per head is the highest in Asia after Japan and Singapore.

Trading, especially as an entrepôt, was the pillar of the economy until the mid-1950s. Since then, manufacturing – first textiles, then electronics – has expanded greatly. The cheaper end of industry is drawn towards China, where labour costs are far lower, and financial services are the new engine of growth. Hong Kong has become the world's fourth largest financial centre. Housing and transport are particular areas of achievement, considering the unexpected increase in population in 1949 and the continued flow of refugees. The largely underground mass transit railway is one of the most advanced in the world.

With its European past and Chinese future, Hong Kong is torn between different values. The British never gave it democracy, yet the new affluent middle class so dreads a Chinese dictatorship that many are emigrating, putting the economy in jeopardy. Although Chinese form 97% of the population, there is a very visible Indian minority and many European, American and Australian residents. Gradually the Chinese are taking over many old British firms, but Australian, American and particularly Japanese corporations are buying in. Hong Kong is traditionally a place where quick returns are expected, so an indication of confidence will be investment in the mid-1990s.

As a large urban area with a small hinterland, Hong Kong depends on others, mainly China, for raw materials and most of its food and water. Its purchases from China, paid for in Hong Kong dollars, account for almost a third of China's foreign earnings. This mutual dependency supports hopes that Hong Kong will continue to enjoy some form of autonomy after 1997. However, the willingness of hardline Chinese leaders to brutally suppress challenges to their power, even at the cost of jeopardizing the country's modernization, may render Hong Kong's economic value an inadequate guarantee of its future.

BALANCE OF PAYMENTS

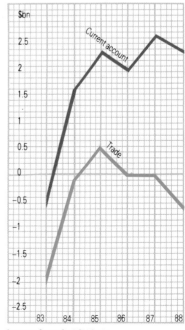

$bn

Current account

Trade

2.5
2
1.5
1
0.5
0
−0.5
−1
−1.5
−2
−2.5

83 84 85 86 87 88

Source: EIU *Country Credit Risk Service*

TAIWAN

Taiwan has been one of the economic miracles of the postwar years. An island about the size of the Netherlands, overcrowded and devoid of any wealth of natural resources, it has achieved astonishing rates of economic growth. Most extraordinary of all, this prosperity has been created under the rule of a government founded on a political fantasy. The ruling nationalist party, the Kuomintang (KMT), asserts that its legitimate authority extends over the entire territory claimed by China's traditional rulers, from the tiniest Spratly island in the South China Sea to Tibet and even the Mongolian People's Republic.

The roots of this bizarre and forlorn claim lie in the Chinese civil war. The communists completed their victory on the mainland in 1949; their opponents, the KMT under General Chiang Kai-shek, moved their seat of government. In the late 1940s, about 1.5m soldiers, officials, camp followers and others descended on this former Japanese colony, a resented influx imposed with considerable brutality on 8m native Taiwanese. The irredentist dream of a return to the mainland gradually faded.

From these unpromising beginnings, the KMT built an economic success. A far-sighted land reform in the 1950s created the agricultural basis for rapid industrialization. From the 1960s, labour-intensive manufacturing became the cornerstone of the economy, fuelling an export boom that produced phenomenal growth rates. The authoritarian KMT has progressively reformed itself, and in 1987 lifted the state of martial law under which it had governed Taiwan for close to 40 years.

By the late 1980s, the economy was dominated by foreign trade and manufacturing. Its success had been built behind a protective tariff cordon, with an undervalued currency and growing dependence on the US market. Pressure mounted on Taiwan to reform its trading practices; it responded with an economic restructuring. It moved upmarket, from the bargain basement to the white goods counter, specializing in consumer electronics and the bottom end of the information technology industry.

OFFICIAL NAME Republic of China.

CAPITAL CITY Taipei.

GEOGRAPHY An eroded central mountain range running roughly north–south plunges steeply into the sea on the east coast but gives way gradually on the west to populous terraced tablelands and alluvial plains. The west coast is lined with lagoons and sand dunes. *Highest point* Hsin-kao Shan 3,997 metres (13,110 feet). *Area* 36,000 sq km (13,900 sq miles).

PEOPLE *Population* 19.1m. *Density* 531 per sq mile. *Ethnic groups* Han Chinese 98% Indonesian 2%.

RELIGION Buddhist 43%, Taoist 21%, Christian 7%.

LANGUAGE Mandarin Chinese. Also local dialects.

EDUCATION Free and compulsory for ages 6–15. There are 16 universities.

CLIMATE Sub-tropical, moderated by the Kuroshio current, giving long warm summers averaging 25–30°C (77–86°F) and mild winters with a mean of 15°C (59°F). Average rainfall is 2,500mm (100ins), around double that in the eastern highlands; typhoon season is Jul–Sep.

CURRENCY New Taiwan dollar (NT$).

PUBLIC HOLIDAYS Jan 1, Chinese New Year, Mar 29, Apr 5, Dragon Boat festival (Jun), mid-autumn Moon festival (Sep), Sep 28, Oct 10, Oct 25, Oct 31, Nov 1, 2, Dec 25.

GOVERNMENT Republic. The head of state and chief executive is a president, elected for a 6-year term by the national assembly, which is dominated by life-term members, as is the main legislative body.

IMPORTS AND EXPORTS

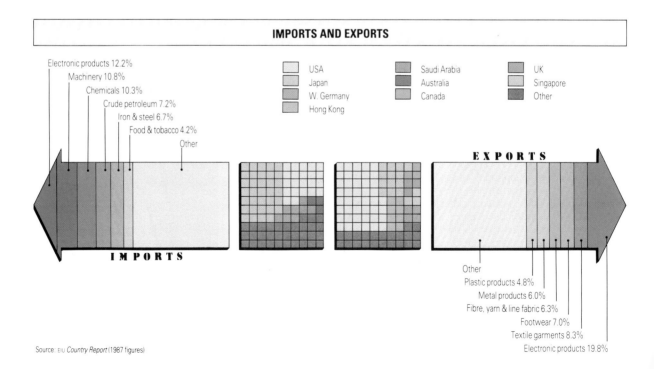

Electronic products 12.2%
Machinery 10.8%
Chemicals 10.3%
Crude petroleum 7.2%
Iron & steel 6.7%
Food & tobacco 4.2%
Other

USA
Japan
W. Germany
Hong Kong

Saudi Arabia
Australia
Canada

UK
Singapore
Other

IMPORTS

EXPORTS

Other
Plastic products 4.8%
Metal products 6.0%
Fibre, yarn & line fabric 6.3%
Footwear 7.0%
Textile garments 8.3%
Electronic products 19.8%

Source: EIU *Country Report* (1987 figures)

With huge reserves of foreign exchange, negligible foreign debt and a versatile and educated work force, Taiwan is well-equipped to make this transition. Living standards have risen fast enough to sustain a soaring import bill. New freedom to remit foreign currency has led to an accumulation of foreign assets. The main threats are beyond Taiwan's control: recession or protectionism in the USA, and – less acute now – mainland intervention. For all its economic progress, Taiwan remains a diplomatic pariah, recognized by only a handful of countries. China now tries the blandishments of a "one country, two systems" approach to woo Taiwan back into the pan-Chinese fold. But Taiwan's rulers and, as far as can be judged, its people remain adamant in favouring the devil of international political isolation to the deep blue sea of reunification on Beijing's terms.

ECONOMIC PROFILE

Transformed in 40 years from a producer of rice and sugar to an economy reliant on manufacturing. Labour-intensive food-processing, textiles, garments, toy and plastic products industries now giving way to newer and more automated industries.

Growth Electronics and computers overtaking food-processing industries as leading contributors to GDP, although textiles holding their own and increasing value added.

Problems Creaking financial system; state-owned banks being gradually privatized. Environment has been ravaged by rapid industrialization; pollution control becoming a major political issue and extra cost to investors.

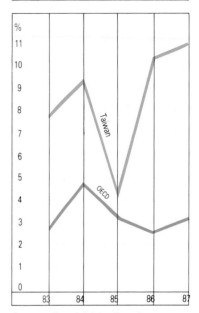

GDP GROWTH

Taiwan

OECD

Sources: OECD *Economic Outlook*; EIU *Country Report*

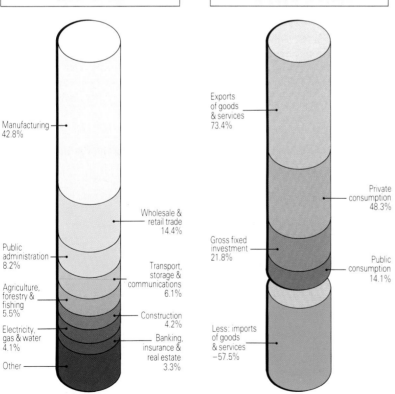

GDP BY ORIGIN

Manufacturing 42.8%

Wholesale & retail trade 14.4%

Public administration 8.2%

Transport, storage & communications 6.1%

Agriculture, forestry & fishing 5.5%

Construction 4.2%

Electricity, gas & water 4.1%

Banking, insurance & real estate 3.3%

Other

COMPONENTS OF GDP

Exports of goods & services 73.4%

Private consumption 48.3%

Gross fixed investment 21.8%

Public consumption 14.1%

Less: imports of goods & services −57.5%

Source: EIU *Country Report* (GDP by origin 1986 figures; Components of GDP 1987 figures)

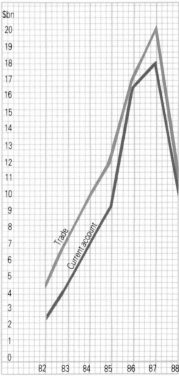

BALANCE OF PAYMENTS

$bn

Trade

Current account

Source: EIU *Country Credit Risk Service*

JAPAN

Japan was the first country outside Europe and America to adopt modern capitalism. It has been so successful that its average income level is now higher than that of the USA. This is despite a social structure quite different from that of Western countries, based on Confucian family values. Japan also cut itself off for 200 years, until the mid-19th century, helped by the 150 kilometres of sea that separate it from the Asian mainland.

The physical nature of the land makes Japan distinctive in other ways. It is subject to earthquakes and so mountainous that only one-sixth of the area can be farmed or lived on, making the population density twice that of Europe and providing the rationale for Japan's concern for social harmony. Another consequence of land shortage is that the average farm is very small, necessitating cooperative rather than individual or household cultivation, and this results today in a surprisingly uncompetitive agriculture. Over a quarter of what Japan eats has to be imported.

Conscious Westernization began in the 1870s. When Japan joined the victors of World War I – having already separately vanquished China and Tsarist Russia and annexed Taiwan and Korea as spoils – it expected recognition as an equal. Instead, it was snubbed by the Versailles peace treaty and at the subsequent negotiations to balance the Pacific navies. Militarists took over in the 1930s, establishing a fascist regime at home and attacking China and Southeast Asia. Their bombing of Pearl Harbor in 1941 triggered American reaction to this aggression, which culminated in the atom bombs on Hiroshima and Nagasaki four years later.

After the war, the Japanese threw themselves into the work of pursuing their economic hopes, helped by US occupation reforms: land redistribution, break-up of monopolies, multiparty parliamentary democracy (under a figurehead emperor) and the rule of law. The almost complete lack of natural resources meant a high dependence on foreign trade, and Japan became, of necessity, the most successful exporting nation as well as, eventually, the world's biggest foreign investor with the largest foreign exchange reserves.

Political stability underpinned these achievements; the conservative Liberal Democratic Party has ruled since 1948 despite scandals involving bribery and corruption at the highest levels of government. Socialist, Communist and Buddhist Clean Government opposition parties have shown no signs of being

OFFICIAL NAME Nihon.

CAPITAL CITY Tokyo.

GEOGRAPHY The archipelago has four main islands – Honshu, Shikoku, Kyushu and Hokkaido – and about 4,000 small ones. Two-thirds of the land area is mountainous and thickly forested; there are more than 1,000 earth tremors a year. Only 15% of the country, mostly the coastal plains, is cultivable, and is intensively exploited for largely arable agriculture. Industrial and urban development is concentrated in a strip along Honshu's south coast. *Highest point* Mt Fuji 3,776 metres *(12,390 feet)*. *Area* 372,313 sq km (143,750 sq miles).

PEOPLE *Population* 121m. Over 75% live in cities. *Density* 324 per sq km. The figure is 1,500 per sq km if uninhabitable areas are excluded. *Ethnic groups* Japanese 99%.

RELIGION Shinto 87%, Buddhist 73% (most Japanese profess both).

LANGUAGE Japanese.

EDUCATION Compulsory for ages 6–15, with plans to increase the leaving age to 18. A third of school-leavers go to one of more than 400 universities.

CLIMATE Pacific coast has hot, humid summers and cold, dry winters. Sea of Japan coast has heavy winter snowfalls. Hokkaido has very cold winters, down to -10°C (14°F), and short, warm summers. Southern Kyushu is sub-tropical.

CURRENCY Yen (Y).

PUBLIC HOLIDAYS Jan 1, Jan 15, Feb 11, Mar 21, Apr 29, May 3, May 5, Sep 15, Sep 23, Oct 10, Nov 3, Nov 23.

GOVERNMENT Constitutional monarchy. The emperor is head of state. Executive power is vested in a cabinet and prime minister, the leader of the majority party in the legislative diet. The 512-member house of representatives is elected for 4 years, and its decisions are largely rubber-stamped by the 252-member house of councillors. The electoral system strongly favours rural constituencies and has kept the Liberal Democratic Party in office for more than 30 years.

THE ECONOMIC MIRACLE

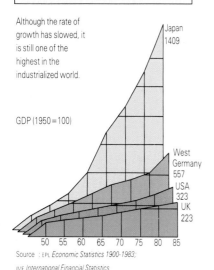

Although the rate of growth has slowed, it is still one of the highest in the industrialized world.

GDP (1950 = 100)

Japan 1409
West Germany 557
USA 323
UK 223

50 55 60 65 70 75 80 85

Source : EPL *Economic Statistics 1900-1983;* IMF *International Financial Statistics*

COMPONENTS OF GDP

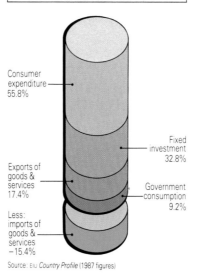

Consumer expenditure 55.8%

Fixed investment 32.8%

Exports of goods & services 17.4%

Government consumption 9.2%

Less: imports of goods & services −15.4%

Source: EIU *Country Profile* (1987 figures)

GDP BY ORIGIN

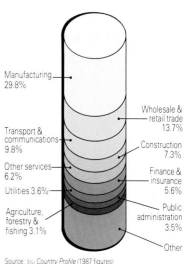

Manufacturing 29.8%

Wholesale & retail trade 13.7%

Transport & communications 9.8%

Construction 7.3%

Other services 6.2%

Finance & insurance 5.6%

Utilities 3.6%

Public administration 3.5%

Agriculture, forestry & fishing 3.1%

Other

Source: EIU *Country Profile* (1987 figures)

Japan's archipelago of 4,000 islands stretches some 3,000 km (1,860 miles) from the 24th parallel, off Taiwan, north to the 45th parallel, just below the USSR's Sakhalin Island.

The four main islands are: Honshu, where 80% of the population live; Hokkaido, a sparsely populated area dependent on agriculture, beer-brewing and tourism; Shikoku, an agricultural backwater; and sub-tropical Kyushu with its spa resorts, where many high-technology industries flourish and the people are reputedly the most outgoing.

Agriculture

Despite scarcity of land, Japan is 70% self-sufficient in food. Farms are small, averaging 1.4 hectares, and labour-intensive. Almost all are worked by owners and their families.

Island disputes

The sovereignty of the Kuril islands, north of Hokkaido, is disputed with the USSR (the Soviets have possession). The Ryukus, south of Kyushu, were only returned to Japan in 1972 after postwar US occupation (Okinawa remains an important US airforce base).

Land prices

Urban land prices nationally have risen by 4,000% (eight times the increase the in consumer prices index) in the three decades since 1955. In Japan's six largest cities the increase has been nearly 8,000%. Property prices and office rents in Tokyo are now the highest in the world.

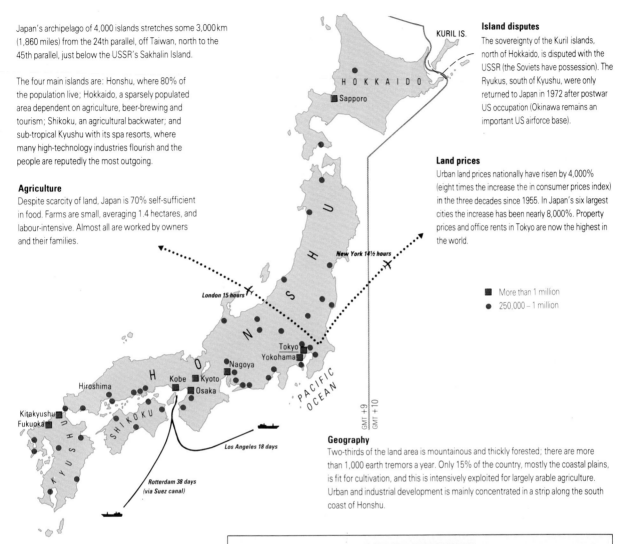

KURIL IS.

H O K K A I D O

Sapporo

H O N S H U

New York 14½ hours
London 15 hours

Tokyo
Yokohama
Nagoya
Kobe   Kyoto
Hiroshima   Osaka
Kitakyushu
Fukuoka
K Y U S H U
S H I K O K U

PACIFIC OCEAN

GMT +9 GMT +10

Los Angeles 18 days

Rotterdam 38 days
(via Suez canal)

■ More than 1 million
● 250,000 – 1 million

Geography

Two-thirds of the land area is mountainous and thickly forested; there are more than 1,000 earth tremors a year. Only 15% of the country, mostly the coastal plains, is fit for cultivation, and this is intensively exploited for largely arable agriculture. Urban and industrial development is mainly concentrated in a strip along the south coast of Honshu.

Major cities

	(population in millions)
Tokyo (capital)	8.3
Yokohama	3.0
Osaka	2.6
Nagoya	2.1
Sapporo	1.5
Kyoto	1.5
Kobe	1.4
Fukuoka	1.2

Travel distances and times

Tokyo to:-	km	air	train
Osaka	552	1hr	3hrs
Hiroshima	895	1hr 30min	5hrs

FOREIGN INVESTMENT

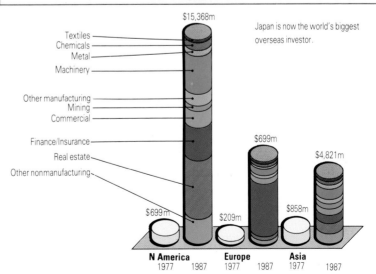

Textiles
Chemicals
Metal
Machinery

Other manufacturing
Mining
Commercial

Finance/Insurance

Real estate

Other nonmanufacturing

$15,368m

Japan is now the world's biggest overseas investor.

$699m

$4,821m

$699m $209m $858m

N America   Europe   Asia
1977   1987   1977   1987   1977   1987

Source: OECD *Economic Survey*

235

able to win power. External stability is provided by the US-Japan Security Treaty, under which the Americans guarantee Japan's defence in the light of the (American-drafted) postwar constitution, which renounces war and the use of force in foreign relations. Until the 1980s, spending on the Self-Defence Forces, as they are called, was kept below 1% of national income (though this was still enough to make it one of the world's biggest spenders on defence). Even after this self-restraint was officially breached by the then prime minister Yasuhiro Nakasone in 1986, Japan's military profile remained far lower than that of other countries. Whether pacifism is entrenched in public life, or whether a new wave of militarism is on the horizon, is a matter of debate.

Japan's diffidence in security terms is matched by psychological unreadiness for a full international role. Few Japanese speak foreign languages well enough or are ready to risk a career outside the familiar domestic mainstream to staff world organizations like the UN. There is also a bedrock of racial prejudice, especially against blacks. Relations with neighbouring countries, notably the Koreas, China and Southeast Asia, where there is some mutual awareness, are often sour. Reliance on imported materials nevertheless leads Japan to a low-key diplomacy that makes few enemies.

WORK FORCE

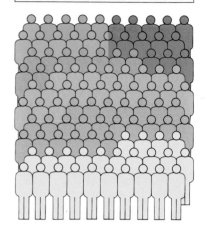

Unemployment stands at around 3% and is unlikely to fall as the contracting heavy industries shed labour. Distribution and service sectors are the main employment growth areas.

- Manufacturing 24%
- Distribution 23%
- Services 21%
- Construction 9%
- Agriculture, forestry & fishing 7.5%
- Utilities, transport & communications 6.5%
- Finance, insurance & real estate 4%
- Other

Source: ILO *Yearbook of Labour Statistics* (1987 figures)

ECONOMIC PROFILE

The world's most successful industrial nation, with steel, ships, motor vehicles and machinery as main products. Most manufactures exported. Until late 1980s few services sold abroad, but now annual exports exceed $50bn. Invests $140bn of long-term capital abroad annually, the most in the world. Agriculture only 3% of GDP, producing mainly rice by inefficient labour-intensive methods. Fishing fleet is world's largest.

Growth Information sector of electronics is fastest-growing industry, along with deregulated telecommunications and financial markets. Banking and securities now moving to foreign centres as well. Atomic energy has doubled capacity in five years to make Japan the fourth largest nuclear generating power. Construction booming.

Problems "Old" industries like textiles, shipbuilding, steel and semi-conductors losing out to Third World producers, especially South Korea and Taiwan. Even Japanese passenger vehicles increasingly made by subsidiaries abroad. Shipping hit by world contraction. Lack of mineral and energy sources: world's largest oil importer. Timber also inadequate as inaccessible.

IMPORTS AND EXPORTS

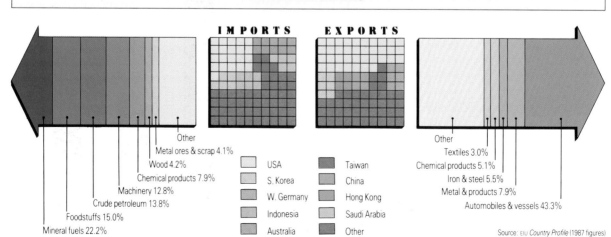

IMPORTS

EXPORTS

Other
Metal ores & scrap 4.1%
Wood 4.2%
Chemical products 7.9%
Machinery 12.8%
Crude petroleum 13.8%
Foodstuffs 15.0%
Mineral fuels 22.2%

Other
Textiles 3.0%
Chemical products 5.1%
Iron & steel 5.5%
Metal & products 7.9%
Automobiles & vessels 43.3%

- USA
- S. Korea
- W. Germany
- Indonesia
- Australia
- Taiwan
- China
- Hong Kong
- Saudi Arabia
- Other

Source: EIU *Country Profile* (1987 figures)

WAGES AND PRICES

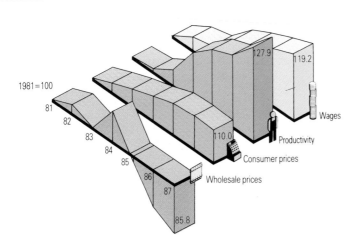

1981=100

81
82
83
84
85
86
87

127.9
119.2
110.0
85.8

Wages
Productivity
Consumer prices
Wholesale prices

Source: EIU *Country Profile*

GETTING OLDER

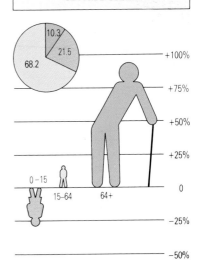

10.3
21.5
68.2

+100%
+75%
+50%
+25%
0
-25%
-50%

0-15
15-64
64+

Longevity is yet another indicator of Japan's high standard of living but spells high welfare bills for the future. The chart shows the population breakdown into different age groups in 1985 and the proportional increase in the size of those age groups since 1945.

Source: EIU *Country Profile*

Japan is the subject of more international misunderstanding than any other important country. The language is highly ambiguous. In finding a way to avoid saying the impolite "no," a Japanese often misleads a foreigner into thinking he means "yes." Law is seen as a means of reconciling two parties, rather than of administering justice. Repression of the individual in the interests of the group – family, company, nation – is carried farther than in most societies. The group ethic is thus the key to Japanese society, and one that not many foreigners comprehend. Lone pioneers like Akio Morita of Sony and Soichiro Honda are generally admired, but others in the literary and artistic fields, like Yukio Mishima, the *harakiri* novelist, are not. Decision by consensus, or by apparent consensus, is preferred to autocratic leadership. Life-long employment is on the wane, given technological advance and rapid changes in corporate structure, but is still an expectation on both sides of industry.

The world first became aware of Japan's "economic miracle" in 1964, when Tokyo hosted the Olympic Games. Since then Japanese industry has raced ahead, achieving leadership in electronic and automobile exports and frightening customers by the size of its trade surplus. The revaluation of the yen, which had been artifically held down, helped to check the imbalance, but complaints continued that the Japanese domestic market remained closed to Western and Third World exports, despite tariff reductions and other liberalization measures in the 1980s. Deregulation of Tokyo's financial market also began. An important consequence of the dearer yen was a flood of Japanese investment and tourism overseas, together with more aid to developing countries.

New problems confront Japan. As the population ages, the welfare burden on industry and on the next generation of taxpaying employees will increase. The work ethic is relaxing, with smaller families, financial affluence, the "leisure boom" and Westernization. The education system, however outstanding, tends to discourage the creativity that the economy will need.

Import dependency, especially in oil, remains a worry. Industrial and commercial success itself brings its own frustrations, with higher costs and reduced international competitiveness, though Japanese corporations have so far proved skilful in absorbing higher costs. The national will that has driven Japan so far will be needed even more in future.

BALANCE OF PAYMENTS

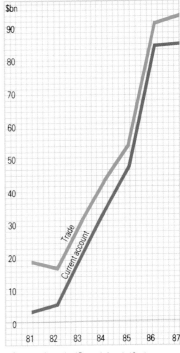

$bn

90
80
70
60
50
40
30
20
10
0

Trade
Current account

81 82 83 84 85 86 87

Source: EIU *International Economic Appraisal Service*

BURMA

In the 1950s Burma exported rice, teak and gems and was self-sufficient in oil. In 1987, the UN declared it a "least developed country." Rice was in short supply and petrol had to be imported. Burma's prosperity was a casualty of the Burmese Way to Socialism, the mixture of Buddhism, international isolation and state control practised since the army took power in 1962.

At independence in 1948 the British colony became the Union of Burma, but never functioned as such. Continuous civil war pitted the army against an unstable alliance of ethnic minorities, a communist underground and drug warlords. Led by U Ne Win, the army took over when the civilian government tried to make concessions to the minorities. The system worked mainly to benefit the military, which formed the core of the ruling Burma Socialist Programme Party (BSPP). The economy, dominated by party-run monopolies, has grown unresponsive, except for a thriving black market. Trade through official channels has almost ceased.

A botched attempt at economic reform in 1987 sent prices soaring and set off an explosion of political protest. Massive demonstrations forced Ne Win's resignation as party chairman in July 1988. The military remained firmly in charge, promising genuine reform and elections while viciously suppressing demonstrations and imposing martial law. Behind the scenes, the ageing Ne Win appeared still to be in effective control.

OFFICIAL NAME Union of Burma.
CAPITAL CITY Rangoon.
GEOGRAPHY Most Burmese live in the valley and delta of the Irrawaddy, which is hemmed in on three sides by mountain ranges and steep-sided plateaus. Area 676,552 sq km (261,220 sq miles).
PEOPLE Population 37.2m. Density 55 per sq km. Ethnic groups Burman 68%, Shan 7%, Karen 7%.
RELIGION Buddhist 87%, Christian 6%.
LANGUAGE Burmese. Also local languages.
EDUCATION Free where available, but noncompulsory.
CURRENCY Kyat (Kt).
PUBLIC HOLIDAYS Jan 4, Feb 12, Mar 2, Mar 27, Maha Thingyan (Apr), Apr 17, May 1, Id al-Adha, Jul 19, Divali, Tazaungdaing Festival (Nov), National Day (Nov or Dec), Dec 25, full moons in Mar, May, Aug and Oct.
GOVERNMENT Military-dominated republic. A state law and order restoration council has abolished all state institutions and the political monopoly of the BSPP, promising multiparty elections.

THAILAND

Thailand alone in Southeast Asia has avoided colonization, a success which owes something to a national pragmatism for which the country is famed. Since the 19th century its kings have been modernizers; in 1932 the monarchy gracefully accepted an end to absolutism when the military demanded it. A succession of military strongmen held sway for most of the next four decades, accommodating in turn the British, French, Japanese and Americans. An unprecedented popular explosion in 1973 took Thailand into democratic territory but the military intervened in 1977, launching a coup – the 13th since 1932 – against a government it thought too right-wing.

"Semi-democracy" has since prevailed. The pillars of the system remain the monarchy, the military, the bureaucracy and the political parties; but the balance has changed. Reverence for King Bhumibhol Adulyadej, on the throne since 1946, is the only constant, ensuring that his rare political interventions are decisive. The military is now less obtrusively involved in politics, but reserves the right to intervene. It claims credit for having blunted Vietnamese expansionism by luring home-grown communists out of the jungle, although schisms among the rebels have been at least as important. Political parties are not well regarded, least of all by the military, but their coalitions have been relatively stable.

A former army commander, Prem Tinsulanond, enjoyed a record uninterrupted term as prime minister from 1980 to 1988. His successor Chartchai Choonhavan, a long-retired soldier with stronger business than military connections, became the first elected prime minister for 12 years and appointed a cabinet drawn from the political parties. Some see this as evidence of the system's maturity, but the bureaucracy and military fear politicians' concern for the public interest will be overcome by their venality.

Well into the 1960s Thailand's wealth rested on growing rice and exporting the surplus. The Vietnam war encouraged diversification into export crops, development of infrastructure and the beginnings of a manufacturing base. By the mid-1980s, political stability had helped Thailand become a favourite Southeast Asian location for foreign manufacturers. Manufacturing has con-

OFFICIAL NAME Kingdom of Thailand.
CAPITAL CITY Bangkok.
GEOGRAPHY The northern mountains, outriders of the Himalayas, extend along the western borders into the Malay peninsula. The east of the country is taken up by the Khorat plateau, 200 metres (650 feet) high, whose rolling terrain gives way to swampland along the Mekong river. In the heart of the country is a great fertile plain drained by the Chao Phraya river, whose wide delta contains the capital. Highest point Doi Inthanon 2,595 metres (8,510 feet). Area 514,000 sq km (198,500 sq miles).
PEOPLE Population 51.3m. Density 100 per sq km. Ethnic groups Thai 54%, Lao 28%, Chinese 11%, Malay 4%, Khmer 3%.
RELIGION Buddhist 95%, Muslim 4%.
LANGUAGE Thai.
EDUCATION Compulsory for ages 7–14.
CURRENCY Baht (Bt).
PUBLIC HOLIDAYS Jan 1, Makhabuja, Apr 6, Apr 13, May 1, May 5, May 9, Visakhabuja, Asalhabuja (Jul, 2 days), Aug 12, Oct 23, Dec 5, Dec 10, Dec 31.
GOVERNMENT Constitutional monarchy. The king is head of state and appoints a prime minister on the advice of a bicameral national assembly. The 268 members of the nonparty senate are appointed by the king for 6 years, while the 357 members of the house of representatives are elected for a 4-year term.

GDP BY ORIGIN

Manufacturing 20.6%

Agriculture 18.8%

Wholesale & retail trade 18.6%

Public administration etc 15.8%

Transport & communications 9.3%

Finance & real estate 9.2%

Construction & utilities 7.7%

Source: EIU *Country Report* (1986 figures)

COMPONENTS OF GDP

Personal consumption 64.7%

Exports of goods & services

Fixed investment 21.2%

Government consumption 13.5%

Less: imports of goods & services −25.0%

ECONOMIC PROFILE

Rice, mainstay of domestic economy and chief export, still covers half planted area, alongside newer crops like maize, sugar, tapioca. Other valuable commodity exports: rubber, tin, teak. Manufacturing at first largely confined to food processing, with some consumer goods produced for domestic market. Export and heavy industries – cement, petrochemicals – now developing.

Growth Foreign investment fuelling boom in labour-intensive export industries – textiles, electronics, shoes, toys – but tourism now leading foreign exchange earner. The only Asean car industry with significant export capacity. Recent large natural gas discoveries offer chance to end dependence on imported oil.

Problems Inadequate infrastructure a constraint on growth. Education system not coping with expanding demand for skilled labour. Rice no longer a reliable earner in glutted world market; new exports face quota problems. Forests destroyed by uncontrolled logging.

tributed more to GDP than agriculture since 1984; a year later textiles overtook rice as the leading export.

For all their recent successes, the Thais are handicapped in their attempt to emulate South Korea in a dash for growth. Economic activity remains focused on the kingdom's traditional hub, Bangkok and the central plain. With a population of 8m, Greater Bangkok is 40 times larger than any other Thai city. Its clogged port and overloaded telephone and road systems are symptomatic of an infrastructure pushed beyond its limits by rapid growth. New investment and dispersion of economic activity have become urgent priorities that will test the capacity, and ultimately the stability, of Thailand's political arrangements.

IMPORTS AND EXPORTS

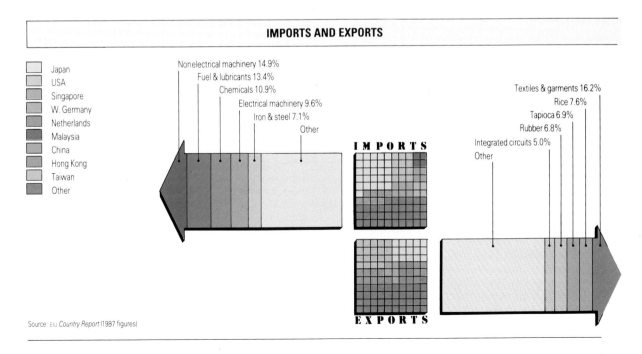

Japan
USA
Singapore
W. Germany
Netherlands
Malaysia
China
Hong Kong
Taiwan
Other

Nonelectrical machinery 14.9%
Fuel & lubricants 13.4%
Chemicals 10.9%
Electrical machinery 9.6%
Iron & steel 7.1%
Other

IMPORTS

Textiles & garments 16.2%
Rice 7.6%
Tapioca 6.9%
Rubber 6.8%
Integrated circuits 5.0%
Other

EXPORTS

Source: EIU *Country Report* (1987 figures)

LAOS

Mountainous, landlocked, sparsely populated, Laos is one of geography's victims. For centuries it suffered from the competing ambitions of two regional powers, Thailand and Vietnam. The French colonized it for strategic reasons. After they left in 1953, Laos endured two decades of civil war, aggravated by the wider conflict in the area. The communist Pathet Lao movement brought stability when it took power in 1975, but also isolation and further stagnation. Now GDP per head is among the world's lowest; 85% of the population are subsistence farmers. Many highlanders, slash-and-burn cultivators and opium growers remain beyond effective government control.

After 1975 Vietnam kept a large military contingent in Laos and packed the ministries with advisers. Late in 1986, the Laotian politburo, in tandem with Vietnam, announced a version of *perestroika*. The chief consequence has been a commercial opening across the Mekong to Thailand.

OFFICIAL NAME Lao People's Democratic Republic.
CAPITAL CITY Vientiane.
GEOGRAPHY The population is concentrated on the east bank of the Mekong and the Bolovens plateau in the south. Area 236,800 sq km (91,400 sq miles).
PEOPLE *Population* 4.1m. *Density* 17 per sq km. *Ethnic groups* Lao 99%.
RELIGION Buddhist 58%, Animist.
LANGUAGE Lao. Also local languages.
EDUCATION Free; state sector only.
CURRENCY Kip (Kp).
PUBLIC HOLIDAYS Dec 2.
GOVERNMENT Communist republic since 1975. The Lao People's Revolutionary Party governs through a supreme people's assembly of 45 members; a president is head of state and chief executive.

VIETNAM

When Vietnam's northern and southern halves were reunited in 1976, a year after the fall of Saigon, the country became the world's third most populous communist nation. A decade later it was still burdened by war, against Kampuchea (Cambodia) now rather than France or the USA, and remained frustrated in its centuries-old struggle for effective independence.

The invasion of Kampuchea in December 1978 made Vietnam a Soviet dependant, crippling the diplomatic opening to the West implicit in Vietnam's 1976 application to join the IMF; doctrinaire policies compounded economic isolation, inhibiting economic recovery from the American war.

Reform became the watchword after the December 1986 party congress, but an entrenched and obstructive bureaucracy ensured that change was slow. A generous foreign investment code promulgated in 1988 aroused some interest, particularly among oil companies keen to resume offshore exploration. But an economic breakthrough depends on withdrawal from Cambodia.

OFFICIAL NAME The Socialist Republic of Vietnam.
CAPITAL CITY Hanoi.
GEOGRAPHY Most is mountainous rain forest, apart from river deltas in the north and south and a coastal plain. *Area* 329,556 sq km (127,240 sq miles).
PEOPLE *Population* 59.7m. *Density* 181 per sq km. *Ethnic groups* Vietnamese 88%, Chinese 2%, Tai 2%.
RELIGION Buddhist 55%, Christian 8%.
LANGUAGE Vietnamese. Also French and English.
EDUCATION Free for ages 6–16.
CURRENCY New dong (D).
PUBLIC HOLIDAYS Jan 1, Tet (Jan), Apr 30-May 1, Sep 2-3.
GOVERNMENT Communist republic since 1976. The Communist Party of Vietnam is the only permitted party. A national assembly of 496 members is elected every 5 years; this elects an executive council of ministers and a council of state.

CAMBODIA

Once the "gentle kingdom" – isolated, but blessed with rich soils and the largest freshwater lake in Southeast Asia – Cambodia has recently gained an altogether different reputation, because of the Khmer Rouge. After their overthrow in 1979 by Vietnam, civil war ensued between the People's Republic of Kampuchea, installed and sustained by Vietnam, and the tripartite Coalition Government of Democratic Kampuchea, of which the Khmer Rouge was the strongest component. The coalition had international recognition and support from China, the USA and Asean. Its most acceptable face was Prince Norodom Sihanouk, picked as boy king by the French who were the first to mistake his smiling adroitness for amenability.

By the late 1980s the economy was barely subsisting on rice. Child mortality was lower only in Afghanistan. Denied hard-currency aid and credits, trade dwindled to a trickle. The exhaustion of the parties and Soviet pressure on Vietnam offered hope of reconciliation, but the promised withdrawal of Vietnamese troops threatened to allow a resurgence of the Khmer Rouge.

OFFICIAL NAME Democratic Cambodia.
CAPITAL CITY Phnom Penh.
GEOGRAPHY Around 90% of Cambodians live on the low alluvial plain around the Mekong and Tonle Sap Lake. East of the Mekong the land climbs gradually to forested mountains and plateaus. *Area* 181,035 sq km (69,900 sq miles).
PEOPLE *Population* 7.2m. *Ethnic groups* Khmer 93%, Vietnamese 4%, Chinese 3%.
RELIGION Buddhist 88%, Muslim 2%, Christian 1%.
LANGUAGE Khmer.
CURRENCY Riel (CRl).
PUBLIC HOLIDAYS Jan 7, New Year (April).
GOVERNMENT A new constitution was promulgated by the Vietnamese-backed government in 1981, providing for a 117-member national assembly to be elected for a 5-year term. The assembly elects an executive council of state whose chairman is head of state and an administrative council of ministers.

MALAYSIA

By the late 1980s, Malaysia's ambition to become a newly industrializing country in the next decade looked within reach. Already, in World Bank parlance, an upper middle-income country, with GNP per head approaching US$2,000, Malaysia is modestly populated and endowed with abundant natural resources. It is the world's largest producer of rubber, palm oil and tin, and has begun recently to exploit plentiful reserves of oil and timber. Successful diversification into resource processing and export industries has made manufacturing a key economic sector. A foray into heavy industrialization followed, with Japan and the East Asian "dragons" consciously adopted as models.

Complicated politics clouds this considerable economic good fortune. Malaysia owes its intricate patchwork of races and religions largely to the British, who in the 19th century imported Chinese and Indians to work on the tin mines and rubber estates of the Malay peninsula. The Muslim Malays remained in the majority but were economically marginalized. In 1963 the 11 peninsular states of Malaya joined with the predominantly tribal Borneo states of Sarawak and Sabah, 530km (330 miles) across the South China Sea, and the overwhelmingly Chinese island of Singapore to form the federation of Malaysia. It was a potentially explosive ethnic configuration.

Three times since independence the delicate social fabric has looked in danger of unravelling. After independence, the three-party Alliance, representing the three main ethnic groups, continued to hold power, dominated by the United Malays National Organization (UMNO). The principle of Malay hegemony was vigorously challenged by Lee Kuan Yew in 1965; Singapore was asked to leave the federation. Four years later, in the heated aftermath of a general election, serious race riots in Kuala Lumpur shocked the communities into a new consensus. This took the form of a broadened governing coalition, the National Front, agreement to avoid sensitive debate, and the New Economic Policy (NEP) which aimed to increase the share of corporate holdings in Malay hands to 30% by 1990.

The third challenge to the system was posed by the ascent of the hard-driving

OFFICIAL NAME Malaysia.

CAPITAL CITY Kuala Lumpur.

GEOGRAPHY Malaysia consists of a mountainous peninsula and the northern part of the island of Borneo. Almost three quarters of the land area is tropical rain forest or swamp forest. The majority of the peninsular population is concentrated on the wider western coastal plain, where short swift rivers flood seasonally. Villages on stilts and colonial cities built on rubber and tin fortunes are typical settlements on the peninsula. The territories in Borneo of Sarawak and Sabah are rugged and forested, and are basically rural, with the few cities mostly populated by Chinese. *Highest point* Mt Kinabalu 4,101 metres (13,450 feet). *Area* 329,749 sq km (127,320 sq miles), of which the peninsula is 131,587 sq km (50,810 sq miles).

PEOPLE *Population* 15.6m. *Density* 47 per sq km. *Ethnic groups* Malay and other indigenous 60%, Chinese 31%, Indian, Pakistani and Bangladeshi 8%.

RELIGION Muslim 53%, Buddhist 17%, Chinese folk religions 12%, Hindu 7%, Christian 6%.

LANGUAGE Malay. Also Chinese, English, Tamil, Iban Dusun, Bajan and other local dialects.

EDUCATION Free for ages 6–19. Education takes up 18% of government spending. There are 7 universities.

CURRENCY Ringgit (Ma$).

PUBLIC HOLIDAYS Chinese New Year, May 1, Vesak Day (May), Hari Raya Puasa, Monarch's Official Birthday (Jun), Hari Raya Haji, Aug 31, Deepavali, Mouloud, Dec 25.

GOVERNMENT Federation of 13 states and one federal territory (Kuala Lumpur). Nine of the states have hereditary monarchs and these elect one of their number head of state for 5 years. The legislature has 2 houses; the 177 members of the Dewan Rakyat are elected for 5 years, while the Dewan Negara has 58 members, 26 elected by the state assemblies and the remainder royal appointees. Executive power is held by the prime minister and cabinet, responsible to the legislature.

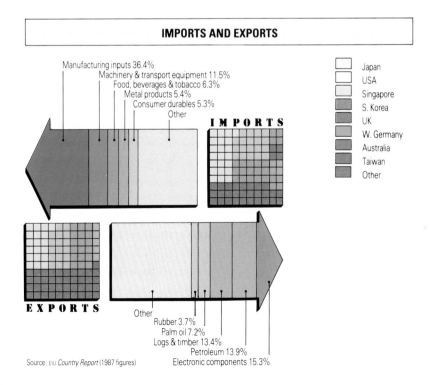

IMPORTS AND EXPORTS

Manufacturing inputs 36.4%
Machinery & transport equipment 11.5%
Food, beverages & tobacco 6.3%
Metal products 5.4%
Consumer durables 5.3%
Other

IMPORTS

Japan
USA
Singapore
S. Korea
UK
W. Germany
Australia
Taiwan
Other

EXPORTS

Other
Rubber 3.7%
Palm oil 7.2%
Logs & timber 13.4%
Petroleum 13.9%
Electronic components 15.3%

Source: EIU *Country Report* (1987 figures)

GDP BY ORIGIN

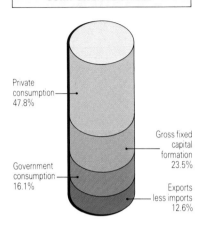

Manufacturing 22.4%

Agriculture 21.5%

Government services 12.3%

Mining & quarrying 10.6%

Wholesale & retail trade 10.5%

Finance, insurance & real estate 8.5%

Other

COMPONENTS OF GDP

Private consumption 47.8%

Gross fixed capital formation 23.5%

Government consumption 16.1%

Exports less imports 12.6%

Source: EIU *Country Report* (1987 figures)

ECONOMIC PROFILE

Rubber and tin traditional mainstays, with rice providing subsistence base. Later supplemented by crude oil, timber and palm oil, and manufactured exports – local resource-based, electronics, textiles. Drive to create heavy industries – the "national car," steel, cement – has lost favour.

Growth Still scope for expansion in wood and latex-based industries. Coal and petrochemicals in early stages of major development programmes; tin emerging from 1985 crash. Several major construction projects – highways, gas pipeline and refinery – to run into 1990s.

Problems Palm oil and cocoa reaching their limits. Healthy trade surplus eroded by services deficit caused by inadequate homegrown shipping, ports and insurance. Rice losing out to export crops and imports rising.

Dr Mahathir Mohamad to the prime ministership in 1981 – the first Malay commoner to hold the office. Amid mounting resentment of the NEP in all communities and growing doubts about the government's industrialization plans, the economy slowed in 1985. The National Front lost much of the Chinese vote in the 1986 general election; the following year Dr Mahathir only narrowly survived a challenge to his leadership of the UMNO, leaving the party seriously divided. Citing growing ethnic and religious tensions, Dr Mahathir arrested opponents and tightened the legislative screw on press and judiciary. Despite growing criticism of his autocratic style, Dr Mahathir retained the support of a substantial parliamentary majority.

For some, the persistence of the split in the UMNO presaged the breakdown of the old system; optimists saw it as offering the hope of real multiracial politics in Malaysia for the first time. Economic pressures meanwhile eased, with export demand and investment recovering and the government taking a more pragmatic approach to achieving the NEP's targets.

BRUNEI

Oil and gas have restored Brunei's fortunes. The once mighty Malay sultanate had fallen on hard times when Shell found oil at Seria in 1929; its lowest point had come in the 19th century, when the British made it a protectorate, squeezed into the present two small enclaves.

Power remained firmly in the hands of the sultan's family after independence in 1984, although technocrats were brought in in small numbers lower down the scale. Deployment of the sultanate's wealth abroad has sometimes looked feckless, but there is a limit to spending on domestic "diversification" and earnings from overseas investments now comfortably exceed revenue from oil and gas.

Political parties have been permitted since independence, but have failed to flourish. Government employees, about two-thirds of the labour force, are banned from political activity and the ordinary Bruneian – enjoying the benefits of a womb-to-tomb welfare state and undemanding public-sector employment – has proved indifferent to politics.

OFFICIAL NAME Sultanate of Brunei.

CAPITAL CITY Bandar Seri Begawan.

GEOGRAPHY Settlements are confined to the river valleys and a narrow coastal plain, where mangrove swamps separate fertile areas of peat and alluvium. *Area* 5,765 sq km (2,230 sq miles).

PEOPLE *Population* 220,000. *Density* 39 per sq km. *Ethnic groups* Malay 65%, Chinese 20%.

RELIGION Muslim 63%, Buddhist 14%, Christian 10%.

LANGUAGE Malay. Also Chinese and English.

EDUCATION Free, and along Islamic lines.

CURRENCY Brunei dollar (Br$).

PUBLIC HOLIDAYS Jan 1, Chinese New Year, Feb 23, Leilat al-Meiraj, 1st day of Ramadan, Revelation of Quran, Id al-Fitr, May 31, Hari Raya Haji, Jul 15, Muharram, Mouloud, Dec 25.

GOVERNMENT Absolute monarchy. The sultan governs by decree through appointed councils.

SINGAPORE

Already too mature to be tagged a newly industrializing country, Singapore has grown at an almost steady 7% a year since splitting from the Malaysian federation in 1965, to become the richest of the Asian "dragons."

Once separate from Malaysia, the island city state was an unlikely front-runner in Southeast Asia. Lee Kuan Yew and his colleagues in the People's Action Party (PAP) found themselves masters of a port city without agricultural hinterland or natural resources, its small population mostly Chinese in a region of Malays. The implications were both economic and political.

Singapore's economic success has depended on agile management to maintain an edge over potential rivals. Singapore was an entrepôt and British military base when it became internally self-governing in 1959, recognizably the child of its founder, Sir Stamford Raffles. Raffles saw what could be made of a muddy Malay fishing village standing astride the sea route from India to China. The British made the island a trading post and base for their foray into Southeast Asia.

British withdrawal east of Suez and the aspirations of Singapore's neighbours forced a break with the past. In the 1960s and 1970s, the strategy was to go for growth through labour-intensive, export-oriented industrialization. This succeeded beyond expectations, helped by a boom in domestic construction and

OFFICIAL NAME Republic of Singapore.
CAPITAL CITY Singapore.
GEOGRAPHY An infertile island at the southern tip of the Malay peninsula, from which it is separated by the narrow Johore strait, Singapore has one of the largest ports in the world. The rugged granitic centre of the island gives way to sandy hills on the east and a series of scarps on the west. Much of the northern sector is mangrove swamp. *Highest point* Bukit Timah 177 metres (580 feet). *Area* 620 sq km (330 sq miles).
PEOPLE *Population* 2.6m. *Density* 4,126 per sq km. *Ethnic groups* Chinese 77%, Malay 15%, Indian and Sri Lankan 6%.
RELIGION Taoist 29%, Buddhist 27%, Muslim 16%, Christian 10%, Hindu 4%.
LANGUAGE Malay, Chinese, English and Tamil.
EDUCATION Free but noncompulsory. English is the main language of instruction. Education takes up 20% of government spending.
CURRENCY Singapore dollar (S$).
PUBLIC HOLIDAYS Jan 1, Chinese New Year, Good Fri, May 1, Hari Raya Puasa Vesak Day, Hari Raya Haji Aug 9, Deepavali, Dec 25 .
GOVERNMENT Republic since 1965. Parliament elects a president as head of state every 4 years. The 81 members of parliament are elected from single and multimember constituencies for 5 years; the People's Action Party has won almost every seat since 1972. Executive power lies with a cabinet headed by a prime minister.

ECONOMIC PROFILE

Entrepôt, financial services centre and commodities exchange for the region. Industrialization based on labour-intensive export processing, shipbuilding and repair, and oil refining. Maintaining competitive edge by moving into high-tech manufacturing and support for R&D. Well-developed infrastructure and government attuned to the needs of multinationals for flexible trade and investment policies.

Growth Export-led growth sustained by strong demand for electronic products and computer peripherals. Bidding to take over Hong Kong's role as secondary financial centre for East Asia.

Problems Dependence on trade, particularly with USA, makes Singapore vulnerable to protectionist pressures. Labour shortages forcing some businesses to move elsewhere.

IMPORTS AND EXPORTS

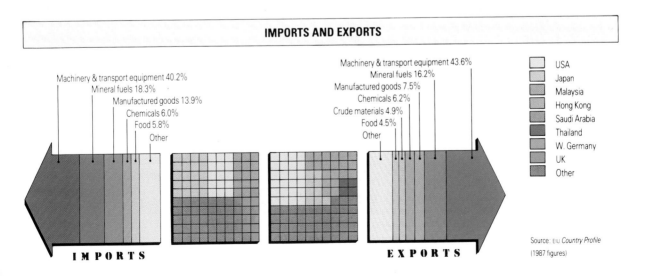

Source: EIU *Country Profile* (1987 figures)

the regional oil industry. In the late 1970s, as mainstays like oil refining began to look shaky and competition loomed from exporters elsewhere in the region, the government launched a second industrial revolution, to hustle the economy upmarket into skill- and capital-intensive industries with high added value.

All went well until 1985, when GDP for once fell. After another bout of self-examination, the course was adjusted. The goal was now to establish a new-style entrepôt, relying on Singapore's efficiency, infrastructure and skills to become a regional hub, a transport and communications centre where multinationals would set up regional headquarters and base their high-tech and R&D operations. The economy took off once more.

Survival has also been the dominant theme in politics. In the beleaguered 1960s, every PAP cadre seemed to believe that he was a Southeast Asian Israeli, under siege in a hostile region. Mr Lee's authoritarian instinct, sharpened in his battles with the left, was that politics was a luxury for Singapore. Social policy has often amounted to social engineering, whether in the famously strict litter laws or in efforts to encourage selective breeding. Some of the consequences are now being felt, as high local wages cut into export competitiveness and government opposition to immigration denies Singapore an easy answer to labour shortages. As it continues to uncover "Marxist" plots, the government's vigilance often seems to shade into paranoia.

Thorough as always, Mr Lee – as yet showing no desire to leave politics – has nurtured a "second generation" leadership team to succeed his own. It will inherit a Singapore of wealthy owner-occupiers that seems assured of a niche in the safer post-Vietnam world of Asean partnership. His successors may, however, find it difficult to abandon the bracing agenda of Lee Kuan Yew, for fear of a crisis of purpose.

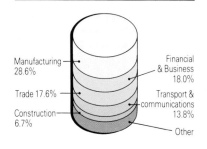

GDP BY ORIGIN

Manufacturing 28.6%
Financial & Business 18.0%
Trade 17.6%
Transport & communications 13.8%
Construction 6.7%
Other

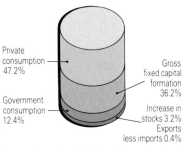

COMPONENTS OF GDP

Private consumption 47.2%
Gross fixed capital formation 36.2%
Government consumption 12.4%
Increase in stocks 3.2%
Exports less imports 0.4%

Source: EIU *Country Report* (1987 figures)

INDONESIA

Indonesia's independent history changed course in October 1965, when troops led by General Suharto put down a supposedly communist-inspired coup. The coup attempt became the pretext for the bloody suppression of what was then the largest communist party outside China and the USSR. Suharto supplanted Sukarno, leader of the bitter independence struggle against the Dutch from 1945 to 1949.

Sukarno's last years had been marked by political turmoil and economic collapse. Since independence, Indonesia had seemed perpetually on the brink of disintegration, with separatist movements throughout the archipelago fighting under regionalist or Islamic banners.

Suharto and the military took depoliticization and development as their watchwords. US-trained technocrats stabilized the economy and ushered in a period of rapid growth, greatly aided by rising oil prices. In the 1970s oil came to account for 70% of export earnings and over half of tax receipts. Not only did income per head improve but so did social indicators like life expectancy, poverty and literacy; some major successes such as rice self-sufficiency and family planning have been achieved largely as a result of government diktat.

Suharto also abandoned his predecessor's anti-Western rhetoric and his bid for international prominence as leader of the world's fifth most populous country and largest Islamic state. A pragmatic, low-key approach was adopted in international affairs, leading to improved relations with the West and with Indonesia's neighbours, partners in Asean after 1967.

Weakening oil prices in the 1980s eroded the economy's most secure revenue base. A series of deregulatory packages have stimulated other exports; oil and gas now account for less than half of earnings. But corruption and nepotism still deform policy-making and since the end of the oil boom Indonesia has accumulated a massive foreign debt.

OFFICIAL NAME Republic of Indonesia.

CAPITAL CITY Jakarta.

GEOGRAPHY There are nearly 14,000 islands in Indonesia, 930 of them inhabited. Most are rugged, sometimes volcanic and covered with tropical rain forest. The larger islands – Sumatra, Java, Southern Borneo, Sulawesi and western New Guinea (Irian Jaya) – contain the majority of the population. Most live in river valleys, alluvial coastal plains or on terraced mountainsides. *Highest point* Puncak Jaya 5,030 metres (16,500 feet). *Area* 1,904,569 sq km (735,360 sq miles).

PEOPLE *Population* 163m. *Density* 86 per sq km. *Ethnic groups* Javanese 40%, Sundanese 15%, Indonesian 12%, Madurese 5%.

RELIGION Muslim 88%, Christian 7%, Hindu 2%.

LANGUAGE Bahasa, Indonesian and others.

EDUCATION Free and compulsory for ages 7–13.

CURRENCY Rupiah (Rp).

PUBLIC HOLIDAYS Jan 1, Leilat al-Meiraj, Good Fri, Ascension, Id al-Fitr, Id al-Adha, Muharram, Aug 17, Mouloud, Dec 25.

GOVERNMENT Military-dominated republic. The president, who is both chief executive and head of state, is elected for 5-year terms. The people's consultative assembly includes a 500-member house of representatives, 400 elected and 100 appointed, but the real power is in the hands of the army and security forces. The left is suppressed.

Java, with 7% of the land area but 60% of the population, is Indonesia's political core; however, most of the oil, minerals, timber and plantation crops that provide the country's wealth come from the "outer islands." Secessionism is now largely confined to the eastern fringe of the archipelago in Irian Jaya and East Timor, both unwillingly incorporated well after independence.

Formal politics has become a sedate affair, dominated by Golkar, the military-backed coalition of functional groups which prefers not to be known as a political party but which wins elections every five years against the two other permitted parties. The real power struggles are conducted out of public view within the military, which invokes the doctrine of "dual function" to justify its involvement in civilian affairs.

Suharto may stand down at the end of his fifth term in 1993, when he will be 72, but no obvious successor exists. Those who hope that Suharto's passing would mean the return of the military to barracks will probably be disappointed, even though its role in the economy has been reduced in recent years, with a civilian for the first time getting the top job at state oil giant Pertamina in 1988. The military establishment reacted badly to the elevation to the vice-presidency in March 1988 of Sudharmono – a soldier who seems to favour a diminishing military role in politics – and saw to it that he was replaced as chairman of Golkar by a retired general more to their liking. The military sees itself as the sole guarantor of stability in Indonesia and, whenever it feels that the people need to be reminded of this, it has only to conjure up the communist bogey.

ECONOMIC PROFILE

Agrarian rice-based economy exporting agricultural commodities – edible oils, coffee, tea, rubber, tobacco – minerals, oil and natural gas. Heavily protected import-substitution industries – textiles, cement, steel, vehicles – tested by trade liberalization and drive to reduce dependence on oil exports.

Growth Export-oriented manufacturing set to grow strongly, with ambitious plans to develop the aircraft industry and electronics; expansion also in minerals processing, furniture and handicrafts. Plans to revive shelved petrochemical projects. Inter-island shipping and ports being modernized and deregulated. Tourism is booming.

Problems Oil production set to decline unless new discoveries made. Financial sector hampered by over-regulation. Capital goods still a major import item. Costs of servicing debt continue to rise.

IMPORTS AND EXPORTS

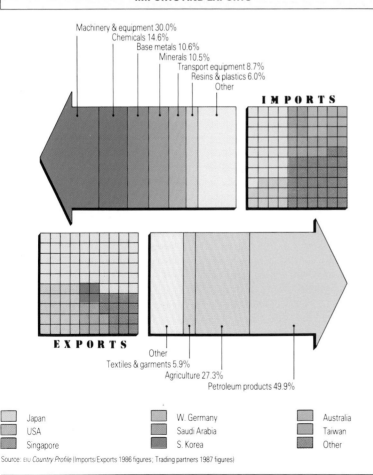

Machinery & equipment 30.0%
Chemicals 14.6%
Base metals 10.6%
Minerals 10.5%
Transport equipment 8.7%
Resins & plastics 6.0%
Other

IMPORTS

EXPORTS

Other
Textiles & garments 5.9%
Agriculture 27.3%
Petroleum products 49.9%

Japan
USA
Singapore
W. Germany
Saudi Arabia
S. Korea
Australia
Taiwan
Other

Source: EIU *Country Profile* (Imports/Exports 1986 figures; Trading partners 1987 figures)

GDP BY ORIGIN

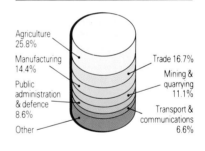

Agriculture 25.8%
Manufacturing 14.4%
Public administration & defence 8.6%
Other
Trade 16.7%
Mining & quarrying 11.1%
Transport & communications 6.6%

COMPONENTS OF GDP

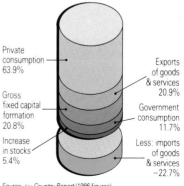

Private consumption 63.9%
Gross fixed capital formation 20.8%
Increase in stocks 5.4%
Exports of goods & services 20.9%
Government consumption 11.7%
Less: imports of goods & services −22.7%

Source: EIU *Country Report* (1986 figures)

EAST TIMOR

For 400 years, East Timor was a neglected backwater of the Portuguese empire, known largely for its superior coffee. Portugal promised self-determination in 1975, but Indonesia's nervous generals, wary of allowing the Fretilin independence movement to establish a communist beachhead in the East Indies, invaded and annexed the territory. Tens of thousands of Timorese died in the invasion and subsequent conflict.

The UN has not recognized the takeover and the government has yet to yield to international pressure to lift restrictions on access to the territory, despite promises to do so. East Timor remains effectively closed to the outside world.

OFFICIAL NAME East Timor.
CAPITAL CITY Dili.
GEOGRAPHY The territory comprises the eastern half of a rugged volcanic island in the chain that runs from Sumatra. *Highest point* 2,920 metres (9,580 feet). *Area* 14,874 sq km (5,740 sq miles).
PEOPLE *Population* 660,000. *Density* 44 per sq km. *Ethnic groups* Indonesian/Malay, Melanesian.
RELIGION Christian 39%, Animist.
LANGUAGE Tetum and other local languages. Also Indonesian and Portuguese.
CURRENCY Indonesian rupiah (Rp).

THE PHILIPPINES

More than superficially Westernized, the Philippines has the cultural marks of 300 years of Spanish rule, followed by nearly 50 under the Americans; Catholicism and constitutionalism run deep. The Philippines was the first Asian country to win independence from Western colonialism, in 1946; economic and security relations with the USA remain strong, if sometimes acrimonious.

Local power brokers are important in a dispersed archipelago. Politics in the two decades after independence revolved around personality and pork barrel. The system survived the rural rebellion of the communist Hukbalahap (1948–53) but not the challenge of one of its own, Ferdinand Marcos.

Mr Marcos was the first Philippine president to be re-elected. He then extended his period in office by declaring martial law in 1972. The pretext was the insurgencies of the communist New People's Army (NPA) and the southern Muslim Moro National Liberation Front; but the armed forces, in a position of real power for the first time, proved incapable of restoring peace. From a localized irritant in 1972, the NPA had become a nationwide force by the early 1980s.

OFFICIAL NAME Republic of the Philippines.
CAPITAL CITY Manila.
GEOGRAPHY Most of the islands in the archipelago are mountainous, with most ranges running from north to south. Some of the islands are coral and some volcanic – there are ten active volcanoes – and many have narrow coastal plains. Most of the population live in intermontane plains in the larger islands, or on the coastal strips. Around 40% of the land is forested. *Highest point* Mount Apo 2,954 metres (9,690 feet). *Area* 300,000 sq km (116,000 sq miles).
PEOPLE *Population* 54m. *Density* 181 per sq km. *Ethnic groups* Cebuano 24%, Tagalog 24%, Ilocano 11%, Hiligaynon 10%, Bicolano 7%, Samar-Leyte 5%, Pampanga 3%.
RELIGION Christian 93% (RC 85%, other 8%), Muslim 4%.
LANGUAGE Filipino and English. Also Spanish and local languages.
EDUCATION Free and compulsory for ages 7–12. Secondary education (13–17) also free in some areas.
CURRENCY Philippine peso (PP).
PUBLIC HOLIDAYS Jan 1, Feb 25, Maundy Thu, Good Fri, May 1, May 6, Jun 12, last Sun in Aug, Sep 11, Sep 21, Nov 1, Nov 30, Dec 25, Dec 30, 31.
GOVERNMENT Republic since 1946. A new constitution promulgated in 1987 provides for a bicameral legislature with a president, elected for a single 6-year term, as head of state and chief executive. The 24-member senate is elected for a 5-year term. The house of representatives serves a 3-year term; it has 200 elected members and up to 50 others appointed by the president to represent various minority groups.

ECONOMIC PROFILE

Agriculture the main employer, producing rice and maize for domestic consumption and coconuts and sugar for export. Manufacturing originally based on local agricultural and mineral resources. Import-substitution industries – notably assembly of consumer goods – developed in 1950s and 1960s, bringing industry's contribution to GDP level with that of agriculture. Ambitious programme to build heavy industrial base launched in 1981 became casualty of economic austerity; most projects abandoned. New emphasis on agribusiness and small-scale labour-intensive industries.

Growth Mining, tourism and financial sector recovering from setbacks of Marcos years. Main motors of manufacturing growth are garments, semiconductors and other export industries. Food and timber processing receiving official encouragement. Buoyant domestic and export demand stimulating investment.

Problems Sugar suffered from low world prices, coconuts from neglect, both from "cronyism." Forests seriously depleted. Continued dependence on commodity exports does little to create jobs. Half of labour force unemployed or underemployed; high level of emigration. Debt service burden has forced rescheduling, making banks reluctant to lend new money. Privatization of government corporations proceeding very slowly.

IMPORTS AND EXPORTS

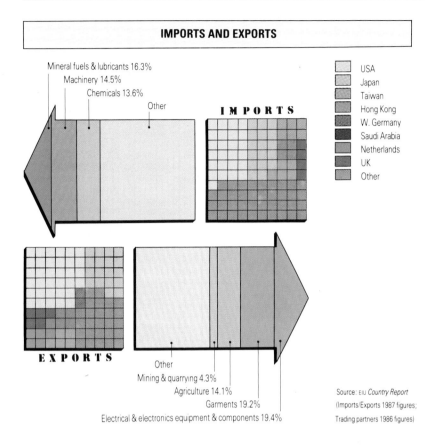

Mineral fuels & lubricants 16.3%
Machinery 14.5%
Chemicals 13.6%
Other

IMPORTS

USA
Japan
Taiwan
Hong Kong
W. Germany
Saudi Arabia
Netherlands
UK
Other

EXPORTS

Other
Mining & quarrying 4.3%
Agriculture 14.1%
Garments 19.2%
Electrical & electronics equipment & components 19.4%

Source: EIU *Country Report*
(Imports/Exports 1987 figures;
Trading partners 1986 figures)

BALANCE OF PAYMENTS

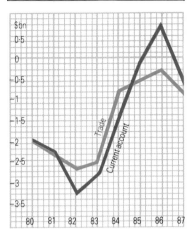

Source: EIU *Country Credit Risk Service*

GDP BY ORIGIN

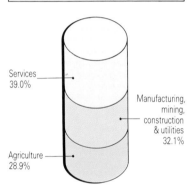

Services 39.0%

Manufacturing, mining, construction & utilities 32.1%

Agriculture 28.9%

COMPONENTS OF GDP

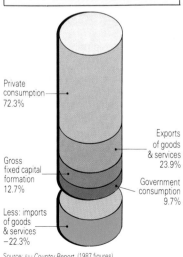

Private consumption 72.3%

Exports of goods & services 23.9%

Gross fixed capital formation 12.7%

Government consumption 9.7%

Less: imports of goods & services −22.3%

Source: EIU *Country Report* (1987 figures)

Confidence collapsed after the assassination of Marcos's chief political rival, Benigno Aquino, in August 1983. The economy went into rapid reverse and by 1985 GDP per head was back at its 1975 level. Poverty and landlessness increased and foreign debt reached an insupportable level.

Blatantly rigged elections in February 1986 triggered popular discontent. Borne on a wave of "people power," Benigno Aquino's widow, Corazon ("Cory"), split the military and supplanted the dictator. A new constitution was approved, elections held and Philippine-style democracy began functioning again.

The new administration quickly wound up the cronies' trading monopolies and rescheduled debts with foreign banks. It was more difficult for Mrs Aquino to weld the disparate anti-Marcos elements in her cabinet into a decisive body. There were five coup attempts in the president's first 18 months, mostly involving soldiers who thought her soft on communism. By shedding the liberals in her cabinet, Mrs Aquino seemed to have won over the military.

No longer seen as an "ordinary housewife" with no business in politics, Mrs Aquino may even seek a second term in 1992. Her critics find her too content to take the moral high ground while disinclined to deploy her prestige against vested interests in the congress. The pressing issue of land reform seems to have defeated her, as it did several of her predecessors. The 10-year Comprehensive Agrarian Reform Programme (Carp), covering both land acquisitions and post-acquisition support services and infrastructure, will be far costlier than originally estimated; and some private commercial farms have already been exempted from land redistribution until 1998.

One item that cannot be neglected is the agreement on US bases, which expires in 1991. The economic cost of sending the Americans home would be high, but many Filipinos resent their continued dependence on the USA.

OCEANIA

SOUTH PACIFIC

Micronesia

Micronesia, the northernmost group of Pacific Islands, stretches in an arc from the Northern Mariana Islands, southeast of Japan to Tuvalu, north of Fiji.

The economies of Micronesia are among the tiniest in the world. Most islands are coral atolls with poor-quality soils; subsistence farming is the main occupation, although copra is a source of export earnings and fishing and tourism are being developed. A select few, notably Nauru, have rich phosphate reserves, whose exploitation is profitable but environmentally destructive.

Spain, Germany, Japan, the UK and USA have all controlled parts of the region at various times. The Northern Mariana, Caroline and Marshall Islands came under US administration by UN mandate in 1947 as the Trust Territory of the Pacific Islands. Most gained effective independence when the trusteeship came to a formal end in 1986, although the USA remains responsible for defence and security and provides economic aid. Guam, largest of the Marianas, elected to remain part of the USA and is an important military base. The status of Palau, an island in the Caroline group but not part of the Federated States of Micronesia formed by the rest, remains unsettled because of a dispute over the USA's rights to store nuclear materials on the island. The populations of most of the islands consist mainly of indigenous ethnic groups. The exception is Guam, whose original inhabitants, the Chamorros, are now outnumbered by other ethnic groups, notably Filipinos and US mainlanders.

Anzus

The Anzus security treaty was signed in 1951 to coordinate the collective defence efforts in the Pacific of the USA, Australia and New Zealand. New Zealand's decision in 1985 to ban ships carrying nuclear weapons from its ports led the USA to suspend joint military exercises under the Anzus pact. This has put the pact's future in doubt, as Australia is also reviewing its defence arrangements.

Antarctica

In some respects, Antarctica is a successful experiment in international cooperation. Nineteen nations, often otherwise antagonistic, have agreed under the Antarctic Treaty of 1959 to keep one-tenth of the global land area demilitarized, nuclear-free and dedicated to research. But the Antarctic "club" is secretive and exclusive; decisionmaking powers are held by the 12 original signatories. Those on the outside, particularly nonaligned countries, would like to see Antarctica treated as a global resource, with fair shares for all in any future development of its potential wealth. Conservationists, on the other hand, want the continent preserved as a "world park" - part nature reserve, part scientific laboratory.

The Antarctic's peace and purity is already being soiled. Offshore, massive concentrations of krill, a rich protein source, are being harvested by Soviet and Japanese trawlers, with unknown effects on future stocks. Huge mineral resources are thought to exist, including an estimated 50 billion barrels of oil - equivalent to 15% of Middle East reserves. Exploitation of these resources, hugely difficult and costly as it would be, would irremediably damage the environment. Even the increasing scale of scientific research, much of it concerned with the depletion of the earth's ozone layer, has brought pollution and destruction with it, whether by accident or design. The pressure will be on the members of the Antarctic club to protect the environment when they renew their treaty in 1991.

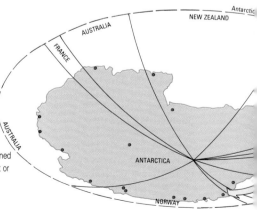

The South Pacific Forum

The South Pacific Forum is the main organization grouping the independent and self-governing states of the region. Established in 1971, it has focused attention on issues such as nuclear testing, fishing rights and the independence of New Caledonia.

Economic and trade concerns are handled by the South Pacific Bureau for Economic Cooperation (SPEC), set up in 1973. This has negotiated duty-free access to the Australian and New Zealand markets for products from the smaller island states. SPEC is also active in trade promotion and coordination of transport and communications policies. Concern is growing among SPEC members about the impact of the "greenhouse effect" or global warming on low-lying atolls.

Exclusive economic zones

The depths of the oceans hold significant mineral resources and the technology to exploit them is rapidly being developed. Attempts to regulate access to the potential wealth of the oceans led to the adoption in 1984 of the UN Convention of the Law of the Sea. This puts 40% of the world's oceans under the control of coastal states, giving them rights over economic activity and responsibility for environmental protection within a 200-nautical-mile exclusive economic zone. Deep seabed areas are designated the "common heritage of mankind" to be controlled by an International Seabed Authority. About 160 nations have signed the convention, but it will come into effect only when 60 have ratified it.

Nuclear tests and nuclear-free zones

France's programme of nuclear tests in the Pacific has united most nations of the region in opposition. The Treaty of Rarotonga, establishing a South Pacific nuclear-free zone, was signed in 1985 by Australia, New Zealand, Papua New Guinea and most of the smaller Pacific island nations. The treaty, which prohibits the possession, testing and use of nuclear weapons, came into force in December 1986. Of the five major nuclear powers, the USSR and China have signed the treaty; France, the UK and the USA have refused to adhere to it.

Equator

ISLANDS

● Papeete

● Avarua   FRENCH POLYNESIA   Tropic of Capricorn

GMT −8½

Adamstown ●

GMT −10   GMT −9   PITCAIRN

Polynesia

The idyllic image of the Polynesian Islands as an unspoiled earthly paradise has been replaced in recent years by the shadow of the mushroom cloud. France governs 120 of the islands, scattered across the South Pacific, and has tested its nuclear weapons at Mururoa Atoll in the Tuamotu archipelago since 1966, despite the mounting protests of Pacific nations and of environmentalist groups. The presence of large numbers of French troops is a boost to the economy of the islands, particularly Tahiti; so, too, is tourism, but high costs and the destruction of the environment caused by the tourists themselves is starting to keep visitors away. Coconuts are the major cash crop, and copra the largest export, but the total value of exports is only about a quarter of the cost of imports each year.

The Samoan Islands, northeast of Fiji, are split between Western Samoa, independent since 1962, and US-administered American Samoa. Tuna-canning plants are a major source of employment in American Samoa but the islands' economies depend on aid, remittances and, to a limited extent, tourism. Western Samoa plans to set up an offshore financial centre.

UNCLAIMED

The populations of most of the Polynesian islands consist predominantly of indigenous ethnic groups. The exceptions are French Polynesia and Pitcairn.

Fishing rights

The Pacific's rich fishing grounds have long been plundered by unscrupulous foreign fleets, often operating illegally in the territorial waters of small island nations. Growing unity in resisting such incursions has led to the conclusion of more formal fishing agreements, such as the treaty signed by the USA with South Pacific Forum nations in 1987. Fish have also been the focus of superpower rivalry, with the fishing agreements signed by the USSR with Vanuatu and Kiribati in the mid-1980s arousing US concern about an extension of Soviet influence in the Pacific.

AUSTRALIA

Long seen as an alien European outpost at the extremity of Western civilization, Australia is increasingly coming to terms with its location and focusing the main thrust of its economy on the fast-growing states of the Pacific rim. The old Anglo-Australian identity is being replaced by one based on a new multicultural mateship, a pride in living in a "lucky country" and an awareness of being part of Asia and the Pacific. The current strategic thinking, too, stresses self-reliance and good regional diplomacy, even though the military alliance with the USA, which took Australian troops to Vietnam, remains axiomatic.

The heritage of education and social reform that gained Australia a reputation as a "working man's paradise" at the turn of the century still has meaning in a highly democratic but also very competitive society. Behind the laid-back image is a country of strivers and achievers, exemplified in recent years by the international expansionism and acquisitiveness of its successful entrepreneurs. Most Australians are descended not from convicts but from free immigrants bent on bettering their lot. Ethnically the population is now 75% British or Irish, though in the majority of cases these links are generations old. The rest are predominantly the product of postwar immigration, which brought in Italians, Greeks and other Europeans and, most recently, Asians, whose arrival marked the dismantling of the infamous "white Australia" policy that had banned nonwhite entry for 100 years. Ironically, the group that has most clearly been excluded from the emerging multicultural consensus is that of the Aboriginal Australians, who form 1% of the population and whose special relationship with the land has yet to be properly recognized.

Australian politics is almost exclusively masculine and unashamedly boisterous. The federal government coexists (uneasily at times) with state governments who guard their independence jealously. In certain instances states have become the virtual fiefdoms of individual political figures. The tension between central and state governments is further exacerbated by the electoral cycle of three years. Whether or not Australians like going to the polls so often, they are obliged to vote on pain of a fine. With a transferable vote system that prevents overwhelming majorities, and the independence of the states, the Australian system has maintained political stability and excitement simultaneously.

Despite its vastness, Australia is among the most highly urbanized nations on earth: well over 80% of its people live in cities, almost all in a belt of well-watered fertile land stretching along the southeast coast from Brisbane to Adelaide and in a pocket around Perth in Western Australia. Their easygoing, egalitarian ethos masks a concern for looking after family needs, reflected in the highest home ownership rate in the world and very high personal savings.

OFFICIAL NAME Commonwealth of Australia.

CAPITAL CITY Canberra.

GEOGRAPHY Australia is by far the flattest and driest of the continents. Its vast, barren and largely uninhabited interior, the outback, is a low, rolling plateau dotted with dry salt lakes. In the south it gives straight onto the sea, but elsewhere it is bordered by coastal mountain ranges. In the south and east the wooded Great Dividing Range separates it from a hilly and fertile coastal region that contains most of the population. The northern coasts and the Queensland peninsula are covered with tropical rain forest and the southern island of Tasmania is cool and mountainous. *Highest point* Mt Kosciusko 2,228 metres (7,310 feet). *Area* 7,686,848 sq km (2,967,910 sq miles).

PEOPLE *Population* 15.8m. *Density* 2 per sq km. *Ethnic groups* Australian 78% (Aborigine 1%), British and Irish 8%, Italian 2%, New Zealander 1%, Greek 1%, Yugoslavian 1%.

RELIGION Anglican Church of Australia 26%, RC 26%, Uniting Church 5%, Presbyterian 4%, Methodist 3%, Greek Orthodox 3%, Muslim 0.5%.

LANGUAGE English.

EDUCATION Free to university level and compulsory for ages 6–15. There are 19 universities. Education is a joint responsibility of state and federal governments.

CLIMATE Tropical and sub-tropical, with wet summers, in north; temperate with wet winters in east and south. Inland is mostly hot desert, with clear skies and extremes of heat and cold.

CURRENCY Australian dollar (A$).

PUBLIC HOLIDAYS Jan 1, Jan 26, Good Fri, Easter Mon, Apr 25, Jun 12, Dec 25, Dec 26. Also state holidays.

GOVERNMENT Parliamentary monarchy. The head of state is the British monarch, represented by a governor-general with limited powers. The 6 states and 2 territories are largely autonomous. The bicameral federal parliament consists of a Senate with 12 members from each state and 2 from each territory, elected for 6 years by PR – and a House of Representatives with 148 members elected from single-member constituencies for a 3-year term. The prime minister and executive council are drawn from the majority party in the House of Representatives.

IMPORTS AND EXPORTS

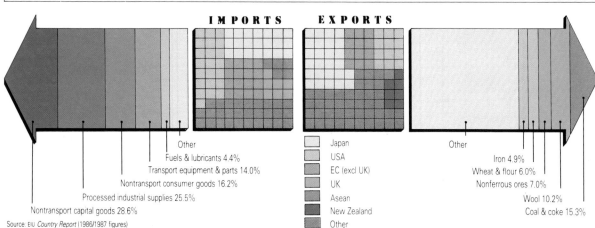

Other
Fuels & lubricants 4.4%
Transport equipment & parts 14.0%
Nontransport consumer goods 16.2%
Processed industrial supplies 25.5%
Nontransport capital goods 28.6%

Japan
USA
EC (excl UK)
UK
Asean
New Zealand
Other

Other
Iron 4.9%
Wheat & flour 6.0%
Nonferrous ores 7.0%
Wool 10.2%
Coal & coke 15.3%

Source: EIU *Country Report* (1986/1987 figures)

Traditionally, Australia depended on its agricultural and pastoral products. It has been the world's leading wool producer since the 19th century; it is also the largest beef exporter and a major wheat grower. Minerals, important since the gold rushes of the 1850s, have boomed in recent years to become the leading export sector. Australia is now one of the world's largest mineral producers: the biggest exporter of iron ore and aluminium; second biggest of coal, bauxite, nickel and zinc; and an important supplier of copper, silver, gold, tin, tungsten and uranium. It is 70% self-sufficient in oil. It is also a continent of natural beauty, and tourism is thriving. By any definition, Australia is resource-rich.

Even so, the country faces a number of economic problems and challenges. With its relatively small domestic economy, it needs free trade to prosper; the formation of trading blocs in Western Europe and the Americas is eyed with concern. Distance makes transport and insurance costs huge in overseas and domestic trade. Drought periodically devastates agricultural output for periods of two or three years. As a supplier of raw materials, Australia is extremely vulnerable to fluctuations in output and prices of its commodity exports. When income falls, the country has difficulty servicing its sizeable foreign debt, although when this has happened – in the 1930s and 1980s – governments have demonstrated considerable skill in carrying through retrenchment.

Australian industry is also vulnerable to external pressures. Manufacturing developed late and focuses mainly on domestic markets; it is still reeling from the reduction of protective barriers in the 1970s and the competition from Asian neighbours is formidable. Restructuring has begun and there have been some modest export successes in high-technology areas. Nevertheless, Australia's manufacturing sector is dangerously weak for a supposedly developed and balanced economy. The last two decades have seen Australia entering a new arena in which to prove its economic resilience and competitive skills. The UK was once the country's principal trading partner, but became rapidly less significant after it joined the EC; its place was taken by Japan, with which trade had been growing since the 1930s. The USA is also now a key partner. Two-thirds of Australia's trade is with countries of the Pacific rim, and relatively long experience in Asian markets also makes Australian expertise a valuable commodity for European companies seeking to expand in the region.

ECONOMIC PROFILE

A major world producer of raw materials. Minerals now main export earner, though agricultural products – wool, beef, wheat, fruits, sugar – still account for 40% of exports. Relatively small manufacturing sector, developed behind protective barriers, beginning to restructure in search of new markets.

Growth Mineral production expanding, as is tourism. Competing effectively and expanding overseas in selected areas: food and drink, media and entertainment, transport, electronic communications. Increasingly important investor and trader in Pacific region.

Problems Manufacturing's contribution to GDP has fallen from 30% to 16% since 1950s. High current account deficit implies heavy borrowing – foreign debt equals 30% of GDP.

BALANCE OF PAYMENTS

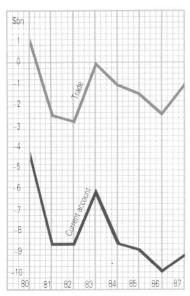

Source: EIU *International Economic Appraisal Service*

GDP BY ORIGIN

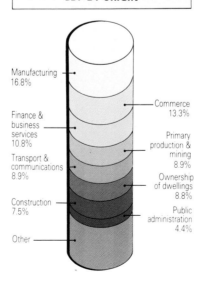

Manufacturing 16.8%
Finance & business services 10.8%
Transport & communications 8.9%
Construction 7.5%
Other
Commerce 13.3%
Primary production & mining 8.9%
Ownership of dwellings 8.8%
Public administration 4.4%

Source: EIU *Country Report* (GDP by origin 1986/87 figures, Components of GDP 1987/88 figures)

COMPONENTS OF GDP

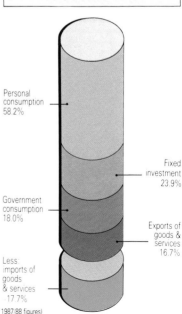

Personal consumption 58.2%
Government consumption 18.0%
Less imports of goods & services 17.7%
Fixed investment 23.9%
Exports of goods & services 16.7%

NEW ZEALAND

Once, New Zealand seemed to have everything to offer: an advanced social democracy, European and Maori cultures in harmonious coexistence, and a land of unpolluted beauty and fertility. The idyll evaporated in the 1970s. The vital relationship was with the UK, which bought 70% of New Zealand's exports and supplied most of its manufactured goods. British membership of the EC has reduced its purchases to less than 10% of New Zealand's exports and even this share is threatened. New markets in the Middle East and East Asia have not properly and permanently filled the gap. Manufactured goods still have to be imported at high cost, and there is a chronic balance of payments problem. New Zealand has also had to think again about its alliances because of its opposition to nuclear weapons. France was alienated by protests about its nuclear tests in the Pacific, while objections to the visits of US nuclear warships led to New Zealand's ejection from the Anzus alliance.

All these changes have forced a formerly secure nation to reconsider its position. With no valuable minerals to help it out of crisis, New Zealand has had to dismantle much of its state-directed economy, float the currency, encourage new industries and import-substitution and hope for success through even greater efficiency. Farm subsidies were slashed, halving farmers' incomes; state industries and utilities were privatized. New markets were aggressively sought and an agreement signed with Australia to introduce free trade by stages. New fish, timber, wood-pulp and iron export industries have been set up and natural gas discoveries have eased fuel shortages.

The free-market medicine has yet to work for the New Zealand economy, despite some success in reducing inflation and improving the current account. Though its farming sector is the most efficient in the world, it faces restricted access to the world's wealthiest consumers in the EC and USA, whose farmers are still heavily subsidized. A weaker New Zealand dollar has made exports more competitive but new sales have not compensated for loss of value.

The social fabric has been affected by economic difficulties. Unemployment and violent crime have increased, as has the traditional exodus to Australia. Race relations have deteriorated, particularly in Auckland, a third of whose population is now Polynesian. Political uncertainties and damaging splits in the reforming Labour government can only make economic recovery harder.

OFFICIAL NAME New Zealand.

CAPITAL CITY Wellington.

GEOGRAPHY Two-thirds of New Zealand is covered with evergreen forest. Of the two major and several smaller islands, South Island is mountainous and scenic, with glaciers, lakes and fast-flowing rivers; most settlement is on the alluvial plains of the east coast. North Island is less rugged but volcanically active, with many hot springs and geysers; the volcanic central plateau, rolling down into Hawke Bay, is the centre of the dairy industry. Auckland, on its isthmus, has harbours in both the Tasman sea and the Pacific; the area to the north has poor soils and sub-tropical vegetation. *Highest point* Mt Cook 3,764 metres (12,350 feet). *Area* 268,676 sq km (103,740 sq miles).

PEOPLE *Population* 3.3m. *Density* 12 per sq km. *Ethnic groups* New Zealander 84% (Maori 9%), British 6%, Australian 1.5%, Samoan 1%, Dutch 1%.

RELIGION Church of England 26%, Presbyterian 16%, RC 14%, Methodist 5%, Baptist 2%.

LANGUAGE English. Also Maori.

EDUCATION Free and compulsory for ages 6–15. There are 7 universities.

CLIMATE Temperate and generally sunny. Average annual temperature 9°C (48°F) in south, 15°C (59°F) in north, with no seasonal extremes. Annual rainfall 600–1,500mm (24–60ins), more in mountains, evenly spread through the year.

CURRENCY New Zealand dollar (NZ$).

PUBLIC HOLIDAYS Jan 1, Feb 6, Good Fri, Easter Mon, Apr 25, 1st Mon in Jun, 4th Mon in Oct, Dec 25, Dec 26. Also provincial holidays.

GOVERNMENT Parliamentary monarchy. The head of state is the British monarch, represented by a governor-general with limited powers. The legislative House of Representatives has 97 members, 4 of them Maoris, elected in single-member constituencies for 3-year terms. The prime minister and cabinet are drawn from the majority party.

IMPORTS AND EXPORTS

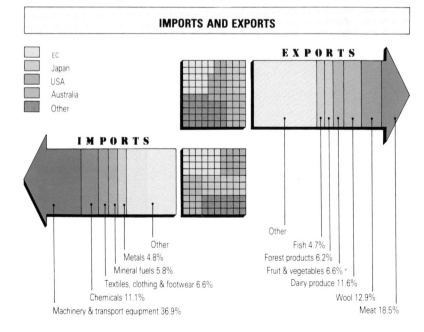

EC
Japan
USA
Australia
Other

EXPORTS

IMPORTS

Other
Metals 4.8%
Mineral fuels 5.8%
Textiles, clothing & footwear 6.6%
Chemicals 11.1%
Machinery & transport equipment 36.9%

Other
Fish 4.7%
Forest products 6.2%
Fruit & vegetables 6.6%
Dairy produce 11.6%
Wool 12.9%
Meat 18.5%

ECONOMIC PROFILE

Overwhelmingly dependent on agricultural exports such as wool, frozen lamb, butter. Few mineral resources, but self-sufficient in coal; hydro-power and natural gas supplies help reduce oil imports. Most manufactured goods imported.

Growth Exports of timber, wood pulp, coal, iron, aluminium, frozen fish and specialized foods, such as kiwi fruit and venison; tourism.

Problems Vulnerable to fluctuating prices and markets for agricultural exports. Policies to diversify and liberalize slow to take effect.

CHRISTMAS ISLAND

GEOGRAPHY *Area* 135 sq km (52 sq miles).
PEOPLE *Population* 2,300. *Density* 17 per sq km. *Ethnic groups* Chinese 55%, Malay 24%, European 12%.
LANGUAGE English.
CURRENCY Australian dollar (A$).
GOVERNMENT Australian external territory.

Christmas Island, in the Indian Ocean, is administered by Australia. Phosphate mining has been the main economic activity; tourism is expected to replace it as the phosphate reserves run out.

COCOS ISLANDS

GEOGRAPHY *Area* 14 sq km (5.4 sq miles).
PEOPLE *Population* 620. *Density* 44 per sq km. *Ethnic groups* Malay 63%, Australian 34%, European 3%.
LANGUAGE English.
CURRENCY Australian dollar (A$).
GOVERNMENT Australian external territory.

Only two of the 27 Cocos Islands are inhabited. Coconuts are the sole cash crop, postage stamps the only other source of revenue. In 1984 the 600 inhabitants voted for integration with Australia.

NORFOLK ISLAND

GEOGRAPHY *Area* 35 sq km (14 sq miles).
PEOPLE *Population* 2,400. *Density* 67 per sq km. *Ethnic groups* European, Polynesian and European/Polynesian.
LANGUAGE English and Norfolk (Old English/Tahitian).
CURRENCY Australian dollar (A$).
GOVERNMENT Australian external territory.

Norfolk Island was a penal colony in the late 18th and early 19th centuries; in 1856 it was settled by immigrants from overcrowded Pitcairn Island. The island has been an Australian external territory since 1913 but has its own legislative assembly.

MELANESIA

PAPUA NEW GUINEA

OFFICIAL NAME Papua New Guinea.
CAPITAL CITY Port Moresby.
GEOGRAPHY The territory includes several smaller islands as well as the eastern half of the island of New Guinea, which has a mountainous interior covered by tropical rain forest. Mangrove swamps and river deltas surround the Gulf of Papua in the south, while the southeastern peninsula has the only extensive plains area. There are few towns; 85% of the population is rural. The other islands have mountainous centres and swampy coastal plains; some are volcanic, some coral in origin. *Area* 461,691 sq km (178,260 sq miles).
PEOPLE *Population* 3.3m. *Density* 7 per sq km. *Ethnic groups* Papuan 83%, Melanesian 15%.
RELIGION Protestant 58%, RC 33%, Anglican 5%, Animist.
LANGUAGE English. Also Pidgin English, Hiri Motu (Melanesian Pidgin) and 700 other languages and dialects.
EDUCATION Free but noncompulsory for ages 7–13. There are 2 universities.
CLIMATE Tropical, with temperatures of 23–32°C (73–90°F) year-round. Annual rainfall of at least 2,000mm (80ins), rising to 7,000mm (276ins) in highlands.
CURRENCY Kina (K).
PUBLIC HOLIDAYS Jan 1, Good Fri, Easter Mon, 1st Mon in Jun, Jul 23, Sep 16, Dec 25, Dec 26.
GOVERNMENT Parliamentary monarchy. The head of state is the British monarch, represented by a governor-general who acts on the advice of the prime minister and the executive council. The council is responsible to a 109-member parliament elected for a 5-year term.

Independent from Australia since 1975, Papua New Guinea is a stable democracy within the Commonwealth, with a fifth of its budget provided by Australia as direct aid. Only 20% of the work force is in formal employment. Although plantation products – coffee, copra and cocoa – are still important, exports are increasingly dominated by mining. Large new deposits have been found of copper, which accounts for a third of export earnings, and other minerals. The Ok Tedi mine and others in the same region have greatly increased the potential for gold production.

The island's terrain makes transport difficult and fosters regional jealousies, but fast-flowing rivers are a valuable source of hydro-power. The main challenges are the equitable use of mining profits and the creation of jobs for the unruly gangs of urban youth.

SOLOMON ISLANDS

GEOGRAPHY *Area* 28,446 sq km (10,983 sq miles).
PEOPLE *Population* 270,000. *Density* 9 per sq km. *Ethnic groups* Melanesian 93%, Polynesian 4%, Micronesian 1%.
LANGUAGE English. Also Pidgin and many local languages.
CURRENCY Solomon Islands dollar (SI$).
GOVERNMENT Parliamentary monarchy. The head of state is the British monarch, represented by a governor-general who acts on the advice of the prime minister and cabinet. The legislative body is the 38-member National Parliament.

The development of the Solomon Islands is hampered by the mountainous and densely wooded topography of the six main islands. Settlements are scattered and transport difficult. Subsistence farming provides a living for 90% of the population. Tuna fish is the main export earner, followed by timber, copra and palm oil, but prices for all these products have been poor in recent years. Faced with persistent trade and budget deficits, the government has been forced to seek finance from the IMF and from the euromarkets. Potential for increased earnings lies in tourism and in exports of spices, coffee and cocoa. Political activity is turbulent, highly democratic and focused more on personalities than policies. Perhaps the islands' biggest challenge is a population growth rate of 3.5% a year; over half the population is under 20.

VANUATU

GEOGRAPHY *Area* 14,800 sq km (5,700 sq miles).
PEOPLE *Population* 140,000. *Density* 10 per sq km. *Ethnic groups* Melanesian 94%, European 2%.
LANGUAGE Pidgin, English and French. Also many local languages and dialects.
CURRENCY Vatu (VT).
GOVERNMENT Republic since 1980. The head of state is the president, elected by an electoral college. Executive power lies with a prime minister, elected by and from the 46-member parliament, and a council of ministers.

A unique colonial history as a condominium – popularly known as the "pandemonium" – governed jointly by France and the UK has left Vanuatu with an independent attitude. The first Pacific state to join the nonaligned movement, it has also opened diplomatic relations with Cuba and China, and with the Soviet Union, which in 1986 signed a fishing agreement giving it access to Vanuatu's ports. Evidence the following year of a Libyan presence prompted Australian criticism, which was roundly rejected as "unwarranted interference" by the outspoken Father Walter Lini, Anglican priest and prime minister since 1980.

Independence was accompanied by a rebellion on the francophone island of Espiritu Santo; in recent years Lini's authority has been challenged by a split in the ruling anglophone party, which sucked in the francophone opposition, leading to an attempted coup in 1988.

Despite its radical political stance, Vanuatu has sought to attract Western investment by setting up as a tax haven and flag of convenience shipping register; but political turmoil has undermined foreign confidence. Most of the people live by subsistence farming; copra is the main export earner.

NEW CALEDONIA

GEOGRAPHY *Area* 19,058 sq km (7,358 sq miles).
PEOPLE *Population* 150,000. *Density* 8 per sq km. *Ethnic groups* Melanesian 43%, European (mainly French) 37%, Wallisian 8%, Polynesian 4%.
LANGUAGE French. Also many local languages and dialects.
CURRENCY Pacific franc (CFPFr).
GOVERNMENT French overseas territory. A high commissioner represents the French government. There are four regional units with limited self-government. 2 deputies are sent to the French national assembly.

New Caledonia is bitterly divided over the issue of independence from France. The indigenous Melanesian people, the Kanaks, mostly support it but now represent less than half the population; French settlers, many of whom came to the island from Algeria, are resolutely opposed. The sometimes violent conflict between the two has been defused for the time being by a plan for increased local self-government leading to independence in 1998; but the low turnout in the French referendum that approved it leaves its future in some doubt.

The economy depends on a single commodity, nickel, which accounts for nearly 90% of export earnings and of which New Caledonia was the world's largest producer during the 1960s. It is still the third largest source, and has about 40% of world reserves. Copra and coffee are also exported, but France continues to provide about one-third of the government budget.

FIJI

GEOGRAPHY *Area* 18,274 sq km (7,056 sq miles).
PEOPLE *Population* 700,000. *Density* 38 per sq km. *Ethnic groups* Indian 50%, Fijian 45%, European 2%, Rotuman 1%.
RELIGION Christian 50%, Hindu 41%, Muslim 8%.
LANGUAGE English, Fijian and Hindustani.
CURRENCY Fiji dollar (F$).
GOVERNMENT Republic since 1987. The head of state is the president. Quasi-civilian government based on presidential decree is in place until the promulgation of a new constitution.

Fiji today is still living with the legacy of colonialism. In the late 19th century, the British brought in Indian workers for the sugar plantations; in time, the Indians came to outnumber the Fijian population but were discriminated against in political representation and land ownership rights. A new electoral system adopted at independence in 1970 aimed to ensure a racial balance in the legislature, but politics continued to be dominated by racial issues.

A crisis was provoked by the April 1987 election, which brought to power the first government with a majority of ministers of Indian origin. Two military coups followed, a republic was declared, the constitution revoked and Fiji's membership of the Commonwealth suspended. A constitution was drawn up designed to give the Melanesian population a permanent majority in parliament. The Indians responded by voting with their feet, many taking their valuable skills elsewhere.

Political instability had a disastrous effect on tourism, a major source of foreign exchange, but the sector has recovered well. Sugar remains the main cash crop; attempts to encourage small-scale industrial development are still in their infancy.

MICRONESIA

GUAM

GEOGRAPHY *Area* 549 sq km (212 sq miles).
PEOPLE *Population* 120,000. *Density* 255 per sq km. *Ethnic groups* Chamorro 45%, Caucasian 25%, Filipino 21%, Korean 3%, Micronesian 3%.
LANGUAGE English and Chamorro.
CURRENCY US dollar ($).
GOVERNMENT Self-governing US territory.

NORTHERN MARIANAS

GEOGRAPHY *Area* 471 sq km (182 sq miles).
PEOPLE *Population* 20,000. *Density* 42 per sq km.
LANGUAGE English. Also local languages and dialects.
CURRENCY US dollar ($).
GOVERNMENT US commonwealth territory.

FEDERATED STATES OF MICRONESIA

GEOGRAPHY *Area* 825 sq km (318 sq miles).
PEOPLE *Population* 87,000. *Density* 105 per sq km.
LANGUAGE English. Also local languages and dialects.
CURRENCY US dollar ($).
GOVERNMENT Self-governing state in free association with US. Formally part of US Trust Territory of the Pacific Islands.

MARSHALL ISLANDS

GEOGRAPHY *Area* 180 sq km (69 sq miles).
PEOPLE *Population* 35,000. *Density* 194 per sq km.
LANGUAGE English. Also local languages and dialects.
CURRENCY US dollar ($).
GOVERNMENT Self-governing state in free association with US. Formally part of US Trust Territory of the Pacific Islands.

PALAU

GEOGRAPHY *Area* 460 sq km (178 sq miles).
PEOPLE *Population* 13,000. *Density* 28 per sq km.
LANGUAGE English. Also local languages and dialects.
CURRENCY US dollar ($).
GOVERNMENT Republic since 1981.

NAURU

GEOGRAPHY *Area* 21.3 sq km (8 sq miles).
PEOPLE *Population* 8,000. *Density* 376 per sq km.
LANGUAGE Nauruan and English.
CURRENCY Australian dollar (A$).
GOVERNMENT Republic since 1968.

KIRIBATI

GEOGRAPHY *Area* 728 sq km (281 sq miles).
PEOPLE *Population* 64,000. *Density* 88 per sq km.
LANGUAGE English and I Kiribati (Micronesian dialect).
CURRENCY Kiribati-Australian dollar (A/K$).
GOVERNMENT Republic since 1979.

POLYNESIA

TONGA

GEOGRAPHY *Area* 747 sq km (289 sq miles).
PEOPLE *Population* 97,000. *Density* 130 per sq km.
LANGUAGE Tongan (Polynesian) and English.
CURRENCY Tongan pa'anga (T$).
GOVERNMENT Monarchy. The king is head of state and head of government. He appoints, and presides over, a privy council which acts as the cabinet. There is a unicameral legislative assembly which comprises the king and 28 members. There are no political parties.

ETHNIC GROUPS For information on the islands of Micronesia and Polynesia, see pages 248 and 249.

TUVALU

GEOGRAPHY *Area* 158 sq km (61 sq miles).
PEOPLE *Population* 8,200. *Density* 329 per sq km.
LANGUAGE Tuvaluan (Samoan) and English.
CURRENCY Tuvaluan dollar (T$).
GOVERNMENT Parliamentary monarchy.

WALLIS & FUTUNA

GEOGRAPHY *Area* 274 sq km (106 sq miles).
PEOPLE *Population* 12,000. *Density* 45 per sq km.
LANGUAGE French. Also Wallisian and Futunian.
CURRENCY Pacific franc (cFPFr).
GOVERNMENT French overseas territory.

WESTERN SAMOA

GEOGRAPHY *Area* 2,842 sq km (1,097 sq miles).
PEOPLE *Population* 160,000. *Density* 57 per sq km.
LANGUAGE Samoan and English.
CURRENCY Western Samoan tala (WS$).
GOVERNMENT Parliamentary monarchy.

AMERICAN SAMOA

GEOGRAPHY *Area* 199 sq km (77 sq miles).
PEOPLE *Population* 36,000. *Density* 182 per sq km.
LANGUAGE Samoan and English.
CURRENCY US dollar ($).
GOVERNMENT Self-governing US territory.

NIUE

GEOGRAPHY *Area* 259 sq km (100 sq miles).
PEOPLE *Population* 2,700. *Density* 11 per sq km.
LANGUAGE Niue dialect (Polynesian).
CURRENCY New Zealand dollar (NZ$).

GOVERNMENT Self-governing state in free association with New Zealand.

TOKELAU

GEOGRAPHY *Area* 12.2 sq km (4.7 sq miles).
PEOPLE *Population* 1,700. *Density* 140 per sq km.
LANGUAGE Tokelauan and English.
CURRENCY New Zealand dollar (NZ$).
GOVERNMENT New Zealand overseas territory.

COOK ISLANDS

GEOGRAPHY *Area* 241 sq km (93 sq miles).
PEOPLE *Population* 17,000. *Density* 72 per sq km.
LANGUAGE English and Polynesian.
CURRENCY Cook Islands dollar (CK$).
GOVERNMENT Self-governing state in free association with New Zealand.

FRENCH POLYNESIA

GEOGRAPHY *Area* 4,000 sq km (1,500 sq miles).
PEOPLE *Population* 160,000. *Density* 41 per sq km. *Ethnic groups* Polynesian 68%, mixed 15%, European 12%, Chinese 5%.
LANGUAGE French. Also Polynesian languages including Tahitian.
CURRENCY Pacific franc (cFPFr).
GOVERNMENT French overseas territory. 2 deputies are sent to the French national assembly.

PITCAIRN

GEOGRAPHY *Area* 5 sq km (2 sq miles).
PEOPLE *Population* 57. *Density* 11 per sq km. *Ethnic groups* European, Polynesian and European/Polynesian.
LANGUAGE English and English/Tahitian.
CURRENCY New Zealand dollar (NZ$).
GOVERNMENT UK colony.

THE MIDDLE EAST

Lebanon

Many Middle East conflicts have been fought out in the suburbs of Beirut: Lebanese Christian against Lebanese Muslim, Israeli against Palestinian, Shia against Sunni. After the Lebanese constitutional crisis of late 1988, the Iraqis supplied the Christian Lebanese Forces with weapons because they shared hostility towards Syria. Meanwhile, Iran restrained its client, Hizbollah, which was in conflict with the pro-Syrian group Amal, to retain the friendship of its only Arab ally.

Lebanese militias

Amal Shia organization set up by Musa Sadr in early 1970s. Support mainly from poor Shias in the south and Beqaa valley. Nabih Berri became leader after Sadr disappeared during a visit to Libya in 1978.

Hizbollah Umbrella organization of radical Shias with links with Iran. Led by Shaikh Muhammad Hussain Fadlallah and Shaikh Ibrahim al-Amin.

Tawhid Radical Sunni movement led by Shaikh Said Shaban and based in Tripoli. Rumoured to have links with Iran.

Kataib Founded in 1930s by Pierre Gemayel. Has traditionally represented the dominant Maronite groups. Military wing, the Phalange, has been absorbed into the Lebanese Forces.

Lebanese Forces Military wing, led by Samir Geagea, of the Lebanese Front, a coalition of Maronite leaders dominated by the Kataib. The strongest single militia grouping.

Fatah The biggest single Palestinian movement, founded in 1957 and headed by Yasser Arafat. Under the umbrella of the Palestine Liberation Organization (PLO).

The Kurds

Iraq capitalized on the end of the Gulf war by turning on its own recalcitrant Kurds, whom Iran had supported. A mass migration of Kurdish refugees into Turkey was allegedly prompted by Iraq's use of chemical weapons against them. A homeland for the 17m Kurds – dispersed in Iran, Iraq, Syria, Turkey and the USSR – remains elusive.

Opec and Oapec

Seven members of Opec – Algeria, Iraq, Kuwait, Libya, Qatar, Saudi Arabia and the UAE – and Bahrain, Egypt and Syria belong to the Organization of Arab Petroleum Exporting Countries (Oapec). Unlike Opec, which is mainly concerned with oil pricing and production issues, Oapec exists to coordinate the Arab industry's activities, by means of joint engineering, transport and services companies.

Gulf Cooperation Council

Saudi Arabia was a prime mover in setting up the Gulf Cooperation Council in 1981. Other members are Bahrain, Kuwait, Oman, Qatar and the UAE. The council aims to coordinate resistance to outside intervention in the Gulf. Progress towards economic integration has been slow during the 1980s economic downturn in the region.

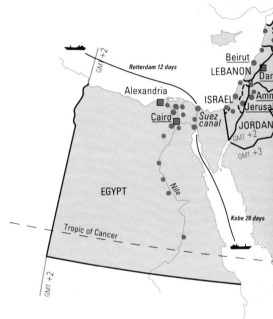

Suez canal

Opened in 1869, the canal is 184km (115 miles) long, linking the Mediterranean with the Red Sea. Nationalization of the canal by Egypt's President Nasser in 1956 precipitated the Suez crisis and war. The canal was blocked during the Six-Day War in 1967 and did not open again until 1975. It has since been widened and deepened to accommodate supertankers. Canal tolls are one of Egypt's largest sources of foreign revenue, bringing in about $1bn a year.

1947 UN approves partition plan for Palestine

1948 Foundation of state of Israel; Arab-Israeli war

1949 Ceasefire leaves Israel with a third more territory than agreed in UN partition plan

1952 King Farouk of Egypt overthrown by army officers, led by Gamal Abdel Nasser

1953 Coup in Iran removes Prime Minister Muhammad Mossadeq, who had supported nationalization of oil industry. Death of King Abdel Aziz Ibn Saud, founder of Saudi Arabia

1956 Egypt nationalizes Suez canal; British, French and Israelis attack unsuccessfully

1958 Iraqi monarchy overthrown

1962 Military coup in Yemen; Egypt and Saudi Arabia support opposing sides in ensuing civil war

1963 Shah of Iran assumes control of government

1967 Six-Day War; Israel occupies West Bank, Golan Heights, Sinai and Gaza Strip. South Yemen becomes independent

1970 Sultan of Oman overthrown by his son, Qaboos. Death of Nasser; succeeded by Anwar Sadat. Civil war in Jordan; Palestinian guerrillas expelled. Military coup in Syria

1971 Bahrain, Qatar and Trucial States become independent

1973 October war: Egypt recaptures part of Sinai; Opec restricts oil supply in response to Western support for Israel

1975 King Faisal of Saudi Arabia assassinated by a nephew. Lebanese civil war begins

1977 Anwar Sadat visits Jerusalem

1979 Iranian revolution; flight of Shah; seizure of US embassy in Tehran. Camp David peace agreement signed by Egypt and Israel; Egypt expelled from Arab League. Muslim extremists occupy Grand Mosque at Mecca

1980 Iran–Iraq war begins

1981 Sadat assassinated; succeeded by Hosni Mubarak

1982 Israel invades Lebanon; massacre at Sabra and Chatila refugee camps

1985 Israel withdraws from Lebanon

1987 Most Arab states restore diplomatic relations with Egypt

1988 Palestinian *intifada* (uprising) in occupied territories; Palestine National Council sets up government in exile and recognizes Israel's right to exist. Ceasefire in Iran–Iraq war; peace talks begin

256

Map Legend

- ■ More than 1 million
- ● 250,000 – 1 million
- ● 100,000 – 250,000

LEBANON

SYRIA

GOLAN HEIGHTS

WEST BANK

GAZA STRIP

ISRAEL

JORDAN

Occupied territories

Tehran

London 6½ hours

Baghdad

IRAQ

New York 13½ hours

Basra

Kuwait
KUWAIT

IRAN

GMT +3½
GMT +3

BAHRAIN

Al Manamah
QATAR

AUDI ARABIA

Doha

Riyadh

Abu Dhabi

GMT +4

UNITED ARAB EMIRATES

Muscat

GMT +4

OMAN

YEMEN

San'a

SOUTH YEMEN

GMT +3
GMT +4

Aden

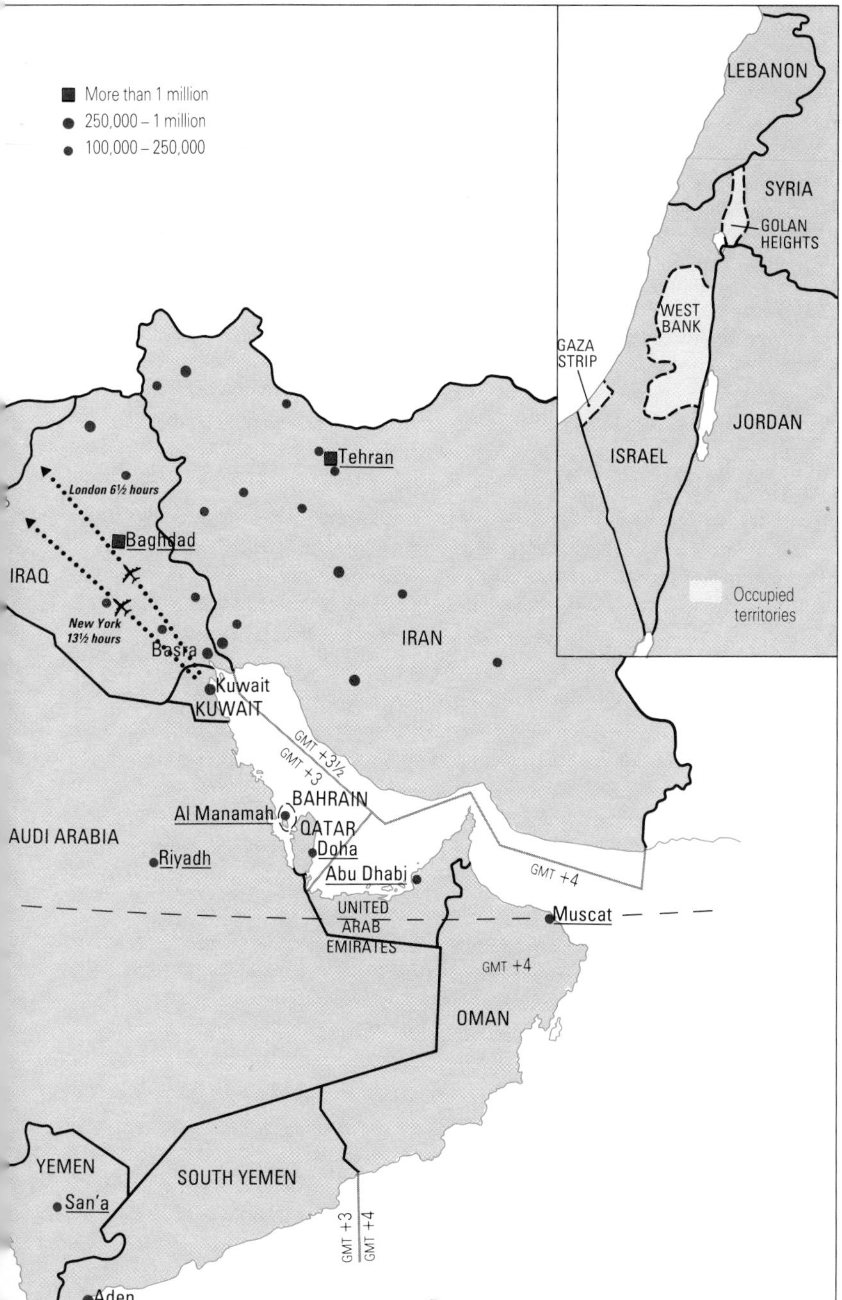

Energy

About half the world's proven oil reserves lie around the shores of the Gulf, but the region's importance as an energy supplier has diminished because high oil prices in the 1970s encouraged exploration and the development of new fields elsewhere. This trend was reinforced by the Iran–Iraq war and worries about the safety of shipping in the Gulf. By 1987, Gulf producers were exporting only about a fifth of the world's consumption, compared with a third in 1979.

THE MIDDLE EAST

SYRIA

Syria's role as peacemaker in Lebanon has restored much of the international respect it lost through alleged involvement in terrorism. Its implication in the attempt to blow up an Israeli airliner in London in 1986 led to the UK severing diplomatic relations and the USA and EC imposing sanctions. But the chorus of condemnation turned to praise as Syria developed a reputation as regional arbiter, using its influence in Beirut to secure the release of hostages and acting as mediator between its ally Iran and the Arab Gulf states. Its rapprochement with both the USA and its moderate Arab neighbours has accelerated since the ceasefire in the Gulf war.

Syria's aim in Lebanon has been to foster unity under its own aegis. In 1976, the Syrian army was sent in to prevent a total Palestinian and leftist Muslim victory over the Christians; the Shia Amal militia has been its main ally, but Syria has also capitalized on splits in the Christian Maronite camp.

President Hafez Assad, Syria's strong-man since 1970, has won recognition for his ability to play off major domestic groups against each other, despite the corruption and nepotism of his regime. Many top positions are held by members of the president's Alawi sect, which represents a mere 11% of the population; opposition is ruthlessly suppressed.

With falling living standards, increasingly acute shortages and a foreign debt of over $4bn, Syria is heavily dependent on Arab aid. Recent oil discoveries should provide greater economic independence.

OFFICIAL NAME Syrian Arab Republic.
CAPITAL CITY Damascus.
GEOGRAPHY The short, sandy coastline on the Mediterranean gives way to a coastal mountain range whose continuation forms the border with Lebanon and merges with the southern Golan Heights. This western sector is by far the most populous region, the rest of the country being a rocky desert plain cut in two by the Euphrates, whose course forms a secondary populated region. *Highest point* Mt Hermon 2,814 metres (9,230 feet). *Area* 185,180 sq km (71,500 sq miles).
PEOPLE *Population* 10.3m. *Density* 55 per sq km. *Ethnic groups* Arab 89%, Kurdish 6%.
RELIGION Muslim 90% (Sunni 72%, Alawi 11%, Druze 3%, other 4%), Christian 9%.
LANGUAGE Arabic. Also Kurdish, Armenian and local dialects.
EDUCATION Compulsory for ages 6–12. There are 4 universities.
CLIMATE Sub-tropical on the coast, with a dry season May–Oct; continental in the interior, with temperatures ranging from below freezing to close to 50°C (120°F). Annual rainfall around 1,000mm (40ins) in the west, less than 100mm (4ins) in the east.
CURRENCY Syrian pound (Sy£).
PUBLIC HOLIDAYS Jan 1, Leilat al-Meiraj, Mar 8, Greek Orthodox Easter (4 days), Id al-Fitr, Id al-Adha, Jul 23, Muharram, Sep 1, Oct 6, Mouloud, Nov 16, Dec 25.
GOVERNMENT Socialist republic. Since the 1971 military coup, Syria has been ruled by the National Progressive Front of five socialist parties. The head of state and chief executive is a president directly elected for a 7-year term. The legislative people's assembly has 195 members.

ECONOMIC PROFILE

Traditionally an agricultural economy, but mineral and manufactured exports increasingly important. Main exports are oil and oil products, textiles and foods. Cotton is main cash crop. Most machinery and spare parts imported.

Growth Recent finds of high-grade crude cut import needs. Emphasis on developing production of chemicals, cement, textiles, leather, paper and electrical goods.

Problems Economy long dependent on large-scale Arab aid. Balance of payments hit by lower oil and cotton prices and decline in migrant workers' earnings. Debt service a heavy burden. Industry suffers from foreign exchange shortages. Flourishing black market; much commerce outside official channels.

IMPORTS AND EXPORTS

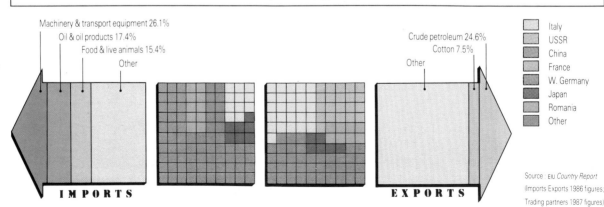

Machinery & transport equipment 26.1%
Oil & oil products 17.4%
Food & live animals 15.4%
Other

Crude petroleum 24.6%
Cotton 7.5%
Other

Italy
USSR
China
France
W. Germany
Japan
Romania
Other

IMPORTS

EXPORTS

Source : EIU *Country Report*
(Imports Exports 1986 figures,
Trading partners 1987 figures)

IRAQ

Ceasefire in August 1988 brought welcome relief to Iraq, battered by eight years of war with Iran. Disputed territory along the Shatt al-Arab waterway, Iraq's outlet to the sea, was the declared reason for President Saddam Hussain's ill-advised assault on his powerful neighbour, but he was also prompted by the prospect of Western support after Iran's Islamic revolution. Although the West's initial fear was of Iranian expansionism, it condemned Iraq when the country used the ceasefire as an opportunity to hit at its separatist Kurds with chemical weapons.

A British mandate after World War I, Iraq remained under effective British influence after independence in 1932 until a revolution in 1958 swept away the Hashemite monarchy. Three coups in the next decade manifested the struggle between communists and pan-Arab Baathists. The Baathist triumph in 1968 led to the rise of the autocratic Saddam Hussain.

Iran's agreement in 1975 to stop supporting Iraq's Kurds in their struggle for independence freed Iraq from dependence on the Soviet Union and allowed it to draw closer to the West at a time when oil wealth was financing an ambitious programme of industrial and infrastructure development. The war halted development but brought Iraq closer to the conservative Arab states, made nervous by Iran's revolutionary fervour. Their financial support helped maintain Iraq's military effort when its oil revenue was affected by Iranian attacks on shipping and oil installations.

Attempts to improve disappointing industrial and agricultural performance began before the war ended, with the dismantling of the apparatus of rigid state control to allow individual enterprises more autonomy. But the war has brought about major structural economic changes, notably the depopulation of agricultural areas, and both the physical infrastructure and industrial plant have been run down. Iraq faces a long struggle to rebuild itself.

OFFICIAL NAME Republic of Iraq.

CAPITAL CITY Baghdad.

GEOGRAPHY The cultivated valley of the Tigris and Euphrates is bounded by mountains to the northeast and desert to the west. *Highest point* Rawanduz 3,658 metres (12,000 feet). *Area* 434,924 sq km (167,930 sq miles).

PEOPLE *Population* 15.9m. *Density* 37 per sq km. *Ethnic groups* Arab 77%, Kurdish 19%, Turkish 2%.

RELIGION Muslim 96%, Christian 3%.

LANGUAGE Arabic. Also Kurdish and Turkish.

EDUCATION Free and compulsory for ages 6–12.

CLIMATE Continental. May–Oct is very hot, averaging 35°C (95°F), and dry, while there are widespread frosts in winter. Generally, rainfall is less than 500mm (20ins).

CURRENCY Iraqi dinar (ID).

PUBLIC HOLIDAYS Jan 1, Jan 6, Feb 8, Leilat al-Meiraj, May 1, Id al-Fitr, Jul 14, Id al-Adha, Muharram, Ashoura, Mouloud.

GOVERNMENT One-party republic since 1958. The chief executive is the president, elected by the 9-man revolutionary command council, which shares legislative power with a 250-member national assembly elected for 4 years.

ECONOMIC PROFILE

Dominance of oil – 98% of exports – reinforced by centralized control of economy. Agriculture employs one third of population but contributes less than 10% of GNP; net food importer. Drive to industrialize in late 1970s emphasized use of oil and gas as feedstock or energy source. State-owned heavy industry produces steel, textiles, cement, bitumen and pharmaceuticals.

Growth Oil sales have risen sharply since ceasefire. Oil refining, petrochemicals, cement and phosphates set to expand.

Problems Economy and infrastructure severely damaged by eight years of war; much industrial plant in war zones destroyed or abandoned. Foreign debt of $50bn; doubts surrounding repayment schedule to 1991 will hamper access to new credit. State interference has constrained industrial efficiency.

IMPORTS AND EXPORTS

Imports

Conventional statistics on Iraqi imports have not been available since 1982, when restrictions were imposed on consumer goods and many other products not associated with the war. Recent statistics only divide imports into civilian and military goods which made up roughly 43% and 57% respectively, and this ratio will almost certainly change now that hostilities have ceased.

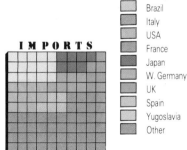

IMPORTS

- Turkey
- Brazil
- Italy
- USA
- France
- Japan
- W. Germany
- UK
- Spain
- Yugoslavia
- Other

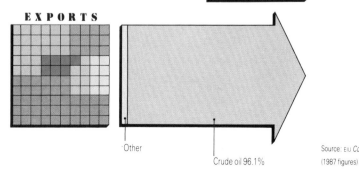

EXPORTS

Other

Crude oil 96.1%

Source: EIU *Country Report* (1987 figures)

IRAN

Iran's Islamic revolution in 1979 created a new threat to the conservative Arab states of the Persian Gulf; it was a beacon for Muslim militants challenging the corruption of their own governments. Iran's Islamic message found listeners throughout the region; every regime has been forced to some extent to face up to the challenge of Islamic fundamentalism. Saudi Arabia, although itself founded on fundamentalist principles, was one of the first to feel the strength of revolutionary fervour when militants took control of the Great Mosque in Mecca in 1979, a violent episode echoed when police opened fire on demonstrating Iranian pilgrims in 1987. Civil unrest outside the Gulf, in Egypt and elsewhere in North Africa, while touched off by economic grievances, often carried the flavour of militant Islam.

The hostility of the conservative Gulf states was, in these circumstances, understandable; the hostility of their Western allies was more carelessly provoked by the siege of the US embassy in Tehran and the hectoring of the West for its imperialism and materialism. The support of both groups for Iraq in the Iran–Iraq war was a natural, and costly, consequence.

The ceasefire in 1988 brought about a curious reversal of roles. War-weary Iran, seeking aid to reconstruct its battered economy, began initially to court the West. Iraq, haughty and ferociously armed, earned international condemnation for its treatment of its rebellious Kurdish and Shia communities.

When the war ended, Iran's oil production was running at barely half the

OFFICIAL NAME Islamic Republic of Iran.

CAPITAL CITY Tehran.

GEOGRAPHY The centre of Iran is a high arid basin dotted with oases and with a vast, dry salt lake, the Kavir, at its heart. The basin is surrounded by a ring of mountains whose fertile foothills are extensively farmed. A marshy coastal plain lies along the south coast of the Caspian sea and a desert strip along the Persian Gulf. Most settlement is in the north and west; the south and east are principally inhabited by nomads. *Highest point* Qolleh-ye Damavand 5,604 metres (18,390 feet). *Area* 1,648,000 sq km (636,000 sq miles).

PEOPLE *Population* 44.2m. *Density* 27 per sq km. *Ethnic groups* Persian 45%, Azerbaijani 16%, Kurdish 8%.

RELIGION Shia Muslim 93%, Sunni Muslim 5%.

LANGUAGE Farsi (Persian). Also Azerbaijani, Turkish, Kurdish, Baluchi, Arabic and others.

EDUCATION Free for ages 6–11. Compulsory 6–14 where available. Mixed-sex schools being phased out.

CLIMATE Continental and dry, especially in summer. Average monthly temperatures range from 2°C (36°F) in Jan to 30°C (86°F) in July, with recorded extremes of -18°C (0°F) and 55°C (131°F).

CURRENCY Rial (RI).

PUBLIC HOLIDAYS Feb 11, Mar 20-24, Leilat al-Meiraj, Apr 1, 2, Id al-Fitr, Jun 9, Jul 14, Id al-Adha, Ashoura, Mouloud.

GOVERNMENT Islamic republic. Since the overthrow of the Shah in 1979, Iran has had an Islamic constitution which revolves around the principle of *velayat-e faqih* (trusteeship of the jurisconsult). The president, who is chief executive, and the 270-member legislature, the consultative assembly, are elected every 4 years. All laws must be approved for their constitutional and Islamic correctness by the 12-member council of guardians.

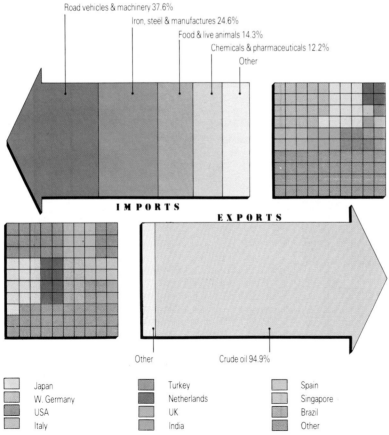

IMPORTS AND EXPORTS

Road vehicles & machinery 37.6%
Iron, steel & manufactures 24.6%
Food & live animals 14.3%
Chemicals & pharmaceuticals 12.2%
Other

IMPORTS

EXPORTS

Other

Crude oil 94.9%

- Japan
- W. Germany
- USA
- Italy
- Turkey
- Netherlands
- UK
- India
- Spain
- Singapore
- Brazil
- Other

Source: EIU *Country Report* (Imports/Exports 1985 figures; Trading partners 1987 figures)

level under the Shah and being sold for less than half the price. The disadvantages of dependence on oil have been hotly debated, but restoring revenue from this source seemed the only feasible way of mobilizing finance for reconstruction. The war promoted the arms industry but little else; shortages of inputs forced the closure of many of the Shah's ambitious schemes. Lack of foreign exchange made countertrade deals the preferred vehicle for new business with overseas contractors. Efforts were made to diversify exports by including large-scale sales of carpets or pistachio nuts in barter trade. Attempts to reverse the serious neglect of agriculture under the Shah's rule have yet to stem the drift away from rural areas that started in the 1960s, adding to social pressures in the cities; around 55% of the population are urban residents, of whom over 5.7m live in the fastest growing city, Tehran, and there is a serious housing shortage.

Iran's ability to finance its war without borrowing on the international market and its scrupulous repayment of interest on pre-revolutionary loans gave it valuable credibility when the postwar reconstruction phase began. Peace also meant that economic and political discontent could no longer be sublimated in the cause of holy war against Iraq. Many Iranians were tired of clerical rule and of the increasingly desperate poverty that the state of war had imposed. Some hoped that control from the mosque and surveillance by the Revolutionary Guards would diminish; others expected a takeover by an alliance of the Revolutionary Guards with the army.

A safeguard against this outcome is Iran's increasingly robust and mature democracy: the country's parliament is open and liberal by regional standards, but is much more controlled than it was in the early 1980s. A delicate balance of power exists between pragmatic moderates, who seek better relations with the West in the interests of economic reconstruction, and radicals, who have little difficulty in finding fuel to feed the fires of Islamic fundamentalism. Relatively moderate leaders seemed to have the advantage after the death of the architect of Iran's revolution, the Ayatollah Khomeini, in mid-1989. The Ayatollah's successor, Ali Khamenei, formed an informal coalition with the powerful speaker of the Iranian parliament and commander-in-chief of the armed forces, Hashemi Rafsanjani.

ECONOMIC PROFILE

Oil and gas production backbone of economy; agriculture recovering from neglect during free-spending years of Shah's regime. Traditional exports – caviar, carpets, pistachio nuts, fresh and dried fruit – a tiny proportion of total. Resumption of industrial development depends on foreign partners' willingness to conclude barter or buyback deals.

Growth Reconstruction offers plenty of scope if finance can be raised. Oil industry and armed forces will initially get priority for funds, followed by housing and power. Plans to complete petrochemical schemes and expand vehicle assembly; possibility of increased natural gas exports.

Problems Recovery from war damage will take years. Poor prospects for increase in oil revenues. Severe shortages of foods and consumer goods; power supplies unreliable. Weak currency raises import costs. Erratic government attitude to private sector discourages investment.

GDP BY ORIGIN

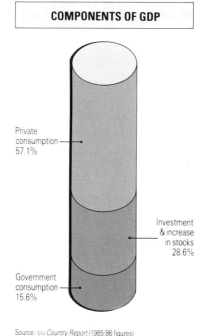

Services 48.0%
Industry 23.0%
Agriculture 21.0%
Oil & gas mining 8.0%

Source: EIU Country Profile (1986/87 figures)

COMPONENTS OF GDP

Private consumption 57.1%
Investment & increase in stocks 28.6%
Government consumption 15.6%

Source: EIU Country Report (1985/86 figures)

BALANCE OF PAYMENTS

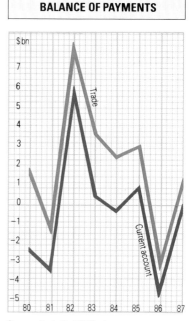

Source: EIU Country Credit Risk Service

LEBANON

The elegance that characterized Beirut as the hub of the Middle East has long gone, destroyed by the hideous violence that has scarred Lebanon since 1975. The conflict which exploded that year had at its heart Muslim resentment at historical Christian pre-eminence, supported by a complex power-sharing arrangement that had not been revised since 1943. Attempts by Syria to impose a package offering Muslims equal representation in parliament failed to satisfy Muslim groups resentful of Christian power. The Syrian invasion in mid-1976 prevented an outright victory for the Muslim leftists and the Palestine Liberation Organization and seemed to have ended the civil war.

In reality this was merely the start of the downward spiral. Two Israeli invasions followed; the first, in 1978, allowed Israel to hand control of the southern border area to its Christian allies. The second, in 1982, aimed at total destruction of the PLO but attracted notoriety when the Christian Lebanese Forces massacred the inhabitants of Palestinian refugee camps. When the Israelis withdrew, Syria resumed its efforts to secure national reconciliation, intervening in strength in 1987. Attempts at reform by President Amin Gemayel failed and his resignation in 1988 left Lebanon without a single government.

The economy survived the 1975–76 civil war thanks to the Arab oil boom, but by 1987 the years of chaos had taken their toll; the Lebanese pound plummeted to 1% of its former value and inflation was running at 200–300% a year. The new generation knows nothing but war and acute poverty.

ECONOMIC PROFILE

Banking and commerce traditionally largest contributors to GDP but badly affected by civil war. Exports of fruit and vegetables much reduced. Industrial base well developed and diversified by regional standards – oil refining, cement, textiles, light industries.

Problems Beirut has lost its role as services and recreational centre of the Middle East. Much of industry and agriculture destroyed or seriously disrupted. Most commerce through unofficial channels, controlled by one or other of warring factions.

OFFICIAL NAME Republic of Lebanon.
CAPITAL CITY Beirut.
GEOGRAPHY Most settlement is along the sedimentary coastal plain and the lower slopes of the Lebanon Mountains. Lying between them and a range on the Syrian border lies the Beqaa valley, another population centre. *Area* 10,400 sq km (4,000 sq miles).
PEOPLE *Population* 2.7m. *Density* 257 per sq km. *Ethnic groups* Lebanese Arab 83%, Palestinian Arab 10%, Armenian 5%, Kurdish 1%.
RELIGION Muslim 65% (Shia 33%, Sunni 25%, Druze 7%), Christian 35% (Maronite 25%, other 10%).
LANGUAGE Arabic.
EDUCATION Free but noncompulsory state schools; secondary and higher education dominated by private schools.
CLIMATE Summers are hot (32°C/90°F) and dry; average winter temperatures 16°C (61°F) on the coast, 10°C (50°F) inland. Annual rainfall is around 750mm (30ins) on the coast, double that on the heights.
CURRENCY Lebanese pound (L£).
PUBLIC HOLIDAYS Jan 1, Feb 9, Leilat al-Meiraj, Mar 22, Good Fri-Easter Mon (both the Orthodox and Western Easters are celebrated), Ascension, Id al-Fitr, Id al-Adha, Muharram, Aug 15, Ashoura, Mouloud, Nov 1, Nov 22, Dec 25, Dec 31.
GOVERNMENT Republic since 1941. Normal political life has been suspended. Formerly, a 99-member legislative national assembly, its seats allocated on religious lines, was elected by PR; and the chief executive was a president elected by the assembly from among the Maronites.

JORDAN

Jordan's identity is inextricably linked with the creation of Israel in 1948. During the first Arab-Israeli war that followed, Jordan absorbed the Palestinian West Bank as well as large numbers of refugees; today at least 60% of Jordan's population is Palestinian. The West Bank, lost to the Israelis in 1967, remains the heartland of any possible Palestinian state and Jordan has continued to wield considerable authority in the region. King Hussain's sudden announcement in August 1988 that Jordan was severing its links with the West Bank caught the Palestinian Liberation Organization offguard, with no effective infrastructure to replace that of Amman.

Natural resources are restricted to phosphates, which account for 30% of exports, potash and oil shale; agriculture is largely confined to the Jordan valley. Jordan depends on remittances from migrants working in the Gulf, service industries, technology transfer and vicarious income such as from rights of transit for Iraq during its war with Iran; Amman competes with Manama and Dubai as a regional business and communications centre.

OFFICIAL NAME The Hashemite Kingdom of Jordan.
CAPITAL CITY Amman.
GEOGRAPHY Four-fifths of Jordan is a rocky desert. Most people live on the northwestern plateaus, on either side of the Rift Valley that contains the saline, marshy River Jordan. *Area* 97,740 sq km (37,740 sq miles) including West Bank.
PEOPLE *Population* 3.5m (including West Bank). *Ethnic groups* Arab 98%, Circassian 1%.
RELIGION Muslim (mainly Sunni) 93%, Christian 5%.
LANGUAGE Arabic.
EDUCATION Free and compulsory for ages 5–11.
CLIMATE Summers dry and hot, winters cold. Annual rainfall 400mm (16ins) in uplands.
CURRENCY Jordan dinar (JD).
PUBLIC HOLIDAYS Jan 15, Leilat al-Meiraj, Mar 22, Id al-Fitr, May 25, Id al-Adha, Muharram, Aug 11, Mouloud, Nov 14.
GOVERNMENT Constitutional monarchy. The king is chief executive, aided by a council of ministers. The legislative assembly consists of the house of notables and the house of deputies, with 142 members elected for 4 years.

ISRAEL

The war that followed the creation of Israel in 1948 left the new state with one third more territory than it had been awarded by the UN partition plan. The flight of Palestinian Arabs was offset by a doubling of the Jewish population in three years through immigration. The 1967 war left Israel in control of more Arab territory, to which it still clings. Today, 60% of Israel's 3.5m Jews were born in Israel; some 2.2m Arabs live under Israeli rule, 1.4m of them in the occupied territories.

Absorbing the new Jewish immigrants presented massive social and economic challenges in the new state's early years. These were successfully met, and the economy grew by a real annual average of 10% between 1950 and 1973. But the legacies of those stressful years, in the form of a centralized and monopolistic economic structure and the enforced integration of people from diverse backgrounds, eventually emerged after the 1973 Arab-Israeli war abruptly ended the era of rapid growth.

The past 10–15 years have seen a transformation in the make-up of Israeli society, with the founding generation, whose roots were mostly socialist and East European, giving way gradually and reluctantly to Israeli-born leaders and managers, many of whose parents came from Muslim countries. The Likud and Labour parties have governed in a series of uneasy coalitions throughout the 1980s, at times joined by some of the plethora of mini-parties created by a proportional representation system that guarantees seats in parliament to any party that gets more than 1% of the popular vote. The price of their support has included the promotion of religious orthodoxy, and the country is generally depicted as becoming more nationalist and religious; but the popular culture and high level of technological achievement underline the strong Western orientation of society.

The external problem of Arab enmity has receded since the peace treaty with Egypt in 1979, but the Palestinian-Israeli conflict, exacerbated by the continued occupation of the West Bank, Gaza Strip and East Jerusalem, has returned to centre stage. The *intifada* (uprising) that began in late 1987 has been a powerful catalyst for Palestinian nationalism and has heightened the split between the Israelis who wish to hold on to the occupied territories and those prepared to yield them in return for a credible peace. Israel's military prowess, built up to resist an external threat, has proved the wrong tool to deal with what is essentially a political problem. The sight of the Israeli army in confrontation with Palestinian youths throwing stones and petrol bombs has severely tarnished the country's image and eroded its support abroad just as the Palestine

OFFICIAL NAME State of Israel.
CAPITAL CITY Jerusalem.
GEOGRAPHY Most Israelis live on the coastal plain – sedimentary in the north, loess in the south – or the hills and mountains of the north and centre. To the east, the Jordan runs in a rift valley between the Sea of Galilee and the heavily saline Dead Sea, the lowest place on earth at 396 metres (1,300 feet) below sea level. The southern wedge of the country is taken up by the Negev Desert. *Highest point* Har Meron 1,208 metres (3,960 feet). *Area* 20,700 sq km (8,000 sq miles).
PEOPLE *Population* 4.2m. *Density* 204 per sq km. *Ethnic groups* Jewish 83%, Arab 14%.
RELIGION Jewish 83%, Muslim 13%, Christian 2%, Druze 2%.
LANGUAGE Hebrew and Arabic. Also Yiddish.
EDUCATION Free to university level and compulsory for ages 5–15. There are 6 universities.
CLIMATE Mainly subtropical, with deserts in the south. Average temperature is around 20°C (68°F) on the coast, 32°C (90°F) in the southern desert. Annual rainfall is often as low as 25mm (1in) in the south, but rises to 2,000mm (80ins) around the Sea of Galilee, almost all falling Oct-Apr.
CURRENCY New sheqel (NIS).
PUBLIC HOLIDAYS Purim (Mar), Passover (7 days in Apr), Independence, Shavuot, Rosh Hashanah (Sep), Yom Kippur, Succot, Simhat Torah (Oct). Muslim and Christian holidays observed by respective minorities.
GOVERNMENT Republic since 1948. The head of state is a president, elected for 5 years by the Knesset, a 120-member legislature elected by PR for a 4-year term. The executive consists of a cabinet, usually representative of the majority coalition, and a prime minister who is usually from the dominant coalition party.

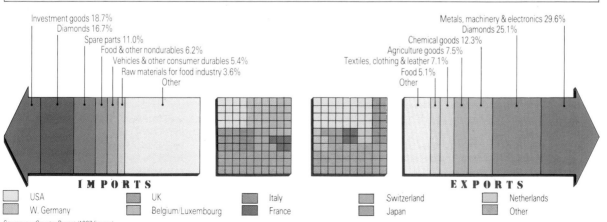

263

Liberation Organization was gaining new international respectability through its decision to recognize Israel's right to exist and renounce the armed struggle in preparation for a peace conference.

The need to find a solution to the Palestinian issue is coupled with the need to prepare for the open international economy of the 1990s. Israel will not be able to align itself with either of its major trading partners – the EC and USA – until it has extricated itself both from its entanglement in the occupied territories and from the overregulated and government-dominated economic structure it has created for itself. Failure to solve these problems will lead to growing political isolation, economic stagnation and a steady loss of human and financial capital. Success will enable Israel to generate or free the resources needed to tackle its social problems and return to a pattern of stable economic growth.

ECONOMIC PROFILE

Intensive high-yield agriculture, much of it on a cooperative basis, has provided self-sufficiency and export capacity. Diversified industrial base, with former export leaders – electronics, metallurgy, weapons – giving way in recent years to textiles, clothing, food products. Major diamond-cutting centre.

Growth Citrus fruit and vegetable exports to European markets. Industry moving to upmarket products as wages rise. High-tech science-based industries –

chemicals, biotechnology, aerospace and agricultural technology – offer growth and export prospects, but face strong international competition.

Problems Military spending a heavy drain on resources. Almost all energy imported. Tourism hit by Palestinian uprising. Delicate political balance has impeded radical economic reform; government dominance of economy still great, although declining.

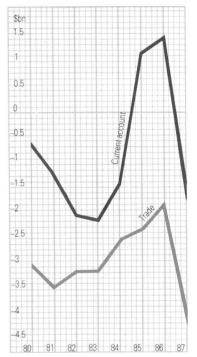

BALANCE OF PAYMENTS

Source: EIU *Country Credit Risk Service*

EGYPT

Egypt, foundation of Arab socialism and solidarity in the 1960s, is today essentially capitalist and pro-Western. Despite this change of character, it has regained much of its traditional authority in the region since late 1987 when most Arab states restored diplomatic ties, severed after Egypt's peace treaty with Israel in 1979.

The death of President Nasser in 1970 ended an experiment that had involved the nationalization of industries, land reform and the takeover of foreign assets, including – most crucially for Egypt's image in the Third World – the nationalization of the Suez canal in 1956. Nasser's influence waned after Egypt's disastrous defeat by Israel in 1967. His successor, Anwar Sadat, expelled Soviet advisers and began dismantling the top-heavy bureaucracy.

In 1974, Sadat moved away from centralized economic management and instituted the open-door policy, aimed at encouraging foreign and domestic private investment. A period of prosperity ensued, although largely dependent on four nonindustrial sources of revenue: remittances from Egyptians working abroad, oil, tourism and Suez canal tolls. The policy is criticized today for having stimulated service industries at the expense of vital agricultural and industrial development.

Sadat's treaty with Israel relieved the country of its military burden and enhanced its credibility with institutions such as the IMF. It also lost Egypt the prestige in the Arab world earned by its performance in the 1973 war with Israel. Anger at the peace treaty was reinforced by the example of the Iranian revolution and reaction to mounting corruption to provide the context for Sadat's assassination in 1981 by Islamic militants.

The new president, Hosni Mubarak, lacked the charisma of his predecessors

OFFICIAL NAME Arab Republic of Egypt.
CAPITAL CITY Cairo.
GEOGRAPHY Egypt is almost entirely desert; a narrow, extremely fertile strip around the floodplain of the Nile and its delta is the only habitable land. Most of the country is flat. *Highest point* Mt Katherina 2,642 metres (8,670 feet). *Area* 1,001,449 sq km (386,660 sq miles).
PEOPLE *Population* 48.5m. *Density* 48 per sq km. *Ethnic groups* Arab 99.7%.
RELIGION Muslim 94%, Christian 6%.
LANGUAGE Arabic.
EDUCATION Compulsory for ages 6–12 and free at all levels.
CLIMATE Dry, with hot summers 30°C (86°F) and mild winters 16°C (61°F). Even on the Mediterranean coast rainfall is less than 200mm (8ins).
CURRENCY Egyptian pound (E£).
PUBLIC HOLIDAYS (*Copts only) Jan 1, Jan 7*, Leilat al-Meiraj, Palm Sun*, Easter Sun*, Sham an-Nessim, Id al-Fitr, Jun 18, Id al-Adha, Jul 23, Muharram, Oct 6, Mouloud, Oct 24, Dec 23.
GOVERNMENT Republic since 1953. The 458-member legislative people's assembly is elected for 5 years by PR. The chief executive is the president, who is nominated by the assembly and approved by referendum for a 6-year term. Parties were banned between 1953 and 1976.

IMPORTS AND EXPORTS

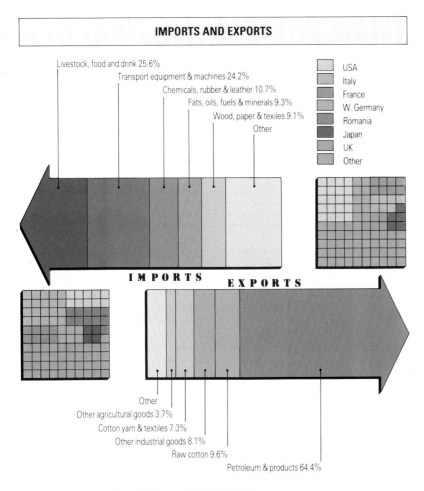

Livestock, food and drink 25.6%
Transport equipment & machines 24.2%
Chemicals, rubber & leather 10.7%
Fats, oils, fuels & minerals 9.3%
Wood, paper & texiles 9.1%
Other

USA
Italy
France
W. Germany
Romania
Japan
UK
Other

IMPORTS   **EXPORTS**

Other
Other agricultural goods 3.7%
Cotton yarn & textiles 7.3%
Other industrial goods 8.1%
Raw cotton 9.6%
Petroleum & products 64.4%

Source: EIU *Country Report* (Imports/Exports 1986 figures; Trading partners 1987 figures)

ECONOMIC PROFILE

Agriculture, leading employer, concentrated in Nile flood plain and delta. Food prices kept low to benefit urban consumers. Cotton is main cash crop, aided by heavy subsidies. Industry, largely import-substitution, developed in public sector, now being slowly privatized and restructured.

Growth Reconciliation with Arab world raising hopes of new investment. Tourism is booming again. Arms industry profited from Gulf war and has found new export markets. Plans to expand vehicle assembly, iron and steel, with Eastern bloc help, and start producing of power station equipment.

Problems Agriculture periodically threatened by low Nile waters, as well as soil salinity and growing pressure on land. One fifth of labour force unemployed. Fears of unrest delaying economic reforms.

BALANCE OF PAYMENTS

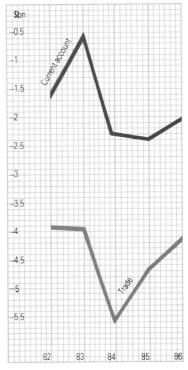

Source: EIU *Country Profile*

but has unhesitatingly fulfilled his pledge to steer the nation towards democracy. A genuine opposition to the ruling National Democratic Party emerged in the first comparatively fair elections in 1984. The press has been liberalized, providing a lively forum for the expression of most political opinions.

A coalition led by the Muslim Brotherhood became the main parliamentary opposition in the 1987 elections. Mubarak seems to have welcomed this, in the hope that the body politic would neutralize the fundamentalists by co-opting them. But the militants remain as violent as ever, and Egypt's middle classes fear an experiment in Islamic government that some see as inevitable, barring a pre-emptive takeover by the army.

Egypt's new regional respectability has given it the confidence to edge away from its strong ties with the USA and be more critical of Israel. These moves betoken a revival of radicalism founded upon support for the Palestinian uprising, discontent with an inflation rate of over 30% and a feeling that the poor are being made to pay for economic measures prescribed by the IMF.

The economy has been boosted by IMF and other loans, a rescheduling of much of its $40bn foreign debt, regular (but controversial) US aid and increasingly favourable trade relations with the Soviet Union. The tourist industry has recovered from a slump prompted by Sadat's death and fears of terrorism. However, Egypt has to import nearly half the food it needs, at a cost of $2bn a year for a population that continues to grow by over 2% a year.

SAUDI ARABIA

Saudi Arabia, with one quarter of the world's oil reserves, has experienced both the benefits and the costs of an oil-dependent economy. It built a modern infrastructure with the extra revenues from the quadrupling of oil prices in 1973, but was thrown into recession when a glut in the market undermined prices in the mid-1980s. No longer prepared to act as Opec's "swing" producer, cutting production to defend prices, it now tailors output and pricing to its own revenue needs.

The slump in oil revenues dislocated plans to adjust the industry. Schemes to replace foreign workers with Saudis and to encourage the private sector to take over the running of industrial projects, particularly in setting up downstream plants at the new petrochemical cities of Jubail and Yanbu, became almost irrelevant.

Rapid development has put growing pressure on a society largely founded on traditional values. Officially, there are no politics in Saudi Arabia. The kingdom is governed by the Al-Saud family; King Fahd and his full brothers form the ruling clique. The conservative views of the Islamic clergy are heeded, particularly since the Iranian revolution of 1979. The occupation of the Great Mosque in Mecca that year by Muslim zealots tested the regime. It responded by curtailing overt personal extravagance and discussing proposals for a quasi-democratic *majlis al-shura* (consultative council). The kingdom's obligation to act as host each year to millions of pilgrims to Mecca exposes it to disruptive influences from abroad; in 1987 Saudi police killed 400 Iranian pilgrims demonstrating against the royal family and its alliance with the USA.

Yet today the kingdom seems relatively stable. There is rivalry within the royal family and discontent among the merchant class, which would like a share in decision-making, but massive social spending helps to keep most of the small indigenous population reasonably content. Iran, exhausted by eight years of war, shows less enthusiasm for exporting its revolution and more interest in getting on with its Arab neighbours.

The kingdom's oil reserves give it considerable political muscle. It used oil as a weapon after the 1973 Arab-Israeli war to garner support for the Arab cause, but it remains torn between support for the Palestinians and its military dependence on the USA. One of the kingdom's main problems has been how to adopt Western technology and economic methods while preserving the strict form of Islam that is its foundation. Contamination by foreign values through, among other factors, an extensive education programme threatens a culture that forbids alcohol, cinema and dancing and imposes Islamic penalties for crimes such as murder, theft and adultery.

OFFICIAL DATA

OFFICIAL NAME Kingdom of Saudi Arabia.

CAPITAL CITY Riyadh.

GEOGRAPHY Basically a sloping plateau, rising sheer – except for a narrow coastal plain in the south – from the Red Sea and sloping gently eastward through sandy deserts to salt flats and marshes on the east coast. There are no permanent rivers. The southeastern quarter of the country is almost totally empty and half the Saudi population are nomadic herdsmen. Mecca and Medina, Islam's holiest cities, are on the high ground to the west. *Highest point* 3,133 metres (10,280 feet). *Area* 2,150,000 sq km (830,000 sq miles).

PEOPLE *Population* 11.5m. *Density* 5 per sq km. *Ethnic groups* Arab.

RELIGION Muslim 99% (Sunni 85%, other 14%).

LANGUAGE Arabic.

EDUCATION Free but noncompulsory.

CLIMATE Summers very hot, with temperatures generally above 38°C (100°F) – average winter temperatures 14–23°C (57–73°F). Although the coast is oppressively humid, rainfall is very low; southern desert can remain dry for years.

CURRENCY Saudi riyal (SAR).

PUBLIC HOLIDAYS Leilat al-Meiraj, Id al-Fitr and next 6 days, Id al-Adha and next 5 days, Muharram, Ashoura, Mouloud.

GOVERNMENT Absolute monarchy with no legislature or organized political parties. The king appoints a council of ministers; the prime minister is invariably a member of the royal family.

ECONOMIC PROFILE

Economy previously based on subsistence agriculture and nomadic herding transformed by discovery of oil. Oil production fuelled rapid development of infrastructure and oil-related heavy industry – refining, petrochemicals, fertilizers, steel. Irrigated agriculture, developed at high cost, has brought self-sufficiency in wheat and eggs.

Growth Banks and industry recovering from mid-1980s slump. Light industry promoted on industrial estates. Continued heavy spending on defence programme. Mineral resources, including gold, silver, copper, coal and bauxite, await development.

Problems Much economic activity still reliant on government spending and hence on oil revenues. Private industry inhibited by small Gulf market and tough competition. New heavy industries entering overcrowded markets.

BALANCE OF PAYMENTS

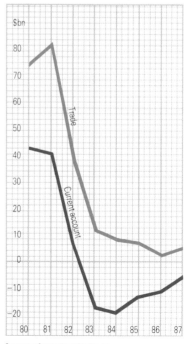

Source: EIU *Country Credit Risk Service*

GDP BY ORIGIN

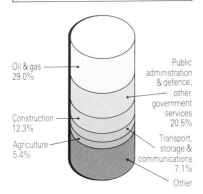

Oil & gas
29.0%

Public administration & defence; other government services
20.5%

Construction
12.3%

Transport, storage & communications
7.1%

Agriculture
5.4%

Other

COMPONENTS OF GDP

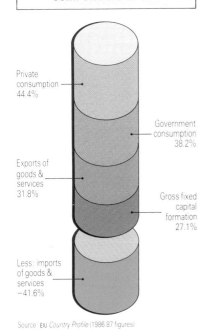

Private consumption
44.4%

Government consumption
38.2%

Exports of goods & services
31.8%

Gross fixed capital formation
27.1%

Less: imports of goods & services
−41.6%

Source: EIU *Country Profile* (1986/87 figures)

OIL PRODUCTION

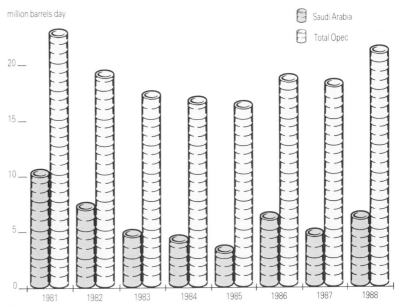

million barrels/day

Saudi Arabia

Total Opec

20 —

15 —

10 —

5 —

0 —

1981 1982 1983 1984 1985 1986 1987 1988

Source: EIU *Country Report*

IMPORTS AND EXPORTS

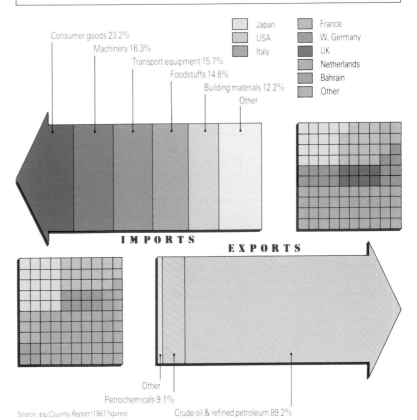

Japan

USA

Italy

France

W. Germany

UK

Netherlands

Bahrain

Other

Consumer goods 23.2%

Machinery 16.3%

Transport equipment 15.7%

Foodstuffs 14.8%

Building materials 12.2%

Other

IMPORTS

EXPORTS

Other

Petrochemicals 9.1%

Crude oil & refined petroleum 89.2%

Source: EIU *Country Report* (1987 figures)

KUWAIT

The discovery of oil in 1938 gave Kuwait financial security to resist the expansionist aims of its three great neighbours, Saudi Arabia, Iraq and Iran. Its oil reserves are the third largest in the noncommunist world, with a lifespan of 250 years.

Tribal loyalty helped the ruling Al-Sabah family develop a welfare state based on free healthcare and education. Kuwait's pioneering status led to complacency and a belief among many Kuwaitis that the country's wealth was due as much to their acumen as to the oil reserves. By the 1980s, the Kuwait stock exchange was among the ten largest in the world. But then, in 1982, the shadow stock exchange, the Souk al-Manakh, collapsed, oil prices fell and the build-up of the Gulf war put Kuwait's entrepôt trade at risk.

Terrorist attacks and threats from Iran created a climate of insecurity in the early 1980s; a generally radical middle class remained quiescent when the government expelled large numbers of Palestinians and Shias. The Kuwaiti oligarchy remains dominant, even though foreigners make up about 60% of the population.

With its small number of people, Kuwait could afford to be more outward-looking in deploying its wealth than some of its neighbours. Income from overseas investments was rivalling oil revenue by the late 1980s and development of refining and petrochemicals at home was linked to the purchase of retail outlets in Europe to guarantee a market. Substantial sums have been invested in experimental agricultural projects, but Kuwait's inhospitable desert terrain prevents much cultivation.

OFFICIAL NAME State of Kuwait.
CAPITAL CITY Kuwait.
GEOGRAPHY Most is flat, rocky desert, with a few low hills and little surface water. The land around the Bay of Kuwait is irrigated and cultivated and supports most of the highly urbanized population. *Highest point* 299 metres (980 feet). *Area* 17,818 sq km (6,880 sq miles).
PEOPLE *Population* 1.7m. *Density* 96 per sq km. *Ethnic groups* Arab 84% (Kuwaiti 42%, other 42%), Asian 15%.
RELIGION Muslim 92%, Christian 6%.
LANGUAGE Arabic.
EDUCATION Free to university level but noncompulsory. There is 1 university.
CLIMATE Hot; daytime temperatures of 50°C (120°F) are common. Annual rainfall 25–200mm (1–8ins); Apr-Sep always dry.
CURRENCY Kuwaiti dinar (KD).
PUBLIC HOLIDAYS Jan 1, Feb 25, Leilat al-Meiraj, 1st day of Ramadan, Id al-Fitr, Id al-Adha, Muharram, Mouloud.
GOVERNMENT Monarchy. The amir is head of state and chief executive. The 1962 constitution provides for a national assembly of 50 members elected by literate adult male civilians. This was dissolved in 1986, when the amir announced he would rule by decree. There are no political parties.

BAHRAIN

Historically a pearling, fishing and trading centre and one of the richest areas in the northern Gulf, Bahrain led the region in developing oil, discovered in 1932. When production waned in the 1970s, the island diversified into communications and banking just as Lebanon, the region's traditional services centre, tumbled into civil war.

Bahrain's cosmopolitan history and industrial sector made for a social awareness shading into political radicalism that persisted after independence in 1971. The national assembly was dissolved in 1975; the Iranian revolution, four years later, sparked off demonstrations among the Shia majority calling for an Islamic republic. The early 1980s were punctuated by Shia agitation, with Iran responding to Bahrain's support for Iraq by repeating historic claims to the island; the ceasefire in the Gulf war in 1988 came as welcome relief.

The oil sector still provides nearly 90% of export earnings, although reserves are running low; heavy use of the refinery by Saudi Arabia bolstered revenue in the early 1980s. An aluminium smelter, iron pelletizing plant and dry dock form the beginnings of an industrial base, and joint ventures with investors from OECD countries are being actively encouraged. The banking sector, which includes both onshore and offshore activity, went through a troubled patch following the recession of the mid-1980s and is having to adapt to increased competition. Since 1986, when the causeway to Saudi Arabia was opened, Bahrain, with its relaxed atmosphere, has become a key recreational centre for the region.

OFFICIAL NAME State of Bahrain.
CAPITAL CITY Al Manamah.
GEOGRAPHY Bahrain island, most of the land area, has a centre of rocky, barren hills and sand and salt marshes to the south and west. The north and northwest is irrigated and contains most of the population. *Highest point* Jabal ad-Dukhan 135 metres (440 feet). *Area* 622 sq km (240 sq miles).
PEOPLE *Population* 420,000. *Density* 670 per sq km. *Ethnic groups* Bahraini 70%.
RELIGION Muslim 85% (Shia 50%, Sunni 35%), Christian 7%.
LANGUAGE Arabic and English.
EDUCATION Free but noncompulsory. Private and religious schools co-exist with state system.
CLIMATE Hot and humid, though annual rainfall is less than 100mm (4ins). Average temperatures range from less than 20°C (68°F) in Dec-Mar to more than 29°C (84°F) in May-Oct.
CURRENCY Bahrain dinar (BD).
PUBLIC HOLIDAYS Jan 1, Leilat al-Meiraj, 1st day of Ramadan, Id al-Fitr, Id al-Adha, Muharram, Ashoura, Mouloud, Dec 16.
GOVERNMENT Monarchy. Independence of the UK was gained in 1971; a flirtation with democracy ended in 1975, and the amir now rules by decree through an appointed council of state.

UNITED ARAB EMIRATES

British interest in the Trucial States in the 19th century centred on its concern to protect the sea route to India. The seven states that eventually formed the United Arab Emirates – Abu Dhabi, Dubai, Sharjah, Ajman, Umm al-Qiwain, Ras al-Khaima and Fujairah – might have been nine, but Bahrain and Qatar decided not to join the federation on its birth in 1971, opting for independence in their own right.

Shaikh Zayed, ruler of Abu Dhabi, the largest and wealthiest emirate, became president of the federation, with Shaikh Rashid, ruler of entrepreneurial Dubai, as prime minister. The dominance of Abu Dhabi, the largest oil producer, was enhanced in 1973 when oil prices quadrupled. Dubai, however, capitalized on its long trading relationship with Iran during the Gulf war, as well as keeping its dry dock in business repairing war-damaged vessels. Despite rapid infrastructural development, the changes brought by the emirates' new wealth have not done away with the old ways of life. Strongly entrenched traditions remain, as does the shaikhs' council, which has held the federation together in troubled times.

Lack of coordination between the emirates has limited attempts to move away from total dependence on oil revenues, leaving the federation with too many banks, too many ports and airports and much duplication of industrial capacity.

OFFICIAL NAME United Arab Emirates.
CAPITAL CITY Abu Dhabi Town.
GEOGRAPHY The area consists of a strip of desert sand and salt flats along the rocky southern coast of the Gulf. *Highest point* Jabal Hafit 1,189 metres (3,900 feet). *Area* 83,600 sq km (32,300 sq miles).
PEOPLE *Population* 1.3m. *Density* 16 per sq km. *Ethnic groups* (residents and citizens) Indian, Iranian and Pakistani 50%, Arab 42%, European 8%.
RELIGION Muslim (mainly Sunni) 89%, Christian 6%.
LANGUAGE Arabic.
EDUCATION Compulsory for ages 6–12.
CLIMATE Hot and dry, with mild winters. Annual rainfall 75–100mm (3–4ins). Average temperatures 18°C (64°F) in Jan, 33°C (91°F) in July; summer temperatures up to 46°C (115°F).
CURRENCY UAE dirham (UAEDh).
PUBLIC HOLIDAYS Jan 1, Leilat al-Meiraj, 1st day of Ramadan, Id al-Fitr, Id al-Adha, Muharram, Aug 6 (Abu Dhabi only), Mouloud, Dec 2, Dec 25.
GOVERNMENT Federation of emirates. Each of the seven shaikhs is an absolute monarch in his own territory, and the seven form the federal supreme council of rulers, who elect a federal president and vice-president from among their number.

IMPORTS AND EXPORTS

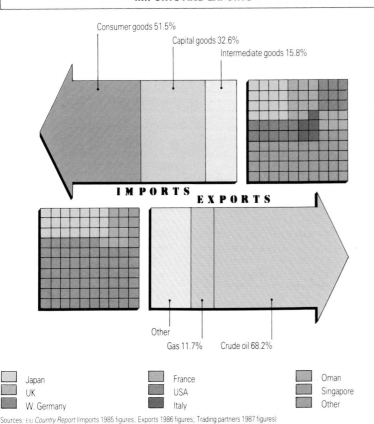

Consumer goods 51.5%
Capital goods 32.6%
Intermediate goods 15.8%

IMPORTS
EXPORTS

Other
Gas 11.7%
Crude oil 68.2%

▪ Japan	▪ France	▪ Oman
▪ UK	▪ USA	▪ Singapore
▪ W. Germany	▪ Italy	▪ Other

Sources: EIU *Country Report* (Imports 1985 figures; Exports 1986 figures; Trading partners 1987 figures)

GDP BY ORIGIN

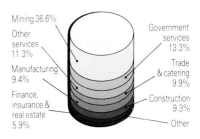

Mining 36.6%
Other services 11.3%
Manufacturing 9.4%
Finance, insurance & real estate 5.9%
Government services 13.3%
Trade & catering 9.9%
Construction 9.3%
Other

COMPONENTS OF GDP

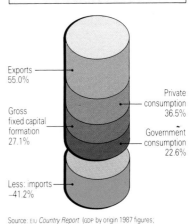

Exports 55.0%
Gross fixed capital formation 27.1%
Less: imports −41.2%
Private consumption 36.5%
Government consumption 22.6%

Source: EIU *Country Report* (GDP by origin 1987 figures; Components of GDP 1986 figures)

QATAR

Qatar was the first Arab Gulf state to start an industrial programme to diversify away from oil. Its cement, steel and fertilizer plants are efficient but cannot compete in glutted world markets. Doha, the capital, where most people live, vies with Bahrain as a business and leisure centre.

Qatar became independent of the UK in 1971, soon after creation of the United Arab Emirates, which disagreements prevented it joining. The country has been ruled by Shaikh Khalifa since 1972 after his cousin was deposed in February that year. Its foreign policy is expressed mainly in concert with the Gulf Cooperation Council (GCC), although it is in dispute with another GCC member, Bahrain, over a series of islands and several border areas; in 1986, the Qatar army raided the disputed Fasht ad-Dibal coral reef, seizing foreign workers who were building a Bahraini coastguard station. There have been indications of increased spending on defence, but there are also signs that relations with Bahrain are improving.

Dependence on oil remains strong, though its share of government revenues had fallen from over 90% to 80% by the mid-1980s. The government, known for cautious management, responded to the unpredictable oil market after 1986 by refusing to produce an annual budget, allocating funds month by month as earnings permitted.

Completion of most essential infrastructure has led to an exodus of migrant workers. New activity will accompany development of the vast North Field gas reserves, set to continue well into the next century, promising a secure income as oil declines.

OFFICIAL NAME State of Qatar.

CAPITAL CITY Doha.

GEOGRAPHY A barren, sandy, almost entirely featureless and waterless peninsula in the Persian Gulf, most settlement is on the eastern side, the location of the capital and oil reserves. *Highest point* Dukhan Heights 98m (320 feet). *Area* 11,000 sq km (4,200 sq miles).

PEOPLE *Population* 320,000. *Density* 29 per sq km. *Ethnic groups* Arab.

RELIGION Muslim 92%, Christian 6%, Hindu 1%.

LANGUAGE Arabic. Also English.

EDUCATION Free but noncompulsory, at all levels. There is 1 university.

CLIMATE Hot and dry, with annual rainfall less than 100mm (4ins). Summer temperatures over 30°C (86°F); winters relatively mild, around 18°C (64°F).

CURRENCY Qatar riyal (QR).

PUBLIC HOLIDAYS Feb 22, Leilat al-Meiraj, 1st day of Ramadan, Id al-Fitr, Id al-Adha, Muharram, Sep 3.

GOVERNMENT Absolute monarchy. The amir is head of state and chief executive, and appoints an administrative council of ministers and an advisory council. There is no legislature.

OMAN

Oman had three primary schools and 10km of tarred roads in 1970 when Sultan Said was ousted, with British help, by his son Qabus. Said, too old to adapt to the changes brought by the start of oil production in 1967, had imposed a nightly curfew in the capital, Muscat, and banned such symbols of decadence as spectacles and radios.

Qabus, trained in the British army, set out to develop Oman rapidly and end the civil war in the southern province of Dhofar. By 1976 the war was over; the return of highly educated exiles from the West accelerated development, which generally eschewed prestige projects in favour of spending on infrastructure, education and health. Oil reserves proved larger than expected and careful management reduced the impact of falling prices. Oil revenues still account for 90% of government income. In addition, copper is exported from mines originally worked by the ancient Sumerians; light industry is expanding; and a stock market has been set up. Rugged scenery offers potential for the nascent tourist industry.

Qabus ended Oman's isolation and developed an independent foreign policy. Previously tense relations with South Yemen gradually improved during the 1980s. Oman has also opened diplomatic relations with the USSR and, like the United Arab Emirates, has maintained close ties with Iran. Defence and internal security eat up over 40% of the annual budget, and Oman has close military links with the UK and USA, which stem from its strategic position at the mouth of the Gulf.

OFFICIAL NAME Sultanate of Oman.

CAPITAL CITY Muscat.

GEOGRAPHY Most of Oman is a flat desert with scattered oases. The Hajar Mountains shield a narrow, settled coastal plain on the Gulf of Oman. There are also settlements on the landward, less steep, side of the mountains. *Highest point* Jabal ash-Sham 3,018 metres (9,900 feet). *Area* 212,457 sq km (82,030 sq miles).

PEOPLE *Population* 1.2m. *Density* 6 per sq km. *Ethnic groups* Arab 87%, Baluchi 4%.

RELIGION Muslim 99%.

EDUCATION Noncompulsory. There is 1 university, but priority is given to provision of adult literacy centres.

LANGUAGE Arabic.

CLIMATE Hot and dry, with high humidity on coasts. Average temperatures around 35°C (95°F) in summer, around 22°C (72°F) in winter. Annual rainfall 75–100mm (3–4ins).

CURRENCY Rial Omani (OR).

PUBLIC HOLIDAYS Leilat al-Meiraj, 1st day of Ramadan, Id al-Fitr, Id al-Adha, Muharram, Ashoura, Mouloud, Nov 18-19

GOVERNMENT Absolute monarchy. The sultan appoints an administrative cabinet and an advisory consultative assembly. There are no political parties.

YEMEN

A stormy history has been played out across Yemen's mountains. Traditional spiritual leaders, the Zaydi imams, held onto power despite repeated uprisings until nationalist officers proclaimed the Yemen Arab Republic in 1962. Civil war followed, with Saudi Arabia backing the imams, Egypt the republicans. After Egypt withdrew, a compromise coalition government was formed in 1970, but violence and upheaval continued. The regime of President Abdallah Saleh, in power since 1978, has proved more stable, reinforced by the first free elections in July 1988. However, even today, control from Sana'a rarely penetrates the craggy hinterland.

Agriculture accounts for 80% of GDP, but the key foreign exchange earner has been an annual $1bn in remittances from 1m migrant workers in Saudi Arabia. This flow of funds, though starting to fall off by the mid-1980s, encouraged the neglect of agriculture, with food crops and coffee displaced by the narcotic plant *qat*. Oil production began in 1986, reducing the huge trade deficit but also threatening to provoke disputes between traditionalists and modernizers over how the new wealth should be spent. Joint oil exploration with South Yemen in disputed border areas promised to confirm a growing *détente* with Aden.

Yemen's geographical position makes it of considerable interest to the superpowers, but the country has managed its relations with East and West to its advantage. In 1979 it concluded a major arms deal with the USSR, with which it has a 20-year treaty of friendship, renewed in 1984; and one of its most important trading partners is the USA, although official trade statistics give only a partial picture, as huge amounts of goods are smuggled in.

OFFICIAL NAME Yemen Arab Republic.
CAPITAL CITY Sana'a.
GEOGRAPHY Population is concentrated in the Yemeni highlands which are cultivated by terracing. To the west is the Red Sea, and to the east a barren plateau slopes away to the ill-defined desert boundary with Saudi Arabia. *Highest point* Jabal an Nabi Shu'ayb 3,760 metres (12,340 feet). *Area* 195,000 sq km (75,300 sq miles).
PEOPLE *Population* 6.9m. *Density* 35 per sq km. *Ethnic groups* Arab 98%, Somali 1%.
RELIGION Muslim 100% (Zaydi Shia 60%, Sunni 40%).
EDUCATION Primary education available for ages 7–13, but noncompulsory.
LANGUAGE Arabic.
CLIMATE Hot and humid, with an annual average temperature of 30°C (86°F). Annual rainfall around 600mm (24ins) in the highlands; coast and eastern sector are desert.
CURRENCY Yemen rial (YR).
PUBLIC HOLIDAYS Leilat al-Meiraj, Id al-Fitr, Jun 13, Id al-Adha, Muharram, Sep 26, Mouloud, Oct 14.
GOVERNMENT One-party republic since 1962. Political parties are banned, though there are competing cliques. A president is head of state and chief executive. Elections for a consultative assembly were held in 1988.

SOUTH YEMEN

The most radical and anti-Western of Arab states, the People's Democratic Republic of Yemen (PDRY) has been edging of late towards the Arab mainstream.

Its militancy began in the 1960s, when the UK's attempt to create a south Arabian federation ran up against rivalry between Adeni merchants and the tribal rulers of the interior. In 1966 the British initiated a two-year transition to independence but the threat of civil war forced a premature handover of power to the National Liberation Front in 1967.

The PDRY's politics has since been both bloody and militantly Marxist. The second president was executed, the fourth ousted in 1986 after fierce fighting which left thousands dead, including most of the leaders of the victorious faction.

The economy has been slow to recover from the events of 1986 but the experience seems to have been sufficiently traumatic to force some new political thinking, encouraged by the Soviet reforms. A noticeable warming in relations with Arab neighbours in recent years has been rewarded with economic aid. Rapprochement with Yemen, allowing free movement between the two countries, has helped create a new mood of openness and self-criticism.

The state plays the dominant role in industry and agriculture. Less than 1% of the land area is cultivable and, until oil was discovered in 1987, fishing was considered the sector with the most potential. Economic performance has been disappointing; remittances from migrant workers in Saudi Arabia help make up the shortfall.

OFFICIAL NAME People's Democratic Republic of Yemen.
CAPITAL CITY Aden.
GEOGRAPHY Most is highland, with a populated strip of coastal plain along the Gulf of Aden. Other settlements cluster along the south-flowing wadis and the few perennial rivers. *Highest point* Jabal Thamir 2,512 metres (8,240 feet). *Area* 332,968 sq km (128,560 sq miles).
PEOPLE *Population* 2.3m. *Density* 7 per sq km. *Ethnic groups* Arab 93%, Indian and Pakistani 3%.
RELIGION Muslim (mainly Sunni) 99%.
EDUCATION Free at all levels and compulsory for ages 7–15.
LANGUAGE Arabic.
CLIMATE Hot and dry. In summer coastal temperatures hover around 38°C (100°F) and humidity is 80%. Annual rainfall is less than 300mm (12ins).
CURRENCY Yemeni dinar (YD).
PUBLIC HOLIDAYS Leilat al-Meiraj, 1st day of Ramadan, Id al-Fitr, Id al-Adha, Muharram, Ashoura, Mouloud, Oct 14.
GOVERNMENT Socialist republic since 1967. The Yemen Socialist Party is the only permitted political organization. The 111 members of the legislative supreme people's council elect a presidium, whose chairman is head of state.

NORTH AFRICA

Western Sahara

The Polisario movement has been fighting for the independence of Western Sahara since 1973, first against Spain, the colonial power, then against Morocco and Mauritania, which divided the territory between them when the Spanish left in 1976. The war continued after Mauritania withdrew in 1979. Morocco gradually extended its control of the territory through construction of a defensive wall of sand and rock. Morocco repeatedly rejected calls for a negotiated end to the war and in 1984 left the Organization of African Unity when the Polisario government-in-exile, the Sahrawi Arab Democratic Republic (SADR), was admitted as a member. The SADR has been recognized by more than 70 governments. Efforts by the UN to end the conflict made some headway in 1988, with both sides agreeing in principle to a ceasefire and the holding of a referendum to decide the territory's future.

The territory's rocky desert was traditionally inhabited by nomads. Since drought and the conflict for sovereignty began in the mid-1970s, most of the Sahrawi have settled; either in the capital, El-Aioun, and other towns under Moroccan occupation, or in refugee camps in Algeria, Polisario's backer.

The rich fishing grounds off the long Atlantic coast have been plundered by foreign fleets. Mineral deposits include a major phosphate works at Bou Craa. These potential riches are one reason for the intensity of the Western Sahara conflict, but it also has deep political roots in the struggle for influence in North Africa between Rabat and Algiers.

Climate

Northern coasts have a Mediterranean climate, with up to 800mm (30ins) of rain falling mostly between November and March; the Atlantic coast of Morocco is cooler and drier. Heavy snow falls in the High Atlas in winter. South of the mountains, the Sahara is hot and without rain.

- ■ More than 1 million
- ● 250,000 – 1 million
- • 100,000 – 250,000

Climatic zones
- Mediterranean
- Steppe
- Desert

- ⌇ Oil pipelines
- Major oil fields
- Major gas fields

Education

The North African countries have invested heavily in education, which is generally compulsory from 7 to 15. Algeria has come close to its aim of providing nine years' schooling for every child and education and training account a quarter of the government budget. There is also strong emphasis on promoting technical skills through higher education, an approach shared by Libya, which had enrolled more than 10% of the population in higher education by the mid-1980s.

Ceuta and Melilla

Two enclaves on the Moroccan coast, Ceuta and Melilla, were retained by Spain when Morocco became independent in 1956. The population of the two cities is mainly Spanish in origin, although the Arab population has grown rapidly in recent years. Morocco formally claims the two enclaves but relations with Spain remain relatively cordial.

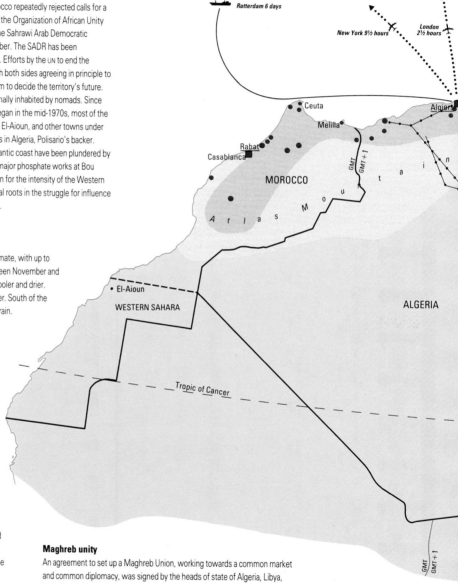

Maghreb unity

An agreement to set up a Maghreb Union, working towards a common market and common diplomacy, was signed by the heads of state of Algeria, Libya, Mauritania, Morocco and Tunisia in February 1989. Previous attempts at Maghreb unity have not progressed very far, due to rifts such as that between Morocco and Algeria over the Western Sahara and those between Libyan leader Muammar Qaddafi and most of his neighbours. But there is plenty of scope for increased trade among the five countries, as well as the need to negotiate as a unit with the EC on the other side of the Mediterranean. Morocco has also applied to join the EC.

Oil and gas

Oil has fuelled the development of two North African countries – Algeria and Libya – and been a valuable export earner for Tunisia. Only Morocco has had to rely largely on imported oil for its energy supplies. Algeria's production from its oil fields in the Sahara has been declining since the 1970s, but it has been replaced as a source of foreign earnings by natural gas. Algeria has become the EC's third largest gas supplier, much of it pumped through the Trans-Med pipeline from Tunisia to Sicily. Libya's oil reserves are expected to last for at least 70 years at present rates of production; the settlement of maritime border disputes with Tunisia and Malta in Libya's favour in the early 1980s gave it access to additional reserves offshore.

Libya's great man-made river

Worried by the increasing salinity and rapid depletion of underground water supplies in the narrow fertile coastal strip, Libya's planners came up with an ambitious solution: a vast pipeline system to tap aquifers beneath the Sahara, up to 900km (560 miles) from the coast. The first stage, costed at $3.3bn, is due to be completed in 1991. Further stages will follow, financed from local resources through a special tax paid by every Libyan.

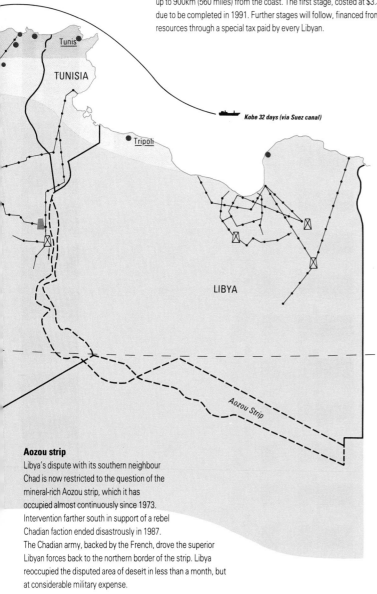

Kobe 32 days (via Suez canal)

Tunis

TUNISIA

Tripoli

LIBYA

Aozou Strip

Aozou strip

Libya's dispute with its southern neighbour
Chad is now restricted to the question of the
mineral-rich Aozou strip, which it has
occupied almost continuously since 1973.
Intervention farther south in support of a rebel
Chadian faction ended disastrously in 1987.
The Chadian army, backed by the French, drove the superior
Libyan forces back to the northern border of the strip. Libya
reoccupied the disputed area of desert in less than a month, but
at considerable military expense.

AFRICA

MOROCCO

King Hassan II has survived several attempts on his life and power since he came to the throne in 1961. As both head of government and the highest religious leader in the land he retains an autocratic hold, although the 1980s saw the emergence of some degree of political expression.

Hassan has established his country as a leading conservative force in African and Arab politics – providing several black African leaders with teams of crack presidential guards – and has made his mark as an active mediator in the Arab-Israeli conflict. His tenacity on the issue of Western Sahara has lost him friends in Africa, however, and has weighed heavily on the defence budget, helping to push external debt up to $22bn in 1988.

The import bill will not diminish unless food self-sufficiency can be achieved. Only a small portion of cultivable land is worked by modern methods, with most still in the hands of traditional farmers. The lengthy depression of world phosphate prices has been partly mitigated by adding value to production, but mineral resources in general are unremarkable. Tourism offers more potential: Morocco is already a popular destination and the sector is attracting foreign investment.

OFFICIAL NAME Kingdom of Morocco.
CAPITAL CITY Rabat.
GEOGRAPHY Bordered on the north by the Mediterranean Sea, the west by the Atlantic Ocean, the south by the Sahara Desert and the east by the Atlas Mountains, Morocco is almost a continental "island." The mountains also constitute a precious watershed, flowing down into the dry, sandy plains and plateaus which cover two-thirds of the territory. The mountains separate the fertile west and north from the near-Saharan south and east. *Highest point* Toubkal 4,165 metres (13,670 feet). *Area* 710,850 sq km (274,460 sq miles).
PEOPLE *Population* 22.1m. *Density* 31 per sq km. *Ethnic groups* Arab/Berber 99%.
RELIGION Muslim 99%, Christian 1%.
LANGUAGE Arabic. Also French, Berber languages and Spanish.
CURRENCY Dirham (Dh).
PUBLIC HOLIDAYS Jan 1, Mar 3, 1st day of Ramadan, May 1, Id al-Fitr, Jul 9, Muharram, Ashoura, Aug 14, Mouloud, Nov 6, 18.
GOVERNMENT Constitutional monarchy. The king rules with a 306-member chamber of representatives. Ministers are appointed by the king and are answerable to him. There are around 12 officially recognized political parties. At the 1984 elections, the Union Constitutionnelle took 83 seats, followed by the Rassemblement National des Indépendants with 61 seats and the Mouvement Populaire with 47 seats.

IMPORTS AND EXPORTS

Crude oil 13.3%
Wheat 12.5%
Sulphur 6.5%
Machinery 5.0%
Other

IMPORTS

France
Spain
W. Germany
Italy
USA
India
Iraq
Japan
Other

EXPORTS

Other
Citrus fruit 7.8%
Phosphoric acid 13.7%
Textiles 13.8%
Phosphates 17.0%

Source: EIU *Country Report* (Imports/Exports 1986 figures; Trading partners 1987 figures)

ECONOMIC PROFILE

Agriculture still employs more than half working population, producing wheat, barley and beans for home market and citrus fruits, olive oil, wine, figs and dates for export. Phosphates are biggest export earner.

Growth Tourism. Strong and expanding fishing and textile industries.

Problems Heavy external debt burden; stagnant world phosphate market. Hopes of extracting oil from shale dissolved as oil prices slumped.

BALANCE OF PAYMENTS

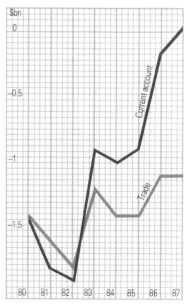

$bn
0
−0.5
Current account
−1
Trade
−1.5
80 81 82 83 84 85 86 87

Source: EIU *Country Credit Risk Service*

TUNISIA

The peaceful overthrow on November 7 1987 of Habib Bourguiba by his prime minister, Zine el-Abidine Ben Ali, ended fears of a convoluted and bitter succession struggle. Bourguiba led Tunisia to independence from France in 1956 and had tried to create a Westernized and largely secular state in his own image. In his last years he had presided over a confused and divided government as the Islamic opposition gathered support among Tunisians who were struggling to make ends meet.

Ben Ali went on to consolidate support by emphasizing national reconciliation: he announced amnesties for thousands of prisoners and invited the opposition to take part both in a "national pact" to draw up policy aims and in a reinvigorated electoral process.

While maintaining Tunisia's commitment to Western alliances and liberal economic policies, Ben Ali has stressed its Arab-Islamic identity, undercutting the fundamentalists' appeal. Relations with Libya have improved sharply, to the benefit of Tunisia's economy and of plans for Maghreb unity.

The mid-1980s' slump in oil prices exacerbated a growing economic crisis and in 1986 the government called for IMF assistance in implementing a structural adjustment programme. The policies required were not far removed from those already in place and Tunisia had less difficulty adjusting than other countries, emerging as one of the IMF's star pupils.

OFFICIAL NAME Republic of Tunisia.
CAPITAL CITY Tunis.
GEOGRAPHY The northern half of Tunisia is the eastern end of the Atlas range. Forests cover the mountains; the fertile valleys and small areas of flat land along the generally rocky and inhospitable northern coast support most of the population. The centre of the country is a depression dotted with salt lakes, and the south is a largely uninhabited semi-desert upland. *Area* 163,610 sq km (63,170 sq miles).
PEOPLE *Population* 7.1m. *Density* 43 per sq km. *Ethnic groups* Arab 98%, Berber 1.5%, French 0.2%.
RELIGION Muslim 99.5%, Christian 0.3%.
LANGUAGE Arabic. Also French.
CURRENCY Tunisian dinar (TD).
PUBLIC HOLIDAYS Jan 1, 18, Mar 20, 21, Apr 9, May 1, Id al-Seghir, Jun 1, 2, Id al-Kebir, Jul 25, Aug 13, Oct 15.
GOVERNMENT Republic since 1956. The head of state and chief executive is a president, elected for a 5-year term, as are the 141 members of the legislative national assembly. A one-party state through the 1960s and 1970s, Tunisia now has a multiparty system.

ECONOMIC PROFILE

Based on Mediterranean produce – olive oil, citrus – plus textiles. Oil, which accounted for half of export earnings in early 1980s, has declined in importance as fields have been worked out and prices have fallen. Tourism now crucial.

Growth Dependent on further expansion of services sector. A number of international banks have set up operations in Tunis. Joint ventures supplying the EC market are being encouraged.

Problems Agriculture has been hit by drought. Economy vulnerable to fluctuating oil and phosphate prices and the volatile tourism market.

IMPORTS AND EXPORTS

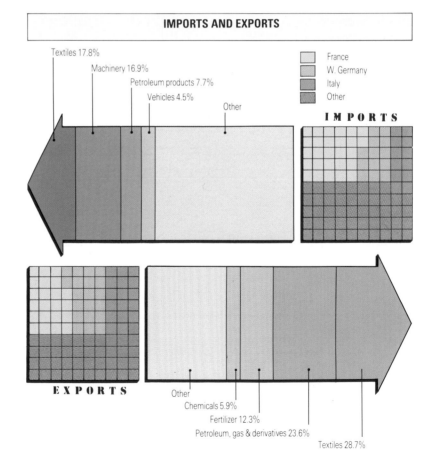

Textiles 17.8%
Machinery 16.9%
Petroleum products 7.7%
Vehicles 4.5%
Other

France
W. Germany
Italy
Other

IMPORTS

EXPORTS

Other
Chemicals 5.9%
Fertilizer 12.3%
Petroleum, gas & derivatives 23.6%
Textiles 28.7%

Source: EIU *Country Report* (1987 figures)

ALGERIA

The riots of October 1988 left hundreds dead and shattered Algeria's hard-won image of political stability. The Front de Libération Nationale remained in power but with its legitimacy, stemming from its role in the bitter 1954–62 war for independence from France, undermined. President Chadli Bendjedid responded with unprecedented political reforms to complement a much-needed overhaul of the socialist economy begun in the early 1980s.

Internal opposition has traditionally been fragmented and weak, despite an upsurge of Islamic fundamentalism. Of greatest concern are the demands of Algeria's youth, by far the majority of the 23m population. Just standing still is difficult with a population growth rate in excess of 3% (outpacing GDP growth in 1985–88) and social expectations which are high by regional standards. This makes reform of the top-heavy bureaucracy and inefficient state industry essential for future prosperity.

Chadli has given state companies more power to make decisions, raising profit to a priority above the social and political factors that previously dominated decision-making. He has also encouraged private agriculture. Hydrocarbons remain crucial: oil reserves are dwindling, but three-quarters of export earnings still come from sales of gas, condensates and refined products. External debt is over $20bn, but the government has made avoidance of rescheduling – and an IMF programme that would challenge "national sovereignty" – a lynchpin of its strategy.

In many respects, the regime is better respected abroad than at home. Charged by Western governments with being a haven to terrorists in the 1960s, it became a leading international mediator in the 1980s, playing a key role in the release of the US hostages in Iran in 1981. Moves towards regional unity in the Maghreb, long an important policy in Algiers, seemed in the late 1980s to be bearing fruit at last.

OFFICIAL NAME Democratic and Popular Republic of Algeria.

CAPITAL CITY Algiers.

GEOGRAPHY Much of Africa's second largest country is a dry sandstone plateau, largely uninhabited, that merges into the Sahara Desert. The Atlas Mountains separate the plateau from the Mediterranean, with a coastal plain where the major cities Algiers and Oran are situated. *Highest point* Mt Tahat 2,918 metres (9,570 feet). *Area* 2,381,741 sq km (919,600 sq miles).

PEOPLE *Population* 21.8m. *Density* 9 per sq km. *Ethnic groups* Arab 83.5%, Berber 16%.

RELIGION Muslim 99%, Christian 0.5%.

LANGUAGE Arabic. Also Berber and French.

CURRENCY Algerian dinar (AD).

PUBLIC HOLIDAYS Jan 1, May 1, Id al-Fitr, Jun 19, Jul 5, Id al-Adha, Muharram, Ashoura, Mouloud, Nov 1.

GOVERNMENT Republic since 1962. The head of state and chief executive is a president. The 281-member people's assembly is the legislative body and its members, like the president, are elected for 5-year terms.

ECONOMIC PROFILE

Exports of oil, natural gas and products still the motor for economic development. Agriculture, mainstay of the colonial economy, fell into deep decline after independence and large-scale food imports are necessary.

Growth Agricultural production gradually increasing, with some products – fruit, wine – available for export. Steel and some other manufactured goods now being exported. New economic policies could open way for development of tourism and service industries.

Problems Insufficient diversification to avoid dependence on shrinking hydrocarbon reserves to pay for food imports and to service debts. Restructuring of industry handicapped by shortages of hard currency, bureaucracy, poor training and overmanning.

IMPORTS AND EXPORTS

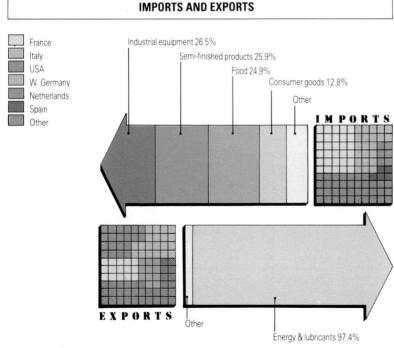

- France
- Italy
- USA
- W. Germany
- Netherlands
- Spain
- Other

Industrial equipment 26.5%
Semi-finished products 25.9%
Food 24.9%
Consumer goods 12.8%
Other

IMPORTS

EXPORTS

Other
Energy & lubricants 97.4%

Source: EIU *Country Report* (1987 figures)

LIBYA

It is not just the revolutionary rhetoric of Muammar Qaddafi that sets Libya apart. An Italian colony until World War II, it was one of the first African states to become independent. Its new ruler, King Idris, took over one of the world's poorest states, with scrap metal left over from the war a crucial export. The start of oil exports in 1961 transformed Libya's fortunes: it soon had the highest GDP per head on the continent outside South Africa.

Qaddafi's 1969 coup was a product of rising Third World radicalism and dissatisfaction with the way oil earnings were spent. Qaddafi's rule is best known for his abolition of conventional government institutions and declaration of Libya as a "state of the masses," his liquidation of opponents, his support for radical movements around the world and his confrontation with the USA and its allies. Some of his international adventures have proved costly, as in April 1986 when US aircraft attacked Libyan cities, or the following year when Libyan forces suffered a humiliating defeat in Chad. There have been occasional stirrings of revolt but a blend of repression and the distribution of considerable resources among a population of only 4m has kept Qaddafi and his supporters in power.

OFFICIAL NAME Socialist People's Libyan Arab Jamahiriya.
CAPITAL CITY Tripoli.
GEOGRAPHY Most of Libya is desert, though there are fertile uplands in the extreme east and west. Inland it is mostly uninhabited, except around scattered oases, and most of the population is concentrated in the cities along the Mediterranean coast. Area 1,759,540 sq km (679,360 sq miles).
PEOPLE *Population* 3.6m. *Density* 2 per sq km. *Ethnic groups* Arab/Berber 100%.
RELIGION Muslim 97%.
LANGUAGE Arabic.
CURRENCY Libyan dinar (LD).
PUBLIC HOLIDAYS Leilat al-Meiraj, Mar 28, Id al-Fitr, Jun 11, Id al-Adha, Muharram, Ashoura, Sep 1, Oct 7, Mouloud.
GOVERNMENT Republic since 1969. Independent since 1951. The Arab Socialist Union is the only permitted party. The head of state is the revolutionary leader, elected by the 1,112 members of the general people's congress.

GDP BY ORIGIN

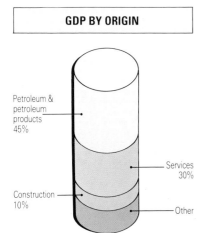

Petroleum & petroleum products 45%

Services 30%

Construction 10%

Other

ECONOMIC PROFILE

Oil reserves are enough to last for 60 years, but revenues running at less than half their 1980 peak. Agriculture is confined to coastal areas and oases.

Growth The project to pipe groundwater from beneath Sahara to coastal areas would transform agriculture if completed. Huge investments in petrochemicals, steel and aluminium industries.

Problems Falling oil prices have hit development of industry and infrastructure. Much food imported.

COMPONENTS OF GDP

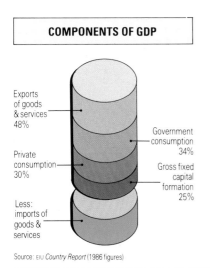

Exports of goods & services 48%

Private consumption 30%

Less: imports of goods & services

Government consumption 34%

Gross fixed capital formation 25%

Source: EIU *Country Report* (1986 figures)

IMPORTS AND EXPORTS

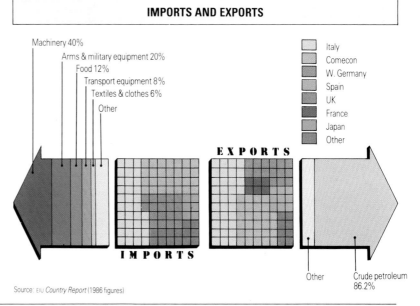

Machinery 40%
Arms & military equipment 20%
Food 12%
Transport equipment 8%
Textiles & clothes 6%
Other

Italy
Comecon
W. Germany
Spain
UK
France
Japan
Other

EXPORTS

IMPORTS

Other

Crude petroleum 86.2%

Source: EIU *Country Report* (1986 figures)

WEST AFRICA

Ecowas and CEAO

West Africa has two overlapping economic communities. The Communauté Economique de l'Afrique de l'Ouest (CEAO), set up in 1974, is exclusively francophone. CEAO's main objective is to liberalize trade among members; its recent history has been marred by allegations of financial irregularities. All CEAO's members also belong to the Economic Community of West African States (Ecowas), established a year later, which has a total of 16 members. Ecowas aims to establish first a customs union and then a full common market. Progress has been slow, hindered by the fact that the region's economies are competitive rather than complementary and by the multiplicity of different currencies used.

Concern to avoid domination of the organization by Nigeria, the region's economic giant, led to the establishment of the Ecowas Fund for Cooperation, Compensation & Development to help redress the balance by ensuring that members did not suffer losses from Ecowas operations and funding development projects in the poorer states. A regional bank, Ecobank, is also being set up.

CEAO consists of Benin, Burkina Faso, Ivory Coast, Mali, Mauritania, Niger and Senegal; Togo has observer status. Ecowas consists of CEAO members plus Cape Verde, The Gambia, Ghana, Guinea, Guinea-Bissau, Liberia, Nigeria and Senegal.

The franc zone

Unlike many African countries, franc zone members – mainly former French colonies – have the advantage of a freely convertible currency. The CFA franc, used by most African franc zone members, is linked to the French franc at a fixed rate of CFA Fr50 = FFr1 and is backed by the French treasury. West African members of the franc zone – Benin, Burkina Faso, Ivory Coast, Mali, Niger, Senegal and Togo – form the Union Monétaire Ouest-Africaine and share a common central bank, Banque Centrale des Etats de l'Afrique de l'Ouest. All are also members of Banque Ouest-Africaine de Développement. Six Central African countries and the Comoros, in the Indian Ocean, are also franc zone members.

Senegambia

The confederation between Senegal and its much smaller neighbour, The Gambia, had its origins in the July 1981 coup attempt against The Gambia's president, Sir Dawda Jawara. Senegalese troops were invited to help put down the coup. Their intervention precipitated discussions on forming the confederation, which were finalized by the end of the year.

The Senegalese head of state is president of the confederation, his Gambian counterpart the vice-president. There is a council of ministers and a parliament, with members drawn from their counterparts in each country. A monetary and customs union is the ultimate objective, but this faces considerable obstacles, as does integration of educational and legal systems based on English and French models.

Desertification

Twenty-five years of declining rainfall and growing population pressures in the semi-arid Sahelian belt have contributed to the gradual southward advance of the Sahara. The world's attention was first drawn to the problem by the Sahelian famine of 1973, when 100,000 people died. That crisis was caused by drought, but the roots of the problem lay in the previous two decades of above-average rainfall, when cash crop cultivation and settlement expanded onto marginal land. Over-grazing, over-cultivation, deforestation and poor irrigation are the main causes of desertification; the process is reversible if the land is given time to rest and reclaimed through tree-planting and terracing, but such techniques have yet to be applied on a large scale.

EXPORT BREAKDOWN

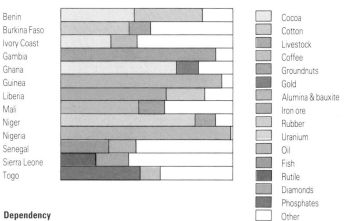

Benin
Burkina Faso
Ivory Coast
Gambia
Ghana
Guinea
Liberia
Mali
Niger
Nigeria
Senegal
Sierra Leone
Togo

Cocoa
Cotton
Livestock
Coffee
Groundnuts
Gold
Alumina & bauxite
Iron ore
Rubber
Uranium
Oil
Fish
Rutile
Diamonds
Phosphates
Other

Dependency

West African countries are particularly vulnerable to commodity price falls. Most are dependent on the export of only one or two products.

Sources: IMF *International Financial Statistics* (1986 figures); EIU *Country Reports* (1986 figures)

London 7½ hours

Tropic of Cancer

NIGER

GMT
GMT +1

Niamey

BENIN

Abuja

NIGERIA

Niger

Porto
Novo

Lagos

né

Climate

Coastal and southern areas have two rainy seasons, in May–June and October; farther north these merge into one, from July to September. The average annual rainfall range is 600–2,000mm (25–80ins); the temperature range is 18–32°C (65–90°F). The dry season is subject to the hot dusty *harmattan* wind blowing from the northeast.

Ethnic and linguistic groups

Colonial frontiers, preserved after independence, took little account of the geographical distribution of African peoples. One of the greatest difficulties faced by African governments has been in building national consciousness and unity from a diversity of ethnic and tribal groups; old loyalties and rivalries live on. Nigeria, for example, has more than 250 ethnic groups; Ivory Coast more than 60. The languages spoken are just as numerous, although most West African languages belong to the Niger–Congo family, spoken by more than 150m people across the west and centre of the continent. The main West African languages include Wolof and Mandinke in the far west and the Kwa languages of the Ashanti people of Ghana and the Yoruba and Ibo of southern Nigeria.

Education

The economic difficulties suffered by many West African countries during the 1980s have threatened their achievements in raising educational standards since independence. The rate of growth of enrolment in education has fallen in the 1980s, as governments have been forced to cut back on education spending and the cost to families has risen. In most West African countries, the majority of children receive some primary education: 77% of the age group in Ivory Coast, for example, 92% in Nigeria. Far fewer go on to secondary schools, less than 30% in both these cases.

MAURITANIA

Mauritania was one of the last countries to abolish slavery, in 1980. After independence from France in 1960, it was led by President Mokhtar Ould Daddah until his overthrow in 1978; a succession of military leaders has followed. The periodic ravages of drought and the development of a mining industry in the 1960s have contributed to the decline of traditional nomadic livestock rearing: as Mauritania entered the 1980s only 25% of the population were nomadic, compared with over 80% in 1965. In order to increase the land area under cultivation, several dam projects were undertaken in the 1980s but arable farming is possible only in the Senegal river valley in the south. Competition for land has provoked racial conflict with the Senegalese. Exploitation of vast iron ore resources began in 1963, peaked a decade later and then suffered from recession in the world steel industry; output began to recover in the late 1980s.

Fishing is now a driving force in the economy; the coastal waters are among the richest in the world, with a potential catch of 600,000 tonnes (660,000 US tons) a year. Regulations ensure that the catch is processed locally to add value.

OFFICIAL NAME Islamic Republic of Mauritania.
CAPITAL CITY Nouakchott.
GEOGRAPHY Around 40% is Sahara Desert, 30% semi-desert. There is a narrow band of fertile land along the Senegal river. *Area* 1,030,700 sq km (397,950 sq miles).
PEOPLE *Population* 2m. *Density* 2 per sq km.
RELIGION Muslim 99%, Christian 0.5%.
LANGUAGE Arabic and French.
CURRENCY Ouguiya (U).
PUBLIC HOLIDAYS Jan 1, Leilat al-Meiraj, May 1, Id al-Fitr, May 25, Id al-Adha, Muharram, Mouloud, Nov 28.
GOVERNMENT Military-dominated republic. The Comité Militaire de Redressement National (CMRN) has ruled since 1978. Army leaders abandoned their plan to introduce a new constitution in 1981 and all political parties are banned.

MALI

In the 14th century, the legendary town of Timbuktu was the renowned religious and cultural centre of a vast Malian empire stretching as far as the Atlantic coast. In 1987, the World Bank ranked the landlocked remnant of that empire as the fourth poorest country in the world.

After independence, the government under Modibo Keita sought to create its own style of African socialism. But economic performance was poor and in 1968 Keita was overthrown by Lieutenant Moussa Traoré. The region's endemic droughts have hit the northern Saharan and Sahelian zones and their main export, livestock. The southern savannah, where cotton, the country's leading export, is grown has fared better. Gold is mined, mainly on an artisanal basis, although a commercial mine at Kalana produced 500kg (1,100lb) in 1987. The early years of independent Mali saw a great expansion of the state's role in the economy but since 1981, as a result of pressure from aid donors, the government has pursued a programme of liberalization.

OFFICIAL NAME Republic of Mali.
CAPITAL CITY Bamako.
GEOGRAPHY Large and landlocked, with two crucial arteries, the Senegal and Niger rivers, which provide vital irrigation, means of access, and a source of fish. *Area* 1,240,190 sq km (478,770 sq miles).
PEOPLE *Population* 7.6m. *Density* 6.1 per sq km.
RELIGION Muslim 90%, Christian 1%, Animist.
LANGUAGE French. Also local languages.
CURRENCY CFA franc (CFAFr).
PUBLIC HOLIDAYS Jan 1, 20, Easter Mon, May 1, Korité, May 25, Tabaski, Sep 22, Mouloud, Baptism of the Prophet, Nov 19, Dec 25.
GOVERNMENT Republic since 1960. The president is the head of state and government and is elected every 5 years. There is an 82-member national assembly which wields little power. The only official party is the Union Démocratique du Peuple Malien (UDPM).

NIGER

Exploitation of the Arlit uranium deposits from 1971 set off a boom that collapsed into sharp recession as demand for uranium shrank in the 1980s. Reserves of manganese, iron ore and molybdenum remain untouched, as does the oil discovered in the Agadez basin in 1982; 98% of the population still make their living from agriculture and trading. Livestock is the second largest export but earnings are understated as large numbers of cattle are smuggled into Nigeria.

The country became independent in 1960 and was run by President Diori Hamani until he was overthrown in 1974. His successor, the sober and autocratic Lieutenant-Colonel Seyni Kountché, died in 1987 and was succeeded by Colonel Ali Saibou. The new president has made it clear that the army would continue its presence in the government following a return to constitutional rule. He has also persisted in a foreign policy which emphasizes links with France and Arab states and in an economic policy which generally reflects IMF prescriptions.

OFFICIAL NAME Republic of Niger.
CAPITAL CITY Niamey.
GEOGRAPHY The largest state in West Africa, Niger is landlocked and two-thirds is desert. Minimal rainfall along the Nigerian border permits limited cultivation while the Niger river provides some pasture land. *Area* 1,267,000 sq km (489,000 sq miles).
PEOPLE *Population* 6.1m. *Density* 5 per sq km.
RELIGION Muslim 88%, Christian 0.5%, Animist.
LANGUAGE French. Also local languages.
CURRENCY CFA franc (CFAFr).
PUBLIC HOLIDAYS Jan 1, Easter Mon, Apr 15, May 1, Id al-Fitr, Id al-Adha, Aug 3, Muharram, Mouloud, Dec 18, 25.
GOVERNMENT Military-dominated republic. Since 1974, power has been vested in the president and in a supreme military council – the CSM – whose members are appointed by the president. A new constitution is being drawn up.

GAMBIA

A narrow strip of land along the banks of the Gambia river, this former British colony is bordered on three sides by francophone Senegal. About half the cultivable land is given over to groundnuts, the major export earner but subject to the effects of Sahelian drought. Output of rice, the staple food, does not meet the needs of a growing population.

Tourism has been the rising star of the economy since independence in 1965. Arrivals, whether black Americans in search of their "roots" or British and Scandinavians in search of sun, rose from a mere 300 in 1966 to 86,000 two decades later.

OFFICIAL NAME Republic of The Gambia.

CAPITAL CITY Banjul.

GEOGRAPHY On average only about 25km wide, much is mangrove swamp and marsh. *Area* 11,295 sq km (4,360 sq miles).

PEOPLE *Population* 700,000. *Density* 61 per sq km.

RELIGION Muslim 85%, Christian 3%, Animist.

LANGUAGE English. Also local languages.

CURRENCY Dalasi (Di).

PUBLIC HOLIDAYS Jan 1, Feb 1, 18, Good Fri-Easter Mon, May 1, Id al-Fitr, Id al-Adha, Assumption, Mouloud, Dec 25.

GOVERNMENT Republic since 1970. Executive power is vested in the president, who is elected for a 5-year term.

SENEGAL

The jewel in the crown of France's African colonies, at independence in 1960 Senegal inherited the region's leading port and its best road network.

The first president, Léopold Senghor, is one of the few African heads of state to have handed over power voluntarily, giving way to his more youthful prime minister, Abdou Diouf, in 1981. Senegal is also one of Africa's few multiparty democracies although, of the 17 recognized parties, only the Parti Démocratique Sénégalais (PDS) offers any real challenge to the ruling Parti Socialiste (PS).

This political stability is in stark contrast to the vulnerability of the country's economy. Senegal is impoverished and drought-prone, suffering from a chronic trade deficit throughout the 1980s due to weak prices for groundnuts and phosphates. Dependence on foreign aid and investment has therefore increased during the period, boosting external debt and forcing rescheduling of repayments. However, tourism is on the increase, particularly in the southern Casamance region, bringing jobs but also the less beneficial aspects of an influx of foreign visitors. Fishing is another growing industry, although the territorial waters are plundered by foreign fleets.

OFFICIAL NAME Republic of Senegal.

CAPITAL CITY Dakar.

GEOGRAPHY Dakar is on the volcanic Cape Verde peninsula, the country's focus. To the northeast is a basin of savannah falling to the Senegal river. To the south is the enclave of The Gambia. *Area* 196,192 sq km (75,750 sq miles)

PEOPLE *Population* 7m. *Density* 35.5 per sq km.

RELIGION Muslim 91%, Christian 6%, Animist.

LANGUAGE French. Also local languages.

CURRENCY CFA franc (CFAFr).

PUBLIC HOLIDAYS Jan 1, Feb 1, Good Fri, Easter Mon, Apr 4, May 1, Ascension, Korité, Whit Mon, Tabaski, Assumption, Mouloud, Nov 1, Dec 25.

GOVERNMENT Republic since 1960. The government is responsible to the president (there is currently no prime minister) and is (constitutionally) controlled by the national assembly. Legislative and presidential elections are held every 5 years.

IMPORTS AND EXPORTS

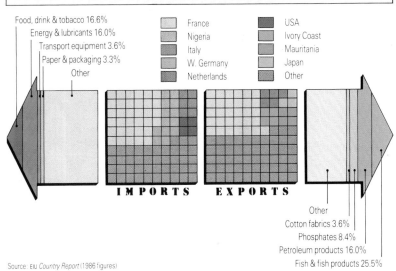

Food, drink & tobacco 16.6%
Energy & lubricants 16.0%
Transport equipment 3.6%
Paper & packaging 3.3%
Other

France
Nigeria
Italy
W. Germany
Netherlands

USA
Ivory Coast
Mauritania
Japan
Other

IMPORTS   EXPORTS

Other
Cotton fabrics 3.6%
Phosphates 8.4%
Petroleum products 16.0%
Fish & fish products 25.5%

Source: EIU *Country Report* (1986 figures)

BALANCE OF PAYMENTS

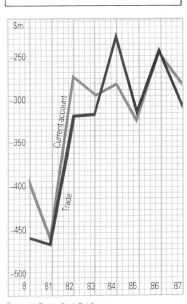

Source: EIU *Country Credit Risk Service*

CAPE VERDE

Twice as many Cape Verdeans live abroad as at home; remittances from the 600,000 expatriates go some way towards bridging the trade deficit. Drought is a fact of life: the most recent one lasted 16 years. The only hope of achieving food self-sufficiency lies in plans to tap ground-water resources. Maize and beans are the staple foods, fish the main export.

President Aristide Pereira, in power since independence in 1975, enjoys support at grass-roots level and is widely respected for his pragmatic handling of the economy and his government's probity and lack of corruption. Plans for unity with Guinea-Bissau, another former Portuguese colony, were abandoned after the coup there in 1980.

OFFICIAL NAME Republic of Cape Verde.
CAPITAL CITY Praia.
GEOGRAPHY An arid archipelago of 10 islands and 5 islets. *Area* 4,033 sq km (1,560 sq miles).
PEOPLE *Population* 330,000. *Density* 81 per sq km.
RELIGION RC 98%, Protestant 2%.
LANGUAGE Portuguese. Also Creole Portuguese.
EDUCATION Compulsory for ages 7–14.
CURRENCY Cape Verde escudo (CVEsc).
PUBLIC HOLIDAYS Jan 1, 20, Mar 8, May 1, Jun 1, Jul 5, Sep 12, Dec 25.
GOVERNMENT Republic since 1975. Executive power is held by a president, elected by the national people's assembly. The assembly is directly elected every 5 years.

GUINEA-BISSAU

Guinea-Bissau became independent in 1974, after 11 years of guerrilla war against the Portuguese. The conflict ravaged agriculture, halving output of groundnuts, the main export. The socialist economic policies of the first president, Luiz Cabral, proved overambitious; since his overthrow in 1980 by his prime minister, Joao Bernado Vieira, a series of stabilization programmes has been carried out with loans from the IMF and World Bank, sectors of the economy have been liberalized and prices for farmers raised.

Output of rice, the staple food, is being expanded; cash crops such as sugar, tropical fruits, cotton and tobacco are being developed. There are untapped reserves of bauxite and phosphates and enormous fishing potential. Oil has been found offshore but boundary disputes with Guinea and Senegal have delayed its exploitation.

The Vieira coup reflected the resentment of black Guineans of the Cape Verdean mestiço elite and, in particular, the discontent of the largest ethnic group, the Balante. The political situation is now reasonably stable but many of the Balante remain disaffected.

OFFICIAL NAME Republic of Guinea-Bissau.
CAPITAL CITY Bissau.
GEOGRAPHY As well as the mainland, with its deeply indented coast, there are many coastal islands and the Bissagos archipelago. The land behind the coastal plain is also fairly flat, much of it covered by meandering rivers edged by mangrove swamps. *Area* 36,125 sq km (13,950 sq miles).
PEOPLE *Population* 907,000. *Density* 25 per sq km.
RELIGION Muslim 30%, Christian 4%, Animist.
LANGUAGE Portuguese. Also Guinean Creole.
CURRENCY Guinea-Bissau peso (GBP).
PUBLIC HOLIDAYS Jan 1, 20, May 1, Korité, Tabaski, Aug 3, Sep 24, Nov 14, Dec 25.
GOVERNMENT Republic since 1974. The 1984 constitution provides for a 15-member council of state, headed by the president. The 150 members of the national people's assembly belong to the only legal political party, the Partido Africano da Independencia da Guiné e Cabo Verde.

GUINEA

This richly endowed country was ruled with an iron fist for a quarter of a century by Ahmed Sekou Touré. After quarrelling with France and being jettisoned into independence in 1958, Touré leaned towards the Eastern bloc and collectivism. Once a net food exporter, Guinea became an importer.

The military government that has ruled since Sekou Touré's death in 1984 has at times been divided by power struggles but President Lansana Conté remains committed to liberalizing the economy and encouraging foreign investment.

Agriculture is the base of the economy, though mining has been the principal source of government funds. Touré recognized this and allowed private investment in the mining industry. The three huge bauxite mines contributed 70% of export revenue in 1987; the Aredor diamond mine has also been a money-spinner since it started production in 1984. Mineral resources and climatic conditions that will support a variety of crops as well as livestock provide the potential for considerable growth.

OFFICIAL NAME Republic of Guinea.
CAPITAL CITY Conakry.
GEOGRAPHY A 280km (174-mile) coastline gives way to four very different regions: the west, with its marshes and snaking rivers; the middle region, with the mountainous Fouta Djallon massif and the source of the Niger; the forests of the southeast; and the savannah of the Haute Guinée region. *Area* 245,857 sq km (94,926 sq miles).
PEOPLE *Population* 6.3m. *Density* 25.6 per sq km.
RELIGION Muslim 69%, Christian 1%, Animist.
LANGUAGE French. Also local languages.
CURRENCY Guinean franc (GFr).
PUBLIC HOLIDAYS Jan 1, Easter Mon, May 1, Id al-Fitr, Aug 27, Sep 28, Oct 2, Mouloud, Nov 1, 22, Dec 25.
GOVERNMENT Military-dominated republic. In April 1984 the constitution was suspended and a second republic proclaimed.

SIERRA LEONE

President Joseph Momoh, hand-picked successor to Siaka Stevens, who retired in 1985, inherited a troubled economy: GDP had fallen substantially since 1980, inflation was high and the debt burden heavy. Smuggling of gold and diamonds was undermining export receipts, and agriculture had been in decline for decades. The government is pinning hopes on a "green revolution" to revive food production, and plans to mine underground kimberlite diamond pipes promise a boost to the balance of payments. Sierra Leone is also one of the few producers of rutile, titanium ore, now its largest export.

The capital was christened Freetown by former slaves returning from England. Their descendants have a sometimes tense relationship with the indigenous population, itself riven by tribal conflicts. Both groups resent the economic power of the Lebanese community. The president has responded to this feeling by discriminating in favour of Africans.

OFFICIAL NAME Republic of Sierra Leone.
CAPITAL CITY Freetown.
GEOGRAPHY Behind a highly indented coastline, the land rises in three distinct zones, culminating in the Loma Mountains. *Area* 71,740 sq km (27,700 sq miles).
PEOPLE *Population* 3.5m. *Density* 48.8 per sq km.
RELIGION Muslim 40%, Christian 9%, Animist.
LANGUAGE English. Also local languages.
CURRENCY Leone (Le).
PUBLIC HOLIDAYS Jan 1, Good Fri-Easter Mon, Aprl 27, Id al-Fitr, Id al-Adha, Mouloud, Dec 25, 26.
GOVERNMENT Republic since 1971. Independent since 1961. Executive power is vested in the president, elected for a 7-year term of office, and in a cabinet appointed by him. The only recognized political party is the ruling All People's Congress (APC).

IVORY COAST

Hailed in the 1970s as Africa's economic miracle, the Ivory Coast found its image as a haven of liberalism and foreign investment severely tarnished during the next decade. The world's largest exporter of cocoa, it has been hit by depressed prices, the disarray of international marketing agreements and its own quixotic efforts to shore up prices by refusing to sell its crop. Offshore oil reserves discovered in 1977 have failed to make the Ivory Coast another Nigeria and output does not even meet domestic requirements.

The economy is predominantly agricultural, with a remarkable range of cash crops. Coffee is the second largest export earner and large volumes of cotton, palm oil, pineapples, bananas and rubber are also exported. But sliding commodity prices coincided with a peak in servicing the $8.5bn foreign debt in the mid-1980s, forcing the government into a series of reschedulings and eventually suspension of debt repayments in 1987.

The country's leader during and after its struggle for independence has been President Félix Houphouët-Boigny – officially born in 1905 but said to be several years older – encouraging a climate of political stability with, for a one-party state, relatively little repression. Ethnic rivalries have tended to be overshadowed by even deeper resentment of foreigners, who form at least one-fifth of the population and a half of the work force.

OFFICIAL NAME Republic of the Ivory Coast.
CAPITAL CITY Abidjan.
GEOGRAPHY The land drops from mountain ranges in the north through savannah lands to the dense tropical forests of the south. The coastline running west from Fresco is marked by high cliffs and rocky inlets; the rest has sandy beaches and lagoons but no natural ports because of barrier reefs. Abidjan port was set up only in 1950. *Area* 322,463 sq km (124,504 sq miles).
PEOPLE *Population* 10.4m. *Density* 32.3 per sq km.
RELIGION Christian 32%, Muslim 24%, Animist.
LANGUAGE French. Also local languages.
CURRENCY CFA franc (CFAFr).
PUBLIC HOLIDAYS Jan 1, Good Fri, Easter Mon, May 1, Ascension, Id al-Fitr, Whit Mon, Id al-Adha, Assumption, Nov 1, Dec 7, 25.
GOVERNMENT Republic since 1960. The head of state and chief executive is the president, elected every 5 years, who appoints a council of ministers. The 175 members of the national assembly, also elected every 5 years, all belong to the only recognized political party, the Parti Démocratique de la Côte d'Ivoire.

IMPORTS AND EXPORTS

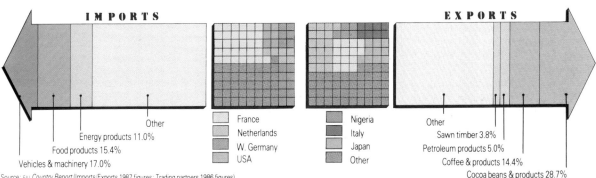

IMPORTS

Other
Energy products 11.0%
Food products 15.4%
Vehicles & machinery 17.0%

France
Netherlands
W. Germany
USA

Nigeria
Italy
Japan
Other

EXPORTS

Other
Sawn timber 3.8%
Petroleum products 5.0%
Coffee & products 14.4%
Cocoa beans & products 28.7%

Source: EIU *Country Report* (Imports/Exports 1987 figures; Trading partners 1986 figures)

GHANA

Ghana was the first British colony to become independent, in 1957. Its first president, Kwame Nkrumah, had a great reputation as a proponent of pan-African socialism and a leader of Third World opinion, but nationalization and a costly industrialization programme wreaked havoc on the economy. Penalized by an overvalued currency, the cocoa industry, key to the country's pre-independence prosperity, went into a steep decline.

A succession of short-lived, predominantly military governments followed Nkrumah's overthrow in 1966, giving way in 1981 to the charismatic leadership of Jerry Rawlings. Rawlings proved an unlikely but effective collaborator with the IMF, his popularity and integrity enabling him to impose tough economic medicine.

Unemployment and the removal of subsidies for essential goods have made life hard for Ghanaians but by the mid-1980s there were encouraging signs of recovery, with a return to real growth rates, a revival of the cocoa and timber industries and new investment in gold mining. With the introduction in 1988 of the World Bank's Pamscad programme, Ghana has also pioneered ways of softening the social impact of the economic austerity policies it has carried through with such determination.

OFFICIAL NAME Republic of Ghana.

CAPITAL CITY Accra.

GEOGRAPHY The Volta basin occupies a vast area in the east, with an artificial lake of 8,500 sq km (3,300 sq miles). It is bordered on the north and south by plateaus up to 600 metres (1,970 feet) above sea level. Much of the central Ashanti region is covered in forest which is now much reduced from its original huge acreage. The Akwapim-Togo mountain range runs from the eastern edge of the Volta basin down to the sea near Accra. The coastline is generally low with little natural shelter. Area 238,537 sq km (92,100 sq miles).

PEOPLE Population 13.4m. Density 56.2 per sq km.

RELIGION Christian 62%, Muslim 16%, Animist.

LANGUAGE English. Also local languages.

CURRENCY Cedi ($).

PUBLIC HOLIDAYS Jan 1, Mar 6, Good Fri-Easter Mon, Jul 1, Dec 24, 25, 31.

GOVERNMENT Military-dominated republic. The constitution was suspended when Flight Lieutenant Jerry Rawlings took power in December 1981. Since then, Rawlings has headed the Provisional National Defence Council (PNDC) which comprises both military and civilian members appointed by him.

IMPORTS AND EXPORTS

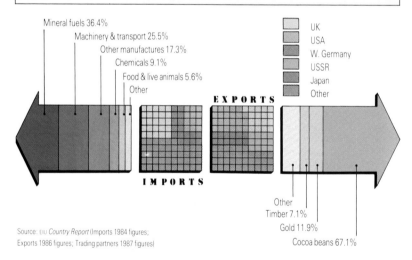

Mineral fuels 36.4%
Machinery & transport 25.5%
Other manufactures 17.3%
Chemicals 9.1%
Food & live animals 5.6%
Other

EXPORTS

UK
USA
W. Germany
USSR
Japan
Other

IMPORTS

Other
Timber 7.1%
Gold 11.9%
Cocoa beans 67.1%

Source: EIU *Country Report* (Imports 1984 figures; Exports 1986 figures; Trading partners 1987 figures)

BALANCE OF PAYMENTS

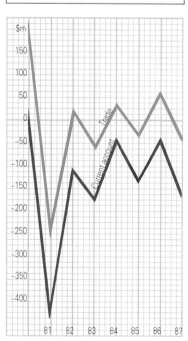

Source: EIU *Country Credit Risk Service*

ECONOMIC PROFILE

Once world's leading cocoa producer, now in fifth place. Diamonds, gold, timber and manganese also exported. Bauxite and offshore oil reserves await development. State-owned industries, developed in 1960s but stagnant in recent years, now being sold off to the private sector.

Growth Cocoa and timber exports recovering fast. New gold rush has begun – exports could bring in $1bn a year in 1990s. Growing foreign investment interest in fishing, tourism and agro-industry.

Problems Depressed cocoa prices. Falling production of diamonds and poor world prices. Loss of much export revenue through smuggling into neighbouring countries. Unemployment and high inflation testing government's commitment to austerity policies.

LIBERIA

Never colonized, Liberia was set up as a republic in 1847 by freed slaves returning from the USA. The US dollar is still the national currency. The slaves' descendants governed until 1980, when Master Sergeant Samuel Doe took power in a bloody coup in which President William Tolbert and many of his cabinet died. Doe's rule has been one of great political unrest. Between 1980 and 1988 there were nine reported coup plots, but General, now President, Doe has successfully exploited divisions among the opposition and thus prevented the formation of a cohesive alternative to his government.

The economy has been in rapid decline since Doe took over, partly because of mismanagement but also because of massive capital flight and generally poor world prices for the main exports, rubber and iron ore. The USA remains an important aid donor, and has used this fact to put pressure on the regime. This has not stamped out governmental corruption or the abuse of human rights but it was probably instrumental in the return to civilian rule. It also resulted, in 1987, in the USA taking more power over the government's spending decisions.

OFFICIAL NAME Republic of Liberia.
CAPITAL CITY Monrovia.
GEOGRAPHY Behind a 570km (354-mile) coastline and plain rise interior hills and generally low mountain ranges. There are some rain forests in the north. *Area* 111,369 sq km (43,000 sq miles).
PEOPLE *Population* 2.4m. *Density* 21 per sq km.
RELIGION Muslim 15%, Christian 10%, Animist.
LANGUAGE English. Also local languages.
CURRENCY US dollar ($).
PUBLIC HOLIDAYS Jan 1, Feb 11, Mar 12, Good Fri, Apr 11, 12, May 14, Jul 26, Aug 24, Nov 6, 12, 29, Dec 25.
GOVERNMENT Republic. On its return to civilian rule in 1986 the by then General Doe was sworn in as president and a bicameral parliament was set up comprising a senate and house of representatives. Doe's own National Democratic Party of Liberia (NDPL) holds the majority of seats.

BURKINA FASO

The former Upper Volta, renamed in 1984, has suffered five military coups since independence from France in August 1960. Income per head is among the lowest in the world, and dependence on Western aid has tempered the more radical left-wing policies of recent governments.

The state is heavily involved in the economy; it owns most of the manufacturing sector and the private business sector is heavily dependent on the goodwill of state officials and employees. Export earnings come chiefly from cotton and livestock (which was badly hit by the 1983–84 droughts) and more recently from gold; there are also reserves of manganese, zinc and silver. Poor infrastructure and low world prices have discouraged investment. Some 90% of the population depend on subsistence farming for survival, and large numbers of Burkinabé seek work in neighbouring countries.

OFFICIAL NAME Burkina Faso.
CAPITAL CITY Ouagadougou.
GEOGRAPHY The north is semi-desert, the south wooded savannah. Rivers generally drain south to the Volta or the Niger. *Area* 274,122 sq km (105,840 sq miles).
PEOPLE *Population* 7.9m. *Density* 29.1 per sq km.
RELIGION Muslim 43%, Christian 12%, Animist.
LANGUAGE French. Also local languages.
CURRENCY CFA franc (CFAFr).
PUBLIC HOLIDAYS Jan 1, 3, Easter Mon, May 1, Ascension, Id al-Fitr, Whit Mon, Id al-Adha, Aug 4, Assumption, Mouloud, Nov 1, Dec 25.
GOVERNMENT Military-dominated republic. The Front Populaire (FP) headed by Captain Blaise Compaoré seized power on October 15 1987.

TOGO

Ruled with an iron hand by President Gnassingbé Eyadéma, who took power in 1967, the former French colony of Togo enjoys relative stability and modest prosperity.

The economy remains heavily dependent on agriculture; phosphates are the main export, followed by cocoa and small amounts of cotton and coffee. Plunging phosphate prices in the mid-1970s created an economic crisis, particularly since the government was borrowing heavily to finance an ambitious industrialization programme, and Togo's foreign debt was rescheduled six times between 1979 and 1988.

The government has a pro-Western outlook and in the 1980s Togo set the pace for privatization in Africa, selling off steel and textile mills and an oil refinery to foreign and local investors. Relations with Ghana are strained; the two countries used to be one until partitioned in 1914 between France and the UK, splitting the main ethnic group, the Ewe, between two nations.

OFFICIAL NAME Togolese Republic.
CAPITAL CITY Lomé.
GEOGRAPHY Behind an indented coastline only 56km (35 miles) wide lies a tableland giving way to wooded mountains and then an infertile, dry plateau. *Area* 56,785 sq km (21,930 sq miles).
PEOPLE *Population* 2.9m. *Density* 52.5 per sq km.
RELIGION Christian 37%, Muslim 30%, Animist.
LANGUAGE French. Also local languages.
CURRENCY CFA franc (CFAFr).
PUBLIC HOLIDAYS Jan 1, 13, 24, Easter Mon, Apr 24, May 1, Ascension, Id al-Fitr, Whit Mon, Tabaski, Assumption, Sep 24, Nov 1, Dec 25.
GOVERNMENT Republic since 1960. Executive power lies with the president, elected every 7 years. The only recognized party puts up multiple candidates for the 77-member national assembly elected every 5 years.

BENIN

This Marxist state, the former French colony of Dahomey, sits uneasily between its market-oriented neighbours, Nigeria and Togo; but politics are tempered by economic pragmatism since legal and illicit trade with Nigeria accounts for at least 25% of GDP.

The economy is predominantly agricultural. Benin's major exports, palm oil and groundnuts, are produced in the south. The timber industry of the central forest belt is declining as reserves dwindle. The arid north survives on growing cotton and raising livestock.

Offshore oil reserves at Sémé, which came on stream in 1982, have failed to live up to expectations. Output peaked in 1985 but has since been dogged by low prices and an unhappy association with a Geneva-based conglomerate. With the deterioration of the economy, Benin's comparative political stability – its president, Mathieu Kerekou, has been in power since a military takeover in 1972 – has been shaken by student unrest and coup attempts.

OFFICIAL NAME People's Republic of Benin.
CAPITAL CITY Cotonou.
GEOGRAPHY Behind a 100km (62-mile) coastline and an area of lagoons lies fairly flat, fertile land rising to mountains in the northwest. *Area* 112,622 sq km (43,484 sq miles).
PEOPLE *Population* 4.2m. *Density* 37.3 per sq km.
RELIGON Christian 20%, Muslim 15%, Animist.
LANGUAGE French. Also local languages.
CURRENCY CFA franc (CFAFr).
PUBLIC HOLIDAYS Jan 1, 16, May 1, Id al-Fitr, Id al-Adha, Oct 26, Nov 30, Dec 25, 31.
GOVERNMENT Communist republic, independent since 1960. The president is elected every 5 years by the 196-member national revolutionary assembly, also elected every 5 years.

NIGERIA

Democratically elected governments have so far proved unequal to the task of managing this unruly nation of more than 100m people; civilians have ruled for a total of only 10 years since independence in 1960. The most recent civilian government, that of President Shehu Shagari, lasted four years before the military took power again in 1983. The idealistic and rigid General Muhammadu Buhari was in turn replaced in a bloodless coup two years later by the more genial and pragmatic General Ibrahim Babangida.

Babangida's task was made more complex by the collapse of oil prices in early 1986. Oil earnings, which accounted for over 97% of export revenue, were halved to $6.1bn in just one year.

Oil production started in the late 1950s, rising steadily to a peak of 2.4m barrels a day at the start of the 1980s. Agriculture was neglected and construction boomed as the oil money flowed in. Cocoa exports were halved, cotton and groundnut exports all but ceased and the public developed a taste for new imported foods. Foreign contractors lined up to build the oil refineries, steel works and vehicle assembly lines that were to ensure Nigeria's industrial future.

OFFICIAL NAME Federal Republic of Nigeria.
CAPITAL CITY Abuja.
GEOGRAPHY The coastline, much of it bordered by mangrove swamp, is intersected by numerous creeks; the southeast coast, dominated by the Niger river delta, is the location of the offshore oil reserves. Inland lies an area of tropical rain forest and bush. Savannah and woodland cover much of the central upland area; the Jos plateau is the watershed of hundreds of streams and small rivers flowing as far as Lake Chad and the Niger and Benue rivers. The far north, bordering the Sahara, is mainly savannah. Spectacular highlands line the eastern border with Cameroon. *Highest point* Vogel peak 2,040 metres (6,690 feet). *Area* 923,768 sq km (356,670 sq miles).
PEOPLE *Population* 100m. *Density* 110.3 per sq km.
RELIGION Christian 50%, Muslim 45%, Animist.
LANGUAGE English. Also local languages.
CURRENCY Naira.
PUBLIC HOLIDAYS Jan 1, Good Fri-Easter Mon, Id al-Fitr, Id al-Adha, Oct 1, Mouloud, Dec 25, 26.
GOVERNMENT Federal republic, independent since 1960. The civilian constitution of the Second Republic, with a US-style president, senate and house of representatives, was suspended when the military took over on December 31 1983.

GDP BY ORIGIN

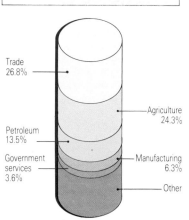

Trade 26.8%
Petroleum 13.5%
Government services 3.6%
Agriculture 24.3%
Manufacturing 6.3%
Other

COMPONENTS OF GDP

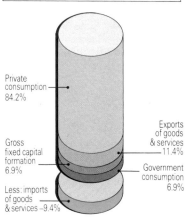

Private consumption 84.2%
Gross fixed capital formation 6.9%
Less: imports of goods & services –9.4%
Exports of goods & services 11.4%
Government consumption 6.9%

Source: EIU *Country Report* (GDP by origin 1987 figures; Components of GDP 1986 figures)

IMPORTS AND EXPORTS

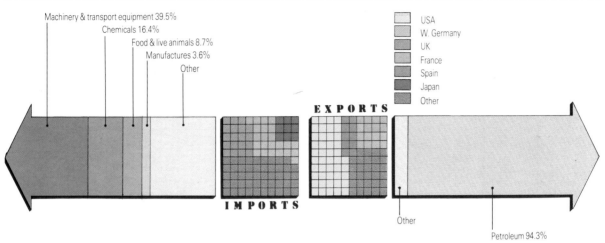

Machinery & transport equipment 39.5%
Chemicals 16.4%
Food & live animals 8.7%
Manufactures 3.6%
Other

USA
W. Germany
UK
France
Spain
Japan
Other

EXPORTS

IMPORTS

Other

Petroleum 94.3%

Source: EIU *Country Report* (1987 figures)

ECONOMIC PROFILE

An agricultural economy, exporting cocoa, groundnuts and cotton, transformed by oil exports. Oil financed development of new industries – refining, petrochemicals, steel, cement, vehicles, agricultural processing – but work on many halted by payments problems.

Growth Agricultural and other nonoil

exports starting to revive. Government pressing ahead with petrochemicals and LNG schemes.

Problems Oil earnings limited by Opec quotas and poor price prospects. Industry starved of spares and inputs. Tortuous debt rescheduling negotiations have delayed new lending and investment.

By the mid-1980s Nigeria was saddled with foreign debt of $26bn with few of its investments in industry or infrastructure starting to pay their way. The Babangida government lost little time in introducing drastic policy changes. Inessential and many essential imports were banned, agricultural marketing was put into private hands, a foreign exchange auction system was introduced, resulting in a rapid devaluation of the overvalued naira, and an extensive programme of privatization was announced. The government's economic measures were generally in accordance with IMF recommendations although negotiations about conditional fund loans had broken down. The relationship between Nigeria and its creditors has been a rocky one, but many foreign aid donors have been sympathetic to its aims and large loans from bodies like the World Bank have helped ease the path to reform.

The new policies soon started to show results. Cash-crop exports revived, as did production of traditional food crops. Industry bore the brunt of recession and the constraints on imports, and was working at barely 30% of capacity in 1988. For the Nigerian in the street, economic adjustment has meant high unemployment, rising inflation and a general decline in living standards.

With its economic reforms under way, the Babangida government is talking of a return to civilian rule in 1992. To this end, it has set out a complex timetable of regional and legislative elections, from which all former politicians have been excluded.

BALANCE OF PAYMENTS

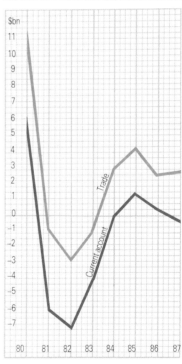

Source: EIU *Country Credit Risk Service*

CENTRAL AFRICA

The franc zone and CEEAC

Six Central African countries are members of the franc zone. All share a central bank and belong to an economic and monetary union, Union Douanière et Economique de l'Afrique Centrale (UDEAC).

In 1983, a new organization was set up, the Communauté Economique des Etats de l'Afrique Centrale (CEEAC), with the aim of creating a common market including all Central African countries. CEEAC's members are the six UDEAC states plus Zaire, Rwanda, Burundi and São Tomé and Principe. Members of the franc zone and UDEAC are Cameroon, Central African Republic, Chad, Congo, Gabon and Equatorial Guinea. CEEAC's members are UDEAC plus Zaire, Rwanda, Burundi, São Tomé and Principe.

The Congo (Zaire)

The second longest river in Africa at 4,670km (2,910 miles), the Congo or Zaire drains the world's second largest river basin. Rising in southeast Zaire, the river crosses the Equator twice before entering the Atlantic. It flows through Zaire for much of its length and forms part of the country's border with Congo; the two capitals, Kinshasa and Brazzaville, face each other on opposite banks.

Ethnic and linguistic groups

Zaireans speak more then 250 different languages, but four predominate: Lingala, Kikongo, Tshiluba and Swahili. There are about a dozen major ethnic groups. Cameroon is similarly diverse: Bantu-speaking peoples dominate in the south, Sudanic and Afroasiatic languages are spoken in the north. The country's colonial history also left it with two official languages: French and English. The largest ethnic group in Gabon and mainland Equatorial Guinea is the Fang.

Tropic of Cancer

GMT +1
GMT +2

London 9½ hours

CHAD

L. Chad

● N'Djamena

New York 17½ hours

CENTRAL AFRICAN REPUBLIC

● CAMEROON

● Yaoundé ● Bangui

Malabo ●

Congo

SAO TOME
AND PRINCIPE ● EQUATORIAL
GUINEA ● Libreville Equator

São Tomé ●

GABON

CONGO
Brazzaville
■ Kinshasa ZAIRE

GMT +1
GMT +2

■ More than 1 million
● 250,000 – 1 million
● 100,000 – 250,000

⊠ Major oilfields
Rain forest

Climate

Most of the region has an equatorial climate, with rain all year and temperatures averaging 28–31°C (82–88°F). Parts of Zaire and Cameroon have a more moderate climate; northern Cameroon is semi-arid. A small area on Mount Cameroon is one of the three wettest places in the world, receiving more than 10,000mm (394ins) of rainfall a year.

Education

Congo and Gabon provide compulsory education from the age of 6 to 16. Both highly urbanized countries, they have been more successful in expanding educational opportunities than vast and diverse Zaire, which transferred responsibility for education to the state from the Roman Catholic church in 1972. In the recent climate of economic austerity there have been hints that this decision might be reversed.

CHAD

Chad has been torn apart by civil war almost continuously since independence in 1960, with violence on a scale that has few parallels in Africa. The growing involvement of Muammar Qaddafi, his eyes on Chadian territory, and the virtual annexation in 1983 of one-third of the country's territory by Libya, at least gave the rival factions an incentive to unite against outside interference. President Hissène Habré's victory in the desert war in 1987, backed by French and US military aid, seemed to curb Libyan expansionism for the time being and offer the chance for internal reconciliation, even though Libya still occupies the mineral-rich Aozou strip in the north.

Average annual income is one of the lowest in Africa and the economy is overwhelmingly dependent on agriculture. Cotton, the main export, was neglected during the war years. Oil reserves in the Lake Chad basin could provide a future lifeline.

OFFICIAL NAME Republic of Chad.
CAPITAL CITY N'Djamena.
GEOGRAPHY Landlocked, it is semi-desert in the north, giving way to savannah in the centre. Most people live in the southwest around the Lake Chad basin. *Area* 1,284,000 sq km (496,000 sq miles).
PEOPLE *Population* 5.2m. *Density* 4 per sq km.
RELIGION Muslim 44%, Christian 33%, Animist.
LANGUAGE French. Also Arabic and local languages.
CURRENCY CFA franc (CFAFr).
PUBLIC HOLIDAYS Jan 1, Easter Mon, Id al-Fitr, Whit Mon, May 1, 25, Id al-Adha, Aug 11, 15, Mouloud, Nov 1, 28, Dec 25.
GOVERNMENT Republic since 1960. The Union Nationale pour l'Indépendance et la Révolution is the sole official party. The chairman of its 14-member executive bureau is president.

CAMEROON

Cameroon's striking diversity extends from its ethnic groupings (over 200 in all), its mixed colonial heritage from the Germans, French and British and its varied climate and scenery to its range of economic resources and activities.

Agriculture is the cornerstone of the economy. Cotton is grown in the densely populated Muslim north; in the anglophone southwest, the plantations of the Cameroon Development Corporation, the country's largest employer, produce rubber, palm oil, tea, bananas and peppers; cocoa and coffee are the major cash crops of the west and centre.

Cameroon is also an oil producer, but oil production passed its peak in the mid-1980s and is scheduled to stop in the 1990s. Industrial development has been patchy and some of the few major projects undertaken, such as the Cellucam pulp and paper mill which went into liquidation in 1986, have not been successful.

Cameroon is officially bilingual but the francophone domination of government and the public sector continues to rankle with the anglophone minority. After more than two decades of autocratic rule, President Ahmadou Ahidjo stepped down in favour of his prime minister, Paul Biya, in 1982. Some moves towards greater democracy have resulted but Biya's looser grip on government has allowed tribal tensions to surface and corruption to spread.

OFFICIAL NAME Republic of Cameroon.
CAPITAL CITY Yaoundé.
GEOGRAPHY The flat, arid northern provinces are sub-Sahelian and frequently suffer from drought. The high area in the west around Mt Cameroon, with its volcanic soils, supports a wide range of crops. The south is generally flat and covered in dense forest. *Highest point* Mt Cameroon 4,070 metres (13,350 feet). *Area* 475,442 sq km (183,570 sq miles).
PEOPLE *Population* 10.8m. *Density* 22.7 per sq km.
RELIGION Christian 50%, Muslim 20%, Animist.
LANGUAGE French. Also English and local languages.
CURRENCY CFA franc (CFAFr).
PUBLIC HOLIDAYS Jan 1, Feb 11, Good Fri, Easter Mon, May 1, Ascension, Djoulde Soumae, May 20, Sheep festival, Dec 25.
GOVERNMENT Republic since 1960. The president, elected every 5 years, is head of state and chief executive. Legislative power is constitutionally vested in the 180-member national assembly, also elected every 5 years. The Cameroon People's Democratic Movement (CPDM) is the only official political party.

IMPORTS AND EXPORTS

IMPORTS

Other
Chemical products 13.4%
Transport equipment 14.1%
Agricultural & food products 16.2%
Machinery & electrical equipment 21.9%

France
USA
W. Germany
Netherlands
Japan
Other

EXPORTS

Other
Coffee 10.1%
Cocoa 14.1%
Crude oil 51.8%

Source: EIU *Country Report* (Imports 1986 figures; Exports 1987 figures; Trading partners 1987 figures)

SAO TOME & PRINCIPE

After a particularly brutal colonization by Portugal, which set up its first colony in 1486 on what were then uninhabited islands, São Tomé and Príncipe was abruptly given independence in 1975. The large cocoa plantations, on which its wealth was based, rapidly deteriorated until a marked about-turn in the government's left-wing policies in the mid-1980s. The cocoa industry is being revived but attempts are also being made to diversify, with exports of palm oil, cinnamon, pepper, coffee and fish, and to develop a tourist industry.

The government has established security ties with Cuba and Angola, but has also sought economic assistance from the West; relations with Portugal, its main source of imports, are particularly good, and France is a major aid donor. The country's president since independence, Manuel Pinto da Costa, has promised economic liberalization and democratization.

OFFICIAL NAME Democratic Republic of São Tomé and Príncipe.
CAPITAL CITY São Tomé.
GEOGRAPHY Both islands are volcanic. *Area* 964 sq km (370 sq miles).
PEOPLE *Population* 110,000. *Density* 116 per sq km.
RELIGION Christian 97% (RC 92%).
LANGUAGE Portuguese. Also local languages.
CURRENCY Dobra (Db).
PUBLIC HOLIDAYS Jan 1, Good Fri, Easter Mon, May 1, Ascension, Whit Mon, Jun 10, Assumption, Oct 5, Nov 1, Dec 1, 25.
GOVERNMENT Republic since 1975. The only party is the Movimento de Libertação de São Tomé e Príncipe. It chooses the single candidate for the presidency.

GABON

Gabon has the highest GDP per head in black Africa and also the continent's lowest birthrate. Its wealth is based on oil, which came on stream in 1957. Output has passed its peak, but new discoveries are still being made. Gabon also has about one-quarter of the world's manganese reserves, as well as uranium and iron ore. Less than 1% of the land area is cultivated and most food is imported.

Oil helped finance ambitious construction projects, notably the 700km (440-mile) Transgabon railway, completed in 1987, which opened up areas of previously impenetrable forest. But falling oil prices and heavy debt servicing brought a new climate of austerity in the late 1980s.

OFFICIAL NAME Gabonese Republic.
CAPITAL CITY Libreville.
GEOGRAPHY An 800km (500-mile) coastline is marked by deep estuaries in the north, giving way to sandy lagoons in the south. There are three quite separate small mountain chains, the Monts du Cristal in the north, Monts de Chaillu in the southeast and Monts de Mayombe in the south; but the overwhelming features are the thick forest, which covers 85% of land area, and an extensive network of rivers and swamps. *Area* 267,667 sq km (103,347 sq miles).
PEOPLE *Population* 1.2m. *Density* 4 per sq km.
RELIGION Christian 95% (RC 64%), Muslim 1%, Animist.
LANGUAGE French. Also local languages.
CURRENCY CFA franc (CFAFr).
PUBLIC HOLIDAYS Jan 1, Mar 12, Easter Mon, May 1, Id al-Fitr, Whit Mon, Id al-Adha, Aug 17, Mouloud, Nov 1, Dec 25.
GOVERNMENT Republic since 1960. Executive power is vested in the president, who is elected for a 7-year term and may be re-elected. The national assembly is elected every 5 years. A formal one-party state was created in 1968 when the Parti Démocratique Gabonais (PDG) was established.

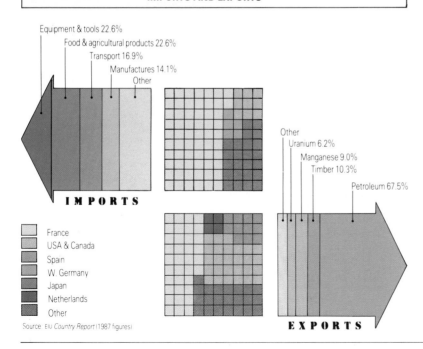

IMPORTS AND EXPORTS

Equipment & tools 22.6%
Food & agricultural products 22.6%
Transport 16.9%
Manufactures 14.1%
Other

IMPORTS

Other
Uranium 6.2%
Manganese 9.0%
Timber 10.3%
Petroleum 67.5%

France
USA & Canada
Spain
W. Germany
Japan
Netherlands
Other

EXPORTS

Source EIU *Country Report* (1987 figures)

CENTRAL AFRICAN REPUBLIC

The lavish ceremony at which former French army sergeant Jean-Bedel Bokassa crowned himself emperor in December 1976 put the country now known as the Central African Republic (formerly Empire) briefly into the international headlines. Bokassa's extravagance and brutality proved too much for France, the former colonial power, which intervened two years later to remove him.

Bokassa's successor, David Dacko, was the man Bokassa had overthrown in 1965 and who had been president of the country since independence. But Dacko himself was replaced in a military takeover in 1981 by General André Kolingba, who has worked hard to stabilize the economy. Diamonds, mainly of gem quality, are the main export. Small quantities of gold are mined but development of uranium deposits must await higher world prices. Cotton, coffee and timber are exported but the country's landlocked position means transport costs are high. Attempts are being made to crack down on smuggling and customs fraud which deny the government much-needed revenue.

OFFICIAL NAME Central African Republic.
CAPITAL CITY Bangui.
GEOGRAPHY Landlocked. Most is a plateau, covered by savannah in the south. The north is part of the Sahara desert. *Area* 622,984 sq km (240,540 sq miles).
PEOPLE *Population* 2.9m. *Density* 5 per sq km.
RELIGION Christian 84%, Muslim 3%, Animist.
LANGUAGE French. Also Sango.
CURRENCY CFA franc (CFAFr).
PUBLIC HOLIDAYS Jan 1, Easter Mon, Mar 29, May 1, Ascension, Whit Mon, Jun 30, Aug 13, Assumption, Nov 1, Dec 25.
GOVERNMENT Independent republic since 1960. The Rassemblement Démocratique Centrafricain (RDC) is the only official party. A 52-seat national assembly was elected in July 1987. The president is directly elected for 6 years as head of state and chief executive.

EQUATORIAL GUINEA

This former Spanish colony was once able to boast the highest income per head in Africa, thanks to the best cocoa in the world, grown on the volcanic soils of the island of Fernando Póo (now Bioko). But 11 years of bloody dictatorship by Macías Nguema left the economy in ruins.

Since the dictator's nephew, Teodoro Obiang Nguema, assumed power in 1979, there has been a very gradual improvement, with rehabilitation of the cocoa plantations. Entry into the franc zone in 1985 brought the advantage of a convertible currency and commercial links with France now rival those with Spain.

Persistent rumours of a South African military presence have alarmed nearby Nigeria, and relatively few of those who fled the country during the Nguema regime have returned. An estimated 100,000 Equatorial Guineans live outside the country and labour shortages are a problem, particularly on the cocoa plantations.

OFFICIAL NAME Republic of Equatorial Guinea.
CAPITAL CITY Malabo.
GEOGRAPHY The capital is on Bioko, a volcanic island off the Cameroon coast. The other principal area is a mainland territory, Río Muni, consisting of a narrow coastal plain and upland plateau. *Area* 28,051 sq km (10,830 sq miles).
PEOPLE *Population* 370,000. *Density* 13.3 per sq km.
RELIGION RC 89%, Muslim 0.5%, Animist.
LANGUAGE Spanish. Also local languages.
CURRENCY CFA franc (CFAFr).
PUBLIC HOLIDAYS Jan 1, Mar 5, Good Fri-Easter Mon, May 1, 25, Dec 10, 25.
GOVERNMENT Republic since 1968. The sole official political party is the Partido Democrático de Guinea Ecuatorial. The country has embarked on a gradual transition to civilian government.

CONGO

In spite of its Marxist-Leninist ideology, the Congolese government has turned to Western interests for help in exploiting its offshore oil fields and to the IMF for aid for structural adjustment.

The 1986 oil price slump imposed a severe toll on development plans, particularly as Congo has a high debt service burden for its size. But oil firms have still found it worthwhile to bring new fields on stream and the country is black Africa's fifth largest producer. Timber is the only other significant export, and its potential is hampered by inadequate transport facilities.

Because of the combined effects of oil wealth, Brazzaville's former role as the capital of French Equatorial Africa, and the huge areas of impenetrable forest, more than half the population live in urban areas, an exceptionally high proportion for Africa. Only 1.5% of the people work on the land, and Congo relies heavily on food imports.

OFFICIAL NAME People's Republic of the Congo.
CAPITAL CITY Brazzaville.
GEOGRAPHY Behind the narrow coastal plain lies very thick rain forest intersected by numerous river gorges. The Niari valley in the east has good fertile farming soil. *Area* 342,000 sq km (132,000 sq miles).
PEOPLE *Population* 1.9m. *Density* 5.6 per sq km.
RELIGION Christian 75%, Muslim 3%, Animist.
LANGUAGE French. Also local languages.
CURRENCY CFA franc (CFAFr).
PUBLIC HOLIDAYS Jan 1, Good Fri, Easter Mon, May 1, Aug 15, Dec 25.
GOVERNMENT Socialist republic, independent since 1960. The Parti Congolais du Travail (PCT) is the only officially recognized party. Its congress elects a central committee chairman who is head of the state and chief executive.

ZAIRE

Zaire is Africa's third largest country, embracing an enormous range of climate and terrain. The capital Kinshasa is as far from the second city, Lubumbashi, as Paris is from Moscow. The country's size creates huge difficulties in developing the resources of this potential economic giant. Its most immediate problem is lack of basic infrastructure, particularly transport.

This lack of communications is one factor that has helped President Mobutu Sese Seko keep his iron grip on the country since 1965. During his presidency, erratic economic policies – with alternating bouts of nationalization and privatization – and rampant corruption have combined with plummeting commodity prices to undermine Zaire's inherent strengths.

These strengths include an exceptionally rich and varied mineral wealth. Copper accounts for 35–40% of export revenue, but has to be transported thousands of kilometres to ports on the Atlantic or Indian Ocean. Shaba, centre of copper and cobalt mining, also produces strategic minerals such as cadmium, wolframite and niobium. Diamond output is mainly of industrial quality, plus the occasional large gem; huge volumes are smuggled out to neighbouring countries. Oil is produced from fields at the mouth of the Zaire river; but the crude is particularly heavy and, as there is no local capacity to refine it, petroleum products are imported.

Several big development projects were started in the days of high commodity prices in the 1970s. Some, like the Maluku steel works, have virtually been abandoned; others, like the massive Inga hydroelectric scheme, which transports power generated at the mouth of the Zaire 1,725km (1,080 miles) to the mining town of Kolwezi, have not yet begun to operate at full strength. The contribution of these "great works" has been to Zaire's foreign debt rather than to its development as a regional industrial power. The government has therefore modified its ambitions in the 1980s. It now leaves responsibility for industrial growth to the private sector and has relaxed controls on direct foreign investment. The new policy promises less superficially impressive but more effective development.

OFFICIAL NAME Republic of Zaire.

CAPITAL CITY Kinshasa.

GEOGRAPHY The country is formed around the Zaire (Congo) river. At its outlet Zaire has a short Atlantic coastline. Up river, the natural vegetation is tropical rain forest. To the south, the land rises to the savannah of Shaba province. The vast forest areas are sparsely populated but, with 3m inhabitants, the capital is one of the largest on the continent. *Highest point* Ruwenzori 5,000 metres (16,400 feet). *Area* 2,344,885 sq km (905,370 sq miles).

PEOPLE *Population* 34.7m. *Density* 14.8 per sq km.

RELIGION Christian 90%, Muslim 1%, Animist.

LANGUAGE French. Also local languages.

CURRENCY Zaire (Z).

PUBLIC HOLIDAYS Jan 1, 4, May 1, 20, Jun 24, 30, Aug 1, Oct 14, 27, Nov 17, 24, Dec 25.

GOVERNMENT Republic since 1960. The head of state and chief executive is the president, elected every 7 years, who appoints the executive council whose members are known as state commissioners. The legislative council has one chamber and is elected every 5 years. Since May 1967, the Mouvement Populaire de la Révolution (MPR) has been the only officially recognized political party. The MPR's central committee wields considerable political power.

IMPORTS AND EXPORTS

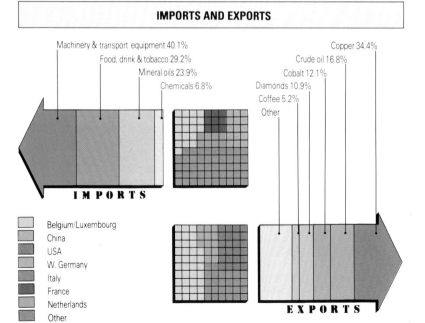

Machinery & transport equipment 40.1%
Food, drink & tobacco 29.2%
Mineral oils 23.9%
Chemicals 6.8%

Copper 34.4%
Crude oil 16.8%
Cobalt 12.1%
Diamonds 10.9%
Coffee 5.2%
Other

IMPORTS

Belgium/Luxembourg
China
USA
W. Germany
Italy
France
Netherlands
Other

EXPORTS

Source: EIU *Country Report* (Imports 1984 figures; Exports 1985 figures; Trading partners 1986 figures)

BALANCE OF PAYMENTS

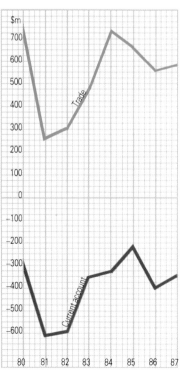

Source: EIU *Country Credit Risk Service*

EAST AFRICA

Climate

Eastern coastal areas have a tropical climate, with two rainy seasons and temperatures averaging 22–32°C (72–90°F); annual rainfall averages 1,200mm (47ins). The Kenyan and Ethiopian highlands are cooler. Lake Victoria, Africa's largest lake, has a strong influence on the climate of the countries on its shores – Uganda, Rwanda, Burundi and parts of Tanzania – bringing heavy rainfall in adjoining areas. Northern Sudan has a desert climate with rainfall of only 160mm (6ins) a year.

Sudanese refugees

Sudan has suffered two civil wars in its independent history. The first lasted 17 years; the second began in 1983. Both have their origins in the African south's fear of domination by the Arab north; an attempt to impose Islamic law is the issue at the root of the current conflict, in which it is estimated around half a million people have died. The war has caused massive suffering and destruction of traditional ways of life in an area prone to drought and famine; at least 350,000 have sought refuge in neighbouring Ethiopia.

Ethnic and linguistic groups

The ethnic groups of East Africa are as diverse as anywhere on the continent. Ethiopia, an empire established by conquest in the 19th century, has 76 nationalities and 286 languages. The Oromo is the largest ethnic group followed by Amhara and Tigrinya speakers. About 40% of Sudan's people are of Arab origin, but there are 19 major ethnic groups. Conflict between the Arab north and African south has dominated Sudan's independent history. A similar divide in Uganda, between the Bantu peoples of the south and the Nilotic groups in the north, has also been a source of ethnic tension. Swahili, originally the language of the East African coast, has become the *lingua franca* of much of the region, spoken as a first or second language by many of the people of Kenya and Tanzania and even parts of eastern Zaire.

Education

Kenya and Tanzania have led the way in expanding education since independence. Primary education in Kenya is free and, although it is non-compulsory, enrolment is virtually universal. Secondary education has also expanded fast, to account for about 20% of the age group. Only a tiny proportion go on to higher education, however. Tanzania, with free and compulsory education from 7 to 14, has achieved enrolment and literacy rates above the African average. Elsewhere the results are less impressive although great strides have been made. Often, too, earlier achievements are threatened by growing economic difficulties and the problems of bringing education to scattered communities in rural areas.

Ethiopian refugees

Ethiopia annexed Eritrea, a former Italian colony on the Red Sea coast, in 1962; Eritrean separatist groups have been fighting for independence ever since. The separatist movement in Tigray, the province to the south of Eritrea, has also been a force to be reckoned with since the late 1970s. Although government forces have held on to the main towns, the rebels have established control over large areas of northern Ethiopia and are often the main channels for relief supplies to famine-hit areas. Around three-quarters of a million refugees have crossed the border into Sudan; thousands more are in Djibouti.

Somali refugees

Ethiopia and Somalia went to war over the disputed Ogaden region in 1977–78; hundreds of thousands of refugees fled to Somalia after the Ethiopian victory. More recently, the movement has been in the opposite direction, as refugees from northern Somalia fled fierce fighting during 1988 between government and rebel forces.

Key:
- More than 1 million
- 250,000 – 1 million
- 100,000 – 250,000
- Major railways
- Refugee concentration

SUDAN

Africa's largest country, Sudan is divided on ethnic, religious and ideological grounds. The civil war has lasted since 1982, at enormous cost to the people of the region, but little will exists on either side to find a settlement; the previous north–south conflict lasted 17 years. The politicians of the north are held together only by ingenious coalitions that make decisive government impossible. Islamic pressure for the reintroduction of Sharia law is opposed by the non-Muslim south, progressives and the left. Prime Minister Sadiq el-Mahdi does an uneasy balancing act between the various factions.

The war, devastating drought and floods have halted expansion. Relief agencies are unable to get supplies through to the starving in the south. In the past, Sudan was called the "breadbasket of Africa," but large-scale mechanized projects, like the Gezira scheme, have failed to realize agricultural potential. Cotton and groundnut exports have been declining for two decades; sugar output has expanded, but most is consumed domestically. The war has also halted development of large oil reserves. Gold mining is being developed on a small scale, but has little impact on the huge payments deficits.

Sudan's debt is the second highest in Africa and the government has long stopped even attempting to service it, which would cost at least 300% of annual export earnings.

OFFICIAL NAME Republic of Sudan.
CAPITAL CITY Khartoum.
GEOGRAPHY Most of Sudan is a plateau through which winds the Upper Nile, with highland to the east, west and south. In the east the Nubian uplands lie between the plateau and the Red Sea. In the west is the barren Darfur Massif. Much of the Nile valley is cultivable, and it is especially fertile around Khartoum and Omdurman. The southern plateau is swampy. *Area* 2,505,800 sq km (967,500 sq miles).
PEOPLE *Population* 21.6m. *Density* 9 per sq km.
RELIGION Muslim 73%, Christian 9%, Animist.
LANGUAGE Arabic. Also local languages.
CURRENCY Sudanese pound (S£).
PUBLIC HOLIDAYS Jan 1, Mar 3, Apr 6, Id al-Fitr, May 1, Jul 1, Id al-Adha, Muharram, Mouloud, Dec 25.
GOVERNMENT Republic since 1956. A supreme council, consisting of the president and 5 others, functions as head of state. There is only one recognized party, the Sudanese Socialist Union. The executive prime minister is drawn from the 301-seat legislative national assembly.

IMPORTS AND EXPORTS

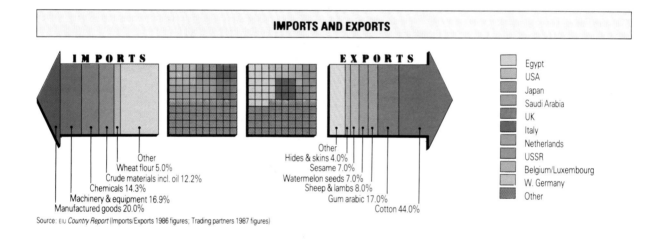

Other
Wheat flour 5.0%
Crude materials incl. oil 12.2%
Chemicals 14.3%
Machinery & equipment 16.9%
Manufactured goods 20.0%

Other
Hides & skins 4.0%
Sesame 7.0%
Watermelon seeds 7.0%
Sheep & lambs 8.0%
Gum arabic 17.0%
Cotton 44.0%

Egypt
USA
Japan
Saudi Arabia
UK
Italy
Netherlands
USSR
Belgium/Luxembourg
W. Germany
Other

Source: EIU *Country Report* (Imports/Exports 1986 figures; Trading partners 1987 figures)

DJIBOUTI

A hot, semi-desert enclave squeezed between powerful neighbours Ethiopia and Somalia, Djibouti has survived through support from France and clever diplomacy by the president, Hassan Gouled Aptidon.

The economy depends on the port, spending by the French garrison and entrepôt trade for the railway to Addis Ababa. The Ogaden war of 1977-78 between Ethiopia and Somalia nearly bankrupted Djibouti by disabling the railway for a year. There are few natural resources and the land is too poor for cultivation; livestock rearing is the main agricultural activity. Over half the population live in Djibouti city. Society has been remarkably stable since independence, with the Issa (Somali) majority dominating the government and the minority Afars forming the opposition.

OFFICIAL NAME Republic of Djibouti.
CAPITAL CITY Djibouti.
GEOGRAPHY Mountainous in the north, with a low plateau in the south. *Area* 22,000 sq km (8,500 sq miles).
PEOPLE *Population* 430,000. *Density* 20 per sq km.
RELIGION Muslim 94%, Christian 6%.
LANGUAGE French. Also Arabic.
CURRENCY Djibouti franc (DjFr).
PUBLIC HOLIDAYS Jan 1, May 1, Id al-Fitr, Jun 27, Id al-Adha, Muharram, Mouloud, Dec 25.
GOVERNMENT Republic since 1977. A one-party state, its president is elected for a 5-year term as are the 65 members of the chamber of deputies, who elect the prime minister.

ETHIOPIA

Ethiopia has exchanged centralized, bureaucratic despotism under Emperor Haile Selassie for the same under President Mengistu Haile Mariam. The ideology has changed from feudal to neo-communist, but the problems of under-development and drought are unresolved. The Eritreans, Tigreans, Oromos and Ogadenis remain dissatisfied with Amhara rule; the state diverts half of its resources to pursuing the seemingly endless Eritrean and Tigrean wars.

Designated by the World Bank as among the poorest countries in the world, Ethiopia remains vulnerable to famine. Collectivist agriculture has failed to cope with deforestation, overgrazing and regular drought. The government's response has been to resettle inhabitants of the chronic drought areas. Since these northern provinces are also those most subject to insurgency, Addis Ababa's concerns are ambiguous.

OFFICIAL NAME People's Democratic Republic of Ethiopia.
CAPITAL CITY Addis Ababa.
GEOGRAPHY Much of the country is mountainous and forested. An arid coastal plain flanks the Red Sea. *Area* 1,221,900 sq km (471,800 sq miles).
PEOPLE *Population* 43.5m. *Density* 35 per sq km.
RELIGION Ethiopian Orthodox (Coptic) 49%, Muslim 31%, Animist.
LANGUAGE Amharic. Also local languages.
CURRENCY Birr (Br).
PUBLIC HOLIDAYS Jan 7, 19, Mar 2, Apr 6, Coptic Palm Sun, Coptic Easter Sun, May 1, Id al-Fitr, Id al-Adha, Sep 11, 12, 27, Mouloud.
GOVERNMENT Military-dominated socialist republic. All candidates for the 835-seat national assembly must be members of the Workers' Party of Ethiopia.

SOMALIA

One of Africa's poorest countries, Somalia has been ravaged by drought, floods and a long-running conflict with Ethiopia over the disputed Ogaden region. It has few natural assets: livestock and bananas are the only exports. After allegations of human rights abuses and Somalia's break with the IMF foreign aid has dried up, exacerbating a serious foreign exchange shortage. President Muhammad Siyad Barre seized power in 1969 and imposed a Marxist military dictatorship. Soviet advisers were expelled in 1977; since then, the USA has been a major aid donor, and has a military base at Berbera in the north. Despite this, ties with Libya are strengthening.

Somalia harbours hundreds of thousands of refugees from Ethiopia; many Somalis live abroad to escape poverty and political persecution at home. Opposition to Siyad Barre is strongest in the north, formerly British Somaliland, the scene of fierce fighting between government and rebel forces in mid-1988. The central authorities have retained control of major towns but much of the area remains in rebel hands. Fighting has spread to the south of the country.

OFFICIAL NAME Somali Democratic Republic.
CAPITAL CITY Mogadishu.
GEOGRAPHY Behind the wide Indian Ocean coastal plain rises a dry, scrubby plateau. The narrow Gulf of Aden coastal plain gives way to montane forest. *Area* 637,700 sq km (246,200 sq miles).
PEOPLE *Population* 4.6m. *Density* 7 per sq km.
RELIGION Sunni Muslim 99.8%.
LANGUAGE Somali. Also Arabic, English and Italian.
CURRENCY Somali shilling (SoSh).
PUBLIC HOLIDAYS Jan 1, May 1, Id al-Fitr, Jun 26, Jul 1, Id al-Adha, Ashoura, Mouloud, Oct 21, 22.
GOVERNMENT Military-dominated socialist republic. Independent since 1960. The leader of the one legal party is president and chief executive.

UGANDA

Once described by Winston Churchill as the "pearl of Africa," Uganda became the pariah of Africa after three coups, two armed invasions, two civil wars, six violent changes of head of state, Idi Amin's bloody dictatorship, and tribal feuds and massacres. Comparative peace was restored when the government of Yoweri Museveni took power in January 1986, but violence has left its legacy: factions in the north carry on sporadic guerrilla warfare, and tribal enmity and corruption have corroded the structure of society.

Museveni's daunting tasks are to restore stability, promote economic growth and ensure a peaceful transition to lasting democracy. Many aid projects started in 1986 faltered as donors waited for evidence of consistent economic management. Stability can still not be guaranteed, although in 1987–88 the president made great strides in this direction.

Uganda is blessed with fertile soils and an equable climate in which most food crops thrive; but production of the major exports – coffee, cotton, tea and copper – has not yet regained pre-Amin levels. Industry, mainly agricultural processing, is only gradually being restored. Inflation is rampant and there is a thriving unofficial economy. Still more serious is the problem of Aids, which has taken a firm grip in some areas.

OFFICIAL NAME Republic of Uganda.
CAPITAL CITY Entebbe.
GEOGRAPHY A landlocked lakeland country, its south and east are filled by Lake Victoria and its basin; from it, through the country's heartland, flows the Victoria Nile. Ice-capped mountains straddle the equator in the west. The north of the country is a high, scrubby plateau. *Area* 236,036 sq km (91,130 sq miles).
PEOPLE *Population* 15.5m. *Density* 66 per sq km.
RELIGION Christian 75%, Muslim 7%, Animist.
LANGUAGE English. Also local languages.
CURRENCY Ugandan shilling (USh).
PUBLIC HOLIDAYS Jan 1, Mar 25, Good Fri, Easter Mon, May 1, Id al-Fitr, Jun 3, Id al-Adha, Oct 9, Dec 25.
GOVERNMENT Republic since 1962. Since the 1986 coup, the head of state and chief executive is the president. Political activity is suspended.

KENYA

Kenya has enjoyed nearly three decades of stable government, first under Jomo Kenyatta and, since 1978, under Daniel arap Moi. Both have been pragmatic, Western-oriented leaders presiding over a free economy. The August 1982 coup attempt, though never a serious political threat, indicated tensions below the surface. Moi responded by imprisoning dissidents, crushing opposition and curbing basic liberties. Kenya today is more authoritarian than at any time since independence in 1963 but the traditions of a free press and – albeit one-party – parliament have not been extinguished.

One of the highest population growth rates in the world – at over 4% – has led to one of the youngest populations in Africa, high unemployment and an exodus from the countryside to the overcrowded towns. But the entrepreneurial spirit is alive and well. A huge unofficial economy flourishes alongside a dynamic service sector which provides much of the real growth.

OFFICIAL NAME Republic of Kenya.
CAPITAL CITY Nairobi.
GEOGRAPHY The African Rift Valley sweeps through the eastern half of the country, filled in the arid north by Lake Turkana. High volcanic mountains around the valley give way to a low, sloping plateau, most of it scrub. The high ground supports agriculture while the drier valley floor and plains are home to herds of game, much of it in extensive reserves. *Area* 582,645 sq km (224,950 sq miles).
PEOPLE *Population* 20.3m. *Density* 35 per sq km.
RELIGION Christian 70%, Muslim 6%, Animist.
LANGUAGE Swahili and English. Also local languages.
CURRENCY Kenyan shilling (KSh).
PUBLIC HOLIDAYS Jan 1, Good Fri-Easter Mon, May 1, Id al-Fitr, Jun 1, Id al-Adha, Oct 20, Dec 12, 25, 26.
GOVERNMENT Republic since 1964. Independent since 1963. The head of state and chief executive is a president, elected for a 5-year term. Since 1982 the Kenyan African National Union has been the only permitted party. The legislature is a 188-member national assembly.

ECONOMIC PROFILE

Coffee and tea are major cash crops, followed by pyrethrum and sisal. Robust light industrial sector, particularly in food and beverage processing and engineering. Tourism, oil refining and entrepôt trade for landlocked neighbours are all important foreign-exchange earners. The most developed financial sector in East Africa. ·

Growth Tourism recently took over from coffee as leading foreign-exchange earner. Horticultural exports, airfreighted to Europe, growing fast. Industry being encouraged to go for export growth.

Problems Shortage of fertile land and rapidly growing population. Heavily dependent on imported oil, although hydroelectric and geothermal power sources are being developed.

BALANCE OF PAYMENTS

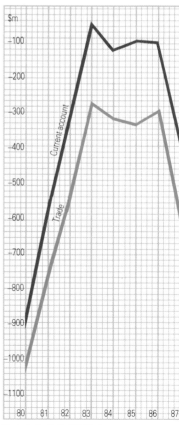

Source: EIU *Country Credit Risk Service*

IMPORTS AND EXPORTS

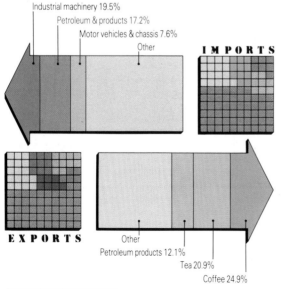

Industrial machinery 19.5%
Petroleum & products 17.2%
Motor vehicles & chassis 7.6%
Other

IMPORTS

UK
W. Germany
USA
Japan
Uganda
Netherlands
Other

EXPORTS
Other
Petroleum products 12.1%
Tea 20.9%
Coffee 24.9%

Source: EIU *Country Report* (1987 figures)

RWANDA

Rwanda has limited natural resources and is one of the poorest countries in the world in terms of GNP per head. It also has a rapidly growing population. President Juvenal Habyarimana, who seized power in a bloodless military coup in 1973, has so far skilfully avoided the tensions inherent in rule by a minority, the Tutsi, over the majority Hutu. In power since 1973, he has won the backing of Western aid donors, whose help sustains the fragile, largely agricultural economy. Coffee accounts for about 80% of exports, backed up by expanding tea production. Pyrethrum and quinquina production have been hit by weak prices and cassiterite mining collapsed in 1985, along with the International Tin Agreement. Being landlocked, Rwanda is vulnerable to disruption of its trade routes.

OFFICIAL NAME Republic of Rwanda.
CAPITAL CITY Kigali.
GEOGRAPHY A landlocked upland plateau. *Area* 26,338 sq km (10,170 sq miles).
PEOPLE *Population* 6.3m. *Density* 238 per sq km.
RELIGION Christian 82%, Muslim 1%.
LANGUAGE Kinyarwanda and French.
CURRENCY Rwanda franc (RwFr).
PUBLIC HOLIDAYS Jan 1, 28, Easter Mon, May 1, Ascension, Whit Mon, Jul 1, 5, Aug 1, Assumption, Sep 25, Oct 26, Nov 1, Dec 25.
GOVERNMENT Republic since 1962. The head of state and chief executive is the president, directly elected for a 5-year term, who appoints his own council of ministers.

BURUNDI

Unlike neighbouring Rwanda – with which it was linked as part of a UN trust territory until granted internal autonomy in 1959, followed by independence after elections two years later – Burundi has suffered periodic eruptions of violence as a result of the divisions between the ruling Tutsi minority and Hutu majority. A massacre in 1988 occurred despite efforts at conciliation by the new head of state, Major Pierre Buyoya, who had overthrown President Jean-Baptiste Bagaza in a bloodless coup in September 1987. In 1988 it was estimated that some 75,000 Burundian refugees were living in Rwanda.

Like Rwanda, the country is poor. Coffee brings in 80% of export earnings. Small amounts of tea and cotton are also exported but most agricultural land is given over to subsistence crops.

OFFICIAL NAME Republic of Burundi.
CAPITAL CITY Bujumbura.
GEOGRAPHY A landlocked upland plateau. *Area* 27,834 sq km (10,750 sq miles).
PEOPLE *Population* 4.8m. *Density* 174.6 per sq km.
RELIGION RC 78%, Protestant 5%, Animist.
LANGUAGE Kirundi. Also French and Swahili.
CURRENCY Burundi franc (BuFr).
PUBLIC HOLIDAYS Jan 1, Easter Mon, May 1, Ascension, Jul 1, Assumption, Sep 18, Nov 1, Dec 25.
GOVERNMENT Military-dominated republic. Independent since 1962. Direct elections are held every 5 years for a president and 52 of the 65-member national assembly. There is only 1 authorized party.

TANZANIA

Since independence Tanzania has been moulded by the homespun socialism of its first president, Julius Nyerere. He pursued experimentation with policies of self-help (*ujamaa*), villagization and state ownership at the highest levels of the economy further than any other African leader. Under his direction Tanzania achieved comparatively high welfare and educational standards, and basic human liberties were respected. But President Nyerere failed to increase agricultural productivity and the state sector let him down badly. Initiative was stifled by an increasingly inefficient and corrupt party bureaucracy. The oil price hikes of the 1970s, world recession and the consequent drop in prices of Tanzania's principal export commodities were the main reasons for the country's economic decline in the 1980s, which huge amounts of foreign aid and the work of international development strategists have not been able to arrest.

An essentially agricultural economy, Tanzania remains dependent on coffee, cotton, sisal, cashew nuts, tea, tobacco and – from Zanzibar – cloves. The light industrial sector, dominated by powerful state corporations, declined under Nyerere through lack of foreign exchange and shortage of spare parts.

Nyerere stepped down as president in 1985 but retained leadership of the party and considerable influence. His successor, Ali Hassan Mwinyi, and a handful of technocrats have done battle against the old guard to restore incentives and the disciplines of a market economy. Revival under the new regime is slow and is hampered – among other things – by an inadequate transport system, but tourism could be a growth sector and basic goods have reappeared in the shops. Gradually, Tanzania's economy is being liberalized.

OFFICIAL NAME United Republic of Tanzania.
CAPITAL CITY Dar es Salaam.
GEOGRAPHY Bounded in the north and west by lakes Tanganyika, Malawi and Victoria, Tanzania is mostly a rolling plateau. Africa's highest peak, Kilimanjaro, lies on the border with Kenya. A narrow strip along the coast and the offshore islands of Zanzibar and Pemba are flat and edged with coral and mangrove swamps. *Area* 945,087 sq km (364,900 sq miles).
PEOPLE *Population* 21.7m. *Density* 23 per sq km.
RELIGION Christian 40%, Muslim 30%, Animist.
LANGUAGE Swahili. Also English and local languages.
CURRENCY Tanzanian shilling (TSh).
PUBLIC HOLIDAYS Jan 12, Feb 5, Good Fri-Easter Mon, Apr 26, May 1, Id al-Fitr, Jul 7, Id al-Adha, Mouloud, Dec 9, 25.
GOVERNMENT Republic since 1962. Independent since 1961. The only recognized party, the Chama cha Mapinduzi, proposes a single presidential candidate for election. The president is head of state and chief executive; there is also a legislative national assembly. The island of Zanzibar has some internal autonomy.

297

AFRICA

IMPORTS AND EXPORTS

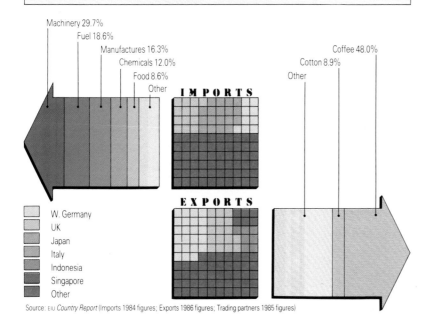

Machinery 29.7%
Fuel 18.6%
Manufactures 16.3%
Chemicals 12.0%
Food 8.6%
Other

IMPORTS

Coffee 48.0%
Cotton 8.9%
Other

EXPORTS

- W. Germany
- UK
- Japan
- Italy
- Indonesia
- Singapore
- Other

Source: EIU *Country Report* (Imports 1984 figures; Exports 1986 figures; Trading partners 1985 figures)

BALANCE OF PAYMENTS

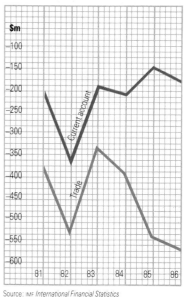

$m
−100
−150
−200
−250
−300
−350
−400
−450
−500
−550
−600

Current account

Trade

81 82 83 84 85 86

Source: IMF *International Financial Statistics*

MADAGASCAR

OFFICIAL NAME Democratic Republic of Madagascar.
CAPITAL CITY Antananarivo.
GEOGRAPHY One of the world's largest islands, its spine is a mountainous plateau covered with rain forest which tumbles into the ocean on the east and slopes more gently down to form a scrubby coastal plain in the west. The south is desert. *Area* 587,041 sq km (226,650 sq miles).
PEOPLE *Population* 10.1m. *Density* 17 per sq km.
RELIGION Christian 51%, Muslim 2%, Animist.
LANGUAGE Malagasy. Also French.
CURRENCY Madagascar franc (MgFr).
PUBLIC HOLIDAYS Jan 1, Good Fri, Easter Mon, Mar 29, May 1, Ascension, Whit Mon, Jun 26, Nov 1, Dec 25, 30.
GOVERNMENT Republic since 1960. The head of state and chief executive is a president at the head of a supreme revolutionary council. A legislative national people's assembly is elected for 5 years.

Madagascar is more a small continent than an island, marooned by some fluke of continental drift off the east coast of Africa. The Malagasy and their language have Indonesian origins; authorities differ about when and how they made the journey. Flora and fauna are unique but have been damaged by widespread deforestation and soil erosion.

The government that took over at independence in 1960 stayed close to France, but Malagasy nationalism, expressed in a bloodily repressed uprising in 1947, rose to the surface again in 1972. French troops and advisers departed and a period of turmoil followed, until navy captain Didier Ratsiraka emerged in 1975 as the strong man of a regime practising "humanist Marxism."

Ratsiraka brought relative stability. All political parties belong to the National Front for the Defence of the Revolution but cover a spectrum from hardline Marxist to Christian Democrat; elections are vigorously contested. Opposition can come from unexpected quarters: in 1985, government forces raided martial arts societies, claiming they planned a coup espousing the principles of Kung Fu.

Madagascar has maintained strong economic relations with the EC (its major trade partner). Its economic policy has been pragmatic. Nationalization, high spending and heavy borrowing characterized the early Ratsiraka years, but poor markets for commodity exports – coffee, vanilla and cloves – threw the economy into crisis in the early 1980s. Madagascar has since become a test case for the free-market reforms being prescribed for many African countries by the IMF and World Bank, and has

liberalized much of its agricultural production and marketing. The unpopularity of the reforms has acted as a rallying point for growing opposition to the Ratsiraka regime.

COMOROS

OFFICIAL NAME Federal Islamic Republic of the Comoros.
CAPITAL CITY Moroni.
GEOGRAPHY A volcanic archipelago, its three main islands, Njadiidja, Mwali and Nzwami, have forested centres and swampy coasts enclosing fertile strips that are heavily farmed for subsistence and export. *Area* 1,862 sq km (720 sq miles).
PEOPLE *Population* 370,000. *Density* 196 per sq km.
RELIGION Muslim 99.7%, Christian 0.2%.
LANGUAGE Arabic. Also French and Comorian.
CURRENCY Comorian franc (CFr).
PUBLIC HOLIDAYS Leilat al-Meiraj, 1st day of Ramadan, Id al-Fitr, Jul 6, Id al-Adha, Muharram, Ashoura, Mouloud.
GOVERNMENT Republic since 1975. An executive president is elected every 6 years, while the legislative federal assembly serves a 5-year term.

Comoros has had two successful coups since it broke free from France in 1975. The first, weeks after the declaration of independence, deposed President Ahmad

Abdallah; the second, in 1978, staged by a group of European mercenaries, brought him back to power.

The mercenaries have stayed on and kept Abdallah in power, with the help of the presidential guard, trained in South Africa. South African developers are investing in the tourist industry and Abdallah's close links with Pretoria have alienated the islands' African neighbours.

Most of the population is engaged in subsistence agriculture, but more than half the islands' food is imported. Vanilla, doves, copra and ylang-ylang are the only export crops, but all face shrinking world markets. Fishing and tourism have scope for growth. The annual balance of payments shortfall is covered by France, which also supports the islands' currency.

MAURITIUS

OFFICIAL NAME Mauritius.
CAPITAL CITY Port Louis.
GEOGRAPHY A volcanic island surrounded by coral reefs, its mountainous, forested centre gives way to vast plantations of sugar-cane in the valleys and around the coast. The territory includes several small island dependencies, up to 1,100 km (680 miles) away. *Area* 2,040 sq km (790 sq miles).
PEOPLE *Population* 1m. *Density* 505 per sq km.
RELIGION Hindu 53%, RC 28%, Muslim 16%.
LANGUAGE English. Also French and Creole.
CURRENCY Mauritius rupee (MR).
PUBLIC HOLIDAYS Jan 1, 2, Feb 16, Mar 12, Good Fri, May 1, Id al-Fitr, Nov 1.
GOVERNMENT Parliamentary monarchy. A governor-general represents the British monarch. A legislative assembly of up to 71 members is elected for a 5-year term.

Mauritius is Africa's great success story. The growth of both clothing manufacture in the Export Processing Zone and the luxury tourist trade has moderated the vulnerability of its economy to a bad harvest of sugar, its only crop. The government aims to diversify further, into financial services and other areas of manufacturing and agriculture. Prosperity and relatively healthy state finances have induced a rare political consensus on increased social service expenditure and staple food subsidies.

A shared socialist perspective has not

prevented fractious parties from playing intricate coalition politics; but these activities appear at least to channel and defuse much of the tension among Mauritius' racial communities.

MAYOTTE

OFFICIAL NAME Territorial Collectivity of Mayotte.
CAPITAL CITY Dzaoudzi.
GEOGRAPHY The coral-fringed volcanic island has heathland in the centre and agriculture in the lowlands. *Area* 375 sq km (145 sq miles).
PEOPLE *Population* 67,000. *Density* 179 per sq km.
RELIGION Muslim 97%, Christian 3%.
LANGUAGE French. Also local languages.
CURRENCY French franc (Fr).
GOVERNMENT Territorial collectivity of France. It is administered through a government commissioner, and Mayotte sends 1 deputy to the French national assembly.

Mayotte voted to remain part of France when the other three Comoros islands declared independence in 1975. Comoros has continued to press its claims to the island, backed by the UN, but Mayotte's politicians limit their ambitions to attaining the status of a department of France.

Ylang-ylang and vanilla are the main exports. The island depends on French aid; it has also received official overtures and private investment from South Africa.

SEYCHELLES

OFFICIAL NAME Republic of Seychelles.
CAPITAL CITY Victoria.
GEOGRAPHY A group of 32 rugged but fertile volcanic islands, four of which – Mahé, Praslin, Silhouette and La Digue – support almost all the population. *Area* 453 sq km (175 sq miles).
PEOPLE *Population* 65,000. *Density* 144 per sq km.
RELIGION Christian 98% (RC 90%), Hindu 1%.
LANGUAGE English. Also French and Creole.
CURRENCY Seychelles rupee (SR).
PUBLIC HOLIDAYS Jan 1, 2, Good Fri, Easter Sat, May 1, Corpus Christi, Jun 5, 29, Aug 15, Nov 1, Dec 8, 25.
GOVERNMENT Republic since 1976. The only recognized party is the Seychelles People's Progressive Front. A president is elected unopposed for a 5-year term as head of

state and chief executive. The 25-member national assembly has 23 elected members and 2 appointees

Faced with the challenge of applying socialist policies in a country largely dependent on upmarket tourism, President Albert René's government has attempted to diversify by expanding fishing, agriculture and light industry through parastatal enterprises.

Tourism brings in more than half the country's foreign earnings but has proved vulnerable to political upsets, like the attempted coup led by South African mercenaries in 1981. President René himself came to power in a coup in 1977, a year after independence from the UK; his exiled enemies continue to plot his downfall.

REUNION

OFFICIAL NAME Department of Réunion.
CAPITAL CITY Saint-Denis.
GEOGRAPHY The volcanic island has a mountainous, forested centre surrounded by an intensively cultivated coastal plain full of sugar plantations. *Area* 2,510 sq km (970 sq miles).
PEOPLE *Population* 530,000. *Density* 211 per sq km.
RELIGION RC 96%, Muslim 2%.
LANGUAGE French.
CURRENCY French franc (Fr).
GOVERNMENT Overseas department of France. It is administered through a government commissioner aided by councils elected to deal with purely local matters. 5 deputies are sent to the French national assembly.

Occupied by France as a penal colony in the mid-17th century, Réunion today is the main French military base in the Indian Ocean. The people of Réunion have consistently opposed complete independence.

The economy has long been based on sugar; its processing and the production of rum are the only industries. Exports pay for only about 10% of the import bill; expatriate remittances and a heavy subsidy from France help to make up the difference.

SOUTHERN AFRICA

SADCC

One of the most successful of African development organizations, the Southern African Development Coordination Conference (SADCC) was founded in 1980 by the nine majority-ruled states of southern Africa: the six front-line states – Angola, Botswana, Mozambique, Tanzania, Zambia and Zimbabwe – plus Lesotho, Malawi and Swaziland. Their explicit aim is to reduce their economic dependence on South Africa. SADCC initially concentrated on freeing its members from the need to use lengthy and costly transport routes to South African ports by raising finance to rehabilitate rail and road links from landlocked states like Zimbabwe and Malawi to the Mozambican ports of Beira, Maputo and Nacala, and Dar es Salaam in Tanzania. These schemes have been a considerable success; around 30% of Zimbabwe's freight, for example, now passes through Beira. Hopes of peace in Angola have focused attention on the rehabilitation of the Benguela railway, once an important export route for the Zambian and Zairean copperbelts.

SADCC does not confine itself to transport projects; the emphasis is on coordination of efforts in a wide variety of areas: agriculture, mining, energy, industry and tourism. Each member country takes responsibility for a particular sector.

The PTA

The 15-member Preferential Trade Area for Eastern and Southern Africa aims to liberalize trade, encourage economic cooperation and create a regional common market. Trade within the region has been stimulated by adoption of a common list of goods from member states to be given preferential treatment, although insistence on majority local ownership has raised objections from countries like Kenya and Zimbabwe, where foreign firms often hold large stakes in local companies. Establishment of a PTA clearing house and use of a common unit of account has reduced the need to use scarce convertible currency in trade between member states. PTA member states are Burundi, Comoros, Djibouti, Ethiopia, Kenya, Lesotho, Malawi, Mauritius, Rwanda, Somalia, Swaziland, Tanzania, Uganda, Zambia and Zimbabwe.

Refugees

Southern Africa has one of the largest concentrations of refugees and displaced people in the world. Over 2m people have been forced to leave their homes in their own countries; 1m more have fled to neighbouring countries. The vast majority are fleeing not from drought or natural disaster but from man-made catastrophes.

Most come from Mozambique, where the Mozambique National Resistance, a guerrilla movement with South African backing, has been causing widespread destruction for most of the 1980s. About 650,000 Mozambicans have fled to Malawi, where they now represent about 10% of the population, placing a huge burden on the country's slender resources. Hundreds of thousands more are in Zimbabwe, Tanzania, Zambia and Swaziland. Close to half Mozambique's population are at risk, deprived of the means to feed themselves.

The civil war in Angola has caused massive displacement of people; the country also supports refugees from Namibia. Most countries of the region have provided a home for some of the thousands of South Africans who have fled their country's apartheid policies.

Climate

Mozambique and Angola have a tropical climate on the coast. Inland, Zimbabwe and Zambia receive most of their rain between November and March. Much of Namibia and Botswana and parts of South Africa have a desert climate. Temperatures average 20–30°C (68–86°F) and annual rainfall ranges from 24mm (1in) on the Namibian coast to 2,000mm (78ins) in Zimbabwe's eastern highlands. In the extreme south there are dry summers and wet, mild winters on the Mediterranean pattern.

More than 1 million

250,000 – 1 million

100,000 – 250,000

Major roads

Major railways

Refugees

25,000

100,000

Ethnic and linguistic groups

Most of the peoples of Southern Africa speak Bantu languages. The Bushmen or San of the Kalahari Desert of Botswana and Namibia are linguistically and ethnically distinct: survivors of the Khoisan linguistic group that dominated the south of the continent 5,000 years ago. Among the largest ethnic groups are the Shona, who make up the majority of the population of Zimbabwe, and the Ovimbundi of Angola.

Education

Most countries in the region aim to provide education for all between the ages of 6 and 14, often free of charge. Zimbabwe, for example, has greatly increased spending on education since independence; in recent years education spending has been equivalent to nearly 10% of GDP and the primary school enrolment rate has reached 90%, up from 50% in the late 1970s. In many countries, however, economic pressures mean that achievements in these fields fall far short of aspirations. In Angola and Mozambique, especially, years of civil war have severely disrupted educational efforts; the Mozambique rebel movement has made schools and health centres a particular target. Provision of secondary education in most countries lags behind that for younger children.

"Homelands"

Variously known as "national states", "homelands" or "Bantustans", these states were created as part of the white South African policy of "separate development." Four of the states – Bophuthatswana, Ciskei, Transkei and Venda – are nominally independent, with their own governments and citizenship, and separate legal and tax systems. In practice, small and fragmented as they are, they lack any real autonomy and are dependent on South African aid. They have not received international recognition.

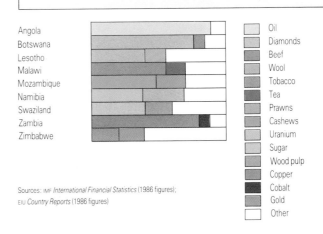

EXPORT BREAKDOWN

Angola
Botswana
Lesotho
Malawi
Mozambique
Namibia
Swaziland
Zambia
Zimbabwe

Oil
Diamonds
Beef
Wool
Tobacco
Tea
Prawns
Cashews
Uranium
Sugar
Wood pulp
Copper
Cobalt
Gold
Other

Sources: IMF *International Financial Statistics* (1986 figures);
EIU *Country Reports* (1986 figures)

SACU

The Southern African Customs Union (SACU) links South Africa with three of its smaller neighbours, Botswana, Lesotho and Swaziland. It dates from 1910, when all four countries were still under British rule. South Africa sets and collects customs duties for all the SACU members and distributes a share to the other three. The union is an important source of income for the smaller states, but it also provides South Africa with a captive market for its goods behind significant protective barriers.

Minerals and cash crops

Southern Africa arguably contains the greatest and most varied concentrations of minerals in the world. South Africa alone has about 49% of the world's gold reserves, 86% of its platinum, 22% of diamonds, 4% of antimony, 83% of chrome, 48% of manganese, 64% of vanadium, plus a whole host of minor strategic minerals like titanium, nickel and fluorspar. Zambia has huge reserves of copper and cobalt; Zimbabwe has a little of almost all of South Africa's range of minerals. Botswana, like South Africa and Zimbabwe, has huge coal reserves as well as some of the world's richest diamond deposits. Namibia has huge reserves of diamonds, uranium, copper, lead, zinc and other metals. Most Southern African countries rely heavily on their mineral wealth and consequently on world mineral prices. Those which do not predominantly export minerals tend to be dependent on a few cash crops.

Kobe 28½ days

AFRICA

ANGOLA

Civil war broke out in Angola before independence in 1975 and has continued ever since. The government, backed by Cuban troops and Soviet military aid, has been opposed by the Unita guerrillas, aided by South Africa and the USA. The international context of the war became less prominent after Cuba and South Africa agreed in 1988, under superpower pressure, to reduce thier involvement.

The economy, ravaged by war and run on austere Marxist lines, has failed to show growth or meet the basic needs of the people. Industry has collapsed and production of export crops has declined since independence. By mid-1988, over 1.5m people were displaced from their homes or destitute because of the war.

Angola is potentially rich. Apart from oil it has gem-quality diamonds and plentiful fertile land; coffee, cotton and sisal are the major cash crops. The 1988 peace agreement promised to allow the government to turn its energies to reconstruction, although Unita retained its capacity for destruction. President José Eduardo dos Santos, more flexible and pragmatic than his predecessor Agostinho Neto, has pressed ahead with economic reforms designed to boost the private sector.

OFFICIAL NAME People's Republic of Angola.
CAPITAL CITY Luanda.
GEOGRAPHY Apart from a coastal plain that merges in the north with the Congo delta, most of Angola consists of high plateau; the vegetation ranges from forest in the north through savannah to near-desert on the southern coast. *Area* 1,246,700 sq km (481,354 sq miles).
PEOPLE *Population* 8.8m. *Density* 7 per sq km.
RELIGION Christian 90% (RC 70%, Protestant 20%), Animist.
LANGUAGE Portuguese. Also local languages.
CURRENCY Kwanza (Kw).
PUBLIC HOLIDAYS Jan 1, Feb 4, Mar 27, Apr 14, May 1, Aug 1, Sep 17, Nov 11, Dec 1, 10, 25.
GOVERNMENT Communist republic. The only recognized party is the MPLA-PT; its leader is president, acting as both head of state and chief executive. The national people's assembly has 223 members elected or appointed by party members.

ZAMBIA

Zambia has had stable government under President Kenneth Kaunda since independence in 1964. Its dependence on copper and its derivatives for more than 95% of export earnings brought above-average prosperity in the 1960s but decline set in as copper prices fell after 1975.

Kaunda's corporatist socialism, expressed through state farms and state-owned corporations, failed to diversify the economy. Agriculture, underdeveloped before independence, was largely neglected – Zambia is now one of the most urbanized countries in Africa – and food production fell, increasing dependence on imports. The average standard of living declined sharply, leading to widespread unemployment and social discontent.

By the end of the 1980s Zambia faced heavy budget and payments deficits and massive debts, with the copper industry, suffering from shortages of foreign exchange and spare parts, in no position to take advantage of a recovery in metal prices.

OFFICIAL NAME Republic of Zambia.
CAPITAL CITY Lusaka.
GEOGRAPHY High and landlocked, Zambia has mountains in the north and east and swamplands around Lake Bangweulu. Most people live in the south. *Area* 752,614 sq km (290,590 sq miles).
PEOPLE *Population* 6.7m. *Density* 9 per sq km.
RELIGION Christian 72%, Animist.
LANGUAGE English. Also local languages.
CURRENCY Kwacha (K).
PUBLIC HOLIDAYS Jan 1, Mar 11, Good Fri-Easter Mon, May 1, 24, Jul 5, 8, Aug 5, Oct 24, Dec 25.
GOVERNMENT Republic since 1964. The head of state and chief executive is a president, elected for a 5-year term, who appoints a prime minister and cabinet. There is only one recognized party, the United National Independence Party (UNIP).

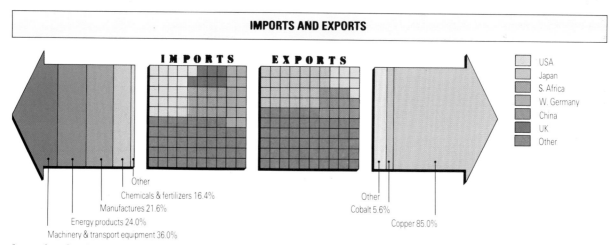

IMPORTS AND EXPORTS

IMPORTS — EXPORTS

USA / Japan / S. Africa / W. Germany / China / UK / Other

Other
Chemicals & fertilizers 16.4%
Manufactures 21.6%
Energy products 24.0%
Machinery & transport equipment 36.0%

Other
Cobalt 5.6%
Copper 85.0%

Source: EIU *Country Report* (Imports 1985 figures; Exports 1987 figures; Trading partners 1985 figures)

MALAWI

President Hastings Kamuzu Banda, in power since before independence in 1964, has refused to pursue orthodox African policies. He has been sympathetic to South Africa, where thousands of Malawians work, and was until recently hostile to most of his left-leaning neighbours. His autocratic rule brooks no opposition; potential successors have quickly fallen out of favour.

Banda has followed conservative, pragmatic economic policies and placed his faith in privately owned agriculture. At first, austere housekeeping and agricultural productivity created an economic miracle in a country with few natural assets apart from plentiful supplies of fish and fertile agricultural land. In the 1980s, balance of payments and budgetary deficits accumulated as prices of the main export commodities – tobacco, sugar and tea – declined. Trade routes have also been seriously disrupted by rebel activity in neighbouring Mozambique.

OFFICIAL NAME Republic of Malawi.
CAPITAL CITY Lilongwe.
GEOGRAPHY Malawi lies at the southern end of the Rift Valley along the eastern shore of Lake Malawi. In the west a plateau rises from the valley floor. *Area* 118,484 sq km (45,750 sq miles).
PEOPLE *Population* 7.1m. *Density* 60 per sq km.
RELIGION Christian 57%, Muslim 16%, Animist.
LANGUAGE Chichewa. Also English.
CURRENCY Malawi kwacha (MK).
PUBLIC HOLIDAYS Jan 1, Mar 3, Good Fri-Easter Mon, May 14, Jul 6, Oct 17, Dec 21, 25, 26.
GOVERNMENT Republic since 1964. The only party is the Malawi Congress Party. The chief executive is the president, elected for 5 years, though Dr Hastings Banda was made president for life in 1971.

MOZAMBIQUE

When the Portuguese settlers fled in 1975 they left behind a bankrupt economy bereft of skilled workers. The Frelimo government, led by the charismatic Samora Machel, set out to provide education and healthcare for all; but the erratic application of socialist policies to the economy did nothing to arrest its decline. Agricultural production was ravaged by drought and floods; by the mid-1980s earnings from the few exports – sugar, cotton, tea, cashew nuts and coal – were at less than half pre-independence levels.

The emergence of the Mozambique National Resistance, a guerrilla group backed by South Africa, set the seal on Mozambique's collapse. The MNR occupied huge areas of countryside and drove nearly 1m people to seek refuge in neighbouring countries; by 1988, almost half of Mozambique's population was dependent on external aid.

Before Machel was killed in a mysterious air crash in South Africa in 1985, he had been opening Mozambique to the West and taking an increasingly pragmatic line on the economy, policies that his successor, Joaquim Chissano, has continued.

OFFICIAL NAME People's Republic of Mozambique.
CAPITAL CITY Maputo.
GEOGRAPHY Most of the country is lowland, cut by many rivers. South of the Zambezi the coastal plain is wide rolling grassland supporting subsistence agriculture; farther north the plain narrows, rising to a savannah plateau on the eastern banks of Lake Malawi. *Area* 801,590 sq km (309,500 sq miles).
PEOPLE *Population* 13.9m. *Density* 17 per sq km.
RELIGION Christian 16%, Muslim 16%, Animist.
LANGUAGE Portuguese. Also local languages.
CURRENCY Metical (Mt).
PUBLIC HOLIDAYS Jan 1, Feb 3, Apr 7, May 1, Jun 25, Sep 7, 25, Dec 25.
GOVERNMENT Republic since 1975. The president of Frelimo, the only party, is de facto head of state, chief executive and chairman of the permanent commission of a 250-member people's assembly.

BOTSWANA

One of the world's poorest countries at independence in 1966, with cattle as the only source of export earnings, Botswana has been transformed by its huge diamond resources. Expanding diamond output during the 1980s generated the fastest growth rate in sub-Saharan Africa, despite a protracted drought that reduced the cattle herd by one-third.

With reserves of $2bn and low external debt, the country's main challenge is to diversify the economy in order to reduce dependence on imports from South Africa and provide jobs for a growing population.

Botswana has managed to combine rapid economic growth with political stability as one of Africa's few multiparty democracies, although the Botswana Democratic Party, founded by the first president Sir Seretse Khama, has not yet lost a general election.

OFFICIAL NAME Republic of Botswana.
CAPITAL CITY Gaborone.
GEOGRAPHY Basically a dry red sandstone plateau, with salt lakes and swamps in the north and desert – part of the Kalahari – in the south. *Area* 600,372 sq km (231,810 sq miles).
PEOPLE *Population* 1.1m. *Density* 2 per sq km.
RELIGION Christian 50%, Animist.
LANGUAGE Setswana. Also English.
CURRENCY Pula (Pu).
PUBLIC HOLIDAYS Jan 1, 2, Good Fri-Easter Mon, Ascension, Jul 15, 16, Sep 30, Oct 1, Dec 25, 26.
GOVERNMENT Republic since 1966. Executive power is exercised by a directly elected president, who is an ex-officio member of a 38-seat elected national assembly.

ZIMBABWE

Zimbabwe underwent the trauma of a decade of civil war before achieving independence in 1980 under the leadership of Robert Mugabe. Mugabe's espousal of reconciliation convinced many members of the white community to stay on but was less successful in winning over dissidents from the Matabele minority. Sporadic guerrilla activity continued until the conclusion of a unity agreement between Mugabe's party and that of his main rival, Joshua Nkomo, in 1987 and a successful amnesty for the guerrillas in the following year.

The economy is remarkably robust. It had become largely self-sufficient in response to sanctions imposed after the government, led by Ian Smith, unilaterally declared independence from the UK in 1965. After official independence, when trade barriers were lifted, there was an upsurge in manufacturing and agricultural and mineral production. Successful agricultural policies have produced massive grain surpluses in drought-free years, enabling Zimbabwe to supply food aid to its less fortunate neighbours. The main challenge facing the government has been to generate the growth to create jobs for a rapidly increasing labour force.

OFFICIAL NAME Republic of Zimbabwe.

CAPITAL CITY Harare.

GEOGRAPHY A landlocked upland rising to a central east–west ridge, most of the land is savannah, save for a forested mountain region in the east. *Area* 390,580 sq km (150,800 sq miles).

PEOPLE *Population* 8.3m. *Density* 21 per sq km.

RELIGION Christian 45%, Muslim 1%, Animist.

LANGUAGE English. Also local languages.

CURRENCY Zimbabwe dollar (Z$).

PUBLIC HOLIDAYS Jan 1, Good Fri-Easter Mon, Apr 18, May 1, 25, Aug 11, 12, Dec 25, 26.

GOVERNMENT Republic since 1980. 80 of the 100 members of the house of assembly are elected; the remainder of seats, reserved for whites before 1987, are now filled by the nominees of the ruling party, Zanu-PF. Of the 40 members of the senate, 24 are elected (10 of them from white-only constituencies) and the rest are appointees. Parliament elects an executive president to govern with the advice of a prime minister and cabinet.

IMPORTS AND EXPORTS

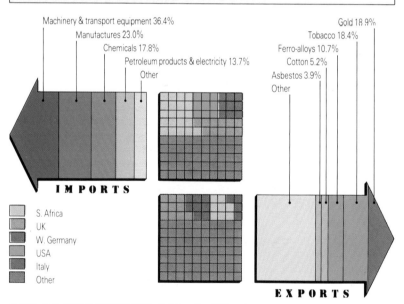

Machinery & transport equipment 36.4%
Manufactures 23.0%
Chemicals 17.8%
Petroleum products & electricity 13.7%
Other

Gold 18.9%
Tobacco 18.4%
Ferro-alloys 10.7%
Cotton 5.2%
Asbestos 3.9%
Other

IMPORTS

S. Africa
UK
W. Germany
USA
Italy
Other

EXPORTS

Source: EIU *Country Report* (Imports/Exports 1987 figures; Trading partners 1986 figures)

BALANCE OF PAYMENTS

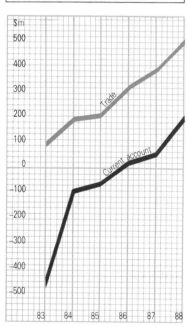

Source: EIU *Country Credit Risk Service*

ECONOMIC PROFILE

Diversified agriculture producing tobacco, sugar, cotton, groundnuts, beef and grains for export; almost self-sufficient in food crops. Rich mineral resources include gold, nickel, copper, tin, chrome and substantial quantities of coal. One of the most sophisticated service sectors in Africa.

Growth Light industries developed under sanctions – vehicles and transport equipment, textiles, agricultural processing – now capturing export markets.

Problems Unpredictability of commodity export prices. Foreign-exchange shortages constrain industrial expansion.

NAMIBIA

Agreements reached at the end of 1988 offered the prospect of independence for Namibia within a year, after more than 70 years of rule by South Africa, which had been given a mandate by the League of Nations after World War I to administer the territory on behalf of the UK. International pressure on South Africa to give up control and allow the country to become independent began in 1946 with the first of several UN rulings. The South West Africa People's Organization (Swapo), expected to form the first independent government, promised to respect minority rights and not engage in wholesale nationalization, despite its commitment to a socialist development strategy. Most trade and industry is controlled by the small white community, whose relationship with the post-independence government will crucially affect Namibia's economic prospects.

Namibia is well endowed with resources, including extensive deposits of diamonds and uranium and rich offshore fishing grounds. The mining industry, largely controlled by South African or multinational companies, contributes 90% of exports and 40% of GDP.

OFFICIAL NAME Namibia.
CAPITAL CITY Windhoek.
GEOGRAPHY Desert predominates: the Namib along the coast and the Kalahari in the east and south. Most settlement is on a central plateau and along the course of the Kunene and the Okavango rivers, which with the Orange are the only permanent watercourses in the country. *Area* 823,168 sq km (317,830 sq miles).
PEOPLE *Population* 1.6m. *Density* 2 per sq km.
RELIGION Christian 96% (Lutheran 50%, RC 20%).
LANGUAGE Afrikaans. Also English, German and local languages.
CURRENCY South African rand (R).
PUBLIC HOLIDAYS Jan 1, Good Fri-Easter Mon, May 1, Ascension, May 31, Dec 10, 25, 26.
GOVERNMENT Under UN administration pending independence, scheduled for 1990.

SWAZILAND

Tradition still rules in this fertile, landlocked state, sandwiched between South Africa and Mozambique. King Mswati III came to the throne in 1986 after the troubled interregnum that followed the death in 1982 of his father King Sobhuza II, who had reigned for over 60 years and seen the country become independent in 1968. The young king faces an uphill task, that of reconciling traditional social structures with the demands of an increasingly urban population.

Sugar, citrus and wood pulp are the basis of the modern export-oriented economy and the country is well endowed with reserves of asbestos, coal, diamonds and hydro-power. Swaziland has been affected by troubles in Mozambique; refugees have fled the fighting and transport links have been cut. South African economic influence remains strong: a growing number of firms are moving in from South Africa or using Swaziland as a base to circumvent international sanctions.

OFFICIAL NAME Kingdom of Swaziland.
CAPITAL CITY Mbabane.
GEOGRAPHY Most of the country is savannah, with agriculture concentrated on the irrigated eastern lowland. *Area* 17,364 sq km (6,700 sq miles).
PEOPLE *Population* 710,000. *Density* 41 per sq km.
RELIGION Christian 77%, Animist.
LANGUAGE English and siSwati.
CURRENCY Lilangeni (Li).
PUBLIC HOLIDAYS Jan 1, Mar 13, Good Fri-Easter Mon, Apr 25, Ascension, Jul 22, Aug 24, Sep 6, Oct 24, Dec 25, 26.
GOVERNMENT Parliamentary monarchy. The king rules through a nominated prime minister and council of ministers. Of the 70 members of parliament 50 are elected by an electoral college of tribal chiefs.

LESOTHO

Surrounded by South Africa, Lesotho, formerly the British protectorate of Basutoland, became independent in 1966. It has one of the world's lowest incomes per head, earned mainly by migrant workers and wool exports; less than one-sixth of the land area is suitable for crop cultivation and agriculture is declining.

South Africa supplies almost all imports. This economic dependence can only increase in the 1990s, with the construction of the vast Highlands water and power scheme; though designed to supply water to South African industry, the scheme will also greatly increase government revenues. Apart from the hydro-electric potential of its rivers, Lesotho has few natural resources.

King Moshoeshoe is nominal head of state but power is in the hands of a military government that took over in 1986 and expelled South African political refugees allegedly involved in cross-border raids.

OFFICIAL NAME Kingdom of Lesotho.
CAPITAL CITY Maseru.
GEOGRAPHY An enclave within South African territory, Lesotho is a high volcanic plateau, more than half of it above 2,000 metres, the source of the Orange and Tugela rivers. Most of the country is savannah, with forests in the deep-cut river valleys. *Area* 30,355 sq km (11,720 sq miles).
PEOPLE *Population* 1.5m. *Density* 50 per sq km.
RELIGION Christian 82% (RC 39%), Animist.
LANGUAGE English and Sesotho.
CURRENCY Loti (Lo).
PUBLIC HOLIDAYS Jan 1, 28, Mar 12, Good Fri-Easter Mon, May 2, Ascension, Jul 1, Oct 4, 7, Dec 25, 26.
GOVERNMENT Military-dominated monarchy.

SOUTH AFRICA

A land divided by racial tensions, South Africa is shunned by liberal opinion and most governments throughout the world; yet the living standard of its black inhabitants is among the highest in Africa. The economy has been shaped both by the natural resources of the country and by its internal political problems. Rich deposits of gold, diamonds and other minerals, and its varied agricultural production, make South Africa a natural exporter; but political isolation and limited economic and financial sanctions imposed by the USA, Western Europe and others have restricted its markets as well as forcing it to become more self-sufficient in manufactures and energy.

The country was settled by Dutch-speaking whites, the Boers (later known as Afrikaners) in the seventeenth century, followed by the British, against whom they fought numerous wars in efforts to retain their independence. The presence of black tribes resulted in battles between blacks and whites.

Just as the Afrikaners wrested political power from the numerically inferior English-speakers in 1948, the blacks, who far outnumbered the whites, began to threaten their position. The second half of this century has seen a prolonged struggle by the Afrikaners to hold on to power, and this has both slowed and distorted economic development.

The Afrikaner-dominated National Party has formed all governments since 1948. Its policy of apartheid or separate development divided the people into four racial categories – white, black, coloured and Indian – with numerous major and minor restrictions on movement and social life. Many blacks have been consigned to "homelands," some of which have been granted a form of constitutional independence not recognized outside South Africa. But growing black political consciousness has inexorably increased the pressure for a reversal of these policies. Support for reform has also come from white industrial leaders, aware of the cost of separate development in terms of the efficiency of their largely black work force.

After P.W. Botha came to power in 1978, the government repealed the pass laws and some apartheid legislation, turned a blind eye to breaches of the Group Areas Act, gradually removed petty apartheid, and devised new schemes to increase the representation of blacks, coloureds and Indians in regional and local authorities. The new constitution of 1984 established three houses to represent the racial categories: for the whites, the coloureds and the Indians. The blacks refused to accept a separate chamber. Their dissatisfaction with the scale of the reform induced the goverment to reconsider a multiracial parlia-

OFFICIAL NAME Republic of South Africa.

CAPITAL CITY Cape Town (legislative), Pretoria (administrative).

GEOGRAPHY Most of South Africa is a wide, rolling tableland, dropping down to a generally narrow coastal plain in a series of dramatic escarpments. Semi-desert in the east gives way to a high central basin covered in savannah and bisected by the Orange River, and to lush grasslands and forest in Natal in the west. A range of mountains lies along the southern coast. *Area* 1,222,161 sq km (471,880 sq miles).

PEOPLE *Population* 32.4m. *Density* 27 per sq km. *Ethnic groups* Bantu 68%, European 18%, coloured 11%, Asian 3%.

RELIGION Christian 59%, African churches 17%, Hindu 2%, Muslim 1%, Jewish 1%.

LANGUAGE Afrikaans and English. Also Zulu, Xhosa and other African languages.

EDUCATION There are separate systems for whites, blacks, Indians and coloureds. Education is compulsory for ages 7–15 for whites, 7–11 for blacks, and varies from state to state for others. The races mix at university level; the 10 white and 9 black universities were desegregated in 1985.

CURRENCY Rand (R).

PUBLIC HOLIDAYS Jan 1, Good Fri, Easter Mon, May 1, Ascension, 31, Sep 5, Oct 10, Dec 16, 25-27.

GOVERNMENT Republic. There are 3 separate assemblies, each passing legislation relating to their own racial groups. The white House of Assembly has 173 members, the coloured House of Representatives 30 and the Indian House of Delegates 40, all elected within their own racial groups. There is no black chamber. Legislation from all chambers has to be passed by the state president who is in addition head of state and chief executive. The president is elected for the duration of a parliament (usually 5 years) by a college of 50 from the House of Assembly, 25 representatives and 13 delegates.

IMPORTS AND EXPORTS

IMPORTS

Other
Scientific instruments 4.3%
Base metals 4.8%
Chemicals 11.1%
Oil 12.6%
Transport equipment 13.2%
Machinery & equipment 27.4%

USA
W. Germany
Japan
UK
France
Italy
Other

EXPORTS

Other
Platinum 5.2%
Food, drink & tobacco 6.1%
Mineral products 9.0%
Base metals 10.9%
Gold 41.4%

Source: EIU *Country Report* (Imports/Exports 1987 figures; Trading partners 1986 figures)

GDP BY ORIGIN

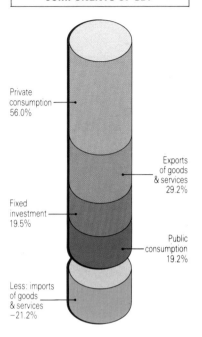

Manufacturing 23.2%

Public administration 13.6%

Agriculture, forestry & fishing 5.6%

Other

Financial services 15.2%

Mining & quarrying 13.5%

Electricity, gas & water 4.4%

Source: EIU *Country Report* (1987 figures)

COMPONENTS OF GDP

Private consumption 56.0%

Fixed investment 19.5%

Less: imports of goods & services −21.2%

Exports of goods & services 29.2%

Public consumption 19.2%

BALANCE OF PAYMENTS

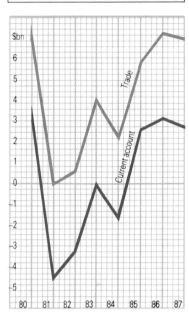

Source: EIU *Country Credit Risk Service*

ment. The replacement of P.W. Botha as National Party leader prompted a broad review of policy.

But the government has found itself in the classic dilemma of all authoritarian regimes at the time when they seek to broaden their support. The reform process provoked a white backlash which gave the anti-reform Conservative Party 26% of the votes in the elections of May 1987 to the white assembly. On the other side of the political spectrum, black opposition groups, which formed the United Democratic Front (UDF) in 1984 to fight the new constitution, have been pressing the government to move much further and faster than their own supporters would tolerate. The African National Congress (ANC), banned since 1960, and other groups have maintained a vigorous opposition and mounted some terrorist attacks. Meanwhile, liberal whites have been split between those supporting parliamentary opposition and those opting for extra-parliamentary methods. With boycotts of white shops, strikes in the mines, school walk-outs and violence, states of emergency have been in force almost continuously since July 1985.

Economic sanctions, which were tightened after 1985, have taken various forms: partial closure or denial of export markets for steel and coal, embargoes on the export of oil to South Africa, and a refusal to renew short-term financial credits. This last measure led to an outflow of capital, and helped to persuade a number of foreign firms either to close down their operations or to sell them, at low valuations, to South African interests. The unrest leading to the first state of emergency in 1985 also had a direct effect on business confidence.

One effect of sanctions has certainly been to impose additional costs: selling exports at a discount in order to find alternative markets, and buying oil at a premium, or producing it at high cost from indigenous coal. But sanctions have not added decisive pressure for political change. Falls in trade with the USA have been compensated for by increased trade with Japan, Taiwan and some other countries. More important than sanctions in explaining the relatively slow growth of the economy in the 1980s has been the combined effect of the world recession, the low prices of commodities, and the drought which seriously affected agriculture between 1982 and 1986. There has been some revival after 1986 with better weather, higher levels of demand in world markets and a recovery in commodity prices.

ECONOMIC PROFILE

Wealth founded on gold and diamonds; also an exporter of agricultural products, particularly fruit and vegetables, and a wide range of strategic minerals unavailable elsewhere. Manufacturing developed to substitute for imports, dominated by iron and steel, engineering, vehicles and chemicals. Coal is major energy source.

Growth Arms exports are thriving. Recent small-scale discoveries of oil and natural gas.

Problems Fluctuations of gold price lead to wild swings in export earnings. Sanctions cutting off export markets and political instability hitting business confidence. Disinvestment has made the country a net capital exporter. Unemployment among blacks a major economic, social and political problem.

GLOSSARY

ACP (African, Caribbean and Pacific) The 66 ACP states, almost all ex-colonies of EC members, receive a large proportion of the Community's overseas aid budget and under the Lomé convention are allowed free entry to the Western European market for 99% of their exports.

Aladi Asociación Latinoamericana de Integración, the 11-member Latin American trade integration organization, based in Montevideo (see pages 101, 144).

Andean Pact The 5-member group of South American states, based in Lima, which aims to establish a free trade area (see page 100).

Anzus The security treaty between Australia, New Zealand and the USA, signed in 1951 (see page 248).

Arab League The organization set up in 1945 to strengthen cooperation among independent Arab states, based in Tunis (see page 256).

Arctic climate No warm season; warmest month below 10°C (50°F).

Ascan Association of Southeast Asian Nations, founded in 1967, based in Jakarta (see pages 101, 227).

Balance of payments The record of a country's transactions with the rest of the world during a given period. The *current account* of the balance of payments consists of:
• "visible" trade: merchandise (see trade balance)
• "invisible" trade: receipts and payments for services such as banking, tourism, shipping and insurance, plus dividend and interest payments
• private transfers, such as remittances from workers abroad
• official transfers, such as payments to international organizations.

The *capital account* consists of:
• short and long-term transactions relating to a country's external assets and liabilities.

Adding the current account balance and the net investment balance gives the "basic" balance of payments. As the overall balance of payments must be in equilibrium, any surplus or deficit in the basic balance is accounted for by changes in foreign-exchange reserves, borrowing from or lending to international institutions and public-sector foreign-currency borrowing. All countries also record errors and omissions (or a balancing item) which in some cases can be very large. (See page 86.)

Benelux Benelux Economic Union (Belgium, Luxembourg and the Netherlands).

Black economy The part of the economy that evades tax and therefore cannot be precisely quantified in official statistics.

Bleu Belgium and Luxembourg Economic Union.

bn billion (used here to mean one thousand million).

CACM Central American Common Market (see Caricom).

Calorie Unit of heat or energy. The quantity required to raise 1 gram of water by 1°C.

Capital goods Assets which are capable of generating income and which have themselves been produced: machines, plant and buildings.

Caricom The 13-member Caribbean Community and Common Market, based in Georgetown, Guyana (see pages 101, 137).

Cash crop A crop grown for sale, generally for export rather than for domestic consumption.

CFA (Communauté Financière Africaine/African Financial Community) Its members, most of the francophone African nations, share a common currency, the CFA franc, which is maintained at a fixed rate of 1FFr = 50 CFA Fr by the French treasury (see Franc zone, pages 101, 278).

CFP (Communauté Française du Pacifique/French Pacific Community) Analogous to the CFA.

CIA Central Intelligence Agency.

CIF (Cost, insurance, freight) Trade statistics usually record imports on a CIF basis, thus including the cost of shipping goods to the country. To determine the visible trade balance for balance of payments purposes the figures must be adjusted to a free-on-board (FOB) basis; the difference between CIF and FOB figures is included in the balance of payments as invisibles.

CMEA See Comecon.

Colony See Dependency.

Comecon The Council for Mutual Economic Assistance, the 10-member Communist bloc trade and economic cooperation organization. Comecon includes Warsaw Pact members and Cuba, Mongolia and Vietnam (see pages 100, 201).

Commonwealth The association of independent states comprising the UK and most of its former dependencies (see page 100).

Communist Used here to identify states that control most or all of the means of production and distribution or those who believe that a state should do so.

Competitiveness The index of a country's labour costs relative to those of its trading partners.

Components of GDP Domestic production by type of expenditure. The categories vary but the usual ones are private consumption, government consumption, investment, stockbuilding, exports and imports.

Constant prices Used to adjust nominal values to constant or real values by removing the effects of inflation.

Constitutional monarchy An independent state ruled by a hereditary head, but controlled by an elected form of government.

Continental climate Hot summers, cold winters: typical of the interior of a continent. Coldest month below 0°C (32°F); warmest month above 10°C (50°F).

Continental shelf The edge of a land mass beneath the sea at depths of up to 200 metres (660 feet).

Convertible currency A currency that can be freely exchanged for another, or for gold.

Countertrade The generic term for trade involving the exchange of goods for goods rather than for money. The various forms of countertrade include *barter*, a straight exchange of goods for goods; *counter-purchase*, where a country selling goods to another promises to spend its receipts from the sale on purchases from that other country within a given period; and *buy-back*, where a company builds a factory in another country and agrees to be paid in output from the factory.

DAC Development Assistance Committee, the OECD committee responsible for promoting aid to developing countries.

Debt rescheduling An agreement between a country and its creditors to spread out debt repayments over a longer period than originally scheduled. Interest payments should continue to flow, although repayment of capital is delayed; the lender is often paid an extra fee for agreeing to the rescheduling. Rescheduling of official debt is negotiated through the Paris Club, that of commercial bank debt through the London Club.

Debt-service ratio A country's interest and capital repayments on foreign debt as a percentage of export earnings in a given period. Used to gauge a country's ability to continue servicing its debt: the higher the debt-service ratio, the more burdensome the payments.

Dependency A foreign territory governed by another country.

Downstream Originally and primarily used in the oil industry to describe activities taking place after the production of crude oil: refining, petrochemical production and retailing. Applied particularly with reference to expansion and diversification.

EC European Community (see pages 100, 158). **1992** Code for the EC project, scheduled for completion by the end of 1992, to establish a single European market without barriers to the movement of goods, people and capital between member states (see page 158).

Ecowas Economic Community of West African States (see pages 101, 278).

Efta European Free Trade Association (see pages 100, 173).

EIU Economist Intelligence Unit.

EMS European Monetary System, created in 1979 to aid the management of exchange rates between currencies of the European Community.

Entrepôt An international trading centre for import and re-export of goods, usually a port.

Factor cost The cost of producing an item, including materials and labour, as distinct from its market price.

Fiscal policy The budgetary stance of central government: the manipulation of taxation and expenditure to control demand for goods and services and the level of economic activity.

FOB (Free on board) Exports are normally valued FOB in trade statistics to exclude the transport costs paid by the importing country (see CIF).

Franc zone The currency zone including former French colonies in Africa and French dependencies in the Pacific which use the CFA (see CFA) and CFP (see CFP) francs, whose value is backed by the French treasury (see pages 101, 278, 288).

French overseas department A subdivision of the French Republic, similar to a department of metropolitan France.

French overseas territory A subdivision of the French Republic, with elected representation to the French parliament.

Gatt General Agreement on Tariffs and Trade, instituted in 1947 to liberalize trade and prevent discrimination. Over 100 countries are signatories. A new round of trade talks, covering agriculture and services, began in 1986. (See page 86.)

GCC Gulf Cooperation Council, the 6-member economic and security organization of Arab Gulf states (see pages 100, 256).

GDP (Gross Domestic Product) The best measure of a country's level of economic activity, GDP is the total value of a country's annual output of goods and services, discounted for depreciation. It is normally valued at market prices; GDP can, however, be calculated at factor cost, by subtracting indirect taxes and adding subsidies. To eliminate the effects of inflation, GDP growth is usually expressed in constant prices.

GDP by origin Domestic production broken down into type of activity. The categories vary but the usual ones are mining, agriculture, manufacturing and government and private services.

GMT (Greenwich Mean Time) Time based on the meridian at Greenwich in the UK. International standard.

GNP (Gross National Product) A country's GDP plus residents' income from investments abroad minus income accruing to nonresidents from investments in the country.

IBRD (International Bank for Reconstruction and Development, generally known as the World Bank) Set up to aid reconstruction in postwar Europe, the IBRD is now mostly concerned with lending to developing countries to finance development projects that cannot obtain finance on commercial capital markets. It is the largest single source of development aid and its lending in recent years has increasingly focused on economic policy reforms, as well as individual development projects, bringing it closer to the role of the IMF (see IMF). The IBRD itself borrows and lends on commercial terms, lending largely to higher-income developing countries. Its soft-loan agency, the *International Development Association*, is financed by contributions from rich countries. It lends to the poorest countries on very concessionary terms. The *International Finance Corporation* aims to promote the private sector in developing countries; it lends and takes equity stakes and encourages participation in companies by other development banks and commercial companies. (See page 91.)

IDA International Development Agency (see IBRD).

ILO International Labour Organization.

IMF (International Monetary Fund) The policeman of the international financial system, the IMF provides short-term balance of payments support to its members. Its assistance is conditional on a country carrying out an agreed programme of economic reforms; other lenders generally make the presence of an IMF programme a condition for aid or debt rescheduling. Members pay subscriptions, or quotas, to the IMF and can borrow up to a certain multiple of their quota (for membership see page 91). In 1970, the IMF introduced the *Special Drawing Right* as a reserve currency (see SDR).

Laissez-faire The belief that economic activity is best left free from government intervention or control.

LDC (Less developed country) Generally used to refer to countries that are not members of groupings of industrialized countries such as the OECD or Comecon.

LLDC Least developed country, a UN category of 29 developing countries which are low-income commodity exporters with little industrial base.

Liquidity Either the speed with which financial assets can be turned into cash, or the volume of turnover in a financial market.

LNG Liquefied natural gas.

London Club An informal grouping of commercial banks responsible for negotiating rescheduling of debt with creditor countries.

m million.

Mediterranean climate Hot summers, warm wet winters, affected by trade winds in summer, westerlies in winter. It occurs on the west side of large land masses between latitudes 30–60°.

Monetary policy Government control of the quantity of money in the economy. Connected to interest and exchange rate policies. The economic doctrine of monetarism maintains a direct link between excessive money growth and rising inflation and holds that the money supply can have no more than a temporary effect on real output. (See Supply-side policies.)

Nato (North Atlantic Treaty Organization) The alliance for the defence of the West against the Soviet Union. Formed in 1949, it includes the USA and Canada and most Western European nations. France withdrew in 1966 from the military command of the alliance. (See page 101.)

Nic Newly industrializing country.

NMP (Net Material Product) A measure of economic performance often used by communist countries. Gross Material Product differs from Gross Domestic Product by excluding the value of services; NMP also discounts for depreciation. (See GDP, GNP, page 212).

Nonsovereign state A dependent state (see Dependency).

Oapec Organization of Arab Petroleum Exporting Countries, set up in 1968 and based in Kuwait (see pages 100, 256).

OAU Organization of African Unity, set up in 1963 to promote unity and solidarity among African states; based in Addis Ababa (see page 100).

Observer status The right to observation at an organization's meetings but not of direct participation.

OECD Organization for Economic Cooperation and Development, the "rich countries' club," established in 1961 to promote economic growth in its 24 member countries and the expansion of world trade; based in Paris (see page 100).

Opec (Organization of Petroleum Exporting Countries), set up in 1960 and based in Vienna (see pages 100, 256).

Pamscad The IBRD's Programme of Action to Mitigate the Social Costs of Adjustment (see Structural adjustment).

Paris Club An informal grouping of Western government officials responsible for negotiation with countries in difficulties with debt repayments. The club is run by the French treasury. (See Debt rescheduling.)

PR Proportional representation, an electoral system designed to allocate seats roughly in proportion to the votes. Several different systems exist. West Germany's 5% vote threshold eliminates the smallest parties. Ireland's Single Transferable Vote (STV) system allows voters to rank their preferences but gives only a rough approximation to proportionality. Israel's parliament, on the other hand, almost precisely reflects the popular vote.

Price-earnings ratio The current market price of a company's shares expressed as a multiple of total earnings per share over the previous accounting year. It provides an indication of whether a company's share price is too high or too low compared with those of its competitors.

Privatization The sale of state assets, particularly state-owned industries, to the private sector.

Producer price inflation The rate of growth of the index of producer prices, the price of goods "at the factory gate."

Productivity The ratios of proportionate changes in inputs of resources to changes in the outputs of goods and services. Labour productivity is measures by an index of man-hours divided into an index of output.

PTA Preferential Trade Area for Eastern and Southern Africa (see pages 101, 300).

R&D Research and development.

Real terms Figures expressed in real terms have been adjusted to allow for inflation.

Republic An independent state with an elected form of government, generally with a president as the head of state.

SADCC Southern African Development Coordination Conference (see ages 101, 300).

SDR (Special Drawing Right) The reserve currency introduced by the IMF in 1970, intended to replace gold and national currencies in settling international transactions. The IMF uses SDRs for book-keeping purposes and issues them to member countries. Their value is based on a basket of the five most widely traded currencies: the US dollar, Deutschmark, pound sterling, Japanese yen and French franc. SDRs are increasingly being used for lending by commercial banks and for accounting purposes by some multinational companies.

Soft loan Money lent on concessionary terms, generally at lower interest rates or with longer maturities than could be obtained in the commercial lending market.

Structural adjustment Shorthand for the package of economic reforms being implemented by many developing countries, particularly in Africa, at the urging of organizations such as the IMF and IBRD and Western donor governments. Policies adopted include trade and investment liberalization, currency devaluation, privatization of state-owned companies, removal of consumer price subsidies, increased agricultural producer prices to stimulate food and export production and tighter fiscal policy. The political cost of adjustment programmes has proved too high for some governments despite help from the Pamscad programme (see Pamscad).

Sub-tropical climate Warmest month above 22°C (72°F); coolest month between 0°C (32°F) and 18°C (65°F).

Supply-side policies Measures to promote the efficiency of production by improving the responsiveness of labour, goods and capital markets. Founded on a belief that the stimulation of demand can have no long-term effect on the real economy, only on prices.

tce tonne of coal equivalent.

Temperate climate Mild winters, warm summers, rainfall throughout the year. Coolest month above 0°C (32°F) but below 18°C (65°F); warmest month above 10°C (50°F) but below 22°C (72°F).

Terms of trade The ratio between import and export prices, measuring the purchasing power of a country's exports in terms of the imports in needs. Terms of trade is expressed as an index to show changes over a period of time. When the index rises, terms of trade improve.

Territory A state under the control of another.

Third World Developing nations. The First World consists of OECD members; the Second World is Eastern Europe and the USSR; and the Third World is most of the remainder. Some call the LLDCs (see LLDC) the Fourth World. The division is arbitrary and its coverage is not universal.

Trade balance The record of a country's exports and imports of merchandise. Sometimes referred to as the visible balance and sometimes used more loosely as a synonym for the current account balance. (See Balance of payments.)

Tropical climate Very hot and generally humid. No winter: coolest month above 18°C.

Unctad United Nations Conference on Trade and Development.

Unesco United Nations Educational, Scientific and Cultural Organization.

Value added The value of output minus the cost of raw materials and other inputs. Used to quantify the contribution of an industry to GDP.

Warsaw Pact The security agreement between Eastern European states and the Soviet Union (see pages 20, 101).

WHO World Health Organization.

World Bank See IBRD.

NOTES ON DATA

Every care has been taken in the compilation of this book, which went to press in June 1989, but no responsibility can be accepted for the accuracy of the data presented.

Figures may not add to totals and percentage breakdowns to 100% because of rounding. In illustrations of percentage breakdowns categories of under 3% are generally not included unless they can be incorporated in another segment, so that statistical discrepancy may be more than that due to rounding. Money figures are generally calculated in dollars and converted from the local currency at exchange rates prevailing during the period to which the figures refer. The way in which statistics are collected and itemized for publication makes precise comparisons between countries impossible.

Recognition of a state by the UN is taken to be authoritative. Thus East Timor is given a separate entry although it has been occupied for several years, whereas the South African Homelands are not. Territories with no permanent inhabitants are generally not included.

Capital city The place named is generally the administrative centre which can differ from the legislative or judicial centre.

Climate See the *Glossary* for a definition of climate types. Temperatures, unless otherwise indicated, refer to the monthly average.

Education Official schooling requirements are given.

Geography The area is rounded to the nearest square kilometre and nearest ten square miles. It includes water recognized as part of the territory.

Government Suffrage should be assumed to be universal unless otherwise specified. For classifications of government see the *Glossary*.

Imports and exports The ultimate source or destination can differ from the country indicated; sources of imports are usually the last country of shipment, which may not be the country of production.

Language Official and widespread languages are given first, then minority and unofficial languages.

Official Name The English translation of the official name is given since, in all but a few cases, this is the name used in international forums such as the UN.

Population Country populations over 1m are given to three significant figures; those under 1m to two significant figures. The statistics are based on the most recent census and not the most recent estimate. They exclude expatriates. Non-nationals are included in some censuses and not in others. Census ethnic categories are used and so style may vary and comparisons between countries may not always be valid. In general Mestizo refers to mixed European/American Indian, Mulatto refers to mixed European/African and Creole is synonymous with mixed. Percentages in each ethnic group are to the nearest 1% unless a figure below 1% or over 99% is quoted. Population density is averaged over the whole area; in many countries density of populated areas is considerably greater because of shortage of inhabitable land or concentration in centres of production or trade. City populations are those for metropolitan districts.

Public holidays Public holidays are given in sequence according to the Gregorian calendar and are correct for 1989. If the holiday is not on a fixed date it is named. Muslim holidays are determined by a lunar calendar and so change position in relation to the Gregorian calendar, occurring 10 or 11 days earlier each year. The Muslim year 1410 began on August 4 1989. Spelling of Muslim holidays has been homogenized where names are already similar, otherwise local usage is given.

Religion Religious breakdowns in censuses vary in degree of detail and the titles of categories. Comparisons between countries may not always be valid. Animism is a general term for nontheistic and tribal religions; since it is often coexistent with other religious beliefs, the proportion of animist in a population is not quantified. Atheists are omitted.

Time zones Time zones are marked by their standard time which is measured relative to Greenwich Mean Time.

Editorial Sources

The Banker
British Geological Survey *World Mineral Statistics*
British Petroleum Shipping
British Petroleum *Statistical Review of World Energy*
Carbon Dioxide Information Analysis Centre
Central Intelligence Agency
Chambers World Gazetteer
Commission of the European Communities
Consolidated Gold Fields *Gold 1988*
The Economist
The Economist Intelligence Unit
  Country Credit Risk Service
  Country Profiles
  Country Reports
  East European Service
  International Economic Appraisal Service
The Economist Publications Ltd.
  Diamonds 1988
  Guide to World Commodity Markets
  World in Figures
Europa Year Book
Executive Office of the President *Budget of the United States Government*
Food and Agriculture Organization
Foundation for Environmental Conservation
Freedom House *Survey of Freedom*
Greenwich Observatory
International Institute for Strategic Studies *The Military Balance*
International Labour Organization *Yearbook of Labour Statistics*
International Monetary Fund *International Financial Statistics*
Lloyds *Shipping Register*
Mining Annual Review
Nasa Goddard Institute for Space
Nuexco Annual Review
Organization of Economic Cooperation and Development
  Development Cooperation
  Economic Outlook
  Economic Survey
Smithsonian Institute *Tropical Rainforests: A Disappearing Treasure*
Statistical Abstract of the United States
Swiss Reinsurance Company *Sigma*
United Nations
  Demographic Yearbook
  Energy Statistics Yearbook
  Industrial Statistics Yearbook
  International Trade Statistics Yearbook
  Map of Desertification 1977
  Monthly Bulletin of Statistics
  National Accounts Statistics
Unesco *UN Demographic Survey*
World Bank
World Bank *World Debt Tables*
World Bureau of Metal Statistics
World Health Organization *World Health Statistics Annual*
World Meteorological Organization *Long-Range Transport of Sulphur in the Atmosphere and Acid Rain*
World Resources Institute *World Resources Report*

GENERAL INDEX

MAP INDEX

A

B

E

I

K

Kizyl-Arvat **50** F 3
Kizyl-Atrek **50** E 3
Kizyl-Su **50** E 3
Kjöllefjord **34** J 1
Kjöpsvik **34** G 2
Kladanj **37** G 3
Kladno **33** F 4
Klagan **56** E 2
Klagenfurt **37** F 2
Klaipėda **35** H 4
Klamath Falls **18** B 3
Klamath River **18** B 3
Klamono **57** H 4
Klarälven **35** F 3
Klatovy **33** F 5
Klerksdorp **76** D 5
Klevan' **35** J 5
Klin **46** G 4
Klina **38** B 2
Klintehamn **35** G 4
Klintsovka **46** J 5
Klintsy **46** F 5
Klippan **35** F 4
Kłodzko **33** G 4
Kłomnice **33** G 4
Klosi **38** B 2
Klotz, Lac **17** N 3
Kluane Lake **14** K 3
Kluczbork **33** G 4
Klyavlino **46** K 5
Klyuchevaya **46** H 2
Kneža **38** B 2
Knin **37** G 3
Knittelfeld **37** FG 2
Knjaževac **38** B 2
Knoxville (IA, U.S.A.) **19** H 3
Knoxville (TN, U.S.A.) **19** K 4
Knyazhevo **46** H 4
Ko Lanta **55** G 6
Koartac **17** N 3
Koba **56** C 4
Koba **57** J 5
Köbe **53** KL 4
København **35** F 4
Koblenz **33** E 4
Kobrin **35** H 5
Kobuleti **39** F 2
Kocaeli **38** CD 2
Kočani **38** B 2
Kochevo **46** K 4
Kōchi **53** K 4
Kochkorka **51** K 2
Kochmar **38** C 2
Kochmes **47** M 2
Kochubey **39** G 2
Kock **33** H 4
Kodi **57** E 5
Kodiak **14** G 4
Kodiak Island **14** G 4
Kodima **46** H 3
Kodino **46** GH 3
Kodžha Balkan **38** C 2
Kofçaz **38** C 2
Köflach **37** G 2
Koforidua **72** D 4
Koggala **54** D 6
Kohat **51** J 4
Kohima **55** F 2
Kohlu **51** H 5
Kohtla-Järve **35** J 4
Koitere **34** K 3
Kojonup **62** B 5
Kok-Yangak **51** J 2
Kokalaat **51** G 1
Kokand **51** J 2
Kokas **57** H 4
Kokchetav **47** N 5
Kokemäenjoki **34** H 3
Kokemäki **34** H 3
Kokkola **34** H 3
Koko Nor **52** D 3
Kokoda **64** E 3
Kokomo **19** J 3
Kokonau **57** J 4
Kokora, Ozero **48** H 1
Kokpekty **47** Q 6
Koksaray **51** H 2
Kokshaga **46** J 4
Koksoak **17** O 4
Koktuma **47** Q 6
Kola **34** K 2
Kolahun **72** BC 4
Kolai **51** J 3
Kolaka **57** F 4
Kolar **54** C 5
Kolar Gold Fields **54** C 5
Kolari **34** H 2
Kolding **35** E 4
Koléa **36** D 4

Kolepom Island **57** J 5
Kolesnoye **38** D 1
Kolguyev, Ostrov **46** J 2
Kolhapur **54** B 4
Koliganek **14** F 4
Kolka **35** H 4
Kollegal **54** C 5
Köln **33** E 4
Kolo **33** G 4
Kotobrzeg **33** G 4
Kolomna **46** G 4
Kolomyya **38** C 1
Kolonia **60** B 2
Kolonodale **57** F 4
Kolosovka **47** O 4
Kolozero, Ozero **34** K 2
Kolpashevo **47** Q 4
Kolpino **35** K 4
Kólpos Ierisou **38** B 2
Kólpos Kallonis **38** C 3
Kólpos Kassándras **38** B 2-3
Kólpos Khanion **38** B 3
Koluton **47** N 5
Kolvitskoye, Ozero **34** K 2
Kolwezi **76** D 2
Kolymskiy, Khrebet **49** SU 3
Kolyshley **46** H 5
Kolyuchinskaya Guba **14** C 2
Kolyvan' **47** Q 5
Komandorski Islands **41** TU 4
Komarichi **46** F 5
Komárno **33** G 5
Komarom **38** A 1
Komatsu **53** L 3
Komfane **57** HJ 5
Komló **38** A 1
Kommunarka **47** R 2
Kommunarsk **39** E 1
Komotini **38** C 2
Kompong Cham **55** J 5
Kompong Chhnang **55** H 5
Kompong Som **55** H 5
Kompong Speu **55** H 5
Kompong Sralao **55** J 5
Kompong Thom **55** J 5
Kompot **57** F 3
Komrat **38** C 1
Komsa **47** R 3
Komsomolets **47** M 5
Komsomol'sk **51** G 3
Komsomol'sk-na-Amure **49** P 5
Komsomol'skiy **47** M 2
Komsomol'skiy **50** E 1
Komsomolskiy **39** G 1
Komusan **53** JK 2
Kon Plong **55** J 5
Konakovo **46** G 4
Konarak **54** E 4
Konda **57** H 4
Kondagaon **54** D 4
Kondinin **62** B 5
Kondopoga **46** F 3
Kondor **50** F 3
Kondut **62** B 5
Konetsbor **46** L 3
Konevo **46** G 3
Kongsberg **35** EF 4
Kongsvinger **35** F 3
Konin **33** G 4
Konitsa **38** B 2
Könkämä älv **34** H 2
Konosha **46** H 3
Konoshchel'ye **47** R 2
Konotop **46** F 5
Końskie **33** H 4
Konstantinovka **39** E 1
Konstantinovskiy **39** F 1
Konstanz **33** E 5
Kontiomäki **34** J 3
Kontum **55** J 5
Konya **39** D 3
Konya Ovası **39** D 3
Kookynie **62** C 4
Kooline **62** B 3
Koolivoo, Lake **63** F 3
Koonalda **62** D 5
Koör **57** H 4
Koorda **62** B 5
Kootenay **15** O 5-6
Kopanovka **39** G 1
Kópasker **34** B 2
Kópavogur **34** A 3
Koper **37** F 2
Kopervik **35** DE 4
Kopeysk **47** M 5
Köping **35** G 4
Koplik **38** A 2
Köpmanholmen **34** G 3
Koppang **34** F 3
Kopparberg **35** FG 4

Koprivniča **37** G 2
Kopychintsy **46** E 6
Kop'yevo **47** R 5
Kopylovka **47** Q 4
Koramlik **51** M 3
Korangi **51** H 6
Koraput **54** D 4
Korarou, Lac **72** D 2
Korba **54** D 3
Korbach **33** E 4
Korça **38** B 2
Korchino **47** Q 5
Korčula **37** G 3
Korčulanski Kanal **37** G 3
Kord Kūy **50** E 3
Kordofan → Kurdufân **68** DE 6
Korea Strait **53** J 4
Korelaksha **34** K 2
Korenovsk **39** E 1
Korenshty **47** N 5
Korets **35** J 5
Korfa, Zaliv **49** V 3-4
Korgen **34** F 2
Korhogo **72** C 4
Korim **57** J 4
Korinthiakós Kólpos **38** B 3
Koriolei **75** G 4
Kōriyama **53** M 3
Korkino **47** M 5
Korkut **39** F 3
Korkuteli **38** D 3
Korla **51** M 2
Korliki **47** Q 3
Korneuburg **37** G 2
Körnik **33** G 4
Kornilovo **47** Q 5
Korobovskiy **47** P 6
Köroğlu Dağları **39** D 2
Koroit **63** G 6
Koror **57** H 2
Korosten **35** J 5
Korostyshev **35** J 5
Korostyshev **46** E 5
Korpilahti **34** J 3
Korpilombolo **34** H 2
Korsfjorden **35** DE 3
Korskrogen **34** G 3
Korsnäs **34** H 3
Korsör **35** F 4
Kort Creek **54** A 3
Koryak Range **49** W 3
Koryakskiy Khrebet **49** VW 3
Koryazhma **46** J 3
Kos **38** C 3
Koschagyl **50** E 1
Kościan **33** G 4
Kosciusko **19** J 5
Kose **35** J 4
Kosh-Agach **47** R 6
Kosi **54** C 2
Košice **33** H 5
Koskuduk **51** K 2
Kosmaj **38** B 2
Kosŏng **53** J 3
Kosovska Mitrovica **38** B 2
Kossou, Lac de **72** CD 4
Kossovo **35** J 5
Kostajnica **37** G 2
Kostamus **34** K 3
Kostino **47** R 2
Kostomuksa **34** K 3
Kostopol' **35** J 5
Kostroma **46** H 4
Kostrzyn **33** F 4
Kos'yu **47** L 2
Koszalin **33** G 4
Kot Kapura **54** B 1
Kota **54** C 2
Kota Baharu (Malaysia) **56** B 2
Kota Belud **56** E 2
Kota Kinabalu **56** E 2
Kota Tinggi **56** B 3
Kotaagung **56** B 5
Kotabaharu (Indonesia) **56** D 4
Kotabaru **56** E 4
Kotabumi **56** BC 4
Kotamobagu **57** F 3
Kotapad **54** D 4
Kotchandpur **54** E 3
Koteasro **51** H 4
Kotel'nich **46** J 4
Kotel'nikovo **39** F 1
Kotel'nyy, Ostrov **49** P 1
Kotka **35** J 3
Kotkino **47** P 4
Kotlas **46** J 3
Kotli **51** J 4
Kotlik **14** E 3
Kotor **38** A 2
Kotor Varoš **37** G 3

Kotovsk **38** C 1
Kotovsk **46** H 5
Kotr-Tas **50** F 1
Kotri Allahrakhio **51** H 6
Kötschach **37** F 2
Kottagudem **54** D 4
Kottayam **54** C 6
Kotturu **54** C 5
Kotzebue **14** E 2
Kotzebue Sound **14** E 2
Koudougou **72** D 3
Koukdjuak **17** N 2
Koulen **55** H 5
Koumac **65** H 6
Koumala **63** H 3
Kounradskiy **47** O 6
Kourou **25** H 2
Koutous **73** FG 3
Kouvola **34** J 3
Kovdozero, Ozero **34** K 2
Kovdor **34** K 2
Kovel' **35** HJ 5
Kovrov **46** H 4
Kovylkino **46** H 5
Kowloon **52** FG 6
Kowt-e Ashrow **51** HJ 4
Koyandy **47** P 6
Köyceğis **38** C 3
Koyda **46** H 2
Koyuk **14** E
Koyukuk **14** F 2
Koyukuk **14** FG 2
Koyulhisar **39** E 2
Kozaklı **39** D 3
Kozan **39** E 3
Kozáni **38** B 2
Kozel'sk **46** G 5
Kozhevnikovo **47** Q 4
Kozhim **47** L 2
Kozhozero, Ozero **46** G 3
Kozhva **46** L 2
Kozlu **38** D 2
Kra Buri **55** G 5
Kragerö **35** E 4
Kragujevac **38** B 2
Krakór **55** H 5
Krakor **55** H 5
Kraków **33** GH 4
Kralendijk **24** E 1
Kraljevica **37** F 2
Kraljevo **38** B 2
Kramatorsk **39** E 1
Kramfors **34** G 3
Kranj **37** F 2
Krapina **37** G 2
Krasilov **46** E 6
Krasino **46** K 1
Kraskino **53** K 2
Krāslava **35** J 4
Krasnaya Polyana **39** F 2
Krasnaya Yaranga **14** C 2
Kraśnik **33** H 4
Krasnoarmeysk **39** E 1
Krasnoarmeysk **46** HJ 5
Krasnoarmeysk **47** N 5
Krasnoarmeyskiy **39** F 1
Krasnodar **39** E 2
Krasnograd **46** G 6
Krasnogvardeyskoye **39** D 1
Krasnogvardeyskoye **39** F 1
Krasnoje Selo **35** J 4
Krasnokamsk **46** KL 4
Krasnokutskoye **47** OP 5
Krasnoperekopsk **39** D 1
Krasnosel'kup **47** Q 2
Krasnoslobodsk **46** HJ 6
Krasnotur'insk **47** M 4
Krasnoufimsk **47** L 4
Krasnoural'sk **47** M 4
Krasnousol'skiy **46** L 5
Krasnovishersk **46** L 3
Krasnovodsk **50** E 2
Krasnoyarsk **48** T 4
Krasnoyarskiy **47** L 5
Krasnoyarskoye Vodokhranilishche **48** F 5
Krasnoye **39** F 1
Krasnoye, Ozero **49** W 3
Krasnoye Znamya **51** G 3
Krasnozatonskiy **46** K 3
Krasnozerskoye **47** PQ 5
Krasnoznamenskiy **47** N 5
Krasnystaw **33** H 4
Krasnyy Kut **46** J 5
Krasnyy Luch **39** E 1
Krasnyy Sulin **39** EF 1
Krasnyy Yar **46** HJ 5
Krasnyy Yar **47** N 5
Krasnyy-Yar **47** O 4
Krasnyy Yar **47** Q 4
Krasnyy Yar **50** D 1
Kratie **55** J 5

O

Q

R

S

Y